Teaching Strategies and Classroom Realities

EDITED BY

Mildred G. McClosky

*For the Graduate Internship Program
in Teacher Education
University of California, Berkeley*

PRENTICE-HALL, INC. Englewood Cliffs, New Jersey

Photograph on page xxi by Vester Dick;
photograph on page 143 by Peter Kleinbard;
photographs on page 223 by Jessica Stanley;
photograph on page 326 by Marianne Hurlbut;
all other photographs by José Gutierrez.

P: 13–896175–1   C: 13–896183–2

Library of Congress Catalog Card Number: 77–115132

Current printing (last digit):

10 9 8 7 6 5 4 3 2

PRENTICE-HALL INTERNATIONAL, INC., *London*
PRENTICE-HALL OF AUSTRALIA PTY. LTD., *Sydney*
PRENTICE-HALL OF CANADA LTD., *Toronto*
PRENTICE-HALL OF INDIA PRIVATE LIMITED, *New Delhi*
PRENTICE-HALL OF JAPAN, INC., *Tokyo*

Printed in the United States of America

Contents

Contents by Subject Areas, xi

Foreword, xix

Dr. Clark Robinson : An Appreciation, xxi

Preface, xxiii

THE GRADUATE INTERNSHIP PROGRAM
IN TEACHER EDUCATION, 1
Clark Robinson

SPAN : A STRATEGY FOR REACHING
THE UNTAUGHT, 7
Ruth W. Mandelbaum

PART ONE

Coping, 13

I : IN THE BEGINNING, 19

1 *In the Beginning, 20*
WINIFRED GIANNINI

2 *Handbook for the Disorganized, 25*
MARILYN JOHNSON HERSHDORFER

3 *Discipline Problems? 29*
JUNE MASTERS

4 *The Interview, 31*
CAROLE LURIE

II : RECURRENT EARLY TEACHING PROBLEMS, 34

**HANDLING DISCUSSION
AND ENCOURAGING ORAL WORK**

5 *Getting the Teacher to Shut Up, 35*
KAREN DRURY NORRIS

6 *The Art of Discussion, 37*
MARY HICKS

EVALUATION PROBLEMS

7 *A Suggestion for the Constructive Use of Grades, 39*
MARCIA PERLSTEIN

8 *Self-evaluation in an Art Class, 44*
ANDREA FISHER

PROBLEMS OF FRIDAY AFTERNOONS

9 *Planning for Friday Afternoons, 45*
CAROLYN MUSKA

WORKING COOPERATIVELY WITH COLLEAGUES

10 *Developing Intradepartmental Coordination, 47*
CHERYL VOLMERT

TEACHING NONACADEMIC STUDENTS

11 *Motivating Underachieving Students
in a Biology Class, 49*
JOAN JAMES SHEFFIELD

12 *Skill in Reading Math, 52*
MIKE HALL

13 *Math for the Disadvantaged, 56*
GARY WAGNER

14 *Algebra for Nonachievers, 59*
JEFF LUEBBERT

15 *Getting Kids to Follow Directions, 61*
DIANE WITTENBERG

PART TWO

Evolving Processes of Instruction, 63

I : INDUCTIVE APPROACHES :
INQUIRY, DISCOVERY, CONCEPT-BUILDING, 64

16 *Inventing Your Own Language, 68*
AL COGLIANESE

17 *Strategy: Imagination, 71*
KATI LYDON QUIBELL

18 *Identifying Living Organisms, 74*
JANET IMAGAWA

19 *Teaching Laboratory Science, 79*
ANNE SMITH

20 *My Use of the Discovery Method*
in Teaching Junior High School Science, 88
WARNER E. FREEMAN

21 *Devising Number Systems, 90*
DORIS TODD

22 *The Function Machine, 92*
JOSÉ GUTIERREZ

23 *Helping Slow Eighth-graders*
to Understand U.S. History, 95
JANET MANLEY

24 *Concepts and Processes in Social Studies, 100*
JANET MANLEY

II : CREATIVITY : PROCESS AND PRODUCTS, 103

25 *The Soul Searchers, 107*
JUDY BEBELAAR

26 *Writing Yields Reading, 110*
ELAINE HAUSER

27 *A French Page for the School Newspaper, 114*
VIVIANE ABOT

28 *An Eight-day Creative Writing Workshop
for High School Seniors, 115*
JULIE RANDALL

29 *Teaching the Reading and Writing
of Short Stories Concurrently, 119*
ELIZABETH AVAKIAN

30 *Dancing: The Joy of Discovering Together, 123*
KRISTEN AVANSINO

31 *Stitchery Project for an Arts and Crafts Class, 125*
ELIZABETH MARKING

III : GROUPING FOR INSTRUCTION, 127

32 *A Grouping Project in Math, 129*
MICHAEL GROSS

33 *An Experiment in Grouping, 131*
ELIZABETH AVAKIAN

34 *Team Learning: The Only Way to Fly, 136*
ANNETTE NORVELLE

35 *Grouping for a Final Exam, 139*
ROCHELLE ESTERLE

36 *Warm-up Activities in a Foreign Language Class, 141*
SUZY NORTON

IV : STUDENTS AS TEACHERS—OF PEERS, OF YOUNGER STUDENTS, OF THEMSELVES, 143

PROCEDURES USEFUL IN MOST CLASSROOMS

37 *Student Involvement in Math, 147*
JUDITH FORCADA

38 *Spanish Teaching by Spanish Students, 150*
NANCY HOLLAND

39 *Students Devise Homework Assignments, 152*
JANET E. BROWN

40 *Strategies for a Seventh-grade String Orchestra, 154*
ANABEL BARAHAL

41 *Individualizing Instruction and
the Use of Students as Teachers, 156*
PAUL CANOBI

42 *Individualized Teaching, 159*
TOBEY SCHWARTZ

SCHOOL TUTORIAL PROGRAMS

43 *A Cross-age Tutorial Program, 163*
PENNY WRIGHT

44 *High School Tutors in an Urban Setting, 166*
MARCIA PERLSTEIN

V : DRAMATIZING DEVICES : IMPROVISATIONAL DRAMA, ROLE PLAYING, AND GAMES, 175

IMPROVISATIONAL DRAMA

45 *Improvisational Drama for Teachers, 179*
ANNE HORNBACHER

46 *Improvisational Drama in an Urban Junior High, 181*
BARBARA GLASSER

47 *Improvisational Drama and Literature, 187*
PETER KLEINBARD

SIMULATION TECHNIQUES, ROLE PLAYING, AND OTHER DRAMATIC DEVICES

48 *The Game, 188*
AL COGLIANESE

49 *The Mock Corporation, 195*
ABBOT M. SCHEER

50 *State versus Santa Claus, 199*
WAYNE CROW

51 *Game Simulation in U.S. History, 201*
JANELLE BARLOW

52 *Drama in Foreign Language, 207*
EVERARDO ALAMILLO

CLASSROOM GAMES

53 *Games for Math, 208*
BONNIE MATHISEN

54 *Gamesmanship, or How to Survive Friday Afternoons, 210*
RITA SCHLAUDT

55 *How to Spice Up an Old Enchilada, 213*
ANITA HALL

VI : USES OF MEDIA AND TECHNICAL EQUIPMENT, 216

PICTURES, PHOTOGRAPHS (STILL AND MOVING)

56 *A Visual Approach to Vocabulary, 220*
JUDY CHAMBERS

57 *Photographed Vocabulary, 222*
JESSICA STANLEY

58 *Using Collages with Literature, 224*
MARCIA JOHNSTON

59 *Look and Write, 226*
ROBERT DAVIS

THE OVERHEAD PROJECTOR

60 *Heavy Heavy Hangs Over Thy Overhead, 228*
GRETCHEN BINGHAM

61 *Uses of the Overhead Projector
for Teaching Geometry, 232*
ROBERT M. SULLIVAN

LISTENING POSTS AND TAPE RECORDERS

62 *Reaching the Nonreader, 233*
STEPHEN AND JACQUELYN BRAND

POPULAR MUSIC IN THE CLASSROOM

63 *Popular Songs and Poetry, 235*
MICHAEL D. THATCHER

64 *Incorporating Music into the English Curriculum, 237*
STEVEN ROSS

65 *An Experiment in Time, 241*
JOSEPH D. FRIEDMAN

USE OF ADVERTISEMENTS IN AN ART CLASS

66 *Commercial Art: Unit for Continuation
High School Students, 244*
LOIS ATCHISON

STUDENT-PRODUCED FILM

67 *Guide to Filmmaking in the Schools, 247*
KENNETH ROSENBERG AND EDWARD TROY

VII : TEACHING FOR VALUES, CONCERNS, ATTITUDES, 252

DEVELOPING SELF-IMAGE

68 *Illustrate Who You Are, 257*
LINDA G. DAVIS

69 *Commonplace Books, 258*
ELIENE BUNDY

PERSONALIZING SCHOOL LEARNING

70 *Personalizing Earth Science, 262*
NANCY S. HARMS

71 *Pool, Papers, and Volleyball:*
A Cooperative Strategy, 265
BROWNLEE SHIREK

72 *Teaching by Discovery, 266*
WILLIE L. WILLIAMS

73 *Does It Relate, Man? 269*
MARGARET ANDERSON BENTLEY

CAREER PREPARATION

74 *Toward a Contact Curriculum, 271*
ROBERT E. KELLER

75 *The Present and the Future, 274*
MARY S. THOMAS

76 *Career and College Guidance in the Classroom, 276*
ROBERT LATHAM

DEVELOPING SOCIAL VALUES AND AWARENESS

77 *Experiences in Teaching for Values, 279*
FREDERICK W. BROCK

78 *Functional Democracy:*
Historic, National, and Personal, 281
RICHARD C. RAINES

79 *Teaching the Social Novel, 283*
BURTON H. GREENE

80 *An Approach to Africa, 289*
KAREN DORN

DEALING WITH RACE PROBLEMS AND ISSUES

81 *Biological Aspects of Race, 293*
ROCHELLE ESTERLE

82 *Black History Week, 296*
RICHARD JONES

83 *Black History, 298*
MINERVA BARRANCO

84 *Black Literature Course, 300*
BURTON H. GREENE

PART THREE

Developing New School Programs and New Public School Models, 305

I : NEW SCHOOL PROGRAMS, 310

85 Student-Teacher Relations:
An Experiment in Cooperative Counseling, 311
MYRNA WALTON

86 Drug Education: Community Education
for a Community Problem, 315
GENE G. DAVIS

87 Evolution of a Black Studies Program, 318
SAMANTHA H. LEE

88 An Interdisciplinary Seminar
in Mexican-American Studies, 320
GINI MATUTE

II : NEW PUBLIC SCHOOL MODELS, 326

89 Opportunity High: Getting It Together, 327
MARCIA PERLSTEIN

90 What Turns Kids On? 338
TERRY BORTON

91 Community High School, 343
JAY MANLEY AND PETER KLEINBARD

Index, 349

Contents by Subject Areas

ART

8 *Self-evaluation in an Art Class, 44*
ANDREA FISHER

9 *Planning for Friday Afternoons, 45*
CAROLYN MUSKA

31 *Stitchery Project for an Arts and Crafts Class, 125*
ELIZABETH MARKING

66 *Commercial Art: Unit for Continuation High School Students, 244*
LOIS ATCHISON

BUSINESS

9 *Planning for Friday Afternoons, 45*
CAROLYN MUSKA

41 *Individualizing Instruction and the Use of Students as Teachers, 156*
PAUL CANOBI

49 *The Mock Corporation, 195*
ABBOT M. SCHEER

74 *Toward a Contact Curriculum, 271*
ROBERT E. KELLER

DANCE

30 *Dancing: The Joy of Discovering Together, 123*
KRISTEN AVANSINO

DRAMA

45 *Improvisational Drama for Teachers, 179*
ANNE HORNBACHER

46 *Improvisational Drama in an Urban Junior High, 181*
BARBARA GLASSER

47 *Improvisational Drama and Literature, 187*
PETER KLEINBARD

72 *Teaching by Discovery, 266*
WILLIE L. WILLIAMS

82 *Black History Week, 296*
RICHARD JONES

ENGLISH

2 *Handbook for the Disorganized, 25*
MARILYN JOHNSON HERSHDORFER

4 *The Interview, 31*
CAROLE LURIE

5 *Getting the Teacher to Shut Up, 35*
KAREN DRURY NORRIS

6 *The Art of Discussion, 37*
MARY HICKS

15 *Getting Kids to Follow Directions, 61*
DIANE WITTENBERG

16 *Inventing Your Own Language, 68*
AL COGLIANESE

25 *The Soul Searchers, 107*
JUDY BEBELAAR

28 *An Eight-day Creative Writing Workshop
for High School Seniors, 115*
JULIE RANDALL

29 *Teaching the Reading and Writing
of Short Stories Concurrently, 119*
ELIZABETH AVAKIAN

33 *An Experiment in Grouping, 131*
ELIZABETH AVAKIAN

34 *Team Learning: The Only Way to Fly, 136*
ANNETTE NORVELLE

42 *Individualized Teaching, 159*
TOBEY SCHWARTZ

54 *Gamesmanship, or How to Survive Friday Afternoons, 210*
RITA SCHLAUDT

56 *A Visual Approach to Vocabulary, 220*
JUDY CHAMBERS

58 *Using Collages with Literature, 224*
MARCIA JOHNSTON

59 *Look and Write, 226*
ROBERT DAVIS

63 *Popular Songs and Poetry, 235*
MICHAEL D. THATCHER

64 *Incorporating Music into the English Curriculum, 237*
STEVEN ROSS

68 *Illustrate Who You Are, 257*
LINDA G. DAVIS

69 *Commonplace Books, 258*
ELIENE BUNDY

73 *Does It Relate, Man? 269*
MARGARET ANDERSON BENTLEY

77 *Experiences in Teaching for Values, 279*
FREDERICK W. BROCK

79 *Teaching the Social Novel, 283*
BURTON H. GREENE

84 *Black Literature Course, 300*
BURTON H. GREENE

FOREIGN LANGUAGES

17 *Strategy: Imagination, 71*
KATI LYDON QUIBELL

27 *A French Page for the School Newspaper, 114*
VIVIANE ABOT

36 *Warm-up Activities in a Foreign Language Class, 141*
SUZY NORTON

38 *Spanish Teaching by Spanish Students, 150*
NANCY HOLLAND

39 *Students Devise Homework Assignments, 152*
JANET E. BROWN

52 *Drama in Foreign Language, 207*
EVERARDO ALAMILLO

55 *How to Spice Up an Old Enchilada, 213*
ANITA HALL

60 *Heavy Heavy Hangs Over Thy Overhead, 228*
GRETCHEN BINGHAM

MATHEMATICS

12 *Skill in Reading Math, 52*
MIKE HALL

13 *Math for the Disadvantaged, 56*
GARY WAGNER

14 *Algebra for Nonachievers, 59*
JEFF LUEBBERT

21 *Devising Number Systems, 90*
DORIS TODD

22 *The Function Machine, 92*
JOSÉ GUTIERREZ

32 *A Grouping Project in Math, 129*
MICHAEL GROSS

37 *Student Involvement in Math, 147*
JUDITH FORCADA

39 *Students Devise Homework Assignments, 152*
JANET E. BROWN

53 *Games for Math, 208*
BONNIE MATHISEN

61 *Uses of the Overhead Projector
for Teaching Geometry, 232*
ROBERT M. SULLIVAN

MUSIC

40 *Strategies for a Seventh-grade String Orchestra, 154*
ANABEL BARAHAL

72 *Teaching by Discovery, 266*
WILLIE L. WILLIAMS

PSYCHOLOGY

48 *The Game, 188*
AL COGLIANESE

85 *Student-Teacher Relations:
An Experiment in Cooperative Counseling, 311*
MYRNA WALTON

86 *Drug Education: Community Education
for a Community Problem, 315*
GENE G. DAVIS

READING

12 *Skill in Reading Math, 52*
MIKE HALL

25 *The Soul Searchers, 107*
JUDY BEBELAAR

26 *Writing Yields Reading, 110*
ELAINE HAUSER

43 *A Cross-age Tutorial Program, 163*
PENNY WRIGHT

57 *Photographed Vocabulary, 222*
JESSICA STANLEY

62 *Reaching the Nonreader, 233*
STEPHEN AND JACQUELYN BRAND

SCIENCE

3 *Discipline Problems? 29*
JUNE MASTERS

11 *Motivating Underachieving Students in a Biology Class, 49*
JOAN JAMES SHEFFIELD

18 *Identifying Living Organisms, 74*
JANET IMAGAWA

19 *Teaching Laboratory Science, 79*
ANNE SMITH

20 *My Use of the Discovery Method in Teaching Junior High School Science, 88*
WARNER E. FREEMAN

35 *Grouping for a Final Exam, 139*
ROCHELLE ESTERLE

70 *Personalizing Earth Science, 262*
NANCY S. HARMS

76 *Career and College Guidance in the Classroom, 276*
ROBERT LATHAM

81 *Biological Aspects of Race, 293*
ROCHELLE ESTERLE

SOCIAL STUDIES

1 *In the Beginning, 20*
WINIFRED GIANNINI

10 *Developing Intradepartmental Coordination, 47*
CHERYL VOLMERT

23 *Helping Slow Eighth-graders*
to Understand U.S. History, 95
JANET MANLEY

24 *Concepts and Processes in Social Studies, 100*
JANET MANLEY

51 *Game Simulation in U.S. History, 201*
JANELLE BARLOW

65 *An Experiment in Time, 241*
JOSEPH D. FRIEDMAN

75 *The Present and the Future, 274*
MARY S. THOMAS

78 *Functional Democracy:*
Historic, National, and Personal, 281
RICHARD C. RAINES

80 *An Approach to Africa, 289*
KAREN DORN

82 *Black History Week, 296*
RICHARD JONES

83 *Black History, 298*
MINERVA BARRANCO

SPEECH

50 *State versus Santa Claus, 199*
WAYNE CROW

(See also sections on Drama and English.)

INTERDISCIPLINARY

7 *A Suggestion for the Constructive Use of Grades, 39*
MARCIA PERLSTEIN

44 *High School Tutors in an Urban Setting, 166*
MARCIA PERLSTEIN

67 *Guide to Filmmaking in the Schools, 247*
KENNETH ROSENBERG AND EDWARD TROY

71 *Pool, Papers and Volleyball:*
A Cooperative Strategy, 265
BROWNLEE SHIREK

85 *Student-Teacher Relations:*
An Experiment in Cooperative Counseling, 311
MYRNA WALTON

86 *Drug Education: Community Education*
for a Community Problem, 315
GENE G. DAVIS

87 *Evolution of a Black Studies Program, 318*
SAMANTHA H. LEE

88 *An Interdisciplinary Seminar
in Mexican-American Studies, 320*
GINI MATUTE

89 *Opportunity High: Getting It Together, 327*
MARCIA PERLSTEIN

90 *What Turns Kids On? 338*
TERRY BORTON

91 *Community High School, 343*
JAY MANLEY AND PETER KLEINBARD

Foreword

This collection of ideas for teachers, written by teachers, is a sensitive documentation of the joys and anguish of teaching and learning, especially of learning to teach. In its substance, the book constitutes a history of the Graduate Internship Program, an adaptive experiment in teacher education that has been operating for fifteen years at the University of California, Berkeley. It is fitting that this book, the dissemination of useful teaching experiences, should be dedicated to Dr. Clark Robinson, the Master Teacher of the Program. During his years as director of the Program, Clark Robinson was the constant exemplar of the internship concept, of learning while teaching. The staff that he selected and helped to train came to share and emulate the concept that governed the Program, responding consistently to the developing needs and skills of each year's group of first-year teachers.

The singular strength of this book is that it was devised and edited by Mrs. Mildred ("Mitzi") McClosky, a member of the Graduate Internship Program staff. During her nine years on the staff, Mrs. McClosky was specifically responsible for the development of a curriculum that was kept relevant to the needs of each year's intern teachers. In her work, she provided a continuing model of the teacher as learner, investing her concerns in each new class of interns and maintaining her interest and support of members of previous classes. Her sensitive awareness of the process by which interns become teachers has borne fruit in the assignment that elicited these classroom-tested strategies, in which interns were required to report candidly on their own teaching and learning in such a way that other teachers might adapt, amplify, and learn from these experiences.

In 1968–1969, Mrs. McClosky was in charge of a year-long series of workshops and demonstrations, a Cooperative Idea Exchange for public school teachers and administrators in the Bay Area of California. The warmth of their response to the opportunity to share some of the ideas in these chapters with others on the front line of education confirms the need for the publication of this and future collections of such materials.

The careful annotations that precede and illuminate the successive entries in this book have grown out of Mrs. McClosky's first-hand observations and discussions of the uses of these ideas. Recurrent empirical evaluations have contributed to the usefulness of these teaching devices for teachers and for teachers of teachers.

In the preparation of over one thousand secondary school teachers, the Graduate Internship Program has been deeply indebted to many persons. At the University of California, William A. Brownell, Dean Emeritus of the School of Education, supported the program through its initial exploratory stages, as an alternate method of educating teachers in more direct contact with the public schools. Others at the University are: Professor James C. Stone, for several years Director of Teacher Education; Dr. Morton Gordon, Dean of University Extension, where the Program was hospitably ensconced for administrative purposes; and Dr. Jane Zahn Edises, former head of Education Extension, who encouraged the publication of this book.

Two educational foundations have made substantial financial contributions. The Rosenberg Foundation of San Francisco has been especially and repeatedly supportive. A first grant in 1955 provided the initial spur for the Program. Another Rosenberg grant in 1958–1962 underwrote the Cooperative Supervision Project, to promote the sharing of responsibility for teacher education between the school districts where interns were teaching and the university staff charged with their education. In 1968–1969, a third Rosenberg grant subsidized the Cooperative Idea Exchange that helped to demonstrate the usefulness of some of these strategies for other teachers in northern California. In particular, Mrs. Ruth Chance, Executive Secretary of the Rosenberg Foundation, has for many years given her perceptive and critical support to the staff of this Program.

In 1964, the Ford Foundation gave a five-year grant to the Program, to seek out and prepare teachers to work with students previously labelled non-achievers. SPAN (School Programs for Academic Non-achievers) is described in detail as "A Strategy for Reaching the Untaught."

The Program is immeasurably indebted to the many working teachers and administrators in dozens of schools in northern California who have welcomed intern teachers into their schools and extended patient guidance to them during the critical period of their entrance into the teaching profession. Finally, there are the hundreds of thousands of students whose participation created the living classroom laboratory for the intern teachers. Their responses have been the reward and the impetus for continuing the commitment to teaching and to teacher education.

RUTH W. MANDELBAUM
Acting Director
Graduate Internship Program
University of California, Berkeley

Dr. Clark Robinson:
An Appreciation

The sweetest path of life leads through the avenues of learning, and whoever can open up the way for another, ought, so far to be esteemed a benefactor to mankind.
—David Hume

Behind the writers of these articles, all secondary school teachers, all products of the Graduate Internship Program in Teacher Education of the University of California, Berkeley, is the influence of a man called Clark Robinson. A vital force in this program from its inception in 1956, and its Director from 1957 to June, 1969, he has been an inspiration to his staff and to the interns whom they have taught, counseled, and supervised.

Clark Robinson is himself a dedicated teacher and learner. His supreme sense of the worth of each individual, his deep belief in keeping the teaching act central in the education of teachers, and his concern for an inter-disciplinary approach to classroom problems are his indelible stamps on both the theory and practice of the Graduate Internship Program. He respects differences in people, in ideas, in teaching styles, in achievements and philosophies. He believes that out of such respect for individuality and variety, wise teachers and learners can develop. The contents of this book clearly proclaim this happy fact. Diversity and growth characterize the teachers who wrote these articles.

Clark Robinson earned his BA degree from Washington State College and an MA and Ed.D. from Stanford University. He taught in the public schools of Washington and California and held administrative positions in elementary and junior high schools as Assistant Superintendent, District Superintendent, Director of Curriculum, and Director of Apprentice Training. During World War II he served as Director of the Curriculum Training Program at the West Coast Ports of Embarcation. For twenty years Dr. Robinson was Director of Publications for the California Teachers Association. From 1957 to June, 1969 he was Associate Head of Teacher Education and Director of the Graduate Internship Program at the University of California, Berkeley. Since 1956 the Internship Program has trained over a thousand secondary school teachers.

Currently Dr. Robinson is directing the initial organization of an internship program in teacher education at the University of California, Santa Cruz. Working on a new program in a new place, exploring new ideas in teacher education, he continues to inspire his staff and interns, both past and present. John Gardner's concept of "self-renewal" describes the way he lives and helps others to live.

Summing up the spirit and works of this man—leader, teacher, mentor, friend—sends us to John Ruskin's thought on education and educator:

> Education does not mean teaching people what they do not know. It means teaching them to behave as they do not behave....It is a painful, continual and difficult work to be done by watching, by warning, by precept, and by praise, but above all, by example....The highest reward for man's toil is not what he gets for it but what he becomes by it.

Clark Robinson, to whom we affectionately dedicate this book, *is* such an example.

MARION S. ANDERSEN

Preface

Enormous Challenges Facing Today's Teachers

Secondary schools in the United States are expected to accomplish Herculean feats: (1) to equip youth with democratic values; (2) to transmit the past; (3) to prepare students for present realities and future problems; (4) to get them ready for jobs, college, family life, and leisure; (5) to inspire them into self-propelled lifelong learning; and (6) to educate more youth of diverse backgrounds and varying aims for longer periods of time than any other nation has yet undertaken. What is more, these tasks are set in an era of social unrest and uncertain future.

Obviously, teaching in secondary schools today is difficult. The pressures are greater now than ever before. Teachers must equip their students for jobs and colleges that require increasingly higher levels of performance. Although education is legally compulsory, teachers are expected to convince *all* their pupils—the nonacademic as well as the college-oriented—that school is a place they would voluntarily attend. High school students grow more restless and rebellious each day. The student protest and minority group movements aimed during the past few years at colleges and universities are now converging on the high schools.

Clearly, the best minds and the best wills are needed if the American dream of quality education for all our youth is to be realized. New types of school programs, various alternatives to present forms of public schooling, must be fashioned in the years ahead. Meanwhile, vast numbers of secondary school teachers are struggling to teach their students effectively.

In these demanding times, dedicated, concerned teachers need to discuss their present problems and pool their wisdom. Unfortunately, such exchanges among teachers do not occur as frequently as they should. Alone of all service careers, the teaching profession has developed historically along the lines of autonomy, academic freedom, and privacy rather than of mutual consultation and cooperative inquiry. Except during student teaching, during an internship, or at yearly professional conferences, most classroom teachers are left to face their instructional challenges pretty much alone. Teachers could profit from periodic joint consideration of new classroom approaches. Certainly, instructional strategies for involving students significantly in the teaching-learning process are needed as never before.

In the Graduate Internship Program at the University of California, we have found that idea exchanges among intern teachers are enormously useful. One intern's enthusiastic report of an effective teaching strategy quickly motivates several other interns to test the same procedure and to improve upon it. Apparently, those who have recently met similar frustrations and challenges are more able to guide others toward solutions.

After years of fruitless search for a comprehensive written collection of practical and creative classroom strategies which could supplement interns' oral idea exchanges, the Curriculum Committee of the Graduate Internship Program eventually concluded that the program itself was the logical source of the innovational strategies we had been seeking. Given the number of gifted interns placed in a large variety of school settings, a supervisory staff that encourages responsible experimentation, a curriculum that provides frequent opportunity for interns to exchange ideas, plus a five-year project,[1] SPAN, designed to reach nonachieving students—the Graduate Internship Program, we felt, was particularly well suited to sponsor the invention, collection, and testing of contemporary classroom strategies.

The Strategy Assignment

In December 1966 the Graduate Internship Program initiated a pilot attempt to crystallize in some permanent form the fresh insights and resourcefulness of new teachers. Interns were asked to review their first months of teaching, and to select and describe the one teaching approach or strategy they had found most helpful either in solving a classroom problem or in improving instruction. Papers were due when interns had been teaching full-time for six months, after they had devised some ingenious solutions to teaching challenges but could still remember why these solutions had been needed.

The "Strategy" papers that resulted were presented in seminars and evaluated by staff seminar leaders and the interns. After further screening by a committee of staff supervisors and former and current interns, thirty-four strategies were selected for a mimeographed edition. In September 1967 the first collection of Classroom Strategies was ready for trial use by interns and other teachers in the Bay Area. Interns for the next two years, 1967–69, used

[1] See "SPAN: A Strategy for Reaching the Untaught," pp. 7–11.

the collection and were asked to write up their own most promising strategies. In addition, we solicited a few strategies from interns of previous years whose special contributions had come to our attention. Then after further evaluation, a new selection was made from all the strategies accumulated and evaluated over the past three years.

Criteria for Selection

Given the assignment to write about the *one* most important solution they had found to a classroom challenge, all of the interns reported strategies of some merit. Consequently, choosing among the many excellent strategies was difficult. For final selection we set up the following criteria:

1. Could the strategy be useful to a number of other teachers in a variety of school settings?
2. Does the strategy have some transferability across subject lines? (We were looking primarily at *process* rather than subject.)
3. Does it incorporate sound principles of teaching and learning?
4. Does it offer possibilities for further variations?
5. Most important, does it show ways to involve students significantly in their own instruction? (We were searching for strategies which could get teachers off center stage and make students partners in the teaching act.)

We also wanted a balance in subject areas, different types of school situations, and instruction for both junior and senior high school levels. We were especially interested in strategies helpful to students not being reached by traditional teaching methods. After continuing scrutiny with all these criteria in mind, the final selection was made for this edition.

Unique Features of the Classroom Strategies

The strategies chosen for publication are geared to today's youth. They demonstrate various ways of helping to prod restless or defeated youth into active learning. These approaches have been found useful both for the alienated or disadvantaged students and for bright, advantaged students who are demanding more vital roles in the classroom.

The written strategies, further, are distinguished for their candor as well as their inventiveness. Narrated in a relaxed, informal, conversational style, the bulk of the strategies included were composed by teachers freshly aware of the initial and recurring challenges confronting today's public school teachers and still acutely conscious of both the little steps and the larger approaches necessary for improving contemporary classroom interactions. Because the interns were encouraged to write honestly about the degree of their success, readers of these strategies should not be misled into false expectations. The aim is not to raise delusive hopes, but rather to guide the reader toward an understanding of both the pains and rewards of classroom experimentation.

Most of the strategy reports are detailed enough for other teachers to reproduce in some form. Too often, teachers are exhorted to reach more students, to make their classrooms come alive, but are not offered specific models that demonstrate feasible ways to translate pious wishes into effective daily practice. The strategies selected offer specific details, precautions, and procedures that could be followed closely for similar courses and students, or adapted in some form to other subjects and other types of classes.

The strategies are designed for a broad range of students and teaching circumstances. The interns who wrote these papers taught many subjects to many kinds of students—in junior high and in senior high, inner-city, suburban, and continuation schools throughout northern California. The various strategies reflect the diversity of the teaching assignments and the special challenges raised by different student populations.

Arrangement of the Book

The collection opens with two introductory essays which explain the professional preparation provided for the teachers who devised the strategies. The first, "The Graduate Internship Program in Teacher Education," is written by Dr. Clark Robinson, whom we invited to do this. Dr. Robinson was the director of the GIP from its inception in 1955 to his retirement in June 1969.[2] It was he, together with the staff he inspired, who gave the program its moving spirit, sound structure, and innovative thrust, and it is, therefore, to Clark Robinson, that this entire collection of strategies is gratefully dedicated. The second introductory essay, "SPAN: A Strategy for Reaching the Untaught," by Mrs. Ruth Mandelbaum, coordinator of the SPAN project from 1963 to 1968, and presently the Director of the Graduate Internship Program, describes the sensitive and thoughtful preparation the SPAN program provided for teachers who were working in the most difficult schools. (SPAN teachers wrote many of the strategies included in this book. In the index, see SPAN for a complete listing.)

Besides offering a framework for the intern strategies, both these essays should be of use to educators of teachers—either pre-service or in-service, and particularly to those involved in urban teacher task forces and in internship programs.

The bulk of the book, the strategy collection itself, is organized under three major divisions:

Part One—Coping
Part Two—Evolving Processes of Instruction
Part Three—Developing New Programs and New Public School Models

Each part contains chapters. Introductions accompany all sections, describe their primary focus, and briefly indicate the special features of each strategy.

The table of contents depicts the categories into which the strategies have been arranged and reflects the GIP's continuing emphasis on processes of instruction. (The categories—such as inquiry, creativity, students as teachers, etc.—were derived inductively after the strategies were assembled. Quite predictably, these categories mirror many of the concerns and innovative directions that the GIP curriculum stresses.) Wherever possible, placement of a strategy was determined by its major thrust, although many could logically belong in

2 Presently he is serving as Chairman of the Committee on Education at the University of California, Santa Cruz.

several categories, and some in almost any. The topical index at the back of the book provides additional clues to contents of the various strategies. Note also that there is an alternative table of contents arranged by subject areas.

Some Suggestions for the Use of the Strategies

1. Most of the strategies demonstrate promising ways of translating current educational theory into more rewarding practice. Too often teachers who know sound principles about classroom teaching may regress under stress to familiar, outmoded methods, or may experiment too haphazardly. Both the procedures and the precautions contained in the strategies may help at such times. Teachers of similar courses and situations should find some of the specific suggestions immediately usable; others might consider mainly the general processes involved in the strategies, and seek individual ways to adapt them to their own style, subjects, students, and community.

2. Now some cautions. The strategies in this collection are the product mainly of beginning teachers who may already have found more effective teaching approaches. They are intended to stimulate other ideas, to help teachers through stressful periods, to afford a pool of experiences teachers can check against their own. They are meant to supplement, *not* to substitute for sound methods books in each discipline and significant readings in the psychological, philosophical, sociological factors in education. Also, bulky as this collection may be, we do *not* claim to have touched upon all the important aspects of contemporary teaching, but only to have pointed the way.

3. However, after two years' trial use of the mimeographed *Classroom Strategies '67,* and after observing the reactions of administrators and other teacher-training programs to that collection, we have reason to hope that the present more comprehensive selection of teaching strategies can make a useful contribution to educators at various levels of experience.

4. We have already found that student teachers and first year teachers can profit from reports of teachers who have recently faced and solved problems plaguing beginners. We expect that more experienced teachers who feel dissatisfied with the adequacy of their habitual methods may find in *Teaching Strategies and Classroom Realities* some new direction and renewed faith. Supervisors, curriculum coordinators, and those who teach teachers should see numerous ways to use the collection. Finally, and most imperative, we hope that the eventual beneficiaries will be the restless and "tuned out" high school students whose motivation to learn may be rekindled by strategies of instruction more sensitive to their needs.

Acknowledgments

The present collection of classroom strategies was made possible by the combined efforts of the Graduate Internship Program staff and the interns of the years 1966–69, together with a few interns from previous years.

As the curriculum coordinator for the Graduate Internship Program and the editor of the strategies, I was helped in several ways by the GIP seminar leaders and supervisors. Clark Robinson and Ruth Mandelbaum worked with me on the original conception of a strategy collection. Anne Hornbacher assisted in the preliminary evaluation of the 1967 classroom strategies. Marion Andersen, Robert Bonnin, Esmer Clark, Lee Crossman, Marie Fielder, Marjorie Johntz, Margaret Lepore, Ray Lippincott, Kati Lydon Quibell, Gérard Poirier, and Paul Weidoff all helped to explain the strategy assignment to their interns, initiated ideas for interns to explore, and later helped to evaluate the strategies which the interns devised.

The publication would not have been possible, of course, without the full cooperation of the interns, who not only wrote about their classroom strategies but also "lived" and evaluated them. The task of teaching is a consuming one, and it is difficult for those who are most involved to analyze and report their experiences honestly. The interns strove admirably to fulfill a difficult assignment. I am especially grateful to interns Marcia Perlstein and Peter Kleinbard, who in addition to their written strategies offered valuable suggestions about the structure of the collection. (Marcia had served as junior editor of the 1967 edition.)

I owe a special debt of gratitude to Jane Zahn Edises, for reviewing the first strategy collection, suggesting useful additions, and encouraging their publication; Ellen Siegelman, for generously offering her editorial skills and wise counsel when they were most needed; and Susan Gangwer, for her patience, competence, and good humor in typing and otherwise preparing this lengthy manuscript for publication.

MILDRED G. McCLOSKY
University of California, Berkeley

THE GRADUATE INTERNSHIP PROGRAM
IN TEACHER EDUCATION

Clark Robinson

The good teacher is never fully prepared for teaching, but is forever preparing. His preparation begins long before he enters a teacher education program and continues long after he completes it. In a formal program he should, concurrently, be both a teacher and a learner, establishing a dual role which he will maintain as long as he teaches.

He must learn to listen and to observe his students so that he can understand what they are thinking, feeling, and doing. The successful teacher must continue to be a learner in his discipline so that his knowledge is current and appropriate to his role. He must keep abreast of the changing times so that his purposes in teaching reflect the changing purposes of education in our society. He must continue to develop new and better teaching techniques. Those that work today may not be equally effective tomorrow; those that work with one class may not be effective with another. A rewarding career in teaching necessitates lifelong learning.

In this lifelong period of professional preparation, a formal teacher education program comprises but a very small segment of the total learning period and provides but a very small part of the total learnings needed for continuing success in teaching. Recognizing this, the strategy of the GIP in broadest terms is twofold. (1) It considers significant factors—personal, academic, experiential—in a candidate's past and selects persons thought to have high potential for success in teaching. What a person has been and what he is as

Clark Robinson is former Director of the GIP, now Chairman of the Committee on Education, University of California, Santa Cruz.

he enters the profession is predictive of what he can become as a teacher. (2) It provides an internship program of preparation in which the member concurrently engages in teaching and in learning to teach. Not only is this dual experience thought to provide the most effective induction into teaching, but it has the further advantage of helping the intern to establish the teacher-learner role, useful in his professional growth as long as he teaches.

There are a number of general principles underlying both the selection and preparation of interns. While the principles in each of these areas will be considered separately in the following pages, it will be noted that a description of the kind of people selected by the GIP serves equally well as a description of the kind of teachers its curriculum is designed to produce.

In this book, interns report teaching strategies which have worked for them. The purpose of this chapter is to introduce these teachers as a group by describing for the reader significant principles underlying their selection and preparation by the GIP.

Screening and Selection

Rigorous screening by the Graduate Internship Program is possible since college and university graduates who apply for membership far exceed the number that can be admitted. This careful screening is essential since most of those candidates tentatively accepted by the Program will be recommended for employment and will be offered teaching contracts by school districts before the interns' professional preparation begins.

How can the GIP staff recommend a person as having the potential to become a good teacher? Of course, staff members must first have a broad conception of the characteristics of a good teacher. Year after year, as staff members instruct, supervise, and counsel the successive intern groups they have screened and selected, their ability to measure promise against fulfillment grows. They welcome diversity, knowing that there can be no single blueprint for an effective teacher. Staff members learn to recognize clues which promise success.

Principles of Screening and Selection

A strong academic background is a basic requirement for success in secondary teaching, and college and university transcripts can provide many clues helpful in screening. Examined carefully by a discerning person, they disclose much more than courses taken and grades received; they reveal even more meaningful personal characteristics, such as breadth of interests, stability, sense of purpose.

High priority is given to all those clues indicative of the candidate's ability to fit the teacher-learner role, a basic ingredient of the GIP. Has he an "open" or "closed" mind? Is he flexible or inflexible? Is he mentally nimble and creative? Will he be able to learn from his students, his peers, and staff members? Has he the ability to communicate in give-and-take situations? Throughout the screening process, answers are sought to such questions as these.

Is the candidate excited about his subject? Does he have the desire to share his knowledge and thinking with others and to share in theirs? Does he find learning an adventure or a chore? Is he primarily interested in ideas or in bare facts? Has he faith in the ability of all students to learn and grow? Does he really see and feel the relationship of his discipline to other disciplines and to life itself? When significant clues are sought to such questions, many will be found during the screening process.

A candidate's commitment to teaching is a vital qualification and should be explored. Is teaching the right vocational choice for the candidate, and is he right for teaching? Approaching their task in this way, staff members assume a vocational counseling, rather than a judgmental role. With the candidate's assistance, pertinent evidence is assembled and assessed. Does he have a realistic view of the teacher's role? Is his motivation superficial or real? Will he find the satisfactions he seeks in teaching? Have his interests and abilities been tested in teaching-related activities? Is he personally and academically qualified for probable success in teaching?

Emotional maturity is important. What are the candidate's self-perceptions? Is he secure enough so that he can view both his strengths and weaknesses realistically? Will he feel secure or threatened in his relationships with students, peers, and administrators? Are his self-expectations as a teacher attainable? When satisfactions are delayed, will he be unduly disturbed? Only as a teacher is emotionally mature can he be an effective adult model for youth, responding in mature ways to the many trying situations he will face.

The ability of a teacher to relate with his students should be predicted. One of the most compelling indications of potential success for teaching in present circumstances may be membership in an ethnic minority group, for with it comes insightful identification with students from that group, and in turn a readier response from those students. Further objective evidence of this ability to identify is the nature, extent, and success of his youth-related experience. What clues do they provide? Will he be comfortable with the age group he proposes to teach? They with him? Can he be an authority without being authoritarian? Is he friendly, outgoing, and warm? Is his attitude toward life negative or positive? How about his sense of humor? Can he show enthusiasm without being embarrassed?

The Screening and Selection Process

Characteristics such as the above most often cannot be objectively measured and recorded on check lists to be statistically scored. Rather, these subjective impressions form interrelated patterns of attitudes, thoughts, abilities, and actions which can be sensed by a perceptive staff, alert to the many clues indicative of teaching potential. When evaluated in conjunction with the more traditional and objective screening criteria—grade point average, breadth and depth in subject matter, work experience, and test scores—these impressions can be translated into a composite prediction of the candidate's teaching success.

The GIP operates on the principle that clues helpful in the screening and selection of interns should come from the perceptions of a number of people who have known the candidates in a variety of situations over an extended period of time. Accordingly, a number of devices are used to aid in the assessment of personal and academic qualifications. All staff members par-

ticipate in the screening and selection process, which includes transcript evaluation, reference letters, a psychological inventory, the candidate's written report
of a school visitation and classroom observations, observed interaction of
candidates participating in a group discussion, and half-hour interviews by
two staff members. Finally, a composite assessment of all the pertinent evidence
is made by staff action.

The staff feels that the hours given to this extensive, time-consuming
program of screening and selection save many hours in the subsequent instruction and supervision of the interns. Further, they believe that the single best
guarantee of superior intern teachers is the selection of superior candidates.

This screening and selection begins in late fall and continues until the
Program quota is filled in early spring. Candidates who are tentatively accepted
are referred in the spring to school districts for final screening and employment,
which begins the following September.

The Curriculum

The Principles

There is no single "right" type of person for teaching and no single "right"
way to teach. Just as diversity is sought in screening, so it is nurtured throughout the Program. Each intern is encouraged to develop his own functional
philosophy of education and his own most effective teaching style.

The best learnings are provided when teaching and educational theory
are experienced concurrently. In the GIP, therefore, classroom teaching is
made the integrating factor in the process of learning to teach. The intern
begins to teach with the beginning of his professional preparation. Educational
theory and classroom practice become mutually supportive. Interns are regarded
as teachers and are encouraged to regard themselves as teachers who are
learning, not as learners who are "practicing" teaching. Being a teacher and
feeling like one speeds growth in teaching competence.

How the intern is taught, it is felt, will influence significantly how he
teaches. Therefore, the staff seeks to make its instructional activities a model
of the teaching-learning process, applicable, when possible, to the intern's
relationships with his students. The adage, "Do as I say, not as I do," has
little relevance to the instructional processes of the GIP.

Since interns learn much from each other, one of the principles of the
Program is to provide numerous ways to encourage and facilitate close intergroup relationships and activities. With the teaching-learning experience they
are sharing as the dominant integrating factor, these incidental and planned
activities provide an enriching, interdisciplinary influence. Persons with diverse
academic and experience backgrounds have much to share when they meet
in heterogeneous discussion and seminar groups.

Members of the staff give their full attention to the Program and meet
regularly to plan, report, and evaluate. They function as a team, with each
member's unique strengths contributing to the effectiveness of the total program. While there is some differentiation of function in the discharge of

Program responsibilities, all staff members participate in the screening, selection, instruction, and supervision of interns.

A warm, close, friendly relationship between interns and staff members is established during the screening and maintained throughout the Program. Often these relationships continue and deepen following an intern's completion of the Program and form the basis for a continuing influence of the Program and its staff in the professional growth of the graduate. Loyal alumni, supportive of the program by which they entered teaching, strengthen the GIP in numerous ways.

A close, cooperative relationship between the GIP and the public schools is inherent in a program committed to the concurrence of theory and practice as the best way to prepare teachers. As has been noted, interns are employees of a school district and members of the GIP at the same time. School districts do the final screening and selection, provide the teaching-learning laboratory, and aid in the supervision of interns.

Structure and Content

The program of instruction extends over a period of two summers and the intervening year of internship teaching. The intern's pre-internship professional preparation begins in a public school summer program with an intensive seven-week period of instruction closely related to his daily part-time teaching experience. During the internship year of full-time teaching which follows, he is supervised by staff members and he returns to the campus on Saturday mornings for instruction. During the post-internship summer, the intern who has not previously met the state requirement must complete six semester units of course work in his major or minor teaching field to complete the Credential Program.

What has been the curricular experience of interns who have contributed to this book? How was the content of their curriculum determined so that it would integrate educational theory and classroom practice? Since teachers tend to teach as they were taught, it is important to examine the master strategy underlying the GIP curriculum for clues helpful in understanding the interns' adaptation of the strategy to their teaching. How have they made the subject content of the curriculum they teach relevant and meaningful in the lives of their students?

In order that professional content may be made meaningful by the interns' teaching experience and that their teaching experience may be illuminated by the study of appropriate professional content, a spiral-type curriculum has been developed. As problem areas are identified in their teaching, interns in their related seminars spiral around the problem, drawing from any or all of the professional content areas (psychology, sociology, growth and development, curriculum, philosophy, etc.) help of the kind needed in the right amount, introduced at the proper time. Thus the spiral curriculum enables interns to visit and revisit these areas, taking at each time that which is helpful and no more, returning for more as it is needed and as it thereby becomes meaningful.

Interns inducted into teaching through such a curriculum apply many of the same principles to their own teaching. At the secondary school level these principles are expressed by such terms as motivation, involvement, interest, relevance, meaning. The strategy underlying the spiral curriculum is reflected in the successful teaching strategies of interns.

How professional content is selected and taught in the spiral curriculum has been described briefly, but nothing has been said about the nature of this content. The curriculum planning must be an evolving process, with the selection of educational theory for seminars geared so as to be responsive to needs indicated by teaching experiences in the classroom. Early in their professional growth, for example, interns may need some content from all the professional content areas as they consider the problems of "classroom management." A week later, as they spiral about the problem of "motivation," they may again draw content from the same educational "foundation" areas, but now in greater depth. Weeks later they may need to spend one or more seminars on a planned consideration of a single background area, such as "adolescent growth and development."

Supervision

As the intern plunges into teaching in his pre-internship summer of preparation, all the resources of the Program support him. Knowing that beginning days in teaching are critical, staff members work closely with interns. Help is available at a moment's notice. It is at this time that the mutual feelings of friendship and confidence developed between staff members and interns during screening and placement activities begin to pay big dividends. When there is a basis of friendship, supervision can be truly supportive. Channels of communication are open. The intern reveals rather than conceals his concerns, and his own perceptions of his problems provide the basis for assistance.

The intern realizes that he has only begun the lifelong process of learning to teach and that no one expects perfection in so complicated a task as the instruction of the young. He knows that some mistakes are expected and can be the basis of valuable learnings, so he tends to mention his mistakes to his supervisor as freely as his successes. As the supervisor helps him to analyze his failures and success and to revise his plans, the intern derives the greatest benefit from his teaching.

The teaching-learning process involves the sharing of experiences. The strategies reported in this book capture in writing some of the teaching techniques shared verbally by interns in their seminars. Just as they should draw from the literature of their profession as long as they teach, so they should contribute to this literature as long as they are teachers who are learning.

SPAN : A STRATEGY FOR REACHING THE UNTAUGHT

Ruth W. Mandelbaum

Underlying all the classroom strategies that comprise this volume is the basic strategy of teacher education that constitutes the Graduate Internship Program at the University of California, Berkeley. As Dr. Clark Robinson indicated in his chapter on that major strategy, for fifteen years the Graduate Internship Program has carefully selected interns who demonstrate high potential for becoming successful teachers and has provided a preparation—the internship—that enables the interns to learn to teach *by teaching* in an atmosphere of supported self-criticism.

It was inevitable that during these years the GIP staff and its interns should become aware of the problems, especially in the secondary schools of the inner-city, of growing numbers of students who are consistently failing in their school work. The compelling emergence of these problems may be attributed, not to a decrease in the national level of intelligence, but to an increase in the number of students who are now required to remain in school for twelve years.

Four or five decades ago there were certainly some students who did not flourish in the classroom. But such students used to leave school and go to work on the farm, in the factory, or at some other job that did not demand previously acquired skills. Today there are no jobs for the unskilled laborer. Now all adolescents are urged to stay in school for twelve years, to get a high school diploma as a minimal prerequisite for a job.

Although the population in the classroom has been changing, the patterns

Ruth Mandelbaum is Acting Director of the GIP, University of California, Berkeley.

of instruction have not been changing in response to the altered situation and to the needs of the growing body of reluctant students. For many of these junior and senior high school students, school has provided only a mounting sequence of failures since the third or fourth grade. No one thrives in an atmosphere that offers no rewards. Nevertheless, society insists that these young men and women remain in school for twelve years, waiting for the exit visa of a diploma that often signifies no greater achievement of purpose or skill than these students had six or eight years earlier. The one skill such students are driven to develop is that of emotional withdrawal, to protect themselves from further hurt in the classroom.

There are many serious social consequences of the growing adult population of academic nonachievers. These men and women are *capable* of learning and they need to learn, but the public school has not been meeting their needs. In 1964 the GIP requested and was awarded a five-year grant from the Ford Foundation to explore four aspects of the problem of nonlearning students: School Programs for Academic Nonachievers (SPAN) proposed:

1. To select for training teachers who were both willing and able to work with students for whom school has been at best a meaningless, continually failing experience
2. To prepare these teachers in a way that might lead to greater success for the nonachiever
3. To help teachers develop new curricular materials and techniques for working with the nonachiever, since the traditional curriculum clearly has been failing
4. To help the SPAN intern teachers to modify the school and community environments, because both have often contributed to the failure of many students

Each year from 1964 to 1968, fifteen of the ninety interns in the GIP were assigned to the SPAN Program. In 1968–69, the last year of the Program, thirty of the total of seventy interns were involved in SPAN.

Selection

How were the SPAN interns chosen? Initially, they were selected by the same screening procedure that has already been described for all GIP intern teachers. In addition, even before their entry into teaching, most of the SPAN interns had been involved in service to the community. Some had worked in the urban ghetto as tutors or playground directors, some in the Peace Corps or in VISTA; all of them specifically chose to work with students whose academic history was heavily marked with failure. Wherever they had worked, these men and women perceived that better education offered some hope for the solution of community problems while the lack of learning threatened to worsen them.

Thus the SPAN interns differed from the other interns of the years 1964–69 chiefly in the extent of emphasis they were to place on the needs of the previously unsuccessful student. Final selection of those who would be identified with the SPAN Program was made by the school administrators who hired them to teach in districts where there were large numbers of "difficult" students.

The fundamental pattern according to which SPAN interns were led to develop each year was the same as that of the other interns of that year. The editor of this collection of classroom strategies, Mrs. Mildred McClosky, has had primary responsibility during the past six years for the intern teachers' curriculum. The table of contents for this volume provides a broad look at the sequence of concerns to which the GIP staff has regularly addressed itself in the lectures, readings, and seminar meetings for its first-year teachers:

ONE. Coping
    I. In the Beginning
    II. Recurrent Early Teaching Problems
TWO. Evolving Processes of Instruction
    I. Inductive Approaches: Inquiry, Discovery, Concept-Building
    II. Creativity: Process and Products
    III. Grouping for Instruction
    IV. Students as Teachers—of Peers, of Younger Students, of Themselves
    V. Dramatizing Devices: Improvisational Drama, Role Playing, and Games
    VI. Uses of Media and Technical Equipment
    VII. Teaching for Values, Concerns, Attitudes
THREE. Developing New School Programs and New Public School Models
    I. New School Programs
    II. New Public School Models

From the start of the Graduate Internship Program in 1956, interns have been encouraged to explore new ways of adapting their materials and techniques to the needs of their current students, and supported in their self-analysis by sympathetic and responsive attention from staff members and from their fellow interns. This self-conscious diagnostic teaching is part of the continuing pattern of instruction in the GIP. While every intern is a teacher, he is also a learner: he shares his experiences with the staff member who supervises his work in the classroom, and with the other interns in the daily seminars of the pre-internship summer and in the bimonthly seminars of the internship year. He learns to seek and welcome critical evaluation and positive suggestions, testing his own and others' ideas in relation to the specific classroom setting where it is to be used. This is the essence of an internship.

Techniques and Materials

While SPAN interns followed the same general curriculum as did other interns in the years from 1964 to 1969, they also enjoyed some important additional services and opportunities, thanks to the Ford Foundation grant. One major service throughout this period was the generous guidance of Mrs. Esmar Clark, a reading specialist whose many years of teaching experience provided invaluable insights into the reading difficulties of the slow learner. In 1965, Al Cunningham, an artist and musician, and Charles Morrison, director of a local theater group, helped a number of SPAN interns to use music and drama as vehicles for teaching communications skills and American history in particular.

Several times during the SPAN years it was possible to bring Dr. Elliott Shapiro, well-known New York school administrator, to share his experiences in the New York City schools and his plans for rescuing students otherwise "Marked for Failure." Mrs. Anne Hornbacher, an intern of the class of 1963, who had participated in experimental summer programs in Philadelphia and Berkeley, worked closely with many interns in exploring the uses of dramatic improvisation to open students to learning.

Especially significant for the SPAN interns were the opportunities in 1966 and 1968 to teach in experimental summer schools in Emeryville and Richmond. These schools were specifically designed to modify the usual secondary school curriculum offerings in response to student needs, and to experiment with classroom techniques that would encourage and involve the reluctant learner. These summer school experiences provided the springboard for a considerable number of the "strategies" that were to be retested, polished, and finally included in this collection.

From the start of the SPAN program, Dr. Jeanne Block, clinical psychologist at the University of California, Berkeley, was attached to the staff as a counselor for the interns and on occasion for their students. Dr. Block was also responsible for devising techniques to evaluate the success of the experimental summer programs and some of the new programs in ongoing school settings.

There are broad variations among these SPAN proposals for helping the teacher to teach and the student to learn. Recurrent in all of them, however, is the value they impute to the individual student, the opportunity they provide for students to become involved in their own learning. The learner's enjoyment of his achievement and the expansion of his competence depend to a large extent on his control of the learning situation. Many of the SPAN interns' strategies develop ways in which the learner becomes self-directed and exploratory in the school setting. In such a role the student is able to internalize his experience; he truly learns.

In many ways, efforts are made to recognize the individual student as a worthy individual. The contract plan sets him up in a one-to-one relationship with the teacher. The variety of groupings helps him perceive himself as a significant member of a group, and helps the teacher distinguish the individual student and recognize him in several possible relationships. The student's self-image grows out of this reciprocity of recognition.

These written accounts of teaching experiences are mature developments from the regular pattern of oral exchange and assessment that characterized the SPAN seminars. The seminars provided a pattern for the kind of cooperative communication that SPAN interns especially hope to follow with the other teachers in their schools, to help build an atmosphere of mutual concern on behalf of all their students. Two of the readings in this book, "Opportunity

High: Getting It Together" and "Community High School" (strategies 89 and 91), describe new school programs developed by SPAN interns to achieve such a school environment.

The SPAN interns have already made significant contributions to the strength of their own schools and shown the way for many other school districts concerned about the problems of the nonachieving students. In keeping with Clark Robinson's philosophy for the good teacher, we can expect that these interns will continue to appear in their dual roles, as both teachers and as learners.

PART ONE

Coping

Under present circumstances, vigorous, alive, intelligent, and socially committed young people often find the schools lonely and intellectually barren places. The social norm which prevails is to treat one's fellow teachers, new or experienced, in a friendly but nonintervening manner. In the first place, the beginning teacher is ordinarily assigned a full teaching load and rarely sees his colleagues except for a brief nod in the corridor or for a few minutes of casual conversation in the cafeteria. In some schools it is still the boiler room which serves as the only forum....[1]

When I speak about the teacher who is new on the job I would like, with the Psalmist, to 'Sing a new song'—a song that expresses the beginner's freshness and anticipation as he ventures into the untried. I would of course have to include in it some old refrains, because the newcomer, in addition to his unique perplexities, shares some basic concerns with veteran teachers. But old or new, these concerns have a special urgency when the beginner puts himself on trial.... The beginner sees himself as on trial before his pupils...on trial before his colleagues and supervisors.... The beginner is mostly on trial before himself, and this is likely to be the toughest trial of all....[2]

Teachers are essentially alone with their problems, not necessarily because they prefer it that way, but primarily because it is not part of the traditions of the

[1] Robert J. Schaefer, *The School as a Center of Inquiry* (New York: Harper & Row, Publishers, 1967), p. 64.
[2] Arthur T. Jersild, "Behold the Beginner," *The Real World of the Beginning Teacher,* Report of the Nineteenth National Teacher Education Professional Standards Conference, New York, June 1965 (Washington, D.C.: National Education Association, 1966), p. 43.

school setting for the staff to meet, present, and critically evaluate their different problems and the ways they handle them. . . . Our work in the public school has made us painfully aware of just how alone a teacher can feel within the school setting. This is true of all teachers, but it is particularly apparent in new or first-year teachers. . . .3

The particular teaching tasks we have selected for consideration in this opening section, *Coping,* are the basic survival problems that besiege new teachers and must be worked through before more sophisticated instructional challenges can be met: How do you get students into their seats after the bell rings? How do you get them to keep quiet without acting like a policeman? What do you do with the kids who obviously hate being in school? How can you possibly plan effective lessons for 150 students daily? What do you do about grades for all of them? Can you get *any* help from your colleagues? These are the perplexing, embarrassing questions new teachers need to ask. Establishing discipline; resolving inner conflicts about freedom, authority, responsibility; organizing for instruction of six classes daily; teaching slow or resistant students; evolving a feasible evaluation system—such problems can overwhelm new teachers who, fearful of exposing early inadequacies, characteristically hesitate to ask their colleagues for help when they need it most. Probably never before have they felt so vulnerable or so alone.

We are hoping that these candid reports of beginning teachers who have met and solved some of these early teaching problems may provide comfort and clues for other neophytes. Somewhat arbitrarily, we have divided this section into two chapters: "In the Beginning" and "Recurrent Early Teaching Problems."

I. In the Beginning

We open appropriately with a paper entitled "In the Beginning," a long, sensitive narration by Winifred Giannini of the staggering classroom control problems which she, a tenderhearted white teacher in an all-black ghetto junior high school had to overcome before anything resembling teaching could occur. Having survived, she offers sensible precautions for new teachers. We turn next to Marilyn Johnson Hershdorfer's "Handbook for the Disorganized," addressed to incoming senior high school teachers. It is a compilation of practical ideas for running classes efficiently, including specific suggestions for basic classroom rules and procedures (use of folders, notebooks, homework, handling of late arrivals, make-up work, etc.), as well as some valuable counsel for planning and pacing instruction. Like Mrs. Giannini, Marilyn Hershdorfer has learned all this the hard way.

We follow these strategies with "Discipline Problems?," a cogent warning by science teacher June Masters, who also teaches in a difficult inner-city school. She warns against blaming students for discipline problems which may arise from the teacher's early anxieties and inability to motivate students. Carole Lurie further points out that in most classrooms little significant learn-

3 Seymour B. Sarason, et al., *Psychology in Community Settings* (New York: John Wiley & Sons, Inc., 1966), pp. 54, 89.

ing seems possible until some degree of rapport is established between students and teacher, and among the students themselves. Sometimes this process takes disastrously long. In her strategy paper, "The Interview," Mrs. Lurie describes her quick and effective plan for (1) bringing order into the classroom; (2) getting students to participate more purposefully; (3) helping teachers and students become acquainted with each other; and (4) finally, creating a community spirit in the classroom.

II. Recurrent Early Teaching Problems

With the first overwhelming concerns out of the way, the teacher continues to face other hurdles. Leading discussions so that more than the usual eager few participate; motivating recalcitrant or defeated students to see some value in academic subjects; encouraging bright but lazy students to make real use of what they learn; getting all students to follow directions; controlling and planning for difficult days and hours (such as Friday afternoon, or the day before a holiday, or the last period of any day); grading and evaluation; working cooperatively with colleagues—these remain continuing challenges for all teachers, especially for beginners.

In this section we have included a series of approaches that thoughtful new teachers have taken to one or more of these recurrent teaching problems.

Handling Discussion and Encouraging Oral Work

Classroom discussion frequently presents a huge challenge for new teachers. Often, eager beginners ask and then answer their own questions. Fearing lack of response, they may actually prevent discussion. The first two strategies we have included here ("Getting the Teacher to Shut Up" and "The Art of Discussion") suggest several ways to draw students into more productive classroom interaction, by reversing the usual balance of teacher to pupil talk, and by providing sufficiently stimulating experiences first.

Evaluation Problems

The way courses are presently set up, grading and evaluation present disturbing problems in many classrooms. Some teachers may use grades as weapons or rewards, depending upon their view of man, and others, nonauthoritarian in philosophy, may hate to grade so much that they end by neglecting all evaluation of student's progress. New teachers, especially, are uncertain about the role evaluation plays for their students. They don't know if students really care about grades. They are confused about whether or not grades should be based more on achievement than on effort, and what they can do about the natural differences in students' ability, speed, or persistence. Ultimately, they want to know how they can lead students toward evaluating themselves.

With all these questions still open, it is often hard to know for whom the grading period is more traumatic, the students or their teachers. As a help to new teachers, we have included here two strategies which describe the typical pitfalls new teachers encounter and then offer several guidelines for ways to avoid them.

In a paper that three subsequent groups of interns now have found especially useful, "A Suggestion for the Constructive Use of Grades," Marcia Perlstein explains how her early fallacious assumptions about the unimportance of grades were exploded. Teaching students in a "Work Studies" program at an urban continuation high school,[4] she found that even with nonacademic students grades were of great significance. She also discovered that teachers must recognize what grades mean to their students, and that students need to know exactly how to earn the grades they desire.[5]

Still other difficult questions remain: how, for example, can a teacher guard against purely subjective grading in aesthetic fields? Should grades be used to reward the talented, lethargic students while punishing less talented but hard-working ones? In "Self-Evaluation in an Art Class," Andrea Fisher, noting the vast differences between students' talents and their industriousness, explains the evaluation scheme she devised to reward students for their efforts as well as their abilities.

Problems of Friday Afternoons

Most teachers recognize that Friday afternoons, the day before a holiday, or the last period of any day are especially difficult for teachers and their students. In "Planning for Friday Afternoons," Carolyn Muska describes a number of planned activities which can make these dreaded times both pleasurable and profitable.

Working Cooperatively with Colleagues

In a strategy called "Developing Intradepartmental Coordination," Cheryl Volmert suggests perhaps one of the most effective but infrequently practiced methods yet known for coping with recurrent teaching problems—namely, joining one's colleagues in sharing ideas, problems, resources, and devising a "division of labor" for meeting common instructional objectives.

Teaching Nonacademic Students

Daniel N. Fader, in *Hooked on Books*, observes:

In the many public schools I have visited in the past five years, the song of success has always had one part a dirge and one chorus the same: We believe we are reasonably successful in the first three grades with most of our children; we know we are doing moderately well with our bright students at almost all levels and better than that in our college-preparatory and advanced placement

---

[4] In California, "continuation school" is the designation given to high schools set aside for students who attend part-time while they work, or for those students who for a variety of reasons could not get along in their regular high school. California has compulsory education through age eighteen or until high school graduation.

[5] Judy Bebelaar (see "The Soul Searchers," strategy 25) was Miss Perlstein's co-teacher for this group. Together they worked out the evaluation system described by Miss Perlstein.

work. But our handling of the general student varies from bad to shocking. We need help. Where can we get it? We need help. . . .[6]

From the loud complaints we hear from one end of the nation to the other, our public schools have obviously not been meeting the needs of non-academic students—more than half of the high school population! New programs, new approaches of all kinds—especially career-oriented ones—are desperately needed, and will eventually be instituted. Meanwhile, for all teachers the greatest teaching challenge lies in providing effective instruction for students who have found little value in school before. We include here several strategies describing the initial efforts and responses of beginning teachers who valiantly tried to meet this challenge head-on.[7]

MOTIVATING NONACADEMIC STUDENTS THROUGH FIELD TRIPS. Biology teacher Joan James was determined from the beginning to make biology intriguing and worthwhile for her less academic "basic" students (as they are labeled in her suburban, college-oriented high school). In her strategy, "Motivating Underachieving Students in a Biology Class," she describes one of her most successful approaches—an all-day field trip to the College of Marin's Marine Biology Laboratory in Bolinas, California. Mrs. James' excursion plan is a concrete example of the instructional procedures that should be taken before, during, and after field trips—if they are to become motivating learning experiences.

READING PROBLEMS. In "Skill in Reading Math," Mike Hall takes on another huge problem in teaching nonachievers: that is, the basic help that many students may need in reading their assigned materials. Assistance with reading cannot be confined to remedial reading or English classes alone. The reading project Mr. Hall devised for his math class could well serve as a model for teachers of other high school subjects. His strategy also contains excellent suggestions for helping all students accept greater responsibility for their own progress.

STRUCTURE. In "Math for the Disadvantaged," Gary Wagner makes a plea for the importance of over-all structure and clear-cut intermediary goals in teaching nonachievers. He found that his early attempts to "provide novelty and avoid routine" were depriving many of his students of the direction and day-to-day achievement which they sorely needed.

APPEAL OF HIGH-STATUS SUBJECTS. Convinced that achieving success in academic subjects makes a substantial difference in nonachievers' attitudes toward themselves and toward school, Jeff Luebbert in "Algebra for Non-achievers" relates how he discarded the usual low level "busy work" given to such students. Starting with what they already knew and carefully guiding them further, he ended by convincing them not only that they could do difficult

---

6 Daniel N. Fader and Elton B. McNeil, *Hooked on Books* (New York: Berkeley Publishing Corporation, 1968), p. 33.

7 Numerous approaches for teaching nonachievers appear throughout the collection of strategies. As Mrs. Ruth Mandelbaum, coordinator of the SPAN Project, points out in her introductory essay, the Graduate Internship Program's five-year SPAN project was dedicated to finding more appropriate curricula and programs for nonacademic students. (See index for entire list of SPAN strategies included in this publication.)

math—the kind usually reserved for college preparatory students—but that they could do it well.[8]

TEST-TAKING. English teacher Diane Wittenberg tackles another recurrent problem for nonacademic students—their attitudes toward tests and their lack of sophistication about ways to take them. Mrs. Wittenberg's paper, "Getting Kids to Follow Directions," contains a description of a unit she devised to help her slower students understand the vocabulary, the mechanics, and the procedures of test-taking.

Although teachers must continually cope with all the basic classroom problems, we hope that some of the ideas and suggestions we have touched upon here may help and reassure beginning teachers through the period of their greatest loneliness and anxiety so that they can confidently set out to create their own improvements and innovations.

[8] William Johntz, Director of SEED (Special Elementary Education Program for the Disadvantaged) in Berkeley, makes this point forcefully in his accounts of the benefits of the discovery approach, especially for the disadvantaged.

1: IN THE BEGINNING

June Masters, science teacher at Castlemont High School, Oakland, California, begins her class in physiology.

In the Beginning

Part I: Fall 1967

Military terms are the most appropriate to describe my first six weeks at H_____ Junior High. The only other time I have had to summon up courage to meet each new day because of circumstances I could not control was during the London Blitz.

The worrisome specific part of my problem had to do with my own feelings toward the children. I was horrified to find that at times I felt violent about them, and felt that if I had a baseball bat I would crack a few skulls. I hated the violence that the children showed to each other, and yet here I was feeling the same way. It did not help to be told by a faculty member to whom I gave a lift one night that I would end up hating minority children as he had after fourteen years of teaching. In the peace of my own home at night I would remember what life in the ghetto was like for these children, and I returned the next day.

So many external factors complicated the situation. The classes were large and all D track students. The room was in the basement, no daylight, and ugly huge pipes crossing the ceiling. Children cutting classes hid down there. They would bang on the door, or open the door and put off the lights. In the Stygian darkness that ensued I was lucky if only a bloodcurdling scream occurred; I was often unlucky, and books, papers, pencils, and anything movable would fly around the room.

Of course, I had made important initial mistakes. I did not make seating charts. I wanted to "know" the children first, so I had to call roll. Six people would answer each name. I tried to reason, but could not be heard above the laughter and noise. It was not until after a GIP seminar that I realized that "where they were at" applied to discipline as well as learning.

I worried about how much time was spent on discipline and how little on teaching. Not only all my waking thoughts, but my dreams were taken up by my problem. I was losing weight and life had lost its savor. If I felt this way, how could I possibly do these children any good? It did me no good to be comforted by a very friendly faculty. The fact that every teacher had gone through such trials the first year made it sound like a prison sentence to me. I decided to give it one more week. My ego would be bruised, and I felt I was letting down people who had faith in me, but I hated that feeling of dread when I awoke in the morning.

My "last" week began like all the others. One class had been sheer hell. I drove home across the bridge, and as so often before I was turning onto Market Street not even remembering passing through the toll booth, when a rage began to burn me up. I awoke next morning feeling almost eager to face that first madhouse of a class. I felt icy angry. I got to my class early and greeted each child as he came in. It was like magic. The children had seen me angry before, but an emotional, hot anger that died very quickly. This was different, and all but four boys realized it. After one cold warning these four were sent out on referral. I announced that I was a teacher, and that I *would* teach them.

I still wince inside when I think of how grateful the children were for the order in the classroom. They had to wait so long for me to get it.

Please do not think that there is always

perfect order in my classes. There is not, but I feel that there will never again be the complete disorder that was causing me to dislike the children. It is no more in my nature to be icy than it is possible for me to say that the children now have an understanding of why they are in school. But I *have* started to teach. This beginning was speeded along by the theatrical device of *deus ex machina*.

Two girls had been muttering insults across the room at each other. I had managed to keep them quiet during class time, but after class a really vicious fight began in the hall. I could not get that fight out of my mind. Next day I asked that class why the fight began, and why there was so much fighting at H_____. For forty-five minutes they talked of the rules of the fighting game. Next day I brought a tape recorder to class, and I now have a very revealing tape on the image of H_____ as a school of "bad" kids, and their own acceptance of being no good because they go there.

After the taping session I got cooperation when I wanted to do something unfamiliar. I was able to take my "worst" two classes to the library to do research on the problems the newly liberated colonies had in writing a constitution. The library staff was very helpful, and the children tried hard to do the work, but were so frustrated by lack of skill.

A delightful incident occurred in one class. I had had to "sell" Georgia when assigning the states, but the girl who had Georgia did a good job. The day the delegates met in class to discuss a constitution, I had taken a pomegranate from a boy. At the end of class it was missing from my desk. "Georgia has it," I was told. Laughing, the delegate from Georgia took it from her pocket. "What do you expect?" she said. "After all, Georgia was started by thieves."

In looking back I feel that it did not take much to bring about the improvement. I shudder when I think how close to giving up I came. I think a brand new teacher in this kind of school should be forearmed as much as possible. "Discipline problems" is vague. You need a blow-by-blow description of what it means. I still cannot think of that first week in detail. It is too painful. And the paperwork! The "cut" slips, the tardies, the adds and drops, the messages from the office that have to be read im-

mediately and signed just when you have got the class settled. These things served to confuse me further.

I just want to add that you do not have to be a masochist or in need of psychiatric help to survive. Even during that horrible first week there was always contact with children outside of the classroom, or a talk with a relative as bewildered by the child as you, who gave a background of rejection and horror right out of the Moynihan report that reinforced my feeling that teaching these students was worthwhile.

As I become more proficient I am sure my children will get something meaningful out of school.

Part II: You Gonna Be Here Next Year?—Spring 1968

Advice to New Teachers

Before you read this section you must read *The Way It Spozed to Be* by James Herndon.[1] It was written about the school I teach in. The description of the faculty is no longer accurate for the book was written ten years ago. But if you take the children of the book and imagine some of the changes, such as daily violence, black militancy, etc., and the influence on the children of West Oakland you will have the feel of the children. The teacher's response to all this is as true today as it was when James Herndon wrote it.

I am sorry that the author is not still at our school. I am sorry he could not answer "Yes" to the question "You gonna be here next year?" I am amazed that I am still around to be asked the question.

No matter how much you read about a ghetto school, it is not until that door closes on you at 8:40 that first morning and you face forty lower track children alone that it means something to you. Baiting the new teacher is a very real part of that first day, and the game is played in earnest. It has to be won by the teacher or it becomes part of the curriculum.

Please keep an open mind while you read this. You are not going to agree with me. I know because I did not like it when I was told these things. I had faith in myself. You need

[1] New York: Simon and Schuster, 1965.

the faith (oh, how you need the faith), but you will not make it by faith alone. The schools seemed to be failing more and more. But teachers can fail children, too.

Find Out "Where They Are"

We accept "where they are" academically, and very soon we are forced to accept "where they are" behaviorally, but there is another very, very important "where they are" and that is the way they see the role of the teacher. There is a way a teacher is "spozed to be," and, like the administration, the children believe you should be able to manage your classroom. That initial baiting period is to see how "good" a teacher you are. They have been in school quite a few years. This is a structure they know. You cannot change these rules and values for the child overnight, any more than you can change attitudes and prejudices of adults overnight. You must work with their expectations; otherwise, in the long run the damage to the children will be as great as your own frustration. Remember, the teacher can always leave—and they do—but the child must go to school.

Establish Order from the First Day On

Every book on classroom management tells you to establish discipline from the very first day. This is hard to do. When you know where you will be, go to the school as often as you can. Talk to any and everyone who is there. Get your list of students as soon as you can. Show this list to other teachers if they are there. Ask them to help with a seating chart if they know the children. All teachers in a ghetto school know that the first year is very difficult and they will help, but you have to ask. They are very aware that each teacher is unique, and they won't give advice until asked. If there are no teachers to give advice, then arrange your seating chart alphabetically or boy-girl alternately. It does not matter how you do it; you will change it later. When the bell rings introduce yourself—name only—then immediately announce you will take roll by seating chart. I was once told not to smile for the first six weeks. I was shocked, but I will try next September.

Your next job is to decide the rules of your classroom. There are definite school rules about gum chewing, radios, profanity, but these are universally ignored. You must make up your mind which ones you can enforce, and enforce them from the beginning consistently. Gum chewing, for me, is unimportant, and I saw an experienced teacher lose the battle.

I would advise you not to worry about giving out books the first day. Order composition books, count out how many for each row, and stand watching as they are passed back. Then do the same with pencils that you have sharpened. Then dictate the rules firmly. Answer no questions. Just dictate, "Rule One, etc." Walk around making sure that they are being written down. Cover everything that may impede the establishment of an atmosphere for learning.

Have the Class Know the Rules and Standards for Classroom Behavior

Please, please, please spend time on the rules of the class. If you are going to an assembly, how is it to be done? How are books to be collected? The floor will be littered after each class. This may seem a small thing, but the ghetto schools are not beautiful, and you will be amazed how depressing litter can be. The children in the afternoon will complain bitterly about the dirty room even as they throw more paper on the floor. I hand the basket around and have each child pick up the paper at his feet.

Dictate these rules every day for at least a week. Our best disciplinarian (who also has a wonderful rapport with her students) told me that she has spent as much as three weeks on the rules with seventh graders. She acts them out, showing the children, for example, that being seated when the bell rings does not mean sliding into your seat. When she told me this last year I thought naively "three weeks wasted." Because I did not listen to her I have wasted weeks and weeks if you add up all the time I have spent (and still do) because I did not start right. I was able to pull up a little this year by announcing that when they returned to school after Christmas not only would there be a new year, but a new Giannini. But you cannot recoup fully.

Find out how the school handles children who have to be sent out. Even if these rules are clear, the students will test to see how much you as a new teacher will stand before you send them out. "Send out the troublemakers," teachers will tell you. Although it is better if you can handle it in the classroom, do not hold the children in the class if too much is happening. It will be understood by the vice-principal, but I suggest that you find time to talk about the behavior with him. Explain that you are establishing rules, and I am sure he will be cooperative.

I find that my troublesome students do not like their parents to be called. I have a desk calendar, and if I have trouble with a student I write down his name and the phone number against it. He will say, "Call my mother. I don't care." I say nothing, but if he calms down then I know I have an ally in his mother. Take a moment to get the phone number of any child who gives trouble. The parents are usually very cooperative in our school, but if the child comes back after school to beg you not to call, check with another teacher. I have two students whose parents "do not know when to stop," in the words of an aide.

Consult Other Teachers

Use your fellow teachers, especially those who are in their second or third year. There is a lot of help in our school, and the helpers were waiting to be asked, but I had to overcome the difficulty of feeling that *I* ought to be able to do it.

Think of Your Students

A word about the children. They are an exciting, vibrant, and delightful bunch, but discipline is their crutch, and without it you can actively dislike them. You will feel a sense of outrage when one of your greatest troublemakers tells you with real anger, "I'm gonna get outa your class. We ain't learning nothing— it's too noisy." One of my students who was sent to continuation school for five months returned to me last week.

"You still here?" he asked me.

"Why shouldn't I be?" I asked.

"I thought they would have kicked you out 'cos your classes is so noisy." This was not said maliciously. This is how he saw me as a teacher. And I wish I could convey the sound of kit-tenish purring in the voice of one of my tough girls as she said to me the other day, "You so mean, Mrs. Giannini. You was so nice once."

One last word. You are "authority." Please use it. You are an adult. You may be the only adult that this child has close contact with. They live with chaos and real violence. The racial tension hits them very hard. They hear anti-white talk and tell you they hate whites. They don't always mean it.

If you work in the ghetto, you too will see violence in your classroom. But you are an adult, and though you may be unable to do much about the outside of your classroom, you determine how much stability there is inside that room.

When I have to write a paper, I feel a little like a front-line soldier who is told to stand inspection all polished up for a visiting general. I think of the mountains of words we have on this subject. I have come to the conclusion that maybe we know too much. I think the danger is that we can immobilize ourselves. A doctor in a big city emergency room is useless if he is so horrified by what has happened to the miscellaneous victims he sees that he cannot give life-saving plasma. I feel that I have shown my concern by *being* there. I see the results of ghetto living; now I must try to give the plasma, using everything I know.

Teachers who stay at our school have a pride of their own. They survived the first year, learned by it, and returned to teach. They rephrase George Bernard Shaw's "those who can, do; those who can't, teach," as "Those who can teach in a ghetto school, do; those who can't, leave and write a book about it."

Publishers now will move to another field since the ghetto school has been well covered, but the ghettoes still need teachers—good ones. Teachers who *can* teach—"cos that's the way it spozed to be."

One Year Later

Looking back to September of my second year, I realize that the fact that it *was* my second year helped immensely. I knew what to expect. I knew that the children are not used to and do not have any security in a permissive

Mrs. Winifred Giannini, now reading specialist at Herbert Hoover Junior High School, Oakland, California.

classroom, so I became highly structured. However, I feel there is another very important component of this second year. I cannot prove it, and you cannot measure it by any test, but I am sure it is there. This important factor is that the children already know who you are. They saw you around school last year. Since you are back again, you are evidently a "real" teacher. Even though I was told several times in each class, "My brother had you last year, but you're not like what he said," I know it speeded my acceptance.

Because I *was* able to teach from the first week, I was able to introduce creative activities. All my classes tried their hand at turning an African myth into a play and acting in it, and one class turned out a newspaper *without my help*.

In all classes we discussed expectations. They wrote what they expected from a good teacher, and I explained fully what I expected from them. I told them my expectations were very

high, and in spite of grumbling at how hard I worked them, they caught the spirit.

Our eighth grade reading teacher resigned at the end of the first semester, and I became the reading teacher. Instead of a basement room I now have a clean, modern portable, and I work with small groups of children.

A few weeks ago a colleague who teaches social studies and is going through new teacher trials told me that there were several children in his classes who were really interested in government, and who would benefit from a more in-depth treatment than he could give in his classroom situation. A day or so later a visitor told us he had really turned on some dropouts when he asked them to read *Animal Farm*.

This gave us an idea. We started a seminar in my portable at lunch time. We gave the group no name. It had few rules. You borrowed or bought the book to be discussed, and everyone contributed to the discussion. No free rides.

If you could not talk about the book you were not welcome; however, anyone could come. We started with five or six, and after a few days we had ten.

Everyone contributes as they munch on their hot dogs, and they amaze each other as well as the two teachers with their insights into the problem of man governing himself. To read *Lord of the Flies* was a natural when we saw how well they understood *Animal Farm.* And now that the pattern is set the children choose their own books. Our current book is Richard Wright's *Black Boy.*

Because of their own observations, we have been able to point out to our group the writer's use of plot, theme, point of view, symbolism, and the different levels of reading, and we are wondering if we could possibly develop an inter-disciplinary team-teaching course next year. We have already had to switch the club from lunchtime to after school because children who did not have the same lunchtime wanted to join.

I do not want this to sound like the happy ending in a fairy tale. It is not. There are many, many days when the enormity of the problems that schools face makes me wonder if it is worthwhile. But during my first year I did not dream a year like this one was possible.

If I can learn as much in every succeeding year I may be close to being the teacher I would like to be in about five years.

MARILYN JOHNSON HERSHDORFER 2

Handbook for the Disorganized

Beginning the Year

I'm a very young, naive-looking girl, small, and I have a way of acting "soft" around my students, so they have told me. Nevertheless, I might have gotten away with this "image" at the beginning of the year but for a further disadvantage: I am by nature extremely disorganized. After creating bedlam in two of my classes the first semester, I have by this time (end of May) pulled myself, my students, and my English course into a profitable working atmosphere. By now my students come to class prepared to work; we share at least the illusion that we are "accomplishing something"; and, most of all, I have time now to enjoy a fuller outside life so that most days I can come to school fresh and enthusiastic.

Because I'm feeling so much happier and excited about my classes, and because I'm looking forward to being a really good teacher next year, I feel that the simple organizational and psychological devices that have painfully evolved in my classes are perhaps more important and useful for a beginning teacher than are more sophisticated educational philosophies.

The most important point I could possibly make is the need for structure in the classroom. The students, despite all their complaints, crave it and are reassured by it; it saves the teacher much unprofitable wear and tear. It was a mystery to me at first why my Spanish classes were running more smoothly than my English classes, and why the students were more cheerful and responsive though the subject matter and daily drilling were much less exciting than the materials for English. I learned later that it was because the students adjusted to, counted on, and then could build upon the rigid structure of the course. English can be such a nebulous, all-encompassing field that it is much harder for the student to achieve a sense of the course and a sense of his ability to cope with the subject. Without this sense of participation in a particular, well-defined course—whether he likes the subject matter or not—the student will remain dissatisfied and restless.

A more experienced teacher with a good reputation might, and hopefully does, arrange his course according to his own precepts from the first day of class. After the first wave of stunned silence or wild enthusiasm, the student will settle down to work. The important element is, again, defining clearly the limitations and possibilities of the course. There are some "freedom" classes at my school involving total student responsibility which are showing some good results. But I believe that it is the extremely presumptuous beginning teacher (as I was) who thinks he has the clearly defined goals and methods necessary to begin such a project without bungling it half way through.

I think I'll begin next year by outlining a relatively structured course, and then gradually I'll begin moving to a new emphasis on my particular interests. On the first day I will mention the key traditional activities which students consider to be "English": book reports, spelling, grammar, objective quizzes to check up on reading assignments. Also I'll mention a string of books we'll be reading, to impress them with how much we'll be doing. (The list can, of course, be changed later.)

As a contrast, I spent the first quarter this year and much of the second quarter on descriptive writing projects, some difficult short stories (but very good stories from a collection called *Great American Short Stories*), and philosophical discussions related to the stories. The students kept complaining that they weren't doing "English." Apparently they are used to judging their progress by a series of book reports, dashed-off essays, and completed units in the anthology. When I finally began to teach sentence structure in the third quarter one boy remarked, "I didn't know you knew what a predicate was!" I have found since that it is easier and more effective at first to prompt original thinking and writing through more traditional guises.

Also, in those strategic first few days, I would list clearly a few handy rules to cover situations that can really mushroom later. A caution: You will immediately put yourself on the defensive by mentioning traditional disciplinary problems such as arriving tardy or talking out of turn.

The students are well aware of these rules and expect you to deal with breaches of them quickly. But, by all means, send a student out at the first hazy indication of sassiness or insubordination. By always waiting for the action to become overt, I allowed other students a great opportunity to subtly test me. Once you allow the "insubordination" to spread, you are lost. After the first week or so, it is usually more effective to establish a system of punishment within your classroom, and to save the dean's office for extreme cases. A satisfactory system for me was to assign half-hour detentions after school in my classroom. The students usually hate this more than the chance to get out of class to visit the dean, and I have to stay at school half an hour anyway. Most of all, it gives me an opportunity to talk with the student about the real problems. A good deal of the most rewarding moments this year have occurred in after-school talks.

The following are some of the rules you should set up at the beginning:

1. *Assigned seating:* You are helpless at first when you don't know names. I let my students choose their own seats for a few weeks so I could check out good working groups and trouble spots. Teach a volunteer to take roll from the seating chart immediately; you simply won't have time. He handles the notation of excused absences and tardy slips as well.

2. *Tardies:* Announce that the roll-taker quietly marks down those who saunter in after the bell has rung. I check the roll book periodically so that habitual latecomers must serve a detention. You have no idea how easily latecomers attract the attention of the class.

3. *Required Materials:* Each student must bring a pencil or pen and the current book every day. Another student quickly looks over the class each period and marks down those who forget the required materials. He distributes "extras" from my desk. Accumulated marks will lower the quarter grade, but if you give "F's" for the day, the student often refuses to work that period.

4. *Homework:* Homework must be in on time. If it is one day late, lower the grade somewhat, and then don't accept any more late papers until a certain date, toward the end of the quarter.

5. *Prompt Beginning:* Students are to be in their assigned seats when the bell rings, with all required materials on their desk: pen, paper, book, folder, or notebook. If this rule isn't enforced, you'll never be able to begin the class period

effectively. While you are struggling to herd students into seats, get them to haul out their books, and quiet them down, others in the class will become restless and begin talking. You have lost your power as the dominating force. It's far more effective to swing the door shut dramatically as the bell is ringing, and have something to say to the class as a whole during the expectant lull. Don't let students fall into the habit of clustering around your desk or confronting you with personal problems until you have had a chance to get the class swinging. Make an announcement, conduct a quick review, anything to make you the leader—then let the class get to work on their five-minute journal entry or short grammar exercises (the reasons for a daily notebook) so that you can issue out-of-class passes, talk to someone, return papers, or quickly review notes for a discussion or short lecture. It's always better to begin class promptly and finish a little early. In a relaxed ten-minute atmosphere at the end of the period, students are always more quiet and orderly than when they first come in; they think about the homework due tomorrow and like to clear up confusions with you, and you may have a chance to relax before the next class comes in.

Planning during the Year

The following procedures, which took me a long, painful time to learn (maybe I'm more disorganized than most people and maybe it simply takes everyone a certain amount of time to work out a smooth-running system), have helped me in three ways. They have:

1. Kept the class running efficiently;
2. Saved me time;
3. Most of all, saved me from the continual pressure I felt at the beginning of the year when I taught from day to day, period to period.

1. *Learn to plan in weekly blocks* as soon as possible, and these weeks will lengthen naturally as you continue. Let's say that I'm coming up through the various "periods" in American literature (students enjoy "finishing" periods) and this week—and perhaps next—I'll be doing Edgar Allan Poe. He will be the loosely held "topic" for the week, and I will try to relate all activities around him: the week's vocabulary words will be "torture words" chosen from his stories; (grouping vocabulary words makes them more fun and they stick—for example "hate" words during the Puritan period); writing exercises during the week will utilize Poe directly as

a model (e.g., ordering detail in a descriptive paragraph like Poe's description of Roderick Usher's study) and for an exercise with style we will work with words that produce "mood" (describe different knocks on doors to produce mood e.g., the knock in Poe's "The Raven" contrasted with a knock by a boyfriend or a fugitive from justice, etc.). You can have discussions on Poe's writing craft (How does he achieve suspense? Unity?), and you can make his stories more topical by, say, showing the importance of emotional effect in modern media. You can bring in related materials. Play a recording of Poe's poetry, contrast mood in two prints or two records. Lastly, a weekly essay might sum up all the week's activities. I had my students "step into" the frame of a factual newspaper article and infuse it with the particular emotional effect they wanted to achieve. In summary, planning in blocks:

a. Saves you time; you can sit down and plan one or two weeks of activity in a concentrated evening;
b. Gives the student lessons in writing skills in a relatively painless way that yet "has a purpose" for him;
c. Channels class discussion constructively;
d. Enables you to plan activities so that no one thing gets monotonous;
e. Allows you to stagger the activities in various periods; trying to conduct the same discussion twice in a day gets very deadly; also, you can plan "rests" for yourself by following a lively class discussion or intense lecture with a writing project;
f. Forces you (this is my problem) to cover the material more efficiently: if I don't see two planned weeks before my eyes, I tend to go on and on with a particular topic;
g. Enables you to make assignments way in advance of date due;
h. Allows you to bring in outside materials before it is too late;
i. Helps you fit in unrelated English activities when convenient, rather than having to shove them into unwieldy corners.

I give diagnostic spelling and grammar tests at the beginning of the year, and these plus weaknesses I spot in themes help me to group students for concentration in various mechanical skills. Students fill up lulls in the period by studying spelling—on their own—for scheduled group tests, or do certain pages of grammar to keep in their class folders to fulfill an eventual requirement. Certain general problems, like sentence fragments and run-ons, I review all year long when I'm stuck for something to do. I keep sets of dittoes for these ready in my drawer. Choice of outside reading for book reports is always limited to the period (or thematic base) of literature we are studying. The reports are oral: For one week, I sit down and talk with a student for five minutes or so about his book when the rest of the class is busy, or I might have a student choose to discuss his book before the class if it ties in with what we are studying. These oral reports (with me or before the class) have been very effective.

2. *The use of folders:* Folders become an essential classroom aid when you learn to plan activities in series or projects. I have found that, once a workable classroom atmosphere has been established, it is most effective to state the requirements to be fulfilled for a given project, and then let the student fill his folder at his own speed. If one assignment isn't completed in class, it automatically becomes homework. The teacher's main job is to structure the project and keep a series of dittoes or materials on hand in the classroom for the relegated periods—and to skim through the completed folders, giving a grade for the entire project. This means a minimum of grading for a maximum of student work. In addition, as I have said before, students enjoy working in terms of projects with goals in sight. The projects are a wonderful break for me: I cease to be the focal point of class activity for a period, and I push the projects to the back of my mind until I have time to grade them. Four folder projects I have done successfully are:

a. A creative writing unit—in which story-writing exercises culminated in writing one's own story;
b. Paragraph organization: I put about thirty photographs around the room (many taken from *Life* magazine's issue on photography) and asked the students to write different types of paragraphs about the pictures, in which details had to be ordered, emotional effect achieved, statements supported by evidence from the picture, and so on;
c. My slow class did grammar exercises which were from an easy workbook—at their own speed; it became a contest which was mapped on a chart: each ten problems equaled one box on the chart, and the winners received prizes as I periodically graded the folders;
d. Daily journal for my "slows": they write about their activities, gripes, opinions, and often a few

weeks of entries will evolve around a particular focus: descriptions in which one of the five senses is especially used, answering teen-age problem letters, writing business letters, and filling in forms.

I've found that for me the best way to teach my slow class is by providing them with a choice of reading, writing, or grammar each day, all to be completed by the end of the week. The slower ones work with one easier novel and answer questions at the end of chapters; the five or six faster students read more advanced novels and do special projects with them. (For example, as fifteen students read Jack London stories, other students read *Light in the Forest* and prepared a debate to present before the class: the white side and the Indian side contested for the right to raise True Son.)

I also use folders in the following ways:

a. My average Juniors keep notes each day—due dates are written down, important notes are taken from my lectures and class discussions, spelling words and vocabulary are listed. I grade these notes.
b. I have a "Past Assignment" folder on my desk for each class; a student who comes in after an absence looks up what he has missed and finds required dittoes in the folder. Without such a folder you will be plagued every day during class with returning students.
c. I keep a "Notes to Myself" folder: As each class files out the door, I jot down where we ended the discussion, announcements to make the next day, papers to ask for, names of persons to be held for detention, and, when I have given a quiz or test, the names of those students who were absent. This is a tremendous help the next day. *I never leave my classroom until this is done.* Using these notes the next day, before school begins, I jot down announcements and the activity for the day for each period on the board so the students will be thinking about the information as I begin class.

3. *Grading:* After much experimentation, I have found that the following procedures seem the most fair and are the easiest for me:

a. *Projects* (collected in folders): one grade for total assignment;
b. *Homework* and brief class exercises: I mark in my book with a quick plus, check, or minus (most are checks) and a few comments;
c. *Tests:* at least one half should be objective ques-

tions, to test knowledge rather than writing ability. If a discussion of ideas is called for, the remaining section should consist of answers of not more than one paragraph. For an average student, an essay test is a frustrating experience, and is usually not a learning experience until he is taught how to write a good essay. This sort of test can be corrected in class by students and the questions discussed at the same time.

d. *Essays*: a student must be *taught* how to write an essay; if you simply assign topics to be written on periodically, the student never really improves writing skills per se. My procedure for teaching essay writing is the following:

1'. Spend a long time on paragraph development.

2'. Make sure the student has been drilled sufficiently in supporting his ideas and narrowing the subject matter.

3'. Spend (at first, at least) the period before an essay is due for in-class writing. The students need individual help.

4'. Require a loose composition plan to be handed in with the essay to make sure the student can identity his topic, central idea, topic sentences, and conclusion.

5'. The following day have each student criticize another's paper by checking off various points on a check list of elements I consider important. This saves me grading time, and helps to make the student a good critic.

Conclusion

I realize that the devices described above may only be useful for my particular personality, interests, and students. I realize also that it is almost impossible to warn a beginning teacher; he seems to learn best through his mistakes. Nevertheless, something here may help someone toward developing his own successful teaching system.

JUNE MASTERS **3**

Discipline Problems?

Background

When I entered Castlemont High School in September, I was still a bit leary about how I was to conduct five classes a day without becoming a policeman. At the briefings the new teachers got before classes began, the emphasis was on discipline problems. (Castlemont was considered a problem school because of its 90 percent black population.) We were enlightened as to what to expect from the students; plans for possible riots were discussed, and we were issued thick booklets of rules and regulations which we were expected to enforce.

I looked at my roll book and discovered that in one class I had 45 students enrolled and in another 39. The smallest class I had contained 30. I also noted that three of the five classes were slow and the other two were average. I knew that the year was going to be a challenge, to say the least. I have been an idealist and an optimist all my life, but now I seriously considered whether I knew what I was doing.

I did not really look forward to school that first day, but there I was, looking into the faces of a sea of students. There was the business of checking in and signing cards and checking to see that students were in the correct classes. We talked a bit about what they expected from biology and my heart sank even further because I discovered that no one really liked biology.

I gave my little speech the second day about how I expected them to behave like ladies and gentlemen and how if that was expecting too much I could just as well treat them as children, but they would not like it. The choice was theirs and they would get the rights and privileges of either group. I went on to say that the class was responsible for the behavior of each member and since they were ladies and gentlemen, they respected themselves as well as each other so that if one person was not acting right the class could bring it to his attention and have him correct the situation or the whole class would be penalized. They weren't too sold on the idea but they went along with it.

The first week went well—getting the clerical details out of the way, finding out about each other, getting them to fill out a questionnaire about their hopes for the future, their past performances, etc., talking about biology in general, and doing observations.

The following week I issued books; BSCS[1] special materials *Patterns and Processes* for the three slow classes and *Elements of Biology* for the other two. To me the *Patterns and Processes* book was extremely boring and I suppose that I communicated it to the students. They became bored and restless. I then discovered why a teacher has discipline problems in her class.

My Solutions to Discipline Problems

I tried punishing, ranting and raving, but that did not help. Then finally it dawned on me that I was at fault; so I tried another avenue of attack. Even though materials were in short supply, I decided to devise more observations, more laboratory experiments, and most important of all, to allow the students to have some responsibility in gathering their own materials. It worked wonders.

Drawing on my intern teaching experience of last summer, I gave ten points for each specimen a student brought in. Soon I was swamped with spiders of all descriptions (students got extra points for identifications and brief synopses of the specimens), frogs, toads, moths, turtles, snakes, lizards, snails, slugs, fishes. The biology room was a hum of activity.

One day I brought in some mice and we spent nearly all day watching the snake eat. It ate six mice. They had to be extremely quiet or the snake would not eat. No one spoke for the entire period and as they left, they cautioned the incoming class against making noise. It was the quietest day I ever had. For their homework assignment, they were required to write a story about a mouse and a snake. The stories were a delight to read; very imaginative and

[1] Biological Sciences Curriculum Study.

humorous. The best story was given a place of honor on the bulletin board.

Another time we were to have a lab in which we were required to examine pond water under the microscope. The students brought in an assortment of water that was alive with all sorts of creatures. The only "noise" that day was the exclamations of delight when they discovered some interesting animals on their slides.

The most exciting experiment of all was when we tested response in some lower animals. I had some brine shrimps and gilaria larvae and snails for the first day of tests. The next day they brought earthworms, fishes, and an assortment of snails and turtles which we tested with electricity, light, chemicals such as salt, weak acid, and weak base. It was a most delightful experience to see them diligently working; when the period ended I could hardly get them to stop.

Then came the moment most of them were waiting for—their first dissection. I explained that the department did not have the money to provide nice juicy earthworms for dissections so we had to use dead ones. Well, next day I had more juicy earthworms than I knew what to do with. More important, they did beautiful dissections, proving to me that they were surgeons and not butchers. I had so many masterpieces that I had much difficulty choosing the winners for the prizes I offered. Not only were their dissections good, but when I gave the practicum exam, everyone was on his toes. Even those who did not like biology were beginning to show some interest. They felt a part of things and so were willing to work. They are becoming more aware that all of these little animals are a part of the same nature in which they are involved. Now they come and ask questions about the little insects and animals they see—and I might add, they see more than they used to. They are more aware of what is going on around them and of how it affects them.

I am not claiming one hundred percent success, but because the students are more involved with their own studies and more in control of what is discussed in class, they are more interested in coming to class, particularly when they come to participate.

Discipline problems? I have very few, if any, because there is a mutual respect between teacher and student, and more importantly, the students are involved in what is going on.

June Masters, leading a class discussion in physiology, Castlemont High School, Oakland, California. (She has few, if any, discipline problems now.)

CAROLE LURIE **4**

The Interview

Problem or Rationale

I teach two classes of medium Freshman English, second and seventh periods. Classes are large, 28 and 34, respectively, so that the largest, most difficult class is seventh period. Students "hated" English and were merely putting in time for the most part. The class, although tracked for medium, represented a wide range of abilities.

Classroom control was a real and present problem. My size (5′ 2″), youth, insecurity, newness, etc., conspired to make adequate con-trol a much sought-after goal. In addition to the problem of control, I wanted to start off with an activity not "Englishy"—students would turn me off very fast if I started with any of the conventional English activities. I also wanted to demonstrate that English is a "gut" subject, a subject which makes one think and feel, and is directly related to the "real" world.

Finally, I needed to buy time. The fact that I did not sufficiently know this age level or their interests meant that I could not plan relevant lessons. I needed a fast way to "psych" out my students.

Goals

Goals are related, of course, to the rationale and include: (1) bringing order; (2) exercising the speaking ability of the students; (3) providing the teacher with information about each student; (4) providing students with information about each other; and (5) providing an activity which would establish feelings of solidarity, continuity, and predictability about classroom procedures and expectations.

Description of the Strategy

Numbers were put in a box and each student picked a number. Since each number appeared on two slips, each student had a partner.

Two students with matching numbers stand before the class. One asks questions, the other answers. Each interview lasts five to ten minutes, and may be followed by questions from the audience when appropriate.

The interviewer uses a list of questions which may be previewed by the teacher. Rules include: no questions should be destructive and the interviewee may refuse to answer by stating "No comment."

Evaluation

I suspect that most of the benefits gained from this exercise cannot be precisely stated, let alone quantified; however, certain impressions remain.

1. Teacher: I thoroughly enjoyed listening to the interviews and learned much valuable information about students. Interviews helped me set a reasonable level of expectation in future lesson planning and, more importantly, helped me to choose relevant materials, insofar as possible. For instance, I learned that students were troubled by an inability to retain written material, and that they wanted to learn to speak before a group, etc.

2. Student: Students almost always enjoyed listening to the interviews, usually enjoyed asking questions, and sometimes even enjoyed answering. By the time the series was over, students were volunteering for additional interviews. I used this excess energy on days when one partner was absent by substituting one of the eager beavers for the absent participant.

The best evidence of increased understanding of self and others was illustrated when interviewers failed to accept the answer "I don't know." Invariably students went on to ask, "Why don't you know?" The answer to that question led to some interesting insight into the person, his background, and his values.

Initially, such questions as "If you could, would you..." would receive a yes or no answer. After brief exposure to interviewing procedures, students were too sophisticated to stop there. They would ask, "Why?" In fact, by the end of the interviews students were fascinated by the answers they received when they asked that very simple question.

Sometimes when answering why, students were forced to question the source of their opinions. Tracing that source back to the original facts—if there were any, and many times there weren't—illustrated to students as no lecture could that intelligent, defensible opinions are based on facts.

The obvious goals were reached. Order was brought to class; students spoke more easily before the group; and we all learned about each other. Incidentally, the teacher had to be interviewed too and play the game by the same rules.

Appendix: Directions for Project

FRESHMAN ENGLISH ASSIGNMENT SHEET

This sheet outlines your assignments for the next few days. Your assignments are twofold:

1. Prepare a list of questions which you will ask a student during your "interview." These questions must be approved by the teacher before your interview. During the interview of others, you will rate the interview. You will give a rating of zero to ten. Ten is highest and is equal to an A, five is equal to C and zero is failing.

Keep your scores and the names of the people on a sheet of paper attached to these directions. Remember: do not ask any question which will embarrass or which is in poor taste.

2. During the interviews, one third of the class will go to the library to gather information from magazines, newspapers, or books for an *oral report*. This report will be delivered to the class at the completion of the interviews. The audience will rate the oral reports. Each student will write the name and score. Again, the range is zero to ten. A committee will grade the oral reports at the end by tallying all the scores.

The oral report will be five minutes long. It will contain information which is useful and informative for the students who listen. Students should use a loud, clear, and pleasant speaking voice; body and hand movements may be used to emphasize points in the talk. The report will be graded in two areas: "Is the information presented in an interesting and effective way?" and, "Is the content of the oral report interesting?"

Five minutes is a long time to fill, so begin work on your oral report immediately. Use your time in the library and practice giving the report at home. Good luck!

II: RECURRENT EARLY TEACHING PROBLEMS

Marcia Perlstein and Judy Bebelaar help their students collect papers for evaluation, Opportunity High School, San Francisco, California. (See "A Suggestion for the Constructive Use of Grades.")

HANDLING DISCUSSION AND
ENCOURAGING ORAL WORK

KAREN DRURY NORRIS **5**

Getting the Teacher to Shut Up

SHUT UP! Would you like to shout this at your class now and then? Maybe you too need to apply this to yourself, as I had to do my first year of teaching. Most of us teachers are devoted to trying to change our students. But sometimes, as in the old proverbs, we need to work on ourselves first.

My strategy was suggested by a valued advisor, Esmer Clark, my supervisor. It is intended to help the beginning teacher give directions, lead discussions, and conduct class with poise and an added degree of assuredness. The strategy consists in simply telling yourself to shut up when you are leading class. Ingenue teachers often explain too much—we even answer our own questions. So the technique is harder to follow than one imagines, but its consequences and rationale are farther reaching and more penetrating than one would guess. "Shut Up" keeps the weeds (tuned out students or discipline problems) down to a minimum in your classroom "garden," and it can also help you root out gigantic beanstalks that have already sprouted.

Situation

I personally applied the strategy out of necessity. I teach high school English (freshmen through juniors) in a small community on the

Sacramento River in the Delta farming region. There are about 450 students in the school and the people there are friendly and not too provincial. I am fairly easygoing so my teaching assumed a somewhat offhanded nature. I had few worries and perhaps was overly familiar with my classes. Also, my student teaching experience was in a reading laboratory, so I had not practiced the give and take which occurs in a normal classroom. Thirdly, I had had only intermittent experiences in speaking before groups and I did not feel I had developed a teaching style.

However, after Christmas I could see that my improvised approach had not been the most efficacious one. Homework assignments did not come in regularly, certain classes were becoming disorderly, and discussions were frequently tedious or trivial. Waiting and continuing did not improve conditions, and I realized that the situation just might be critical.

The Strategy Works

Probably admitting the existence of a serious situation is the first step for correcting any dilemma. Next came analysis, which brought hope and gave me more conviction in taking the actions which Esmer and I deemed necessary. We discovered that my basic problem was a case of an overactive jaw. I talked too much.

Using the Strategy

One step in becoming more objective about my talking was to be observed by others such as Esmer and a school counselor. I also made tapes of my classes. Most important, though, was my journal book in which I logged daily experiences. This gave the whole project a scientific character and allowed me to note trends and to see progress later. Also, to make changes one needs to analyze details and specific events which can only be remembered this way or through the use of tapes—which I did not do often enough. Tapes are painfully honest.

Other approaches were used to remind me of my motto, such as a card on my desk which had "shut up" in Swedish. Before each class, too, I primed myself to be in the correct, sober mood needed—just as a revolutionary would repeat his slogan for courage or as an actor would prepare to go onstage. (In a sense teachers are both.) To keep my sanity I answered personal questions only after the class was underway, and never just before the bell.

As for class discussions, which are fundamentally important in English class, I gained tips from the tape about when to speak and when not to. I had the habit of answering my own questions or of saying "good" to student responses. So my new assignment was to ask a stimulating question and then to wait. Yes, the pressure would grow, but the mistake I had made before was giving up too soon and being overly sensitive. The uncomfortable quiet can actually be a time for thinking; also, I discovered happily that if the teacher outwaits the students, one of the latter will begin speaking. Then, after the discussion ball started bouncing, I was supposed to say "hmm" or "That's interesting," or an encouraging "Yes…" to get others involved. When the teacher says "good" he is making a value judgment and indicating that the answer is satisfactorily completed, which it need never be in many cases. The system of silence really was effective, though it took endurance to initiate it. Sometimes I repeated the question again. If there was not much response after several questions, I would stop the discussion and say, "We will pick this up tomorrow. Be thinking about some ideas for these questions," which showed that I had faith in their ability to eventually answer the questions.

An advantage of the technique was that it helped me evaluate myself and to revamp my questions. No test and no discussion is effective if the teacher tells all the answers. I also began to see more clearly the advantages of planning rather than of talking impromptu so much.

An example of how "Shut Up" can work for giving instructions came at the end of my poetry unit with the juniors. My room was papered with intriguing magazine photos for the class to write poems about. I explained this to them, but when nothing happened I panicked and continued expounding on how they should take ten minutes to look at pictures and formulate an idea. "There are some more pictures on my desk and you should use rhyme and a definite meter since this structure would help you move from one line to the next…" ad infinitum. An observer later said that they had shown interest in the poems and needed a moment to start, but that I had stifled them. With the next class, I made a short statement, presented the pictures, and then simply demanded silence for thinking after the first ten minutes. Good results!

General Results

My "Shut Up" campaign is still in effect. It grows more rewarding daily. My students seem to appreciate the new atmosphere that has been created, and the class runs more smoothly. I do not think that one of them would write today that "There is no control over the class and not enough effort put into the teacher's lectures," as one girl did two months ago. Homework is coming in much more regularly and discipline problems are less flagrantly obvious. Mainly, I listen to my students, and I can enjoy them more.

But the main boon from a "Shut Up" strategy is that it inspires confidence in both the students and the teacher. If the teacher asks a question and then attends a response, he is showing that he believes his students are capable of thinking and of answering; he has faith in them. As the teacher experiences success in bringing about the actions he desires, he becomes surer of himself—and almost everyone needs success to be more effective.

If the teacher keeps still to obtain initial results, then he becomes more confident and feels less threatened, and he can be more natural. He knows that he will be listened to, and talked to, for he knows how to listen himself—and to talk sparingly—and that, my friend, can make *all* the difference.

MARY HICKS **6**

The Art of Discussion

I. Introduction

Discussion, conversation, dialogue, oral participation—call it what you will. My strategy was to develop a particularly quiet, attentive, and terribly serious class into a lively, talkative group. I challenged myself to break down some barriers that had evidently been up for some time.

Last fall, when I first entered my five English classes, I met five combinations of students that made me realize how differently you must approach each class. But I also learned something that startled me. My average students (or the ones placed in the M track, if you will) were *not* reluctant to speak. On the contrary, they were happy to do so, although seldom on the subject. The ones who would *not* talk were my A track, college prep students, juniors looking ahead. They came in each day for fifth period, read their assignments quietly, wrote beautiful papers, and froze up in any attempt at discussion. For several weeks we went on like this, and I began to concern myself with just getting them to talk.

II. Using Individual Projects to Thaw Out Students

The second novel we read together was Hemingway's *The Old Man and the Sea*. The students loved the story, but when I told them that for three days they would be doing special individual projects before the class, they were horror-struck. I gave them great freedom, only suggesting possibilities when asked—write a poem about the sea, draw a picture, do a dramatic reading, find some interesting facts about Hemingway. Do anything as long as you present it to the whole class and talk about it. I worked with anyone who asked for help, but left them alone otherwise. I forced myself not to remind or prod and when the time came, only two students would not participate. The others came up with some great things. One boy, painfully shy, presented a small painting he had done of the old man in his boat. Everyone was so taken with his picture, he later brought other pieces of his work to class and talked about them with much less effort. Two girls had great talent for reading dialects and were very popular with the class. But, above all, I noticed that once the students were up in front, none of them really seemed to mind the spotlight. After the unit was over, we evaluated it, and for the first time there seemed to be an *open* discussion.

I realized soon after that part of the trouble was my *own* seriousness. When my college prep class was there in front of me, I became concerned with teaching them things that were valuable for college English classes. I felt I had to get down to business and be very serious. But the atmosphere was strained and I wasn't getting to know the students as people. Small wonder they didn't want to talk. I didn't, either.

The projects were a step in the right direction. Later in the first semester, when I had them write an evaluation of the class so far, they seemed to agree on one thing—the projects were great.

I watched the papers for editorials and magazines for interesting articles. I brought controversial issues by the score and we discussed them. But, to a great extent, it was still teacher-student question and answer time. They talked to me, *not* to each other. When someone got into an argument or even a discussion with another student, they would be stopped by mean looks from class members who thought I wouldn't like it.

During the semester break, I thought about it a great deal. These kids needed to exchange ideas and not remain in their individual shells, keeping the same opinions and ideas they had always held. They wouldn't challenge each other or me, and I wanted them to know how serious this position was.

III. Trying Debates and Panels as Stimulators for Discussions

In January I took one day and had them decide on a number of topics that concerned them. I told them that we would be organizing debates, panels, and discussions on these topics. At first they listed smoking on campus, student court, cafeteria food, and I let them make the suggestions. But then a boy said, "Those are silly suggestions. We talk about those all of the time. How about something like the draft, something that really concerns us." Then the topics changed to marijuana legalization, gun legislation, birth control pills for unmarried girls under eighteen, and the fairness of the draft. Each person chose the topic he preferred to work on.

The class spent several days in the library, gathering material. They interviewed people, took surveys, and read widely. We scheduled the debates in order to give full class periods to each of them.

The first debate, on the captured *U.S.S. Pueblo,* was a good one, but not very spirited. The next day the class talked about it and decided they needed to do more preparation, and that *everyone* needed to join in the discussion. I sat in the back of the room, watching as they worked on their problems.

The debates got better and better. More and more students took part; it even reached the point that the audience frequently got exasperated when the debaters were talking because, as they put it, "We can't get a word in." Our debate on gun legislation was an exciting time. Students got so involved they would go

out the door arguing and attempting to convince each other.

My part in all this was to stay out of it, except when asked for help. Students must be allowed to pick subjects, choose their own sides, take enough time to prepare, and speak freely. In the case of marijuana legalization, I simply let them know that admitting something personal was dangerous, but opinions were another matter.

Students must be allowed to evaluate frequently. They are quick to criticize and should learn to accept criticism. But they also must cooperate or little will be accomplished. A teacher must remember not to reprimand those who are unprepared. The others who are working with these people will let them know, and it's far more effective coming from their peers.

While we were doing the debates, I assigned little homework or reading. I told them to spend time reading articles on their subjects. Consequently, everyone (myself included) learned a great deal from the well-informed debaters.

The debates took about a month in all and were a success in the students' opinions. We decided that we needed more classroom discussion. I promised them that whenever they had something they wanted to discuss, we would discuss it, regardless of lesson plans. So far, this has worked beautifully. I have found that if students are given the freedom to discuss, they are more willing to do regular assignments.

IV. Conclusion

College prep students are under great pressure for grades, and college entrance exams worry them. They are sometimes so serious they are frightening. I am still trying to let them know that they can show weakness or have unpopular opinions and live to tell about it. (We have a "glare" system for anyone who makes fun of another class member who is trying to venture a serious opinion. Everyone glares at him in unison. Fortunately, this is taken in good humor.)

When I think of last fall, I can see improvement and, best of all, so can the class. Before I wrote this paper, I told the class members that they were the subjects of my attempt. They laughed and then talked seriously about it. A boy said, "The beautiful thing about this class is that we're all comfortable and nobody's afraid to talk." A girl wrote in her debate evaluation, "I've always been afraid to talk in a class before, but in here I forget that, and I'm afraid I won't get a *chance*."

I still have students who are so reluctant to talk that they may never do so. They say beautiful things on paper, but they don't really *want* to talk. I won't force them. We need quiet, steady people, too.

Once after I had been ill for two days, I came back to school rather unprepared for this particular class. You should have heard the serious offers I had from students who wanted to take over!

Appendix

ENGLISH V, SPECIAL PROJECT

In conjunction with our study of *The Old Man and The Sea,* you will each be expected to prepare or help prepare a project to be presented before the class. The project may be a paper, a drawing, a dramatic reading, anything that you would like to prepare that pertains to Ernest Hemingway or his novel.

Please be prepared to turn in a brief outline of your project *this Thursday, November 2.* The projects themselves will be presented before the class on *November 8 and 9.*

You may decide to work on an individual project or prepare something with a group. Please keep these groups at no more than four people.

Some Suggestions

1. Biographical report on Ernest Hemingway with perhaps some pictures, interesting anecdotes, etc. (There is available a very good book written by his brother.)
2. Dramatic reading from his works—novels, short stories, etc.
3. A drawing of something in the novel (e.g., the old man in his skiff).
4. An original poem of the sea.
5. Perhaps a series of poems with illustrations—the sea, man's endurance, etc.

EVALUATION PROBLEMS

MARCIA PERLSTEIN **7**

A Suggestion for the Constructive Use of Grades

The Boys

The boys I teach in a self-contained team-taught class are part of an experimental project, "The Work Experience Program." They are boys who, for reasons as diverse as their number, are not part of the regular departmental arrangement. They attend school for as few as four or as many as sixteen hours per week. Some read no more than their own names, while others are grappling with the complexities of Dostoevsky, Camus, and Hesse. All of them have experienced failure in the traditional learning situation. Even the ones who are able to read far above grade level find themselves never passing courses. I feel that Judy Bebelaar, my teaching partner, and I have worked through many significant changes in attitude with this group. The grading question involves itself with some of the important aspects of our work.

The First Grading Day

The day that our first set of grades was due (a school requirement) came all too soon; we were unprepared for the responses which greeted us. Although the boys' attitudes had changed significantly, we did not feel that we could give them good grades. They still had problems in truancy, starting assignments, following through on difficult tasks, etc. We thought they'd understand all this.

We distributed grades by calling the students to our desk, holding a short conference with each one, and assuring each that we felt he could do better the next time around. Boys who the day before had smiled and joked with us, who had been prodded into serious views of their own work, were now shouting pejorative comments from all directions. We were told that our class was a "looney class," that we didn't know how to teach, that they hadn't learned anything, and that they all wanted out. Some made derogatory remarks about us personally: Judy was too skinny; I was too fat; we were sloppy; we were late; we kept their papers too long. The room was a pigpen; there wasn't enough space to operate; there were not enough books; we hadn't given tests. The remarks were hurled too quickly and directly for me to do justice to the entire range in this small effort at reproduction. There were no positive comments; the closest that any came to this phenomenon was neutrality. Some were gazing at their more vocal colleagues and not saying anything at all.

One boy sputtered out a chain of obscenities, stormed out of the room, and disappeared for several days. One of us cried and left the room; the other screamed for control and finally dis-

missed the class. Boys were streaming into the counselor's and the Work Experience Coordinator's offices clamoring for change.

Fallacious Assumptions

Needless to say, we knew something was wrong. Their strong reactions forced us to examine carefully what we had done. Although we hadn't voiced our assumptions, we were obviously operating under some fallacious ones. Any action (even a passive one) manifests a corresponding attitude.

We had rejected grades as part of a whole network of experience which might make people bitter, competitive, grasping, and dishonest. Several things were wrong with this attitude. For one thing, it was a distorted one because grades do not have to do these things to a person. The more important error we made was in not taking enough time with grades. By our attitude and by not preparing the boys for evaluation, we had implied that grades were not significant. By minimizing their importance, and almost denying their existence until grading day came upon us, we were trying to eliminate a part of experience for our students which could not be eliminated at that time. Even if it could, we had no right to make that choice. Perhaps one first needs to succeed with grades before choosing to accept or reject them. We had projected our own feelings about grades onto our students and fallaciously assumed that they did not care about grades.

Our actions on that fatal grading day also indicated that we thought that the boys did not feel judged by the grades they received. This too was incorrect. They took their grades very personally; they felt that we were telling them that they were bad. They saw no relation between their performance and our ostensibly arbitrary evaluation of them. Therefore, they replied in kind with all the offensive and defensive material at their disposal.

The last fallacious assumption underlying our actions was that grades cannot motivate. Thus, we had never used a grade as a device for encouraging them to work. We'd never mentioned grades before the first report card. We later realized that the work they'd done for the first six weeks seemed to them to bear little relation to the grade which they'd received. Thus, the rating came as a shock.

After carefully examining what we had done to provoke their reactions, it seemed a wonder to us that they'd not thrown us around the room along with the words, paper clips, and paper airplanes.

The First Step

After our deep "soul searching" we decided to wait about a week before trying to rectify the situation. During the week that followed the grading debacle we were as friendly as we could be. We quietly worked and spoke with them and absorbed all the hostility that came our way. We won them back quickly because we'd made fairly good contact prior to the crisis.

The purpose of our first step was to hear from them. We'd examined the situation from our own perspective (which was bound to have had its limitations). Before we proceeded we had to find out what grades meant to them, how grades made them feel. We asked them to write compositions on the subject. Their papers were to include anything they thought of when they thought about grades. We never mentioned their grades in this class; we presented the idea as the concept or abstraction of grades. We thought that writing was a good way to begin because they'd experienced some success in this area and they'd have an opportunity to express themselves without making us verbal targets.

Their Responses

Their responses helped shape the program which we launched. The major complaints they had about grades revolved around unfairness, competition, and pressure. Jim B. seemed to hit on all the points which summed up the others' responses:

I believe that grades are basically a bum deal, because parents tend to put pressure on a child to get better grades. Teachers also put pressure on students to get better grades.

I honestly believe that too much emphasis is placed on grades and when a student has pressure he'll break if he can't stand it. Why don't they let a student work at his own speed. That way he'll learn more. Because he'll do his work only as fast as he can do it that way he won't be pushed and he won't skip anything and what he learns [sic] he'll remember.

The class's points were well taken. We were now headed in an entirely new direction.

New Set of Assumptions

Based on our postgrading day perceptions and the writing the boys had done, we evolved a new set of assumptions upon which we founded the stratagem with which this paper concerns itself. The ideas which emerged seemed so simple that we wondered why we hadn't thought of them sooner. However, they represented the distillation of a complex thought-teaching process which evolved rather slowly and painfully.

We decided that, despite their poor self-images, our students *did* care about grades. Any other attitudes were merely very elaborate defense mechanisms, many of which had been perfected over long periods of constant use. They could not easily separate the grade which they received from our conception of them as people. Their own opinions of themselves (or their self-images) were integrally related to our opinions of them as people (as symbolized by the grade). When they felt unable to succeed, they felt pressure. Each assumed that others were doing better than he was (i.e., that others were better people), and a feeling of competition and a sense of frustration resulted.

Although grades do all of these negative things to them, it is possible that if these conditions are removed, the opposite may occur. Thus we worked on the assumption that grades can motivate positively if used carefully and as an integral part of curriculum, attitude development, and self-awareness. Ratings can be handled on an individual basis as long as there is some framework into which disparate elements can fit.

We'd set ourselves quite a task. We now had to integrate our new set of assumptions into a successful stratagem. Success would be measured by the way the students felt about themselves on the next report card day. If they did not react as violently as they had on the first, we would be on our way.

Strategy

The boys could not perceive our assumptions through osmosis. We had to incorporate them in an obtrusive manner; they had to learn to handle various mechanical things (which were results or symbols of our assumptions) by themselves. We wanted them to see the relationship between the things they did and the things that happened to them.

We decided to use their writing as a starting point. As mentioned earlier, they were on pretty firm ground in this area. We'd emphasized honest expression, the ability to put on paper what you were actually thinking. (This is dealt with in depth in Judy Bebelaar's paper, "The Soul Searchers," strategy 25.) They all knew that they could write about anything they wanted to. Thus, we told them that for the next report card they would each be responsible for one page of writing per day. We made no comment on quality at this time, as far as the grade was concerned. We still had lengthy discussions with them about their work, in which we elicited their feelings and criticisms and when prodded gave ours. However, for grading purposes this was not the issue. They had to produce a page of writing each day. They always had the option of choosing their own topic if they were not "turned on" by the one which we assigned. At the end of each day they signed a small index card, writing what they had accomplished and the appropriate grade. If they'd written a page, they gave themselves an A. If they had slept or read or played with the tape recorder, they indicated their activity and gave themselves an F. It was fine for them to do these other things *after* they had finished their writing. They all knew that in order to get credit for each day's work they had to produce a page of writing; if they didn't write, they didn't receive credit.

The system was simple. They could manage it by themselves. They could measure their own progress. We were quite flexible about giving them opportunities for make-up work. However, no grades were given on credit. If the work was not in on a particular day (even though two or five or twenty were promised on the next), they had to give themselves the F. The system was totally objective. The grades were a true reflection of the amount of work they'd accomplished. Anybody who wanted to succeed could.

They soon began to realize that these grades were not in any way related to our feelings about them as people. For example, a boy might give himself three Fs in a row and still find us talking to him, joking with him, and helping him when he wanted us to. We emphasized our availability. We were there to facilitate the learning process for them, to help them get better grades, to act as moderators when they tried to rationalize an A for a blank page.

We thought at first that we'd use this system only for several days. However, we found that it took three weeks at the rate of one card per student per day for them to really see that what mattered was what they *did,* not how much or how little they knew, or many nice or nasty things they said, or how much or how little they promised to do. We discussed the idea on different levels. We told our Camus man that he had an existential choice; he was free to earn anything in the spectrum from A to F. We told our immature ninth grader that he was old enough to handle his own grades and that he knew when he'd finished his work.

The next step was to tell them on Monday of the fifth week that they would not be getting an index card until Friday. That still meant that they were responsible for a page of work each day, but they would not grade themselves until the end of the week. At that time they would simply count the pages they had done; five were required for an A.

The final part of the process came with the second report card. We prepared them for this every day during the three days preceding grading time. They burst into a last minute flurry of make-up activity. We thought this was healthy. They knew exactly what to do in order to earn the grade they desired. They saw the day as imminent and wanted to prepare. Up until this time their classic reaction was to give up when something for which they were unprepared was on the horizon. Those last three days were really fun. They were writing in every imaginable position. They were on the floor, on the desks, leaning against bookshelves, spinning, squatting, squealing, but always writing. They grabbed their folders and counted and recounted and then recounted again. They screamed if we held onto a paper to show someone; their security lay in having those papers in their folders. They measured and weighed their folders; they rearranged their work many different ways; they spread their papers out and looked at them from different directions. Their own work for the first time was a constant source of pleasure to them.

The day before grades were to be handed in they each got an orange index card (not to be confused with the white ones they had been using all along). They each were to have twenty-four pieces of writing for an A; all other grades were to be awarded proportionately. They wrote the number of papers they had and the grade they deserved. We collected the cards, discussed the grades, and then returned to our work. On report card day they were not required to work; they played Scrabble and scribbage, listened to music or talked about cars while we attacked the massive pile of paperwork. This day was dramatically different from the first.

Introducing a Notion of Quality

We were not entirely satisfied. It was true that we had come a long way, but we were far from getting them to examine themselves seriously. They were still looking at their work through our eyes. During the next six weeks we continued with the cards on a once-a-week basis. We added math and reading to the cards quite easily. One page of written math was required each day, as well as different numbers of pages of reading for each student (ranging from the learning of five language experience cards for some to reading several chapters and examining certain thematic strains for others). They were able to accept the idea of different reading requirements for each one of them. There was no stigma attached to a low reading level because they had been tutoring each other for a long time. These other quantitative arrangements took care of themselves since the pattern had been carefully worked through in the writing experiment of the preceding weeks.

For the next few days we discussed quality. They readily admitted that there were times when they just wrote anything in order to satisfy the requirements. They pointed out that they knew when they had written something good. Some felt that it was better to do something bad than nothing at all. There were no answers; they batted several questions around for a long time. Some volunteered to discount low quality work for the next several weeks, provided that they

could be the judges of quality for their own compositions. They confessed that they were annoyed when we didn't evaluate their work, merely discussing points which they had brought up. We finally reached a compromise; they would submit the work which fulfilled the requirement of a page per day, while we would make an effort to be a bit more critical, to give the individual spelling lists and grammar lessons. We reluctantly agreed.

For their final grades we asked them to fill out cards with the number of pages they'd written all term and write the grades they deserved. In addition, they all were *required* (the only required topic of the term, for they'd always had the option of choosing their own, as mentioned earlier) to write a full page evaluation of their progress. They were asked to consider everything other than quantity: the things they thought they'd learned, their attitudes, their feelings—in short, anything which they felt was important for someone to know which couldn't be found on their index cards.

Ben talking, in this class I have learned more in this class than in others. I think, What I like in the class was that I had a little freedom. My writing has at least improved as far as I'm concerned. I really can't say you've taught me any math because you haven't. I knew the math when I came in this class. Going to the beginning you haven't really used power over me. I would of defied you.

Sometimes I sit in this class. All of a sudden I think to myself what hell am I doing here and start getting carried away by lifting chairs and other things. I feel like why don't I get the hell out of here. Because when I'm in the mood I know that I'm not going to do work. When I get the urge to write I write.

Like it would be a song in my head I get my own rhythm to the words I write I get deep feeling in some of them they some time make me feel happy and then depressed.   BEN B.

I think that I have done all of the work that is to be done. I have done all of my conflict work that is. I think that all of my work is very, very good. The work I have done is from the bottom of my heart. The work is some of the best in the class. My attendance is almost perfect. I have missed one day. I have learned to do all of my work in one period. In my attendance at that school has made me the editor of our class. I have learned to express myself in the class as well as at home. I have made more friends in this class than in all of the classes in all of the schools that I have been in.   CURTIS B.

These papers speak for themselves. Each one is honest, thoughtful, and unique. To say that we were touched and delighted is a gross understatement. Flying around the room in place of the obscenities of the first day were our high spirits. They had indeed begun to see the relationship between the things they did and what happened to them; they had reached levels of self-awareness that many people never reach. They were happy with their successes, but realistic about their failures. Together we had worked through a major problem.

ANDREA FISHER **8**

Self-evaluation in an Art Class

The grading of student art projects is usually quite subjective. In high school it is often the case that good students receive the good grades and the mediocre artists remain unmotivated. A teacher's grading is often far too sensitive to the teacher's taste and sophistication. The teacher determines the projects and the criteria for grading them. In the case of stitchery, for example, the teacher has the personal choice for grading on the craftsmanship of stitches, the force or movement within the project, the color combination, the variety of textures, or other aesthetic or technical qualities.

My past teaching experience had been discouraging because I had felt forced to give good grades to the talented but lethargic students, and poor grades to the untalented yet hard-working students. This is the dilemma of the art teacher; how can she reward the good students and simultaneously stimulate the relatively ungifted ones?

The weekly "use of time grade" has alleviated some of these difficulties. The weekly "use of time" grade is given to each student at the end of each week and is based upon tardiness, classroom behavior, the degree to which students work toward their individual capabilities, and the student's willingness to cooperate with both the teacher and with other students. Since the problem of hourly cleanup is especially important to the art teacher, the "use of

time" grade applies here as well as to the students' willingness to perform their own jobs and to be out of the classroom on time. This grade constitutes 50 percent of the students' semester grades, while artistic ability exhibited in projects as well as in outside reports constitutes the other 50 percent. I have found it most effective for the students to evaluate their own "use of time" grade during an individual conference with me. In the beginning I graded them myself and set the pace for the course. During the later conferences I reminded the students of the concepts of the weekly "use of time" grade. In the beginning of the semester I tried to set high standards, so that when they began to grade themselves they were aware of the appropriate goals.

When the students then came up to give me their "use of time" grades, I found that they most predominantly underestimated themselves. They were usually unduly harsh. If, however, the students weren't too far off from the accurate grade (in my opinion) I would let their suggestions become grades.

I have been criticized by some of the good art students (and by their parents) for this grading scheme. Some of the less motivated talented students are so accustomed to "getting by" on their talents alone, that it seemed unimportant for them to function in the classroom. They have told me that this grade simply protects the people who do not have as much talent as they do, and that it isn't fair. I feel that my purpose as a secondary school art teacher is to prepare the majority of students to be able to tastefully select the objects that they will live with, and to be visually aware of their environment. This, to me, is more important than preparing the few talented students for further art education or for art careers. I feel that my system offers both groups of students a reasonable challenge since it also encourages the talented students to produce.

The results of the weekly "use of time" grade are very encouraging. The classroom atmosphere and the quality of the projects both compare very favorably to my observations of other classes. Even classroom behavior problems have now become trivial.

PROBLEMS OF FRIDAY AFTERNOONS

CAROLYN MUSKA **9**

Planning for Friday Afternoons

I. Background

One book on methods points out that a teacher who delays getting his class started until five minutes after the bell each period is cheating his students of 15 hours of learning each year (180 day $\times$ 5 min. $\div$ 60 min. = 15 hrs.), an equivalent of over three weeks of class meetings during the year. I'm still trying to figure out a good way to save those weeks, but with roll to take, class entry slips to sign, and the various requests and complaints to listen to at the beginning of a period, at least two and a half weeks have already slipped through my fingers.

There is another block of time that may be lost at an even more alarming rate—whole periods on Friday afternoon. Not only were my students being "cheated" of learning time, but I was carrying around a defeated, Somewhere-I-failed feeling all weekend as a result of a Friday afternoon when nothing seemed to go right. It was just after such an afternoon that a teacher with many years of experience told me that one of the first things she tells a student teacher is, "Plan for Monday, Tuesday, Wednesday, and Thursday—and *then* plan for Friday."

In the summer seminar group we had discussed the possible need of special planning for the day before a holiday and the need for making allowances in the fall for behavior on the days of football games, especially if some of the players are in your classes. Even so, I had never before quite connected the problems I had on Friday with the way students were feeling about the weekend just ahead. How could I have forgotten the special feeling I got as a child just by thinking "It's Friday!" And how I must regret, as a teacher, that mine is not the classroom attributed to Tolstoy's peasant school where "The children spent entire days at their studies and were reluctant to leave the schoolhouse."

Judiciously asking questions and contriving conversations concerning student behavior and lesson plans on Friday, I gathered the following impressions from experienced, tenured teachers:

1. A surprising number of teachers questioned admitted to more difficulties in teaching on Friday than on other days. (I overheard a teacher at the end one Friday complaining bitterly about the "bunch of squirrels" he had in his seventh period World Backgrounds class.)
2. Those admitting to difficulties did not seem to relate the difficulty to their lesson plan for the day; nor did they seem to vary the plans from other days of the week.
3. With many of the teachers there seemed to be an unconscious acceptance of the need for special planning for Friday and a correspondingly unconscious adjustment to the situation.
4. When I asked for specific information concerning the kinds of plans they made for Friday, they mentioned most frequently either tests or films. A teacher of General Science B has described on more than one Friday morning before class a particularly flashy lab demonstration she had planned for the day. An English teacher, one of the few I talked with who specifically plans for Friday, said she frequently uses Fridays as a time for conferences with her students.

The specific remedies for turning Fridays into the highlight of the week instead of a kind of doomsday for the teacher are not easily prescribed. There may be no need for special planning; the regular pace set for the rest of the week may work just as well for Friday. If there is a need, it will soon be evident. The one general rule that could be applied to any class, however, is simply this: Friday is a good day for a change of pace. The need for a change of pace seems to have a direct relation to at least three conditions of the class:

1. Age level (the younger the class, the greater the need).
2. Academic motivation (the less academically inclined, the greater the need).
3. Period of the day (the later in the day the period, the greater the need).

II. Plans for Fridays

My last period class, Typing I, is made up of forty students, thirty-two of whom are freshmen. It's a very friendly, outgoing class with a keen competitive spirit. My first attempt at anticipating the mood of the class just before a holiday showed me how keen this competitive spirit was. The class was divided into teams by rows. One sentence was selected and the first typist in each row started the game by typing the sentence as fast as possible, removing the paper from the typewriter, and passing it to the next typist. The process was repeated by each typist in the row, with the row finishing first winning. The pressure to win was terrific and those who were not typing were jumping up and down cheering their teammates on. My reaction was mixed—I enjoyed the enthusiasm but I felt uncomfortable when I thought of how the noise would sound to the principal or department head. Still, if discipline is a matter of getting the attention of the class when you want it, I suppose discipline was being maintained because I simply didn't want their attention until the game was over.

This particular exercise in speed has undergone some needed changes but I frequently use it in a modified form on Fridays. I have found that interest is still high and order is a little better when each typist in the row is given a specific length of time (10 to 20 seconds) for typing and then the total words typed for each row is calculated to find the winning team.

Certain Fridays are designated in advance as periods for personal typing and students are able to type reports for other classes or do personal letter writing. Special drill books and a variety of ditto material with suggestions for composing at the typewriter are kept on hand for those who do not provide material of their own for these periods. One suggestion for an interesting exercise in composing is to have students interview the person next to them and then type an interview report. Students who have been absent during the week are given an opportunity on Fridays to make up work. Drill assignments emphasizing speed or accuracy, according to the individual's need as shown by a five-minute inventory writing at the beginning of the period, are very useful in breaking through skill plateaus and have proved quite successful as a change of pace for Friday.

I have felt the difference in the behavior of this particular class to such an extent that I am already looking for special material for my next year's Friday afternoon classes in Business Math and Record Keeping. Since these classes meet all three requirements for predicting difficulty in maintaining the usual week's pace on Friday, I feel confident that my efforts will not be wasted.

Bibliography

Books

1. Boynton, Lewis D. *Methods of Teaching Bookkeeping.* Cincinnati: South-Western Publishing Co., 1955. Gives some interesting information on the history and popularity of bookkeeping in high school but is somewhat out-of-date. Specific lesson plan suggestions are given for the first week of teaching, as well as detailed plans for teaching the work sheet, adjusting entries, and closing entries.
2. Russon, Allien R., and S. J. Wanous. *Philosophy and Psychology of Teaching Typewriting.* Cincinnati: South-Western Publishing Co., 1960. If you can ignore the title and read the book, you will find many helpful suggestions for teaching typewriting. I found the suggestions for introducing the keyboard and emphasizing technique in early lessons very useful, as well as the section on composing at the typewriter. Each chapter ends with an annotated bibliography which is almost as interesting as the book.

Periodicals

Following is a list of magazines and pamphlets published specifically for business teachers. Articles by high school and college business teachers covering specific subject area and specific problems within the subject area have contributed a great deal to solving my own problems during the year. I have included the addresses as a reference for ordering.

1. *The Balance Sheet,* South-Western Publishing Co., 5101 Madison Road, Cincinnati, Ohio 45227. (free) (branch office in Burlingame, Calif.)
2. *Business Education World,* The Gregg Publishing Co., 8171 Redwood Highway, Novato, Calif., 94947.
3. *Business Teacher,* The Gregg Publishing Co. (free)
4. *California Business Education Journal,* School of Business, San Francisco State College, San Francisco, Calif. 94132.
5. *The Journal of Business Education,* 34 North Crystal St., East Stroudsberg, Pa.
6. *Typewriting News,* South-Western Publishing Co. (free)
7. *United Business Education Association Forum,* UBEA, 1201 Sixteenth Street, N.W., Washington, D.C.
8. Agencies and sources of information
   a. Vocation Educational Department, San Mateo County Board of Education, 590 Hamilton St., Redwood City, Calif. 94063.
   b. Curriculum Library, San Mateo County Board of Education.
   c. The Bureau of Business Education, California State Department of Education, Coastal Regional Office, 1111 Jackson Street, Rm. 4075, Oakland, Calif.

WORKING COOPERATIVELY WITH COLLEAGUES

CHERYL VOLMERT **10**

Developing Intradepartmental Coordination

The Problem

A German major, I began my intern year teaching two classes of World History. My background in this field was deplorably inadequate. I found myself caught up in an exhausting, unending struggle to learn both the subject matter and teaching techniques of Social Studies. I spent hours searching for supplementary materials, duplicating this information for my students, and concentrating on varying the approach in class from day to day.

It was all I could do to stay on top of my preparations from one day to the next. I was dissatisfied because I had neither the time nor the experience to map out long-range course objectives. I also had no time to evaluate the merits of the new materials I introduced and the new techniques I tried.

My frustration was compounded by a lack of departmental coordination. The other Social Studies teachers had ideas and materials they were willing to share, but more often than not, their help came *after* I had presented a less-than-successful lesson in class.

Although I, as a new teacher, felt the lack of departmental coordination most acutely, the system—or absence of one—seemed to me to be absurd even for the most experienced teachers. We *all* were caught in the same whirlpool—defining goals, looking for materials, devising tests, and duplicating supplementary information. Each of us spent days producing for ourselves what we could have accomplished together in hours.

The Solution

After defining the problem, the solution was obvious to me. Somehow the Social Studies "department" had to be induced to start acting like one! All of the teachers could gain a great deal if, instead of duplicating each other's efforts, we worked together.

In attempting to bring about intradepartmental coordination, I had two major objectives:

1. to create a reliable source of new ideas on materials and techniques relevant to a well-defined course of study;
2. to implement a "division of labor" among teachers (researching, typing, dittoing, etc.) to create new free time for specific delineation of objectives and evaluation of how objectives are being met.

Procedure
(or, How to Get the Ball Rolling)

All of the World History teachers had a common problem. Our school was new and our budget was limited. The only reference material provided by the district for our students was the textbook, and the text, we all agreed, had serious limitations. The book attempted to cover World History through an unimaginative series of area studies. The organization and presentation of all the units was identical, so that the students, when beginning to study a new area, had the uncomfortable feeling that they had been through it all before. In addition, the scope of each study was much too broad. All of the teachers recoiled from the "blitz" approach to Russian geography, history, economics, politics, and culture, designed to be presented in six weeks; each teacher was attempting to compensate through his own efforts for the text's inadequacies.

Recognizing that the textbook was our common enemy, I decided that the best way to pull all of the teachers together was to come up with a feasible alternative to it. I spent a couple of weekends looking for new materials which could be adapted relatively easily to our use. Having amassed the raw materials, I roughly outlined a potential unit which could be developed from it. I worked out in great detail the first two lesson plans. Finally, I calculated *exactly* what each teacher would have to do (in terms of researching, typing, mimeographing, etc.) to contribute to the development of the unit.

With my material and outlines in hand, I confronted each teacher individually with the "hard sell." Playing on the general dissatisfaction with the text, I pointed out that my unit was an alternative *only* if we all adopted it and worked together to implement it. (The material was too extensive to be reproduced for the students by one teacher.) I stressed the potential advantages to be accrued through a group effort—new ideas, help with the busy work of lesson planning, more free time, and hopefully a more exciting course of study for our students.

Results

After agreeing to try to work closely together, the members of the Social Studies department met regularly before school. Each teacher completed his share of the necessary preparations to be made for the unit and participated enthusiastically in discussions evolving from classroom experiences. My two major objectives were fulfilled. The group itself became a reliable, continuing source of ideas on methods and materials for each teacher. By pooling our labor, we acquired more free time to reflect upon the progress and focus of our lessons.

Additional benefits which I had not anticipated resulted from intradepartmental coordination. The group has developed a new interest in curriculum. As we evolve a cohesive, well-organized unit, we find ourselves planning ahead for a cohesive, well-organized four-year Social Studies program which we now believe we can cooperatively achieve.

We are finding that as a group we have more power to request new materials and equipment from the district.

Finally, and most importantly, we agree that our students are much more enthusiastic and involved than they were when we were grinding out lesson plans and materials individually. This is partially because we are no longer ex-hausted when we enter class. We are more alive and purposeful as a result of intradepartmental coordination.

Postscript: Four Months Later

Four months have elapsed since the foregoing part of this paper was written. During this time the Social Studies teachers have continued to cooperate in the planning and implementation of each unit. Together we have been able to overcome the limitations of the textbook as *the* source of knowledge for the students. During our unit on Latin America, for example, we shelved the text completely and focused the course around sixteen mimeographed readings from original sources. Working together on this project, we cut a total of fifty stencils and assembled three hundred student pamphlets. It was a monumental task which any one of us, working alone, could never have accomplished.

TEACHING NONACADEMIC STUDENTS

JOAN JAMES SHEFFIELD **11**

Motivating Underachieving Students in a Biology Class

Background

One of my first assignments for my first year of teaching biology was to teach a Basic Biology course. There are nineteen students in the class, predominantly freshmen, with "lower intellectual abilities" and various emotional problems. These two categories themselves lend to behavior problems in most classrooms.

Since these students generally have quite low reading abilities, almost anything they learn must come from doing. I find them able to handle a laboratory situation very successfully. I try diligently to make biology relevant to them in these laboratory exercises by continually relating it to the environment we live in.

Unit on Marine Biology

About the fifth week of school we began a unit on marine biology. I decided to leave the

duration of the unit up to them, to let it run as far as their interest span held them. As it turned out, this unit lasted two and a half weeks.

We decided that we could relate a marine biology unit easily to the natural environment of Marin County where they lived. We began by observing preserved specimens of marine life. We saw films borrowed from the school's Instructional Materials Center. At the center there were numerous films on marine life. I previewed many of them at home over two successive weekends and chose those films that best presented the material that we wanted to study. Besides the resource materials in the classroom on marine life, we pretty well drained the school library of the more visual books, and I chose about a dozen books from my own community library. The students' only writing assignment was to write a short research paper on a sea animal of their choice. They had two weeks to accomplish this, with ample time in class to peruse the books. (In this course I very seldom assign homework; everything is done in the class hour.) However, they were motivated enough in this unit to ask if they could take

books home overnight and over the weekend. Out of eighteen students, ten produced beautifully written papers. The subjects were varied, but starfish proved to be the most popular. Some students went to their own community library and checked out additional books.

Field Trip—High Point of the Unit

The terminating activity of the unit was greatly anticipated by the students. This was a class field trip to the College of Marin's Marine Biology Laboratory in Bolinas. The trip had to be arranged early in the school year so that we could coincide the trip with the end of the unit. We did not have enough students in the class to warrant a school bus, so we arranged for three other drivers and myself to provide the transportation. The three drivers were mothers active in PTA who had expressed willingness to assist teachers in field trips.

The day of our trip finally arrived. Although the weather was clear at 8 A.M. when we departed from school, rain was predicted. Everyone was warmly and ruggedly dressed for beach weather. The chance of rain was not an upsetting factor to them. We took the "back" roads to Bolinas through the beautiful Lucas Valley. The light rain had arrived and we could observe the lush green hills of the countryside. We passed numerous dairy farms and observed a deer in one of the meadows. Many of these students had not been exposed to much of the natural beauty of this area even though they live nearby.

Arriving in Bolinas about 9 A.M., the marine lab technician was ready to conduct us on the tour of the laboratory facilities. For the class it was most exciting to observe the living forms of sea life in the aquariums. Here at the marine lab the sea water is piped in from the ocean and is always circulating. In the ordinary school-room setup these salt water aquariums are difficult to reproduce. Sea water can be made synthetically, but since this does not always produce an ideal set of conditions for sea life, schools have to be content with preserved speci-mens of sea animals. So for many of the stu-dents this was their first opportunity to observe living specimens. They now had the chance to carry a crab in a safe manner, to put their fingers near the center of a sea anenome and to feel its sting. They could touch a spiny sea urchin and see a starfish move on the glass of the aquarium. The marine lab technician had an easy and relaxed manner in dealing with the students. He interested them by his way of describing the oddities of these sea animals and answered their many curious questions.

We spent about an hour and a half at the laboratory and then ventured down to the beach area to stretch our legs. After an hour's automobile ride and an hour and a half of observing, they needed this break.

The tide was high and not much of the beach was accessible for walking. One of the students did find a giant chitin which we took back to the marine laboratory for identification.

Back into the cars and off to Point Reyes National Seashore. There a park aide met us and in about twenty minutes related some of the natural history of the area. At this particular time we were standing in light rain, but not one complaint arose from the group. The park aide's presentation was pleasant and informative for the students. Many found that there were camping facilities and various trails to hike. There is a species of white deer, not natural to the area, that has been brought into Point Reyes. One of the films we had seen was *Island in Time,* a Sierra Club production which was concerned with the ecology and conservation of the Point Reyes area.

A picnic was being anticipated at this time and we found shelter under the redwoods as it was still raining lightly. Girls in the class had baked dozens of brownies and I had enough cold soft drinks for all in my camper.

From Point Reyes we started our drive in-land to return to school. Although it didn't apply to marine biology, we made a stop at Samuel P. Taylor State Park in the San Geronimo Valley. There we walked through the redwoods and along the stream with the lush green moss and ferns growing beside it.

Our final activity was not on the itinerary. It was now raining too hard to remain outside. Since my home was on the way back to school, I decided it might be fun to stop in, build a fire in the fireplace, and make some popcorn. We had two hours before we were due back in school. I was a bit doubtful of this venture since my house is small and we were many. However, everything went very well. Two fel-lows built a fire and two others made popcorn. Students discovered the stereo phonograph and played records. They even found some of their favorites among my collection! Others sat at the kitchen table and played games such as Clue, Lie Detector, and Scrabble. In this way we created a lot of warmth and friendliness among the class. There was no visible antago-nism among the students or between the stu-dents and teacher.

Results

I feel, and the students agree, that the whole unit was most successful in many ways. They did learn. I feel biology was made relevant to them through this ecological approach. Also in the coming years, all of us will have so much more leisure time. I feel the field trip intro-duced them to possibilities available to them in their own area.

The next day the students reflected on the unit and field trip. I find that even weeks later in our study of biology they are able to relate many experiences in this unit to others. A follow-up trip to the tide pools is planned for spring when the tides are low enough.

Bibliography for Students on Marine Life

1. Beebe, William. *Adventuring with Beebe.*
2. Brown, Vinson. *Exploring Pacific Coast Tide Pools.*
3. Carter, Samuel. *Kingdom of the Tides.*
4. Darling, Louis. *Coral Reefs.*
5. Fisher, James. *The Wonderful World of the Sea.*
6. Hedgpeth, Joel Walker. *Common Seashore Life of Southern California.*
7. Hedgpeth, Joel Walker. *Introduction to Seashore Life of the San Francisco Bay Region and the Coast of Northern California.*
8. Hull, Seabrook. *The Bountiful Sea.*
9. Hylander, John Clarence. *Sea and Shore.*
10. Kovalick, Vladimir and Nada. *The Ocean World.*
11. MacGinitie, G. E., and Nettie. *Natural History of Marine Animals.*
12. Miller, Robert C. *The Sea.*
13. Miner, Roy Waldo. *Field Book of Seashore Life.*
14. Smith, Lynwood. *Marine Biology, Common Sea-Shore Life of the Pacific Northwest.*
15. Yasso, Warren E. *Oceanography.*

Motion Pictures

Borrowed from Instructional Materials Center, Marine County, California.

Island In Time	MP2145
Life In The Ocean	MP901
Life In The Sea	MP1317
The Sea	MP1906
Seashore Oddities	MP293
Marine Biologist	MP2793
Mollusks	MP483

MIKE HALL **12**

Skill in Reading Math

I. Introduction

Our freshman General Math class is typical of such classes at almost every high school in the country. The students range in ability from those who need only a little more preparation before beginning algebra to those who have met nothing but failure in math, and are being forced to take one more course before they can finally forget it.

The students are generally poor in mathematical skills. I was forcibly struck, however, by two more vital deficiencies which they all seemed to share: the first was a general inability to read and comprehend mathematical writing, and the second was a wide-spread lack of any sense of responsibility for their mathematical progress.

A math teacher is tempted to say that these are not our concerns; reading belongs in the English department and irresponsibility is the concern of the Dean. Any teacher, though, who gives this idea more than a fleeting thought is missing a chance to teach lessons that will be remembered long after the quadratic formula is forgotten.

I decided that by approaching the first problem, I could eventually develop a classroom situation that would also serve to solve the second. Therefore, I started out on a reading project in my General Math class—which, of course, shocked the students considerably, not to mention some of the faculty.

II. Developing Skills in Reading Mathematics

The majority of these students did not have reading problems in the usual sense. They could pick up the book and read all the words in any section, and make sense out of the more or less nonmathematical sentences. Their deficiency was in the special techniques of reading *mathematics,* which is in many ways very different from other material.

I decided that they needed to master two new skills. First, they had to learn the importance of definition to mathematics. A mathematical word cannot have connotations. Its meaning does not depend on the context. Its precise mathematical meaning may differ from its common use. Thus, the reader of a mathematical text must devote special attention to the definitions, and learn exactly what they do (and do not) mean. Secondly, they had to become proficient in actually *using* the examples in the text. An example cannot be just skimmed along with the rest of the page. It must be carefully studied and often worked out independently as it is read.

Fortunately, our textbook (SMSG,[1] *Introduction to Secondary School Mathematics*) is ideally adapted to these two goals. Important words are underlined when they are first defined, and all of the definitions are summarized at the end of each chapter. Examples are clear and complete, and frequently are presented as "discovery" exercises with instructions to the student to follow carefully on his own paper.

The first semester (before I began this project) had been devoted to a review of topics from elementary school arithmetic. The third quarter materials, however, are basic geometric ideas which were totally new to most of the students. With a plenitude of new ideas and definitions, this seemed to be the appropriate place for a new approach.

The first step was occasional reading assignments as a supplement to the class lectures. The students would be told to read the next section and assigned one or two problems not covered in class. Thus, they were broken in gently to reading on their own.

In order to emphasize the importance of definitions and examples, they were required during their reading to copy each definition (which could be readily identified because the word was underlined) as they came to it and also to work out on their own each example from the text. Both of these papers were turned in along with the homework.

After several of these assignments, I omitted the problems but required the students to turn in a summary of the section in their own words. They ranged from "Summary—it tells you how

[1] School Mathematics Study Group.

to add and measure problems" to a precise and well-written half-page including all of the important ideas. I was pleased to see that almost all of the students realized that definitions were an important part of their summary.

These summaries were reviewed and discussed in class in order to increase the student's perception of their importance and to emphasize the basic parts of a summary.

In order to test the effectiveness of the project this far, I gave a pop quiz on a section which they had just read; this section included several important definitions (very difficult ones) and I asked the students for those definitions. Most of them did very poorly.

Immediately after collecting those papers, I asked the students to give me the same definitions with their books open. I was pleased this time to see that almost all of the answers were exactly right.

This test showed, at least, that they had begun to see the text as a reference, and to note the important definitions so that they could refer to them again. They had not yet learned to memorize them, but the very fact that they could benefit from the text in an open book quiz was a long step from where they had started.

Most of the quarter continued in this fashion. The summaries became very complete, and the students began to benefit greatly from their reading. Few of them benefit from a group lecture, but the reading on their own makes it much more personal and they learned much more. By the end of the quarter almost all new material was presented first by reading, although I still guided it on a day-to-day basis.

III. Developing Responsibility for Learning

For the last two weeks of the quarter, I made a long-term assignment: read an entire chapter, do the exercises, and prepare for a test. The chapter was about twenty pages; I collected the homework a week and a half after they began. We then had one day for review, and then a test. The scores on this test were uniformly as good or better than before.

With this assignment, I had begun to deal with the lack of responsibility many of the students exhibited. Their class time during the week was their own, to use in reading and doing problems to prepare for the test. The majority (but not all) responded well to the challenge, and began to feel that their mathematical progress was up to them.

The fourth quarter material is preparation for algebra, and here I was ready to put the students entirely on their own. Now that they had the ability to read mathematics with comprehension, I turned them loose. Each student proceeds through the book at his own speed, doing the exercises and taking the tests as he comes to them. (See Appendix for class procedures.)

Now each student is fully responsible for his progress. He knows that it is up to him to succeed or fail. Goofing off, playing games, or sleeping in class hurt only him—and he is fully aware of how and why they do. Again, most of the students (including some of my "class problems") have responded enthusiastically to this system. They accept their responsibility in a very adult manner. I have begun to suspect their lack of a sense of responsibility was due to the failure of many teachers to give them any responsibility.

The advantages of this free-reading method are many, especially in a mixed ability group such as I had in my General Math class. The slower students can devote more time to a section, and need not hurry through it half understanding in order to "keep up." The more capable students are not slowed down by the class, and consequently devote their extra time to more work rather than to disruption and mischief.

These lower level math students, in general, get very little from large group work. Class time and lectures are largely wasted, and it is necessary to repeat the material individually to almost every student in the usual classroom situation. With most of the class reading at their own rate, however, the teacher has much more time to devote to individual help. Each student can talk to the teacher for a few minutes daily, which is usually enough to get him over his personal rough spots. Often three or four students will have the same problem at about the same time, and they can work effectively in a small group without disturbing the classwork as they would in a lecture situation.

The teacher is also, freed, I have found, from much of his "baby-sitting" time. Disciplinary problems have dropped immensely, since the students are diligently exercising their newfound responsibility. This provides more time for individual work without the constant disciplinary worries.

It is, of course, no breeze. I can't just sit there at my desk and let the class read while I am oblivious. I have to constantly circulate, help out here, prod a little there, provide encouragement somewhere else. Usually a student needs only to be reminded of his personal responsibility in order to respond favorably. Only one or two are still unmotivated and must be prodded constantly.

IV. Conclusion

In general, then, I feel that I have accomplished two major objectives by this strategy, with very few appreciable drawbacks. I have added to my traditional 'Rithmetic class three *other* R's: Readin', 'Ritin', and Responsibility. Perhaps this last is really the teacher's most important job.

Appendix

CLASS PROCEDURES

This quarter will be devoted to elementary Algebra. The classwork will provide a look at higher math for the student who will not be continuing in Math, and will be a "head start" for those students preparing to take Algebra. This sheet outlines the procedure and grading which will be in effect.

The responsibility will rest with YOU, the student, to determine the grade you want and the amount of work you will have to do to achieve that grade.

    I. Procedures
        A. Read carefully each section of the book. (Each section is numbered and titled: i.e., Section 17–2, "The Negative Half-Line," begins on p. 242 and goes to p. 247.)

1. Summarize the important ideas of the chapter. Define all underlined words.
2. Do ALL exercises in the section. (One section may include more than one set of exercises: e.g., Section 17–2 includes Exercises 17–2a, p. 243; 17–2b, p. 246; and 17–2c, p. 247.)
3. Get the answer book and check your work. Mark an "X" by each wrong answer.
4. Return the answer book to the desk, and correct all wrong answers. Then check your corrections.

B. When you have completed an entire chapter, take the following steps:
1. Do the Chapter Review exercises which appear at the end of each chapter. Check and correct this test.
2. Hand in the following:
   a. all exercises from the section
   b. your summaries of each section
   c. the chapter review exercises
3. Take the test on the chapter. The test is closed book and is available from the teacher's desk.
4. If your score on the test is 70 percent or better, go on to the next chapter. If it is less than 70 percent, consult the teacher for study assignments to prepare you to take the test again.

II. Grading

A. Forty percent of the grade will be on the number of chapters completed by the end of the quarter, as follows:

5 chapters completed   A
4 chapters completed   B
3 chapters completed   C
2 chapters completed   D
less than 2 chapters   F

B. Forty percent of the grade will be the average of the scores on ALL tests taken. (This includes tests not passed!) The usual percentage scale will be used.

C. Ten percent of the grade will be on the chapter summaries and homework. They will be graded as follows:

5 points   A
4 points   B
3 points   C
2 points   D
less than 2   F

D. Ten percent of the grade will be on Application and Citizenship. These grades will be determined as explained below.

E. Please note that the policy on TARDIES will be strictly enforced. Quarter grades will be lowered by $\frac{1}{2}$ letter grade for each three tardies.

III. Application and Citizenship

A. ALL rules will be strictly enforced. No exceptions will be made.

B. Each violation of a rule will be recorded. The quarter application and citizenship grade will be determined from these records as follows:

5 or less   A
6 to 10   B
11 to 15   C
16 to 20   D
21 or more   F

C. Each student is expected to bring to class all of the necessary materials (textbook, pencil, paper, etc.). Failure to bring the materials will be handled as follows:
1. If the book or materials is at school but not in the room, the student will go get it, and will receive a truant tardy.
2. If the book or materials are not at school, 5 citizenship violations will be

recorded. The student is then expected to sit quietly and allow the other students, who are prepared, to study. Citizenship violations during the period will be penalized doubly.

PLEASE SAVE THIS SHEET FOR REFERENCE DURING THE QUARTER!

GARY WAGNER **13**

Math for the Disadvantaged

I. Rationale

For most students, school is a bore. Classrooms are, in general, cold, impersonal, overcrowded, and generally uncomfortable. Where children are tracked, the lower track students are made doubly uncomfortable by being asked to listen to some joker who is often only one or two steps ahead of him talking about a subject which has little or no immediate connection to his daily "real" life—his life outside of the schoolroom, his life in the corridors, at home, on the basketball court, or in his dreams. Every nine weeks he receives a written condemnation of his inattentiveness which he and his parents, if he is living with them, interpret as (1) a certificate of stupidity and/or (2) a testimony to both the inadequacy of the teacher and the predestined futility of trying any longer.

It has been noted that children are eager for school when they first enter but that their enthusiasm is inversely proportional to their length of exposure to the school system. They become "unmotivated," enmeshed in a web of apathy, failure, and frustration.

II. Some Suggested Procedures: A Weekly Work Schedule

Why, then, advocate a regular weekly work schedule—especially in a ghetto school where frustration and failure (and therefore boredom) are practically a way of life? Midway through my first teaching year, I discovered that in my efforts to provide novelty and avoid routine in the classroom I was depriving many of my students of a sense of direction and the feeling of accomplishment which is so essential for a healthy self-image. I was providing a secure classroom situation in which students did not fear me and did not anticipate familiar failure situations, but the students' security did not spring from a sense of learning, or progress as *they* conceived it. I could see some progress but they had no clear-cut standards by which they could gauge it. I felt that a more regularized curriculum, including homework, tests, etc., would provide some standards and more clearly delineate immediate and long-range goals.

Once I had decided to use this more traditional approach, the main problem I had to face was assuring flexibility in planning without sacrificing the structure. I chose three elements as indispensables: (1) a Friday quiz, (2) a Thursday review session, (3) three nights of assigned homework. It was in this rather rigid framework that I decided to try to avoid boredom, both for me and for the children. It was not overly difficult to provide novelty in the assignments themselves. We made frequent, but not constant, use of the overhead projector. I assigned some problems in the text and made up dittoes for others. For review sessions and for introductory lectures, I frequently required note-taking. We played games and I made up crossword puzzles where topics permitted. But the greatest amount of variety came from two other sources. First, each Monday represented a fresh start on a new topic because the "old" one had been tested on Friday. I didn't want my students to feel that math, like the rest of their education in public schools, had to be fragmented, but I did want them to feel that, after their freedom on the weekend, they had a new lease on their mathematical lives on Monday. (I have found that Mondays tend to be more productive and exciting than any other day of the week.) I wanted the students to open a clean notebook on this day. Therefore we generally review the previous week's test on Tuesday or Wednesday. I can think of few things more demoralizing than beginning a week by focusing on things one has done wrong in the week that preceded. As a by-product of the weekly test then, a sense of novelty and freshness was found in the mathematics itself!

III. Use Grouping

The second, and most successful, change I made at midyear was the institution of a grouping program in which autonomy was the key. I divided the class into five groups, each of which represented a range of talents and achievement. I chose a leader for each group on the basis of maturity, ability to articulate, and peer respect. Not infrequently I bypassed the "better" student in favor of one who seemed most likely to be able to accept responsibility and delegate authority. (Out of twenty-five choices in five classes, I made two rather serious blunders.) The class was given two assignments for each week; they were to turn in an original review worksheet on Thursday and take a test on Friday. The tests were based on their own worksheets which were graded primarily on selection of problem types from the material which they were asked to cover during the week. I did not allow them to choose their own topics for study, but I did allow them to learn the material in any manner which they saw fit. They made their own assignments, graded each other on participation in the group, and kept their own records. I served as an advisor, primarily to the team leaders, but not exclusively. I was freed to combat the problem students more than ever before, and for the first time really began to see my students as people. The classroom buzzes with frenetic (and occasionally chaotic) activity—most of it related to mathematics.

IV. Have Students Keep Record

There are several additional mathematical advantages to emphasizing group autonomy which might be noted here. My students found it imperative to develop and organize data logically and clearly in order to grade one another accurately. Many had never kept records before. There were a large number who had no conception of what it meant to get 70 percent on a test. They knew only A, B, C, D, and F. By requiring percentage grades to be recorded for all tests, I was able to make percentage a practical doing-thing rather than a passive practical receiving-thing. Often the case for relevance in the curriculum is misstated. It is one thing for students to do problems from a text involving dollars and cents and quite another for them to make change. I had been giving percentage grades in lieu of letter grades to my students for four months, explaining each week why four out of six was 67 percent and not 46 percent. Certainly these grades were relevant to them. But until they had to give themselves percentage grades and record them in a permanent record themselves, most were nearly totally ignorant of the functional relations between fractions, percentage, and test grades. Finally, because the students were making their own assignments and therefore had a personal stake in them, very few assignments went undone, which was not always the case when I gave the assignments.

V. Avoid Excessive Lecturing

The temptation to state the obvious is presently overwhelming, so I shall succumb. Most new teachers, many experienced teachers, and nearly all math teachers talk too much. J. R. Suchman, Director of the Illinois Students in Inquiry Training, noted that a recent study of one (presumably typical) school system showed that 97 percent of the questions asked in the classroom were asked by teachers. The lecture method is hardly suited to the dispositions of active young teen-agers. The vast majority of their learning is still largely motor-oriented, and much of it seems to flow from the pencil to the brain rather than the other way around. The implications of this state of affairs are impelling, but in their zeal to make the material clear, most teachers refused to be impelled. Ten well-chosen circumference problems which can be completed during class are worth two hours of brilliant blackboard presentation, probably much more because the student can see and feel what he has accomplished when he writes. He can walk out of the class with the feeling that his hour has been productive of more than a headache and a stiff back.

I have found that students are generally grateful for a fifteen minute presentation before moving into groups where the real learning takes place. Probably 75 percent of the significant questions I am asked come after the class has dissolved its rows and the students are free to wander about the room. Again, the reasons are obvious. The most sure-fire way to insure having a student lie is to ask him in front of thirty of his peers if he understands what you have just spent fifteen minutes patiently explaining. Still the lectures drag on, ineffectual and interminable. Teachers tend to be slow learners.

This suggests another advantage in autonomous groups. Since the students have become the teachers, the teacher can become a student, observing how his students communicate. It is amazing how quickly one student can learn a difficult concept from the impatient explanation of one of his peers. Finally, one can often see his own techniques mirrored in the teaching techniques of his students. The parody is often as shocking as it is informative.

VI. Use Textbook

I stated earlier that the student requires some form of physical confirmation of his progress. One of the most effective I have en-countered is the cardinality of the set of pages he has turned in a text. Ghetto children (and their parents) hold especially traditional views of what a school and its curriculum should be. While I tend to disagree, there is no question that little is to be gained in either the short or the long run by trying to convince a thirteen-year-old that he and his parents are wrong in their assessment of what constitutes success for the student. The student seems to require a feeling that school is a place for business, not play. It is for this reason that seventh and eighth graders, the ghetto children especially, resent an unstructured—or what appears to be unstructured—approach to mathematics. If they cannot see and feel that what they have done constitutes an education as they conceive it, they feel that they are being cheated because the teacher has "given up" on them.

This is the sole reason for my use of the State-issued text (*Mathematics*, by E. T. McSwain, *et al.*, Laidlaw, 1963–64, California State Series). It is a well-structured, ingenious, and mathematically excellent text. Unfortunately, most children cannot read it. Its language is rather sophisticated and its explanations lengthy. This is of little concern to the students, however. Books provide problems—teachers provide explanations. However unfortunate this may be, it has become a fact of life for me and the other teachers of lower-track students with whom I have talked. Removing the mountain which stands between reading and learning mathematics continues to be a process of erosion rather than explosion. Still the book is invaluable. On Monday, page 293 is established as the target for the week. The child knows where he is going and he begins to believe that he can do what the experts say he should be doing. By Friday he can feel the weight of 292 pages of math which he has "done." He is moving and he knows it. It is a pleasurable sensation.

14

Algebra for Nonachievers

Background

Math is traditionally the nightmare of all students. They don't understand it, they can't do it, so they hate it—it's that simple. And if this is true of normal students, one can just imagine the reaction of students who have never made it in school.

I teach a special class of ten students whom the state has labeled "educationally handicapped" (EH). Despite the theoretical baggage about neurological handicaps and brain dysfunction that the EH program picked up on its trip through the state legislature several years ago, in practice my class contains a superb variety of educational misfits. Many are known to juvenile court, several are chronic runaways, most have experimented with drugs. Eight out of the ten have at least one parent missing, and the remaining two homes apparently more resemble battlegrounds than places of rest and security. They have a variety of emotional problems, difficulty in concentration, or hatred of anything that smacks of authority, including teachers. But without exception they have at least normal ability; that ability has simply never borne fruit in academic achievement. To the contrary, all have been expelled from school at some time for either behavior or attendance problems.

After spending three unsuccessful weeks with an arithmetic workbook, I decided, under the influence of a workshop I had attended, to try to teach these kids basic algebra. They needed something (1) that they could be motivated to do; (2) that they would be able to do; and (3) that they could not only do, but do well. I found that the first was no problem once they had recovered from the shock of my telling them that they were going to start doing ninth-grade math. (Most of them are ninth-graders who have grown accustomed to working below grade level.) The problem lay in distilling the ninth grade material into a more comprehensible form. I attempted to do this by starting with the already-known arithmetic processes and slowly moving into new areas.

Strategies

My first math sheet consisted entirely of combining terms containing two unknowns. The first reaction, of course, was "What in hell do these crazy letters mean?" I told them they would represent a number they didn't know and were trying to find; they would be actually working with such numbers only after they learned how to do arithmetic with them. Their response was, "That's easy!" and I was off and running.

The first sheet was all addition, the next three contained both addition and subtraction. At that point I felt I could try to introduce negative numbers. I placed a series of strips of masking tape on the floor of the classroom, representing a number scale from $+10$ to -10. I first explained it as a new way to do the problems on the sheets we had been doing. Then I asked what would happen if, instead of taking, for example, $3y$ from $6y$, I did the reverse and took $6y$ from $3y$. "You can't do that!" was the reply. I responded that this was true, but assuming that we could, how could we represent the answer we'd get? I had one student walk off the problem by starting at 0, going up three strips, then back six. Minus 3 was his answer. That, I said, was all there was to negative numbers; they were merely a way of keeping track of what we were doing if we happened to take away more than we had to begin with.

For the first day or two, everybody was enthusiastically pacing off the answers to their problems. When their feet got too tired, I gave them a dittoed representation of the small scale, which they could use with their fingers.

Next I wanted them to start familiarizing themselves with letters as representing unknown numbers, rather than merely as labels that they had to tack onto their answers in order to get them right. I gave a letter a value, and then provided a coefficient to multiply that number by (e.g., $y = 3$; $3y = ?$).

At last, I turned it around and had them actually find what number y or z represented. (I didn't use x because it could be confused with the multiplication sign.) I asked them what number plus one equals two, etc.

The whole class had followed along pretty well up to this point. The novelty had worn off and there was some day-to-day reluctance, but it was nothing like the way I almost had the arithmetic workbooks thrown back in my face the first three weeks I had worked with them.

The previous week I had enrolled a new student who had already had some algebra. I found out, however, that when he was faced with an equation like $y + 5 = 13$, he would just "psych" it out. He had no idea that what he was really doing was deducting 5 from each side and isolating the unknown. I didn't want my students to also get stuck in this rut, and so although I let them get started by merely "psyching" out the answers, I wanted to switch them over to the longer, but more correct, method.

I did this by literally setting up the whole operation for them, so all they had to do was the subtraction. The next day I told them I'd gotten lazy and left it up to them to set up the subtraction. But, I told them, they couldn't go wrong if they took the number on the same side of the equation as the unknown, reverse the sign, and add. Although it did take several days, they did catch on and were able to get the signs, as well as the numbers, correct.

Next I complicated things a bit by adding coefficients to the unknowns, but they surprised me by catching onto this almost immediately.

This is about where we are at this point. I have thrown in several sheets on exponents and graphing to provide variety, but my goal is still to increase their ability to handle and solve algebraic expressions and equations.

Some Tentative Conclusions

My students had experienced so much failure that any inquisitive spirit, any willingness to experiment with their own ideas and hunches, had long been extinguished. I felt I had a better chance of succeeding with them if I started with what they already knew, if imperfectly: arithmetic. All along I had suspected that the problem was their unwillingness, not inability, to do arithmetic. Given the motivation, I thought that much of the difficulty would disappear. As a precaution, however, I duplicated addition and multiplication tables for them to use if they needed them. I wanted to be sure the focus was on what they were learning they *could* do, not on what they had learned they could not do.

What is most important for the purposes of the class is the ego boost that several of my students are getting by being successful for once in math, and having a string of perfect or near perfect papers to prove it.

This points out the most paradoxical thing I seem to have learned from teaching this class; no matter how much a kid has been pushed around by the educational system, he has to know that he can get along in it if he wants to before he will be willing to depart very much from it. My kids will go along with any departure from routine that I may allow, but they will insist, "This isn't schoolwork!" and act as if they're getting away with something. For this reason, I believe a lot of changes would have to take place before I could let them grade themselves (a goal I would like to work toward). At present they still need the security of someone else's evaluation of them.[1]

But more to the point, this need for security made it necessary to start a new approach to math from the point at which they had all failed repeatedly before. For such students, the known, even if unpleasant, appears preferable to the unknown and its attendant insecurity.

[1] ED. NOTE—Cf. Miss Perlstein's approach in "A Suggestion for the Constructive Use of Grades," strategy 7.

Getting Kids to Follow Directions

Adams Junior High School in Richmond covers only grades seven and eight, so several times a year batteries of standardized tests are given to the eighth-graders for high school placement and counseling. The tests are given by having teachers pass out booklets and answer cards in a classroom, while direction-giving and timing are carried out via intercom. Teachers cannot help after the test begins.

I happened to have a very slow group of eighth-graders during several tests, and I noticed that many of them did not even try to do the test. What might have been low scores would be zeros because the directions were given in a strange manner, were not repeated, and used unfamiliar language. There was a time for questions before the actual test began, but these students didn't grasp enough of the directions to know how to question them.

Watching their bewilderment and inability to cope with the mechanics of directions, I decided to develop with them a unit on following directions.

This has turned out to be an ongoing daily exercise rather than a self-contained unit. I now plan to continue "direction" exercises several times a week all year.

The goals in the project are manifold, and they keep increasing. We began working on listening and following a direction only being repeated once, and will work up to no repeats. We also work on mastering directional words[1] and on following sequential directions.

There has been slow but steady progress in these skills, and in my larger goal for these stu-

[1] I use the word to designate a term used in sets of directions which the direction givers assume the reader knows.

dents—to help add some order and sense to their lives.

Strategy

The first assignment was a dittoed sheet of nonsense directions which the students all enjoyed doing and did fairly well. They all made some careless mistakes, however, and we talked about being careful in little things. Their interest was piqued.

For the next few weeks I gave short daily oral exercises. Each day I introduced one or two new directional words, explained them, and immediately used them in the exercise that day and days following. Some words the students now know include *alternate, consecutive, diagonal, sign, print, asterisk, chronological,* and *margin.* We are still working with these words and others and interchange oral with written tests so the students recognize the word in print. (After hearing it often, they can recognize/read the "big words," which has also a side benefit of ego-building.) Another important reason for written tests is that seeing the corrected answer with the question lets them see their mistake. This is not possible with merely a corrected paper of answers from an oral test.

I always try to make the directions I give them a little whimsical so that they continue to enjoy these few minutes of the period. Being able to believe that the teacher is sometimes a bit silly, and they a bit wiser but willing to humor me adds a nice balance of give and take to the class, too.

We have now expanded into sequential problems and are learning how not to be confused by extraneous material. An instance of the two combined: "If we are in room 304, divide 112 by 4 and add the answer to your age. If not, write the alternate letters of the first half of the alphabet."

They have to go through several deductive steps, understand a directional word, and note that I only want half the alphabet dealt with. I also sometimes ask for wrong answers and nonsense answers to make sure they read closely.

By chance, in looking for new material, I've added another dimension to the directions—incorporating their knowledge of the immediate world and our other studies in the directional tests. It sometimes helps to reinforce other class lessons, and just nudges them to be more observant sometimes (e.g., If Sherlock Holmes smoked a pipe,... If Miss McVittie is principal of Adams,... If the bulletin board I took down yesterday had a picture of...).

This unit has been successful with both the class and me, not only because it is useful and enjoyable, but also because I see tangible progress in the students' learning. More important is that they too can *see* that they know something today that they didn't know yesterday, and it is a concrete gratification to them and an incentive to enjoy school.

Appendix

SAMPLE DIRECTIONS TEST

1. Draw a triangle. Inside the triangle draw a rectangle which touches each side of the triangle. Make an X inside the rectangle.
2. Write in numbers: sixty seven hundred; and six thousand, seven hundred.
3. In the lower left corner draw a symbol of war and print your first name backward below it.
4. Give the wrong answer to this question: Are owls birds?
5. If three days before tomorrow was Wednesday, draw six diagonal lines. If it wasn't, draw a striped elephant.
6. Put the following in alphabetical order: ringer, rinse, ring.
7. Write the symbol used in comic books to show someone is sleeping.
8. Put in chronological order: childhood, old age, teens.
9. What are the initials of the United States of America?
10. Write down the fourth number in the following series: 67, 99, 1088, 21, 12, 60, 42.
11. Put an asterisk 3 lines below your answer to question four.
12. If $12 \times 6 = 74$ write "Christmas is coming soon." If not, write "Santa goes ho, ho, ho."
13. Draw 5 squares in the middle of the page. Color 3 of them in, leave one blank, and draw a face in the other one.
14. Write yes no matter with what letter your last name begins.
15. If Egypt is in Africa, write the shorter of the words *orange* and *blue*. If not, draw a bottle tilted against the left margin.

PART TWO

Evolving Processes of Instruction

To be sure, teaching—like the practice of medicine—is very much an art, which is to say, it calls for the exercise of talent and creativity. But like medicine, it is also—or should be—a science, for it involves a repertoire of techniques, procedures, and skills that can be systematically studied and described, and therefore transmitted and improved. The great teacher, like the great doctor, is the one who adds creativity and inspiration to that basic repertoire...[1]

Part Two, *Evolving Processes of Instruction,* is a survey of promising instructional practices that Graduate Internship Program teachers are currently using—processes for encouraging inquiry, discovery, conceptualization; methods for promoting creativity; ways of grouping students, and using them to teach other students; techniques for enriching learning via dramatic devices and games; uses for technical equipment and the mass media in the classroom; and most important, processes for helping students develop personal, social, and intellectual values.

For convenience, we have divided Part Two into seven separately introduced chapters, each focusing predominantly on one of the above processes. We have tried to select strategies that are both useful in their own discipline and transferable across subject lines.

[1] Charles E. Silberman, *Fortune* (August, 1966), 124.

I: INDUCTIVE APPROACHES:
INQUIRY, DISCOVERY, CONCEPT-BUILDING

Science students at King Junior High School, Berkeley, California, discover habits of fish in a mini-aquarium.

...Discovery, like surprise, favors the well prepared mind....Our aim as teachers is to give our students as firm a grasp of a subject as we can, and to make him as autonomous and self-propelled a thinker as we can....The hypothesis that I would propose here is that to the degree that one is able to approach learning as a task of discovering something rather than "learning about it," to that degree will there be a tendency for the child to carry out his learning activities with the autonomy of self-reward or, more properly, by reward that is discovery itself.[1]

Curriculum builders of the late fifties and through most of the sixties have devoted considerable attention to the processes of inquiry and discovery. Jolted by Sputnik and financed by the federal government, public school curriculum coordinators were propelled into establishing project centers for developing instruction more appropriate to the Space Age. With Jerome Bruner's now classic *Process of Education* clarifying the emerging focus, the new approaches emphasized the necessity for generating processes of discovery and inquiry in American classrooms.

For a decade now, teachers have been exhorted to develop their students' ability to inquire, to discover, and to think productively. Have they been able to carry out these ambitious commands? Regrettably, after visiting a hundred schools in and around major cities in thirteen states, John Goodlad, Dean of the Graduate School of Education at UCLA, reports a huge discrepancy between teachers' intentions and their actual practices. He writes that "as far as our sample of schools is concerned,...we are forced to conclude that much of the so-called educational reform movement has been blunted on the class-room door...." He insists that "if teachers are to change, they must see models of what they are to change to...."[2]

From our own work with beginning teachers, we know that their urge to stimulate students to think critically and creatively is strengthened when specific and workable models are available. We have noted that when lectures on inquiry and discovery were followed with demonstrations of actual teaching strategies, other teachers were eager to try out variations and new possibilities. Many of the strategies included in this section were inspired in this way. We have included samples of various discovery and inquiry approaches which Graduate Internship Program teachers have attempted in several disciplines. Although they cannot be as compelling as live demonstrations, we hope that these written strategies are concrete and detailed enough to suggest further ideas to the reader.

Discovery and Language

We begin with Al Coglianese's strategy, "Inventing Your Own Language." By having each of his three classes first create and evolve their own languages (known to their inventors as Kovich, Vaca-lode, and Bazouborfle), and then compare them with each other and with the English language, Mr. Coglianese demonstrates a singularly effective way to help students discover basic prin-

[1] Jerome S. Bruner, "The Act of Discovery," *Harvard Educational Review*, XXXI, No. 1 (Winter, 1961), 22, 23, 26.
[2] *Saturday Review* (April 19, 1969), 60–61.

ciples of language development and usage. The same approach could be used equally well in any foreign language class or as an introduction to more sophisticated linguistic studies.

Moving next into foreign language teaching, we have included "Strategy: Imagination," in which Kati Lydon suggests various "pretending" activities which can prompt language students to imagine and discover the meaning of words and concepts in a foreign tongue.

Discovery in Science Classes

The next three strategies, by Janet Imagawa, Anne Smith, and Warner Freeman, illustrate discovery and inquiry methods for science classes. (While science teachers usually praise scientific thought, they do not always know how to promote it, especially with unmotivated students.) In "Identifying Living Organisms" Janet Imagawa describes how a concept-formation exercise she devised with varied geometric figures helped a group of high school freshmen in a lower track biology class formulate basic principles of classification—useful to biology or to any other subject. Anne Smith's strategy, "Teaching Laboratory Science," details the activity-oriented approach she used in a physical science class. Daily laboratory investigations, with only minimal readings and lectures, encouraged even her slow and reluctant students to discover for themselves some patterns in the nature of matter and its relation to energy. We have included her teaching plans and dittoes for an entire week, for they offer teachers of all subjects a heartening example of the step-by-step planning that helps students think critically, make sound judgments, and develop the habits of inquiry that foster discovery. In his strategy, "My Use of the Discovery Method in Teaching Junior High School Science," Warner Freeman, another inventive science teacher, includes a few easily replicable classroom experiments and devices for helping students enjoyably discover scientific facts.

Discovery and Mathematics

The discovery method, by its very nature, forces the teacher to focus on the culture-free aspects of any discipline: concept, process, and approach. Rote fact and technique, areas in which the disadvantaged child is notably weak, are not susceptible to discovery. Discovery removes the demands of rote fact and technique from the disadvantaged child's educational experience and frees him to fulfill his maximum intellectual potential.

How ironic, not to say delightful, if our new concern for the disadvantaged learner should direct education in general away from rote learning and toward conceptual understanding. . . .[3]

We move next to two strategies which demonstrate the use of the discovery approach in mathematics. Doris Todd, working with top-ability but noisy seventh graders, explains in her strategy paper, "Devising Number Systems," how having her students devise their own mathematical symbols channeled their energy and directed them toward a genuine grasp of arithmetic operations.

[3] William Johntz, Director of SEED Project (Special Elementary Education Programs for the Disadvantaged).

José Gutierrez,[4] exploring the discovery process with disadvantaged students, illustrates his own invention—a set of visual devices for leading students into mathematical understandings and discoveries of their own. His strategy, "The Function Machine," explains these readily reproducible visual aids and offers a sample unit to demonstrate their use.

Discovery and Concept-Building in Social Studies

The last two strategies in this section, both by Janet Manley, offer specific techniques for promoting inquiry about historical events, politics, and social institutions. In "Helping Slow Eighth-Graders to Understand U.S. History" Mrs. Manley recounts how she encouraged her students to work out their own rules of government first for the classroom, then for the early American colonies. Next the students compared the governments they had created with those the colonialists had actually established. Mrs. Manley pursued further inquiry approaches in a pilot summer social studies program sponsored by the Vallejo School District, primarily for disadvantaged students. She describes these efforts in "Concepts and Processes for Social Studies." Building on her students' areas of greatest initial interests—such as guns and cars—she guided them up the conceptual ladder (e.g., from guns to licensing laws to present social controversies about guns, violence, etc.) to a greater understanding of contemporary social problems.

In all these strategies the teachers stretch their students' minds by involving them directly in inquiry and discovery processes, by creating activities which beguile their students to conceptualize and to hypothesize. We are reminded of Alfred North Whitehead's injunction:

> Whatever interest attaches to your subject-matter must be evoked here and now; whatever powers you are strengthening in the pupils must be exercised here and now; whatever possibilities of mental life your teaching should impart, must be exhibited here and now. That is the golden rule of education, and a very difficult rule to follow. . . .[5]

[4] José Gutierrez, an intern in 1965, worked as a teacher-coordinator in the California state-sponsored SB28 Demonstration Project for the Disadvantaged, 1966–68. Presently he is serving as a math supervisor in the Graduate Internship Program.

[5] Alfred North Whitehead, *The Aims of Education* (New York: New American Library, A Mentor Book, 1953), p. 18. Originally published 1929.

AL COGLIANESE **16**

Inventing Your Own Language

Introduction

Recently I overhead one of my sophomore English students muse as he translated a love letter, "Smork makes the zinx go round." He was hesitantly corrected by one of his classmates, "Zort, flot pab schlink zinx zem zam." The second student's objection was based on the mixing of two languages, English and Kovich. However, his correction was ironic because it was delivered in Bazulborfle mixed with Kovich.

Both Kovich and Bazulborfle are languages invented by my high school English students. Kovich is the senior language; Bazulborfle is the sophomore language. The freshmen have also invented a language; they call it Vaca-Lode.

This invention of languages was an experiment in language studies. It was the result of a search for a way to make grammar more palatable to my students. At the same time I wished to take the study of English grammar out of isolation and put it into a context which would make it immediately useful.

Language Invention

At the beginning of the experiment each class began to develop a vocabulary. They did this by role playing a series of social situations in which the players communicated with one another verbally without using words from any known language.[1] The class watched the players to guess the situation and to transcribe the sounds that were made. After the role playing situation was identified, the class and the players collectively decided upon the meaning of the sounds. After thirty or so sounds were assigned

[1] See Viola Spolin's *Improvisations for the Theatre* (Evanston, Ill.: Northwestern University Press, 1963), especially the section on Gibberish, pp. 120–27.

meanings, the class wrote a three sentence paragraph in their new language. Of course, this paragraph was very difficult to write, but afterward the students felt the need to invent more and particular words. They discovered immediately that they needed words for conjunctions, prepositions, and other function words. All their subsequent inventions were based on the need to express something that they could not otherwise express. It is to be noted that while the classes delighted in inventing "weird" sounds, they were hesitant to waste time with other than the most basic words, words indicating human relationships, basic artifacts, days of the week, common actions, etc. It is interesting to further note that when a senior student suggested that his class invent a word for "time" he was condemned for becoming too abstract.

The vocabularies were being developed for several days when someone in the freshman class decided that she wanted to write of more than one of a particular object. The first grammatical rule came about. "What do we do in English?" I asked. "Add 's,'" she said. "What would you like to do to form plurals in your language?" "Add 's,'" she decided. I passed the news of the rule on to my seniors and sophomores; they condemned the freshmen for being unimaginative. The seniors added a "k" or "ak" to the root word to form plurals; the sophomores added "i."

The *tense* rules followed immediately. They took almost a period to develop. Rules for possessives followed the tense rules; then came rules for comparing adjectives.

In each case when the problem of rules would arise, I would ask, "What do we do in English? What would you like to do in your language?" The freshmen and sophomores seemed satisfied with four basic grammatical change rules; the seniors found a use for seven. All three languages retained the basic word order of English. It was found, however, that Bazulborfle and Kovich, because of the lack of auxiliaries, could not easily distinguish a statement from a question unless something was done with word order. It was decided in both cases that to form a question the word order of a statement be reversed. All the classes decided that case distinctions (except for possessives) were an unnecessary bother. The freshmen voted to do away with the articles. The freshmen also developed two forms for the present tense and the present perfect tense. One form is for common usage, the other for formal usage.

Assignments in the use of the languages fell into two categories—compositions and teacher-prepared translations. The students wrote short poems and paragraphs in their respective languages; they wrote letters to one another, both to members of their own classes and to the members of the other classes. They translated teacher-prepared sentences, expository paragraphs, and stories from their languages to English and from English to their languages.

Results

The translating from English languages proved to be the most valuable exercise for the examining of English grammatical rules. The students worked in small groups so that possible mistakes could be discussed. Many times errors such as the following would occur: "He beats his mother" translates into Kovich as "Ha nur hazo kooti." Many students confuse the English distinction between "beat" and "beats" as being essentially the same distinction between "car" and "cars" and thus they mistakenly translate "beats," a verb not distinguished in Kovich from "beat," as a plural noun. Thus, "He beats his mother" erroneously becomes "Ha nurk hazo kooti," although "nurk" is an impossible form in Kovich. Within the small group, the dealing with such errors caused a close and valuable examination of the basic workings of the English language.

One interesting and unexpected side effect of the invention of languages came about as a result of the necessarily small vocabularies. In an effort to work within the limitations of the language, the students had to resort to extreme economy. This economy gave most resulting English translations a poetic quality. The following are translations from students' letters:

"The moon is old. The winds laugh. Are you sleeping? The sun is an island. The time calls you and me."

"You are sexy and young, and you are my love-teacher."

"Today is the twenty-fourth of the month. It will rain from the cloud now. The rain is water from heaven. It is clean. Rain may go from the heaven day or night."

"I like parties. Parties swim from early night into early moon-go."

"It is a black day. I think the sun is in hell."

"The day is early. Clouds go over. The wind brings them. See the sun? It calls the night a dead time. All is joy to me."

The device here which seems to abound is the one that yokes together two unrelated words to form a third—like the Old English kenning. Two are illustrated above (in the second and fourth selections). They are "love-teacher" and "moon-go." Others I have noticed are "sky-tear," "water-brother," "river-tiger," "world-father," "forest-tiger," "fire-sky," "mind-music," and "devil-tongue." I have seen none of the obvious neologisms like "forest-fire" or "dog-house." Probably these are "no fun."

Student Responses

Eighty percent of the students who participated in the experiment said that they enjoyed it. Not quite so high a percentage thought that it was more effective than the traditional approach to grammar. Below is a chart indicating student opinion on the effectiveness of this method as compared to the traditional approach. Of the seventy-two students polled, twenty-five are seniors, twenty-five are sophomores, and twenty-two are freshmen.

	More effective than the traditional approach	Equally effective as the traditional approach	Less effective than the traditional approach
Seniors	56 %	24 %	20 %
Sophomores	52	28	20
Freshmen	72.7	9.1	18.2
Total	59.7%	20.9%	19.4%

Appendix A: Samples of Grammatical Changes

TENSES

English	Kovich	Vaca-lode	Bazulborfle
I am	mur ploo	ome fa (nepa)	gramft barf
I was	mur pl`oó`	ome fa orla	gramft barfin
I will be	mur plòò	ome fa torta	gramft barfa
I have been	mur plooid	ome conga fa (nepa)	gramft barft
I had been	mur plooid'	ome conga fa orla	gramft barfint
I will have been	mur plooid	ome fenga fa torta	gramft barfat

PLURALS

eye = eyes	carftel = carftelk (add "ak" for pronunciation where needed)	erk = erks (add "es" for pronunciation where needed) includes personal pronouns	eh = ehi Includes personal pronouns

DEGREES OF ADJECTIVES

happy	moosh	tunor	gleesh
happier	mooshdo	anod tunor	gleesht
happiest	mooshda	bor tunor	gleeshy

POSSESSIVES

man	zork	meop	tonk
man's	zorkzo	meop'	tonku
men	zorkak	meops	tonki
men's	zorkakzo	meops'	tonkiu

ADJECTIVES FORMED FROM NOUNS

water	kish		
watery	kishav (add only "v" in pronounceable cases)		

Appendix B: Sample Page of Vocabulary

English	Kovich	Vaca-lode	Bazulborfle
a	daba	—	ruf
above	deesoo	-trop	-zie
about	-korfu	bunta	-zam
afternoon	—	trooter	-raz
aflame	—	parde	—
all	zalempy	opt	aa
also	dukzeldit	-dil	fooba
an	daba	—	ruf
and	yorkoavesky	dop	sorinch
animal	—	—	gasger
as	-tsin	dal	lom
at	rit	dem	-onki
baby	—	—	puc
bad	—	-noj	banf
be	ploo	fa	barf

English	Kovich	Vaca-lode	Bazulborfle
beat	nur	naru	-bradowf
beard	richee	—	—
because	carpi	gemou	-upledoon
black	morky	-Meomu	—
blanket	bloch	—	—
blue	inal	Kurnt	glock
boat	zormestrianite	—	—
body	og	—	boval
booze	fleena	-Zasch	—
boy	-lib	-yob	wang
break	—	sha	daba
bright	-mot	glick	—
bring	tago	-rono	—
brother	—	arle	font
build	sach	—	—
burning	—	parde	—
but	uh	amef	urt
by	-ebu	-retep	oolu
call	dwip	—	—
can	glik	-mup	—
cat	knig	—	—
center	rin	—	—
chair	rach	—	gloop
child	—	—	unk
clean	humple	cesif	bask
clock	ool	—	—
close	—	-oit	slorbol
clothing	lairk	—	—
cloud	zopo	—	—

KATI LYDON QUIBELL **17**

Strategy: Imagination

One of the things that language teachers constantly hear their students say in the process of learning a language is: "Why do *they* say it that way? That's stupid." It certainly would

ED. NOTE: Kati Quibell was an intern in 1961–62. She has since become head of the Foreign Language Department at El Cerrito High, and has served as a master teacher for interns during the Summers of 1965, 1966, and 1968. In the Spring of 1969, while on her sabbatical, she was asked to serve as a Graduate Internship Program Supervisor of foreign language interns. We asked her to describe the approach to teaching which she felt most strategic in her field.

be a mistake for language teachers to ignore the fact that the "other" languages may sound strange and different to their students. The question is how to handle this attitude without just telling the students that their language is just as strange, but rather helping them to expand their horizons and their understanding of "other ways." One of the approaches that I have found most essential is to teach students to use their *imagination*.

Imagination as defined by Webster is: "the formation of mental images of objects not present to the senses, especially of those never perceived in their entirety; hence, mental synthesis of new ideas from elements experienced separately." In our day and age when most youngsters have grown up with space shots taking off in their living rooms, it is difficult to see how one could develop their incentive to imagine. It's all done for them already. It seems, however, that in the audiovisual environment in which we are teaching foreign languages, to be able to imagine is a *must*. Most of us are involved in a method of language teaching which is both global and immediate and in which the major objective for learning a language is to provide more communication. We are concerned with teaching spoken language above all. We have to lure our students into a "game" situation where the world becomes French or Spanish, or whatever language is being taught. For this, we will need as our major ally imagination.

In the classroom we attempt to reproduce "foreign life" so that our students can learn how to act in the new cultural context. We would like the student to be immersed in the situation so that he is compelled to be drawn into the new environment and thus to become part of it.

We often ask ourselves how we can best explain words to students, especially abstract words for which we cannot use pictures. Hopefully, they will be explained in terms of a situation, not in terms of another word in their native language. Why should I go through all that trouble of creating for them a situation within which the word can be explained, if the first thing the student does when he has understood the word or group of words is to translate it in his mind into English? I am afraid that the teacher who is still asking this question has not really been convinced of the absolute necessity for making language learning an active experience where meaning is not something independent of actual linguistic behavior. It *is* linguistic behavior. Thus students must learn to use the words(s) significantly and appropriately. They should learn to discover meaningful language behavior by noting the situation in which the language occurs, and from the intonation and rhythm with which it is expressed. For example, the simple phrase "I am a girl" can serve as a beautiful model of the value of intonation and rhythm when stress is put on different words. The student will, in the case of a simple translation of the word *by* the teacher, have only that other word as a point of reference. If the word has been explained within a situation, his frame of reference will be much richer and more meaningful. The teacher allows the student to discover the word. And any teacher who has seen the spark of light in a student's eyes when he has just discovered what the teacher or another student has been trying to explain, knows what discovery means.

In order to successfully draw a student into a situation with which he is not at all familiar, the teacher has to teach him how to imagine. This takes time and patience, both on the side of the teacher and of the students. It has been my experience that it is well worth it. I have very often found that at first a student even hesitates to answer how many rooms there are in his house because he has not learned the number seven and that is the number he needs to deal with reality. When I begin by giving them a fantastic description of the house in which I live, they soon learn that my major concern is with whether or not they have understood my question and that after that, they should give free reign to their imagination. This process is slow but absolutely necessary if later we are going to ask our students to imagine that they are walking down a street in Paris and must confront a policeman in order to find this or that landmark. At first the imagining does not take them too far from reality: Imagine your mother has three daughters, how many sisters do you have? Imagine you are your father, how many daughters do you have? Imagine I am your sister. What color are your sister's eyes? Paul is your next door neighbor. Where does he live? We are going to New York this afternoon. How will we get there? and on and on. In one of my classes a student took so well to this "game" that she had us all believing that she was an only child. Later she told me that she really liked the sound of the phrase "ein einziges Kind" much better than "ich habe 3 Bruder and eine Schwester." In our "class world" she also had a bright red motorcycle and a boyfriend with one brown and one green eye.

Sometimes a picture can be very helpful in

Mrs. Kati Quibell helps her French students imagine the meaning of words in Le Petit Prince, El Cerrito High School, Berkeley, California.

this pursuit to help the student exercise his imagination. For example, while showing a picture of an old man to a student, I nod my head quite emphatically and say, "This is a picture of you, yes?" "Yes, it is my picture." Generally the answer is accompanied by a smile, for they can tell the "game" is about to begin. I proceed, "Who are you?" "I am an old man." "Why do you say you are old?" "Because my hair is white." "Any other reasons?" "My skin is not young." And so on. I can then go to another student and say, "Do you know this old man?" pointing at the picture. "Yes." "Where is he?" "He is sitting there," etc. It probably need not

be pointed out that the students are conjugating the verb "to be" while going through this exercise.

Imagination becomes little by little a most helpful tool in the teaching of a language. Eventually the classroom can become Paris or Madrid, and the students can imagine themselves in a sidewalk café ordering a refreshing drink after a long day of sightseeing.

One of the principles that goes hand in hand with the freedom to imagine is the freedom to guess. Students learning a foreign language have to learn that sometimes there are no "good" reasons for some of the "peculiar" ways in which this or that is expressed. The teacher has to be ready to accept that there might be more than one answer to her question and allow the students to guess, imagine, discover by trial and error.

Students sometimes are asked to look at a picture and try to imagine what action it could suggest to them. A simple picture of a girl carrying a pair of shoes to the shoe repair shop (one could see that the soles had big holes) brought forth a marvelously imaginative story of some tiny animals who were living in the shoes and whose door was going to be closed by the cobbler. They decided to have a big party before the tragedy came about. The student then went into great detail as to what "everybody" was going to wear. The lesson that had just been studied dealt with clothing and the students had been encouraged to incorporate as much of the new material as possible into their stories. Her imagined situation thrilled us all.

As their vocabularies become richer and their minds are more at ease when asked to imagine, I try to have them explain an expression or words by imagining a situation where the word or expression could be used. They then describe this to the class, and often their initial effort becomes enlarged and enriched by the contributions of other class members. It is in this way that the student is asked to imagine a situation with which best to demonstrate his understanding of the words, and also the possible cultural implications that accompany their usage. We all know how difficult it is for some students to correctly use a typical foreign language pattern. It is only through the skilled use of imagination that the teacher can allow the student to go beyond the words to communicate to them the feeling of a French, Spanish, etc., situation. The student should, while mastering the different linguistic patterns, also get into the habit of imagining himself in all sorts of situations. He will then find himself in a position of imagining a world different from his own, thus going beyond the usage of foreign words toward a more significant need to communicate and understand the attitudes and feelings of other people who have grown up immersed in a different culture, using another language.

JANET IMAGAWA **18**

Identifying Living Organisms

Setting

This unit was planned for a Life Science class made up mostly of high school freshmen. Since this was the lower track biology class at the school, many students were taking it as the easiest way to satisfy their high school science requirement. Many were also taking it because they were freshmen and their counselors thought them too young for the tougher biology course. The students' abilities varied greatly, from gifted on down to almost nonreaders.

Taxonomy has never been my strength. When I was confronted with the task of teaching taxonomy, I felt the need to expose my students to the importance of taxonomy, and the major problems it presents to the biologists.

Since taxonomy is so difficult to make interesting because of its factual and seemingly trivial nature, I had to try extra hard to find a fresh way to present it. The lesson plans that I finally evolved have an underlying philosophy that experience and discovery offer the most effective ways of learning.

Preparation for Learning Taxonomy

Before we could make progress, my students had to be helped to see the importance of taxonomy. We discussed the reasons we have a binomial system of nomenclature and the value of using the universal language of Latin. My students were quick to point out the fact that, even within one country where the same language is spoken, different populations may confuse each other with different common names for the same organism. Perhaps the fact that many of my students were from families who were stationed at Hamilton Air Force Base and who had done much traveling helped. Also, several of my students often go hunting in the woods around their homes and are familiar with some of the common flora and fauna. It became evident to all that confusion would arise when people from different areas tried to talk about a particular organism if they did not standardize their language.

As a basis for our discussion we used a chapter entitled "Classification of Living Things" (Chapter 7) from their textbook, *Biological Science for High School,* by William H. Gregory and Edward H. Goldman.[1] The chapter included a discussion on Charles Darwin's contribution to classification. Most of my students were already aware of the impact that Darwin's ideas had made on taxonomy. The controversy which his theory of evolution stirred in the last century in its application to the evolution of man still has not subsided. The concept of *time* in taxonomy was therefore already imbued in my students.

The question arose, "How can you tell if a plant or animal is primitive or advanced?" This question led to discussion of the clues that a taxonomist can use, such as the fossil record, comparisons of morphological features and habitats of the living and dead, and biochemical aspects of the living.

This was the setting for the beginning of my strategy.

Creating a Taxonomic System

To acquaint the students with the difficult process involved in classification, I gave them a set of twenty-one geometrical figures which I

[1] Boston: Ginn and Company, 1968.

had constructed. The students were given specific directions in class to divide these into no more than two or three groups. Since no two figures were alike (see Appendix A), they were forced to give precedence to a few characteristics. They next divided the figures according to similarities they'd decided to focus upon, ignoring differences for the time being.

They were hesitant about doing this, and asked me which characteristics they should use. I then reemphasized that they were to pick their own, and that it didn't matter what they picked as long as they did not tell anyone else in the class what they were doing. They worked alone, quietly.

When they were finished, they were asked to divide each large group into two or three smaller ones. The reason for giving them a choice of division into two or three groups was to allow flexibility for individual preferences. I even had a few students who insisted they could divide each group into no less than four smaller groups. I gave in and allowed this if their reason was convincing.

I kept having them divide the groups into smaller ones, despite their groans, for the task was not as easy as it appeared.

For every category they were asked to write a brief description of the distinguishing characteristic of the group. To decide which characteristic was to take precedence over the others was a task which the more conscientious students took with surprising responsibility and, as a consequence, with some agony. Several commented, "This is hard!"

After about half an hour a few were still not finished, although most of the students were. Some students had several pages filled with writing, which they showed to me, surprised by the complexity of their job. At this time I had them quit their work for the time being and asked for volunteers to tell what criteria they had used for the first division. There were at least five different methods which we listed on the board, each with good reasoning behind it.

Some had used essentially the same criteria, but used different words to express them. For example (see Appendix A) the circles with the scalloped or ruffled edges were called by several different names. There was always some discussion before it was decided which word they would use to describe something, so that they would know if two criteria were the same. In this way they learned the value of a standardized system for describing the same thing. At this point I was unable to resist the temptation to step in to settle all disputes, and give the correct geometrical terminology for describing these figures. I think the exercise would have been better if I had just let them argue it out themselves.

We all came to the final conclusion before the bell rang at the end of the fifty-minute period that there were several systems that could be used equally well for classifying the figures, and I emphasized to them that in biology, also, taxonomists did not always agree on classification. As a consequence there are many systems in use, each slightly different from the others.

Making a Key

The next day I gave a dittoed sheet (Appendix B) of one system which could be used to classify the twenty-one figures. The main difference between mine and theirs was that I had given each figure a number, once I had classified it down to itself.

After drawing one of the figures on the board, I asked them to tell me what its number was. Using the dittoed sheet, they were quick to find the answer; but each time a student gave an answer, I asked him to outline aloud the thought processes that led him to his conclusion. Example:

I looked at Roman numerals I, II, and III, and decided that it fitted II because it had straight edges. Then I looked at A, B, & C, D, and E under II and decided it belonged under A because it was a square. Since it was a plain square, it is number 5.

This was a tedious way of going about it, but was important for laying down the essentials of using a biological key. The students had fun telling me the numbers of figures I put up on the board, but I cut them off after about four figures and, while their appetites were still eager for this "game," I gave them a real biological key (Appendix C) which I had composed from examples of green algae illustrated on page 107 of their text. I then explained to them how to use the key.

I had made up pictures which I could hold up in front of the class and they could all see. I had them use their key and write the name of the algae on a piece of paper. When all were finished, students who volunteered answers were asked to go through the process by which they had arrived at their conclusion. Their thought processes were of course similar to that used in finding the numbers of the geometrical figures.

After four or five algae identifications, all the students seemed to understand very well how to use the key. When we finished all eleven of the algae, they clamored for more algae to identify; they (and I) had had such a good time!

This particular exercise was effective because there was opportunity for the slower students to be called on and prodded, and yet it still held the interest of the brighter ones.

Final Statement

I felt that my students had learned a lot about the processes involved in taxonomy in an enjoyable way that was thorough yet not boring to them or to me.

They learned very important concepts and skills:

1. That a classification system is not easy to construct, but requires careful investigation and weighing of characteristics.
2. That classification is not rigid, but can differ with each individual taxonomist, and with new information.
3. That a universal language of communication is vital.
4. That there are ways to use and construct a key for identifying living organisms.

Appendix A

Life Science
Imagawa
11/14/66

Classify the following figures according to directions given in class:

Appendix B

Life Science
Imagawa
11/15/66

CLASSIFICATION

I. Figures with curved edges
  A. Figures with the edge as one continuous curve
    1. Circle with a circle in center
    2. Plain circle
      a. Small
      b. Large
  B. Figures with ruffled edges
    1. With circle inside
    2. Without circle inside
II. Figures with straight edges
  A. Four sides

1. Squares
    a. Square within a square
    b. Plain square
2. Diamonds
    a. Plain
    b. Diamond in a diamond
3. Trapezoids
    a. Side lines of equal length
    b. Side lines of unequal length
B. Three sides
    1. Skinny
    2. Very small
    3. One right angle
    4. Two equal angles
C. Five sides
D. Six sides
E. Ten sides
III. Figures with curved and straight edges
    A. Three straight lines at right angles and one semicircle making the fourth side
    B. Three sides with semicircle making the fourth side
    C. Two sides and semicircle making third side

Appendix C

Life Science
Imagawa
11/16/66

GREEN ALGAE KEY

1. Cells elongate or boxlike and forming a filament (single row of cells stuck together)—2.
1a. Cells not boxlike or forming filaments—8.
2. Filaments unbranched—3.
2a. Filaments branched—6.
3. Spiral-shaped chloroplasts—*Spirogyra.*
3a. Chloroplast not spiral—4.
4. Cells elongate and large—*Oedogonium.*
4a. Cells not elongate—5.
5. Cells short and squarish—*Ulothrix.*
6. Branched filaments with all cells same size—*Cladophora.*
6a. Cells not all same size—7.
7. Cells get narrower toward free ends of filaments (pointed at ends)—*Stigeoclonium.*
8. Cells round or irregular in shape, and organism unicellular—9.
8a. Organism not unicellular—10.
9. Organism with two flagellae—*Chlamydomonas.*
9a. Organism without flagellae—9b.
9b. Organism small and round—*Chlorella.*
9c. Organism not small and round, but divided by a constriction into two mirror image halves, giving the organism the appearance of a two-celled plant—*Micrasterias.*
10. Organism multicellular, and cells with flagellae—11.
10a. Cells without flagellae—12.
11. Organism with about twenty cells, and cells compactly held together—*Pandorina.*
11a. Organism made of hundreds of cells, and held far apart from each other—*Volvox.*
12. This organism is made of many cells, all without flagellae, compactly held together and outer cells with humps—*Pediastum.*

Teaching Laboratory Science

The problem with which I have been faced this year involves the teaching of physical science to low track (i.e., disinterested and/or marginally intelligent) students. The course, as arranged in our school, is a semester course. In January the physical science classes change and each teacher gets a new set of students. At our semester change, I reviewed what had been accomplished in my first semester and decided it was most unsatisfactory; we had learned some rather trite facts, had some good days but more dull ones, and in general both my two classes and I were not sorry when the course was over.

Something had to be done! After attending a workshop led by Harry Wong of our district, in which he outlined an "all-lab" course which he had designed for his general science students, I decided to try a modified course of this type in my classes. We would aim at having lab each day, "trying" to apply discovery methods to our scientific learning, and at eliminating as much as possible the lecture-demonstration routine.

This, of course, is an idealized aim which is not as rosy in reality as it may seem on paper, but to my surprise the all-lab idea *has* proven feasible, at least most of the time. I will briefly sketch the details of how the course is run and will then spend some time discussing pros, cons, pitfalls, and delights of this strategy (as I see them).

On the first day of the new semester, the students in my physical science classes were greeted with two pages of rules and much sternness. (In spite of my natural tendencies, I have found that this is beneficial for the kids, and makes life easier for us all from the first—especially for a teacher who tends to look about sixteen years old, as I do.) "THIS is the way

it is," I said, unsmiling. "We *will* have notebooks and pencils every day, and will attend class or else make up work after school. There will be no homework in here, and thus you are doubly responsible for your work in class. This is a lab course." Then came the rules of the lab. "Thou shalt, thou shalt not." And then an outline of what would happen to the unlucky person who failed to comply with these rules. (In our science department, such people become "slaves" or "volunteers" who wash glassware, clean tables, staple papers, etc., after school for a given amount of time.)

After this half-hour indoctrination I announced that there would be lab every day starting now, and showed them a tricky little demonstration using alcohol and water and ice, to test their powers of observation. (Ice floats in water, sinks in alcohol. Why?) We had talked already of hypotheses and of trying to prove your own ideas wrong. They were intrigued.

On the second day, we were off to lab work, and, with perhaps one day a week for catching up, have been "labbing" ever since. In our course, we steal heavily from other San Carlos teachers, from college chemistry experiments, a bit from the BSCS[1] *Patterns and Processes,* and much from a new book, *Physical Science, A Laboratory Approach.* We also take anything else which will fill the bill, including a few original ideas. At the beginning of each investigation the students receive a dittoed lab sheet, usually one to three pages in length. As you can see in the Appendix, these sheets vary in the amount of information given and requested of the student. Where an experiment requires new

[1] Biological Science Curriculum Study.

techniques or somewhat complicated setups, or where the results are somewhat difficult to interpret, I may go over the routine and show it to them first. Other times I say nothing, but force them to read the instructions and to work out the lab entirely by themselves. The students work in pairs. I shift seats every three weeks to keep lab partners constantly changing. Part of the reasoning behind this is that there are "good" and "bad" lab partners, and it is unfair to keep an average student too long with either kind.

At the end of each small "unit" of our course, I hand out a summary sheet (one is included in the Appendix). This is written in class using notes for help, and the sheet aids the students in pulling their thoughts together. It also aids me by showing where the ideas have gotten through.

Until the end of the first quarter I graded each lab write-up simply with A, B, C, or D, reserving Ds for incomplete papers or those which showed that some of the work had been "faked." I am presently changing this policy for several reasons to a point system based partly on the actual lab write-up and partly on spot quizzes which cover lab work. More on the reasons for this will be found in my evaluation.

In running a lab course such as this, a number of problems arise, many of which can best be solved by organization. I include here some rather small details of my organization, since I have found myself floundering more than once for lack of such little things.

1. *Lab setups.* On each dittoed lab write-up sheet I have a list of materials. I have a set of small plastic planter trays, numbered 1–15, and put an identical set of equipment into each tray. It is worth the effort to put reagents into small beakers or dropping bottles and include some in each tray. This helps prevent wasted materials. You will also begin to set up the reagents for experiments for years to come, so that the initial work will be many times repaid. Each lab pair has a number and is responsible for the items on their tray. Using the write-up sheet as a guide, my student clerk, of no more than average ability, can set up the trays before a lab. I always take along a spare tray with extra parts!

2. *Lab Cleanup.* We have a seating arrangement in which there are five horizontal rows of tables. I label the front row Monday, the next is Tuesday, etc., and the youngsters in the "row of the day" are responsible for cleanup of sinks, hardware cupboard, and so forth. This way the labor falls equally and with minimum need for memory on my part.

3. *Notebooks.* Silly as this may sound, much of the notebook problem is helped if I make sure to punch holes in everything I hand out. This takes extra time but is worth it. I also color-code all handouts (pink for film note sheets, white for labs, green for straight information) to make them easier to index. For notebook check time, I make up a check list of what should be included, hand it out ahead of time, and then on the day of the check have the students trade books and go through them with a second check list. At the same time they check for neatness, crumpled pages, pencil writing, etc., and fill out a score sheet. I then put the final grade on the score sheet. The students do a much better checking job than I ever could, and with minimal effort!

4. *The time problem.* We are all aware that some students finish lab work in less time than it takes others. We handle their free time in several ways. Some students are willing and able to help the others finish the lab. Others I give the option of doing extra investigations, looking further into the problem. Actually, the time problem has not been as bad as I had expected. Often, as long as everyone is somewhat motivated, work of manipulative nature can be done at about the same speed by most pairs of lab partners. Figuring out why something happened often takes a bit more time, however.

5. *Theme.* The theme of this course is twofold in subject matter. We are studying the particulate nature of matter and its relation to energy. We are also studying the nature of the classification process, this being a more basic and less narrowly "physical science" objective. We started out seeing how we classify substances and reactions on the basis of easily observable facts and are progressing toward less easily observable phenomena as means of classification (i.e., we started seeing, touching, smelling; now we measure solubility, heat of reactions, crystal formation). The subject matter is broad but based on chemistry, my own

favorite branch of physical science. One lesson I learned in my first quarter of teaching was that it is difficult to develop enthusiastic labs for subjects which leave you cold.

In the Appendix you will find the lesson outline for a week's work, and the dittoed sheets which accompany it. With a few modifications in format, this is the way we do it.

Evaluation

1. *Problems.* The problems with a system like this one, as you may well have already imagined, are several. First, it is a hell of a lot of work. The physical labor of setting up and running lab investigations every day is exhausting. The actual running of the lab is in some ways more tiring than lecturing: you are always on call, showing, listening, trying to ask good questions to help the students answer their own. You are constantly aware of *equipment,* its use and misuse, its movement. As a teacher in two rooms, I must load each day's equipment on a cart and brave the traffic in the halls to get to my classes. These problems I lump in the WORK group and dismiss them as solvable with organization, experience, and a good student clerk.

The second group of problems is somewhat more troublesome: this group I call the HONESTY group, and I mean by that cheating and nonworking students. There will be many students who will be delighted at the chance to work in lab and who will give you their wholehearted support, but there will also be a few (in my classes these are mostly girls) who think labs are the worst bore in the world. These girls will try very hard not to work, on the assumption that they can't do it and it isn't worth doing anyway. Copying on lab reports is a common problem among these students. For this reason I am shifting my grading system from straight lab grading to short quizzes and spot checks as well as a subjective appraisal of lab competence. This treats the symptoms. I have found that the best cure for the disease is personal attention, whenever possible, and have had some good success with some unhappy girls, showing them that it is possible and maybe also desirable for them to do well.

Before approaching the third problem, which

I, as a lover of science, feel most deeply, let me say that these problems are only the large ones, and you would undoubtedly find many new and exciting categories of your own.

My most distressing problem is the feeling that many of the deeper concepts and ramifications of basic ideas are not being handled well. We can discover many things in lab, but when it comes to working through these things, to finding the beauty of their relationships, we seem to miss all but the most obvious. Occasionally we do break through; sometimes I am amazed by the ability of my so-called slow students to see the meaning of a physical fact. There are times when I feel that perhaps I am not stretching these kids enough. Perhaps in trying to give them a way of success I am making that success too easy, too much fun. I am denying them the grimy delights of hard thinking. Maybe because they become so quickly tired of a problem we often drop the problem too soon. Here I need more time to experiment with the minds and feelings of these young people and to learn more about how far to pull them and where to relax.

2. *Pleasures.* Enough of the problems for the moment. Here I want to sing a little about the joy of teaching this type of course. It is *fun.* The kids look on their science class as a highlight of the day; this I have been told directly and indirectly. They get to be good at something, whether it is weighing on a balance or adjusting a bunsen burner or drawing a meaningful graph. They help each other out. They have bad days and good days, although they are never allowed to give up on bad days. They move from step to step in lab work and become skilled in spite of themselves. (Of course, in my ignorance some of the steps are too big, some too small.) We have dull labs and mysterious ones (meaning those in which nobody seems to understand what happens or why). They find a lot of my questions on lab assignments vague and devious, and I think it pleases them when I agree with them and ask them how to reword the questions. They like being able to suggest improvements in lab procedure or to come up with some new idea. This, of course, is rather too common this year. As my experience increases, I expect that a lot of the unintentional goofs will iron out, and the ques-

tions will be less ambiguous, but I plan to leave some goofs, some ambiguities in the structure, because it is good for my students to find them.

3. *Assessment*. In testing this type of curriculum, I have fallen down a bit. I "test" very seldom. The tests are thought tests, open notes, with questions to test the ability my students have acquired to apply their knowledge. They don't do remarkably well. Some have learned to think, some have not. Most are still plodders. The biggest accomplishment seems to be that they are finding this type of plodding worthwhile, and, to the extent that they can, are discovering a certain pleasure in using their brains to try to "figure out" the physical world.

Bibliography

These books were useful in finding ideas for interesting and worthwhile lab investigations:

1. Marean and Ledbetter. *Physical Science: A Laboratory Approach: Investigating Matter and Energy.* Reading, Mass.: Addison-Wesley, 1968.
2. *Biological Science: Patterns and Processes* (Biological Sciences Curriculum Study) New York: Holt, Rinehart, & Winston, Inc., 1966.

Most of the other labs are taken from other teachers or made up out of diverse suggestions.

Appendix

In the following few pages you will find the plan for a week's work under my system, and the dittoed material which accompanies it.

WEEK OF APRIL 15-19, 1968

Monday	Tuesday	Wednesday	Thursday	Friday
Complete lab on calories in food. Turn in at end of period.	Discuss calorie lab. Begin lab on conductivity of materials.	Finish lab on conductivity. Turn in questions.	Discuss labs. Discuss all heat and implications. Summary on heat, due at end of period.	Lab on using new methods of classification (a small-time qualitative analysis lab, using solubility and heats of solution. Works marvelously!).
Assignment:	Assignment:	Assignment:	Assignment:	Assignment:

NO HOMEWORK ASSIGNMENTS IN THIS COURSE.
OCCASIONALLY STUDENTS FINISH UP WRITTEN WORK AT HOME.

General Science B: Physical
Mrs. Smith

Name _____
April 4, 1968

LAB ON HEAT CONTENT OF FOODS

Purpose: _____

_____

Materials: Tin-can calorimeter   10 ml graduated cylinder
          Test tube   3 pieces of walnut (each about .2 gm)
          Small cork   3 pieces of peanut (each about .2 gm)
          Needle   3 pieces of potato chip (same weight)
Drawing of equipment setup:

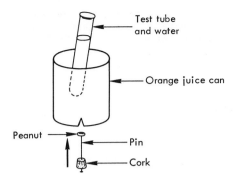

Procedure:

1. Assemble equipment.
2. Measure 8 ml of water and put it in the test tube.
3. Measure the temperature of the water and record it on the table. Remove the thermometer before the next step.
4. Ignite the nut and quickly put it under the test tube inside the calorimeter. Burn the nut to ash. If the fire sputters and goes out, ignite the nut again. If this problem persists discard the partially burned nut, refill the tube, and start over with a new piece.
5. After the piece of nut has burned completely, measure the temperature of the water and record it on your table. Repeat this for three pieces of walnut, three peanuts, and three potato chips. Record all data on your table.
6. Be sure to use new water for each trial.
7. Now convert your figures to the quantities desired for comparison (see below).

Data Table:

Substance	Temperature at beginning	Temperature at end	Difference in temperature	Average
Walnut				
Peanut				
Potato chip				

General Science B: Physical   Name_____
Mrs. Smith   April 4, 1968

QUESTIONS FOR LAB ON CALORIES IN FOOD

1. You have written down your data for the experiment on the previous page. Now it is time to turn these measurements into calories.

Rewrite your data on the following table so that it will be convenient to calculate your calories:

Substance	Amount of water	Temperature change (average)	Calories of heat used
Walnut			
Peanut			
Potato Chip			

2. Why was it important to use the same amount of each type of food you used?

_____

3. Which type of food had the most calories per gram?_____

4. Which had the least calories per gram?_____

5. Do you think all the heat produced by burning these substances was used to heat the water? If not, where did it go?

_____

6. Which type of food would a person on a diet most want to AVOID? _____

_____

7. Why do we need to know how much water was in the test tube each time?

_____

8. Why do we not leave the thermometer resting on the bottom of the test tube while the food is burning?

_____

9. State the difference between a calorie, which measures amount of heat, and a degree, which measures intensity of heat? When is each one used?

_____

10. State one improvement in equipment or method which would have made this lab more accurate.

_____

General Science B: Physical   Name_____
Mrs. Smith   Date _____

LAB ON THE HEAT CONDUCTIVITY OF MATERIALS

By now we have talked about several qualities of heat. We found that heat is measured in calories, and that the intensity of heat in an item can be measured by degrees with a thermometer. We have found that the quantity of heat, or the amount of calories, required to raise the temperature of a given quantity of water will be higher than the quantity needed to raise the temperature of a smaller quantity of water.

In this lab we will test several types of materials to see in which type heat can be transferred the fastest.

Heat is transferred through the collisions of fast-moving molecules with one another. When heat is transferred through a solid, we say it is *conducted*. When heat is transferred through a gas, such as the air, we say it is traveling by *convection*. When heat simply radiates out from a hot object through the air or water or nothing at all, we say it is traveling by *radiation*.

We will be working with examples of conduction in this lab. Think right now about the other two methods of heat travel.

Write a common example of convection: _____

Write a common example of radiation: _____

Problem: In this Lab, we will study the rate at which heat travels by conduction through several different types of material.

Hypothesis: (Which type of material do you think will conduct the best?)

_____

Materials: graduated cylinder   metal can
bunsen burner   plastic drinking cup
ring stand and ring   100 ml beaker
thermometer   beaker tongs
clock   wire gauze

Procedure: For each separate trial you will do the following:
1. Measure out 50 ml of water with the graduated cylinder and place in beaker. Heat this water until it reaches boiling.
2. When the water is boiling, but before it gets much chance to boil away, pick up the beaker with the tongs and pour the boiling water into the metal can. Immediately read the temperature of the water.
3. Now read the temperature again every 30 seconds and write it in the data table. Do this for a total of three minutes.
4. Now you will start again with fresh water, and do the same thing, except that you will pour the water into the plastic cup.
5. Finally, do the same experiment but leave the water in the beaker. Be sure to take the beaker off the ring stand. (Why?)

Data Table:

Type of Container	Temperature						
	0 sec.	30 sec.	60 sec.	90 sec.	120 sec.	150 sec.	180 sec.
Metal							
Plastic							
Glass							

Which type is your best heat conductor? _____

Now graph your results on the graph paper provided. On the vertical axis, put the temperature. On the horizontal axis, put the time. Use red pencil for the metal container, pen for the plastic, and a broken line for the glass. Remember to have labels and title and a key.

If we refer back to our old idea that matter is made up of particles, how do you explain the movement of heat through any type of matter? _____

_____

In which type of matter, according to our lab, do you think the particles are the easiest to move about? _____

This lab has shown us one more way in which different types of materials act. Eventually we will use all these differences to classify materials in new and better ways than we had back at the beginning of the semester.

General Science B: Physical　　　　　Name _____
Mrs. Smith　　　　　　　　　　　　　Date _____

SUMMARY SHEET #4: *HEAT*

1. After all our labs, try to give a good over-all definition of heat:

_____

2. What quality of heat does the degree measure? _____
3. How does heat intensity differ from heat quantity? Give an example.

_____

_____

4. For each of the following pairs, tell which has the more intense heat, and which has more quantity of heat:

_____ nail heated 3 minutes in bunsen burner flame
_____ beaker of 100 ml of water heated 5 minutes in b.b. flame
_____ 100 ml of water raised from 20 to 40°C.
_____ 50 ml of water raised from 20 to 50°C.

5. Calculate the calories involved in each of the following problems:

_____ 1. A peanut burns up and in doing so it brings the temperature of 9 ml of water from 25°C to 60°C. If the peanut weighs .2 mg, how many calories per gram does the peanut have?

_____ 2. It takes five minutes for a bunsen burner flame to bring 100 ml of water from 25°C to 100°C. How many calories per minute of heat is the bunsen burner giving to the water?

6. Why does water evaporate more slowly from a container with a top on it?

_____

7. In which case do you think water boils "hotter," a closed pan or an open pan, and why?

_____

_____

8. What causes an explosion? _____
9. Explain why it is impossible to "conduct cold." _____

_____

General Science B: Physical　　　　　Name _____
Mrs. Smith　　　　　　　　　　　　　Date _____

PROCEDURE FOR DETERMINING UNKNOWNS

We will classify in this lab using two main criteria: solubility and *heat* of solution.

For best results, FOLLOW DIRECTIONS EXACTLY.

Before you begin, read *all* of the directions.

1. Take the five test tubes and measure 3 cm from the bottom of each tube. At this point mark a line. Then measure 1 cm from the bottom of each tube and mark a second line. Lastly, put one letter, A through E, on each tube. Place them upright in the test tube rack.
2. Put enough water into each tube to reach the higher mark.
3. Take a *small* amount of powder A on the tip of your spatula and drop it into test tube A. Stir with the stirring rod and record on your record sheet whether the powder dissolves or not. Do the same for the other four powders in the proper test tubes.
4. Wash all five test tubes. You should have found that three of the substances dissolve in water and two did not. Take the test tubes for the two which did not dissolve and fill them to the upper mark with alcohol. Drop in a small amount of each of the two substances and record which will dissolve in alcohol.

YOU SHOULD NOW KNOW THE IDENTITY OF TWO OF YOUR POWDERS.

5. In the three test tubes you have left put enough water to fill to the *one cm* mark.

Now into the first one put a *large* spatula full of your matching unknown, stir gently with the thermometer and note and record whether the substance raises the water temperature, lowers it, or leaves it the same. Any change should be of about 3 to 5°. Do the same for the remaining unknowns.

6. If you have worked carefully, by now you should know the names of all the unknowns. If you are uncertain of any, repeat your work.
7. When you are sure you are right, put the number and letter of each vial and the name of its contents in the summary part of the record sheet.
8. GOOD LUCK!

General Science B: Physical   Name_____
Mrs. Smith   Date _____

RECORD CHART FOR UNKNOWNS

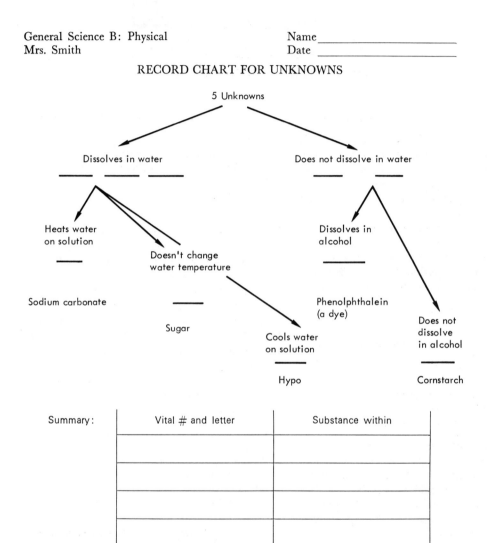

Summary:	Vital # and letter	Substance within

My Use of the Discovery Method in Teaching Junior High School Science

Introduction

Ideally one should attempt to teach in such a manner that each individual student can relate in his own way, making use of previously learned skills and acquiring new ones. I find the "discovery" approach very useful for the teaching of science.

This paper consists of several experiments and one self-testing quiz or game which was enjoyed by most of the students in my science classes. I gave them a push in the right direction and tried to stay out of the way until they needed me.

Detecting Energy

Materials needed:
1. One lemon (fresh)
2. One carbon rod from the inside of a pencil
3. One copper or zinc coated wire
4. Two pieces of thin, insulated copper wire

DO NOT EAT LEMON WHEN FINISHED!

Place electrodes (*copper* or *zinc* wire and carbon rod) at either end of a fresh lemon and attach wires as you would to any battery. See if you can detect *electrical energy* by placing both free ends of the wires to the tip of your tongue at the same time.

Cooperate with some of your fellow students and put your *Lemon Batteries* in *parallel* and *series*. Detect *voltage* on a *voltmeter* sensitive enough to detect voltage in the millivolt range (1/1000th of a volt). Record results.

Question: How many lemons are needed to produce 0.5 millivolts, 1, 2, and 2.5 millivolts?

Transmitting Energy

Materials needed:
1. One tin can (top should be cut away cleanly)
2. Several pieces of string (10, 16, 34, and 52 feet)
3. Nail
4. Hammer
5. Paper clip

Punch a hole in the end of the tin can. Thread the string through the hole and tie it to the paper clip so that the paper clip will be on the inside of the can.

Attach the other end of the string to a friend's tin can in the same manner. Pull the string fairly tight between the two of you. Transmit the voice through the string by speaking into the can in a normal manner.

Record results when cans are 10, 16, 34, and 52 feet apart. (Record if voice is: *very strong, strong, medium, weak,* etc.)

Questions:

1. What is the limit for this type of voice transmission in feet?
2. What happens to voice transmission if the string is broken and then tied back again?
3. Can you explain why or how this type of telephone works?

Matter and Energy in Motion $(E = mc^2)$

Materials needed:
1. One beaker (1000 cc)
2. 20 cc cooking oil (the smokeless kind)
3. Popcorn (several ounces)
4. Bunsen burner or hot plate
5. Wire gauge (if using bunsen burner)

Mr. Warner Freeman and student observe sex differences in male and female guppies, King Junior High School, Berkeley, California.

6. Heavy cardboard to cover the beaker
7. Ringstand

Adjust ring on the ringstand so that the bottom of the beaker is about 3½ inches from the top of the Bunsen burner's flame. Adjust flame on the Bunsen burner until it is about medium hot. Turn air intake on the bottom of the Bunsen burner's barrel to adjust the heat of the flame. Put oil into the beaker until it covers bottom (about 3 mm deep). Heat over flame until a drop of water dances on the oil. Then test the popcorn by dropping one kernel into the hot oil. If the kernel cooks for about 5 to 10 seconds and then pops with a good snapping action, then the oil is just about right. (A weak, wet pop should mean what?) When oil is hot enough, cover the bottom of the beaker one kernel deep with the kernels of corn. Put top on with something to weight it down.

Questions:

1. Record all reactions observed in the beaker.

2. Can you think of any laws used in your scientific studies explaining the actions of the popping corn?
3. What causes the popcorn to explode with such force?
4. What is the corn kernel's outside covering called?
5. What is the substance on the inside called?
   a. Before it is popped?
   b. After it is popped?

Acidity and Alkalinity

Materials needed:

1. Several feet of pH paper
2. One notebook
3. Scotch tape or paper tape

Get some pH paper from your lab. Cut the strip into *one inch long* pieces. Test water from all of the water sources you can find around your neighborhood and your school. Make several tests for each water sample at different times of the day. After taking the *pH* of the water, record time and tape the strip into your notebook. Take the color chart found on the roll of pH tape and find out the *pH* of each water sample.

A pH of 1 means lots of acid. A pH of 12 to 14 means very basic or alkaline (like the taste of soap). A pH of 7 means neutral, no acid or base (like good pure water).

Flame Test

Materials needed:

1. One Bunsen burner and hose
2. Five test tubes, small beakers or such, and a test tube rack
3. Chromium or iron wire (not copper)
4. Several chemicals containing Na, Li, Ca, Be, Sr, Fc, Ni, Zn, K, Cu, or Pb.

Bend wire at one end until a small loop forms (⌒̶̶̶̶̶̶̶̶̶⌒). Heat wire in the flame's outside cone until it is red hot. After wire has cooled, wet the looped end and stick it into one of the chemicals that you received from your teacher. When some of the chemicals stick to the wire, put the wire back into the flame's outside cone. Record anything that happens to this chemical. Do the same for each chemical, making sure that the wire is cleaned after each test.

Who Has the Fact?

Materials needed:

1. One ball (rubber)
2. Large open space (room size)
3. Students (they may stand or sit)

First form your students into a large circle around the room. (They may be standing or sitting.) The starter begins the game announcing the chosen topic (any choice). He then throws the ball in an *underhand fashion* to some unsuspecting person who must catch the ball. If the ball is caught, then he in turn throws the ball to some other person. If the ball is missed then that person is penalized and he must produce a fact *within five seconds.* The statement must deal with the chosen topic. Failure to do so gives him one *out* or *miss.* Two such misses put him out of the game.

Any infraction such as *throwing the ball overhand, interfering with another person's catch, coaching another person, or giving the same fact twice* carries the same penalty as a miss. The penalty question must be answered in five seconds.

The game can be played down to the last man.

DORIS TODD **21**

Devising Number Systems

Course and Class Description

My third-period mathematics class of top ability seventh graders is large and noisy. It is an interesting contrast to my first period class of students of the same ability level. They perform equally well on tests, but they are quiet and accepting, polite, and somewhat lethargic. Third period is always jumping from beginning to end. Unfortunately for me, sometimes the enthusiasm of the students is not directed toward mathematics. A large proportion of the

class is made up of highly individualistic and imaginative students who apparently have known each other for some time. Competition is keen in both social and intellectual accomplishments. The most vocal students in the class will not accept a particular subject merely for the sake of pleasing the teacher. They want (and demand) to know its value, now and in the future, and at times have me hard-pressed for good answers when standard arguments leave them unimpressed. However, a certain amount of material must be covered by these students to prepare them for the courses which they will be required to take in the future—unless the system changes.

One section of the curriculum which had to be "covered" had to do with learning how to express numbers in numeration systems other than base ten. I conjecture that even bright students when openly competing with classmates are reluctant to depart from familiar subject matter in which they feel comfortably superior, to go on to new material which is at first confusing. I have noticed repeatedly that these students love to compete at computations but exhibit hostility toward unfamiliar concepts.

Rationale

I chose my strategy to capitalize on the native competitiveness of the class members as well as on their enthusiasm and inventiveness. I wanted to overcome the hostility which many of them felt at being required to learn how to express numbers and compute in numeration systems other than base ten.

Strategy

Each student was asked to make up a base four numeration system, giving names to each of the four symbols he intended to use. The symbols could be anything satisfying the definition of the word "symbol." The names for them could be anything the student chose to call them. Using his own four symbols, each student was to make up an addition sentence in such a way that someone else could determine the value of each of the symbols. For example, in base four,

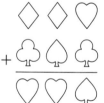

could be shown to mean 223 plus 101 equals 330.

Student Responses

At first there were quite a few errors. Students were more interested in drawing elaborate symbols and giving them amusing names than they were in presenting foolproof arithmetic sentences. Gradually, however, as more and more began to catch on to the game, the problems became more elaborate; some even decided to use subtraction and multiplication. During the two days that I had planned to do this as part of the lesson, enthusiasm mounted, so that students were begging me to let them present their problems long after I felt they had adequately understood what they were doing, and after everyone had had at least one turn.

My Attitude

It was a pleasure for me to see these bright students so imaginatively involved in learning arithmetic, and enjoying it so much. Also, it gave me an opportunity to stand in the back of the room and to observe my students in direct relationships with their peers. While I gained a great deal of insight into the various personalities of my students, a rather strong camaraderie developed amongst them. Since then I have sometimes wished that it were not quite so strong.

Value

In order to make up an arithmetic sentence in base four, it is necessary to understand the principles involved in expressing numbers with different symbols. The value of having each student present such a sentence encouraged all of them to understand the principles involved, and also provided the class with a variety of teachers and a variety of drill in computation which the students would never have accepted from one teacher. It astonished me, also, how easily these students were able to generalize their knowledge about addition in base four to competence in other arithmetic operations in base four and then to generalize further to computation in any other base I could name.

The Function Machine

In the discovery-oriented classroom where the teaching of concepts is a major mathematical objective, the function machine serves not only as a model, but because of its shape and bright colors, as a motivational device as well. In working with ninth-grade low achievers, I found that they enjoyed figuring out what happened between the time of input and output from a particular machine. What is more, the students were eager to manipulate the machines themselves and to give each other practice in arithmetic.

The function machine can have many forms. The diagrams below represent two of the most common.

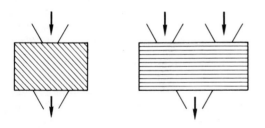

The inner workings of these are mysterious, Attempts to explain these workings lead into the realm of definition (e.g., why $2 + 2 = 4$) and confuse the problems we are dealing with. Let us not concern ourselves with how the machine works, but go quickly to the use of the machine.

The first type of function machine, called the single input or unitary machine, takes a single number as input and emits a single number output.

Example:

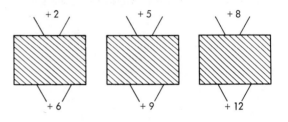

This particular machine adds four to the input. Another example:

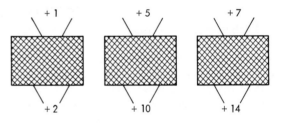

This machine, called a doubler or a 2-er, simply doubles the input. Other examples are machines that take the opposite, subtract 5, take the absolute value, divide by 3, or square.

The second type, called the double input or binary machine, takes two numbers as input and combines them somehow to give a single number as an output. Once again by example:

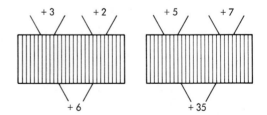

This machine, called a multiplier, does simple multiplication.

Examine the following machine:

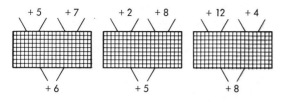

This is a simple averaging operation. Other binary machines can do addition or subtraction, take the largest input, double the first and add it to the second, or as many other combinations as a teacher may want to create.

A feature of these function machines is that they can be physically linked together in innumerable combinations to provide skill building activity that students have fun doing. Each machine must have been used by the student and he must be familiar with its operation *and* its common name.

Example:

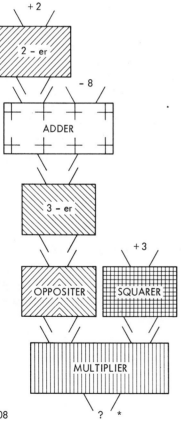

After students have experimented with combinations of machines they may well come up with questions such as these:

1. What is the effect of putting a doubler upside down? A tripler?
2. If a combination of machines has three adders, what is the minimum number of inputs?
3. What happens when a binary machine is used upside down?
4. Some machines cancel the effects of others. Which do this?

These are questions that come out of student "free play" with the machines. The teacher should be able to answer questions like these before attempting to use these machines with students.

The following sample unit is a lesson using the function machine to help students discover prime factorization.

We assume that the class has had experience with the single input machines such as the doubler (2-er). The class is asked to imagine the following hypothetical situation:

A factory is in the business of building machines like doublers (2-ers) triplers (3-ers), 4-ers, etc., and they are interested in cutting the cost of production. The biggest cost is the *designing* cost for new machines, and the problem is to eliminate the building of *new* machines if the job can be done by a combination of the old machines. (Note: The teacher can decide on the various embellishments for his class— e.g., the best math student could be the factory manager and could veto certain ideas.)

Having described the situation, the teacher gives the first necessary machine, the doubler or 2-er. The class quickly follows with a tripler or 3-er. The operation of these two machines is illustrated in several quick examples.

The next multiple necessary is multiplying by four.

QUESTION:

Do we need to construct a 4-er? The response is "no" because most students will understand that two 2-er machines are the equivalent of one 4-er, and one or two examples will convince the class if necessary.

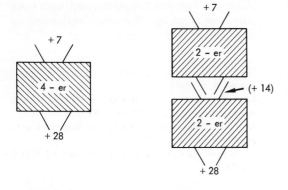

We can now begin to construct a list on the blackboard.

To multiply by 2 use 2-er
3 use 3-er
4 use 2-er, 2-er
5 use......

The placing of 5 on the list usually causes some disagreement. Some students will suggest that you can use a 2-er and a 3-er to reproduce a 5-er. This provides a chance to follow up a wrong answer.

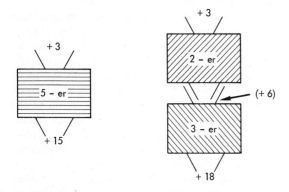

This example, done by the students, is sufficient to convince them that a 2-er and a 3-er are not equivalent to a 5-er. Some student may suggest changing the order of the 2-er and 3-er; if not, the teacher should suggest it. The teacher could direct the class to some conclusions about commutativity of multiplication by 2 and 3.

The conclusion that a 5-er is necessary is inevitable, but the class should argue out and demonstrate any idea, with the teacher strongly supporting all experimentation.

The students should at this point start thinking ahead and make conclusions about whether or not a 6-er, 7-er, or 8-er is necessary. The chart on the board should now look something like this:

To multiply by 2 use 2-er
3 use 3-er
4 use 2-er, 2-er
5 use 5-er
6 use 2-er, 3-er or 3-er, 2-er
7 use 7-er
8 use......

At 8 many students will want to fill in a 4-er and a 2-er to get 8. They should be guided to the discovery that a 4-er does not exist. Once it is clear that some machines do not exist, a criteria question can be formulated.

QUESTION: Do you need to build a 100-er? If not, what machines would you use to be the equivalent of multiplying by 100?

Once a student is able to deal with such a criteria question, it seems apparent that he has discovered prime factorization.

The "manufacturing" of a function machine for classroom use can be as easy as drawing a simple sketch on the blackboard. A far more effective machine may be created for use with an overhead projector by this simple procedure:

1. Make a pencil sketch of several machines (no larger than one by two inches).
2. Prepare an overhead transparency from this pencil sketch.
3. Cut a piece of 3M colored adhesive film to size and place this on your transparency for added color.
4. Cut the individual machines from the transparency.

You will now have a set of colored machines which are attractive and easily arranged in any combination on the overhead projector.

Helping Slow Eighth-graders
to Understand U. S. History

Introduction

The primary distinction between man and other animals is said to be man's capacity to think, to reason, to solve problems in an intelligent manner. It has been alarming to me how the public schools have neglected the development of this capacity. Consequently, the most difficult task that I have been presented with has been that of how to begin, and in a few cases, continue the development of many students' thinking capacity. This has been particularly difficult in low track classes because the students in these classes have generally been conditioned to assume that they can't think—at least not on a meaningful level.

Needless to say, the task has been difficult and complex. Success has been limited and often nonexistent. Nonetheless, I have reached the conclusion that it is impossible to teach anything meaningful unless the thinking mechanism is shifted into gear. Therefore, my primary approach to teaching has become one which focuses on getting the students to create, imagine, and think constructively, not one which requires them to accumulate information. The rationale for this focus is that without some broader, more meaningful structure to relate to, the information becomes virtually useless.

The foremost problem in this task is getting the students involved, or at least somewhat involved. If they become involved then they become motivated. So, how can one make information immediate and meaningful? The step I finally took after some depressing failures was to avoid beginning with information. I learned not to confront the students with a body of material that will "turn them off" before they begin. I learned to begin with the kids and to let them build their own structure. I've found that if I let them build something, the chances of their relating to it are increased. After they've created the basic structure, they can be given access to information that they can use to complete the structure. My hope is that the information becomes something that they will use and not something that they will merely accumulate and forget.

I've chosen to illustrate this approach by describing a unit on government that I've done in my eighth-grade U.S. history classes. The objective of the unit is to have the students grasp some broad ideas of why societies, and groups within societies, have governments, how governments are formed from the needs and specific situations of these groups; and how governments function to meet their needs. Further, the objective is to apply these general ideas to the specific situation of the United States. The emphasis is on having the students themselves discover the broad basic ideas, and on their being able to mold specific examples and circumstances around them. First, the students decided that a government was necessary, even for themselves. Then they created a government. Next they applied this principle and decided that the colonies needed a government after the Revolutionary War. They created governments that would fit this situation and then compared their governments to the Articles of Confederation. They have analyzed the problems of their governments and have gone on to try to solve them. They have researched and role played the Constitutional Convention and have developed the Constitution along broad lines. We are now in the process of looking at the actual Constitution more carefully and specifically.

The unit, from the beginning through the role playing, has taken five weeks.

Unit on Government

The two classes that have been using the unit described in the introduction are eighth-grade U.S. history classes. The school is a junior high school which services a low-middle income area of Vallejo. Approximately one half of the students are Caucasian and one half are minority groups—primarily black and Mexican-American. One class is a track three class in a four-level tracking system and the other is a track four class. The track four class is about one third Caucasian and two thirds minority groups. Reading comprehension is low, as is writing ability. There is almost no leadership in this class, partially because of lack of ability and partially because of lack of confidence. The I.Q. scores in this class range from 73 to 103, with the majority of the class falling in the 87–90 range. The track three class is mainly white middle-class students. Here there is a noticeable improvement in reading and writing ability. There is some leadership in this class, although there is an immaturity which inhibits the effectiveness of this leadership. The I.Q. scores range from 82 to 110. The average is 98. Both of the classes are small. Each has twenty-five enrolled, and usually two or three students are absent each day. Consequently, the groups are very workable in terms of size.

The initial problem in reference to this unit was introducing the concept of "government." From other references that I had attempted to make toward government, I had realized that the majority of the students had little or no concept of what "government" meant. In keeping with the main approach which I discussed in the introduction, I began by having the class read and discuss an excerpt from *Huckleberry Finn* (the passage describing Tom Sawyer's organization of his band of robbers). I found that the selection was good to use initially because the majority of the students had heard of *Huckleberry Finn*. (They had not read the book, but they had seen the movie.) The major-

ity had liked it, and so the project began on a positive note. It is important to read the passage aloud to or with the class. It is also a good idea, since some of the students may not have heard of *Huckleberry Finn,* to let them discuss the plot of the book as much as they are able to, so that the passage has some concrete frame of reference.

The question that I asked after we had read the passage was simply, "What are the boys doing?" The initial responses were ones which retold the specific action. This type of response needed to be guided toward more general ideas. For example, in reference to the oath, I asked why the boys had to have an oath. The classes eventually came up with the idea that the oath was needed to make things definite and to keep everyone together. The signing of the oath with blood, they said, made everything final. Out of this line of discussion the classes came up with the idea that people need to be organized if they are going to do something together. From this point, I asked them what this sort of organization could be called. At this stage it became something of a word game and eventually someone said "government."

We then moved the discussion toward giving examples of government. This was not too successful because most of the students had never participated in a government. Some had participated in some club governments, however, so it was not a total loss. I then tried to focus the discussion on the school government. This was also somewhat remote to most of the class. However, they at least knew that it existed, so I brought the focus directly upon the classroom and asked them if they thought that if they were isolated from the rest of the world they would have to have a government. Since the overwhelming answer was "yes," I asked them to justify the necessity. In order to do this they had to begin thinking about what a government does. The general response was that they needed to have a government to protect themselves because they didn't trust everybody in the room. This was the primary justification. They themselves had come up with one major function of a government—making laws to protect the people.

From this point, I asked them to organize a government for their classroom which would do the things that they wanted it to do. (Here I reached a stumbling block because they had to write.) Since the task of creating a government was not an easy one, I tried to provide some guidelines for them. I gave them three basic steps to take: (1) define the situation, (2) given the situation, what problems need to be solved? (3) given the problems, create a government that will best solve them. Even these are fairly broad guidelines; consequently, the assignment had to be made very clear. Even so, many students didn't follow this pattern, but they did come up with something workable.

Most of the students created very basic, simple governments. They had a president and a policeman and they could vote. The fault of most of the papers was not in their simplicity, but rather in their lack of any definition of power. We worked on this concept some. They began to suggest the problem of money and giving certain people certain powers and things to do. They began to become much more definitive and clear. The problems of money and power, of course, led beautifully into the Articles of Confederation.

After we had dealt with an immediate situation, we took a step backward about two hundred years. They became colonialists (see Appendix A). We began working the same pattern: knowing the situation, figuring out the problems within that situation, and then solving them. I gave them a worksheet which they worked on in groups. The task was to describe the situation in the colonies after the Revolutionary War. The students came up with spotty descriptions, but with more thorough written work than they had in the past. I typed up the best answers to each of the questions that the classes had handed in and dittoed them. We then went over their descriptions very carefully in class. Needless to say, everyone was not at the same point of progress, and I think that this specific type of review was necessary. Also, I had to keep in mind that this was a difficult and extensive project and that it was necessary to refocus and summarize constantly.

The classes then took the second step and discussed some of the problems. The main problem that was brought up in both classes was that of how to unite thirteen colonies into one nation without having some sort of a powerful figure like a king. I deliberately focused on one

large problem so that the scope of the task was not too large. However, they did bring out several other problems that were very important and we dealt with them to some degree (see Appendix B). Their job at this point was to create a government that would solve these problems.

After they had done this individually, we looked very specifically at the Articles of Confederation from a comparative standpoint. We talked about their governments in class and I wrote about five different plans on the board. (A better way to handle this phase would be to ditto their plans off. I've found that notes are very difficult to get taken unless very definite outlines and structures are used.) We discussed the weaknesses of the Articles of Confederation and at this point I gave a quiz. I did this to provide some definite mark of achievement and also to provide an opportunity for review.

I then gave out a ditto which summarized the failures of the Articles of Confederation, and the problems that loomed ahead. We had discussed all of these things in class so this was another point of review and restatement of what they, for the most part, had come up with. This set up the organization of a Constitutional Convention which was to design a government that would be better than the old one. (The assignment sheets are in Appendix C.) The details of the organization are explained fully. I took the liberty of simplifying the issues and had the classes working primarily on one problem: how to balance the power on the level of states versus nation and on the level of the national government itself. The students used the Virginia and New Jersey Plans as their guidelines for proposals and demands, and they went on and compromised to the extent that they set up the legislative branch with two houses, one based on representation, the other on territory. They also corrected the tax problem and the currency problem. (See Appendix D for examples of student thought.)

The classes are now in the process of looking at the Constitution in more specific detail. They are essentially looking at it to see how *their* plan was perfected. I plan to go into the actual functioning of the government by conducting some mock trials and mock sessions of Congress.

GOVERNMENT PROJECT

Time: Right after the Revolutionary War has ended—1783.
Place: Philadelphia.
Who you are: A leader in the colonies.
Your job: You are attending a convention. You are to figure out the best government for the colonies.

Remember the steps that must be taken in order to do this. They are the same steps that you took to make up your own government.
1. You must describe the situation of the colonies. Answer questions like:
    a. How many colonies were there? How big is your territory?
    b. Were they all the same size?
    c. Which ones were big and which ones were small?
    d. Did the big colonies want the same things as the small ones?
    e. Do you colonial leaders want to have separate colonies at all or would you rather just be one big country?
    f. What kind of government did you have before the Revolution?
    g. Do you want the same kind? If not, why not? What didn't you like about it? What did you like about it?
    h. What things do you believe in? (Look at the Declaration of Independence.)
    i. How do you make your livings?
2. List three big problems that the colonies had to think about and solve. (Think about the things that we have talked about in class—all the things a government might have to do.)
3. How are you going to organize a government that will fit the situation that you have described and solve the problems you have?

TRACK 4: PROBLEMS THAT THE CLASS COMPILED AFTER DISCUSSING THE SITUATION IN THE COLONIES AFTER THE REVOLUTIONARY WAR.

1. How to satisfy everyone
    a. Big states
    b. Small states
2. Keep colonies separate or have one big country—how to do it.
3. How to set up trading laws
4. Who are going to be the leaders? King? Congress? Mayor? Governors?
5. Money—who is going to make the money?
6. How to give equal powers
7. Mail—postal system
8. Taxes—how much, how to get them, what to spend them on.

Constitution #2
Name _____

You are to be one of the delegates to the Constitutional Convention. Your job at this convention will be to figure out a better form of government for the United States than the Articles of Confederation.

Your first step is to elect a President. The person who is elected President will work with the state group that he is from and he will run the convention meetings.

As a delegate you have a big responsibility. It is your duty to see that your state is well represented. In order to do this you will have to know about and be able to protect the interests of your state. You have to know where you stand on the issues and problems that we have talked about in class. The first thing to consider is: "Are you a big state or a small state? What do the big states want and what do the small states want?" Then you have to have an idea about what went on at the Convention. In order for you to do this, you will have to do some research—READING!!

Story of the American Nation—pages 169–184
The Growth of America—pages 165–172

As you do the reading, take notes on anything that you think is important to the interests of your state. Then prepare a short statement in your group that says what your interests are. Be sure that you use the dittoed sheet that explains the Virginia Plan and the New Jersey Plan when you to this. If you think that it is necessary, you may work with other groups and their delegates. For example, if you are a large state you may want to work with some delegates from the larger states. Also, the delegates from the Southern states may want to get together to see if they have any special interests.

When these reports are finished, we will have a meeting and see if one plan can be worked out that will satisfy everyone.

The slogan for the Convention is COMPROMISE.

Note: Your report should explain some of the main interests of your states and it should also give some definite ideas for a plan of government. The plan should be figured out according to how it will help your state. Again, remember that you have the two basic plans to work from: The Virginia Plan and the New Jersey Plan.

Appendix D

TRACK 3: EXAMPLE OF ASSIGNMENT RECEIVED WHEN THE CLASS WAS ASKED TO CREATE ITS OWN GOVERNMENT.

I live in Mansley city we have a population of 22 people. We have to have some kind of government. I am one of the council members who have to elect what kind of government would be suitable for the city. Our city is two small to have a big type of government so we have president, tresury and two senators. A president jobs is to say what's best for the people like taxes to make the country bigger and they could get stuff like hospitals, schools, stores and job training. A tresury job is to give the president brief information on how much money they have and how much money it would take to build houses, apt., schools, churches, stores, hospitals, and pit people for on the job training. A senators job is to keep count of how many people are in the city or country. So you can see that our government we want is hard job and you have to be in good health and in good temper, they don't pay much because they don't have enough money. You have to be a honest member of the city and you have to be popular. And if you tax the people just so you can get rich and rule the country you will loose your job or you will be assinated and they would not let any of your family into the city.

TRACK 3: EXAMPLE OF ASSIGNMENTS RECEIVED WHEN THE CLASS WAS ASKED TO CREATE A GOVERNMENT FOR THE COLONIES AFTER THE REVOLUTIONARY WAR.

The kind of government I would have after the war is: a person who is head of the country: a president, then I would have a governor for each state and a mayor for each city or town, etc. The president would be a head of the whole country. He is supposed to organize the governor's and tell them what their supposed to do, while the governors tell the mayor's how to organize the people in the towns and cities.

I would have my government this way because I don't think there should be a lot of people governing. The president is ahead of everything, he just has mayor's and governor's because he can't be everywhere at once. 1 big country would be too much for him to handle. He can't do the whole job by himself.

We will need a President to take some of the big Problems of the United States. And to take care of foreign afairs and trading. We'll need a Vice-President to attend meetings and to run the country when the President is ill or when something happens to the President. We will need some secratary of states to take mostly care of letters and stuff like that and to take some of the problems. We will also need to pass and veto laws. We'll need to run each state. We'll need senetors, counsilmen to help with some of the problems with each State and Country. We will also need a mayor to run the cities.

TRACK 4

One student with a recorded I.Q. of 80 handed in his government proposal and then added a P.S. which said, "The reason which people need a government for is they don't trust other people and the reason they don't trust other people is that they don't trust themselves."

JANET MANLEY **24**

Concepts and Processes in Social Studies

Background

Facing increasingly serious tensions among its different racial groups and increasingly serious student dissatisfaction with what many students considered a largely irrelevant curriculum, the Vallejo School District began in 1967 to take steps to cope with its many and varied problems. One beginning step in this process was the attempt to revise its social studies program as it existed in the fifth, eighth, and eleventh grades. As in all public schools in California, these are the three grades in which United States history is presented to students.

There were two very pointed objectives to this new curricular approach. One was to deal with the history of minority groups in the United States thoroughly, honestly, and meaningfully. The second was to somehow make the curriculum more relevant to the students. Neither of these objectives was being widely accomplished through the traditional textbook-memorization approach. I do not mean to make a blanket condemnation of all social studies programs and teachers. I do think, however, that whatever relevant teaching and learning is being done is being done in spite of the traditional type of curriculum, not because of it.

The curriculum revision was to be based on a process approach to learning. That is, students were going to learn thought processes as opposed to just names and dates. These thought processes would hopefully give the student a basis for coping with many given problems. They would enable him to use data effectively, not simply to memorize it for a test. These processes would enable him to look at a given problem from a variety of viewpoints based on the different disciplines in the social studies field, i.e., geography, economics, political science, history, anthropology, psychology, and history. Further, they would give the students a basis for continued learning and investigation of future social problems—a basis for coping with the increasingly complex problems that our world faces. Learning the dates of the American Revolution would not help a student understand current revolutionary action. However, an understanding of some of the social forces that contribute to any revolutionary situation may provide some basis for comparison, evaluation, judgment, and perhaps needed action.

The trend toward this process-oriented type of curriculum is growing and, in fact, the new California State Social Studies Framework is based almost entirely upon this approach. Also, some of the most practical and concrete work was done by Hilda Taba for the Contra Costa School District.[1]

The Summer Project

The Vallejo School District had used Taba's Contra Costa Guides as a broad guideline during the school year 1967–1968. Subsequently, three pilot projects were run during summer school, 1968. I was directly involved in the development of the eighth grade curriculum and the summer school pilot project for that grade level. The pilot class was ideal in that it provided a basis for experimentation in heterogeneous classes and team teaching. The students included all track levels (Vallejo has four) plus students who had just finished three grade levels—sixth, seventh, and eighth. The class was four hours long, so that we had approximately the same number of hours that would have been involved in an entire year of regular school. Also, our budget was relatively liberal, so we had enough money to buy new materials and to rent films. The availability of a fairly large source of resource materials is important to this type of approach to social studies since the students must find differing viewpoints and material not commonly found in textbooks provided by the state.

Central to our project and to the implementation of Taba's type of curriculum is an understanding of the term "concept," or "main idea," as Taba phrases it. Basically, a concept can be defined as a fiber or thread that is woven throughout the different disciplines and that can, at any given time, be found as a force working within the fabric of a given period of time. For example, one might deal with the concept of "social change." Briefly, social change is a process that always has and probably always will be taking place within any given group of people, be it a relatively small organization or an entire civilization. During the six-week summer session we were to deal with six concepts that touched upon various social studies disciplines:

1. Input-output
2. Social change
3. Conflict
4. Man and his environment
5. Technology
6. Morality and choice.

Some of the concepts were rather specific and some very general. For example, input-output dealt with the discipline of economics, whereas conflict was much more general and involved many disciplines.

Concept-oriented Teaching

How does this conceptual, process-oriented approach make social studies more relevant to students? How does one begin? The four teachers who were involved in the junior high class began, most importantly I think, with the students themselves. We tried as much as possible to require that the students build their own areas of study out of their own interests. Consequently, we asked that the students think of some things they were interested in and wanted to learn about. Since we were concerned with processes, the subject matter was not set and we could be very flexible. For example, some of the boys were interested in guns, so they spent time during the six weeks investigating the recent controversy connected with gun laws. Again, the most important thing was not that they be able to recite the gun regulations of all fifty states when they finished, but rather that they have some idea of how to investigate a given problem. However, to simply allow a freewheeling, unstructured atmosphere for investigation is not sufficient, especially for junior high age students. Since for the most part the students had not had experience in this new approach, our job as teachers was to help them establish a meaningful structure upon which they could build their investigations.

Exploring the Concept

We began by dealing with the concept of social change. We started by asking them very simply to specify any change that they had seen taking place recently—in any area. The question was broad enough so that most of the students could respond. After they had made some observations about change ("Cars are more

[1]For a detailed description of Taba's approach, see John S. Gibson, *New Frontiers in Social Studies: Action and Analyses* (Detroit: Citation Press, 1966).

expensive," "It's sunny today and it wasn't yesterday," "Vallejo is bigger than when I moved here," etc.), we asked them how they would go about finding out why these changes had taken place. They decided that they'd have to ask questions and then look up the answers in books—which brought us to the first key process that needed to be developed—*asking analytical questions*. This is a difficult process to develop because most students are so used to asking only factual types of questions. Such questions are not useless, however, if they can be expanded to help answer the more difficult "Why?" type of question.

The task, however, was not impossible and, in fact, very often the students asked analytical questions without even knowing it. For example, after having made their own observations about change, we asked them if they could make any general statements about social change. From their amazingly perceptive and complex generalizations came the questions which they later used to study the process of change more specifically. Some of the generalizations were: Things change too fast. Things change when someone invents something. Things change because of forces affecting them that they can't control. The corresponding questions that could be built from these generalizations are, I think, obvious. Also, these three generalizations were not all that the students came up with. By the time they were finished, the list numbered about fifteen.

After the students, to a large extent, had established their structure for investigation, they broke up into small groups based on interest. We had provided further structure by asking that they investigate change as it related to the family structure in the United States. They then chose what family group they wanted to work on, the black family, the pioneer family, the white middle-class family, etc. Their specific goal was to present the results of their investigation to the rest of the class.

Results

By way of warning, the first presentations were just short of disaster, but as the six weeks progressed, the ingenuity of the students in devising new ways to present their findings was very encouraging. Among other things, they began to devise useful audiovisual aids plus some effective role playing.

The small group technique was used a lot, although we varied the criteria for grouping. Small groups were the major method we used to individualize instruction in a very heterogeneous class, and, I think, the results based on student evaluations and some standardized tests were generally very positive. The students were required to work within a specific structure and toward developing the types of process discussed earlier, but they had partially helped to establish that structure. The structure was flexible enough to allow them to follow their own interests to a large degree. However, also very important was the fact that they could not succeed by simply doing "their own thing." They had to communicate with the rest of the class by teaching the others what they had learned.

Minimal Bibliography

Gibson, John S. *New Frontiers in Social Studies;* Vol. I: *Goals for Students;* Vol. II: *Action and Analysis.* Detroit: Citation Press, 1966. Contains detailed descriptions of the social science concepts alluded to in this paper.

II: CREATIVITY:
PROCESS AND PRODUCTS

Creating life forms in a beginning art class, Berkeley High School, Berkeley, California.

The process of working on a task is not the only aspect that can give pleasure. There is also the product to be considered. Many of the tasks that are used for learning experiences end up with some outcome of a strictly physical nature. There are written stories, geometrical constructions, arithmetical computations, paintings, sculpture, and the whole gamut of artifacts created in connection with units in social studies. Because these products represent the end point of the child's performance, inevitably they have high value for him. The extent of this value determines, in at least some small way, the reinforcement value they can have for the learning experience through which the child has just gone.[1]

Along with inquiry and discovery, creativity has been a major focus for educators of the past decade. Centers have been established for studying the correlates of creativity in artists and scientists. The creative process itself has been assiduously investigated by university scholars. Careful recommendations have been given to both teachers and businessmen about ways to nurture creativity in schools and industry. But again, as with the interest in inquiry and discovery processes, creativity has been more honored in statement than visible in practice.

Happily, this has been less true for Graduate Internship Program teachers. Partly because of the philosophy of the Graduate Internship Program with its encouragement of creative experimentation, and largely because of the people selected, our teachers make valiant efforts to develop the creative potential of their students. They often strive to give their students first-hand experience with the creative processes and the pleasure that comes from completing carefully wrought products—poems, stories, magazines, newspapers, dance productions, classroom films, scientific projects, or whatever possibilities their imagination or the subject might dictate.

In this section we have selected a few examples of the many ways such teachers have fostered creativity in their students: first, a group of strategies centering around creative writing, and second, some experiments with creative class projects.

Creative Writing (Newspapers, Magazines, Short Stories, Poems)

Creative activity is a constructive quest for a sense of meaning in experience. . . . The child of low intelligence, or one who is emotionally unbalanced, needs to indulge his phantasy more than a bright child, often recklessly, and totally, becoming quite involved in his own imaginings. He benefits from a contact in which a stable adult holds the ring, respects his expression, stimulates it, and helps him towards closer apprehensions of reality. Only good can come from this controlled and sanctioned phantasy. . . .[2]

"Me write? Just try to make me," say most nonacademically oriented students. It is so easy for teachers to become intimidated. But Judy Bebelaar's and Elaine Hauser's strategies show several ways that hardy teachers can

[1] Robert Sears, "Product Pleasure," in *Learning About Learning* (Washington, D.C.: U.S. Government Printing Office, 1966).
[2] David Holbrook, *English for the Rejected* (London: Cambridge University Press, 1964), pp. 210, 205.

overcome the natural resistance of their students. Mrs. Bebelaar reports the lure a student-written newspaper can provide if a teacher is willing to coax and convince students that they can write something worth publishing. The "Soul Searchers," (so named by her students), the class newspaper which resulted from her prodding and their writing, proved to be a strong motivating force, well worth the initial efforts.

Elaine Hauser's paper, "Writing Yields Reading," describes the creative writing laboratory which she devised to raise the self-image and reading skills of senior high students who were reading two years or more below grade level. Her strategy contains specific suggestions about the topics and procedures which proved most evocative, such as having her students write police descriptions of someone in the class, or imagining that they had one thousand dollars to spend.

These are followed by a set of strategies designed to provide creative challenges for all types of students—from bright to slow. Mrs. Abot's "A French Page for the School Newspaper" shows how to transform traditionally dull classroom assignments into exciting creative activities. Mrs. Randall and Mrs. Avakian in their respective strategies, "An Eight-Day Creative Writing Workshop for High School Seniors" and "Teaching the Reading and Writing of Short Stories Concurrently," each illustrate effective ways to lead students toward genuine appreciation of good poetry or literature. By having their students write poems or compose stories as they study each genre, both teachers provide their pupils first-hand experience in the discipline, joy, and sense of power that go into artistic creation. Elizabeth Avakian combines the usual academic study of short stories with an inspiring, carefully sequenced short story writnig project, culminating in a magazine enthusiastically compiled and edited by her students. Julie Randall's crash program, an eight-day creative writing project, beginning with Haiku composition and ending with free verse, served to loosen up her students' usual inhibitions against creative writing and to rid them of their negative attitudes toward poetry.

Creative Class Projects

We proceed next to a strategy which used a group project to change attitudes of students toward others. In "Dancing: The Joy of Discovering Together" Kristin Avansino describes the way an unusual interschool dance project, involving the creation of a far-out modern environment (including tin cans, elastic-linked chairs, posts, etc.,) plus the invention of group dances appropriate to the mod scene, brought harmony and pleasure to groups usually torn apart by racial conflicts and tensions.

We close this section with an example of the creative process at work in an art class. With her "Stitchery Project for an Arts and Crafts Class," Elizabeth Marking shows a way to use the more talented students in an art class, and to help all students experience the texture and colors of their environment.

We have, of course, only begun to suggest the endless variety and the powerful benefits of creative teaching and learning. Teachers who stimulate creativity report the tremendous appeal that creating something has for both educationally disadvantaged and bright, unchallenged students. Creative classroom activities are not only involving and pleasurable in themselves, but generally, through providing joy in accomplishment, lead to a desire for further mastery, learning, and self-discovery.

> The peculiar mark of the creative teacher—as different from all other businesses of man is not his learning alone but his ability to transform others by the contagion of his peculiar creative powers. . . . Good teaching is not solely the business of instruction: it is also the art of uncovering and enlarging native gifts of insights, feeling, and thinking. . . .[3]

[3] Hugh Mearns, *Creative Power: The Education of Youth in the Creative Arts* (New York: Dover Publications, Inc., 1958), p. 267.

The Soul Searchers

The Soul Searchers is a project which is still in the process of "becoming," as are the teaching methods we are using to encourage the writing in the publication. Although I don't suppose there has ever been a teaching project which one could describe easily, this one seems to me particularly difficult to analyze in a simple and straightforward fashion. Yet I feel that it is important to attempt to capture the experiences which led to the first two publications of *The Soul Searchers,* and that it is important to describe those experiences in the rather loose and perhaps unorthodox manner I intend to employ in this paper.

The Work Experience Program is a self-contained program set up this year for students who work part-time. Most of the students attend school for half a day, although some come only one day a week. Many of them were recommended for jobs because a full day program seemed too much for them, or because they were failing courses or were otherwise showing a lack of interest in school. The fact that these students have not very often succeeded in a school situation, of course, does not mean that they were all students who simply had no academic ability. Some of them have rather severe emotional problems; some have just fallen into a pattern of rejecting all authority figures—and of course teachers are included; some are what are commonly known as "the culturally deprived"; some are students who needed jobs to help support their families; some seem to have recognized the many inadequacies of education today and have simply refused to cooperate in a situation that seems meaningless to them. Most fall in two or more of these categories. In addition there are some students who are known at Samuel Gompers as "American-ization students"—students who have recently immigrated and whose command of English is poor. A few of our students are fairly sophisticated intellectually—they read and can discuss Camus and Hesse. Some are extremely naive in almost every way. As is evident by now, such a range of abilities and attitudes would require a corresponding range of teaching methods and styles.

Marcia Perlstein[1] and I chose a newspaper-type publication as a way to allow for the wide range of interest and ability, and hoped that the promise of doing something "different," something to be done for themselves and other students rather than to satisfy the requirements of teachers, would motivate these students. I don't think they really believed, at first, that a publication would result. The day we chose a name for the paper, the class showed little interest. It took us almost an entire period to elicit three or four suggestions for a title, and it was only after a great deal of coaxing, pleading, and prodding that we got the class to vote at all. I must admit we helped swing the election toward *The Soul Searchers* (the suggestion for the name was theirs)—that was just what we'd hoped they'd come to do, and what we meant to do ourselves, too. I think we have succeeded in encouraging them in this direction. Following are some excerpts from some papers the students wrote this term about the newspaper project:

I think that *The Soul Searchers* newspaper is the best thing that has happened to Samuel Gompers since it opened up...because it tells about what the kids say about themselves.

[1] See Marcia Perlstein's "A Suggestion for the Constructive Use of Grades," strategy 7.

It is good for the one who reads it and is good for the one who writes it, because you can tell anything you like, and anything you feel.

This project I found very interesting because of the challenge, but it really became bad when people lost interest and the teachers had to push it. Which I thought was really a bad show—it was our paper and we quit when it got down to the nitty gritty, but then I shouldn't complain, because I flop out too at the last moment. But writing the pieces was really a good thing. It gave us a chance to make our ideas public and our philosophies made known, which seems to make them worth more because I had shared them.

I wood say it wood be a good ting to do in a clas it maake you tink and kepe you out of troble and wot you fell you can say and it make the porsons fell good. If I could read and write beter I wold to do it. [This is a new student, Jeff, who has not yet had a chance to contribute.]

I think these comments give you some idea of the varying writing abilities of these students, as well as an indication of their success in "soul searching."

What these comments do not show you is the difference in attitude, in willingness to write, between the beginning of the program and now. Although the first period of the day was meant for writing, it was often not until well into the second period that words were actually being written on paper. Students are given a topic for the day, but are always permitted to choose their own alternative. The only requirement is that they write. But even with this allowance, most of the students found it difficult to write at first. Most of them were used to failing in English classes and had long ago simply resolved not to enter the contest any longer. Most of them, too, were still trying to treat Marcia and me as authority figures—try as we would to convince them that we weren't. (Here I use "authority figure" as they do: not necessarily someone who has authority and is to be respected and obeyed, but someone who is *trying* to retain a position of authority, and who is to be resisted in every manner possible.) And we experienced all kinds of resistance: silent refusal, noisy refusal, protests against the assignment, and then protests that they couldn't think of anything else to write about, complaints of sore hands, no pencils, being too cold to write, too hot to write, too tired to write. There

was even an organized strike complete with placards! But now they will write on almost any topic, and often have very good ideas of their own. Andre, who was also a student who would not write at all at first, just this week brought in a paper about a man who had to throw some people from a life raft in order to save the others from drowning. He had heard about the incident in class at the beginning of last term, and had just begun to want to write about it (may I say to search his soul?). He thought he would get no credit since he had written his paper at home, but wanted to show it to me anyway. He also told me that for the next newspaper he would like to write about a friend who had died in Vietnam. Even new students, who should have problems about writing similar to those the other students had at the beginning of last semester, seem to write much more easily and willingly, because the classroom atmosphere, the attitudes of the students are so different from what they were.

This is where I must discuss the "teaching methods." One of our best "methods" arose out of a kind of desperation on our part. When students would not write, they were usually talking. So we would sit beside them and act as stenographers, taking down every word they said. Here is a transcript of one of those sessions:

HERBERT: Some people here, Curtis. (Marcia and I sit down by them) What Y'all doin'? What Y'all fittin' to write? What Y'all writen that fer? (Scornfully) They think they could write fast. Tryin' to make me go on a trip with them, but thas dead! (Then ensued a conversation about Curtis' ring.)

HERBERT (again, looking over my shoulder): I know what yer writin' now. (Someone makes a comment about Curtis' money and asks him if he's planning to take it to heaven with him.) They can't bury you with no money Curtis. Fifty cents—thas all. (Someone comments that Curtis and Herbert aren't going to heaven, but to some place else.) Yeah, we goin' to be pitchin a ball downstairs too, while you upstairs prayen.

This method often convinces students that they do have something to say, and somehow their words become much more important when they are put on paper. It has worked very well with several former nonwriters, and has encouraged them to write down their own ideas, since we are not always available as "secretaries" (their term) and we often miss words and make mistakes.

This method was used in conjunction with another device. We sometimes play music—Cannonball Adderly, Bach, Ravi Shankar—and have the students write whatever comes to mind: words, phrases, bits of memory or imagination—telling them to pay no particular attention to complete sentences, grammar, spelling, etc. They will always listen and comment on the music, even if they won't write, and it's very easy to sit by the nonwriters and record. Usually, they are soon peering over our shoulders and making corrections. And often they turn out some astonishing poetry.

If you come to think of it, it's like
How somebody's tip toin', man—
Now he's movin' a little faster
    Comin' out of his sleep

He's runnin' now—
    See, he's runnin'?
He's gettin' tired now—
    He's slowed down
    Threw his coat over his back.

June dandelions and July apples
Warm sunny summer—morning milk—
    angelic and innocent
Four feet high, no need to shave
High voice of young boy.

It's like a butterfly which flits and skips
    and grooves
Then it rests.
It lands and then comes on solid as it finds
    the wind and sunlight
It goes high and then slides low
Then away it skips again.

Interesting pictures, as in *Stop, Look, and Write,* will often encourage good writing too—stories and poetry, when students are told to describe, to free-associate, *not* to write in sentences.

We used several other "gimmicks" which resulted in varying degrees of success. Students were told to close their eyes and describe an object by sense of touch. They were given the tool of simile and asked to apply it to one another, to school, to war, to buildings around them, etc. We sometimes evolved interesting and relevant problems, and let the students provide the solutions. For example, we let them act out a store robbery in which one boy was abandoned by

his companions. They were to complete the story. Discussions about topics that interest the students—the trouble at Hunter's Point, welfare, Juvenile Hall, Governor Reagan, peace and civil rights demonstrators, etc., usually led to some good papers. Now we rarely get a chance to formally assign a topic after a discussion. There is usually a resigned but good humored chorus of "I know—now *write* about it!"

I think one of the most effective means of encouraging cooperation in class and writing was hardly any method at all. Marcia obtained many free admissions to performances at San Francisco State. And although the tickets were originally meant for her drama class, at first one or two, and now several of our W.E.P. students attend every play. One would hardly expect that a very sophisticated performance of Racine's *Le Cid* would interest our kind of students. But they thoroughly enjoyed the play and between acts they discussed the problems with real understanding. But perhaps even more than the plays themselves, the idea that teachers would want to spend time with students outside of school hours, that teachers could be real people, and the joking and talking on the bus to and from the play were important in contributing to the change in the class atmosphere, which in turn contributed to more writing—which resulted in more articles for *The Soul Searchers.*

Perhaps here I should also discuss briefly the "units" we used—the themes around which we organized the writing assignments. We tried to pick concepts which were important to the students, but which were broad enough to apply to different backgrounds and interests. For instance, we used "Conflict," which meant using pictures of fights, of angry people, of war, etc. It also meant discussing gang fights, Vietnam, the Nazis, and war in general. We spent some time on self-conflict and conflict as they felt it in a school situation. Here is one of my favorites from the conflict unit:

The colors are arguing. They hate each other. The colors have destroyed each other's beauty. Some of the colors have united to make new colors. The yellow, the green, and the brown have turned to rust.

People of different colors unite to make a new color. A black person and a white person make a new color—not gray. The colors will always fight. There will always be colors. There will be more colors tomorrow.

"Choice" was a unit which developed from "Conflict." And here we used some poetry about choice, discussion about choices in their lives, choice as viewed by conscientious objectors, choice in school, etc.

All of these "methods," if they can be called that, resulted in what we call *The Soul Searchers*—something that is not quite a newspaper, not quite a literary journal, and not quite a magazine of opinion, but a little of all of these and something else too. What is important about it, I think, is that it has a place for many levels and kinds of expression, and what is perhaps most important of all is that the students have come to realize their own ability to produce something they see as good—even excellent— that they have come to see that each of them has a right to express himself, and should, no matter how unsure he is of his ability to express himself well. One final anecdote, I believe, will illustrate this last and most important point. Marcia and I chose the articles for the first paper because at that time the students didn't know how good they were and hadn't yet moved from the ordinary English class concept of "good" (neat papers, spelled correctly, written easily) to what has become our concept of "good" (honest papers, written after introspection or discussion, and evidencing a willingness to learn to express themselves better). The students themselves chose the articles for the second paper, going through each student's folder and picking the best work. When they came to Ronnie Johnston's folder (Ronnie was absent that day), they paused for a discussion. Ronnie is a very immature ninth grader who writes very little and poorly. He has moved a great deal, and hasn't ever really learned to read and write. They decided they must include something of his, even though the quality of his work did not meet their standards, because he should be allowed to have his say, and have his share of pride in their common effort.

ELAINE HAUSER **26**

Writing Yields Reading

San Lorenzo is an overcrowded four year high school. It is located in San Lorenzo District and designated as a target area for federal funds. The vast majority of its students come from white, middle-lower-class homes. According to the latest estimates, 60 percent of its students read below grade level and thirty percent go on to (junior?) college.

The Reading Lab in which I teach five classes (approximately fifteen students per period) of remedial reading is funded by E.S.E.A.[1] The lab is housed in a well lighted and cheerful temporary building separate from the main structural complex of the school. It is admirably well stocked with overhead projector, tachistoscope, and fifteen individual reading stations containing controlled readers, headsets for a tape recorder, and dictionaries. The book collection is inadequate though varied, and both the librarian and I recognize few restrictions regarding book selection for these students, either in the library or elsewhere.

Lab classes are supposed to be composed of students reading two years or more below level (see above), referred by teacher and counselor recommendation. This "mode" of composition makes for a heterogeneity manifested in its broadest terms since *each* class, furthermore, contains some freshmen, sophomores, juniors, and seniors, bright kids, limited kids, disturbed

[1] Elementary and Secondary Education Act.

kids, severely disturbed kids, kids with hearing problems, perception problems, motor problems, high potential students, kids with no potential as *students,* "tough guys," foreign language-speaking kids, and a fledgling Hell's Angel who occasionally brings guests to class.

The prevailing attitude in the lab has become one of cooperation and mutual pleasure. I am convinced that these students, by their own admission, feel that the rest of the school considers them "dummies" but that their reading teacher does not. My most successful single method for fostering their positive feeling is not really a method. It is a belief. I *know* they are not "dummies." The second most successful method, this strategy, is writing.

Every Monday my students *know* that they will write from a choice of subjects (usually two or three) for approximately forty-five minutes. The willingness and therefore the ability to concentrate for that length of time is the real substance of this strategy. This result was carefully planned and prepared for from the beginning. The topics and the forms of their expression and evaluation are crucial to the success of this strategy.

Topics

The first writing assignment given (from David Holbrook's *English for the Rejected*) was "A Police Description" of someone in the room. The lab was new to many of the students, as were most of their fellow labmates. They were asked to observe and to become aware of one another's unique traits and mannerisms, style of moving, sitting, speaking, rather than what they were wearing. I announced that I would read as many as time allowed to the class, without mentioning the writer's name, and the class would then try to determine which person was described in the paper. They understood that pointing out merely hair color or weight problems, etc., would give away the identity too early, so they were forced to more subtle distinctions for the sake of the "game." One boy described the "sad, silent" woman in a picture on the wall. Several students described me with disconcerting accuracy. At least one point, idea, or word from each paper was thoroughly and publicly praised on each paper (see evaluation). I said nothing of a corrective or cen-

sorious nature about these earliest writing attempts unless another student in the room was insulted in them. If anyone could not or would not write, I listened to that student privately and wrote down whatever it was that he finally said.

As the precedent for a pleasurable, regular assignment became established, I found that a variety of choices satisfied the various moods, concerns, and abilities of my highly variegated students. Invariably I had ulterior, pedagogical reasons for providing these choices. The topics had to be provocative and evocative, to begin with. Along with each went little "nudge notes" (labeled "hints," "suggestions," "tips") encouraging the students to recognize that *this* topic required description and imagination or examples (one to a paragraph) or proof (logical order for the sake of persuasiveness), etc. Occasionally I gave no suggestions at all—carefully pointing out this fact—on such subjects as "My Last Day on Earth" (mind-expanding without drugs).

The subjects fall into three major categories: objective or familiar; personal or relative; abstract or discursive. Though these are broad and overlapping categories, certain students consistently refuse to brave the second and third categories, whereas all will attempt the first. The more able and confident students can do remarkable things with the ostensibly "simpler" subjects. More and more often the fearful ones dare to take on the difficult themes as the semester progresses. Many find it hard to resist any of them!

I have listed below some of the most successful subjects in each of the three categories:

1. *Objective*
   A Police Description
   The House I Would Like to Live In
   Adults Think Teenagers Are...
   Are There People Like Us on Other Planets?
   Schools Should Be Improved
   Appropriate School Clothes
   What's Good or Bad about TV?
   What Would You Do with $1,000?
   Cars or "Bikes"?
   Do Teachers Confuse Students?
   Is LSD "For Real" or Just a Fad?
2. *Personal*
   The Wife I Would Like
   or
   The Husband I Would Like

My Best Friend or My Worst "Friend"
I'm Not Really Like That!
The Hardest Thing for Me to Do
Who Gets Hurt More, a Boy or a Girl?
What Kind of Career Would You Be Able to Stand—or Love?
My Son Is in Jail?!
Perfect Parents
What Is School?
The Fight (Describe It to the Dean, Parents, a Friend)
3. *Abstract*
Can a Person Really Hate Himself?
My Last Day on Earth
Is There a Difference Between Conceit and Self-respect?
If I Can Create, Why Should I Destroy?
What Causes Prejudice?
It Takes Strength to Be Happy

Form of Expression

At each writing session the students are reminded that the best and strongest ideas are the honest ones. They are asked to think deeply before they write and then to write what they really feel or visualize. This encourages some to highly amusing accounts of situations that others take very seriously and which still others take as pure fantasy. A few use the occasion to employ four-letter words, more to test *my* honesty than for any other reason. I hardly react or, if I do, it is to admit that though they may need these words to write their thoughts, I cannot read their thoughts out loud without blushing. This sounds like the truth to them (it *is*) and the phase soon passes. Insulting remarks about other students for the purpose of hurting them are not tolerated.

At the earliest of the wrting sessions, I told the classes often and vehemently that spelling was merely a skill which anyone could develop. I told them not to worry about the spelling of the words they wanted to use but merely to put them down as they sounded or, if they wished, to ask me to write them on the board. (I am still constantly amazed at the verbal knowledge these students have. They know so many more words than they will dare to write for fear of misspelling them.) At this time in the school year (beginning of the second semester) the blackboards are literally covered on Mondays with the words the students have asked me to write.

More and more often I hear someone say very softly, "That's what I thought," after the word goes up.

Once their ideas were found to be interesting to me and enjoyable for them to write, I was able to point out that certain collections of words were impossible to say out loud. I asked them to try out certain written combinations of words in order to "hear" whether or not they could be *said*. This is a routine way to test for sentences now that my students believe that written thoughts and oral ones are not hostile strangers to one another.

These students now believe that often they have valuable ideas which deserve to be stated clearly so that others may recognize their value, too.

Form of Evaluation

For approximately the first four weeks, no corrections were made on the papers and grading ("good try," "good," "very good," and "excellent") was based solely on ideas, strong expressions, clever observations, or good individual work. In short, I found something of value in everything but a blank paper. Once relaxed in this way, students could say what they had in them to say and they could remain at it for longer and longer periods of time. This production enabled me to see where some problems were, what they were, and therefore to plan for the resolution of some of them. No rewards were given for fancy handwriting or "goodie-goodie" remarks. The latter very soon disappeared.

Now my students ask me if I have *corrected* their papers, not graded them. Many study these corrections carefully. I still bracket good sections and thereby point them out as "well done" or "well thought," but I do not hesitate now to show that I feel other sections are less well done. Certain words are marked for closer examination. Certain constructions are designated as "incomplete" or "too many words here —put in a period where *you* have to breathe!" I usually place one inclusive remark at the top of the page (which stands for a "grade," I suppose) and this remark may be anything from "You've done better than this," to "O.K." to "I've shown this to all my friends!" Most of the time I still rely on "good," "very good," and "excellent," with the corrections in plain sight.

I am quite convinced that sheer quantity (practice) and the type of involvement that the students are revealing with regard to their ideas is bringing about a marked improvement in their control of language. Fulfilling all assignments (noted with a check in their folders) entitles them to a "B" in the lab. Their self-appreciation is still, to me, the highest purpose of evaluation of these students.

Other Activities

At least one day during the week is devoted to concentrating on a certain prevailing problem revealed in the form of the writing. It may be sentence structure, vocabulary building, spelling drills (not always based on the writing), punctuation, or paragraphing. Friday discussions often center on themes written on the previous Monday or prepare for the writing exercise of the upcoming Monday.

Occasionally I pass out individual photographs or ask the students to choose one on impulse from a stack on the table. These photographs are clipped from *Life* and *Look* magazines and are mounted on poster paper. I ask the students either to describe in great detail exactly what they see or to create a story about what they think they see. They almost always choose the latter.

The Magazine (see sample in the appendix) is a collection of the best writing by each student in the Reading Lab between September 1966 and December 1966.

I corrected spelling, the structure of sentences where necessary to reveal meaning, and punctuation. I added titles to each article.

The students did not and do not write primarily for "publication." (Our second magazine will appear in May.) They write for the pleasure and interest their work affords them. It was the majority opinion that the magazine was good but that some modifications would have to be made in the second edition. The most important of these modifications would be adding the name of each writer to his work! (They had absolutely refused to have this before they saw the finished production.) Their main concern on Mondays is whether or not the subjects offered are sufficiently interesting. They know they write best when they are involved and stimulated by the project at hand.

The Magazine turned out to be a delightful tangential benefit. Most important, however, has been the change in the students' attitudes toward writing and toward themselves.

Bibliography

Holbrook, David. *English for the Rejected.* London: Cambridge University Press, 1964. (Available in paperback.) This is the most useful reference book I have found for convincing and instructing teachers in the uses of writing for remedial students. It seems a small point to mention but, in this book, Holbrook makes it very apparent that a reading teacher must have a genuine gift for "translation." Without the patience or ability to decode the students' early writing attempts, the teacher will be at a great disadvantage.

Appendix: Sample Page from "The Magazine"

SOME THOUGHTS ABOUT COURAGE

Self Discipline

I feel discipline without deans or parents could happen but teenagers would have to become a lot more mature. With parents and deans always there, teenagers let their responsibilities go and figure "my parents or the dean will fix me up."

Deans, to my way of thinking, are just there to scare you into being good and not "messing around." For instance a teacher will say, "sit down before I send you to the dean" or "shut up or you're going to the dean."

Teenagers need discipline most in their freshman and sophomore years. After that, most teenagers start to grow up.

It's fun to "goof" around. You'll do it all your life. But there's a limit. There could be discipline without deans or parents, but it's a long time coming.

Self Dignity

Self dignity is what you think is right and not what everyone else thinks.

Belief in Self

Self dignity is what you see in yourself. It is what you believe in and your pride in what you believe. A high standard of dignity has importance.

You can achieve dignity when you believe in something, keep believing in it and have respect for it and never let anyone "put it down."

Helen Keller

Helen Keller was a great woman. She was fortunate to be able to tell people how she lived in the dark. She was the kind of person you would like to know.

In a way, I wish I were in her place right now.

Why can't we see what they are going through?

I Learned How to Fight

When I lived in Oakland, I learned how to fight.

I let people push me around until one boy said something about my mother. I fought and won.

After that, I stood my ground. Now I'm not afraid of anyone.

Watts Riots

I can't really describe my feelings about the riot itself, but the Negro boy that killed the white man was under gang rule.

I mean that he thought he could show everybody he was a big brave man, being able to carry a gun and shoot a man.

I think that seeing a man being beat up caused him to get excited enough to pull the trigger.

VIVIANE ABOT **27**

A French Page for the School Newspaper

Introduction

Our school newspaper, having a monthly foreign language section, makes it necessary for the French department to come up with new ideas to be included in it. Being in charge of the French page, I have the responsibility to find material students would be curious about and like to read. I decided that one sure way of attaining this goal was to have them devise the means by which this could be accomplished.

Strategy

My first period eighth graders are, on the average, more advanced than any others I have. Not only do they seem more mature, but they also are more motivated. (I realize this latter fact may be due to the time of day, but it never-theless remains a pleasure for me to meet this class.) Consequently, they were the natural choice for the newspaper project in which I involved their talents.

I asked the students to write some practical ideas for the school newspaper as a homework assignment. Upon reading these, I discovered they were divided into a few general classifications: crossword puzzles, scramble words, stories, and fill-ins. There were a few noticeably different ideas—usually stemming from a special talent, such as poetry, drawing cartoons, etc. I had these students bring in samples of their work. As they were all quite good, I had them do the finished copy to be used for the newspaper. Next I divided the class into "family groups." I tried to use as leaders those who had given me good representations of their ideas,

assuming that since they had been well organized on paper, they would also be able to
lead a group.

In some cases I actually changed a few students around so those who had similar ideas
would all be working together, even on several
crossword puzzles or fill-ins at a time, if necessary. As it turned out, about half the class was
working on stories—first in English, then translating them into French, with my help. Some of
these became a lot funnier than I had anticipated, with titles such as "Clarence l'éléphant,"
"Les trois petits cochons," "Mademoiselle Bee
Bop." The students would insert their own little
variations to the stories, making them rather
individual. The crossword puzzles and the
scramble words were easy enough for the
seventh graders to work out from the newspaper.
(This is desirable, as it keeps the French page
from being exclusively on the eighth-grade
level.)

We spent a Monday and a Friday working
out these ideas, plus half a period on Wednesday. The students were all finished by then,
except for a few sentences in a couple of stories.
In such cases, I asked them to finish on their
own time, especially when the incentive was
strong. They respected a newspaper deadline.
They really seemed to enjoy what they were
doing, and the pride of having their work
"published" was very much present.

Since there was a great amount of material
to be used, I divided the contributions and
spaced them out over several issues. The reason
for all this material in one big lump was that
some of the ideas took longer to expand and
to be written out than others. The students
working on the "quick" ideas (i.e., scramble
words) were naturally finished much faster than
the others, so I had them do several.

On the whole, the monthly French page
came out satisfactorily, and the result pleased
me as much as it did my students.

JULIE RANDALL 28

An Eight-day Creative Writing Workshop for High School Seniors

The strategy I am going to describe involves
teaching an eight-day creative writing unit to
a group of thirty-two students in my senior
composition class. The purposes of this unit
were twofold: first, to get the students to
"loosen up" and really express themselves freely,
and second, to try to change their attitudes
toward creative writing, and toward poetry in
particular. (We devoted the greatest amount of
time to writing poetry. We began with haiku,
then went on to the ballad, then to free verse.)
For five of the eight days the students wrote,
analyzed, and criticized their own and their
classmates' poetry. (No names were affixed to
the poems typed up for critical analysis.) On
the seventh day of the workshop the students
wrote in any form they wished. Many wrote
using a "stream of consciousness" technique,
and while they wrote, Tchaikovsky's "Romeo
and Juliet" was played in the background, followed by Ravel's "Bolero." Their work was
typed up on a ditto and each student received
a copy of the booklet of poems and prose that
the class produced. Their work has been submitted to the *Ilium,* the school's literary magazine, for publication, and also in the competition
for the *Ilium's* annual poetry contest. The
work of the students was not graded, and they
were free to write or not as they chose. All the
students participated—most of them with enthusiasm. I felt the workshop was enjoyable and
successful for both myself and the students.

Description of Class and the Setting

This was a class of thirty-two (sixteen Black, three Oriental, thirteen Caucasian) seniors, most of them having evidenced a high level of ability in their academic subjects. It was an ebullient group, containing the school cheerleaders, Pom Pom girls, and two of the football stars, not to mention the staff of the literary magazine, various student council members, several members of the welfare commissioners' board, two band members, one of the school's track stars, and several students who at one time or another had been nominated for various popularity contests. Reading test scores (Gates, Ml form) indicated that almost all were reading at or near grade level (several reading above grade level), with only five of the thirty-two reading at tenth-grade level or below. No one scored lower than eighth-grade level. I would describe the class as one having very high potential, average skills, but below average motivation in some cases, as far as academic subjects were concerned. Many of the students were not willing to sacrifice the pleasure of the moment for the gains to be gotten in the future —i.e., scholarships to college—by hard work and study in the present. At first, they had to be frequently reminded of the importance of doing their homework, turning in their assignments, not socializing in class, etc. As it turned out, all but about four became quite diligent about doing their work after the first quarter grades came out!

Significant Events Preceding and Following the Strategy

Preceding this strategy, the students in the advanced composition class had followed a very heavy schedule. They had one composition a week (no less than three hundred words, usually five hundred words). In addition to this, they had daily in-class writing and reading assignments, and reading to do for homework (in Warriner's *Advanced Composition: A Book of Models for Writing*). Immediately preceding the creative writing workshop, they had just completed a six week research paper on which they had worked very hard. So, psychologically, this was a good time to have a creative writing workshop, for the students needed to relax and loosen up after their heavy schedule, and they

were ready to do so. They also knew that while participation in the workshop was not compulsory, and no grades would be given on their work, they would submit their writing to the *Ilium* for publication and schoolwide circulation.

Rationale for This Strategy

The rationale behind this strategy was threefold:

1. To offer the students a chance to express themselves freely after the rigid and disciplined schedule they had followed for most of the semester.
2. To help them overcome the negative feelings many of them had about creative writing and poetry in particular.
3. To let them experience success in writing creatively. By beginning with haiku, and letting them compose their own haiku (with the emphasis on feeling, or emotion, rather than form), they had a chance to write poetry that was not difficult, and that in almost all cases sounded good. In other words, the most uncreative students surprised themselves (and, on occasion, me) by writing some very nice haiku.

The Strategy

The day before the workshop was to begin, which was also the day the class handed in their research papers, I announced the plans for the next eight days. We had an informal class discussion, and I called for students' suggestions for the workshop. At the same time I presented a tentative outline that we might follow unless they had suggestions to the contrary. They were willing to go along with my suggestions; only a few students were indifferent to the whole idea. There were no suggestions or comments by the class as to what they wanted to do. Throughout the workshop they relied on me to set things up.

On the first day of the workshop I gave each student a ditto sheet containing several haiku by well-known Japanese poets. We did not discuss the mechanics of haiku, but went right to a discussion of the feeling the poem was intended to convey. (Throughout the entire workshop, the emphasis was on emotional content of a poem, rather than metrics, form, etc.) Students were asked to silently study all the poems, then volunteer to read the poem of their choice aloud, trying to convey by tone of voice, expression, etc., what the mood of the poem was—or what mood the poem produced in the student. The students did this, and as we proceeded, they became quite enthusiastic. Almost everyone wanted to read one of the poems and have the rest of the class indicate the mood the student conveyed through his reading. By the end of the first session of the workshop, all the students were interested in haiku and familiar with the form, although there was no discussion of form. What is more, those who read had achieved a feeling of success because all interpretations were accepted and praised. They were ready for the activity to be carried out on the second day of the workshop.

On the second day of the workshop the students were given two strips of paper, on which were printed the first lines of a haiku by a famous Japanese poet (Issa, Basho, Buson, etc.). They were asked to compose their own haiku from these first lines. For this activity the class was divided into two groups, and members of Group I received the same set of first lines as members of Group II. The students were told that on the third day of the workshop we would compare and discuss the haiku produced by the two groups. Group I was then taken to another room by my student teacher to compose their haiku and discuss the poems in a small group, and I did the same with my group. Students spent about twenty minutes writing, then we put our chairs in a circle and discussed some of the poems. Many students asked for more first lines, while some wrote original poems of their own. At the end of the period, Group I joined us, and we spent the last three minutes of class time recapitulating the proposed assignment for the next session.

On the fourth day of the workshop we read poems composed by both groups. I had, meanwhile, dittoed up all the haiku written by both groups, so that each student had a copy of the entire set of poems. Poems were compared and discussed. This took about half the period. During the remainder of the period a new activity was introduced. Students were given a brief description of the form and structure of the ballad. I read some examples of the ballad form, and my student teacher sang a few stanzas of "Barbara Allen" to further illustrate the rhythm and the beat of the ballad. The assignment for the next session was to write an origi-

nal poem in either haiku or ballad form—or any other form that the student was familiar with—and submit this poem at the end of the period—to be typed up and presented to the class on the following day for small group analysis. (Students were assured that no names would be affixed to poems submitted for critical analysis.)

On the fifth day of the workshop, the students worked on their original poems, with the student teacher and myself assisting when help was needed. Most of the students by this time were really caught up in the spirit of the workshop and were writing with a great deal of gusto and enthusiasm.

The sixth day we broke up into small groups again, Group I going with the student teacher and Group II remaining with me. I had collected all poems from the day before and dittoed them up, so each student had copies of the poems. In our separate groups, we analyzed and criticized the poems. Questions came up, such as: What is a poem? What distinguishes poetry from prose? Must a poem have form? Are some of the poems we are analyzing poetry? Why or why not? Interest was high, students participated eagerly in the discussion, and the fifty-five-minute period seemed to go by in five minutes. I felt the students got more out of discussing their own poetry, and a better understanding of poetry in general through analyzing their own work than they would have if they had analyzed Shakespeare's sonnets or Milton's epics. In the small group seminars students felt free to express themselves and everyone had a chance to do so. Again, no one was "wrong" in his interpretation—therefore, the students experienced success in groups, and this reinforced positive feelings toward poetry. The students whose poems were analyzed readily identified themselves (although, as I mentioned, no names were affixed to the poems) and were eager to interpret their own poems and to get their classmates' opinions. This session of the workshop was perhaps the most successful of all. Everyone felt good about what had been written and discussed when the period ended— including the teacher and the student teacher. The two groups met together during the last five minutes of the period, for the next assignment to be announced.

On the next to the last day of the workshop,

students were told they would be asked to write anything they wished, in any form they wished, while music played in the background. They were told they could write haiku, ballads, prose, using stream-of-consciousness technique, free verse, or whatever they could think of.

On the seventh day of the workshop, students came in prepared to write. I first put Tchaikovsky's "Romeo and Juliet" on the phonograph. The students wrote with a great deal of intensity during this selection. Several sat and listened for quite a few minutes before beginning to write. Before the selection was halfway through, they all seemed completely caught up in the spell of the music, and in the writing they were doing. The next selection was Ravel's "Bolero." The class relaxed during this music, seemed less contemplative and more detached as they wrote. At the end of the period, they handed in what they had written. That night I typed up their work and dittoed it. The next day I handed out copies to the class.

On the eighth and final day of the workshop we read and discussed the work of the previous day. The two "stream-of-consciousness" works were read aloud and compared. Attention was given to a poem depicted pictorially, which led to a discussion of Lewis Carroll and E. E. Cummings.

The last ten minutes of class time was devoted to getting student's permission to submit their work to the *Ilium*; the student teacher and myself circulated among the class, took down names of students who wished their work to be submitted for publication, and noted any special instructions the students had pertaining to their writings.

We all felt the workshop had been good. The students were pleased about their work. They were very candid in expressing their delight at seeing their work dittoed up and their names in print. They responded positively to all phases of the workshop, and although there were two or three students who did not write, these students nevertheless participated in discussion and analysis, and showed interest in certain phases of the workshop while it was in process. When it had ended I felt both the students and myself had learned something, not only about poetry and creative writing, but about each other. We all experienced success.

Appendix A

HAIKU

So far... so low...
a drowsy thrush? A waking nightingale?
Silence. We do not know.

Clouds come from time to time—
and bring to men a chance to rest
from looking at the moon.

Song of the cuckoo:
in the grove of great bamboos,
moonlight seeping through.

The tower high
I climb; there, on that fir top,
sits a butterfly!

Won't you come and see
loneliness? Just one leaf
from the kiri tree.

A trout leaps high—
below him, in the river bottom,
clouds flow by.

How cool the breeze:
the sky is filled with voices—
pine and cedar trees.

Green fields of grain:
a skylark rises—over there,
comes down again.

The rain of spring:
in the carriage that we share,
my dear one's whispering.

Where the stream bed lies,
only there is darkness flowing:
Fireflies!

Tarnished is the gold—
with young leaves round us, we look back
to days of old.

In these dark waters
I dreamed of battles
Women planting rice
Ballet in the air
One fallen flower
Arise from sleep, old cat,
See, see, see! Oh See!
Twilight whipperwill...
Mountain-rose petals
Take the round flat moon
Why so scrawny, cat?
Standing still at dusk
In silent midnight
Dead my old fine hopes
Black cloudbank broken
Wind-blown, rained on
White cloud of mist
Green shadow-dances...

Many solemn nights
My good father raged
Seas are wild tonight
Life? Butterfly
Moon so bright for love!
A saddening world:
Pretty butterflies...
Such utter silence!
A white swan swimming...
Come out! Come out!
Sadness at twilight
Must Springtime Fade?
Afternoon shower...
Ah, unrequited love!
Far across low mist
Old dark sleepy pool...
A lost child crying
Silent the old town

ELIZABETH AVAKIAN **29**

Teaching the Reading and Writing of Short Stories Concurrently

This unit came about in an attempt to teach the reading and appreciation of short stories to a track two (average) college preparatory group of sophomores at Berkeley High School. After a rather unsuccessful bout with Greek tragedy, which the students found irrelevant to their lives, I was seeking to involve them more immediately in the literature we were reading. It occurred to me that true appreciation of a literary form comes only when one is forced to grapple with the creation of it oneself, and I felt that my students would be far more concerned with understanding the structural principles of the short story if they themselves were in the process of writing them.

We began by discussing the concept of conflict, which is at the root of all fiction. The class arrived at a definition of conflict and was then asked to bring in pictures from magazines, newspapers, etc., illustrating any kind of con-

flict—either man against man, man against his environment, or man in conflict with himself.[1] Each student brought in a picture and then wrote a brief description of the conflict involved. These were then exchanged and the students commented in writing on each other's interpretation of the conflict, adding their own ideas as well. After I had also commented on the descriptions, the pictures were numbered for reference and posted around the room.

Concurrently with this activity the class read

[1] The idea of using photographs as a stimulus for writing came from the book, *Stop, Look, and Write,* by Hart Day Leavitt and David A. Sohn (New York: Bantam Books, 1964) and from a weekend extension course in "Seeing and Writing" based on the same book. The advantage of having the students choose their own pictures is that they generally have a strong interest in the subject they choose, and are, therefore, more eager to write about it.

the first short story in our anthology,[2] "The Catbird Seat" by James Thurber. We analyzed the structure of the plot, identifying the rising action, the turning point, the climax, and the dénouement. Definitions of these elements of the story were evolved by the class. These concepts, as well as the concept of conflict and its resolution, were then applied to the plot of "First Confession" by Frank O'Conner, the second story in the anthology.

The students had been informed that the conflict they had described in connection with the pictures they had chosen would form the basis for the short stories they were going to write. Many of them responded with terror or disbelief. They were highly skeptical despite my assurances that I would guide them step by step through the writing process and that they *would* each be able to write one.

As we discussed the first few stories in the anthology (which, incidentally, includes a rather good text on the structure of the short story and challenging study questions for the stories themselves), I constantly called their attention to details they would want to remember when composing their own stories. With the reading of "First Confession" we began to discuss the various methods of characterization and the different points of view from which a story may be told. Using some of the text questions, the students rewrote sections of the story from different points of view in order to discover the effect point of view has on the nature of the story. We then discussed the advantages of using various points of view for different purposes.

When I felt fairly sure that the class understood the basic structure of plot and the need for establishing a particular point of view from which to tell the story, I had them each write an outline of a short story plot based either on the conflict they had previously described or on a conflict suggested by another picture.[3]

Next we tackled tone and setting as they operate in the short story. This was done in groups, with each group formulating its own definition of setting or tone and applying it to one of the stories we had read. Finally each group reported back to the class for a general discussion of the two topics.

During the time that the groups were meeting and preparing to present their conclusions to the class, I was able to talk with individual students about their projected outlines. I tried to have individual conferences with each one before the class actually began to write, but since I was conducting this unit in two classes, each with approximately thirty students, this was clearly unworkable. I think that a more feasible and possibly more productive way to have conducted this part of the writing unit would have been to have the students meet in groups to discuss their proposed outlines, thereby giving them a chance to exchange criticisms and ideas.

As the students began to work on their rough drafts at home, we began in class to discuss the concept of theme in connection with the story "The Lottery" by Shirley Jackson. In leaving the discussion of theme for last, I was following the progression of the text, but I also feel that it made sense pedagogically. If the students had started out with the idea that all stories have to make some sort of point, and if they had built their stories around the theme, rather than the conflict underlying the story, I think most of them would have written thinly disguised essays. Instead, in stories which had themes, the themes grew naturally out of the conflict that had originally attracted the students.

In teaching about theme, I made use of the definition in *Story and Structure*,[4] an excellent college text. I gave the students the ground rules that Perrine sets down for determining the theme of a story, and we discussed possible themes for "The Lottery." The idea that more than one statement of theme could be right was stressed, and each class came up with a slightly different statement, a composite of the suggestions of several students.

Next the students were asked to hand in their first drafts. After I commented upon ways that they might be improved, they began to write the final drafts. I think more exchange of student papers would have been valuable here, too, but I was pressed for time (grades had to be in) and did not attempt this.

2 Robert W. Boynton and Maynard Mack, *Introduction to the Short Story* (New York: Hayden Book Company, 1965).

3 See Appendix for a sample instruction sheet.

4 Laurence Perrine, *Story and Structure,* (New York: Harcourt, Brace & World, Inc., 1959).

Four different activities terminated the reading portion of the unit. At the beginning of the marking period, students were told that for their outside reading reports they could choose *any* work of fiction. Since we would be studying the structural principles underlying fiction, they would be asked to write about their books with reference to structure; consequently, any work of fiction would be applicable.

After we had completed our extensive analysis of the first three stories in the text with relation to the aspects of the short story described above, I passed out a description of additional literary terms and ideas. We discussed those concepts that were still unfamiliar—character types, symbol and irony, the difference between escape and interpretive literature—applying them to the short stories we had read.

I then asked the students to write an essay about the book they had chosen, answering questions related to all of the structural concepts we had discussed in class. These essays were due a week before the final versions of the short stories. For the most part, the students showed an understanding of literary terminology and an ability to apply it to new works of literature. They were able to distinguish between escape and interpretive literature, and to distinguish between good and bad escape literature.

The second culminating activity involved the middle section of the text, which divides stories by "types" into stories of terror, crime, fantasy, and humor. Students were allowed to choose the story type they wanted to work on, and each group of students was responsible for presenting the two stories listed under its type to the class. The class was to have read each pair of stories before the panel discussion took place. Each group made up a short objective quiz to test whether or not the class had, indeed, read the stories. This provided some incentive to read carefully, and gave the students practice in making up questions. The panels were responsible for devising a set of criteria for judging a story of the type they had chosen and for evaluating the two stories in terms of their criteria.

Finally, students were given a test on the short story, in which they were required to demonstrate their understanding of the terms used in class by presenting illustrations from any of the short stories we had read. The last writing assignment involved a comparison of "Paul's

Case" by Willa Cather with any of the other "Stories Grouped by Theme" in the final section of the text, all of which deal in some way with adolescents adjusting to adult life. These are all excellent stories, and I think if I were to teach the reading portion of this unit again using this book, I would skip over the second section, in which the selection of stories is not as good, and concentrate on the last, possibly by having panel discussions dealing with each story.

The writing portion of the short story unit culminated with the publication of a class magazine, in each class, containing the five or six best stories as selected by an editorial board elected by the class. This four-man board was given the responsibility of determining the criteria by which each story should be judged.[5] Each story was read, graded, and commented upon in writing by at least two members of the board, and then read and graded by me. The final grade for the story was an average of our three grades. (I was surprised to find that the students were consistently rougher graders than I.)

After all the stories had been read and graded, the editors selected the stories that they felt should be published. These were then duplicated and distributed to the class for Christmas presents. If Christmas hadn't intervened, I think it might have been fun for the classes to have read each other's stories and perhaps voted on the best. Because of the sheer mechanical difficulties, not all of the stories that the board selected could be duplicated (I ended up typing most of the ditto masters myself), but I have submitted them all to the school magazine in the hope that at least one will be published.

The entire unit lasted about eight weeks, although the writing portion of it was done over a period of about six weeks. In evaluating the unit, I would say that contrary to the contention of Mary Hiatt,[6] my students were not inhibited by the fact that they were reading professional stories at the same time as they were writing their own. Rather, I feel that they were stimulated by the stories we read and discussed in class. Moreover, the writing of the stories motivated the students to learn about

---

5 See Appendix for sample evaluation sheet.
6 "Teaching the Writing of the Short Story," *English Journal,* LIV: 9 (December 1965), 810–18.

the structure of short stories. And what is more important, by *experiencing* rather than only *studying* the relationship between form and content, they were able to truly assimilate information that is usually simply memorized.

Bibliography

1. Boynton, Robert W., and Maynard Mack. *Introduction to the Short Story*. New York: Hayden Book Company, 1965.

2. Dick, Thomas. *Fiction: Notes on Literary Terms and Ideas* (a study guide for use in junior high). Prepared for Berkeley Graduate Internship Program, 1965 (mimeographed).

3. Hiatt, Mary. "Teaching the Writing of the Short Story." *English Journal*, LIV: 9 (December 1965), 810–18.

4. Leavitt, Hart Day, and David A. Sohn. *Stop, Look and Write*. New York: Bantam Books, 1964.

5. Perrine, Laurence. *Story and Structure*. New York: Harcourt, Brace & World, Inc., 1959.

Appendix

ENGLISH III.2

HOW TO MAKE A PLOT OUTLINE FOR A SHORT STORY

I. Thinking process
  A. Define your main conflict.
     For this use the picture you have already described, IF you think it is a suitable conflict for a short story. (The conflict between the North and the South in the Civil War is NOT a suitable conflict for a short story, whereas a conflict between two individual soldiers or within one soldier's mind is.)
     If you would prefer to find a new picture expressing conflict, or if you would like to use one of those posted on the bulletin board, be my guest.
  B. Decide what led up to the conflict in the picture and what is likely to be the outcome.
  C. Give the picture a title. This will help to focus your attention on the main conflict. The title can also serve as the title of your story.
  D. Decide on the climactic event in the story—the event to which all the others will lead and in which the conflict will be resolved.
  E. Decide at what point you want to begin telling the story. Are you going to tell the events in the order in which they happened, or are you going to use the technique of the flashback in which the main character will remember or the narrator will relate the events which have gone before the story opens?
  F. What are the main scenes or events that will lead up to the climax?
  G. How will the story end?
  H. From whose point of view will the story be told? You have essentially three choices:
     1. Told by one of the characters in the first person.
     2. Told from the point of view of one of the characters but written in the third person (as in "The Catbird Seat").
     3. Told from an *omniscient* point of view—that is, the narrator does not tell the story from the point of view of any one character, but is able to shift from one perspective to another or to view the situation objectively (as in "The Lottery").
II. Writing process: How the outline should look
  A. Title it with the title of the story.
  B. State in the introduction who will be telling the story.
  C. List the main events of the story, pointing out where your telling of the story begins, what events (if any) are going to be treated in flashbacks, which is the climactic scene, and which is the turning point. (These last may be the same.)
  D. Tell how the story will end.
  E. Identify what the major and minor conflicts in the story are and how they are resolved.

CRITERIA FOR EVALUATING SHORT STORIES: Period IV

Name of story _____

Author _____   Grade _____

Evaluator _____

1. Is the plot well constructed and logical? Does the ending follow logically from the rest of the story?
2. Are the characters realistically and consistently developed?   _____
3. Is the tone of the story appropriate and consistent?   _____
4. Is the point of view from which the story is told effective and consistent?
5. Is the setting of the story appropriate and well described?   _____
6. Is the title well suited to the story? Is it effective?   _____
7. Is the over-all grammar, spelling, punctuation, etc., good?   _____

COMMENTS:

Should this story be published?   _____

KRISTEN AVANSINO **30**

Dancing: The Joy of Discovering Together

I. Background

Racial conflict permeates our society. Large urban centers are the melting pots for sizzling emotions. To this fact San Francisco is no exception. My dance classes have been, I think, representative of most urban high school classes.

Through the media of dance, I have experienced great satisfaction. My goal has been simply to reduce friction between the students so that the common objective of learning can be pursued. My prime objective has been to develop project experiences in which the students must work in harmony in order to create and finally realize an artistic goal.

Basically, my strategy to achieve this goal has been to employ the many available techniques of dance. Although my teaching experience has been brief, my success has been rewarding. The students have had to utilize interrelating move-

ments to perform their dance phrases. At first, this was met with consternation and apprehension. Through time, the common jealousies and antagonisms have subsided. The necessity of a common goal has become evident to most of the students. They have realized, sporadically at least, that working together precisely is imperative in the art of dance.

The Polytechnic High School dance studio is a laboratory for the creation, implementation, and evaluation of novel dance techniques. Experimentation has yielded unique interpretations of grouping, team learning, student teaching, and problem solving concepts related to dance. These strategies help students relate more harmoniously with themselves and other human beings through exposure to the beauty and joy of dance. Excuses such as "I can't do this" or "I don't want to work with that group" no longer exist in my classroom.

II. Interschool Dance Project

It was a motley collection of tin cans, pieces of elastic, tissue paper, and small bells that provided the setting for one such creative dance experience. The occasion warranted special consideration; my advanced class had invited representatives from other high school dance departments to participate in a dance class. I was apprehensive about this event, having viewed similar efforts which had fostered competitive hostilities between representatives of schools. The span of the school year had alleviated intraschool feelings of self consciousness and jealousy in my classes; I wanted this lesson to be a memorable interschool event—a happy, harmonious experience.

As a prelude I opened my eyes wide to look at the environment. I focused, too, on the type of learning I wanted to occur. First, I knew that I must provide dance activity which could be individually interpreted; involvement and success must erase feelings of inferiority and failure. I must appeal to all—beginners and ballerinas. Then I thought, "Let's have some fun. Let's do something different, creative, way out." Thirdly, I wanted to promote natural movement and natural personalities. Also, I hoped to ignite minds into thinking about the world around them and about themselves. Lastly, there must be rewarding relationships with others to kill preconceived notions. My eyes scanned the environment seeking a vehicle for dance. Junk, cans and paper, was amazingly beautiful waste. My query was resolved! The vehicle and rationale must now be articulated.

I met with a group of students, and we laid the groundwork for the dance experiment. All were anxious to create an environment in the studio; each was responsible for bringing certain items. The big day came, and all decorated with gusto. Tin cans were tied together with string. Bells jingled on pieces of elastic. Newspaper and tissue paper were crumpled and stacked. Elastics linked chairs and posts in the room. The group was proud! It was their creation!

Upon arrival, the visitors' fascination with the environment was evident. Energies concentrated on the articles strewn about the studio. Individuals were unified from the start. My role as teacher ended with the completion of a short welcome and introduction. Then I became a participant.

Three students taught the entire class. Their vitality and naturalness contributed a special charm. First, the girls demonstrated various movements characterizing the items in the room. Their arms and legs extended as the elastic stretched; they collapsed as the elastic popped. They rolled as cans do; they clanged against each other as if they were cans tied together. They did flat movements and then crumpled up like newspaper in motion. They performed vibratory movements to jingle imaginary bells. The leader asked everyone to mirror her movements, to concentrate upon the circular and angular shapes she was creating. Next, under the direction of the "teachers," each individual was to interpret his own papers, cans, and bells. Each movement was unique; everyone was concentrating on the concept of becoming the object. After this was completed, small groups revealed their explorations to the others in the class. No one was hesitant about performing, and all watched intently.

The next development surprised and elated me. The freedom I had allowed my "teachers" resulted in a new dimension of the movement material. One girl asked the class to look at the bells and cans and to link their movements to someone else's just as the string and elastic linked the objects. This assignment brought strangers together, happily solving the movement problem.

Next, the "teachers" placed girls from various schools together to form four groups. Each was assigned a particular object. Their instructions were to capture the movement qualities of the object, to use the sounds produced as musical accompaniment, to "become" the object. The girls went immediately to work—laughing, talking, and creating. It was difficult to realize that these individuals had met a mere half hour before.

The dances which emerged were movement "gems." The bell group tied their objects on arms, legs, necks, and waists; the vibration from bodies in constant motion, interspersed with sporadic pauses, created a lovely effect. Then the cans clamored onto the stage. One girl kicked, rattled, and rolled the cans; the other members portrayed these movements in dance at the same time. The paper dance was a delicate blend of straight and crumpled movements. Girls enclosed their bodies in paper and closed by throwing paper into the air, running into it, and floating downward with it. Girls formed weblike designs with their elastics. This ended when all members released the elastics and collapsed to the floor. The elastics fell upon them.

At the completion of the dances, we asked the papers and bells to spatially relate their dances without altering the movements. The cans and elastics also joined forces. The movement contrasts were stunning.

At the conclusion an exhilarated, harmonious group departed from our dance environment. My goals had been met. The nature of the lesson provided opportunity for individual and group success. Individual interpretation at the beginning of the lesson evoked personal learning and confidence. Later, teamwork produced art, unified in intent and content. The objects intrigued everyone; the dancers' involvement with the objects promoted a fresh exploration of movements and feelings. The girls had experienced the joy of discovering, of learning, and of dancing together. An old orange juice can just won't be the same again!

ELIZABETH MARKING **31**

Stitchery Project for an Arts and Crafts Class

This lesson plan worked well in a class of both boys and girls, grades ten to twelve. Briefly, it consists of making a collage to serve as a working model for a stitchery project.[1]

My objectives were: (1) to encourage the students to look for flat shapes, patterns of line, and texture—elements particularly relevant to this art form; (2) to introduce unusual subject matter; (3) to try to teach the students to consider the lines and shapes as abstract forms; (4) to keep everyone busy at all times in order to reduce discipline problems; (5) to have everyone learn the techniques involved without having to teach *each* person *every* single thing.

The plan started out with a series of drawing exercises to accomplish my first three objectives. The first day I projected out-of-focus slides onto a screen, using reproductions of portraits, landscapes, etc., which were suited to my purpose

in that they had a wide range of value contrasts. The students were to analyze what they saw in terms of lightest tones, darkest tones, and medium tones. In brief, five-minute studies, they then quickly sketched the forms on newsprint, with charcoal or conté crayon. Since they could not discern the "subject matter" of the slides, the students avoided the trap of drawing the subjects according to preconceived notions. This exercise forced the students to "see" flat shapes in terms of tone.

Next the exercise was expanded to include not only the "out-of-focus sketch," but also a study of the focused slide in terms of *line* only. This is very different from the former exercise in that *no* tone is indicated; only the outlines of forms are shown.

The next day we went outside and made sketches of the landscape, trying to employ the techniques introduced previously. We also made rubbings of weeds and leaves and of the cracks in the floors and sidewalks as examples of line patterns.

---

[1] It is important that this project be called "stitchery," not "embroidery," since the latter term can turn off the boys.

The following day we did another exercise. Students were instructed to imagine themselves in an airplane flying over the land. They were to draw what they would see of the landscape as they looked down: the pattern of plowed fields following both straight lines and hill contours; the clusters of trees and buildings; the flowing lines of roads and rivers, etc. Then I told the students to forget about trying to reproduce these features exactly and realistically. Instead, they were to treat the "landscape" as a series of flat shapes and line patterns, a two-dimensional abstraction of a three-dimensional reality. They were urged to find stylized ways of illustrating the features in terms of *design*. For example, trees could be represented by simple circular shapes, or by spirals, or by radiating "star" patterns, or by amoeba-like shapes, or whatever. These ideas often led students off in opposite directions; namely, instead of showing a *macrocosm,* as some students chose to do, others decided to show a *microcosmic* world of the tiny plants and animals they had observed under the biology microscope.

From these many exercises, the students were to select their own most interesting sketch, or part of a sketch, and enlarge it to a full-size drawing. This drawing was then to be used as the basis for a collage.

The collage represented a model for the stitchery project. The students were encouraged to collect things with interesting textures to use on the collages. The only restriction imposed was that whatever was glued down—string, paper, leaves, etc.—had to be translated into yarn and fabric. For example, construction paper could become felt appliqués; transparent tissue paper overlays could be translated into nylon net; paper doilies suggested lace trim motifs; areas of glued-down crumpled tissue could be indicated by closely stitched loops of yarn, etc.

When the student had finished this collage, he was given a small piece of burlap, a needle, and yarn. I then taught him several stitches to practice. I required that every student master a group of about a dozen stitches, from which each was to select six to use on his own stitchery.[2] As others finished their collages, they were assigned to those who knew the stitches, who in turn taught them what they had just learned. The chain process, the "each one teach one" approach, had several good effects. It involved everyone in activity at all times (no waiting for my individual instruction); it was good practice for the students, since it was a good test of whether they had *really* mastered the techniques; and in several cases it enabled me to evaluate my teaching process, since often the student who had just struggled with the problem had more insight into how to explain it to a beginner than I did.

Finally, using chalk and tissue paper patterns traced directly from the collage, the stitcheries were laid out on pieces of burlap. Appropriate yarns, raffia, fabrics, buttons, pearls, laces, etc., were selected by each student and the final project was completed.

Each student would advance from one logical step to another, at his own rate, and everyone was busy at all times. This reduced discipline problems and the class went well.

As for timing, I allowed one week for the preparatory drawing exercises; the collage took one to two-and-a-half weeks, depending on the student. The practice sampler took two days to two weeks; the actual stitchery required two to four weeks to complete. The students who finished early were allowed to select a project of their own to do or they could elect to learn how to weave on a small table loom, a project closely related to stitchery.

2 I distributed a dittoed sheet of diagrammed stitches to serve as a convenient reminder.

III: GROUPING FOR INSTRUCTION

Grouping project at King Junior High School, Berkeley, California. Students in a seventh-grade history class construct a questionnaire to survey attitudes of King students toward junior high school.

It has long been argued that teachers should individualize their instructional practices. This generalization is the cliché of all clichés, often heard at professional meetings and PTA Programs. The question is, of course, "How?"[1]

How can one teacher deal with the wide range of differences in any classroom of thirty students? Even with students grouped homogeneously according to academic achievement there remain great differences in emotional maturity, aptitudes, motivation, and styles of learning. The conscientious teacher who wishes to plan appropriate classroom instruction for each of his students faces an almost impossible task.

In what ways can grouping within the classroom help? What are some of the benefits of small groups? Some of the possible dangers? What are the guiding principles upon which small groups can be formed?

For this chapter we have selected examples of various types of grouping which can be used effectively in almost any classroom—from voluntary grouping to structured team learning. In "A Grouping Project in Math," Michael Gross describes the procedures and precautions he used to make grouping most beneficial. Elizabeth Avakian explains "An Experiment in Grouping" which she tried in an English composition class of students with widely different abilities and interests who had one thing in common—a mutual dislike for the subject. Through voluntary groupings around interest areas and required groupings around needed skills, Mrs. Avakian tried to work out a balance between the students' personal interests and their academic needs.

Using another system of grouping, team learning, Annette Norvelle describes the benefits her students derived from this more structured system— clusters of six students each, with a leader, a co-leader, two average, and two below average students. Team learning, she reports, provides a means of freeing the teacher from center stage and assigns to teams of students greater responsibility for teaching each other. With its unique mixture of competition between groups and cooperation within the groups, team learning can provide individual instruction and motivation for all types of students—the achievers, the average, and the below average.[2]

In a science class for underachievers, Rochelle Esterle shows a way to use group examinations as a motivating experience. Suzy Norton next explains how she combined team learning with games in order to discipline and interest restless students in a foreign language class.

No single method of grouping, of course, will serve all needs. The wise teacher will use combinations of these approaches and will construct new ones for his particular situation.

[1] James Raths, John R. Pancella, and James S. VanNess, *Studying Teaching* (Englewood Cliffs, N. J.: Prentice-Hall, Inc., 1967), p. 132.
[2] Dr. Gérard Poirier, Supervisor of Teacher Education, University of California, Berkeley, introduced this method of team learning to the Graduate Internship Program teachers.

A Grouping Project in Math

I. Background

Several times during the school year I had placed the students in my five freshmen "Foundations of Algebra" classes in small groups to work on materials when I felt that they could clearly benefit from one another's information. After each of these sessions I felt that it had gone quite poorly. The students did the work they were asked to do, but they were certainly not utilizing the group situation. Instead of groups, I had individuals sitting close together functioning as individuals. I felt that there were two basic reasons for this lack of group communication: (1) the students were not used to functioning in the group situation, especially in a math class; (2) the assignments were really oriented toward individuals and hadn't been designed for a group. I think we too often take an ordinary assignment and ask students to work as a group. Instead of structuring a group assignment, we "implore" the students to work as a group.

II. The Project Design

To force the students to work together profitably, I designed a special statistics project. If they didn't work together they would quadruple the work each had to do.

I divided each of my classes into groups of four (some five) to work on the assignment. Each group was designed with two purposes in mind: (1) I wanted to keep friends together as much as possible; (2) I wanted each group to have a cross section of student personalities and *abilities*. I did not select a group leader, and deliberately refused to select group leaders when asked to do so by the students. Each group developed its own leaders as it began to function; many of the leaders who emerged were rather surprising. In no case did the leadership hamper the group's progress.

III. The Project Assignment

On the first day of the project I gave each student a copy of the project requirements. The following is the information on the handout:

FOUNDATIONS OF ALGEBRA
GROUP STUDY ASSIGNMENT

TABULATING AND ANALYZING

Material:

Chapter 11, *Foundations of Mathematics,* Wiebe.[1] Read Chapter 11 and work some problems from each problem set. Decide the number of problems you should do from your understanding of the material. If you feel that you understand the section very well, it will only be necessary to try a few problems. Sections that are more difficult will require more practice. (Please label each problem you work with page and problem number.)

Report:

1. Write a general summary of the material covered. This part of the report should include the major ideas covered in the chapter. Include your ideas about the importance and uses of the material. You may go to the library for added information.
   In this part of the report, you may include an evaluation of the chapter.
2. Include the problems you have worked.
3. Create a test that you feel would adequately

---

[1] Arthur J. Wiebe, *Foundations of Mathematics* (New York: Holt, Rinehart & Winston, Inc., 1962).

cover the material in this chapter. Please work each problem you've written.

The topics the students covered in Chapter 11 of the text were the following:

1. Preparing frequency distributions and histograms
2. The arithmetic mean
3. The arithmetic mean for large sets of numbers (a method of approximating the mean through a frequency distribution)
4. The median and the mode
5. School census. Here the students had to design and administer a questionnaire to a realistic sample. The material was then analyzed and presented, using the material they had studied in the chapter.

IV. Use Of Optional Daily Lectures

When I designed the project I was unsure of how well the students would be able to develop an understanding of the material from the book. They have had very little experience and less success in reading mathematics texts. After the first day it became clear to me that they needed help in deciphering the text. I didn't want to go back to the traditional class setting to help them with the material, so I designed a short optional daily lecture to cover different sections of the chapter. The students were invited to attend these lectures. Students who wanted to attend brought their chairs to the back of the room; students who did not feel the need to listen could continue their independent work. Several interesting things developed during these lectures. Many students who had elected not to attend the lecture went through the strangest contortions to put themselves into a position which allowed them to watch without appearing to participate. Many of these students gave me more of their attention during these lectures than they ever had in the past. Another interesting thing was the feeling of warmth I felt during these lectures. This was particularly pointed out to me on one occasion when, after an entire day of group activity, I decided to deliver my lecture to my entire last period class. I felt lonely in front of the room all by myself.

The lectures were kept short and to the point. If needed, further illumination of the material was handled within the individual groups.

V. Group Meetings

I met individually with almost all of the groups (at their request) to discuss the format of the chapter summaries and school census. Many interesting ideas developed in these group meetings. Many of the groups decided that they would interview people who used statistics in their jobs to learn about the practical applications of the materials they were studying. This suggestion came autonomously from several groups and I suggested it to others. As source material, the students used parents, friends of their families, teachers, and the school's principal.

The project was carried on for approximately three weeks. Students were given three days each week to work on their reports. The other two days were spent in a more traditional class setting, working on the algebra we were studying as a class. I found that after several days of group work the students were much more attentive to the normal class routine. They enjoyed working in groups, but were relieved to occasionally turn the responsibility for their learning back to the teacher. I often used this perception to good advantage by presenting particularly important material to my classes after several days of group activity.

Each group was required to turn in one report. All members of the group received the same grade. This created problems, as some students did more work than others. I felt that this was an inequity that had to be accepted if my goal of a totally group-oriented situation was to prevail.

VI. Results

The results were quite varied. Some reports were creatively designed; others were haphazardly done. The majority of the reports were quite good and demonstrated that the students had learned the material well. On the day that the projects were due, I spent most of the period giving the classes an oral discussion test on the material. Some of the questions were computational but most were conceptual. I asked questions, called on students to respond, and then had other students evaluate the responses. In this way I was able to get a fairly good idea of what the students had learned in the project. I feel that they developed a broader conceptual understanding of the material than they would have if the material had been presented in a more traditional fashion. I don't think that their computational skills were as highly developed as they would have been (but I question the importance of this ability). Many students articulated sophisticated ideas pertaining to the material. For example, in each class several students developed the idea that by graphing information, one sacrifices accuracy for communication.

I feel that this project accomplished the goals I had in mind. The students developed an understanding of elementary statistics, and more important, they learned to work together toward a common goal. I think the subject matter of the project was particularly appropriate for freshmen. These students will be taking three years of social studies while in high school and will often be called on to interpret material presented in graphic form. At the beginning of the project I had been amazed by how few students had any real understanding of simple graphic methods of communicating information.

I used grouping in several other ways after this project was completed. I find that if the assignment is really a "group" assignment, the students are now able to work quite well together. At this point I allow them to form their own groups and am usually quite satisfied with the results. I feel that group activities are an excellent way to vary the class experience.

ELIZABETH AVAKIAN **33**

An Experiment in Grouping

I. Description of the Class

The experiment was tried in a composition class composed of twenty students, fifteen boys and five girls, most of whom are second semester juniors from track 1 and 2 English classes (all college prep). They have been placed in Comp. A rather than in the next sequential literature course (a high-powered survey of the English novel) because they either showed deficiencies in writing skills, failed to turn in writing assignments, or simply were barren of ideas about literature.

It is a diverse group composed of hippies, social clubbers, foreign-born students, and black students who have worked their way up from track 3. I have discovered that many of the students feel threatened by this diversity. Although there are some friendships within the class, there is more hostility than warmth between the students. They feel that they have little in common, and those who vocalize generally show contempt for those who don't look, act, or think the way they do. What makes the class even more difficult to teach is the fact that it meets tenth period—the last period of the day, when teacher and students alike have all had it. I had just about had it with this class when I turned to this project.

II. Objectives

A large problem had been the inability of the students to communicate in class. Discussions always dragged, but tension was nonetheless high. I hoped that by working in small groups the students might come to know and understand each other better, and consequently be able both to help each other with their writing problems in the small groups and to communicate more effectively in discussions when the class again met as a whole.

I also hoped that they would produce more and better writing when working on a project they had both chosen and played some role in developing.

Finally, I wanted them to develop some sort of an understanding of their own educational needs and processes. How much could they learn on their own and from each other? What things did they need a teacher for? Were they capable of enough self-discipline to carry on their own projects without the constant surveillance and supervision of a teacher?

One of my secret objectives was to prove to them that they had ideas and that they were capable of mature, responsible behavior. They could not learn this as long as I was in front of the room "instructing" and they were sitting in their seats "learning." They needed to be involved in the total process of teaching and learning. Arthur Pearl says;

We have to build in the gratification which comes from having a sense of contribution—a sense that you are of value to someone else. The student role as a passive sitter and absorber of knowledge is not particularly gratifying. The teaching role is. So one of the things to recognize is that it would be better if teachers did some learning and the learners did some teaching right from the beginning.[1]

Although I do not remember reading this before I started, it was actually the theoretical basis for my experiment.

III. Procedure

I divided the class into several groups, each working on a different project for a week at a time. Students chose the project they wished to work on and could stay with the same group the following week, but no changes were permitted in the middle of the week. If a student had an alternative suggestion to those offered, he could form a group of his own. There was only one limitation on this freedom of choice: every member of the class had to spend at least one week in the skills group working on fundamentals of writing. (Five people were assigned to this group by the teacher each week, although others could join if they wished.)

Each group had a chairman and secretary appointed by the teacher. The chairman was responsible for the proper functioning of the group; he communicated the weekly and daily plans and assignments to the group and made sure that the members kept up their work. The secretary was to take notes during class and submit a written progress report to the teacher at the end of each period.

All groups, with the exception of the skills group, were to turn in one paper, relating to their project, on Mondays. The skills group was given a test, made up by the teacher and covering the skills they had studied that week. These skills were chosen by the students themselves, after looking over their back papers to see which mistakes were the most frequent. Each member of the group had the responsibility of teaching or helping to teach one skill to the rest of the group, leading exercises in it, and assigning homework from the grammar book in that skill. This procedure remained constant throughout the three weeks that the project was in operation.

The other suggested groups for the first week were a creative writing group and a current affairs group. The creative writing group was given an assignment involving the reading and writing of short stories, according to a plan I had worked out in one of my tenth grade classes the preceding semester.[2] Although I worked out the sequence of lesson plans and assignments, the chairman had the responsibility of conducting the lessons, and the students had the responsibility of coming to their own conclusions about the stories they read and of criticizing and helping each other devise the stories they wrote.

The current affairs group was given a choice of topics, from which they were to pick and formulate a specific question relating to it and research, discuss, and write about it. They were given class time for all three activities.

IV. Results : The Project
as It Actually Happened

Week 1

Having prepared carefully for each day for each group, to the extent of having daily typed lesson plans ready, I found everything went

[1] Arthur Pearl, "Educational Change: Why—How —For Whom?" from unpublished speeches distributed by the Human Rights Commission of San Francisco, 1966 (1254 Market Street, San Francisco).

[2] See strategy 29.

according to schedule. Although the class had greeted my enthusiastic proposal of the project with what I can only describe as "critical apathy," they seemed quite happy to give it a try once they were settled in their groups.

The skills group functioned pretty smoothly, thanks largely to an excellent chairman, and all did fairly well on a rather difficult exam I made up for them at the end of the week. The current affairs group was provided with literature on their chosen topic and a tape of a talk given on radio station KPFA. They all produced fairly good essays. The creative writing group was a bit too rushed in their project, and their stories were largely uninspired, with the exception of two which were quite good.

At the beginning of the second week, I had the students grade and evaluate the other members of their groups, including themselves, on the basis of how well each student performed as a member of the group. These grades were more revealing as an indication of interaction between students than as an objective measure of performance. They were averaged together and entered in my book as the "group grade" for the week. We also had a brief discussion on the project thus far—brief because, as usual, the students were reticent. But when I asked for a show of hands, all but one girl wanted to continue.

Week 2

Although I did less planning for the second week and thought it had gone poorly, in retrospect it seems that things went better than they had the first week, with the exception of the skills group which contained some of the most difficult people in the class. The students had become accustomed to the routine of coming in and getting to work on their own projects. The creative writing group, most of which remained intact, devised its own assignment— writing a story from the point of view of a button—and turned out some very imaginative pieces. A new group was also established—the Reading Comprehension group, made up of three students (later expanded to five) who wanted to improve their reading speed and comprehension. They were set up with an SRA text and charts that they could keep individually. The only writing they were required to

do was one précis a week, which gave them practice both in writing concisely and in reading comprehension. The current affairs group wrote papers on the draft—that is, two of the three members wrote papers. The third, an extremely withdrawn hippie-looking boy whom I have yet to reach (he always pulls his hair over his eyes when I try to talk to him) still doesn't produce anything.

The project was continued for a third week, after which evaluations were written. These essays were graded only to give the students an incentive to take them seriously, but since they were writing about something they had actually experienced together and, in fact, helped to create, I think there would have been a high degree of involvement anyway. One girl even took hers home to finish and corrected every sentence fragment in it (her nemesis). Most worked for the entire period on their papers, some even stayed after school to finish, which was highly unusual for this class. This degree of involvement in the evaluation indicates to me that something fairly significant must have happened to the class during the time the project was in operation.

V. What Didn't Happen
That Should Have

1. Because students were allowed to choose a different group each week, and I assigned new people to skills each week, in some cases there wasn't enough continuity or time to develop a satisfying piece of work or enough time for revision.

2. The skills group in particular had difficulty functioning without direct supervision since they were at a loss to know how to *teach* the material and felt frustrated at their inability to help each other learn. Bordeom and apathy were also a problem in this group, since most of the students had not chosen to be there. I think I probably should have taken charge more in this particular group.

3. Those students who had not written much or at all during the year or who were absent more than they were present did not increase significantly in their output, with only two exceptions, one of whom is a black student who was, until this point in the term, extremely hostile toward the class and had even stopped

coming. His essay on capital punishment was a beautifully heartfelt piece of work, as was his evaluation.

4. The more conscientious and compulsive students in the class, of which there were but a few, found working in this way with other students a bit frustrating. They apparently found it difficult to do their own work because they were aware that other people weren't doing theirs. One girl was particularly upset by the authoritarian role she had begun to play in her group.

VI. What Did Happen That Should Have

1. The students got to know one another and even to appreciate some people whom they had rejected before.

2. The writing produced was on the whole better, as a result of increased involvement in the subject matter. Output also increased, largely because of group pressure, which, from several comments, proved to be stronger than any pressure I as a teacher had been able to bring to bear.

3. Many students who had never participated in large group discussions found their voices, and some self-respect too, in the small groups.

4. The students developed an increased awareness of the entire educational process—how they learn and why. They also developed an appreciation of the teacher's problems. A classic remark by the chairman of the creative writing group after the second day: "Now I know what you go through! I read the directions at least three times, and then somebody asked me a question about something I had just said! Now I know why you're doing this!"

5. I learned a great deal about the students as individuals. Since I was freed from the front of the room, I could travel around and talk to various students. From the choices they made, the things they wrote, and the talks we had, I was able to get to know them better than I know most of my other students, and was thus able to help them more effectively.

6. The period did not drag as it used to, but was, for the most part, busy and productive, if a bit noisy.

VII. Observations

The project could really be tried in any subject field on any level, either on a limited basis as I did (for three weeks, while the class was reading Kesey's novel, *One Flew Over the Cuckoo's Nest,* on their own, preparatory to a class discussion), or for an entire semester. No prior knowledge of the students or of their probable interaction is necessary—except in the matter of choosing chairmen—since the groups are purely voluntary. The results have shown me that choice is an extremely important commodity to all human beings, and no less so to students, and that, in most cases, once a student feels a sense of personal commitment to a project because *he* has chosen it, he will take the responsibility of seeing it through.

Appendix A

Comp. A.
Mrs. Avakian

TENTATIVE PLAN FOR GROUPING

Ground Rules:

1. Each student must choose his group for the following week on the preceding Friday. He must remain with that group and do all the assigned work for the following week. No switching groups in midweek.

2. At the end of each week you will be given an opportunity to change groups. You may remain with the same group if you like; however, EVERY student at one time or another MUST join the skills group for at least one week.

3. A chairman and a secretary for each group will be appointed by the teacher. The chairman's job is to make sure that members of the group accomplish the tasks assigned to them and that the group as a whole accomplishes its tasks for the week. Chairmen may expect to stay after school for a few minutes each day to report to the teacher on the progress of the group. The secretary's job is to make notes on

the group's activities each day, and to sum up in writing the week's activities. The secretary should also make note of any tasks that are assigned to individual members of the group, and to make note of whether they are done.

4. Each group, with the exception of the skills group, is to turn out one fairly good-sized piece of writing a week. Writing should relate to the work being done by the group. In some cases, topics will be assigned by the teacher; in some, they will be devised by the group itself. These papers will be graded by the teacher and must be handed in no later than Monday of the following week. The group may make an earlier deadline.

5. On Friday of each week, groups will report to the class on what they have been doing and make recommendations and suggestions to future groups of their kind. If time allows, part of Friday will also be used for students to help each other revise their papers.

6. Grading for work done in groups will be based on the following:
   a. Grade on paper;
   b. Self-evaluation on participation in group;
   c. Evaluation by other group members on participation;
   d. Observation by the teacher of your participation.

Appendix B

Composition A

ESSAY AND EVALUATION

Write a well organized, carefully thought out essay evaluating the grouping project in which you have been involved for the past three weeks. In writing the essay, consider the following questions. You may not want to answer all of them, or you may think of others which I have not raised. Use these as a guide to the kinds of things I would like you to be thinking about. Your essay will be graded for logic, organization, and effectiveness of presentation of ideas, not for what you say, so speak your mind. Please use the whole period; if you finish early, use the time to check your paper carefully for mechanical errors. Do your best thinking and writing. Consider these questions in writing your essay:

1. How helpful was this project to you in developing writing skills? From what you have been able to observe about others, how helpful was it to them?
2. How interesting and valuable were class periods? Did you look forward to the class with eagerness, dread, or indifference? Why, in each case, was this so?
3. How much do you feel you learned about the other people in the class? Do you like them more or less now? How much do you feel you learned about yourself? (In answering this, please feel free to give specific examples; these essays will be kept confidential.)
4. As a result of the project, did you write more, less, or the same amount as before? Why, in each case? Did you enjoy writing what you wrote more or less? Why?
5. Was your attendance in class more or less regular during the time the project was going on? Was the change in regularity due to what was going on in class?
6. Can you think of ways in which the system could be modified to strengthen its good aspects and eliminate its weak ones? Would you like to try this again later in the term, incorporating your suggestions?
7. Did this project teach you anything about education in general, and if so, what?

N.B. THIS IS NOT A QUESTIONNAIRE, BUT AN ESSAY. YOU ARE EXPECTED TO DEVELOP YOUR ANSWERS WITH SPECIFIC EXAMPLES, SUGGESTIONS, ETC. NO GLIB GENERALIZATIONS, PLEASE.

THE SKILLS GROUP WILL BE GRADED SPECIFICALLY ON THOSE SKILLS WHICH THEY HAVE PRACTICED THIS WEEK, IN ADDITION TO THE OTHER CRITERIA. THIS IS IN LIEU OF A TEST.

Team Learning: The Only Way to Fly

Introduction

Team Learning is a system of grouping in which students of varying abilities are placed in groups with a leader and co-leader who act as assistant teachers and coordinators.[1] The groups must be carefully chosen according to members' strengths and needs, personalities, and ability to relate to others. Leaders are chosen for their leadership qualities, maturity, and ability to relate sympathetically to other group members.

My purposes for beginning this system were multiple. I was saddened at the lack of concern for others which I saw in evidence in many of my students. I was appalled at the peer pressure I saw applied so many times to insecure students, and at the self-destructive actions which usually followed. There is, especially during the early teen years, an overwhelming fear on the part of many students to participate or take total responsibility for their individual participation, for fear of failing and being ridiculed. So, what can a teacher do?

First, find a way for children to trust one another, rather than jabbing at and ridiculing one another. Make it rewarding for one person to help another. Take the full responsibility for success or failure off the individual's shoulders and place it on a foundation strong enough to support it—the group. Find a way to keep the class somewhat orderly so that learning can go on without the presence of constantly suffocating questions and searchings on the part of each

[1] My strategy is based upon Dr. Gérard Poirier's conception of team learning. See his book, *Students as Partners in Team Learning* (Berkeley, Calif.: Center of Team Learning, 1970), for complete description of the Poirier method.

student. Try to get everyone once again involved in the process of learning by giving them a means to success and an active role in the activity of learning. In short, begin Team Learning.

The Class

Although I have introduced and have been using Team Learning in four of my five classes, I will use only one of my classes as an example for this paper. My class consists of fourteen boys and sixteen girls; eight black, ten Caucasian, five Mexican or Philippino, one Greek, seven Chinese. Some of the latter three groups are foreign-born, or first generation, bilingual students. The blacks are both standard speakers and dialect speakers. The reason I'm pointing all of these things out is to show that my group is diverse, both culturally and linguistically. Our school has a foreign-born language program and many of my students take both an English for the Foreign-Born class and a regular English class simultaneously. With this fantastic mixture of ethnic and cultural backgrounds, there are some recognizable animosities among the more verbal students and many more repressed prejudices and suspicions among the other, more quiet students. Aside from these emotional responses, the Cantonese youngsters have picked up black dialectal changes, which further complicate their learning of standard English. The various problems which these dialectal speakers have are different from the problems of the bilingual Spanish speakers, and both of these groups have different problems from the immigrant Cantonese or the first generation bilingual Cantonese-English(?) speakers. Confusing? Well, just try teaching grammar (linear-style) to a group like this.

Introducing Team Learning to the Class

After randomly placing students in groups one day, and finding the students pleased and excited with the results, we discussed doing a team activity on a continuing basis. I tried to get my students to discover what a team can do better than an individual. We ended up with these answers:

1. Win a game.
2. Get more right answers.
3. Help each other.
4. Be stronger.
5. Protect each other.

We talked about what else is needed to make a group of people into a team and they came up with (1) a captain, (2) a coach, and (3) backing (money, equipment, a place to play). Finally they discovered that a team must have another team with which to compete before the team would really have strong reason for mutual support.

After much pleading on the part of my students, I finally consented (happily) to honor their requests. It was, admittedly, "hornswaggling" on my part, but there is nothing students like better than talking their teacher into something they think is "fun." I only consented after stipulating that I choose the teams and captains. We all agreed this would be our "experiment."

Grouping

I spent a few days writing information about each individual on 3 × 5 cards in this manner:

Francis, Elaine

A	S	C
2	1	2 = 1.6

Personal:

Keep away from Cookie and Susan. Absent more than average. Needs to succeed and be recognized. Doesn't take any crap from anyone.

Ability:

Very verbal, strong minded. Likes to compete. Good leader with able boy co-leader. Is understanding of others, but has quick temper.

Rating Scale:

1—leader
2—above average
3—average or below
4—below average to weak
5—very weak
A—academic
S—social
C—creative

These cards took a long time to complete. The next step was preparing the groups. Placing compatible people together took the better part of an evening. I tried to keep talkative buddies separated while putting achievers and underachievers, verbal and nonverbal people, shy and troublesome people together in groups. I also wanted to put people with little self-control into groups with understanding members, put strengths and weaknesses together for mutual support, and separate clots of snobs, ingroups, and "clingers" from one another.

I next chose group leaders who were conscientious and understanding, who could get along with others and understand the members of their groups who had grave skill or personality problems. If I had two students of like ability, I chose the one with the most compassion as the leader and designated the other as co-leader.

After I chose the leaders, I spoke to each one individually. I told him the reasons I had chosen him as team captain or leader and showed him the names of the people in his team. We discussed the kinds of difficulties some of his members had, and the kinds of problems he felt he might have. Each captain seemed pleased, though in some cases shy, about being chosen. Each one accepted the position.

The next day I divided the class into teams and we began an exercise.

Discipline

An interesting sidelight to Team Learning is a decrease in outlandish showoffery. Students who had been behavior problems and had been constantly irritating to the class and to me stopped some of their antics when they found out the group could lose points because of such displays. Every two weeks each team starts with one hundred citizenship points. Excessive noise or arguments, lack of attention, or insufficient work done on the part of team members can lower the team's score. At the end of the two weeks, scores are tallied and the winning team gets candy bars—a small expense for the change in behavior observed (eighth-graders can be hard on one's eardrums and patience). If a group worked particularly well, or if a student who had been troublesome was working and managing to use self-control, the group was awarded points and he was commended as the one responsible for the gain. This technique can be used whether you are doing a team activity or not. It also keeps the teams cohesive during those times when you have something planned which might not be a team activity.

Activities

When I began this project, my class was working on improvisational drama.[2] I decided to unite creative writing with pantomime. I did a pantomime for the class. They were supposed to follow the action as closely as possible and note down quickly what they thought the actions were. The teams formed "huddles" and manufactured a story. One member was the recorder who wrote it down and put it in order. Each member added what he had seen. Then each group chose a member to tell the story to the class. All groups rated all other groups but their own on a six-point scale. (The following aspects were to be kept in mind by each person: Well-written, well-spoken story; members had been aware of detail and expression; imagination was evident.)

6 = excellent
5 = very good
4 = average
3 = below average
2 = poor
1 = ugh

Each member rated the team, then the coordinator averaged the scores and gave me that score. Each team had five scores at the conclusion which looked like this:

	Team					
	1	2	3	4	5	6
Member 1	4	6	3	5	6	4
Member 2	5	4	4	3	6	2
Member 3	3	6	4	5	5	4
Member 4	5	5	4	4	6	4
Member 5	5	5	5	5	5	3
Total	22	26	20	22	28	17

[2] Viola Spolin, *Improvisation for the Theater* (Evanston, Ill.: Northwestern University Press, 1963).

Thus, team 5 was first, team 2 second, teams 1 and 4 tied for third, team 3 was fourth, and poor old 6 finished last. There was high interest evident during the entire period, and the activity took the whole fifty-four minutes. We continued with other activities.

One of them was a story unit in which I had assigned six short stories in the space of two weeks to be read by everyone. Then I assigned one story to each team. They were to review it and make an oral review to the class, then they were to think up twenty questions for a test. Of those twenty I chose the five best ones and made up a thirty-question test. All the members of the group were to help each other to get as many right answers as possible.

We have done team learning spelling tests where the leaders and co-leaders quiz and drill the other members on their words and then have a spell-down. The captain picks a member whom he believes can spell the word correctly. Each member may only be picked once until all of the members have had their first turn. As soon as a member misses a word he is out. The team with the last surviving member wins the record, while that team with the most points (one for each correct word) wins the score. The activity can go on for the whole hour too. Class interest is astounding.

Another successful game we have played is called Sixes.[3] It is a game which builds concentration, awareness, grammar, and sometimes vocabulary. I also use it to relax some of the students who are hypernervous in front of others. It goes like this: Each group gets up in front of the class. One student is chosen to stand in the middle of the circle which they form. The center member closes his eyes while the other members pass an object from one to another in the circle. When the center member claps his hands, the person who is holding the object must name six words which the center member or the teacher designates—for example, six form-class II words (verbs) beginning with the letter D, or six noun determiners, etc. While the person names these words the object continues to be passed around the circle slowly. He must stop when the object returns to him. Every correct word named is worth a point. Each team has a time limit. At the conclusion of the game the points are tallied and go down as

[3] *Ibid.*

part of the all-over score for the week for each team.

The variations are innumerable. This kind of method makes learning an active rather than a passive thing. Students get involved in the team, in the effort, and in the learning.

Conclusion

Team learning can be used, or modified for any kind of class; math, foreign language, science, history. Almost any quiz you give can be turned into a team-learning activity. The leaders can be assistant teachers when you are introducing new material. Teach them while the students are working on individual reading or are studying; then they teach the rest. The teacher can then spend time with individual problems, or can hold a small class for those students with special problems.

Students love to compete when they have confidence. They can gain it from their team, who start cheering for each other. Students can also commit themselves if they know there are others who will back them up. Pretty soon they will no longer need Dumbo's magic feather, they will soar all by themselves. It's the only way to fly.

ROCHELLE ESTERLE **35**

Grouping for a Final Exam

The Teaching Situation

I undertook this project with my biology class, which consisted of tenth- to twelfth-grade students with varied levels of ability. All but five of the students in the class were repeating the course. Their reasons for failing ranged from absences and tardies to personal conflicts with the teachers. Many lacked self-discipline or were just restless. Some of the students in the class were definitely slow learners, while others were quite bright.

Description of the Project

The project I will describe was an experiment with taking the final examination in small groups rather than individually. These groups could discuss each question and submit answers which they mutually decided upon.

What I Hoped to Achieve

The purpose of this project was to give a meaningful and challenging exam which would promote thinking and support one's answers without a competitive, working-for-a-grade situation. It was hoped that this type of situation would force the children to think in a new perspective, where they were judged by their peers. There would be no authority figure whose answers were always right; instead, a correct answer was one that could be supported by valid arguments.

Account of the Project

Grouping

The students were allowed to divide themselves into groups of three to take the final. Anyone who preferred to take the exam alone was allowed to do so. The students for the most part stayed in the groups they sat in at their lab tables. This worked very well, because the students at the tables knew each other and worked well together, so no strange, artificial setting was imposed upon them, and also because students were to some extent grouped with others of similar ability. Peculiarly, the two slowest students in the class preferred to work alone. The brighter students debated about working alone or in a group, and some decided that they could profit from pooling their knowledge. No slow students tried to join the bright groups, even though they were aware of the difference. Perhaps they would have felt conspicuous in that position.

Rules

1. Every student was required to participate.
2. Students were not allowed to leave their seats to see what other groups were answering. They had to decide upon the correct answer within their group. Students seemed very willing to cooperate.
3. Each group could turn in only one answer to each question. They were not allowed to say "John thinks A is correct, but Bill thinks B." They had to agree on one answer. Their agreement was extremely important to the group testing method, and was most difficult for the students to do. This was the key point which made it necessary for the students to discuss their answers and support them against criticisms from their peers.

Questions: The questions were of the multiple choice and essay types—about twenty-nine multiple choice and six essay type. Selection of questions was done carefully so that all of the multiple choice answers were feasible, but only one was correct. It was hoped that the students each would choose different answers and then argue why their choice was the best. This is very important, also, as questions must stimulate debate. The essay questions were of the type where students listed several possible answers in paragraph form. Sample questions will be found in the Appendix.

Evaluation

I felt this method of testing was extremely successful. One reason was that the idea of the group final was presented very seriously. The rules and groupings were strictly enforced, and students abided by them willingly. They saw the exam as a way to check their own ideas against those of other students. It was a real pleasure to walk around each table and hear the students arguing for their answers. On several occasions, the students became so concerned about a certain issue that they'd promise not to change their answers if I'd tell them who was right. The next day all the groups were anxious to get their papers back; they had never been so concerned with their daily quizzes.

The multiple choice questions were more stimulating than were the essay questions. Perhaps the essay questions could have been answered individually, rather than having one student write the entire group's ideas.

One problem I had was that the groups or individuals finished at very different times. I needed some meaningful work for them to do until the other groups caught up—work which would not be completely anticlimactic.

I feel that it was very important that the students be given the option to work alone. This allowed a margin for both bright students and quiet students who wouldn't work well in a group situation. It encouraged slow students to work alone rather than be put down by their peers. Students should perhaps be exposed to all types of learning situations; however, the option did allow some flexibility for various personalities. Perhaps one could try enforced grouping on a less important examination to see how it worked.

All the students did extremely well on the examination. Each multiple choice question was worth two points, with half credit given in some cases where students explained their answers and were almost right. The essay questions were worth from five to ten points. Most scores fell between 80 and 96 percent.

I feel this experiment was very successful. There were none of the usual cheating problems, as talking was legal. The students enjoyed the exam and their interest was stimulated by it.

Appendix

SOME SAMPLE QUESTIONS

1. The eye spots on a butterfly are examples of adaptive coloration because:
   a. they camouflage the butterfly.
   *b. they scare away birds by looking like predators' eyes.

c. they tell us which butterflies are males and which are females.

d. they make the butterflies more attractive.

2. The reason why Western Fence Lizards (blue bellies) exhibit their blue coloring is:

   a. to attract females.

   b. to scare away predators.

  *c. to scare away other lizards invading their property.

   d. to resist sunlight.

3. Vampire bats get the blood they eat by

   a. inflicting a deep wound.

   b. always biting into a large blood vessel.

  *c. secreting a substance in their saliva which prevents blood from clotting.

   d. attaching themselves to the victim for long periods of time.

4. A rattlesnake can detect its prey by

   a. sense of sight.

   b. sense of smell.

   c. change of surrounding air temperature.

 *d. all of these.

5. The race of man which is resistant to the disease malaria, but more vulnerable to anemia, is

   a. Australoid.

   b. Caucasoid.

  *c. Negroid.

   d. Mongoloid.

6. A barbiturate is

 *a. a drug which induces sleep.

   b. a stimulant.

   c. any drug which affects the nervous system.

   d. another name for marijuana.

7. List the arguments *against* legalizing marijuana.

8. Discuss in a paragraph several of the ways which venereal diseases can be prevented.

SUZY NORTON 36

Warm-up Activities in a Foreign Language Class

As I evaluate my first few months of teaching, I feel that I am now able to assess more accurately the successful and unsuccessful areas of my teaching. One of the first problems which faced me as a new teacher was how to motivate the students and how to instill in them a desire to learn a foreign language.

After much experimenting, I discovered what I found to be an effective means of "warming up" a language class in ten to fifteen minutes. The effectiveness of the activities which I shall discuss lies partially in the activities themselves, and to a great extent in the fact that my classes are grouped in teams.[1] The presence of teams in the classroom automat-

[1] ED. NOTE: See strategy 34 by Annette Norvelle for a description of team learning processes.

ically creates an atmosphere of cooperative competition, excellent in any learning situation.

Procedures

As soon as the bell rings, class is ready to begin. I write the teams' numbers on the blackboard in two vertical columns. Next to one column, I place the total number of points accumulated for each team, while the other column is reserved for the score for that day's activities. This, in itself, serves as an incentive for the teams to earn as many points as possible. One of the most successful warm-up activities which I have discovered is "Twenty Questions" (ou "Vingt questions" en francais.) I ask a volunteer to think of a word (preferably a noun) which the class must guess. He will tell me the word, ask for questions from the class, and keep track of the points at the blackboard. For example, he might choose "happiness" (bonheur). The class must ask questions (in the foreign language, of course) which can be answered "yes" or "no." To help them get started, I dittoed about thirty questions which categorize words. The following are a few of these:

1. Is it a noun? Adjective? Adverb? etc.
2. Is it an animal? Vegetable? Mineral?
3. Is it found under the surface of the earth? On top of the ground? In the sky? etc.
4. Is it natural? Manufactured?

Whenever a team member asks a question that can be answered "yes," then that team receives one point. If the team has the correct answer, their team earns two points; however, if it has arrived at the wrong answer, it loses two points. The team which has scored the greatest number of points in this activity then receives one point toward its total score.

Another activity which has been equally successful is "Mathematics" in the foreign language. I usually begin by presenting a problem orally, such as: "How much are $30 + 30 + 30 - 9 \times 10 + 2 - 8$? If they cannot do this in their heads, they grab a piece of scratch paper. I can count on about five hands shooting up almost simultaneously, to which

I must pay close attention so that I can determine which hand was first. If he can give me the correct answer then his team receives a point. I generally ask several questions before turning it over to the students. Then I ask students to present a problem. This is difficult for them at first, but they learn quickly. The students take great pleasure not only in being the first to answer a problem, but also in presenting difficult problems to their peers.

A third activity which has worked out well is "Anagrams." I take ten or fifteen new vocabulary words which have appeared in a recent lesson and scramble the letters. I place them on the blackboard one at a time; the students must then decipher the word. A team receives one point for pronouncing the word correctly, one point for spelling it correctly, and one point for the correct definition. Thus, if a person pronounces it correctly but cannot spell it, his team receives only one point and another team is given the opportunity to spell it correctly for a point.

Another enjoyable yet valuable activity is one I call "Design." A volunteer goes to the blackboard. I ask him to draw or represent in some original fashion a word, a phrase, or even a sentence. The more artistic and creative student will usually do well at getting a word across to the class, while other, less talented students will have some difficulty—which is always amusing. The person who eventually guesses the word or phrase earns one point for his team and the privilege of taking his turn at the blackboard.

A few other activities which can be used to launch a foreign language class are the following: "Hangman," "Bingo," "Question-Answer," "Spelling Bee," and "Tick-Tack-Toe."

Evaluation

As I observe the effectiveness of these activities, I see many positive results. The fun which the students have in trying to "beat out" the other teams serves to motivate them. Closely related to motivation is involvement. Regardless of whether or not a student has a good background in the language, he somehow always wants to help his teammates.

IV: STUDENTS AS TEACHERS—
OF PEERS, OF YOUNGER STUDENTS,
OF THEMSELVES

Berkeley High School student tutoring sixth-grader in drama, Berkeley, California.

The thing I like best about the tutors was they were young and understood us [Summer Tutee, JFK High School].

I really didn't realize how hard it was on a teacher until I had the opportunity to stand in front of a class with all kinds of eyes staring at me. So now I see how it is and the *big* hassel they go through for us. So I don't think I'll give any of my fall teachers any hassel cause I wouldn't want them to do me like that [Summer Tutor, JFK High School].

In the old rural one-room schoolhouse, advanced students often shared responsibility with the teacher for instructing younger or less able students. A revival of this once common procedure, in addition to lessening the teacher's heavy burden, might provide both intellectually stimulating and character-building activities for many students, while offering to the slower students far more individual help.

From our own observation, and from all contemporary reports on experimental tutorial programs, both the academically gifted and the educationally disadvantaged students profit from the youth-tutor-youth experiences. Not only do the tutored students often make surprising improvement when tutored by someone closer to their age, but the tutors themselves also gain measurably. For example, in "Studies in Tutoring" (*Journal of Experimental Education,* 1967), Robert D. Cloward concludes about one typical tutoring program on the Lower East Side of Manhattan:

Perhaps the most startling outcome of the program was its impact on the tutors themselves. Not only did they help their pupils to read better, but they showed marked gains in their own reading proficiency. In a seven month period the tutors showed a mean growth in reading skills of 3.4 years, as compared with 1.7 years for the controls.

Reports about increases in academic gains for the tutors should not be startling to those who have taught. For teachers often assert that by all odds the best way to learn something is to teach it. Why shouldn't teachers themselves profit from this awareness, and exploit the many benefits that using students as teachers can offer?

In this section we will focus on the various methods enterprising young teachers have evolved to use students profitably as teachers—of each other, of themselves, and of younger students. We have divided the section into two parts: first, several techniques and procedures which can be used by a single teacher and her students in ordinary classrooms; and second, two well-detailed and documented school tutorial programs—one involving cross-school tutoring, and the other a schoolwide use of students as tutors.

I. Students as Teachers: Procedures Useful in Most Classrooms

We begin with several methods which thoughtful and harassed teachers have devised to give their students increasing responsibility for instructing themselves and each other. The strategies which follow can easily be adapted to many subjects and to most classrooms. We start with possibilities for using students as teachers in math classes.

First, Judith Forcada, in "Student Involvement in Math," describes several procedures she found useful for transforming passive students into involved participants. Through regular use of student instructors, plus group work in problem-solving, and a math laboratory, she managed to change completely the usual "one facing thirty" pattern she had found so unprofitable.

A further illustration of the use of students as teachers is seen in "Spanish Teaching by Spanish Students." In this paper, Nancy Holland demonstrates how using students to teach vocabulary and to review grammar reduced the boredom that had generally attended those activities in her classroom. The students were conscientious about their teaching, used varied approaches, and the whole class welcomed the break in their usual routine. Janet E. Brown, in "Students Devise Homework Assignments," describes another simple way to involve students—have them construct and correct homework assignments for each other. Her strategy, which she found useful in both her math and German classes, could be equally effective in other subject areas as well.

Faced with the problem of teaching music students who were at widely different levels technically and musically, Anabel Barahal, in "Strategies for a Seventh Grade String Orchestra," tells how her use of more advanced students to help those less advanced raised the level for all of them and solved several instructional problems. She discovered that while teaching his pupil, the student was "learning how to watch for faults in his own playing." Paul Canobi, teaching business education to students who also differed widely in abilities and concerns, was overwhelmed at first with the job of providing adequate and varied instruction for students in a small rural school with limited staff, few course offerings, and scant resource materials. He found one solution to be a combination of student teachers and independent study programs designed to offer a stimulating and practical program in business and office practice. In an entirely different setting—a large, sophisticated, college-oriented school—English teacher Tobey Schwartz successfully employed some of the same methods. Her strategy paper, "Individualized Teaching," tells how by using students as teachers, by pairing and grouping students, and by offering individual study projects, she was able to individualize instruction effectively and provide more challenge for all types of students.

We have merely touched upon the various possibilities for coopting students into the educational enterprise. We turn now to larger scale tutorial programs which extend many of the same principles as those reported in the preceding classroom strategies.

II. Students as Teachers:
School Tutorial Programs

From among the several tutorial programs that interns have developed in various settings, we focused on two different models—the first, a cross-age tutorial, and the second, a high school peer-tutorial program serving students and teachers within a school.

1. A Cross-School Tutorial Program

We have asked Penny Wright to write about a tutorial program that subsequently became a model throughout the Bay Area. In her report Penny

Wright describes the program she initiated and administered at Emery High School SPAN Experimental Program in 1966 (see the introductory essay by Ruth Mandelbaum, pp. 7–11). Her primary aims were to raise the self-image and achievement of high school students who were reading below grade level by having them tutor first grade students at a nearby elementary school. She found that the self-concepts of poorer or educationally disadvantaged students improve dramatically when they realize how significant they can be to others.

2. A School Tutorial Program

In another tutorial effort, Marcia Perlstein developed and coordinated an all-subject, all-school peer-tutorial program at the John F. Kennedy SPAN Experimental Summer High School, in Richmond, California, 1968.[1] Her report shows how the use of thirty-four high school age tutors by the school staff helped considerably with the problems of teaching the educationally disaffected, especially in motivating both the tutor and the tutee. She found further that by observing how the students were teaching each other, formerly discouraged teachers could get a subtle form of in-service education. In the hope that future organizers of tutorials might find their task simplified thereby, we have included most of the materials Miss Perlstein used in organizing, implementing, and evaluating the John F. Kennedy tutorial program.

[1] As an intern in summer 1966, Marcia Perlstein had Penny Wright as her SPAN master teacher. In the summer of 1968 Marcia Perlstein herself became a master teacher and tutorial program coordinator for a SPAN experimental summer school.

PROCEDURES USEFUL IN MOST CLASSROOMS

JUDITH FORCADA **37**

Student Involvement in Math

Background

I have been very bothered in certain of my mathematics classes by the teacher-student relationship—the teacher giving answers, answering questions, solving problems, and introducing new material. It was the "one facing thirty" situation, a situation in which the only really active participant was the teacher. All action revolved around the teacher. It was easy for students not operating at the same pace as the instructor to lose interest.

I found this situation occurring in my survey of mathematics (pre-algebra) classes. These students are primarily freshmen and sophomores who are planning to take algebra or are completing the two-year mathematics requirement for graduation. They have not been recommended by their previous teachers for algebra.

I wanted to make my classes situations in which there would be interplay between myself and my students—where they could be active participants, not passive listeners. I wanted to create much greater involvement for the students, hopefully leading them to a mathematics laboratory situation in which there could be maximum learning through participation and sharing. I wanted the instruction to become "student-centered"—to be *their* class, not mine.

My Plan for Student Involvement

I proceeded to involve my students in various ways: (1) regular use of student instructors; (2) group work in helping with problems, writing problems, discussing ideas, problem-solving competition, and making reports and projects; (3) a mathematics laboratory consisting of regular sessions in which individual and group work projects are completed and review is accomplished.

My plan took various forms, some being successful and free of problems, others requiring more development in both time and materials. The following is a fairly detailed description of the various methods I used to involve the students. Along with each description I have included brief evaluations and suggestions. The ideas for the most part are not novel,[1] but I feel strongly that through increased and better organized use of them my pre-algebra students could become involved with mathematics.

1. Student Board Work for Homework Answers and Discussions

Originally in order to review assignments I would give answers or call on individual stu-

1 Jerome D. Kaplan, "Classroom Management," *The Mathematics Teacher,* LXI: 8 (December 1966), 749–52.

dents to read particular answers or have them place solutions on the board. The students liked putting their work on the board but they were passive and did not pay attention to the material when I was discussing it. We then began to increase the work presented by students on the board. They liked "performing" and I noted that they would pay much more attention and at least complete part of the assignment to have something to present. I also have been asking capable students to give an entire solution set, but the problem here is to make sure the student can answer some basic questions. It may be necessary to meet with him briefly beforehand to go over bothersome points. I have noticed not only that the students in the class show more interest, but also that the student presenting the solution develops his ability to teach.

2. Student Instructors

During the semester, two students returned to class after long absences. At that time I asked two of my better students to take charge of them, and during work sessions to teach them any material they had missed. The two returnees were thus able to go over missed material, discuss it with another student, and master it faster than I would have been able to teach it to them during class time. This worked very well, and is at least a partial answer to what to do with students returning from absences, who have to make up new material.

Some of my better students have also presented new material to the class. Many of them have seen much of the pre-algebra material before, and it takes only some review work with me to refresh their memories. These students take great pride in teaching the class, and their classmates pay close attention to the new speaker in front of them. I would hope these student instructors could teach on a regular basis. It is an impressively good break in the routine for the class, and the student teachers must do much worthwhile thinking, preparing, and presenting.

3. Using Students for Clerical Duties

In order to totally involve students in all aspects of the classroom, I have had students handle most of the clerical duties such as passing out corrected homework and collecting exams. I ask different students each day so as to spread participation around and to give quieter students a more active part. I find that students who are very shy and otherwise inactive in class will take pride in passing out papers, which is at least a step toward involvement.

4. Involving Students in Grading

The students also participate in the grading procedure. They are given a point sheet on which to record earned points. About every two weeks we confer and compare our point totals and discuss their work. Hence, there is some student involvement in the grading procedure.

5. Mathematics Laboratory

My attempt to involve my students with mathematics is most fully represented in the mathematics laboratory I've developed. At this point in my teaching I feel this is the best possible way for my pre-algebra students to learn mathematical ideas and develop skills. Here students can work at their own rates and really become involved with the material, by doing, not just listening. Raymond Sweet summarizes the reasons for a mathematics laboratory:

There are a number of reasons for operating a mathematics laboratory. One is that the laboratory method of teaching is a pedagogically sound technique. It utilizes an experimental approach that requires each student's participation, but allows him to work at his own rate. This leaves the instructor free to administer more individual help. Also, because the laboratory is usually conducted on a less formal level than the regular classroom, it provides an opportunity for more discussion among the students, and they learn from one another. Most of all, it adds variety as a change from the usual classroom routine.[2]

Because I have not been able to have completely separate lab times, I have been attempting to hold a lab period two or three times

[2] Raymond Sweet, "Organizing a Mathematics Laboratory," *The Mathematics Teacher*, LX: 2 (February 1967), 117–20.

weekly in which we work on problems, review, do group and team work, preview new material, and work on reports and projects. The students are free to use the lab period for whatever they need. Daily problem sessions at the end of the hour are coordinated with this so as to provide maximum time for individual work. Below I have given brief descriptions of some of the main points of my laboratory technique this year. Again, it is not a complete lab setup, but an attempt to combine the traditional classroom situation with laboratory techniques.

a. Daily problem sessions. Daily during a portion of the period students in my classes have a chance to work individually or together on problem work. It is my feeling that they do not learn mathematics well until they get thoroughly involved in it, in a situation in which they can study, question, and get help.

b. Group and team work. During the laboratory periods we have been having group work in which students work together in self-chosen or prearranged groups on problem sets or in writing their own tests. I have also done something that has been quite successful in the quieter classes. I divide the class into teams which I have chosen in order to afford balance. Each team has a portion of the blackboard and each chooses a captain. Someone gives a particular problem and each team solves it and places it on the blackboard. Points are awarded for speed, accuracy, and for instructing every member of the team on the correct solution. A running score is kept throughout the semester or quarter. I have had some difficulty with noisier classes in teams because the noise level does increase so, a point that must be definitely considered.

c. Reports and projects. Like most students, my pre-algebra students had always seen mathematics as strictly a problem-solving subject. I felt that regardless of whether the students would be going on in mathematics or not, it would be of value for them to see the subject as a part of the development of civilization—to learn something about the background of mathematics and its different branches. So this last quarter of the year I have assigned reports for students to do in groups, pairs, or as individuals. I have given them about one-and-one-half months to do research for these reports, allowing some class library time, after

showing various mathematical references (books and magazines) in the classroom. Their topics range from general history of mathematics to forms of number systems, to mathematics in nature. (See Appendix.) They are using the overhead projector, filmstrips, dittoes, and posters for presenting their topics.

One project is worthy of noting separately. A group in one of my classes was joking one day about writing a play and was quite surprised when I showed them some mathematics plays from a book called *Colorful Teaching of Mathematics*.[3] They became very interested and are in the process of working on parts and making scenery for a presentation of a six-act play called "The Pageant of Numbers," based on the history of the different fields of mathematics.

At the time of this writing the final presentation has not been made, but judging from the enthusiasm generated thus far in the play, it is bound to be successful. Not only are the students having fun with the play, but the content of the play is such that they and the class audience will gain a good deal of insight into the development of mathematics—in a way much more palatable than the lecture method.

These reports and projects have probably generated more involvement than any other procedure would have. This I expected. They represented a drastic break from normal mathematical routine for these students, many of whom are "putting in mathematics time" for graduation. I have found their enthusiasm in many respects much higher. I encourage others to make use of mathematical library resources. Our school librarian was surprised and delighted to help my students with projects.

Some Problems

Generally in the laboratory situation the main problem for me has been the big one, classroom management. The workable noise level is bound to increase, and at times other teachers are annoyed. I would hope that in a maximum laboratory situation a separate or at least larger room would be provided. There are always students at certain levels of maturity

[3] J. Weston Walch and Cristobel M. Cordell, eds., *Colorful Teaching of Mathematics* (Portland, Maine: 1955).

who are not going to settle down to work—but I found that they do not cause any more bother than in the normal classroom situation. At least in the lab technique there is a chance of getting them involved. There is also a problem with student attitude. Both the students and myself have become conditioned previously to not becoming deeply involved in a class that to *some* the transition from a traditional classroom to a "lab" situation is a difficult one. There are complainers, but generally they are becoming increasingly more used to the new pattern.

The only other problem I feel is my inadequate storehouse of materials. I do not, as a beginner, have enough worked out so that I have sufficient review sheets and new material prepared for individuals at their own paces. This is something that must be organized in the mathematics laboratory setup.

Conclusion

Generally, I am happy with the development thus far. The slant has been toward the "student-centered" laboratory technique coupled with the traditional classroom situation. There have been successes and failures, as mentioned above. Student responses have been generally good. It is obvious that they feel greater individual responsibility, but many also mention how much they like having a break in the routine. Alternating the project days with the new material days has also been favorable.

Although my strategy to involve students in mathematics needs more development and has been limited by the boundaries of a traditional school setting, I believe it has been a successful attempt to transform passive listeners into more active participants.

Appendix

EXAMPLES OF REPORT TOPICS

1. The origin of zero
2. How to use the slide rule (with background of development)
3. Mathematics and electronics
4. Mathematics and woodshop
5. Developers of geometry
6. What is trigonometry?
7. Early numeration systems
8. Probability
9. Logic
10. Mathematics and nature
11. Mathematics and music
12. Primitive methods of counting

NANCY HOLLAND **38**

Spanish Teaching by Spanish Students

Foreign language instruction requires the teaching of long lists of vocabulary and constant review of grammatical points. This can be extremely boring for everyone concerned. As a break in the normal routine is always welcome, one day I decided to let the students do all the teaching. The results were unbelievable! Boredom vanished as new faces began to review the daily lesson. The students generally made very good teachers. They were not only more demanding of their peers, but they also shared the same enthusiasm. The dullest material became exciting to the student who was to teach it to his friends. Each student-teacher felt important.

My first venture was to let them teach extra vocabulary, such as the parts of the body, road signs, many items of food, and idioms. All seventh- and eighth-grade classes were given the same vocabulary. Surprisingly, the seventh-graders learned much faster. Individual 3 × 5 cards were handed out with the Spanish word or words and their English translation written in groups of two or three. For example, one card might read: Puente angosto = narrow bridge; Hombres trabajando = men working. Each student received at least one card. (There is no problem here. Just make certain that there are plenty of cards to meet the demand.)

Every day I asked for several volunteers near the end of the period to introduce their words. They received a plus or a double plus if they were good teachers. Here are several ideas they used in their presentations. The students wrote their words on the board in Spanish and in English. Many showed pictures from magazines. Then they had each row repeat the Spanish. They erased the Spanish at the end and had volunteers rewrite it on the board. The good students often asked questions of the class, using the new vocabulary.

Students kept lists in their notebooks of all the new words. I also maintained a list of the different words taught in each class. If the students were absent they could find the words they missed from other students' lists. That was always their responsibility.

I had one student review all vocabulary daily by reading the English aloud and having the class give the Spanish equivalent. This exercise went very quickly. There were frequent quizzes which the students themselves administered.

The strange part of all this was the tremen-dous number of words that were learned in one month. The students had increased their vocabulary by sixty words or phrases beyond those learned in the regular lessons. Above all, they not only knew the words, but they could spell them.

My next venture was to allow volunteers to review the homework assignments. These were generally sentence translations to be written on the blackboard. The volunteer assigned each sentence to a different student. When all the sentences were completed on the board, the teacher would discus them with the class. Every teacher was urged to mention written accents, difficult spelling, and to clarify grammatical questions made by the class. In general, the teachers performed marvelously. The class often participated vigorously, arguing the correctness of a sentence. I sat in the back of the class and tried only to comment when they failed to correct an error after all discussion had ended. (It was often very difficult for me to be restrained and let the students analyze the sentence variations slowly.)

The students also enjoyed conducting the oral drills in the ALM (Audio Lingual Methods) book. They were most successful when they wrote the drills on cards without holding the book. Frequently I would have them repeat the same drills on several other days. The experience students gained was valuable, since the initial presentations were usually rough and slow.

A final venture was to allow my more advanced pupils to explain new grammar. I always selected easy material, but it was nevertheless challenging to those advanced students. The class always seemed more than patient with each teacher and responded heartily to a new face.

As a final comment I might add that I learned many fresh techniques from observing these student-teachers. After all, they know best how to communicate with their own friends.

Students Devise Homework Assignments

While working with the Holt-Rinehart German language series second-level book, *Sprechen and Lesen,* and with an *Introduction to Mathematics* book for a pre-algebra course directed at freshmen, I discovered the material in these books, especially the German text, needed to be supplemented. Besides making up my own problems or consulting another text for supplementary problems, I assign my students to write up exercises to present as class-work for a classmate, whose work the first student will then correct. The language students need much drill and review, more than is provided in the text. The math students also profit from additional exercises, as well as from the attempt at making up a problem which will "work." This is necessary, since they are to correct their classmates' work.

When presenting such an assignment for the first time, the teacher must give several examples and be very specific about what is a good finished product. The format must be neat, legible, and widely enough spaced to allow for the answer to be written. The class should know that each student will be evaluated both on his exercise set and his work on someone else's paper. The person doing the set is to write his name at the bottom of the page. The students may use exercises in their books as well as examples on the board as models, but theirs should only be similar, not the same. In a language class the teacher can assure himself that a variety of words be used by assigning to certain rows specific vocabulary-dictionary pages. He should also tell the class to stick to the one grammatical point emphasized and to try not to do more than they know how to do.

The exercises can be formulated in class or, preferably, as homework to be used in class the next day. It is also possible to treat these as a quiz, especially if such exercises have been done many times before.

The teacher will evaluate each student in two ways: (1) on the format of his exercise set, the grammatical errors in the exercises themselves, neatness, and following directions; and (2) on his performance on the exchanged exercise set. The problem has come up about what to do with *those* students who have no exercises for another student to do. While the rest of the class is working on the exchanged papers, these students begin to formulate a paper for which they will get partial credit; they are to turn in *something!* With a variation of the plan, these students can still be asked to "perform." Before handing in the papers, the class can use them as the basis for oral drill (concentrating perhaps on those who have no set ready). Most of the grammar as presented in the Holt book can be adapted to oral work. However, the additional oral drill is not always appropriate for the math course. Some problems from the math papers could be presented as board work for further discussion and review.

When using this idea as homework and for use in class the following day, I usually assign ten to twenty different excercises, not all on the same grammar point.

For example:

I. Write down two infinitives and three persons addressed, for each verb. The other student is to give the correct imperative.
   lesen—das Buch
     Rolf,
     Herr Schmidt,   } 6 point total
     Gisela and Fritz,

II. Nominative
Accusative
Compose six sentences using a noun with a modifier, as a subject, and six sentences using the same noun in the accusative case—omitting the modifier(s). (I give the directions in German.)
1. Der Brunnen-Platz is in der Stadt-Mitte.
Ich kann_____Brunnen-Platz nicht finden.
The other student is to fill in the blank.
III. Singular
Plural
Give eight nouns that we have studied, either in singular or plural. The other student is to give the other form, with definite article.
der Ruder
die Stadt

In the math class the number of problems can be reduced if there are problems where neatness counts more than usual and is time-consuming (drawing diagrams, graphing, etc.).

I have spent a whole period working with these exercises—fifteen to twenty minutes for the students to do the problems, ten minutes to correct them, and ten minutes for oral drill from these papers with students asking and answering while I supervise, and the last few minutes for a quick practice dictation using some of the original sentences (correcting grammar if necessary). Incidentally, if a teacher has an overhead projector and a good supply of blank transparencies, most students enjoy writing a dictation down for the screen and class discussion. The attention is thereby focused on the screen and everyone sees the corrections at the same time.

Outside of class, the teacher has a more time-consuming job with the corrections because each paper is different and there seem to be more possibilities for mistakes in original papers.

However, I believe it is worth the time, for he gets a general picture of other poorly understood grammatical points not covered specifically in the exercise set.

I am pleased with the students' reactions to these assignments, especially German students, who are eager and concerned about what they do with them. They have not been composing overly difficult exercises, for, of course, they themselves must be sure of the answers, but their exercises are challenging to the other students. I have varied the grading procedure by deducting points for mistakes not corrected by the student-teacher. (I have only tried this once with the math class, with mixed results. Many of these students do not do their homework regularly.)

I find that now, since my German class knows what I expect, I can also use this as a quick in-class assignment. For example, at the end of a restless day, I have given them five minutes to compose as many exercises as possible on a given grammar point (an easy one), and five minutes to do it, with one or two minutes to discuss some of the exercises to be given only orally. Perhaps it seems that this is all unnecessary trouble which the teacher could ignore by presenting exercises of his own to the class. On the contrary, I feel that this helps the students more, for they must recognize other students' mistakes. They must know the answer to the problem and demonstrate that knowledge.

There will always be those students whose work is difficult to read or filled with mistakes, but I can always hope for their improvement. And I do believe that most of the students both profit from and enjoy these "homemade" exercises.

ANABEL BARAHAL **40**

Strategies for a Seventh-grade String Orchestra

I. Introduction

The class discussed here is a seventh-grade string orchestra made up of fourteen violinists and four cellists. These boys and girls are at extremely different levels musically and technically. Ways had to be devised to keep the interest of the more advanced players, and at the same time to provide material which would not be too difficult for the less advanced players. The advanced players had to be challenged if discipline problems and chaotic situations caused by boredom were to be avoided.

Two main problems presented themselves at the beginning of the school year:

1. How to teach technique to students of widely varying capacities and levels.
2. How to keep from boring the more musically advanced and still relate to the less advanced.

The strategies devised for a relatively successful solution to these problems evolved after several inadequate attempts made during the first two months of the fall semester. Although they were particularly devised for the instrumental make-up of fourteen violins and four cellos, variations of these strategies can be used in other classes. Perhaps the most successful element of these strategies is that they are directed toward the individual and the satisfying of his particular needs.

II. Technique Building

The first step was to find a way to expand the technique of each student at his own level. At first an attempt was made to teach scales and position work to the entire class. This was partially successful but it was necessary to con-

centrate on the separate problems of each instrument while the players of the other instruments had to wait. Since the cello players were all taking private lessons and were more advanced than most of the violinists, their needs were mainly to learn ensemble playing. Therefore Monday was made technique day for the violins while the four cellos were allowed to work alone in a practice room on an ensemble piece. Full attention could then be devoted to the violins and their technique. In addition to music class, about half of these students were taking private lessons. I used them as student-teachers on a "buddy" system. The technique problem of the day was introduced to all. The main difficulties were explained. Ways of overcoming poor positions (holding the instrument incorrectly) and faulty bow handling were discussed. The student-teacher was to work with his students, attempting to follow through on the correct methods. While teaching his pupil, the student-teacher was learning how to watch for faults in his own playing. (The teaching process clarifies the mechanics of a technical process to the teacher as well as to the student because of the need to analyze every detail.) The technique period was also used to show the students how to practice at home. Difficult passages for the violins taken from the music we were playing on other days were taken out of context and worked on.

Solos were heard at times and grades for achievement were recorded. Testing of individuals was used mainly as an opportunity to give each student pointers on how to improve his playing. Testing sessions were always quiet. The entire class listens attentively while one student is being tested. Testing should not be done so often that it becomes routine because it would then lose its suspense and special excitement.

Generally the best way to teach technique to string players is by doing and not by talking. Too much talking can lead to a noisy classroom.

III. Keeping Up the Interest of All

Challenge and responsibility help most to keep the more advanced players interested, occupied, and helpful to the remainder of the class. When these students were not challenged or occupied they quickly became noisy and talkative and tended to tease and be generally mischievous.

One way of challenging the two most advanced cello players was to give them the viola parts to play. They had to play mostly in the higher positions and read in three different clefs. Since there were no viola players in the group, these two cellists were really helping out the whole group. The two remaining cellists were challenged by having to carry the cello and double bass parts by themselves, when they were used to being "followers."

The music was selected to contain both difficult and easy parts for the violins. Advanced violin parts were used to give the better players more position work. A concerto for four violins and string orchestra gave the group a chance to compete for the solo parts. The entire class selected the solo players who tried out by playing in another room with the door open. The most valuable experience was the practice for the tryouts. Several weeks were given over to the playing of these parts by the entire group so that all had a chance to play the parts prior

to the final selection of the soloists. Two runners-up were chosen to replace absent soloists when necessary.

The selection of music from different periods helped to give all a chance to play music of their preference. The playing through of a variety of pieces was often done not only in order to give practice in sight reading, but also to pick out pieces that were most liked for further study.

A written test was tried once. The emphasis of the test was on music theory, all of which had been explained at least twice in class. The best players were not in all cases the best at music theory. At this age they seem to learn most by doing. Writing and discussion have not been too successful. Nevertheless, this test was valuable as a means of determining how much each student learned and what needed to be more thoroughly gone over so that they could have a better understanding of the construction of music. As a rare change in the usual program, written work seemed to interest most of them. Requests were made such as "Can we do this again?" or "Do we get a chance to do better next time?" Those advanced players who didn't do too well seemed determined to try to understand and pay more attention when explanations were given in class.

At the beginning of the year the class seemed unruly, noisy, and hard to handle. They are working hard now on pieces that are both beautiful and difficult. Their goal is to perform well at the music festival toward the end of the year. The four cellos will perform at an ensemble concert. Somehow the noisiness and unruliness seem to have decreased and the interest of the class is high. Most important of all, they are a pleasure to teach.

Individualizing Instruction and the Use of Students as Teachers

Introduction

Since I have every level of student from MR (mentally retarded) to extremely bright, and since I have a multitude of functions to perform, ranging from counselor-disciplinarian to administrative assistant of the superintendent, my obligations to students are not altogether easy to meet.

In our small, rural high school the students do not have enough choice of courses and there is a great variety in their abilities and achievement levels. I've decided to handle these problems with a dual solution.

First, through an independent study program, more courses are being offered, individualized for the students and their needs. The courses are in business math and clerical office practice. Students with a "free" or study period take math or office practice, working at their own convenience and pace, using the business machines and typewriters for their practices, problems, and exams. I make myself available during the day to discuss problems, progress, and general goals, in addition to planning for speakers and group discussions. My prep period is used for math.

Second, existing courses are improved by using student-teachers, thereby allowing for more attention to the needs of each student. The student-teachers do lesson plans, set up timings and exams, grade papers, and teach the typing students. The students seem to enjoy this for it gives more individualized attention to particular students' needs. Otherwise, I get spread too thin and cannot give help where and when it is needed.

I. Course Individualization in Clerical Office Practice

In clerical office practice, the class happens to consist of only seven senior girls. I do feel that only seniors, and possibly some juniors, should be allowed to take this course. However, the maturity level of some students and the possibility of their dropping out of school earlier might suggest including them in such a class.

The textbook is up-to-date and generally covers all aspects of the duties a girl will have in an office. There is an accompanying workbook which has office assignments covering the many aspects of office work, such as applications for employment, invoices, business letters, etc. The textbook has units of study and sections within the units. Tests and the workbook are correlated with the text. Class periods are supplemented by the use of speakers, discussions, and films which should prove helpful to students when they seek employment. Field trips are used when possible. Lesson plans are only of a very general and broad nature and allow for individual student needs.

The students in clerical office practice are assembled generally during seventh period each day, but many of them do their work at other times, also, especially in typing class. The room is well lighted, modern, and has machines available for use most any time of the day. The students come and go freely in doing their work.

Each student does her assignment by units of work, proceeding at her own rate. The way things have been working out so far, individual students can take unit tests when they feel ready.

Some of the students are way ahead and probably will finish a one-year course in one semester.

Business Math

In business math, I have seven students, ranging from grades ten through twelve. Again, my preference in such a course is for juniors and seniors, mainly because of their maturity and proximity to graduation, when the subjects learned to be used occupationally are freshest in the students' minds. However, in special cases some students from lower classes are included also.

Here, too, the textbook is a modern, up-to-date workbook which embraces all the fundamentals of arithmetic, including decimals, fractions, and the like. In addition, the book covers social security, income tax, payrolls, checking accounts, bank financing—the many practical aspects which every student will normally encounter in life. This, I think, adds to the value of the course, because the school does not offer a senior problems or consumer economics course, and most of the students know absolutely nothing about "what it's like out there."

The tests cover a block of chapters consisting of several units each. They are timed, but flexibility is the key word in my courses, and discretion is used because timing is not always a good idea for all students. If a student is Spanish-speaking or not vocationally oriented toward bookkeeping or math work, for instance, what's the necessity for timing? The tests are correlated to the workbook, however, and this eases the burden on some of these students. Help is given wherever and whenever needed.

My planning for course activities is very broad and not detailed. This allows for the greater flexibility in meeting student needs that I feel most essential for this type of program. Since this is first and foremost in my mind, I waste less time on lesson plans and paperwork and devote more of my time to individual students and their problems.

Math Class

The students are assembled in no one period for math. My fourth period, my prep period, I have set aside for four math students. I also have a math student first period, one sixth period, and one seventh period. They work quite independently, but when help is needed, it is available. They have access to the same room that the office practice students use, and machines are used at their discretion whenever they want to work on their lessons. They work virtually at their own pace and take the tests when they feel ready after completing the necessary units of work. These students are in and out of the room periodically each day, working on their math and asking help as needed. The experience so far indicates that most of the students are progressing well ahead of a normal schedule. Any pressure comes from within each student, not from external sources.

Some Conclusions

I believe there probably is no necessity to restrict this type of program to a certain grade or course, although I can speak only from my very brief and limited experience. Any use of such an approach, of course, varies with the user, the environment, the students, and many other factors. However, the whole idea behind individualized instruction is its extreme flexibility. It allows for more student choices, more independent study and work, development of self-discipline, greater individual incentive, a sense of personal achievement, and because of all this, it perhaps helps to create better persons and better students. Also, it gives students a taste of what's coming in college for those who are going on.

Judging from past records of some of these students, I think it's safe to say they've improved in their grades on tests and in their course work. I think the fact that they are being allowed to use their own initiative and are being treated with enough respect and teacher confidence in them—some for perhaps the first time—has been a positive influence. It is really amazing to look at the results. I had students whose grades normally were C's or D's who moved into the high B category, even on a comparative level. Two students received incompletes but made up their work within three days at their own prompting.

Student response to the program so far is great. They like the independent study approach. They like to proceed at their own rate without having to produce under a standard classroom situation. As a matter of fact, enthusiasm is so high that I feel the students are doing much better than they otherwise would. I don't feel that this is really a biased view, either, because I've taken the time to compare these students with others, and have studied their past records and talked to them and to their other teachers. Indeed, my enthusiasm is so great that I want to use the same approach with general business, consumer economics, and senior problems, just to mention a few possibilities. So far, the response of the students to this idea is one of great excitement. I feel, also, that evidence indicates there is a real need for an expansion of this program. Any expansion, however, must be keyed to restraint—that is, a teacher must not end up having too little time or energy to carry on such a program successfully.

II. Use of Student-Teachers

I use two students for teaching typing. They each take a separate period, one first and one sixth. The classes are about the same size and have about equal mixtures of students from grades nine through twelve. Since they have both had two years of typing and deal primarily with Typing I students, their knowledge and experience is quite sufficient. The students are selected on the basis of aptitude, potential, ability, and desire. They have not been restricted because of grades, however, as this is not always the best criterion for selecting student-teachers.

As mentioned in the introduction, the duties of the teachers are multifaceted and cover the full range of activities that teachers normally pursue. Initially, the student-teachers may have had some difficulties with acceptance by their peer groups. However, as the students relaxed and became accustomed to the new situation, they came to rely on the teachers and have more confidence in their ability to answer questions and help with problems. One of the main difficulties has been the fact that the teachers are probably overworked—that is, they have too much work to do in the areas of planning and grading. I intend to implement a plan I am considering whereby each Typing I student will grade all the period's Typing I papers for one

night and each Typing II student will grade all the period's Typing II papers for one night. This will involve all the students in operating the class. Perhaps this involvement will give them a greater appreciation of the role of a teacher and allow them to see things from a different perspective. Since all the students have a copy of dittoed grading standards, the work shouldn't be too difficult. Also, some directions can be easily given initially.

The over all goal is to give all students some valuable experience in new approaches to learning. Also, many students interested in a teaching career would be allowed the opportunity to try it. Of course, with this system I also have more time in the classroom to devote to individual students and their needs. The students who are teaching are not first "thrown to the wolves." We sit down and plan the week's lessons in advance with all the areas to be covered. The point that each and every item planned is not a "cut and dried" rule to be followed is stressed. The teachers prepare in advance how they will approach the subject to be covered and study the material carefully. Also, what is not covered one day can be carried over and covered the next. Assistance is given in setting up tests and in making them up. Grading is done according to a dittoed standard which will be amended as needed. Help is given in how to go about teaching or presenting areas to be covered. Conferences are held in order to discuss ideas, approaches, goals, grading, or anything else they need or want to cover. Evaluations are from both the student-teachers and myself. Hopefully, enough flexibility exists to allow for freshness and originality in teaching.

Some Conclusions

In the final analysis, the important thing is that learning is taking place. The relationship of student to student-teacher and vice versa seems to be good. Valid experiences are being gained by both students and teachers. The students are responding well. They seem to enjoy the working atmosphere in the classroom, and since the student-teachers are more aware of the likes and dislikes of their peer group, they probably have a sharper feel for the group. Because of these factors the classes may be doing better than they normally would. I know that the two classes with student-teachers are doing better than the class without one.

My enthusiasm is high because the one thing I really needed was time, especially with my multiple duties and the fact that this is my first year of teaching. I now have much more of it. Also, some of the students have special need for help. I fully intend to utilize this approach much more fully next year because of its popularity with students, especially with those interested in trying their hand at teaching. If I am able to add more courses, I will use as many students as possible. This may be the only opportunity for some of these students to approach the "teaching game," and for some may make the difference between a good, secure career or a life of failure and despair. That is not as farfetched as it may seem, especially with the large percentage of Mexican-Americans in the student body. The stimulus of success cannot be replaced by anything, and the self-confidence gained from teaching may well be the turning point in the lives of many of these students.

TOBEY SCHWARTZ 42

Individualized Teaching

Introduction

Individual prescription simply means the prescription of materials and methods for the individual student—that is, teaching that recognizes the unique capabilities, needs, and interests of each student. IP[1] also means the recognition that people teach themselves. Teachers guide; they are a resource material.

Students do not come in the flavors our school systems advertise. Many freshmen in high school, for instance, are capable of the activities we limit to seniors, and many seniors would benefit from what we consider freshman fare. It is clear to any thoughtful teacher that each student ("ability-grouped" or not) has unique characteristics as a person and as a student. Even if every student in a class is reading *Julius Caesar* at the same pace, with the same study questions, participating in the same discussions, taking the same tests, and watching (or not watching) the same teacher, there will be no uniform learning experience. There will be as many things learned, or not learned, as there are students in the room, all the way from how to throw the better spitball to why Antony can sway an audience, and there will be as many ways of learning, or not learning, as there are students in the room.

Most of the methods in this paper involve grouping, and they require careful planning of both the teacher's and the student's time, but the main objective of all these methods is to encourage the student to inquire and explore in any area at his own pace and on his own steam. IP can be used to teach anything. Ultimately IP should produce in the student the capacity to learn independently; its real educational goal is self-reliance.[2] One way to think about it is this: if the teacher becomes a guide, the student, we hope, becomes an explorer. Finally he may learn to make his own maps, and then there are always other countries and he needs no guide but himself.[3]

[1] Hereafter I will use the initials IP for individual prescription.

[2] See Thoreau's *Walden*. Classrooms can turn into ponds; exploration can take place anywhere, if process rather than content is stressed.

[3] See S. I. Hayakawa, *Language in Thought and Action*, (New York: Harcourt, Brace & World, Inc., 1939).

There is really nothing new about IP except the increased attention being focused on it everywhere. Good teachers have used IP methods for years. IP requires the teacher to relinquish the spotlight at the front of the room, requires him to talk less and let the students talk more, and requires him to accept a view of himself as guide or resource material rather than as the ultimate authority. The beginning teacher should attempt IP only when he is reasonably certain of himself in a classroom and has found out what techniques seem to suit him best as a teacher.

Pairing

Probably the easiest kind of IP to start with is pairing. The teacher may introduce a unit or body of material to the whole group, lecture on background material, present basic terminology or vocabulary, and outline the objectives of the unit. It is most important that the student understand the goals of a unit or activity. Let him in on the secret of what he's supposed to learn; later he'll tell you whether he did or didn't. The teacher may or may not have access to a variety of materials, and this will partly determine the diversity and pacing of the pairs to come. After the introduction, the teacher explains that work will be done in pairs, and that the students themselves will have a say in their pairing off. A few students require direction in pairing, but in most cases it should be a voluntary choice. Here the teacher needs faith and patience. Part of the learning that goes on in pairs involves a student's assessment of his own characteristics and needs. For instance, let's say two close friends choose each other. They discover as they work that one becomes tutor and the other student, and one or both of them object. (It may work the other way; they may both like it and benefit from the relationship.) If the avenue is open for flexibility in pairs, they will request a change and a new pairing off will take place. The teacher may also suggest the change himself. Or some students may not want to work in pairs after a certain trial period. These students should be allowed to work alone. Therefore, constant mobility may occur between the pairs.

At first students may be hostile to the idea of pairing.[4] To forestall insecurity and confusion in himself and the students, the teacher must have the following things well in mind: everything needs time and patience to work smoothly; students must have been adequately prepared, both for pairing and for the material they will explore in pairs; the teacher himself should be constantly circulating from pair to pair, helping, commenting, correcting, or just listening; the teacher must communicate his faith in the students' ability to learn; and again, the teacher must be able to allow the students to work out their own problems to some degree without constantly giving answers or forcing conclusions to get it done more "quickly" or "efficiently."

When the students are paired, the teacher supplies each pair with the working material it needs. Every pair may be working on the same set of discussion questions on a book all the students have read in common, or each pair be working with different materials or on different projects. The limiting factors are materials and the availability of the teacher for consultation, but the technique of pairing itself offers practically limitless variety. For instance, pairing may be used in a writing unit in an English class for only a short time, if that suits the goals the teacher (or the student) has set. After preparatory work on creative writing, pairs of students take photographs cut out of magazines to use as a starting point in their writing. Each pair of two writes its description, poem, or short story, using the photograph. The two people in one pair work together, producing one product. If the teacher wishes to make a competition out of the exercise, he sets a deadline when all the assignments must be turned in, and the class as a whole then discusses the written work and chooses the best. Or pairs may exchange the assignments and write critiques. Or the teacher may simply grade each assignment as it is turned in, setting no deadline and encouraging consultation with other pairs about ways to improve one piece of writing.

4 The students' attitudes depend a great deal on the teacher's attitude. If you are uncomfortable, they will be too. However, confidence can be slowly gained by both teacher and pupil if there's no necessity to hurry anywhere.

In other words, pairing may be used for a long or short period of time, may be simply an interlude between group discussions, may generate larger groups or precede individual study, and may be used to teach many skills. In English, a teacher may use pairing to present anything from spelling practice to literary analysis. The students teach themselves.

I have spent a great deal of time on pairing as one method of IP because the same variety and diversity of application are available in other IP techniques. A more rapid explanation of small groups and individual counseling follows.

Small Groups

Individual Prescription in groups larger than two can happen in a number of ways. Again, the same prerequisites in attitude and organization are important as were mentioned above for pairing. Groups generate themselves, given the proper classroom environment. When the teacher encourages consultation between pairs, larger groups will generate spontaneously out of the pairs. The teacher may also present alternative activities to a class and let students choose activities. If the suggested activities don't draw participants, let the students suggest activities. They will. The teacher may or may not limit group size, according to the activity. In general, the larger a group becomes, the longer it takes for the group to organize itself for productive activity, although the experience of organizing group activity may be fully as important for the students as the production of a written or oral assignment. Free-flowing discussion, where the discussion itself is the goal in mind, is very important, too.

As with pairs, a packet of material may be given each group, or each group may be asked to develop materials of its own, given adequate preparation and aid from the teacher. These may be study questions, tests to write, rules for writing topic sentences, criteria for evaluating poems, illustrations, or anything else germane to the area the students are exploring. When students produce their own tests, criteria, and teaching materials, they should be allowed to test them on one another to evaluate the usefulness of the product. But students should not

be asked to use skills they have not yet developed or do not feel confident about without some guidelines. The teacher suggests methods, encourages, corrects, and provides adequate resource materials (written or oral), whether the task is set by the teacher himself or by the students. In addition, the teacher has the responsibility of guiding sequence. Before a student can write a test on a novel, he must read and understand the novel in his own terms, and before a student can tape record questions for the rest of the class, he must understand how to work a tape recorder. If these comments seem obvious, they seem so only because the part the teacher plays may seem minimal in reading this. Actually, being a walking resource material is quite a full-time job.

If students are working individually on a number of different materials, and the teacher encourages consultation between students working on similar or related material, the students will come together with one another on their own and request of the teacher a forum to air a group idea or project. In my program, students working in similar areas individually have themselves requested of the teacher class time to present a play, lead a discussion or panel group, give a lecture, or even work with other interested students on vocabulary and spelling problems. Although the initiative often comes from the more self-reliant and aggressive students, students with less self-confidence and less experience of success join up and may even begin to lead or organize others. It is very hard to fail when there is no one to work against but yourself. In the case of student-generated groups, the students learn how to focus and organize their own learning activities themselves. Students often learn a great deal more from each other than they do from a teacher, though a teacher may be able to select, organize, and articulate material better than most of his students. However, good selection, organization, and articulation of material does no good unless the students learn, one way or another, how to do it themselves.

Individual Counseling

The last kind of IP I want to discuss is individual counseling. In discussing both pairing and grouping I have already mentioned individual projects in a number of places; all kinds of IP encourage individual learning. Individual counseling, however, requires the teacher to consult with the student on a one-to-one basis about a program or project tailored to his individual needs and interests. This may take place once every two weeks for each student throughout a year, may be a one-shot deal at the end of the year, or any gradation in between. The counseling may take place practically anywhere—office, lawn, or in the back of a busy classroom. If the teacher must see students individually in one part of the classroom during the class period, the rest of the students *must* be occupied while the teacher counsels each in rotation. If the teacher wishes to begin individual counseling sessions for all the students, pairing or grouping or study sessions should be functioning in advance. Activities for the rest of the students, however, can be as simple as a free reading session. Or some students could be listening to tapes or records, some reading, some talking. But careful planning is necessary so that the teacher can be prepared for what will actually take place in the classroom, whether it is paired learning or a bull session. Again, the limiting factors are environmental: noise levels tolerated by school or teacher (noise generally doesn't bother students much if they're interested in what they're doing), the flexibility of the teacher (who has become part of the en-

vironment), and the size and adaptability of the room.

In individual counseling, some students may progress very quickly to entirely self-directed tasks. They will use the teacher as a guide: "How can I find out whether Ray Bradbury's scientific data in his stories is realistic?" Some students will want the teacher to outline activities for him: "I don't like English. What can I do?" But *no* student, when given the chance to work individually, will actually choose to do nothing. He may announce that he's going to do nothing, but if interesting and varied enough activities go on around him, he will eventually participate in some way, even if it is only to listen or to disagree.

In any IP, there is one thing both students and teacher have to get used to: there is no necessity for every student in the room to be working away at a task with a furrowed brow. Pauses, discussions that get off the track and lead to new topics for exploration, just talking or dreaming are all things that take place in any classroom and should be part of the *accepted* learning experience, because they are all part of learning. If a student can learn to throw a better spitball, he can learn what you want to teach him, provided it is something worthwhile to learn and provided you give him the chance. IP is one way to make it very hard for the student to fail. What's there to fail?

SCHOOL TUTORIAL PROGRAMS

PENNY WRIGHT **43**

A Cross-age Tutorial Program

The Project

As part of the 1966 SPAN[1] Summer Demonstration School at Emery High School, this special class involved eleven junior high and high school students, each tutoring a first grader in reading. The program ran throughout the six week summer session and required two class periods of fifty minutes each. The first period was devoted to a seminar and workshop in the high school where tutors discussed learning problems and teaching techniques and where they prepared materials for the tutoring session. During the second period they met with their tutees in the cafeteria of Ralph Hawley Elementary School. They worked on a one-to-one basis in language development and reading improvement and cooperated in group activities with other tutors and tutees.

Its Objectives

The project had three main objectives for the tutors. First, by giving them real responsibility as teachers, we tried to improve the self-image of students with histories of behavior problems and low academic achievement. Second, we hoped that the teaching process might help them gain personal insights, particularly as

[1] See introductory essay by Ruth Mandelbaum for further description of SPAN's Emeryville Demonstration School.

they might see their own behavior patterns and learning problems reflected (or exaggerated) among the younger children. Third, although we did not expect measurable reading growth in such a short period, we hoped that new, pleasant experiences with easy reading (in the role of teacher instead of pupil) might provide some remedial assistance and perhaps create more favorable attitudes toward reading.

For the tutees our goals were to give additional reading and language experience to children who were having difficulty, and to provide each child with the friendship and personal interest of his own special teacher.

Orientation for Tutors

The students who showed up at the first orientation meeting had all volunteered to take part in the tutorial program, but after ten minutes of discussion, I began to suspect that only three or four of them had come because of interest in teaching a younger child. Later, some told me the real reasons they had signed up as tutors was a chance to "get out of English" or "to do easy work and no homework." One boy volunteered because of the free bus trip every day to the elementary school. His note said, "I get to my house fast and also not paying busses." One of the first girls to sign the list of volunteers recruited two other friends. They both had some reservations. One wrote,

"My first reason was my friend. Reason number 2 was a question on my mind. Would you *really* let us be teachers or just more or less baby sitting." Although these confessions came later in the program I had a pretty good idea of their feelings and I was worried. I had no power over them if they decided to quit the program in midstream, leaving the tutees stranded. I was sorely tempted to pick only the most dependable, enthusiastic members of the group, but that would mean screening out the very students the SPAN program wanted most to reach. Still, it was very important that they realize their responsibility to the younger children. Since I couldn't decide what to do, I just waited. At least I had some time—a whole week before the elementary school began. First, I asked them to talk about their own experiences in first grade—what they remembered especially liking or hating; what made them feel proud of themselves or what experiences might make a child bored or unhappy in school. As they talked I made a list of the general criticisms they had about schools and teachers and asked them to describe what a teacher ought to be.

The need for responsibility, sympathy, and a real interest in the child was a recurring theme in their statements. I realized I had no need to remind them of their obligations to the tutees. (Some even suggested that a tutor be "fired" if he goofed off or was absent more than three days.)

The orientation was too long. After the first skepticism and shyness, everyone was confident. "When can we start?" "When will I get my kid?" But gradually the eagerness changed to restlessness and worry. Maybe this won't be much after all. Maybe the kids will be hard to handle. Maybe they will ask questions we can't answer. My whole plan had been to build the seminars and workshops directly around the events of each tutoring session. Without the children it was hard to make any activity seem relevant. Out of desperation, I invented some games for them to play involving auditory and visual recall of patterns or tasks in motor co-ordination and spatial judgment. I wanted them to see how hard it really is to learn to read and to demonstrate that each person may have his own style of learning which depends on his perceptual strengths or disabilities. The games

got them moving around and immediately began showing up individual differences among the tutors. Some of the poorest readers were delighted to find games in which they did better than anyone else. I think perhaps these activities helped to rid them of the notion that a person was either "smart" or "dumb" because he had trouble. After these games, all but two of the tutors were beginning to talk freely about their own learning problems.

The Tutoring

On the first teaching day the tutors were just like any other new teachers, overprepared, anxious, and eager to be accepted.

The tutees huddled together in one corner of the cafeteria, tremendously excited and a little bit "scared of those big kids." For a minute the two groups just looked at each other across that big room. Then David, one of the oldest tutors, walked over and put his arm around a first grade boy. Tutors and tutees suddenly began finding each other, and staking out a working space at one of the tables. Heads bent together over a book; sometimes a small arm slipped around a tutor's waist. Now and then I saw a first grader climb onto a tutor's lap in order to see better. After the first week tutors needed only to appear on the playground and the tutees would come climbing down from the jungle gym, running for their teachers. I have never seen, before or since, quite this response from children.

Of course there were problems. Even the tutors' magical power over their first grade pupils waxed and waned, and keeping things from bogging down required tremendous energy and concentration from the tutors as well as from me. And we were not always up to the demands. One tutor said to me plaintively, "You never have enough time to just *be* with us." The problems were mostly of a logistical nature. Never were there any serious conflicts between tutors and tutees, and many seemed to have formed deep attachments for each other.

Evaluation

At the end of the session both the tutors and tutees were unanimous in stating that the program should become a part of the regular curriculum. Four of the tutors continued to see their tutees for informal activities after summer school ended. Of those who initially volunteered for reasons other than interest in tutoring, only one said that the tutoring had not helped him in any specific way.

Staff members from both the high school and the elementary school frequently noted improvement in the behavior of tutors and tutees in classes other than the tutorial.

In our final evaluation sessions tutors were very helpful in suggesting activities which should be included or emphasized in another tutorial. Here is a partial list of techniques we tried and felt were worth repeating.

Photo Stories (An Idea Suggested by a Tutor)

Two of the tutors had Polaroid Swinger cameras and the school bought film. Each child pasted his own photograph in a book and dictated the captions to his tutor who then used vocabulary from the captions to make flash cards and helped the child build a reading vocabulary. Tutors loved the pictures almost as much as the little children did.

Machines and Gadgets

Another time I would make better use of machines. Machines themselves are attractive to these kids. Tape recorded interviews with the children were very successful and I would do much more of it next time. Both typewriters and tape recorders were useful to transcribe stories the children dictated.

The opaque projector can be used to show "movies" which the children make on rolls of shelf paper. (This is something we talked about but never tried.) I would like to see each child use the Language Master several times a week—better still, every day. We did make use of all these machines at least enough to recognize their great value, but we were not consistent or analytical enough. With care and planning, though, I think these machines can be used with enough discrimination to get at the individual needs of each child.

Group Activities

We found one-to-one tutoring was greatly enhanced by the group sessions at the end of each day. One tutor read a story to all the children, or children read the books they had made to the class and we played back the taped interviews and stories. Once, tutors put on a puppet show and a music program for the children. Everyone seemed to enjoy it, but group preparations took up much class time and might not have been as useful as individual projects. Music and dancing activities were suggested on several occasions, but the group was never sufficiently organized to carry this off.

Programmed Reading

Although our work with Sullivan Programmed readers had some definite advantages for the tutors as well as the children, I am not sure that I would use these materials another time. For one thing, until a tutor really masters the teacher's guide, the whole process can be terribly tedious and the child may even be held back by the tutor's inefficiency. Another, more important reason is that use of programmed materials does not take full advantage of the intimate personal qualities of the individual tutoring situation.

MARCIA PERLSTEIN **44**

High School Tutors in an Urban Setting

Introduction

Tutoring programs have, in the last three years, been tried in many different ways. Some stop when the funding ends; others are discontinued because of minor flaws. I think that the philosophy behind these projects and the value to both tutors and tutees are important enough to warrant working through the difficulties. I believe that the gradual inclusion of tutors on school staffs can help solve several problems in teaching the educationally disaffected.

The 1968 summer tutorial program at John F. Kennedy Summer School in Richmond, California, represented one ambitious attempt to incorporate student tutors into the instructional program.

As part of a special project, thirty-four tutors entered Kennedy Summer School in June of 1968. They brought to an already unique experimental summer program verve and vision which were refreshing and thoroughly theirs. They were up and down stairs, in and out of classes—scurrying, scrambling, and *involved*. They progressed from simple notions about teaching and teachers to a refined, highly complex educational philosophy. Just as in adult faculty situations, not all tutors agreed. However, all used personal experience and observation as the particulars from which they developed generalizations about teaching. This report will concern itself with a short survey of the tutors' contributions to the summer school. It is the intent of this paper to present enough detail that some replication of this project will be possible.

Objectives

Our aims were threefold: we were interested in the tutors, the tutees, and the teachers. We hoped that each tutor could discover his own worth through participation in concrete success experiences for others. In addition, tutors would be motivated to improve their own skills in order to teach the students in their charge. With increased competency in communications skills, they might begin to see new possibilities for themselves in the future. High school diplomas and even college education could become a reality; paraprofessional careers in all phases of community service would be a possibility.

The tutees were generally students for whom little help had previously been available. They could now learn from people close to their own age, people who really understood the difficulties they were having.

For the teachers the tutoring program offered additional classroom resources. We also hoped that the tutors' presence would provide a subtle kind of in-service training experience for the teachers. The teachers would be able to note in exaggerated fashion what kind of methods did or did not work with disaffected students.

The Selection Process

A nucleus of math, science, English, and social studies teachers had been meeting for several weeks to plan the curriculum of the school. This group was composed of staff members from most of the secondary schools in the district. They brought applications back to their campuses, publicized and described the program, and recruited potential aides. Their active recruitment of tutors was most significant. The publicity and announcements would have attracted mostly high achievers; recruitment by teachers who had met and formulated a set of criteria made possible the inclusion of other kinds of students—those who would be helped as much as they would help. The effect of having teachers suggest that certain students apply also promoted others to volunteer. Word soon got around that "A" students would not necessarily be selected; other qualities were being seriously considered.

What were these qualities? Initially the committee was looking for students who had some feeling for one of the four subjects, status among their peers, a sense that all wasn't right with education, but at the same time a desire to make positive improvements, and finally, an intuitive understanding or feeling for others who were experiencing difficulties. We had a number of applicants to choose from; by the end of the process we were more than satisfied with the group we'd selected.

The Selected

The group we finally chose consisted of high school students who would be returning to the Richmond schools in the fall. To some extent they mirrored the racial proportions found in the community. There was one Latin American, seven Caucasians, and twenty-six blacks. They were a microcosm of the student body. Each was what almost any student could become— given support, encouragement, and status. Specifically, they were that side of every student who is beginning to like himself. Many of them became self-fulfilling prophecies. We told them that they were special and could teach others. Those qualities surfaced and they *did* teach others. Although they varied greatly, both students and teachers recognized them as models, as someone tutees could emulate with pride. One student wrote:

I like the tutors, they make pretty good company. The thing I like about them best is they act natural. They don't come in wearing dresses down to their knees, and talking all proper; ready to make you shut up. They come in acting natural, talking natural, and like any other teenager.

A teacher wrote in a final evaluation:

D. is friendly, well-liked, educated, and very bright. I am sure many of the students use her as an unconscious model for their ideas and ideals.

A junior high school tutee described her tutor in these words:

I.G. is my tutor and she is nice, bold and has a sophisticated air about her, she knows how to dress and she also knows how to talk to people and puts them in their place, when they should be in it.

In the Classrooms

The tutors' teaching assignments varied according to the teacher, the subject, the tutees, and any special talents and interests the tutors revealed. Most of the tutors developed their own styles of teaching and some even brought in their own materials. Every teacher provided a structure within which the tutors were asked to work. Some gave the tutors considerable freedom.

She, to a great degree, defined her own role in the classroom. She worked primarily with a "hard core," a "clique" of boys whose main goal seemed to be to conspire to disrupt the class. She was excellent. Outside of that, she just did whatever I needed done. She was always *there*.

Many tutors had their own small group of students to work with. They would both help students complete assignments given by teachers and develop their own. In one case, a tutor's one period activity developed into a classroom project:

One week R.'s group (gradually expanded to include other interested students) wrote and videotaped a play. This was probably the most consistently motivating group activity of the summer.

Several worked with one or two individuals who had severe reading difficulties. They brought them to the library of the tutoring staff room where, away from the pressures of the classroom, the tutees could respond more positively to the help offered.

Some teachers grew to respect tutors enough to ask them to lead the entire class for short periods of time. They either presented a lesson they had prepared in advance or moderated classroom discussions. One tutor described this experience on a reflection sheet:

One day Miss_____ gave me the class for a twenty minute discussion. To even capture their attention I had to give more of myself than I ever imagined I could. But I got through. A person must be willing to give everything with the idea of perhaps never receiving anything if he wants to teach. A teacher has to be an unusual person, someone who can bounce back and continue to give. Many times students are in the wrong, but all the blame seems to fall on the teacher.

Moving beyond the Classroom

Since we remained fairly flexible, several things developed spontaneously. Helpful changes were then included in the regular program. For example, some teachers needed tutors only sporadically. Thus, we developed the idea of the floating helpers. There was a pool of two or three tutors who were available on call. They were housed in the Counseling Co-op with teachers and served as translators who assisted in the communication between teacher and student. They greeted students at the door, where they could speak quietly with them until a teacher could see them.

After the first week of school, the position of tutor became such a valued one that other students wanted to participate. Teachers were so pleased with their tutors that requests came in for more. All except the few floating tutors had been given regular assignments; the demand soon far outweighed a supply which remained constant. We soon figured out a way to satisfy our customers. In addition to the tutors other students were permitted to tutor two or three days a week, as long as they kept up with their classwork. The student-tutors received credit rather than salaries. We had six students working in this capacity. The teachers who released them from their classes found that they worked harder than ever on the days they returned to class.

One tutor who had not been working harder than ever was found to have been poorly placed in an art class. He felt extremely ill at ease and unimportant because there were no serious remedial skills he could help students with in an art class. He began cutting that period, and started hanging around with the student hired to run the videotape equipment. After talking for a while with this tutor and getting some notion of his feelings, we withdrew him from his tutoring assignment and paid him for the time he put in as a videotape operator. The transformation was classic. He began taking a genuine interest in what he was doing, worked extra hours without pay, and learned every technical detail he could. He started videotaping tutors

in the classroom and in seminar sessions. Tutors could set up appointments and bring groups of students down to make use of the videotape. Thus, the tutor became an instructional as well as a technical resource. This experiment became such an integral part of the tutoring program that I would not run another similar operation without a videotape "expert."

The Tutors as a Group

Since there was a sizable number of tutors and they had several activities in common, they began to develop an important identity as a group. They were asked to send representatives to both student council and faculty meetings. As a body they could support many kinds of school activities.

One spontaneous activity caused the faculty to become aware of the special service tutors could provide. The junior high school students were a source of concern to the rest of the school. The tutors became aware of this and decided to concentrate on this problem at one of their seminars. The younger students, in their view, were having problems because they were forced into a high school time and class schedule which they weren't emotionally mature enough to handle. After coming to this general conclusion, the tutors made concrete proposals for rectifying the situation. After several of their representatives presented their observations at a school faculty meeting, a modified version of their ideas was put into practice the following week.

The staff now knew that the tutors could be a valuable resource. It wasn't long before they were called upon again. The school experienced some disturbances where police had to be called in and classes canceled for several days. Parents, teachers, tutors, and students submitted proposals for handling the reopening of school. The tutors attended all faculty meetings throughout the time that school was officially closed and shared their insights. Although not all teachers were overjoyed by the tutors' presence, none made an attempt to prevent them from making useful contributions.

The last contribution the tutors made as a group was to join a number of students, a psychologist, and several teachers in what developed into a "Get Hip" movement. They spent many long afternoons before videotape cameras trying to deal with interpersonal problems of students and teachers. From their unique vantage point, they were able to make some important observations. Several district administrators have asked the tutors and other students who participated in these sessions to attend teacher orientation and in-service courses to share their views with teachers in the district.

Seminar

The seminar was conceived of as a combination faculty meeting and in-service course for tutors. The tutors were treated as a professional staff of adults who were being given the opportunity to share experiences and ideas so that they could more effectively do their job. In large part these meetings were modeled on the seminars of the Graduate Internship Program of the University of California.

The beginning of every meeting was devoted to exchanging both ideas and problems. The group would focus on the problems and offer alternatives. If the tutor was very anxious and requested my intervention, I would agree to visit his class the next time it met. Many difficulties, however, were resolved through the combined efforts of the entire group. I used this time to gather curriculum ideas. If there seemed to be concerns central to a large part of the group, we would devote the entire session to these concerns. In addition, I tried to gather articles and bring in resources whenever they seemed appropriate.

Reflections of Tutors

Part of every Friday was set aside for writing "Reflection Sheets." Tutors were asked to look back over the week in any way they wished. From these I gained more ideas for seminar content and classroom visitations. A paragraph from a reflection sheet often provided the basis for extended discussions. From the first sheet to the last, the tutors sounded like mini-teachers. Subjects extended the entire gamut from discipline problems to pay scale, from feelings about themselves to insights on technique. Here are a few statements culled from their first reflection sheets:

The first week of school I was very eager to get to my class. I enjoyed the first three days when we did desk work. When we finally did get our classes it was very disorganized. On Thursday, I was beginning to feel a part of what was happening and it was terrible. The children were rude, mean and bad. On Friday I was ready to give up and quit. I decided to try again on Monday. The first week was very discouraging.

Things seem to be getting better all the time. The classes don't seem quite as wild as they were at first. From a student's point of view it's interesting to see how sincere the teachers are about reaching students.

The first week I didn't know what to do. I thought it was going to be very hard to do things just like a teacher. I was going to go home at first, but I stayed and found out that all you needed was a little nohow. I am glad that I am here because it's lots of fun working with the students. And that's all I have to say right at the moment.

I was troubled basically with discipline the first week getting the kids to get used to me and that I wasn't going to take any stuff. Now I'm cool down to where I can help the kids more by not getting angry so fast, by watching the other tutors and I try their way and try to add a little originality on my part. It seems to work so now I'm getting along better with the kids. And things are working much better. I've found the situation in the classroom depends on the teacher and tutors and I've learned not to make big things out of small ones.

By the end of the six-week session tutors had the following insights:

Maybe it's because I'm black and don't look upon them as problem kids so they don't respond as problem kids. Sometimes when you relate to students as problem kids, this is exactly what the kids want you to do so they play the "game."

If you had a student that didn't want to work if you made it seem more interesting to them they will start. Take a student off by himself and talk to him about all what's on his mind. Don't talk as a teacher but another student.

I learned that you can teach a person better if you don't call him a name like stupid or dumb because if you do he'll think he's stupid or dumb.

My first period teacher tries to hard to reach the students by coming down to their level as a means to get them to listen to her or as a basis for communication (at least this is the impression I got).

My second period teacher is, well I wouldn't say she does a better job because both are teaching the same thing and it does depend on how willing the student is as far as learning goes, but my second period teacher is boring for she is like regular school. And I feel she should do something different. My suggestions are: (1) to the first teacher is to be a teacher, that is kind of strict as far as discipline but conscious of a need to be on the level of students but to really come down means to lose a certain amount of respect. This is where the tutors can be made most effective but where we aren't being used. (2) To the second teacher—to continue as she is doing that is be a regular teacher but use the tutors more as a form of variety, for her class is just like regular school and this in itself turns students out.

As for the seminar, the concerns at the beginning centered around the following: a definition of the role of tutor; discipline problems; the difficulty of being "in the middle" (between teacher and student); materials which would stimulate their tutees.

They next moved to consideration of deeper problems: motivation; making content relevant versus teaching academic skills; changing teacher and student attitudes; their own ego involvement; the influence of racial concerns on curriculum and attitude.

The discussion concerning "skills versus relevance" has been preserved on tape. In terms of maturity and insight, I would equate what the tutors did with any in-service teacher education discussion on the same topic. They hit on every major issue covered by the literature on this question. To me, this session represented the concrete fulfillment of the prophesy—treat students as teachers and they will *be* teachers.

The last week, after a large group meeting we broke down into four task-oriented groups. Although these were numerically unbalanced (since the tutors chose their groups according to their interests), all the tasks were completed. One group worked on setting up a more refined Time/Pay System; another developed an evaluation form which supervising teachers could use to view progress their tutors had made (these were placed in their permanent folders to be used for job and college recommendations); the third group worked on evaluating the tutorial program from the tutor's point of view; and the last group turned its attention to recommending ways in which the district

could implement tutorials during the regular school year. Let's turn to what they found.

The Results

The surveys developed by the tutors were combinations of quantifiable questions and those which required comment. (Samplings of the comments will be found in the Appendix.) More than 80 percent of the tutors felt that tutors were very helpful in class; the rest thought they were of some help. About 75 percent thought that tutors were helpful in getting students and teachers to understand each other better; the others were divided between a "no help" and "very helpful" attitude. All but one felt that most students had welcomed the use of tutors. More than 80 percent felt they were most effective with students younger than they. One hundred percent of the respondees felt orientation meetings ought to be held before tutors are assigned; in like manner, all tutors thought supervising teachers ought to meet with the group of tutors periodically. About 80 percent of the tutors felt the seminar was of some value, while the remaining few were split between feeling that it was very helpful and no help at all. Over 80 percent felt that their teaching experience itself was very helpful; the rest felt it was of some help. On the question of whether their tutoring experience would make better students of them in the fall, the group was spread all along the spectrum. About 40 percent felt they'd be much better students, 40 percent felt they'd be better, and 20 percent felt they'd be no better. A person who felt she'd be a much better student in the fall explained her answer in this manner:

I really didn't realize how hard it was on a teacher until I had the opportunity to stand in front of a class with all kinds of eyes staring at me. So now I see how it is and the BIG hassel they go through for us (some, some). So I don't think I'll give any of my fall teachers any hassel cause I wouldn't want them to do me like that.

In comparison to the tutors, the teachers were far more complimentary about the program. All of the teachers said that their tutors were punctual, attended class regularly, and should be recommended for fall tutoring assignments. Although the questionnaire was a rather exhaustive one permitting the teachers many opportunities for lengthy comment, most took the time to add a very special one on the last page of the survey. (See Appendices for sample comments of teachers.)

The last group of evaluators was the tutees. Several teachers included a question or two on the tutors in their final class surveys. Some of the typical comments were:

I like them because they help me with my work. I would like them to work with me during regular school also because I think I could learn more about the classes.

I like best of them is that they don't boss us around like some tutors do. Their alright and they don't think their so smart.

I worked with Roland making a tape and reading a play. I think Roland would be a good tutor. I liked the way Roland joins in with the kids in his group instead of trying to boss them around.

The thing I like best about the tutors was they were young and understood us.

I think of them (the tutors) as a very nice and smart group. They are smart, not mean and very quick about things.

I like them because they are helpful and I always need and always will need help.

And Now...

And now I'd like to do it again. I'd like to build on the strengths of this program, re-fine some segments, and expand the use of tutorials. I'd like to see student self-help pro-grams become an integral part of urban edu-cation. I would give the tutors and teachers a more extensive orientation, at which time tutors would be presented with shiny new attaché cases. Their practical and symbolic value would launch the self-fulfilling prophesy cycle in high gear. Videotape equipment, in the capable hands of a tutor-operator, would be used sooner and more extensively. Materials such as flash cards, word games, typewriters, and tape re-corders would fill the tutoring staff room. A full-time coordinator would be hired to handle tutor assignments, orientation, seminars, and individual tutor visitations and conferences.

These few changes do not veer radically from the pilot program. They might, however, make the difference between success and "su-persuccess." If multiplied, such tutorial pro-grams could play a leading role in drowning out the dirge of failure in urban schools.

Appendix A

Name_____ School _____ Age ____ Grade (as of Sept., 1968)____
Home address_____ Telephone number_____

1. In which subject would you like to tutor?   _____
2. What special area of that subject do you like best?   _____
                                          least?   _____
3. What are your special qualities which would help you to be a good tutor?
4. What do you think a tutor's *role* in the classroom ought to be?
5. What do you think makes students fail?
6. What things usually go on in a typical classroom which you believe ought to be eliminated?
7. What do you think the ideal classroom setup would be?

Appendix B

TEACHER'S EVALUATION OF TUTOR*

Mechanics
1. Is the tutor always punctual to class?
2. Does the tutor attend class regularly?

* This questionnaire was constructed for the teachers by a committee of tutors.

Attitude
1. Does your tutor ever show impatience toward students?
2. How does the tutor work with you in planning and teaching?
3. Does the tutor take sides during a disagreement between the teacher and students?
4. Does he tend to give you the idea that he enjoys his work or does he give you the idea that he has to do it?
5. What is the tutor's reaction to outbreaks of violence in the class?

Teaching Ability
6. How does the tutor handle the class when the teacher is absent or while momentarily taking over?
7. What kinds of methods does your tutor employ in teaching students?
8. How much success does the tutor have in motivating a student?
9. Does the tutor make it easier for the students to understand the work when they are in doubt? If so, how?
10. Is the tutor too forceful or not forceful enough toward the students?
11. What was the main job of your tutor? Did he fulfill this job as best he could?
12. Can your tutor work with any type of student? (slow, fast, black, white, etc.)
13. Do you think that your tutor should be one of the fall tutors?

Miscellaneous
14. Would you have any objection to having this paper read by your tutor?

Thank you.

Teacher's name _____
Tutor's name _____
Subject _____

Comments

EXAMPLES OF TEACHERS' COMMENTS

D. is the closest thing I have ever seen to a natural teacher. She seems to have an intuitive understanding of good teaching methods. I have a very high regard for D.'s intelligence and for her strength of character. I weep for the nation in which she may not become all that she could be. We need her talents very much. I would do all I could to encourage her to go on in her studies and to put that perceptive mind of hers to good use.

D. has helped me a lot in frankly telling me some of the things I didn't realize about the feelings, opinions, and expectations of the students. She is tactful and gracious, and I only wish she and I could have had more dialogue about interclass relationships, because here again I respect her judgment.

The only difficulty which J. had to face was the slightly defensive attitude of the students (some of whom were older than he). For a few days at the beginning, a few students seemed to resent his being paid to do a job that they saw no need for.

However, J's knowledge of the details of geometric proofs won the class's confidence almost immediately. In correcting their work, he did an extremely thorough job.

The class soon realized the value of a second person circulating around the room during work periods. They gained respect for J. as a "teacher."

J. waited for the students to ask him questions rather than force things down them. This was an ideal approach in this situation—as it made the class realize how truly helpful he was.

From the first day D. came into the classroom she seemed to know exactly what to do. I have never seen anyone (including any teacher I have known) with such an immediate grasp of good teaching techniques. D. does naturally what many good teachers must learn through years of experimenting. Perhaps this is because she understands the children so well, but I am inclined to believe that she also has a very unusual intuitive understanding of what learning is all about. In any case, she is an outstanding teacher.

Yes. D. displayed great initiative in helping students to understand their work. She was able to give help because she was alert to the opportunities to give help.

It is hard to be forceful enough for difficult eighth graders. R., as well as the teachers and other tutors, could have been more forceful. However, students' responses to a questionnaire indicated that they appreciated the tutors' friendliness and gentle discipline, whereas they felt that the teachers should have been more strict and less kind to disruptive students.

I feel the black-white factor enters in. They related to her more, but I think when they saw that C. and I worked as a team they would respect me more eventually.

He seems to enjoy tutoring and most important, relating and being with people. I highly recommend he enter teaching as a profession.

He explains well—speaks their language.

G. immediately goes to a group of students who are acting out in any manner and helps to settle them down. He is not afraid to try to discipline them.

Great success. Many times I have seen her work the entire period with two youngsters, and they were completely engrossed in their success. At the end of the period, they have rushed up with pride to show me their work.

He seemed to have an attitude that the work was simple and that each student could understand it. I believe this attitude rubbed off on some of the students. Many of them had never had the attention we could offer in the summer session. I'm perhaps being greedy, but I believe a few more A.'s in the classroom would have enlarged our successes further.

When she asks a question of a student, she is patient enough to wait for a reply even if it is slow in coming. She doesn't put a student down. She doesn't force a student. She has a good calming effect on her small group of students so that they do settle down and allow themselves to concentrate on schoolwork.

She employs a very old teaching method: genuine enthusiasm and a sincere interest in relating to individuals.

Appendix C

TUTOR EVALUATION OF TUTORING PROGRAM*

1. List the most important things you did as a tutor.
2. How much do tutors help a class?
   _____ Very helpful   _____ Some help   _____ No help
3. Did you help students and teachers understand each other and get along better together?
   _____ Very helpful   _____ Some help   _____ No help
4. How much of your tutoring time did you spend with:
   _____ Individuals?   _____ Small groups?   _____ The whole class?
   (Give answers in fractions or percentages.)
5. Do most students seem to welcome or resent the use of tutors?
   _____ Welcome   _____ Resent
6. Do you feel you worked better with students who were
   Younger than you? _____ Your own age? _____ Older than you?
7. Give an example of how you helped one student.
8. Give an example of how you helped a small group or a whole class.
9. In selecting tutors, what characteristics (kind of person) should be looked for? (List the most important characteristics first.)
10. *Who* should evaluate the tutors' work?
11. *How* should the tutor be evaluated?
12. Is team tutoring a good idea (for example, a boy-girl team)? Give your reasons.

* This questionnaire also was written by a committee of tutors.

13. Is the present rate of pay an adequate amount?
14. During the school year, should tutors be paid or be given credits?
15. Should orientation meetings be held before classes are assigned?
    _____ Yes   _____ No
16. Should all the tutors and all the teachers using tutors meet as a large group now and then?
    _____ Yes   _____ No
    If you think they should meet, how often should it be, and for what purposes?
17. How much has the tutor seminar helped you to be a better tutor?
    _____ Very helpful   _____ Some help   _____ No help
18. Has your work as a tutor been helpful to you?
    _____ Very helpful   _____ Some help   _____ No help
    Explain your answer.
19. When you go back to school in the fall, will you be
    _____ a much better student   _____ a better student
    _____ no better student
    Explain your answer.

SOME SAMPLE COMMENTS OF TUTORS

I got to understand the teachers and how some of them really are.

Helped individual students having difficulties with classwork. Led small group discussions. Had a small group read "A Raisin in the Sun." Helped a boy learn phonetics, interested him in reading African books. I also, as a white girl, became friends with black students—people friends, not on color lines; which was important to them and me, to life.

Helped some guys who were just terrible around the first of summer straighten up and I've also picked up a couple of friends doing so. But I still got respect from them.

Learned a lot about teachers—methods—ideas and things on the other side of the fence at school.

Helped students in trouble.

Learned what teaching really is behind the scenes.

Took them to the library to help them with reports.

Helped the teacher to understand the kids.

V : DRAMATIZING DEVICES:
IMPROVISATIONAL DRAMA,
ROLE PLAYING, AND GAMES

Miss Judith Forcada leads innovative mathematics games to challenge and stimulate creative abstract thinking, Serramonte High School, Daly City, California.

Modern adolescents are not content with a passive role.... Games have...a peculiar motivating quality.... This perhaps derives from the close connection they provide between action and outcome. A player sees the consequences of his moves, and is immediately able to test them against a criterion: the moves of the opponent.... To put the matter briefly, if secondary education is to be successful, it must successfully compete with cars and sports and social activities for the adolescents' attention, in an open market. The adolescent is no longer a child, but will spend his energy in the ways he sees fit. It is up to the adult society to so structure secondary education that it captures this energy.[1]

Given the ceaseless competition of television, popular music, movies, newspapers, magazines, and more recently, the potent competition of mind-expanding drugs and youth protest movements, teachers are compelled to find bolder ways for making classroom activities more involving and meaningful. Clearly, today's students are unwilling to suffer silently in dull classrooms.

Wisely applied, improvisational drama, role playing, simulation devices, and learning games can bring a spirit of excitement and challenge into any classroom. By the use of games, even routine skills and the dullest materials can be learned with some pleasure. In this section we have assembled samples of various types of classroom games and dramatizing devices—from improvisational drama courses and full-scale simulation techniques to simple classroom games for rote learning. The chapter is divided into three sections:

1. Improvisational Drama
2. Simulation Techniques, Role Playing, and Other Dramatic Devices
3. Classroom Games

Improvisational Drama

Everyone can act. Everyone can improvise.... We learn through experience and experiencing.... The game is a natural group form providing the involvement and personal freedom necessary for experiencing.... Any game worth playing is highly social and has a problem that needs solving within it,... an objective point in which each individual must become involved, whether it be to reach a goal or to flip a chip into a glass. There must be group agreement on the rules of the game and group interaction moving towards the objective if the game is to be played....[2]

For this section we asked Anne Hornbacher, an accomplished practitioner and proponent of improvisational drama, to describe briefly the improvisational drama courses she now gives (at the University of California, Santa Cruz, and elsewhere) to help teachers develop self-awareness in themselves and their students.[3] Following Mrs. Hornbacher's paper is a detailed report by Barbara

---

[1] James S. Coleman, *The Adolescent Society* (New York: The Free Press, 1962), pp. 315, 324, 329.

[2] Viola Spolin, *Improvisations for the Theater* (Evanston, Ill.: Northwestern University Press, 1963), pp. 3, 4, 5.

[3] Anne Hornbacher (intern 1963; GIP supervisor 1967–68) taught improvisational drama in the Philadelphia Cooperative School Program described in Part Three, "Developing New School Programs and New Public School Models." Later she expanded some of these ideas in the Berkeley High Summer Workshop, 1967.

Glasser of the improvisational drama courses she evolved for an ESEA (Elementary and Secondary Education Act) project coordinated and supervised by Anne Hornbacher for two junior high schools in Berkeley. As an aid for inexperienced but interested teachers, Miss Glasser has included a full set of the exercises and improvisations that she found most successful with junior high school students. Next, Peter Kleinbard recounts the special uses he found for improvisational drama in the teaching of poetry at the senior high school level.

We suggest, also, that the reader note the strategic part improvisational drama has played in the curriculum of the schools described in the New Schools section of this book.

Simulation Techniques, Role Playing, and Other Dramatic Devices

One of the loves of all children, anywhere, is this activity we call drama. It has a central function in their lives, for through it they experience growth and change.... These young men and women...acting adjustments in their groups, experience beforehand the demands that will be made on them as adult creatures in society.... But in freeing children to enter into other possible experience, entering into the lives of others, gaining self-possession in mind and body, and stirring the imagination, drama...changes children more quickly than any other "subject."[4]

The ingenious strategy, "The Game," describes in detail the dramatic format Al Coglianese created for a twelfth grade psychology class. By inventing several imaginary countries (Amazonia, Utopia, Merada, Alexandria), and working out their internal and external problems, Coglianese's students learned how to examine and cope with the various psychological and social relationships that can exist between individuals, groups, and nations. Next, Abbot M. Scheer relates his application of the dramatic principle to a business class. Transforming his class into a mock corporation (Funny Cars, Incorporated) complete with stocks and bonds, he propelled his students into genuine insight into business practices and into new responsibility for their own learning. Speech teacher Wayne Crow was also able to use an enveloping dramatic format successfully. In his strategy, "State Versus Santa Claus," Mr. Crow shows how students' attendance at a real jury trial, followed by a simulated trial in the classroom, enabled them to learn the usual speech course materials much more pleasurably and meaningfully.

We follow these strategies with a few examples of occasional role-playing in other subjects. Janelle Barlow in "Game Simulation in U.S. History," demonstrates how role-playing and simulation techniques impel students to discover basic insights into historical and contemporary social problems. She offers a few replicable examples of role playing which proved particularly stimulating, including detailed plans for a mock Greek forum debate about whether or not the Melian citizens should fight or submit to Athens during the Peloponnesian Wars, and an "Integration of a White Neighborhood Game"

4 Geoffrey Hawkes, quoted in David Holbrook, *English for the Rejected* (London: Cambridge University Press, 1964), p. 248.

aimed at having students discover how to solve the various community problems likely to arise.

Next we turn to foreign language teaching, an area in which role playing and dramatic devices can be used extensively. Everardo Alamillo outlines in his strategy, "Drama in Foreign Language," the increased motivation and improvement that came from having his students write, rehearse, and act out their own skits. His most advanced class worked out a complete two hour mock trial in Spanish; and, he reports, previously indifferent students were willing to give up lunchtime for practice.

Classroom Games

No compulsion then, my good friend, in teaching children; train them by a kind of game, and you will be able to see more clearly the natural bent of each. . . .[5]

In this section we have selected a series of simple games used for a variety of instructional purposes. In "Games for Math," Bonnie Mathisen explains how experimental games, such as Matho-Bongo, can be exciting to junior high school students—a restless age group which perhaps most requires novel and varied classroom activities. Also working with junior high students, Rita Schlaudt found that games could rescue Friday afternoon classes from the usual boredom and control problems. Her strategy, "Gamesmanship on Friday Afternoons," includes a useful description of the ingenious literary and grammatical games she and her students invented—"Guru Says," "Smilies," "Potato Power," and others.

These math and English classroom games are followed by several games for foreign language senior high school classes. Anita Hall in "How to Spice Up an Old Enchilada" explains how such well known games as Bingo, Hangman, and Simon Says, when played in a foreign language, can alleviate the tedium of audio-lingual drill, and motivate students toward mastery of necessary language skills.

The strategies included in this section only hint at the countless ways in which creative teachers can use dramatic devices and the spirit of play to enliven school learning and help bridge the chasm between education and delight.

[5] Plato, *The Republic,* Book VII.

IMPROVISATIONAL DRAMA

ANNE HORNBACHER **45**

Improvisational Drama for Teachers

A tall young woman stands poised and quiet before a circle of adults. All watch her intently as she brushes strands of an invisible cobweb away from her face. Imperceptibly her breathing quickens. The audience tenses and pulls forward as a deep flush rises from her neck and sweat shows on her forehead. Her hands are tearing now at the air-web, frantic and appalled. Her eyes are frightened and frightening. Several people in the audience turn away. One lady hides her eyes. "You can stop when you want to. It's up to you," the leader's voice cuts softly into the tension. Her contortions, now punctuated by small cries of distress, continue for a painful moment. Then slowly the mood changes. Anger and determination begin to push back fear; ineffective, hysterical gestures become purposeful. Seconds later, the woman breaks the dreadful silence she has created with a laugh. She looks at the audience, surprised, all cobwebs conquered. The audience sighs, grunts, and shifts back. Bodies open again.

The young woman and her audience are teachers who came to Santa Cruz to take a week long course called *Improvisations for Self-Other Awareness*. The class was learning about improvisation by doing it. I provided the necessary structure and tone, a considerably easier task than the one which faces me now. Writing about improvisation is difficult because it is primarily a nonverbal experience with a wide and highly personal range of effects. Like "loving" and "living," it resists easy definition.

I chose this incident to explore with you because it was relatively simple, yet contained all the elements crucial to learning by improvising. The experience began with a problem—one of a long series designed to develop improvisational skill. (For a complete discussion of method and an excellent sequence of problems, see Viola Spolin's *Improvisation for the Theater,* Northwestern University Press.)

The player was to imagine herself entangled by or in a large object of her choice. She was to concentrate on making this object real for the audience. "Improvisation is finding out that you can see and sometimes even touch the invisible," wrote a perceptive young Upward Bound student. Joann, the player in this exercise, did concentrate on making the cobwebs real. We saw them and felt her aversion. But she also touched her own fear. When this happened, the frontier between appearance and reality began to dissolve, and the audience became frightened. Such an intense personal experience is not the goal of improvisation, but it is a frequent result of the process of learning to improvise.

While the focus of the activity is on acquiring skill and control, the player must also learn to explore and make use of his instruments: his body, senses, experiences, thoughts, feelings.

179

Students at Opportunity High School, San Francisco, in a spontaneous improvisation. Gary, as the dean, tries to deal with Ruth, as an insolent teenager.

The first step in learning to improvise is learning to "be yourself," free from those masks and roles that customarily are assumed in social situations. Sudden personal discovery often comes with this exploration, but it is to be treated as a welcome bonus in the discipline of acquiring greater skill and confidence. Improvisation, then, is therapeutic in the same way that writing or painting may be, and is not to be considered a variant form of T-group or psychodrama.

For this group of teachers it was a painful first experience. They were gripped and hung on the wall of Joann's tension, embarrassed to see real emotion, afraid of their own responding feelings. Several moved as if to stop the exercise. The sense of danger was strong and all the defenses which operate to keep things light and amusing were clamoring for the end. Joann,

however, had chosen this response to the problem and opened herself to the experience. To stop her would have been to freeze her in her fear, preventing resolution. It would also have been patronizing, showing a lack of trust in the process and in her ability to handle it.

This lesson wasn't lost on the teachers. We talked for a long time about "protection," about how we too often keep anything real from happening in the classroom, how "for the good of the class" we send out a youngster who becomes angry, how we hide our own emotions in order to maintain the rigid mask of authority. Honesty, the pain sometimes necessary to growth, the trust which permits learning to take place without intervention—how all are forfeited in the name of protection.

With this new understanding also came articulation of deep concerns. Many teachers felt inadequate to cope with problems that might arise through improvisation; they imagined mass rioting and violence, a loss of control. They wondered when they might be justified in stopping an improvisation. Experience is the best answer to these questions, but I was able to reassure them that I had never seen an improvisation go out of control, with one exception when a real temper was lost along with the improvisation. (This happened in a tense interracial class of eighth-grade boys. We later used improvisation to explore the problem and to help the boy who had lost his concentration. "It teached me to keep my temper better," wrote another belligerent.) I told the questioners that the teacher is certainly justified in stopping an improvisation when it is dull, unbelievable, or sloppy, and to remember that the first step in learning to trust students is beginning to trust oneself. Perhaps they are the same thing.

Joann's face was shining when she finished. She laughed. She was ready for more. The fear was there, but she had found out she could not only face it, but also control it. And each of us who went through the experience with her shared her triumph as well. We felt good, alive, moved. I was deeply struck at the time by the need that we all have for such activity and reassurance, the need for this practical magic that can give tangible expression to our fears, and then the skill to slaughter those fears one by one. The hero returns to the group carrying the dragon's head, and for the moment of celebration at least, everyone lives happily ever after.

I suspect sometimes that all the talk about relevance in education boils down to this: that we all need to learn to live more honestly with ourselves and with each other. And we all need to live more in the present because the present moment is the only one in which we are alive. There is literally a world of difference between a class which talks about experience (usually someone else's) and the class which does something together. Although the former is certainly appropriate in many cases, it has become the only way most of us know how to teach and to learn. No wonder we were bored and bore our students. "We learn only through experience and no one ever teachers us anything," wrote Miss Spolin in the introduction to her book. Experience daily teaches me the truth of this statement. Improvisation is simply one effective way to learn by doing. There are many others.

It was predictable that these teachers began, as teachers will, by asking me what improvisation is and why it is important and how were they supposed to use it. I kept my peace and by the second day the questions had stopped. They were finding out for themselves. I suggest that you do the same.

BARBARA GLASSER 46

Improvisational Drama in an Urban Junior High

The bell rings. There is excited chatter as I take the roll. I am smiling at some conversation overheard and thinking how good it is that I can smile, be myself, in a class with students who, for the most part, want to be there. The class is integrated—truly heterogeneous, with ten white and eight black students from all the various academic and socioeconomic groupings. I call attention. Carmen, a school behavior problem, loudly tells the boys in the front to shut their mouths and the class begins.

"Let's start with an Orientation game." A

few hands shoot up. (This is a game in which one student begins an activity and others join when they know what is happening. Donald begins in a space ship. Others join as strange flying creatures and objects. Finally the ship lands on Mars—confrontation with the Martians—"Keep it real, remember you are weightless. React to the players," I side coach (see Appendix). "Two minutes to end it." Martians are very funny; they turn out to be greedy, suspicious, jealous, and aggressive, especially about their property—strangely like earthlings. Brief evaluation follows: Did they work together? Was the concentration complete? Why did you like it?

Next: I am experimenting with the use of modified psychodrama in the solution of conflict problems. Conflicts have been up to now too trivial or very funny, treated lightly and without seriousness, as is common with this age group. Today I want them to think more seriously, deeply. The group seems ready. There is a feeling of trust. "Think of a problem you've had, or know about, that is important to you. Choose your own partner to work with. If you can't think of or don't want to do a problem of your own, work with someone who has one." Initial reluctance and then slowly students are seeking each other out, talking, planning. Some are still sitting, sullen, isolated. "Ron has a problem with his father being too bossy and strict. Daryll will you help him?" Now everyone is involved. Seven minutes later I call for attention and the first group begins. We get a manipulative little sister always getting older sister in trouble—worried mother, punishing father. Ron and Brad act out a school problem Ron had in kindergarten—black student gets into fight with white student and black student is always blamed by "prejudiced" teacher. This develops into playlet of about thirty-five minutes and has to be continued the next session. Parent-child relationship evolves and finally Parent conference with Principal and teacher. Black confronting white; "He's always disrupting the class." The atmosphere is electric, it is real and I don't need to make any side comments. It ends—silence. Yes, we believed it. Everyone concentrated. Did this really happen? That's just the way my father acts! Bell rings—students scatter to their next class. I feel an inner excitement, an affection for all the people in this class. They learn from each other and themselves. How I wish the rest of my classes could be like this.

Why Improvisation?

This is my second semester of the second year. It has not always been this way. I began last year as a first year teacher with only one summer of apprenticeship behind me to teach four experimental classes in an Improvisational Drama project. Funded by ESEA, its purpose was to provide creative experience learning for the heterogeneously grouped classes. Through the process of improvisation, the class would learn to work together as a group, while also providing success experience for otherwise alienated, nonachieving students. The improvisation technique, it was hoped, would diminish students' feelings of alienation by encouraging the development of positive self-images, the ability to communicate more openly and honestly with others, plus an increased sense of community and group responsibility. Improvisation is relevant to student needs, since it is experientially based. The experience is here and now; the subject matter is indeed the student; and improvisation provides the means for the student to relate to himself and others.

Mechanics: Early Problems and Solutions

The mechanics of achieving a racially balanced heterogeneous class were solved by taking volunteers from study classes and from a reading workshop. Students whose contacts had been limited to P.E. classes and school corridors were brought together in a small class atmosphere. Evaluation procedures were set up by the use of questions about students' feelings toward school, each other, and themselves. These would be given at the beginning and then at the end of the semester. A major problem for me as a new teacher was facing a potentially hostile and explosive group, one that many new teachers have to face. How does one maintain a free enough atmosphere to further creativity, while maintaining the discipline necessary to prevent chaos and destructive behavior? My problems were aggravated by poor working conditions—i.e., a poorly lighted, poorly heated bungalow, or the teachers' cafeteria. However, despite the difficulties, I had some significant success even in that first semester.

An especially memorable victory was a class which began completely divided and hostile. Difficult behavior problem boys, mostly black, comprised half the class, while the other half consisted mainly of high potential students, mostly white. The class, initially impossible, became workable and exciting when improvisation began to catch on with the boys. Problems of control and behavior were reduced to a minimum as the activity at hand became more rewarding than the disruption.

The boys who soon were tremendously good at improvising, became sought after as class leaders, and received great status and approval from other class members. Other students who had previously regarded these boys as disrupters now saw them as persons of talent and worth, from whom they had much to learn. Thus, attitudes of class members changed toward each other, as well as toward the teacher. Some problems continued to exist and problem students were not magically transformed into "model" angels, but the experience shows that in a situation in which they could receive the rewards of success, recognition, status, and acceptance of who and what they were, previously hostile and alienated students became active class participants. Two of the students were later selected for demonstrations of improvisations outside the school and were used the following semester as teacher aides. Other classes were not so dramatically successful, perhaps due in part to lack of strong leaders in the class, but on the whole there were positive gains for most students. Some comments of students' first semester evaluations were:

I enjoyed the class, especially the scenes we did. I like the orientation games, where you have to join to make it work. You accomplish something if you can make it work.

It's very good. Expression was in abundance, much freedom and social comment. It made you know people more.

Greater tolerance and respect was also evident, especially between racially divided groups.

Black student: When I first came I didn't like nobody. I used to pick on them. Now I don't do that no more. I used to bother them and now I can talk to them.

Caucasian student: Yes, I'm not so wary of people. I say "hi" when I pass them. I understand them more now.

As far as personal or academic gains other than drama:

I became freer and more sure of myself.

Yes, I help teachers more than before. I used not to say very much and now I say quite a lot.

I see things more beautiful.

Emphasis on concentration also helped some students who had reading problems to begin to enjoy reading.

While second semester was considerably smoother than the first and more successful in terms of over-all achievement of goals in classes, outside factors, such as the death of Martin Luther King and the subsequent rise in black militancy, increased classroom tension. It succeeded in tearing apart one class, polarizing improvisations into "black drama" and "white drama." This did not happen in the three other classes; some students were unaffected; others pulled closer together, perhaps in part because of this tragic event. We gave demonstrations of improvisations to faculty groups. A videotape was made of the process of teaching improvisations. All in all it was a hectic, sometimes depressing, but ultimately rewarding year.

Methods and Materials

Much of the exercises, games, and ideas for improvisation problems come from a book with a wealth of technical information and methods called *Improvisation for the Theater* by Viola Spolin. Some of the following suggestions come from there, while others have been developed on my own or gleaned from other drama teachers (Anne Hornbacher, Jay Manley, and Peter Kleinbard at Berkeley High). The following are a few of the exercises I found most successful with my junior high school students.

1. *Orientation games*[1]
   a. Emphasis on either who or where person is

[1] See Appendix for definition of terms and explanations of key activities for the teacher.

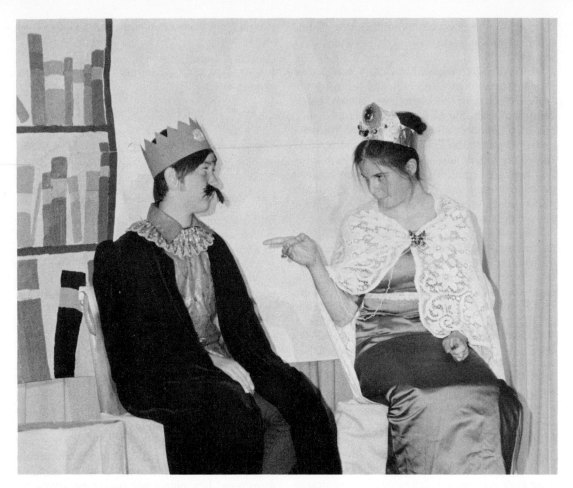

"It was your great Aunt Malkin," says the queen accusingly to the king in a student improvisation based on A. A. Milne's The Ugly Duckling. Adams Junior High School, Richmond, California.

One person begins an activity, showing where and/or who he is. Others join when they know what is being done to create a scene. As they join they may alter the nature or direction of the scene, but they must never break the game—i.e., by responding inappropriately or not taking cues from others. Through such initial games, students learn to give form and direction to group activity. It also allows great creativity and unplanned spontaneity. Recommended to begin or end a class.

b. Hat game variation

A box full of hats is provided. Starting student selects a hat and takes on a character appropriate to the hat he has chosen. Others join, with the stipulation that they too choose a hat and an appropriate character to go with it. A wide variety of hats, especially those indicating occupation, different regions, is desirable. Beginning students stop playing themselves and begin spontaneously to take on different roles.

c. Tableau orientation game

One student freezes in a position or attitude. Other students join to create a picture or tableau. The teacher can freeze or unfreeze the scene or individual players as well. Students see the value of giving and taking focus, and will begin to do this naturally after some training.

2. *Sculpture exercise*

2–4 players or (or more, depending upon space available).

In groups of two:

A is the sculptor

B is the material to be sculpted or the "blob."

Point of Concentration for A is to be as imaginative as possible in shaping his blob.

Point of Concentration for B is to be totally neutral.

Side Coach (Teacher's comments) "Be entirely neutral; don't move unless you are moved. It's up to the sculptor to maintain your balance." After sculptors are finished, call "freeze" and reverse the process. Next have two groups join together to mold the two blobs into one sculpture. You may vary the exercise by having them mold the blobs into an emotion, a relationship with each other, etc.

This is a good nonverbal exercise which usually arouses enthusiasm, as well as some initial resistance. It is a good means to get students to make acceptable physical contact with each other.

3. *Object exercise*

Two or more players

A group of two or more players begin a scene. After the scene has been established, the audience may call out different objects.

Point of Concentration: to use these objects in an unusual or unconventional way.

I usually limit the number of objects to be incorporated in the scene to three or four. A player must use the first object before the second can be called.

4. *Change of emotion*

Groups of 2–4 players

Students decide who they are, where they are, and what they are doing. Then either the teacher can assign a change of emotion, or students can decide that for themselves (example: anticipating disappointment).

Point of Concentration: the change of emotion which the players go through.

Evaluation: "Did they solve the problem? What was the change of emotion? Did you believe it?"

Of course this can be varied. Students can go through more than one change or can just portray one emotion.

NOTE: Any scene in which the players are obviously not concentrating seriously should be stopped and started again. Similarly, if the audience is being disruptive, the scene should not be allowed to continue. Concentration by both player and audience should always be a prime requirement or the exercises are worthless.

5. *Transformation of relationships*

2 or more players

Players decide on a beginning relationship with each other. Through spontaneous association this relationship changes during the course of a scene. Begin orientation game; then, once the game has begun, call out changes of time or form; for instance:

Transform players into animals;

Move players back in age to children or up to adults or old people in the same situation;

Move players back in time to prehistoric days, the sixteenth or eighteenth century, or forward to a *2001* type situation;

Sometimes players change roles or entire relationships, such as fathers and sons, doctor-patient, lawyer-client.

Point of Concentration: On transforming the relationship. This can be very successful once students catch on to the nature of the problem and let themselves associate freely.

6. *Opening and closing lines*

Two or more players

To stimulate interesting or different types of scenes, teacher or students can provide opening and closing lines which students must use to begin and end their scene. Just giving an opening line can also be used. This has the advantage of providing some structure while still leaving room for spontaneity and imagination.

7. *Other useful exercises* in Spolin are: mirror exercise (A is a mirror and imitates all B's movements); tug of war with an imaginary rope; gibberish, dubbing, hands, back, feet alone.

8. *Play ball*

Large group

The group decides on the size of the ball. The members toss it among themselves on the stage. Once the game is in motion, the teacher-director calls out the ball as being of different weights.

Point of Concentration: weight and size of the ball.

Side Coaching: "The ball weighs two pounds; it's normal again; now the ball weighs forty pounds."

Evaluation: Did all players concentrate on the weight of the ball?

Improvisation in Subject Areas

English

Improvisation can be done with success in many different kinds of classes. If a teacher is willing to risk himself, the rewards can be great in increased interest and class enthusiasm.

1. Improvising plays, stories, or parts of novels
   A good way to get students to relate to and understand the characters and the problems they face. Various techniques can be used:
   a. Improvise a scene after the play or story has been read.
   b. Stimulate interest in a book by presenting a problematic situation and ask students to act out their solution. Then read what actually happened and compare.
2. Improvisation to build plays
   With a low-track English 7 class this year, we produced and later wrote a play entitled simply, "My Black Play." The play took four class periods of improvisation. It started with a simple conflict between brothers and grew to a family drama involving the return of a father to the home. This greatly stimulated a previously difficult and uninvolved class. Two of the students took on the bulk of the writing of the play, which was then mimeographed and distributed to class members.
3. Other useful exercises which can be found in Spolin are storytelling, poetry building, and relating an incident (useful to liven up a grammar lesson on adjectives and adverbs). Give the bare facts of an incident and have students embellish it orally with color, size, etc.
4. Working from myths and fairy tales
   a. Take well known fairly tales like Cinderella, Fisherman and His Wife, Jack and the Beanstalk. Have students act them out in a variety of ways: literally; modernize it (Cinderella in a miniskirt?); or satirize it (the wolf in the Three Little Pigs as tax collector, urban renewal?).
   b. Try African myths with open endings. I have read myths to students from a book called *African Myths and Tales* by Susan Feldman. There are myths called "Dilemma and Moral Fables" which have problematic endings. Have students act out tales and provide their own endings. Have students discuss the various possibilities.

Social Studies

Act out problems in history. Present an actual historical event, without telling the real outcome. Let different groups of students work it out and discuss what the students chose to do and how they came to their decision, as opposed to what actually happened. This can help students better understand historical conflict as well as the people of the period they are studying.

Some Final Thoughts

Be brave—dare to disrupt the order to create new order. Be patient. Don't be afraid to fail and you'll succeed. Play with students. Break the teacher-student role. Step into their shoes and have them try on yours. Remember, the process of improvising is more important than the end product!

Appendix

IMPROVISATIONAL DRAMA

Definition of Terms and Class Procedures

Improvisation: Improvisation is something which all of us do throughout our daily lives. We are improvising when we cook without a recipe, make a dress or boat without a pattern, or speak without a written speech. Each day we do not plan exactly what we are going to do or say but rather respond naturally to people and situations. Thus, improvisational drama uses a skill which we all have and channels it to solve dramatic problems. In an improvisation class, students work together to solve problems presented by the teacher. The problems are at first simple but later become more difficult and complicated. The student provides the content of the drama (i.e., the characters and situations) from his own experience, but must work within the limits of the problem set by the teacher.

Point of concentration (POC): Each problem will have a POC. This is a main point to which we direct our attention and energy. For example, if the problem is to play ball, the POC might be on showing the weight and size of the ball.

Side coaching: During the exercises done by the class, the teacher's voice will be heard giving directions, helping the students solve the problems or keeping them working on the POC. "Concentrate!" "Make it real!" "Share your voices with the audience," are frequent examples of this.

Evaluation of problems and the audience: In order for improvisation to be successful, the whole class must work together. The performers work to solve the problem, the audience must also be involved in solving it by paying close attention and then evaluating how completely the problem was solved. Members of the audience who call out or otherwise disrupt the scenes break the concentration of the class and destroy the possibility of successful improvisations. In evaluation of the performers we do not judge them as "good" or "bad," but rather as "complete" or "incomplete." "Did they solve the problem?" "Was it real?" "Did you believe them?" These are some of the questions the audience will be expected to respond to.

PETER KLEINBARD **47**

Improvisational Drama and Literature

The following are two adaptations of improvisational exercises for use with literature. It should be noted that they are advanced exercises and should be used only with students who have mastered many less difficult exercises.

The first problem was done in preparation for a unit on Yeats' plays. Images are crucial for an understanding of Yeats' work. One must not only read and understand the image, but have many alternative interpretations in mind in order to be able to place it within the new domain of logical relationships which Yeats will often switch to in the course of a poem or play. Furthermore, the image is often Yeats' means of taking the poem from the rational verbal level to a nonrational experiential level. Thus, it becomes the crucible out of which his logical statements are inspired and molded. But because many of his images are quite bizarre— "weasels fighting in a hole," "honey of generation," and materials taken from Irish, Japanese, and other mythologies—the student is tempted to pass them over rather than to try to deal with and understand them.

One way I worked with the images was to pass out mimeographed sheets full of them and ask five students to plan an "improv" around one of them while the rest of us did other work. At the end of the class, the group presented their improvisation. The rest of the class then discussed what was communicated to them. Finally the image was read and the class compared what they saw on the stage with what was evoked in their imaginations. Many good things happened as a result of this work. For one, it caused a tremendous intensity of focus on the images and the different ways they could mean—as visual image, as sound, as logic. Secondly, students were amazed at the ability of their mates to communicate complex materials or to create attractive movement on stage. Thirdly, girls who had been trained in dance movement were driven by the complexity of the problem to communicate this more complex type of movement to the rest of the students.

A second adaptation of the improvisations was based on a dubbing exercise. In this, two students go to the back of the room and two go on stage. Either group can begin a scene. The two in the back are the voices, the two in front are the bodies. The point of concentration is to maintain a close interrelationship between sound and movement. We used this exercise with plays that we read. Students read more closely in order to be able to anticipate the kind of movement and sequence of movement that might be asked of them by their dubbers. We were able to explore different ways a scene might look and the kinds of meanings that different presentations could give to the words. Thus students got a sense of the richness of possible interpretation of the written works.

This suggests only two of many possible adaptations of improvisational exercises to specific content. In all cases, provided the adaptation has been carefully thought through beforehand, it will result in a deeper, more organic sense of meaning and of how meaning is communicated. For what you are doing is asking your students to actually experience the work of art. Given the remoteness of the surface aspects of much literature that is central to our tradition, it would seem to me there is great value in attempting this kind of work. I see no reason why improvisational techniques might not be tried in almost any subject field. The limitation is really the teacher's imagination.

Bibliography

Spolin, Viola. *Improvisation for the Theater*. Evanston, Ill.: Northwestern University Press, 1963.

SIMULATION TECHNIQUES, ROLE PLAYING, AND OTHER DRAMATIC DEVICES

AL COGLIANESE 48

The Game

I. Abstract

The concern of this paper is a teaching device that has proved itself particularly successful in my twelfth-grade psychology class.

"The Game" is a simulation of a real-life situation on a large scale. It is concerned with the functioning of individuals in a given though increasingly complex social situation. Through playing the game the student comes first to "live" and then to examine the psychological and social relationships that exist between individuals and groups.

In the game the teacher functions as the coordinator of all proposed actions—he never prescribes. His main function is, when needed, to introduce into the situation specific problems related to psychology. (Most problems, however, are caused automatically by the interaction of the groups and their members.)

II. Preliminary Preparation

A. Grouping

The game is designed in such a way that random grouping is possible and even desirable, but the students in this psychology class had been previously divided into three groups for purposes of performing experiments. These previous groupings were maintained at the outset of the game.

The reason that random grouping seems desirable is that the students are thus allowed to realign themselves as they see fit. Since a cooperative spirit is essential to the advantageous functioning of a city-state, the freedom to determine one's colleagues becomes important; this freedom is an integral part of the game as it is now set up. When a student finds that he does not get along with other members of his group he may either stay and work out his differences or he may break away from that group altogether. As the game goes on, however, the decision to break away seems to be increasingly more difficult to make because of the stake that the student builds up in his city-state.

B. Choice of Site

Before it was announced that the class was to play the game, the students were presented with an hypothetical area relief map and asked, first as a class, to discuss the prospect of locating the best possible site for a major city. Many questions were asked concerning location of resources, fertility of land, weather conditions, etc. Their questions were answered without revealing the location of most of the resources. The class then divided into the three groups for the purpose of deciding upon one site per group. Happily each group chose a different site.

C. The Social Institutions

The day before the initial playing date I explained how to play the game. I also gave a short lecture on the function of the six basic social institutions and explained that these were to be considered in meeting the needs of the populace of the city-states. These six institutions are the economic, the political, the educational, the familial, the religious, and the recreational.

D. Materials Used at Outset

1. The Aero Relief Model of Geographical Terms, Aero Service Corporation, 1958. Map area is 42″ × 30″. Scale: 1″ = 10 miles. (Any relief map will do.)
2. Mimeographed replicas of the above map.
3. Three sheets of heavy white drawing paper, 18″ × 15″ to represent each city-state. Scale: 1″ = 1 mile.
4. Three paper rectangles, 1.8″ × 1.5″, to be taped onto relief map to indicate the sites of the three city-states.
5. Mimeographed sheets of symbols with cost of various items symbolized. (This list of symbols is added to constantly.) See Appendix.
6. Colored pencils: each city-state is assigned a color. Symbols indicating sites of material expansion are drawn in on appropriate maps in appropriate colors and returned to the groups just before their next playing date.
7. Mimeographed lists of eight job titles.

E. Materials Added to Date

1. Mimeographed maps of a large area containing the relief map area. Scale: 1″ = 360 miles.
2. Blank mimeograph paper to represent the area of each city.
3. Appropriate maps and pencils to facilitate constructing another city-state.
4. Colored yarn to be used on relief map to indicate borders.

III. Input

There are six factors given at the beginning of the game. These are (1) a population of 1,000,000; (2) a population increase rate of 2 percent; (3) modern technology; (4) an average income of $5,500 per family of four; (5) natural resources (mostly unknown); (6) a one-year time period between playing dates. The last three factors need further explanation.

For practical purposes, all finances are figured from the average income per family of four. If, for example, inflation occurs, the price of materials and objects remains constant, but the average income per family of four will decrease. If, on the other hand, a city-state drills a successful oil well, the price of oil does not decrease, but the average income per family of four increases—in this case by ten dollars. I realize that this method does injustice to economics, but I wish to emphasize psychological problems and keep the reality of other problems at a minimum.

I have placed on the area map (or rather, under it) many natural resources: gold, silver, oil, gas, copper, iron, etc. Although I have studied somewhat the correlation between types of terrain and natural resources, most oil, gas, and ore fields are placed arbitrarily. It is the responsibility of the members of the city-states to devise means to find and to exploit natural resources.

The one year period between playing dates is so set because this time period allows the city-states time to collect taxes so that they may operate. On the other hand, certain actions which would quite obviously terminate in considerably less time than a year are necessarily dealt with over several playing dates. For example, certain military operations, which in reality would take a few days, require reaction from other city-states. This reaction cannot take place until a subsequent playing date. However, this dual system of reckoning time seems to disturb no one.

IV. How to Play

After the sites are determined, each group is directed to choose its form of government, to appoint an individual or a subgroup to submit a masterplan for the city (to be sketched in lightly on the 18″ × 15″ drawing paper), and to determine who is to be responsible for each of the following job categories: Head of State, Head of Housing and Agriculture, Head of Entertainment and Recreation, Head of Welfare and Education, Head of Culture (i.e., the arts), Head of Transportation and Communications, Head of Economics, Head of Military. In the event that any other job categories should spring up, the members of the city-state decide who is to bear the responsibility for them.

The game is now played once a week. Each week the teacher returns to the city-states the results of their proposed actions of the week before. These result sheets are studied and discussed by the various groups to determine what further proposals are possible and desirable. Each member of each city-state then draws up and submits proposals appropriate to his job category. No proposal is denied if it is financially and logistically feasible. (For sample proposal and result sheets see Appendix.)

V. General History of the Game Thus Far

The three groups named their city-states Merada, Alexandria, and Amazonia. To get the game under way, I had the groups play it three days in succession. On the second day two members of Alexandria and one of Merada chose to break away from their respective city-states and form one of their own which they named Utopia. With them went one fourth of the population of Alexandria and one tenth the population of Merada.

All the city-states promptly made land claims. The claims of one were not recognized by the others. Two members of Merada were influential enough to determine for that city-state a policy of armed aggression against the other city-state in order to secure land. Until recently this aggression took the form of threats and troop movements only. In the face of this warlike policy, the other city-states chose to set up defenses; they also drew up and signed a nonaggression and mutual defense pact.

All the city-states except Merada chose to form democratic republics. Merada is vaguely socialistic. All the city-states except Merada collect 10 percent of total income each year for operating expenses. Merada collects annually sometimes 30 percent, sometimes 40 percent. The people of Merada were initially quite upset over this high tax rate and threatened to stage costly riots, but the government of Merada pacified the people by more than adequately providing the necessities of life.

Merada was the first city-state to initiate a farm program, to stockpile atomic weapons, and to mobilize troops. Amazonia was concerned mostly with erecting hospitals, providing institutions for the mentally and physically handicapped, maintaining an effective police force, building bomb shelters, developing parks and resorts.

Alexandria's emphasis has been in the direction of transportation. It is very interested in connecting itself by rail and by road with Amazonia and Utopia, partly to facilitate trade and partly for ease of troop movements. Alexandria's leaders seem to be greatly in fear of Merada. Alexandria is not very interested in expansion, but it will not compromise on land disputes. Two members of Alexandria do not get on well with one another, but they choose to remain in the same group.

Utopia, because of its location, is relatively free of the turmoil caused by Merada. Utopia moves cautiously. Its city plan is greatly detailed. Its military is small. It is interested mainly in internal development. Instead of wildcatting for oil, gas, or ore as did the other city-states, Utopia sent out a fact-finding team to determine as closely as possible the locations of resources. Utopia is interested in expansion to some degree, but it avoids conflict with the other city-states.

Because of its high tax rate, Merada was able for a long time to get a great deal more done than the other city-states. It plunged into debt, however, when it built a doomsday machine (they are going for $1,000,000,000). As a result, by the playing date, January 13, 1967, Merada found itself with a deficit of $81,826,393. Merada had company, however; Amazonia had a deficit of $311,016,458, and Alexandria had a deficit of $3,423,995,908. Utopia was the only city-state working with a surplus, namely, $114,224,950. The three in debt are trying to pull themselves out by deficit spending. Merada and Amazonia seem to be succeeding, but Alexandria spends in the wrong places and adds a growing employment problem to its growing debt.

Recently I added another dimension to the game by running off maps of a large area, a small part of which contains the area representing the relief map. The city-states are now expanding into this large area, discovering what it is like as they expand. In this large area I have placed other countries and communities. These are controlled by the teacher and will inevitably be discovered by the city-states. These comunities have various cultures developed to various degrees and various attitudes toward outsiders. As the game goes on, then, expansion widens, Merada's warlike policy is subsiding, and the search continues for food, shelter, clothing, and "the good life."

VI. Modifications

Because the coordinating of the actions of the city-states was taking from six to eight hours preparation before each playing date, I had decided to allot time to each city-state to make its proposals orally. I tried this plan once, and it did not work out. After conferring with one city-state, I would confer with a second, thereby leaving the first with nothing to do. I plan now to return to the written proposals, but intend to have the groups keep the records of their own expansion rather than to continue to keep the records of it myself. I will, however, keep master maps of all areas and continue to keep financial records. Because much of the preparation time was spent in dealing with the expansion records (i.e., the maps for each city-state), I expect to reduce preparation time by two or three hours.

Although all students are progressing well with their specific tasks, often the accomplishments of some of them are overshadowed by the large problems being dealt with in other fields. For this reason I am going to introduce into the game a chart indicating the relative progress of each job category in each of the city-states. The chart will be made up in terms of percent of accomplishment, with 100 percent representing optimum accomplishment, except in the case of the economics category, where raw figures of surplus or debt will serve as a better indicator.

Several students have tried to call formal conferences of one sort or another, but, because of the degree of competitiveness in the game, they have not succeeded. Although there is no problem in getting students to initiate discussion here and there as they work, the formalization of student initiated discussion would be a great asset to the game. If they do not produce this formalization themselves after the next few playing dates, I will do so myself, and make it a regular feature. Undoubtedly the addition of one more playing day per week will be required.

VII. Evaluation

In terms of the game per se, the students evaluate themselves, both individually and as groups. Several standards have emerged. First, a premium has been put on cooperativeness. It was quickly discovered that a cooperative attitude among the members of the city-state is a must for efficient functioning. Second, the students found competitiveness very desirable because the nature of the game is such that the city-states will compete with one another for several things—so far only for land and resources, later for trade. Third, the students have recognized the value of the ability to devise effective and cheap methods to accomplish specific tasks which they found desirable. This ability calls for creativity. Any member of a group which does not have a spread of cooperative, competitive, and creative people to teach others in the group to develop these qualities has the opportunity to realign himself with another group or to learn these qualities from observing the functioning of the other groups. I have found that it can be helpful to occasionally suggest to a student that he ask or see so and so on a specific point. If a group or a student is unable to cooperate, compete, or figure out a problem, the city-state will suffer automatically by the nature of the game. But with each suffering there is a lesson that the students quickly learn, and the lesson is basically the same: to function well as a group it is necessary to cooperate, to compete, and to think. That the students evaluate themselves in these terms is of great importance, and one of the primary aims of the game.

I am, however, equally interested in evaluating the students in terms of learning the matter of psychology, in terms of how well they can draw principles of psychology from the game and how well they can apply principles of psychology, to the game, or rather, to that which the game simulates. The fact that through the game the students actually experience the matter of psychology seems to have been a great aid to their ability to learn the matter better. And, because of the large scope

of the game, transfer seems to have been greatly facilitated.

VIII. Advantages of the Game

1. Aside from the limitations of the context of the game, the groups possess total freedom.
2. Interest and involvement are very high.
3. The students "live" their subject.
4. The game is extremely flexible: problems involving a great many studies can be injected and telescoped to almost any degree desired.
5. Transfer is easily facilitated and almost automatic.
6. It is an excellent way to come to know one's students.

IX. Disadvantages of the Game

1. As it now stands, teacher preparation is very time consuming.
2. Teachers do not know everything that there is to know. Inaccuracy in unemphasized studies is probable.

X. Application to Other Subjects

Anyone searching for a method to integrate several departments or subjects may find this game useful. Of course, modifications would be in order to fit specific needs. On a grand scale it is conceivable that the city-state motif could serve to integrate geography, civics, economics, history, psychology, any other social studies, and possibly, all sciences except the life sciences.

I think that the game works very well with the study of psychology, but I think it would work better with civics, economics, or history. With these subjects the game could teach more directly, by its own operation, and there would be less necessary reference to theory than there is with psychology.

XI. Source

The game is my invention (I think). I understand, however, that IBM has a training program wherein the trainees form several mock corporations and compete with one another for nine weeks. IBM uses computers.

SYMBOLS IN USE THUS FAR

Notice that almost no attention is paid to the reality of the economic situation of the world. Most figures are totally arbitrary.

Designation		*Economic data*
——	Road	$7,000 per mile in flat terrain
⚓	Ship	$2,000,000
🛥	Submarine	$10,000,000 with missiles
🏃	1000 troops	
▰	Farm area	$1,000,000; feeds 100,000; employs 5,000
▲	Factory	Cost and employment varies with type
●	Ground observation post	(Requires presence of troops; range, 20 miles)
Ⓡ	Radar station	$1,000,000 (range, 60 miles)
Ⓐ	Atomic stockpile	$80,000,000
Ⓜ	Exploding mine	$800
→	Indicates direction of movement	
✕	Marks the exact spot	
◐	Missile station	$900,000 (an arrow stands for missile in flight)
⌁	Railroad	$4,000 per mile in flat terrain
⌷	Bridge	$180 per foot
⎵	Gas well	$100,000 to drill to maximum depth
⌐⊙⌐	Oil well	
⌢	Dam	Cost varies
⊤	Power plant	$3,000,000
⌇⌇⌇	Power lines	$1,000 per mile
↑	Air squad (9)	$9,000,000 (an arrow stands for a squad in flight)
↓	Mine	Cost varies
⌂	Housing complex	$75,000,000 (houses 20,000)
Ⓟ	Police complex	$5,000,000 (serves 100,000)
Ⓗ	Hospital complex	$50,000,000 (serves 50,000)
Ⓢ	Retail stores complex	$6,000,000 (serves 50,000)
Ⓖ	Cultural center	Cost varies (serves 100,000)
Ⓣ	Entertainment area	$5,000,000 (serves 100,000)
⌸	Water works	$25,000,000
Ⓔ	Education complex	$20,000,000 (serves 30,000 students)

⊔	Docks	$20,000,000
▭	Bomb shelter	$250,000,000 (serves 300,000)
▭	Park	Cost varies
Ⓕ	Fire station	$5,000,000 (serves 100,000)
Ⓒ	Communications center	$10,000,000
Ⓓ	Doomsday Machine	$1,000,000,000
⊣⊢	Tunnel (for road)	$200 per foot
(No symbol)	Military training center	$30,000,000

Changes in income correspond to cost and employment; in turn, these vary arbitrarily, except where indicated.

SAMPLE PROPOSAL: AMAZONIA—DEPARTMENT OF ENTERTAINMENT AND RECREATION

I propose a city park next to the proposed government buildings and business area. I want it to be one mile wide, with trees, shrubs, grass, flowers, cement walks, a fountain in the middle, a swimming pool in the lower left corner, swings, slides, seesaws, monkey bars toward the upper right corner; benches and garbage cans distributed throughout the park. I propose that it have a zoo toward the upper left hand corner with a quarter admittance to the zoo and a fifty cents admittance to the swimming pool.

(Because a drawing of this proposed park was not indicated on an accompanying map, it was not granted. On the next playing date the map was submitted and the proposal granted.)

SAMPLE RESULT SHEET: AMAZONIA

Housing: The two proposed housing complexes were not indicated on the city map. Therefore not granted: I don't know where to put them (and your people are in great need of housing). After your 10 percent tax you have this time a working fund of $146,292,504. Dock granted (see attached maps). The city park must be indicated on city map—an admirable project. Farms granted and all to do with them (see map). (You put your farms rather close to Merada, you know.) As you set it up, the post office pays for itself—very good. Fire house and police station granted (see map). Telephone company: indicate on city map, please. Social welfare program very good: Please indicate on city map where the facilities are to go. Also work out a welfare budget more precisely for the entire population.

Weather—same as before
Population—1,061,208
Total expenses since last time—$159,958,950
Leaving after 10 percent tax a *deficit* of $13,666,446
Income per family of four is $5510

Please return these sheets.

The Mock Corporation

By using a mock corporation setup in my high school business classes, I attempted to determine answers to the following three questions:

1. Do students gain insight into who they are by interacting with each other in the simulated business environment of a classroom mock corporation?
2. Is the student's insight enhanced by interaction with fellow students who play roles of subordinate, peer, and boss?
3. If the students do gain new insights into themselves, do these insights result in their taking increased responsibility such as:
   a. Showing initiative?
   b. Being creative?
   c. Behaving maturely?

Procedures

The mock corporation situation was organized out of three different classes in an upper middle class suburban school.[1] Bookkeeping I, about thirty students in first period, became FUNNY CARS, INC. Business Law, second period with about thirty students, chose the name of THE BLUE FOX LAW FIRM. The sixth-period Business English class became secretaries to the various employees in the first two classes.

The basic or key organization was FUNNY CARS, INC., which was a multimillion dollar corporation producing "Funny Cars"—a type

[1] See Appendix.

of racing car with which the students are familiar.

Boss relationships were created by such positions as Chairman of the Board, Vice President in Charge of Production, Chief Accountant, and so forth. Peer relationships were created among vice presidents, among various middle managers, and among those reporting to the managers. Subordinate relationships obviously existed throughout the organizations—e.g., managers to vice presidents and secretaries to managers.

The BLUE FOX LAW FIRM was organized as an independent firm, but its main function was to support FUNNY CARS, INC. in matters of law suits, contractual arrangements, trademarks, and other legal arrangements.

The students in the sixth-period Business English class were assigned as secretaries (on an individual basis) to provide typing services to all employees of both the period one and period two mock corporations. Handwritten memos, letters, schedules, and charts were transmitted to the secretaries from the two corporations by the instructor. Each secretary typed an original and duplicate of each item. The duplicate was stapled to the rough draft and mounted on the right side of a manila folder which was tabbed with her boss's position and name. The original item was left loose inside the folder to be reviewed, signed, and delivered by the student boss the next day. A separate set of manila folders was kept in a box for each of the two mock corporations.

Grading was done every two weeks. Secretaries were graded on composition, grammar, format, and quantity of work. Employees of FUNNY CARS, INC. and THE BLUE FOX LAW FIRM were graded on initiative, follow-through, conferences held, and quantity of work. Every effort was made to make the students realize that this was "a real corporation situation and that when you get a job in a corporation you cannot keep that job by sitting around and waiting for someone to tell you what to do." Initiative was placed at a premium. The students were told that they needed to show initiative and to come up with ideas, letters, conferences, and reports if they were to "keep their jobs."

Since the whole mock corporation idea was to let the students interact, take initiative, and be creative, no strict assignments were given. However, in order to get the thing "off the ground" and in many cases to keep it going, "pump priming" of ideas and suggestions by the instructor were necessary.

Results

Students definitely gained insight as they accumulated experience in their new roles. The students' work clearly revealed that their learning, involvement, and self-awareness were stimulated by their various "real-life" roles. Their behavior bore out Watson's comment that opportunity for fresh, novel, stimulating experience is a kind of reward which is quite effective in conditioning and learning.[2]

I believe the results of the interactions via the mock corporation bore out my original hypothesis that as students gain more insight into themselves and their own patterns of interacting, they grow in responsibility and initiative.

Interestingly, the students with behavior problems in most cases chose the top "boss" jobs, while many "A" students were content with less involved clerical or desk type jobs. Furthermore, the behavior-problem students

were accepted by the other students in their leadership roles in spite of the fact that the bosses may have been getting low grades before. Obviously, the students gained insights into their own behavior by seeing themselves interact with fellow students in roles of subordinate, peer, and boss. In many cases those who had previously seen themselves as taking a leadership role in grades—i.e., being "A" students—now found themselves willingly taking a back seat to the aggressive, commanding, and outspoken manager-type student.

Wherever possible, the students assumed roles much in keeping with their sense of who they really felt they were. If the student didn't like his job, he was free to change, and in many cases did so in order to more clearly identify himself with his growing insights. This desire for gaining self-insight is in keeping with Erikson's statement: "What we have described...is identical with *the need of young people anywhere* for ideological affirmation. Young people may try to find various forms of 'confirmation' in groups that range from idealistic youth movements to criminal gangs."[3]

The simulation of the adult world of business broke students away from their usual isolation into small teen-age societies which focus teen-age interests and attitudes on things far removed from adult responsibilities.[4] The "real-life" mock corporation seemed to bring the students out of their teen-age world and then confront them with new and exciting insights into their own capabilities and potentialities.

In summary, the mock corporation environment proved to be a very successful learning tool. The fact that the teacher was not the "kingpin," but served as coordinator and resource person freed the classroom from much of the usual student-teacher relationship and allowed the student to freely develop his own insights, take initiative, be creative, and assume responsibility in his own way.

2 Goodwin Watson, *What Psychology Can We Trust?* (New York: Teachers College Press, 1961), p. 4.

3 Erik H. Erikson, *Insight and Responsibility* (New York: W. W. Norton & Company, Inc., 1964), p. 65.
4 See Grace and Fred M. Hechinger, *Teen-Age Tyranny* (New York: William Morrow and Company, 1963), p. 28.

ITEM IN SCHOOL NEWSPAPER

Vol. IV — No. 13   Campolindo High School, Moraga, California   May 5, 1967

Funny Cars Inc. Growing In Business Law Classes

Learning by doing is the motto of the Campolindo students involved in Mr. Bud Scheer's business classes.

A mock corporation, Funny Cars Inc., has been set up by the first period bookkeeping class, in which students go about the regular duties of such a corporation. They buy land, bill customers, and hold board of directors meetings, to name only a few of these duties.

The business law class, alias Blue Fox Law Firm, handles the legal affairs of Funny Cars Inc., such as making contracts, and fighting legal suits. Also included in this class are students who set up the State Kangaroo Court, and the Private Eyeball Agency.

The paperwork of both Funny Cars Inc. and the Blue Fox Law Firm is processed by the students in Business English. Each member of the corporation and the Law Firm has his own secretary.

CORPORATIONS PROJECT: GENERAL INSTRUCTIONS

1. Place all items received on LEFT side of folder. Place all items you create on right side.
2. Date all items, e.g., Job Descriptions, rough drafts, etc.
3. All bosses must have the Job Descriptions of those *immediately* under them in their folders.
   a. Boss's own Job Description is placed on right side of folder.
   b. Job Descriptions of those immediately under the boss are placed on the left side of folder.
4. Extra copies of memos and letters (except those intended for later multiple distribution) must be removed from folders.
5. Memos (or letters if very important) are used for communication *within* an organization.
6. Letters are used for communications *outside* of an organization. All letters leaving Campolindo must be cleared, by all parties concerned, with your instructor.
7. All correspondence, whether written or typed, must be in good taste and written in a manner acceptable to similar actual business situations.
8. Secretaries are to staple the typed copy of all memos and letters to the *top* of rough drafts, punch and mount these items on the Acco fastener in the folder. The original is left loose in the folder for later transmittal by the manager or employee.
9. All folders are to be fixed with a blue tab. The manager's name is on the front of the tab and the secretary's name on the back.
10. All folders are numbered in consecutive order. They must be returned to the file in that same order.
11. If a manager receives a letter which requires action by one of his employees, he

should write (in pen) a note at the top of the letter telling his employee what he wants done. The note should be dated.

12. All correspondence received by a manager should be initialed and dated in the upper right hand corner on the day received.

13. Secretaries are responsible for mounting items in folders and maintaining folder material in proper date order. Managers and employees should inform secretaries of problems with material in folders but *should not rearrange or remove* filed material.

Appendix C

SAMPLE JOB DESCRIPTIONS

Vice President in Charge of Production

1. Keep plant managers informed of increases or decreases in production.
2. Keep in constant touch with Purchasing Department—Supplies and materials ordered and coming in.
3. Maintain the supply of labor—keep an adequate number of workers.
4. Work with Vice President of Finance in determining profit and loss, money for supplies for plant.
5. Work with Vice President of Finance to make sure there is sufficient payroll money.
6. Keep in constant touch with Production Department accounts so as to control overproduction costs.
7. Attend Board Meetings. (As a member of the Board, I am directly responsible to the stockholders who elected me.)

Vice President in Charge of Marketing

1. Boosting sales.
2. Approving advertising.
3. Making market ideas.
4. Looking over sales ideas.
5. Making sure salesmen are doing job.
6. Supervising programs.
7. Taking clients out to dinner.

Appendix D

ARTICLES OF INCORPORATION FOR FUNNY CARS, INCORPORATED

1. The name of this corporation is Funny Cars, Incorporated.
2. The primary business in which the corporation is to engage is the manufacture of commercial automobiles. The corporation may engage in any other business, whether related or unrelated to the foregoing, in which natural persons may lawfully engage and which is not prohibited to corporations.
3. The county in this state where the principal office for the transaction of the business of the corporation is to be located is the city of Moraga and county of Contra Costa.
4. The corporation is authorized to issue only one class of shares of stock. The total number of shares which the corporation is authorized to issue is 3 million. Each share is to have a par value of $100, and the aggregate par value of the total number of said shares is $300 million.
5. The number of directors is four, and the names and addresses of the persons who are appointed to act as the first directors of the corporation are:
   Steve Romelt, 67 Blank Street, Moraga, California
   Jim Bergfeld, 148 Blank Street, Moraga, California
   Ross Costa, 268 Green Avenue, Orinda, California
   Andy Cayting, 99 Oakland Street, Orinda, California
The number of directors may be changed from time to time by a bylaw changing the number.

6. Bylaws (other than one—or any amendment thereof—changing the authorized number of directors) may be adopted, amended, or repealed by the Board of Directors, subject to the right of the shareholders to adopt, amend, or repeal bylaws.
7. Each shareholder will be allowed to purchase and acquire any shares that may be issued after the first offer.
8. In case any shareholder desires to sell his share or shares of the stock of this corporation, he shall first offer them for sale to the remaining stockholders at book value. Any sale in violation of this provision shall be null and void. A stockholder desiring to sell his said share or shares shall file notice in writing of his intention with the secretary of the corporation and unless one or more of the shareholders exercises a request to purchase the stock within 30 days thereafter, they shall be deemed to have waived their privilege of purchasing, and he will be at liberty to sell to anyone else.

IN WITNESS WHEREOF, we have executed these articles of incorporation this 4th of May, 1967.

Steve Romelt	Jim Bergfeld	Ross Costa	Andy Cayting

WAYNE CROW **50**

State versus Santa Claus

I. Introduction

Role playing, game simulation, and other dramatizing devices have made it possible for high school speech teachers to achieve a higher degree of student involvement by presenting old materials in new ways. In my speech class, I employed the role playing of a jury trial in order to teach some basic concepts of law used in courtrooms today.

Today's high school student is more aware of the court of law than was his father twenty years ago. With such television shows as "Divorce Court," "Day in Court," "Perry Mason," and others, which show fictional or recreated courtroom scenes, the mass media of today exude an increasing amount of exposure to all the elements of law. It is also surprising to note how many students in any given school have had first hand experience with the courts either through parental divorce or juvenile delinquency. Personal experience has not always left the student with the proper respect for law and its battlefield, the courtroom. The following unit was designed to show students how law is

decided upon by evidence and supportive testimony, not by emotions and hearsay.

II. Description of the Unit with Suggestions for Possible Users

A. Preparation for Role Playing of the Trial

1. Arrange for field trip to the county courthouse. Give the students an opportunity to witness actual courtroom trials in operation. The Alameda County Courthouse is accessible and offers the students a chance to see a hearing as well as a jury trial. Close attention should be paid to the court's calendar, which is available to teachers through the clerk's office.

2. Familiarize the students with the roles to be played in a courtroom. The judge, bailiff, court recorder, counsel for defense, prosecuting attorney, jury foreman, and jurors are positions that should be explained fully to the class before the trip is made so that the students can identify the persons occupying the roles.

3. Explain to the students how the jury system works and how jurors are selected to serve.

4. Assign television shows to be viewed for classroom discussion. See local papers for listings.

5. Break the class into workable groups of twelve to fourteen members. Teachers should make the selection of groups carefully in order to give balance to each group. Habitual absentees should be evenly dispersed, so that their absences don't interfere with the work of the group.

B. Requirements for Groups

1. Choose an intriguing person to place on trial. This is a vital point, and a miscalculation here was the main reason why some groups didn't carry off the assignment as well as others. Examples of subjects my students selected were the following: try Robin Hood as a thief; try Abraham Lincoln as a war criminal (assuming the South won the war); try John Wilkes Booth for murder; try Santa Claus for breaking and entering.

The introduction of humorous topics was not of my choosing, but in the end the humorous trials came off best because of higher interest and total group involvement.

2. Groups must select members to fill certain roles of the court. The selection of qualified attorneys and judges is so important to the success of the trial that this should not be left to group choice alone. The attorneys play the biggest part and must be able persons with quick minds and leadership abilities. Each member of the group fills either a court position or automatically becomes a witness for the prosecution or defense.

3. Each group must serve as a jury while waiting for its trial to come to court. Members listen to testimony and pass judgment on the accused. This provides valuable experience in developing critical listening abilities.

C. Daily Work Activities

MONDAY. The trip to the courthouse is the starting point for the actual unit. Each group should visit one of the trials in process to take notes on procedures and observe the activities within the courtroom. Students should be aware of the tension created by the human conflicts and strained relationships within a courtroom.

The group members should begin to choose their roles or recommend other members for certain roles when they see them performed in the trial. (This is a vital point for the success of the mock trial.)

TUESDAY. In class the groups must move quickly into action to select a topic and to assign members to the various roles. The teacher should meet separately with the judge and attorneys of each group to impress upon them the importance of their leadership. In order for the judge to direct action during the trial, the attorneys should present to him a legal brief outlining the case.

WEDNESDAY. The groups begin to rehearse. On this day it is important to have separate rooms for each group to rehearse in. The jury should be composed of members from the other groups. Jury members should not be informed in advance of the case. The rehearsal should concern itself with the order of events, sequence of witnesses, and the staging of the trial, not with testimony. The witnesses are to write their own testimony, keeping in mind the relationship their role has to the trial. Spontaneity is necessary for a successful trial and too much rehearsal will take away the unexpected responses. Rehearse procedure, but do not rehearse testimony!

THURSDAY. Set up your classroom to simulate a courtroom. The tape recorder must be centrally located to catch all of the voices during the trial. Allow the full period for the trial. I found the following arrangement useful:

FRIDAY. Repeat the procedures, using the Thursday group as jury.

MONDAY. Play the tapes back to the students and have them write a one page summary of the assignment. This can be exciting for the students, because even the normally shy individual likes to hear his voice on tape.

III. Looking Back

My attitude toward the unit underwent a change about Wednesday as the groups began to rehearse their trials. Whereas my original goal had been to keep a firm hand on the proceedings and make certain that my objectives were fulfilled, my feelings began to loosen up when I realized how much fun the students were having. The injection of humorous topics saved some trials from being half-hearted performances.

The real learning experience was the field trip to the courthouse. This made a lasting impression on the students that could never be duplicated through any series of carefully planned, well presented teacher lectures. Whether this trip would have been more beneficial if it had come after the unit I haven't resolved yet.

Role playing filled a real need in my class. A full year public speaking course, in my opinion, is too long, and it is extremely difficult to avoid periods of low interest and boredom when listening to the performance of individual speakers. Some type of group activity is a necessary part of this course, and I intend to use simulated court trials again next year.

JANELLE BARLOW 51

Game Simulation in U.S. History

Introduction

One of the most successful activities I have used during my first year of teaching has been role playing or *game simulation*. Students are assigned roles, sometimes vaguely and sometimes quite specifically, within a particular framework. Generally a specific problem is outlined for the game, though many times the students can be left to determine for themselves the limits of their activity.

I have found that when a student is asked to role-play instances that are outside his ordinary daily activities, not only can he learn certain facts and institutional arrangements, but he can also discover his own values and draw the kinds of relationships which are meaningful only when he makes them for himself.

Social studies provides a host of opportunities for this kind of activity, which takes on added value when the student realizes that his high school social studies class can be exciting. Certain aspects of game simulation are closely related to the concept of discovery learning— that is, in Bruner's terms, "discovery of regularities of previously unrecognized relations and similarities between ideas, with a resulting sense of self-confidence in one's abilities."[1] One of the more exciting "discoveries" happened when a notorious low ability student indicated to me that the large states which have more votes in a convention can control outcomes. The simplicity of this statement is evident once stated, but discovering this fact while participating in an actual political nominating convention was important for that particular person.

Evaluation of the results of a game simulation is the most difficult aspect of this kind of activity. One might think that constructing the situation might be the most taxing, but in the final analysis, the question that the teacher must constantly be posing deals with the understand-

[1] Jerome S. Bruner, *The Process of Education* (Cambridge, Mass.: Harvard University Press, 1961), p. 20.

ing acquired by his students. Since people learn in different fashions, and learn different items at different rates, evaluation is a particularly difficult task in role-playing situations, where all students are reacting, both *to* the group and *within* the group.

The only generalization that can be offered is that each different kind of game simulation must be evaluated in a manner related to the particular game. For example, some situations are best evaluated through written work based on the knowledge the student is expected to have acquired. Those game situations interested in articulating values can perhaps best be evaluated by discussing the values in question. In some instances a simple question asked of a group can make the group aware of the purposes of the game, and can make the individuals aware that they have participated in a learning experience. (One very important aspect of role playing is making the student recognize that he is in a learning situation. If he looks upon the game as merely being fun, his attitude toward the role-playing situation and the total class can change, and the student may become a discipline problem.) Some evaluations can best be achieved through observation of the students' actions while they participate in the game. And, of course, some game situations are best evaluated through a combination of the above.

Game Simulation Theory Problems
(Some Tested Examples)

This section is divided into three subsections: historical simulation, institutional simulation, and current social problems simulation. One point should be made before dealing with specific examples. Novato High School has a modified team teaching program. Not only is there a large group lecture hall, but there is also a great deal of interaction between the member teachers in the social studies department. Consequently, it is relatively easy to get large numbers of students available for game simulations. Although it is not always necessary to have large numbers of students for many role-playing situations, sheer numbers can sometimes have a positive effect upon the activity.

Historical Simulation

The first experience I had with game simulation this year occurred on the sophomore level. I arranged for a simulation of the open democratic forum debate between Melian citizens as they decided whether to fight Athens or submit to her power during the Peloponnesian Wars. Appendix A is an outline of this activity I arranged for in a lecture hall situation. Cooperation among teachers was fantastic; one teacher saw so much in the Melian-Athenian dialogue that she spent one whole period discussing it.

Several important results were noted. First, although this particular activity was received with tremendous success in the lecture hall, the conclusion reached by all involved teachers was that this activity could also be handled in individual classrooms. Many students participated to an unprecedented degree—low-track students as much as the upper-level ones. When the debate had been concluded and the vote taken, the students were asked if this was a good way to make a decision. For each class, the answer was a resounding "No!" I think many of them were shocked to discover that a "pure" direct democracy has some severe limitations.

This event was reported by the students to their parents as the most outstanding event of the year to date. The impression was significant; students discovered their own values, the values—and actions—of their fellow students, and learned factually of a situation they had hitherto not known about. This last point proved to be very significant, for many students argued in the open debate that the battle must be fought for the sake of future generations.

Only four or five pupils out of about six hundred had heard of Melos before entering the classroom.

Institutional Simulation

I have used several activities in which the primary purpose of the participating students was to enable them to see firsthand the mechanics and structure of the institution in question. The following activities were among several I set up for senior government classes.

1. *Congress.* The mock Congress used in

three separate classes was set up according to the desires of each class. Two classes chose to be the Senate and one the House. Bills were then exchanged between the various classes. Each student became either a Democrat or a Republican.

Considerable time was spent explaining the procedure involved in having bills become laws. John F. Kennedy's aid to education bill was traced through Congress. At each point that something needed clarification, I felt free to break in and explain the point at issue. At the beginning of each period, I discussed the previous day's events.

This activity proved to be highly successful for purposes of evaluation. A small objective test and essay were assigned. The students were asked to take one of the bills used in class and explain why that particular piece of legislation would or would not get through the 1966 Congress. Also, on the basis of class discussion, I was able to determine that many students had learned for themselves several important facts about Congress: that extremely controversial pieces of legislation are almost doomed in committees; that the bulk of the work accomplished in Congress takes place in committees; that the chairmen of committees have almost unlimited power; and that the Rules Committee is an extremely important link in the House.

As a side benefit the students underwent a rigorous introduction to parliamentary procedure. I have since been talked into setting up a successful school club with the purpose of teaching parliamentary procedure.

2. *Political convention.* This activity created the greatest amount of active participation among the students. The entire senior class was involved for a period of four days. The first day was spent explaining what goes on at a political convention, and having the students choose the particular state they wanted to represent. Not all states were represented, but each state had at least six members on its rolls. A committee of four from each period was selected to choose committee members and convention officials. The second day was spent with the students role-playing in their committees, holding caucuses, or meeting with their states. (Examples of the directions to each committee can be found in Appendix B.) Since the convention involved about three classes for each period, the success of the activity depended upon the cooperation of the other government teachers. (Once again it should be noted that this activity does not require a team teacher effort. This past summer I conducted a similar activity with only twenty-six students.)

The convention played was for the Republican Party, and students were asked to choose possible candidates for the nomination. Although some students wished to play the Democratic Party, this suggestion was rejected because it was thought that the Republican Party offered more choice this year (1967).

Two days were allowed for the actual convention. Very few limitations were imposed upon student action. Bass drums were allowed, Hawaiian representatives "hulaed" up and down the aisles; special clothing and accents were acquired. The more capable and more vocal students were given key assignments, though by no means was anyone barred from talking. The participation of almost everyone was quite evident.

Evaluting this activity proved challenging. My three classes spent an additional day evaluating the convention as an efficient and appropriate means of nominating the presidential candidates. A sheet containing brief statements about conventions was distributed. Arguments pro and con were listed on the board, and then some attempt at fusing them was made. The general conclusion reached was that the U.S. party system and national nominating conventions complement each other. That is, the decentralized nature of American political parties dictates the means for nominating candidates.

Current Social Problem Simulation

The social problem handled was that of integration of a white neighborhood by a black family. The activity was handled entirely in each separate classroom, though there was interaction between the classes. The purpose of this activity was to make the students aware of a current problem and allow them to discover whether they could solve this kind of problem. The students involved were juniors in U.S. History; the unit being discussed was that of Black History. This idea originated with one of my colleagues, though I was instrumental in carrying it out.

Each student was handed a printed sheet containing information about a situation involving a black family moving into an all-white neighborhood. (See Appendix C.) Those students interested in joining the Protect Property Values Association (PPVA) were invited to an organizational meeting in one of the classrooms. A civil rights group was established, as was a PTA. The more capable students were asked to be the real estate company that sold the property, a local Chamber of Commerce President, and a local city councilman.

After planned action by the various groups and individuals, the students were asked to resolve the problem by any means. The majority of the class could only engage in emotional debate; one group went so far as to stage a sit-down strike. The referee that period then arrested the students and one of the vacated classrooms became a jail. Several newspaper articles and propaganda sheets were printed and distributed.

The following day an additional element was introduced into the game. The local "newspaper" reported that the black family's home had been attacked and the real estate men had received threatening phone calls. It became quite apparent that three of the four U.S. History classes were unable to solve their problem. The class that was successful had set up negotiators representing each side. These negotiators met in private conferences.

The classes that had failed to resolve the problem were set up for discussions primarily centering around the questions: Why was the group unable to resolve the problem? Is it likely that a problem of this type can ever be solved?

Evalution of this activity was exceedingly difficult, though there was a majority agreement that time was well spent. As a teacher, I was able to view emotions and values that later proved invaluable as the unit on Black History progressed. We did encounter some difficulty with adverse public opinion. Apparently, two telephone calls were made to the principal's office, condemning the use of the school for demonstration purposes. We countered by calling the local newspaper, which then wrote a laudatory letter praising the use of game simulation as a learning device.

Game Simulation Theory Problems
(Proposed Examples)

I have three additional major game simulations planned for the remainder of the year. A Supreme Court case is going to be held while the class covers a unit on civil and human rights.

A subsequent activity will involve students with the local Novato City Council. The council has agreed to set up four city governments—one for each period in which government classes meet—allowing the students to solve some local problems and propose a master plan for Novato's future. The actual involvement of students in local government should acquaint them with their community's particular governmental problems, and should allow the students to form hypotheses about urban problems in general. A series of important readings are to accompany the activity.

The final major game simulation planned for the year is an international game. My plans are vague as yet; tentatively, I plan to have students choose nations to represent. Each day that the students are negotiating with each other, new items will be interjected into the game. It is hoped that some awareness of the implications of nations' actions, the complexities and the pressures of modern-day politics will be recognized by the students.

Conclusions

After six months of teaching, I have noted that role playing is one of the more successful devices for getting students to the point where they are not only capable but also willing, indeed eager, to draw their own conclusions. Let me, however, warn the beginning teacher who attempts to duplicate these situations in his own classroom. I have been quite successful in innovating new ideas in Novato High School's Social Studies Department, and have considerable support from faculty members, including the department chairman. *If this support were not apparent, I might have hesitated to conduct such boisterous activities.*

LECTURE HALL GROUP ACTIVITY FOR THURSDAY

Suggested Procedure

I. Group activity

    A. The group activity in the lecture hall would simulate the open democratic forum debate between the Melian citizens on the question of whether Melos should fight for honor against the Athenians and lose, or submit to colonization by Athens and thereby save themselves.

    B. The success of this debate will depend on what is accomplished in the sections and how actively the X classes can be inspired. The following outline is recommended:

MONDAY. Review in the sections the History of the Peloponnesian War. This should not take too long and would be just one activity on that day.

TUESDAY. Each student should choose the role of a particular kind of citizen. It is assumed that citizenship will have already been discussed. The girls—because of their general verbal superiority at this age—should also be allowed to choose roles, as long as these are male roles. The student should be aware of the "vested interests" of the role he has chosen.

The students should begin work this evening deciding which stand they will argue for. It might be a good idea to have them come up with a tentative written argument.

WEDNESDAY (THE NEXT WEEK). The dialogue between the Athenians and the Melians should be read in the sections. It might be necessary to explain the dialogue to Y classes. Each argument could be covered in class. Debate and Discussion should *not* take place in the section. Save this for the lecture hall.

THURSDAY. The dialogue should be reread at the beginning of the class and then the debate should commence in an open democratic forum. At the conclusion of the period a final vote should be taken, and the students should be told how the actual decision was made.

II. Purposes

    A. This group activity should enable the students to use the lecture hall in a direct participation manner.

    B. The brighter students will also have the opportunity to demonstrate their skills.

    C. Parallels of this activity to current world problems and to the theme of this course—the individual's relation to authority—are also present.

    D. The students will see how the open democratic forum operated and they will also realistically see the historical events of the Peloponnesian Wars.

PLATFORM COMMITTEE

Members:

Chairman:_____

Duties: Draw up the party platform and recommend that it be adopted by the convention. The chairman of your group should be prepared to announce the decisions of your committee to the convention floor.

You might want to address yourself to the following items:

Civil Rights	Social welfare programs
Inflation	The importance of the individual
Taxes	in America

Vietnam	Foreign policy in general
Military defense	Crime
China	Education

U.S. HISTORY: INTEGRATED NEIGHBORHOOD GAME*

You are a resident of Sunny Hills, a suburban neighborhood in Megalopolis, a major American city. Homes in Sunny Hills are ten years old at the very most. Current market prices range from $23,000 to $32,000.

Most houses are painted in pleasant pastel shades and all have well-kept lawns, shrubs, flowers, and trees. Utilities are underground; sidewalks and streets are all paved and well maintained.

Almost all the houses are occupied by people under the age of fifty. Almost all homes have twenty- to thirty-year mortgages.

Recently, a $23,000 home on Arrowhead Drive was sold. Last week, neighbors noticed a black family moving some furniture into the home. Two days ago, a circular was placed at every door in the neighborhood. It read as follows:

Protect Your Investment

1. Do you want to protect your most important investment?
2. Do you want to keep property values high?
3. Do you want your neighborhood to maintain high standards in education and community development?
4. Do you want to be able to live in a distinctive community?

If you answer *yes* to all these questions, come to a Protect Property Values Association (PPVA) meeting tomorrow room 32, periods 4 and 5; room 33, periods 7 and 8.

Groups and Individuals Involved

1. Leaders of PPVA
2. Real estate company which made transaction. (A partnership of three real estate brokers who knowingly sold the house to the black family. There has been an unwritten understanding among Sunny Hills real estate men that houses would be sold only to Caucasians.)
3. Megalopolis Council of Civil Rights Organizations. (Five years ago, Megalopolis civil rights groups—CORE, NAACP, SNCC, and the Urban League—agreed to merge their efforts in a united front. Efforts of the MCCRO have included city legislation creating a police review board, redrawing school boundaries, and two well-publicized demonstrations in a local department store and bank in order to encourage equal employment.)
4. The PTA (a typical school PTA)
5. President of the Sunny Hills Junior Chamber of Commerce
6. Megalopolis City Councilman from Sunny Hills

* The idea for this game originated with a colleague of mine—J.B.

Drama in Foreign Language

Instructional material is well outlined in the table of contents of any Spanish book. The teacher of Spanish can look at the contents and be able to form his weekly and daily lesson plans. How the material can most effectively be taught, however, is a totally different matter. Although foreign language teachers may be well aware of the various available methods, such as daily dialogues and repetition of grammar drills, they must all explore other more imaginative ways to have students learn a foreign language. For this reason, I designed a few teaching strategies which have proved useful in my second year Spanish classes. (Of course, these were only supplementary to standard methods.)

Strategies Used

I began with having students present to the class descriptions of people. In this assignment, I did nothing more than to tell the students to bring to class pictures of people who were interesting to them and to prepare a three minute speech about these people. They presented the speeches and pictures to the class the next day. Their reaction to this exercise was very positive. Some students gave informative speeches; others related themselves to the people in their pictures by imitating them. The students enjoyed speaking and acting in the Spanish language. This exercise we later performed every two weeks.

The second part of my strategy was to have students rewrite scenes from a book and to perform them in class. The scenes were taken from *Graded Spanish Readers, Books I–V* (published by Heath). I divided the class into five groups. Each group chose a scene from the novel *El Periquillo Sarniento*. I gave the groups fifteen minutes each day, for a week, to work on rewriting the scenes. The groups handed in to me a preliminary copy of their scene; I corrected it and gave it back to the students. During the second week, the groups met fifteen minutes daily to practice their scenes. By the third week the groups were ready to act five scenes spoken in Spanish. This intrigued the students; they were eager to learn vocabulary and to live the life of the "picaro" Periquillo.

The students became so involved in dramatizing that they asked permission to create their own skits and to present the skits to other Spanish classes. I then chose directors who were interested in writing a play and in directing a group of students to perform it. This time the students had more time to perfect their plays because the plays were more extensive. Some of the plays that were written ranged from simple adaptations of television programs, or of "Smokey the Bear" and "The Three Little Pigs," to an adaptation of one of Cervantes' *Entremeses*. The success of this activity can be evaluated only by the fact that the students were willing to perform their work for other classes and for parents during an Open House Night. It should be noted that in this part of my strategy the students were left very much on their own. They were not satisfied with the time they were allowed in class; so they met further during lunchtime.

The fourth part of the strategy was to have an advanced class create a trial. The two best students were chosen to act as lawyers for the prosecution and the defense. The prosecution wrote a general description of the crime; this was dittoed and given to the rest of the students. The various roles of witnesses, jury, policeman, clerk, and judge were assigned by the two lawyers. Each lawyer met with his group of witnesses. They worked two weeks preparing their cases. In class they were allowed to meet in groups during the last ten or fifteen minutes of the class. The trial was presented on the third week; it lasted two hours.

I have tried to give the reader an insight about the possibility of using drama in the classroom. I believe it is important for foreign language teachers to supplement their material with the use of drama. It is important because it gives the students an opportunity to learn by living the language. I am very pleased with the results obtained from using drama with my classes; I saw students actually enjoy learning Spanish.

CLASSROOM GAMES

BONNIE MATHISEN **53**

Games for Math

A former mathematics teacher now teaching science remarked that math is such a boring, dull subject to teach: "It is all the same. There is no variety." I have discovered many students also feel this way about mathematics. Therefore a math teacher must be especially careful not to fall into a dull and unimaginative routine.

My efforts are directed more and more to showing students that math really is fun—that math class can be an exciting place.

The textbooks at our school do not emphasize the more fascinating aspects of mathematics; they are not fun. Therefore as a teacher, I have sought supplementary materials, devices, and techniques to remove the fears of my students about math, to catch their attention, and to spark their imagination. I have accumulated some useful ideas and am searching for more.

The following pages illustrate techniques I have tried on upper middle-class seventh- and eighth-grade students. They have worked well; I am confident they can serve as springboards to better and even more effective ideas.

Mathematics Laboratory for Experiments

Have the students do experiments in class. They can work alone, in pairs, or occasionally in small groups. For one experiment, the students copied plane figures, dissected them, and rearranged them to form squares. We then expanded and tried to find the areas contained in triangles, parallelograms, trapezoids, and other figures. The actual work with the figures helped the students understand the meaning of area and relate the new geometric forms to the familiar square and rectangle.

For another experiment, make polyhedrons

after a unit on solids. Use Tangrams. Do picture graphs after you have discussed graphing. Give the students points to plot which when connected will make a picture. If they can, give them equations of line segments which when graphed make a picture. Then encourage the students to create their own graphs.

Do line designs in a geometry unit. Seventh and eighth graders love them. Don't limit yourself to your own ideas—borrow them from books, magazines, and other teachers. The reward for the time it takes to get started and to set up the experiments will be the enthusiasm and the increased understanding of the students. Be careful to set up each experiment so the student can do it himself. Then, step out of the picture and let him solve the problem.

I hope to structure my class as a mathematics laboratory for at least one quarter next year.

Think Sheets

These are fun sheets with logic problems, algebra problems, magic squares, topology, and other puzzles. Have them to work on after tests or to spark up the week. These are not for grades, just for fun.

Contests

Arithmetic races or arithmetic baseball are good, especially for review of computational skills. I "pitch" the problem to the batter, who must solve the problem correctly for a base hit. If he solves the problem before anyone else in the class fields it, by solving it, he has a home run. Seventh graders especially enjoy this competition.

Games

Play Matho-Bongo. Have the students number bingo-type cards. Make up, beforehand, problems which when solved will equal the numbers on their cards. Problems can be made to stress the unit you are covering. Play for rows, corners, and whole card.

Make up cross number games. Let the students make up the clues and have the class solve the puzzles.

Ask your school to purchase games such as *Instant Insanity, Pythagoras, Euclid,* and many others.

Dice

Buy a pair of dice. There are a variety of games which can be adapted to learning situations. One game is to build numbers based on the roll of the dice. Specify the number of digits. (Example: ⬚⬚⬚⬚⬚.⬚) Roll the dice. Each student puts the number rolled in whichever square he chooses. The object of the game varies. The students may compete to create the largest number or the smallest number. This can be expanded to the largest even or odd number, the largest multiple of 3, etc. I use it to emphasize, reinforce, or introduce new topics. The game works beautifully for teaching place value. Move the decimal point back and forth and play games to create the largest or smallest number. When working on different bases, create the largest number, base eight or base seven. For the slow students, the adding of the dice is good practice, and again, the students love it.

Reflection Sheets

Be a human teacher. Have discussions in class. Mathematics is often thought of as an impersonal subject. Discussion can help to establish a rapport between students and teacher that might not otherwise exist.

Find out about your students. In math this is sometimes difficult. I use reflection sheets to give students an opportunity on Friday to tell what they did not understand in math for the week. They can write what they liked or disliked about the class, what they have done that they are proud of, or how they disappointed themselves or others. This gives them a chance to reflect about the week and what they have accomplished. It also gives them the opportunity to communicate with you on an individual basis, and affords you the opportunity to respond.

Conclusion

I have seen two major problems as a beginning teacher. One is getting the student interested enough in the subject to want to learn. The second is developing an accurate means of evaluating a student's day-to-day learning rate and comprehension. I tend to believe that my students understand more than they actually do.

The above techniques are helping me solve both of these problems. My students are involved and discovering all by themselves. They are excited when they are playing games, and ready to learn so they can get their Bingo square or "hit" in baseball.

All of these techniques require action by the student and all I need do as a teacher is watch the action carefully. It is then possible to better discern where there are gaps in the students' understanding. Watching them provides me with immediate feedback.

These techniques also offer variety important in any classroom, and especially in mathematics, where so much variety is possible.

Bibliography

1. Eason, Oliver. *Graphing Pictures*. Portland, Maine: J. Weston Walch, 1966.
2. Pearcy, J. F. F., and K. Lewis. *Experiments in Mathematics Stage 1, Stage 2, and Stage 3*. Boston: Houghton Mifflin Company, 1966.
3. Seymour, Dale G., and Richard B. Gidley. *Eureka*. Palo Alto, California: Eureka Publications, 1967.
4. Seymour, Dale G., and Snider. *Line Designs*. Palo Alto, California: Creative Publications, 1966.

RITA SCHLAUDT **54**

Gamesmanship, or How to Survive Friday Afternoons

Description

The problem was a matter of control on Friday afternoons. It was aggravated by two scheduling factors which were not changeable and one factor of my own making. Vallecito Junior High School in San Rafael runs on a modified core system for its four hundred white, upper middle-class, suburban students. That means each teacher has a "home room" and the same students for at least three out of eight periods (history, English, and reading, in my case). My problem class was English, which follows an elective activity period (golf, knitting, Broadway Musical, etc.) and a lunch period followed by games. As a result, the kids are usually six feet off the ground during English class, and Fridays are especially frantic.

I chose Fridays as test days because tests require some concentration and enforced control. The problem was, however, what to do with those students (my class is a heterogeous one of thirty) who finished early. The following approaches were tried with little or no success:

1. "Read a book" or "Study." (Didn't bring book, or "...on Friday afternoon?!?")
2. "Do homework." (Homework, per se, is frowned on by the principal, and I rarely assign it over the weekend.)
3. "Get a head start on next week's assignment." (The kids who finished first usually didn't need it.)
4. "Go to the library." (Well, they were sent back. After all, the librarian has to survive, too.)
5. "Free write." (This worked, but it was such a valuable idea exchange and composition tool that I hated to see the slow finishers deprived of the opportunity.)
6. "Shut up." (This, of course, worked least well.)

All the above strategies achieved were hard feelings and frustration. I tried moving testing to other days, and planning my most scintillating lecture or discussion (an unqualified flop) or showing *the* great film short on Fridays. (There aren't that many great shorts, and word got out about Friday Film day, and so did control.)

Then, one Friday after a test, I saw two students playing a word game called "Hangman." They were so intent that they ignored me as I sauntered by in teacherly strides. "Well!" And then I thought, "Well, why not?" So, for the last few minutes the entire class played "Hangman." One of the words used, to my surprise, came straight off the spelling list of that week. Therefore, finding a way to capitalize on the game idea(s) and to relate that game, however tenuously, to what we were learning became the survival strategy for Friday afternoons.

Materials

The following is a descriptive sampling of games used in my class which may be creatively "adapted" or pilfered at will for use in others.

1. *Word puzzles, scrambles, anagrams:* All these games use words we've had in class, gussied up in puzzle form. This can work in reverse, too. Given words, make your own puzzle to stump your neighbors.

a. *Word puzzles*

_ _ _ _ _ _ _ _	Use of harsh-sounding words
_ _ _ _ _ _ _	Ability to take in or hold
_ _ _ _ _ _ _ _ _	What someone does for a living

b. *Scrambles*

U O S H N D	_ _ _ _ _ _ _	Name of river in U.S.
R U S E O P R I	_ _ _ _ _ _ _	Name of lake in Africa

c. *Anagrams. Add to each word the letter at the end to form a new word.*

I D E A with S _ _ _ _ _ _
V E A L with G _ _ _ _ _ _

2. *Crossword puzzles:* These are always good when there's nothing else available. *Read Magazine, Scholastic Scope, Current Events,* and *Practical English* are good sources. Also, Scholastic Book Club puts out several good collections of puzzles. Some of the more able kids will enjoy making up their own, using vocabulary words or words from the history chapters assigned that week.

3. *Initial game:* The idea came from *Read Magazine's* "Language at Play" section, and can be adapted for use in either history or English classes. We played it during the 1968 presidential campaign. You take the initials of candidates and make up a slogan which says something about the candidate. Examples given to the class were:

Harry S. Truman (HST)—"Had Some Temper"
Abraham Lincoln (AL)—"Assassinated Leader"

The best sample my class found was for George C. Wallace—"Get Cops Working."

4. *"Guru says":* This game was inspired by the book *The Raft,* a dull book popular with the kids. It uses the art of writing proverbs. Starting with one character's "God helps them who help themselves" we updated proverbs with our own Guru sayings. Examples: "He who hits older brother gets hit back." Guru says, "He who eats eye of lizard expects acid indigestion." Guru says, "He who skis backward runs into tree."

5. *Rigmarole:* This, too comes from *The Raft.* Once when we stumbled over a tongue-twisting passage we stopped to give examples of great twisters (try "six thick thistles"). The next Friday out came the ditto with "Rigmaroles" or counting twisters. Everyone wrote at least one sample (from one to ten, making each line alliterative with the number). The best were dittoed off and read aloud on Monday. We also made up others on the spot, and tried to listen carefully to repeat each line in correct sequence.

Examples: One old octopus oozing oil
Two trilling teenagers tripping through the tulips

6. *Potato power:* This game followed a grammar lesson on nouns or nominals and a reading of Lewis Carroll's "Jabberwocky." To play the game, take a noun (like "potato") and substitute it in all the sayings, commercials, ads, or graffiti you can think of in place of the given noun.

Examples: "Take a potato to lunch"
"Potato power"
"And so's your potato"
"Potatoes—when you care enough to send the very best"
"Things go better with potatoes"

7. *"Similies":* The game is to write imaginative comparisons, using *like* or *as* to introduce the phrase. Give several examples of funny similies and encourage class to write their own. Example: "As funny as a flood in a fizzie factory."

8. *"Who Am I?"* Another oral game on the order of "What's My Line" and "Twenty Questions." Kids assume the identity of one of the "people to remember" in the history text and try to stump a panel of experts (usually four). Each panel member has two questions to ask, but one wrong guess ("Are you Alexander Hamilton?" "No.") results in forfeit. The game can be adapted to English classes, using fictional characters or authors.

9. *Punny-punny:* In our election study in history we ran across a cartoon in which Agnew remarks to Nixon: "Don't worry, Dick, we're a shoe in." So history turned to English and what puns were, and on Friday out came the ditto sheet with examples of funny puns, or punny-punnys. Puns were beyond some of the class, but those who wrote their own got together to judge them on a knee-slapping scale (with five knee-slaps at the high end).

10. *John Underwood:* This is one just for fun, found in another teacher's typewriter and hidden away for a Friday afternoon when patience and inspiration run out before the clock. Given the letter below left (which was supposedly delivered by the Post Office to John Underwood, Andover, Mass.), figure out the well-known phrases in the samples below. If there is time, make your own samples.

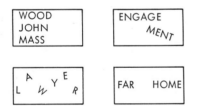

The strategy was twofold: get control and relate the controlling technique to the learning experience. Games were quite effective on both counts.

There were a few questions when I introduced the games. Some wanted to know if they "had" to do it. I said that I would like them to try. Almost all did, and it became a matter of routine to get a game ditto after finishing the quiz. The room was relatively quiet, control was established, and Fridays became just another day in the week. The games were collected but not graded. If the game was open-ended, calling for their contributions, I gave a check or plus. Also, I made a point of always summarizing the best samples on a ditto to hand back to the class on Monday. Kids were delighted to see their work in print, and were anxious to share the games with classmates, kids in other classes, and even parents. They brought in their own games, which we promptly used.

Many of the game ideas were so "hot" that we did not wait for Friday for an official ditto, but did them on the spot. In addition, the game idea proved useful the day before the big dance or field trip or whenever the normal lesson proved unworkable.

Not all the games grew out of, or were related to, the curriculum (even as wide and flexible as mine is). Many were just for fun, a way to "amuse them today," as Christopher Robin would say. They were, however, a positive learning experience which could be shared. And I guess that's the name of the game.

How to Spice Up an Old Enchilada

Nothing is more uninspiring to a teacher or her students than a dull, colorless textbook. The so-called audio-lingual approach to Spanish is just what it claims to be and no more. Not only is our A-LM text lacking in visual interest; it undermines any interest in the written page by its constant repetitions and drills.

One of my main challenges these first few months has been to try to enrich the A-LM approach so that a high level of student interest and motivation could be maintained. By the time students reach their third and fourth years of Spanish, as they have in my classes, they have generally attained an admirable mastery of Spanish pronunciation, but are generally bored with the same old learn-by-drill technique. I have listed below several strategies which have proven quite successful in alleviating the boredom of the A-LM routine and in motivating mastery of necessary skills.

Contests are usually highly motivating; my students are always eager for them. The class is normally divided into two or more teams, which are determined each by different physical factors. For instance, the boys may team up against the girls, the brunettes against the blondes, the tall students against the short ones, the ones with dark eyes against the ones with light eyes, or one side (or row) of the room against the other(s). This variety in the composition of the teams does seem to have a positive effect on the participation of the students. Most of the contents I've used have been at the board. The students are given a verb to conjugate, a word or phrase to translate, a problem in agreement of subject and verb or noun and adjective, or some other short question. Whichever of the two students at the board is first to answer correctly two out of three questions wins a point for his team.

(Often the winning team members each receive a lemon drop or some other small prize.)

Spelling bees and Password, both played in Spanish, have also proved instructional as well as fun. The spelling bees are very good for reviewing recent vocabulary words and the names and pronunciation of the letters of the alphabet in Spanish. Password serves the dual purpose of forcing the students to think in Spanish and helping them to enlarge their vocabularies.

I have found it very helpful, as the students are coming into the classroom, to put some question, problem, or riddle on the board for them to work on while I take roll. For instance, I may scramble the letters of some Spanish words or proper names—for example, the capital cities of the Latin American countries—for them to unscramble. Or there may be several words on the board in no particular order with which they are to construct a sentence. Occasionally I write one long word in Spanish on the board, and they are to make as many small words in Spanish from it as they can. Once I listed several words in English on the board, and as a prize for telling me the Spanish for each word, I excused the winning student from that night's homework assignment.

Bingo (or Lotería in Spanish) is very good for teaching numbers. Each student who wins receives a lemon drop or similar treat, and then he calls the numbers until someone else wins. The game can also be played with words from a particular unit or vocabulary list. Hangman (La Horca) is very good for teaching letters of the alphabet. Crossword puzzles and a jumbled word game have also proven successful in reviewing words. (See Appendix.)

A final strategy which most of my students thoroughly enjoy is that of singing songs in Spanish. It's a wonderful way to introduce the

Spanish culture, and the students can pick up many new words. They also enjoy learning the words in Spanish to a song already known in English. (See Appendix.)

The strategies I have included here have excited me because they have excited my students and shown them that learning another language can be meaningful and fun.

Appendix

SONGS LEARNED IN SPANISH CLASS

Round

Mi gallo se murió ayer (repetir)
Ya no cantará co-co-ri co-co-rá, (repetir)
Co-co-ri-co-ri co-co-ri-co-rá. (repetir)

Mi Querida Catalina (O My Darling Clementine)

Un minero en una mina
Una hija poseía,
Era bella y era fina
Mi querida Catalina.

Era esbelta pues en kilos
De noventa no pasaba,
Y su piececito chico
El nueve y medio calzaba.
De mañana muy temprano
Con sus patos se paseaba
Por las orillas del río
Pero nunca se banaba.

Me miraba, se reía
Y por verme tropezó.
Las burbujas si salían,
Pero Catalina no.

CROSSWORD PUZZLE

1 Y	2 O	3 S	4 O	5 Y	▨	6 P	7 A	8 N
9 O	R	E	J	A	10 S	▨	11 L	A
12 C	A	R	O	▨	13 I	Z	A	R
14 A	C	A	▨	15 O	N	▨	16 B	I
17 N	I	▨	18 T	I	▨	19 V	E	Z
20 T	O	21 M	A	R	22 I	A	N	▨
23 A	N	I	S	▨	24 P	R	▨	25 D
26 R	E	▨	27 C	28 A	S	A	29 D	A
30 E	S	P	A	N	O	L	E	S

Across
1. I am (2 words)
6. Bread
9. Ears
11. Article
12. Dear
13. Tonight
14. Here
15. Argumentative suffix
16. Two (combined form)
17. Neither
18. Personal pronoun
19. Time
20. They would take

23. Sweet liqueur
24. Introduction to a written book, (abbr.)
26. Prefix meaning repetition
27. Married
30. Spain's citizens

Down
1. I shall sing (two words)
2. Prayers
3. He will be
4. Eye

5. Already
7. Form of
8. Part of the face
10. Without
15. To hear
18. Cheap restaurant
19. Long pole
21. My
22. _____ facto (by the fact itself; Latin)
25. (You) give
28. Verb ending
29. Preposition

VI: USES OF MEDIA AND TECHNICAL EQUIPMENT

Language master machine helps students learn correct German pronunciations. University Demonstration Secondary School, Oakland, California.

There is a world of difference between the modern home environment of integrated electric information and the classroom. Today's television child is attuned to up-to-the-minute "adult" news—inflation, rioting, war, taxes, crime, bathing beauties—and is bewildered when he enters the nineteenth-century environment that still characterizes the educational establishment where information is scarce but ordered and structured by fragmented, classified patterns, subjects, and schedules. . . .[1]

From all the emphasis in recent years on educational technology and media, one might assume that today's classrooms have been inundated by the technological revolution affecting the rest of our society. But although there are occasional evidences of some of the new technical equipment—teaching machines, educational television, videotapes, language labs, films, and so forth—many teachers remain glued to more traditional tools—blackboard, chalk, paper, pencil, textbooks, and teacher talk. Yet students obviously learn not only from these usual means, but from sights, sounds, tactile experiences— from movies, popular music, from television, magazines, and daily newspapers. Why should not teachers take advantage of *all* these means for extending and enhancing academic learning?

In this section we have included a few simple models for using technical equipment and the media to meet instructional problems more effectively.

Pictures, Photographs (Still and Moving)

We begin with an uncomplicated, easily replicable strategy. In "A Visual Approach to Vocabulary," Judy Chambers describes her use of pictures from popular magazines to illustrate and teach vocabulary. Having read Miss Chambers' strategy, Jessica Stanley was able to build on it and adapt it for uses in her own classroom. Her paper "Photographed Vocabulary," shows how she used the camera and photographs of students to extend her pupils' stock of words and abstract concepts. Marcia Johnston, in her strategy "Using Collages with Literature," explains how she encouraged her low achieving students to use visual means to communicate their understanding of literature. Robert Davis next demonstrates several ways to use pictures, both still and moving, as a compelling basis for a seventh-grade English program. His strategy, "Look and Write," indicates how relevant English can be when students study the subject in the context of contemporary television and films.

The Overhead Projector

In more and more classrooms today, teachers are finding the overhead projector a useful ally. For one thing, it allows the teacher to face his students while he is writing—an important consideration in some classes. Gretchen Bingham's Spanish class was one of these. We have included here her poignant description of an all too familiar ghetto classroom situation—a roomful of unmotivated, rebellious students in awkward physical surroundings, confronting a subject in which they see little relevance. In "Heavy Heavy Hangs Over Thy Overhead," Mrs. Bingham explains how her use of cartoons on the over-

[1] Marshall McLuhan and Quentin Fiore, *The Medium Is the Massage* (New York: Bantam Books, 1967), p. 18.

head projector helped solve some of her most overwhelming classroom problems. Mr. Sullivan, in his strategy, "Uses of the Overhead Projector for Teaching Geometry," describes several other ways to use the projector for greater flexibility in the presentation of course material—including its use as a tool for competitive classroom games.

Listening Posts and Tape Recorders

Also working with underachieving urban students, Stephen and Jacquelyn Brand describe the use they made of listening posts and tape recorders for motivating their classes of slow readers. Although setting up listening posts and taping appropriate materials takes time and careful planning, the results seem to justify the additional effort.

Popular Music in the Classroom

Anyone carefully observing the activities of today's students outside the school must be impressed with the hold that popular music has on them. Rock music has become the art form of this generation. Yet in most classrooms, teachers take little advantage of the opportunity such music offers for reaching students. Here we have included three different ways to use music in the classroom.

First, Michael Thatcher demonstrates his use of popular songs to teach a progressively more difficult unit on poetry. For example, by examining the thematic content, rhythm, and imagery of such popular songs as the Beatles' "Fool on the Hill," he brought his students to a genuine appreciation of poems like Wordsworth's sonnet, "The World Is Too Much With Us." Next, in his strategy, "Incorporating Music into the English Curriculum," Steven Ross details several kinds of writing assignments for which selected tapes and records of popular music can be used as stimuli—ranging from free association exercises to scenario script writing. He reports that with a combination of music and composition experiences, his class of average and below average English composition students—the kind who usually hate English—increased both their writing and listening abilities, and were extremely enthusiastic about the course.

Following this, we see how popular music can be used in social studies. For a class of eighth graders, in which the usual problems of motivation and control loomed large, Joseph Friedman decided to use popular songs as a motivating vehicle for teaching concepts about time and history. His strategy, "An Experiment in Time," explains how, beginning with songs like the Chambers Brothers' "The Time Has Come Today" and Otis Redding's "Sitting on the Dock of the Bay," the teacher can pleasurably demonstrate alternative responses individuals can make to their moment in history—attitudes either of active engagement, defeat, apathy, or sublime indifference.

Use of Advertisements in an Art Class

In her strategy, "Commercial Art: Unit for Continuation High School Students," Lois describes how she made her students conscious of the art items which fascinated them—the posters, car designs, clothes fashions, advertisements—all the art of Madison Avenue. By having them analyze the human emotions and values to which commercial art appeals—including an exercise in creating their own advertisements—she brought her pupils to a greater understanding both of their environment and of themselves.

Student-Produced Films

For teachers who have some mechanical aptitude and sufficient drive to use one of the most potent of all tools available for today's teacher, the student-made film we have included Kenneth Rosenberg and Edward Troy's brochure of directions for classroom filmmaking. Mr. Rosenberg started making films with junior high school English and French classes in his first year of teaching. These films proved so motivating for his students that he was asked to introduce cinematography courses in his school, and two years later to become the school district coordinator for cinematography programs at both the junior and senior high schools in his district.

Surely, in the years to come, more and more teachers will find important uses for mass media and technical equipment in extending their instructional efforts. Here we have only touched on the many possibilities awaiting the enterprising teacher. In the next chapter, "Teaching for Values, Concerns, Attitudes," and in Part Three, "Developing New School Programs and New Public School Models," there are further examples of ways to bring the world into the classroom and the classroom into the world.

PICTURES, PHOTOGRAPHS
(STILL AND MOVING)

JUDY CHAMBERS **56**

The Visual Approach to Vocabulary

Introduction

In the following paper I will attempt to explain a very simple and effective vocabulary technique—that of using pictures to reinforce vocabulary words. I have found this technique superior to rote memorization of words in that it engages the student actively in the discovery of words and gives him a concrete sense experience on which to base his association of word and meaning.

The technique of the visual approach to vocabulary is very flexible and readily adjustable to the level of a class. I teach one section of advanced sophomores and four sections of average ones, but the technique can be used with other grade levels with some minor adaptations.

Procedures with an Advanced Class

My advanced class already possesses a fairly large vocabulary. They are quick, aggressive, and responsive. For them I had a group of fourteen pictures—a picture of a model in an orange and magenta dress, posed against an equally bright background, to suggest "flamboyant"; a picture of a watermelon to suggest "succulent"; two women's profiles to introduce "juxtapose"; a dreamy young woman for "pensive"; etc. With the advanced class I merely held up the picture and let them guess the word that fit, in a free-for-all, "Twenty Questions" method. Usually the quiet students are engulfed by the louder in this type of situation. Student involvement reaches such a peak, however, that when the right word is finally associated with the picture, all who thought of it want recognition and inform you that they had already "thought of that." Also, since the instructor remains quiet during the guessing, it's possible "not to hear" the brighter students until one of the slower ones says the word. He or she then receives the immediate reinforcement of a "right" answer. It is often necessary to placate the brighter students with "I wanted to see if someone else knew it," but they understand and enthusiasm grows throughout the whole class.

It is also beneficial with a bright class to give the first letter of the word during the guessing period. This exercises their speaking vocabularies. For example, I held up the "pensive" picture and said it began with *p*. "Pining" and "poignant" immediately came forth, both good associations with "pensive."

At any rate, the brighter students love the activity and demand that they not be helped into finding the word. They often evaluate the aptness of the picture with the word and apply other vocabulary words that fit.

As a follow-up to the guessing, the words are put on the board and the students are to look up their meanings in a dictionary and write a sentence with each. Usually, they are stimulated enough to try including most of the words in a paragraph, an activity which they would not approach while I used the memorization method.

For My Average Classes

The technique used for my average classes is quite similar, except that I put the list of words on the board before we begin. I'm not sure of the efficacy of this. My reasons for doing it are the following: (1) the class would become quickly frustrated if they had to draw the correct word from their own vocabularies; and (2) there are words with which the class is totally unfamiliar, such as "euphemist." If they are staring at such a word during the guess period, they become curious about it before its picture appears, and the connection between word and meaning seems more effective as a consequence.

It is best to go through the list orally with the whole class, pronouncing the words before you begin the guessing session. This way they are not so shy about saying them out loud.

Of course, having the words on the board can lead to random guessing, merely for the chance of being right. If I think a student was lucky, I ask him why he associated the word with the picture. I ask if anyone in the class can tell why, for instance, the picture of two people dining together in a penthouse "means" *intimate*. Someone will then come up with, "Well, they're alone together and it's *cozy* and *friendly*"; thus the connotations are established.

With my average classes, once the word has been correctly guessed, I put its meaning on the board in the vernacular, rather than in "dictionarese." The students appreciate this very much; dictionaries confuse them, for they only add unfamiliar words to define the original unfamiliar one.

When I grope to define a word in the vernacular, the students are drawn to define it themselves. When I overdefine one, they insist on a concise meaning.

It is beneficial in these sessions to run a loose class. A show of hands need not be strictly enforced, as it inhibits. Some of the best definitions come from the unconscious verbal associations of the students. It is doubly reinforcing

for them to verbally conjecture about the uses of the word and to be praised for it. ("Flamboyant? Oh, you mean like Mod clothes are *flamboyant*?" "Exactly." etc.)

The average class follow-up is almost the same as the follow-up with the advanced class. They copy words and definitions and then make a sentence with each. I then display the words of the week on the bulletin board, with their meanings printed below them. There they are assimilated through preclass tours of the room and pencil sharpening trips.

Testing

The testing method I use is orthodox. One method is to give the students a mimeographed list of the words and a paragraph with appropriate blanks left for the words. This tests comprehension of meaning. Another method involves administering the test orally. I read a sentence, substituting a blank for the correct word. The student is then to write the word on his paper. This tests both his comprehension of meaning and his spelling, and is the more difficult of the two methods. I have also used matching word with meaning and multiple choice. I prefer the more thorough method of comprehension in context.

One incident remains in my mind about this method. I was talking with Bill, one of the slowest, most conscientious students I have. We were looking at something, and I was telling him an anecdote, unrelated to vocabulary. He stopped me and said, "That reminds me of one of our vocabulary words. The one with all the blue and two people all alone having dinner— *intimate*, that's what it is!" I was delighted with his associations, and with the successful aid to his memory that the recall of the picture had provided.

I have found the visual vocabulary technique extremely effective. The students look forward to the sessions and demand pictures now. Their comprehension has improved considerably; no student who has been present during the presentation of the words misses more than three. Besides, the visual approach to vocabulary is fun. Try it.

Bibliography

Hackett, Maryann. "The Word of the Day," *English Journal*, LV: 9 (December 1966).

Photographed Vocabulary

I teach two eighth-grade "regular English/ Reading" classes in a school where reading has been declared a target area because of the enormous percentage of students who are reading below grade level. My two classes are hardly comparable except in the fact that they represent two extremes: in the case of vocabulary, one group is a glutton for sophisticated-sounding words and the other has a shocking paucity of even the most basic vocabulary. But one thing, I found, can be counted on in early adolescence no matter what the state of intellectual development: unabashed vanity. That discovery plus the suggestion from Daniel Fader in *Hooked on Books* that vocabulary development is part of the self-improvement instinct at this age led me to use the strategy of photographing a word in action—i.e., a student in the act of being that word. This technique evolved from Judy Chambers' strategy paper on the use of pictures in studying new words.[1] (I had used her intuitive approach to vocabulary several times and found that it worked marvelously.)

In preparation for a three-day lesson, I made up a dittoed list of thirty "actable" words complete with definitions; thinking that a unifying theme might tie things together, I chose words all of which described people in some way. As it turned out, the words were grabbed up immediately and what I had carefully prepared as a pep-up speech was not even needed. So and so was loudly called "garrulous," everyone claimed to be "studious" though suffering seriously from "ennui," and I became "eccentric."

After they had read through the several

[1] Strategy 56 in this volume.

pages more or less silently (I kept hearing "Hey, look on page 3, that fourth word—that's Miss Roberts"), I used each word in context, having them "fill in the oral blank." (E.g., "The graffiti writers at Downer are so _____ that they keep the custodians busy every weekend cleaning the walls." The word was "prolific.") The sentences were relevant to them so the interest level remained high. This took an entire period.

The next day I explained to them that each person would be responsible for demonstrating to us the meaning of one word from that list, and that they must do this only in a tableau because I had procured the services of a photographer (my husband) for the next day to photograph their frozen representations. At the same time, the rest of the class would be taking a test on the words by writing down what word they felt each was acting out.

The remainder of that period was spent in signing up for words, using each word on the list in a sentence, and suggesting possible ways of acting out these words. I encouraged them to bring props and even wear costumes if that would help.

I hardly believed we would be able to get to everyone in one day, but they were so organized and needed such little encouragement that a complete performance took less than thirty minutes to do in each period. I had put their names in order on the board so they knew exactly when they were to pose, and up they went. The quality of the acting was certainly mixed, but the ingenuity was often very entertaining. What turned out to be most amusing was their eagerness to be photographed. After the initial stage fright you couldn't keep them away. We got many renditions of "sinister," but "hirsute" seemed to be the day's winner.

My plan for testing them on the spot didn't work out because they were too excited and half of them didn't even remember to write down the words because they were too busy consulting with their neighbors. Though it may sound chaotic, and I will admit I wondered at the time just what they were absorbing, when we went over the names on the blackboard at the end I got beautifully choralled answers for each name.

The attractive aspect of this project seems to me to be what will come with the follow-up. I am returning their pictures after Christmas, and hope that the pictures' pull will also draw them to the word beneath it. I plan to use the room as a portrait gallery and will test them further to see just how much they learned from the experience.

It was an enjoyable approach for all concerned. Rarely has a day gone by without my having to report on how the printing of the photographs is coming along. (I'm doing the printing—that's why it's taking until after Christmas.) The entire project made words literally come alive.

Studious.

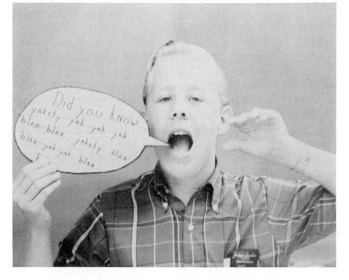

Garrulous.

Students illustrate words. Downer Junior High School, Richmond, California.

Using Collages with Literature

Last year I taught junior English to low achievers (third of four tracks) who had little interest in excelling in either reading or writing. To get them to read a novel was barely possible and to write about it bordered on the impossible. I was discontented with their written work because I felt that it did not reflect the depth of their understanding. By giving the students a written exam on their reading, I was trying to measure two things at once: the students' understanding of the work and their ability to express their emotions in writing. Class discussions of the events and characters in the novels revealed that the students understood what was happening in the book, but their written exams did not match the quality of their conversations. I wondered if there might be another means by which the students might express their interpretation of the novel, a medium which did not involve the written word, but which would still reflect the students' sensitivity to the work.

It occurred to me that since today's society is increasingly visually oriented, people might be able to express themselves more accurately in terms of what they can see, rather than what they can write. Since most of my students watched a great deal of television, they were able to compare many of the situations in the novel to typical television drama situations. As the students described the scenes and character actions that occurred in the television programs, they seemed to talk from a picture in their minds. From this impression I got the idea of having the students actually express their impressions of the novel in a collage. Instead of trying to find words to represent their ideas, the students would use pictures from magazines, colored paper, drawings, or anything else to depict their understanding.

I divided the class of thirty-three students into four groups and gave each group a pair of scissors, a jar of glue, a white poster board, and access to about forty magazines. I literally begged and confiscated the scissors, glue, and poster board from the art teacher and the secretaries in the main office. At first I asked students to bring in magazines, but I found that few did, partly because of their skepticism about the entire project, and partly because the students came from low income families where having magazines around the house was not commonplace. I brought in old magazines from our garage and solicited others from teachers; a few students brought in others. Obviously, the picture magazines worked best, such as *Life, Look, Glamour,* and *Sports Illustrated.*

Each group could choose one topic from the following selections to portray: a character from the novel, the relationship between two characters, a decision a character had to make, or a theme in the novel. We had read *The Ox-Bow Incident* and *The Red Badge of Courage,* and many students portrayed cowardice and bravery in either novel, the decision the youth made to go back to camp in *Red Badge,* or the dominant father-meek son relationship in *Ox-Bow.* To construct the collage, the members of each group had to discuss what aspects of their topic they wanted to stress, what kind of material they wanted to use, and how to combine the pictures to portray the idea they wanted to express. In these discussions, students exchanged their ideas heatedly and argued about which impressions were most accurate; each student inadvertently became "involved" with the novel by trying to persuade others to paste the pictures his own way. Within each group most students looked through magazines for possible material and tore it out; one trimmed and two or three pasted. A few, of course, did not do any of these, but simply sat and read the magazines—but they were *reading,* and these were generally the slowest students, many of whom had not even read the novel. I tried to get them to tear out material occasionally, but generally let them read all hour. I made a mental note to stock the back of the classroom with old magazines in the future and frequently to allow a day or so for free reading (novels for the faster students, magazines for the slower ones). Perhaps it also would have been a good idea to have allowed students to take some of the older, class-worn magazines home to keep or to pass on to their friends.

The cutting, arguing, and pasting took about four days. On the fifth day, we mounted the finished collages around the room, and students were encouraged to walk around the room and to inspect them carefully to judge their worth. After about fifteen minutes of this inspection, the class discussed each one in great detail, explaining the strong and weak relationships that were in the work. The students were surprisingly quick to spot a lazy job and did not hesitate to criticize the students who were responsible for it. Apparently many felt slighted that they had put forth their best efforts and were willing to share them, while a few others had been slacking off and thus had little to offer. This concern with a student's academic responsibility to other students in the class was rather startling to discover in these low achieving juniors, and the peer criticism had a deeper effect on the fun-loving students than mine would have had.

Christmas vacation interrupted us, or I would have extended the unit to include a writing exercise on the collages. After the full class discussion of each work, I would have asked the students to write a short explanation of what he "saw" in one of the collages. I would hope that seeing his ideas expressed visually

would help the individual more easily find words to express those same thoughts. I might have varied the assignment by asking for a short paragraph on one aspect of one of the collages, and then repeated the assignment for several days, using different collages. I think I would be most concerned with how faithfully the student thought the collage represented the novel, thus placing him in the role of the critic. This role would allow both him and the teacher to assume he knew the plot and basic characters of the novel; he would be called upon to judge how well the collage interpreted the work, which necessarily calls for *his* critical interpretation. This role might also restore some sense of work and success to students who are used to being categorized as "dummies" and "failures."

Like any other device, this approach can be worn thin if used for every novel read in class. It is also rather time-consuming (one week for the construction and evaluation, two weeks if you include the writing section) and involves some organizing of materials. I had two junior classes in two different rooms (three floors apart), but I solved the problem by having two of the heftiest fellows go to the other room at the beginning of the hour to haul the magazines to our room. Incidentally, I also found it useful to show each class how the other was progressing; this not only gave them new ideas and whetted their creativity with their sense of competition, but also gave them a new respect for their companions' talents and insights ("You mean *they* did that?"). Although I used this idea with low achievers, I am also going to use it with college preparatory students to try to awaken a new way of appreciating literature and expressing ideas. I would like to stress that both art and literature spring from life, and each is simply a different means for expressing the same feelings.

Look and Write

My approach is a variation and development on the theme of *Stop, Look, and Write*.[1] I use pictures, first still, then moving, as a basis for a seventh grade English program. Composition, grammar, and reading are derivative, and are the fruit surrounding this core.

The students involved are predominantly white, middle and working class, average kids in Pittsburg, California.

My assumptions are as follows:

1. These students, who are probably typical, have a contradictory relationship to the mass media. On one side they are deprived: good literature, good films or good television programs are rare in their world. Consequently, their ability to perceive critically is undeveloped. On the other side, they are extremely rich; they see a continuous succession of movies and television programs.
2. For them the English class is surrounded by a *cordon sanitaire*. It has little or nothing to do with their real life. It's just school.
3. Before students can be taught to write well, they must be able to write.
4. It is easier to teach analytical reading skills in familiar media (visual media) than in an alien medium (literature).

My first objective is to get the students writing and seeing. I begin by showing photographs to the class. The first few days we look at pictures with a twist, with something going on that students don't see at first (like the pickpocket photo in *Stop, Look, and Write*[2]). This is a game, and the students get involved in really scrutinizing the pictures.

The pictures themselves are shown with an opaque projector. This is the easiest and cheap-

est way of showing them. The room is darkened, except for a spotlamp that is directed at the ceiling. Thus the image is visible on the wall, but the room is still light. The purpose of this is twofold; first, the students can write while they scrutinize the photo; secondly, they are aware that this is a classroom laboratory.

The next phase runs for three or four weeks. We look at interesting photos three times a week for about fifteen minutes a day. The students are asked to describe everything they see in the photo, and to write a page of description in the fifteen minute period. All that counts is accuracy of description and quantity of writing.

A few papers are read back to the class. Most papers are not read by the teacher. A half page rates an "OK." A full page rates a "Good." If a student finishes his description in less than fifteen minutes, he is asked to make up a story about the picture in the time remaining.

By the end of three or four weeks every student has broken the one page barrier at least a few times. This means that we can begin to study grammar, using our own papers as raw material.

We also begin to discuss certain pictures. "Did you notice what the man was carrying?" "Where do you think this picture was taken?" "What do you think these people were talking about?" In this way critical discussion is introduced. At first, as here, it is on the simplest level. Everyone can participate at this level, even the poorer readers and those who have formed the habit of not participating. We carry this type of discussion over to the stories we read in our anthology.

Each student keeps a folder of all his papers. The folders will be graded by the teacher. But,

[1] Hart Day Leavitt and David A. Sohn, *Stop, Look, and Write* (New York: Bantam Books, 1964).
[2] *Ibid.*, "The Power of Observation," p. 21.

more important, students are encouraged to evaluate their own progress in writing. Also, all photos used in class are later put on a bulletin board for further reference by the students.

In the next phase we begin to write ourselves into the photos. For example, I show a man on a tightrope, and say, "Imagine that you are on the tightrope. What do you see, hear, smell, feel?" The idea is to increase our sense awareness, to involve and evoke our personal feelings and emotions, to expand our descriptive vocabulary. We begin to write short, personal experience papers for homework. We read related stories in the anthology.

The third phase is to use the photos merely to inspire our own stories. By this time everyone can write some kind of a story. The old excuse, "I don't know what to write about," has disappeared because the students have written so frequently that they have lost the fear of writing.

I see no definite time limits for phases two and three. But probably the class is ready to leave the opaque projector after about six weeks. My use of still photos now becomes more limited, infrequent. Later we will compare photos, write characterizations.

I want to point out again that this is an extremely simplified version of *Stop, Look, and Write*. I have modified the ideas of that book to fit the needs of seventh-graders. All sorts of modifications are possible.

The next stage of my strategy is to graduate from photos to films.

There is a wealth of short but good films available—for money. My use of films thus far has been restricted to those I could get free. My eventual goal is to put together a coherent, well-organized plan for seventh grade, a plan which would be coordinated with specific reading material. In lieu of such organization, my method has been to improvise. But I have found that if I know in general what I want to get out of a film at a particular time, I can usually find, with a minimum of previewing, the kind of movie I need.

I have two objectives at this stage. First, I want to build on the perceptual skill we have developed by looking at photos. I want to raise this skill to the level of "reading" a film. From here we will transfer this ability to reading literature. Secondly, I want to use films as addi-tional stimuli to encourage thoughtful writing.

Students are at home and confident with this medium. I find that we can immediately begin discussing deep films at a high level of maturity.

Let me emphasize the fact that the spotlamp is on and the room is well lit while we are watching a film—the same conditions as when we looked at photos. Tricks like this help the students to change their formerly passive approach to films. And, of course, they can take notes during the film.

I use the following procedure. When a film is over, the students write for two or three minutes to collect their thoughts. Then we discuss the film. We always begin by verbally establishing the continuity of the film: How did it start? What happened next? Then what happened? Then I ask questions directed toward those aspects of the film that I want the class to consider.

At least as frequently as we view and discuss films, we read and discuss short stories, using the same procedure in discussion. It is easy and even natural to discuss a good movie which we have just seen and enjoyed. Why should it be any more difficult with a short story?

Here are some examples of the level of critical discussion we achieve. Besides showing what this technique is about, these examples contradict, in my opinion, certain assumptions about the intelligence of seventh graders.

Discussing "Occurrence at Owl Creek Bridge," a movie the kids go nuts over: The man comes up out of the water, and there are these shots of trees and spiders, and we hear a song. Why? What does this mean? (This is our first acquaintance with the term "symbol." Everyone gets the idea that the trees, and later a flower, represent life.) Most of the film is just a dream, and takes place in a split second. How do you know it's a dream? What hints does the film give us before the ending? (The students have picked up the smallest details from the film, and remember them in the light of the surprise ending. This is something that almost never happened before when they read stories.) What correspondence can you see between what the man dreams is happening to him and what is really happening? (This is a tough one. But many of the kids get it.)

As a writing assignment I ask the class to

rewrite the middle of the film, but to keep the same beginning and ending. They are to write the things *they* would see in the last second of life, in the context of escaping.

In discussing "A Chairy Tale" I ask: "How did the man finally get to sit in the chair?" (Even though the film moves very quickly, the class follows it and understands. "He let the chair sit on him.") "Do you remember the flower in 'Occurrence at Owl Creek Bridge'? What did we call it?" (Everyone: "A symbol.") "And do you remember the idea of 'A Time Out of War'?" (It was an allegory about war.) "Now, do you think this chair was symbolic? Do you think this movie is an allegory?" (Shocked silence. The idea that this funny film could have a moral to it needs some time to sink in. But it's obvious once the question is posed so that they understand it.)

As a writing assignment I ask the class to write a similar story, substituting a different object for the chair.

We don't read every film. Some films just stimulate incredibly good writing. The papers written after seeing "Dream of the Wild Horses" are among the most exciting I've read so far.

Here then is the outline of a rather far-reaching strategy. There are so many modifications and variations possible that a teacher can get really excited. I have barely scratched the surface.

I stated earlier that students tend to see English as irrelevant. It is obvious that so much life can be brought into the classroom via the visual media that the class can become a kind of laboratory for examining life.

The power of this strategy is that it uses the students' strength, their familiarity with the visual media, as a lever to develop language skills. I have even started referring to the class as a "Communications" class. Written English, when seen in the context of other media, becomes relevant, because it has a place in life and isn't just something you get in school.

I'll conclude by mentioning a couple of related possibilities opened up by this strategy. Comic strips can be viewed as films laid out spatially. The kids know them, love them, and can learn a lot by making up their own. Films can and should be a bridge to critical television viewing. And now we begin to transform some of those hours spent in front of the television into an educational experience.

THE OVERHEAD PROJECTOR

GRETCHEN BINGHAM 60

Heavy Heavy Hangs Over Thy Overhead

Even though I had the advantage of being placed in a school in which there had been an intern the year before (which meant full briefing beforehand), still, as a white teacher in a 99.6 percent black junior high, the problems were far more than I bargained for. Teaching foreign language is generally thought of as one of the "luxury" teaching jobs, I've been told, but I've found that there are obvious exceptions —particularly when discipline is an almost insurmountable problem.

The problem of discipline combined with a text which makes little hit with the instructor (and very little sense at all to the students) plus a classroom with zero flexibility has made it tough, to say the least. It is hard to determine whether the problems of discipline are a result of the method and text used, or whether, because of the inherent discipline problems, the audio-lingual method of teaching a foreign language is a near impossibility with this particular combination of students and their current attitudes.

From the first day the challenges were there: "Miz Bingham, how long do you think you will stay at Hoover?" (The students seemed delighted that they had been through three Spanish teachers in the same number of years.) The last Spanish teacher literally had been driven from the school. "Miz Bingingham, you got a car?...Not any more." (Clearly, most students are not there through any choice of their own.) Each day presents new, unpredictable problems. Each class, each day, brings a different combination of frustrations: from card-playing to throwing paper; from potential fights to tipping over chairs; from thumb tacks to spitballs. There is more inexhaustible energy pent up in one school than I ever dreamed—all slanted against learning.

Since the audio-lingual method relies almost entirely on oral repetition and drill, it is essential that the class work together as a unit. Considering the previously mentioned handicaps, this presents more than a slight problem.

The classroom in which I find myself and my students captive consists of nine tables divided by an aisle down the middle leading to the front of the room. The tables to the right seat three people and the tables to the left seat four—all riveted to the floor and quite immobile. The tables on the right are flush with the wall, thus making it impossible to use the blackboard space provided. The blackboards in the front of the room are about 75 percent obscured from view by the tape recorder console, so blackboard space is rather limited. This means that board drill is nonexistent for the students and teacher, and games which involve any special formations are completely out.

The Beginning of a Solution

To cope with the physical problems of the room and the discipline problems of the class, the overhead projector has become a partial answer. Although the setup of the room does not lend itself readily to this either, at least it does give a central visual focus to each student. It has been a great help for presenting the following:

1. Dialogue presentations and drills
2. Grammar presentations and drills
3. Vocabulary drills
4. Telling time

Since ALM includes a dialogue at the beginning of each chapter which the students are supposed to memorize, with the help of records and tapes, I have found that the additional use of visual stimuli aids greatly in the memorization. The text provides a series of rather bleak, unimaginative posters which I found to be of little use at all. I decided to make my own drawings. After the dialogue has been introduced and explained orally, my stick figures depicting as well as possible the action of the conversations along with the captions written beneath do seem to capture the focus of the class. They serve as an aid to students for recognizing the words in combination with the sounds. For the beginning classes it is easy to cut slits in the plastic overlays and insert a piece of cardboard to "erase" the writing. These can easily be removed and replaced without much fuss. (See Figure 1.)

For grammar presentations the overhead has been a great help. By making up transparencies with the rules first, then sentences utilizing the rules, followed by another transparency leaving out the point stressed for reinforcement (such as the $A + EL = AL$ and $DE + EL = DEL$) the attention of the whole class is drawn to the screen. (See Figure 2.)

By drawing pictures of the vocabulary words presented in the various lessons, with the articles and words beneath, the oral, visual, and aural can be reinforced simultaneously. The picture can then be removed for oral drill alone or the picture can be shown without the writing by using the cardboard insert to cover it up. (See Figure 3.)

The students enjoy the pictures and seem to be eager to see what you're going to do for the

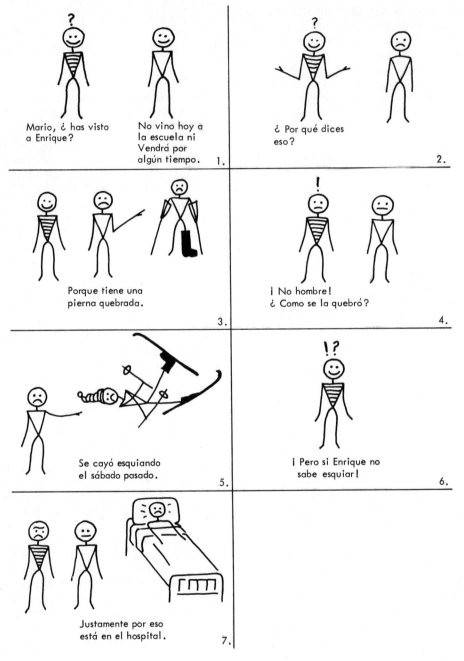

Figure 1

A + EL = AL
DE + EL = DEL

Vamos a la escuela.
Vamos al cine.

Tú quieres los discos
de la muchacha.
Tú quieres los discos
del muchacho.

Voy a la iglesia
_____ fútbol.
_____ tienda.
_____ hospital.

Es el libro de la madre.
_____ padre.
_____ hermana.
_____ hermano.

Figure 2

next dialogue. They often have comments to make about the quality and have even taken to drawing them themselves. Things like "papas fritas" and "albondigas" are a little hard to get across, but a few laughs don't hurt the class any.

The overhead has also been useful in telling

time. By drawing a clock and cutting cardboard hands, fastened with a braid, it is easy to see the time "move." This is particularly helpful in stressing the time as it progresses to the next hour. Subtracting from the hour coming up next as soon as the minute hand passes the halfway mark seems to be a difficult concept for the new Spanish student to grasp, and the visual aid which the whole class can see helps tremendously.

The students have reacted favorably to the use of the overhead and often ask to be "quizzed" with the vocabulary pictures. Since no one else at our school seems to make much use of the overhead, I have had an ample supply of the plasticene squares. Magic markers (which are not supplied by the school) seem to work best. They come in many beautiful colors. It helps to write the grammar point which is being stressed in a contrasting color. Often I include a design of some sort at the top of the page or as a border. There are books available which include Aztec and Mayan designs to add a little culture as well.

The use of the overhead is, of course, not the answer to the frustrations and rebellion of our students, but it has proved a help in my situation.

La silla
Las sillas
Una silla
Unas sillas

El libro
Los libros
Un libro
Unos libros

La casa
Las casas
Una casa
Unas casas

Figure 3

ROBERT M. SULLIVAN **61**

Use of the Overhead Projector for Teaching Geometry

My first attempts to teach geometry without an overhead projector were largely unsuccessful. My writing on the blackboard is not very legible; time was wasted as I wrote theorems and drew diagrams on the blackboard; occasionally I had to consult my notes so as not to forget parts of a proof. Consequently, I would seldom cover all the material I had planned for a lesson. Some more efficient method of presentation was clearly indicated.

The use of the overhead projector solved all of these initial problems. I could print on the transparencies instead of write, diagrams could be neatly drawn with a straight edge, and notes could be kept beside the projector for ready reference without the students' being aware of them. Although there is probably more over-all time spent in preparation of a lesson plan involving the projector, there is much less time wasted in the classroom.

The general routine I have established for teaching geometry is as follows: students volunteer to present solutions of assigned problems on the blackboards. When a student completes his proof, I ask the class for questions and comments. I also comment on the student's work and presentation. Next I show on the overhead projector a prepared solution of the problem, which may or may not agree with the student's. All students are offered an opportunity to ask questions or make comments on my solution. After the assigned problems have been reviewed, I discuss new material. For this I use the overhead projector in conjunction with a blackboard. The basic outline of the new material—such as definitions, theorems, and the main ideas of the lesson—are presented on the overhead projector. Discussion of the material and answers to students' questions are carried to the chalkboard.

The use of transparencies allows for flexibility in presentation of material. A complete or partial solution of a theorem may be displayed. Sometimes I give only a statement of the theorem; then development of a proof is done together by the class. The discussion period is normally ended by working two or three problems together with the class using the overhead projector. Students seem to enjoy this method of presentation much more than a traditional blackboard lesson.

I have found the overhead projector also useful in playing a game similar to "College Bowl" for review of definitions, postulates, and theorems. To play the game the class is divided into two teams. Questions such as "Define a Parallelogram" are flashed on the overhead projector. Following the students' verbal answers, whether correct or not, the written answer is displayed. Both the questions and answers are prepared ahead of time on sheet transparencies. This game has proved to be a stimulating means for helping to learn by rote the material which can all too often be dull.

The above uses of the overhead projector require only a marker pencil and sheet transparencies for preparation. These are materials normally available in any school. The confidence given a new teacher by knowing he has his lesson already prepared is of tremendous value. Use of the overhead projector is recommended for all teachers of geometry, but especially for new teachers who are still gaining confidence and competency in the art of teaching.

LISTENING POSTS AND
TAPE RECORDERS

STEPHEN AND JACQUELYN BRAND **62**

Reaching the Nonreader

Introduction

Many students at Samuel Gompers High School, a continuation school, have failed so many times that they strongly and loudly resist regular school assignments. Those who read below the fourth- or fifth-grade level cannot comprehend most junior high or senior high school textbooks. They have been unable to do their assignments for so long that they prefer to ignore any school work rather than demonstrate their inability to do it.

We believe that most of these students desperately want to learn to read, but they must be encouraged to learn with a variety of materials which are not as threatening to them as the textbooks which have always been the cause of their failures. By using instructional materials like the listening posts and dictaphones described in this paper, combined with an individualized teaching approach, we have been able to provide students with successful reading experiences which are also interesting and enjoyable.

Listening Posts

To provide our students with enjoyable reading experiences which would build the foundation for follow-up classwork, we set up a listening post area in our classroom. Listening posts are sets of earphones connected to a tape recorder. Students can read along with recordings made by the teacher. This technique is particularly effective with students who read below the fourth-grade level, and absolutely critical for the total nonreaders in our classes. Each student sits at a small desk provided with earphones. The students listened to a wide range of stories and articles while following along on dittoed sheets or books containing the taped materials.

Use of listening posts has been effective in several ways: (1) the students have enjoyable reading experiences, some for the first time. (2) Meaning and continuity in a story is transmitted to students who otherwise cannot read well enough to understand much of the story. (3) The slower students are able to work on the same materials the faster students are working on (without the tape, usually); thus they do not feel they must work on different or less exciting material. (4) Since the student's listening comprehension is much greater than his reading comprehension, he is able to successfully answer questions about the reading selection which would otherwise be extremely difficult for him. This helps build the student's confidence in his reading potential, as indeed it should, since listening comprehension is recognized by reading teachers as a good index to potential reading ability. (5) While students are listening to a taped story, the teacher is free to work with students individually without worrying about other students who have difficulty working independently; students, almost without exception, listen quietly and attentively to the tapes. (6) With the high absentee rate at our school a major problem, it is important that students may hear the tape whenever they come to class, without the need of the teacher. The students' success with the material presented at the listening posts has greatly contributed to their self-confidence as well as to their desire to work on improving reading skill.

Allowances must be made for the initial reactions of the students to the listening posts. In our case, some immediately began to imitate pilots radioing in for landing, to the amusement of the entire class. Others took delight in pulling one wire or another, which caused a breakdown in the system. Many toyed with volume controls on other students' desks, causing periodic screeches from the victims. However, the desire to fool around decreased as the interest in hearing the tapes increased, and we rarely experience these problems any more.

This technique may, at first glance, appear to be a lot of work for the teacher, who must be constantly preparing new tapes for class. It does, in fact, require additional out-of-school time so precious to a first year teacher. (We have now begun to have students record the material.) However, the resulting increase of meaningful activity within the classroom combined with the development of sustained interest among the students more than justifies the preparation time.

The Language Experience Approach

What I can think about, I can talk about. What I can say, I can write or dictate. What I can write, I can read. I can read what I can write and what others can write.[1]

For extremely poor readers, we have found the language experience approach to be most successful. "In the language experience approach

the student's account of his own experience or thoughts is used as reading material."[2] Even students with extremely limited sight vocabularies are able to read their own stories. Since the student easily remembers his story, he is able to recognize words based on the limited phonetic or visual recognition skills which he does have.[3] This gives him a successful experience in reading and helps him to develop his sight vocabulary and word attack skills. Furthermore, the reading material is of extremely high interest value to the student since it is his own work.

Implementing the Language Experience Approach: Using the Dictaphone

We have used dictaphones in the classroom to implement the language experience approach to reading. Dictaphones are tape recorders often used in businesses for dictating letters. Students who cannot or will not write can dictate essays into the dictaphone which can later be transcribed by a typist. Not only does the dictaphone facilitate language experience learning without requiring much individual teacher time, it also adds some of the advantages of the listening posts to the language experience approach.

The student dictates his story into the dictaphone just as he would dictate it to the teacher. Since he has complete control over what is recorded, he may erase portions or make changes if he chooses. The teacher may tell the student that corporation executives use these machines to dictate letters to secretaries who are not there in the same way the student will be dictating to the "teacher-secretary" when he cannot be there. The teacher may wish to record some instructions for the student to listen to before he begins his dictation.

Later that day the teacher, or perhaps an advanced student from a typing class, types the dictated story. The next day the teacher asks the student to read the story back to him, and/or the student can read along with the

---

[1] R. V. Allen, "The Language Experience Approach," in Warren G. Cutts, ed., *Teaching Young Children to Reaa*, U.S. Department of Health, Education and Welfare (Washington, D.C.: Government Printing Office, 1964), p. 59.

[2] Ruth Strang, *Diagnostic Teaching of Reading* (New York: McGraw-Hill Book Company, 1964), p. 30.

[3] The only student we have who cannot read back his own words has virtually no phonetic ability and can get no clues by looking at the word to help him remember what he said.

recording. This provides an individual listening post with the best reading material available!

The dictaphone is a very attractive machine to our students. Even our most reluctant non-readers use it with little persuasion. They enjoy listening to themselves over and over. It offers some temptation to sing and play around, and it would be best if the distaphone could be placed somewhere where the noise would not disturb the rest of the class, but its advantages are great.

A major obstacle to widespread use of the dictaphone is the teacher preparation time in typing the student dictation, but this might be overcome by sending the dictaphones to a typing class for transcription, which would also provide useful experience for the typists.

The listening post and the dictaphones are two important aspects of our reading program. Also critical to the success of a reading program is the presence of many attractive alternative activities from which a student can choose. On any given day, a student in our reading workshop can read from a large selection of paperback books displayed on a revolving book rack, write or type a journal, read a newspaper or magazine, work on improving reading skills at the Controlled Reader or Language Master, work on programmed instruction in Sullivan workbooks, work with a teacher or a tutor on assignments from this or another class, use the listening post, or work with the dictaphone.

We have focused on two aspects of our reading program which have been most successful with nonreaders. In both techniques, an important outcome has been the building of self-confidence in the student. Unlike methods which group according to reading ability, and therefore emphasize the nonreader's inability to read, these approaches draw on our students' strengths, their listening comprehension and verbal ability.

POPULAR MUSIC IN THE CLASSROOM

MICHAEL D. THATCHER **63**

Popular Songs and Poetry

Approaching poetry through the use of popular songs is one way to get around the common reaction many students have toward poetry ("You mean we're going to study poems? Ugh!"). Poetry is far removed from their environment. Popular music is an important part of it, so it's a good place to begin since you'll already have their interest. I began this unit by showing my classes how poetry has its roots in song: the *Odyssey* was originally sung, for example, and the lyrics of Provençal troubadours, Shakespeare's songs, many love lyrics of the seventeenth century are all part of this tradition; and the song-cycles of Schubert, Beethoven's Ninth Symphony, etc., show the same cross-fertilization between musical and literary achievement.

I then asked my classes to suggest songwriters and poets whom they would like to study, and in each class I got a list long enough so that I could choose from it those names that I would have chosen myself anyway (e.g., Dylan, Donovan, Simon and Garfunkel, the Beatles). We were all happy. At this point I found it necessary to emphasize that we would study songs *as poems,* concentrating on the words; otherwise they would have tried to turn me into a disc jockey. Also, I let them select the artists, but I selected the songs, so they had some choice but not a free hand in deciding what we would do.

Usually I would select a song, then transcribe it and ditto off copies. In many cases this was made easier by the fact that recording artists like the Beatles and Simon and Garfunkel have their song lyrics printed on the album jacket—a testimonial to the literary value of their music. Then I would pass out copies of the song. We would listen to it and discuss what it meant and *how* it meant; this led us naturally to consider tone, imagery, repetition, figurative language, etc., and the students gradually became more accustomed to these and other critical terms.

As we moved from song to song, I tried to preserve a thematic continuity; that is, we would often consider two songs that had a similar "message"—like the Beatles' "Fixing a Hole" and "Fool on the Hill"—and compare them, both thematically and stylistically. I found that this was a good way to introduce poems which the class might have choked on otherwise. For example, when we considered those two Beatle songs, I included Wordsworth's sonnet "The World is Too Much With Us," and we compared all three as rejections of society. When we got to the Rolling Stones' "Paint it Black" we contrasted it with Wordsworth's "She Dwelt among Untrodden Ways" as two elegiac statements. Simon and Garfunkel's "Dangling Conversation" can be compared with any of George Meredith's *Modern Love* sonnets. And so on, depending upon the teacher's interests and breadth of experience.

One way that songs are especially helpful in demonstrating poetic techniques is in the shadowy area of sound and sense, and the rela-

tion of form to content. The musical variation in a well-constructed song often emphasizes, by means of a change of key, of chord structure, of voicing, a change in the meaning of a poem. For example, in "Fixing a Hole" the music goes up to a sustained dominant chord whenever the speaker talks about the world outside his own private world. Similarly, the matters of line length, organization into stanzas, use of repeated lines, phrases, and verses, as well as rhyme, meter, and so on are exaggerated in a song and therefore easier to isolate and discuss. This came out especially well when I asked my classes to write their own poems or songs; I was able to collaborate with the music teacher so that my students worked with his students in setting some of their own literary efforts to music.

After a few weeks my classes got to where they could interpret a song or poem pretty well, and then I passed out a dittoed list of questions which we had most often discussed in relation to a specific song or poem:

1. Who is the speaker? What is he like?
2. Whom is he speaking to?
3. What is the setting or occasion?
4. What is the tone of the poem? How is it achieved?
5. What poetic devices are used? To what effect?
6. How does the form of the poem illuminate the content?

Their final project was then to select a song or poem of their choice and write an essay explicating and analyzing it, using the questions to spur their thinking. Because they got to choose their own poem they were caught up in the assignment, and I got many interesting essays. I might add, however, that it was a difficult and time-consuming set of papers to correct, because of the diversity of topics and approaches. By the end of the unit I felt gratified that both my students and I had learned something about the language of poetry, and I was heartened by their enthusiasm; they had found that poetry is not just a pastime for old ladies and schoolteachers, but a fascinating part of their everyday experience.

Incorporating Music into the English Curriculum

The Teaching Situation

The course I taught was a summer school course in English Composition. My students were from all high school levels: ten sophomores, ten juniors, and seven seniors, and were mostly "average" to "low average" in ability according to school categories. About half of these students were Caucasian and half were black; well over half were male.

What I Hoped to Achieve

The purpose of the summer course was twofold: to provide a supportive environment where writing could be an easy and natural means of self-expression; and to encourage each student to become a more thoughtful, aware, and responsive individual. I chose music, an important daily experience for them as well as for me, as the main vehicle to achieve these ends.

Procedures

The tape recorder is nothing new in the classroom, yet its potential has been only partially tapped. I would hope that those who read this paper might try using a tape recorder in the manner suggested, and then proceed from there to further possibilities.[1]

I divided my summer composition course into three parts. The first was free creative writing with instruction in description and narration, and the development of listening skills (which includes span of attention). The second part consisted of formal instruction in the structure of paragraphs and sentences (using the work of Francis Christensen[2] for the latter). The final two weeks reverted back to creative writing, this time with the emphasis on creating richer sentences and better organized paragraphs.

The purpose of the first part of the course was to get my students accustomed to writing and translating abstractions (e.g., jazz) into concrete thoughts. I also used Leavitt's *Stop Look and Write*[3] (*SLW*). A typical assignment for the first week was to pick a character out of *SLW* and write a story about him or her, using the taped music I brought to class for mood or theme. I was careful to use songs which were very clear in meaning and with which the students were all familiar. I was also careful to choose those artists who would appeal to the tastes of all my students. (White students do not always care for "soul" music, while black students often care for little else. By presenting all kinds of music in class I tried to break down these highly categorized tastes.) As time went on the assignments became more demanding. One day during the second week I prepared a long and varied assignment. The first part of

---

[1] I would like to suggest two other uses for the tape recorder in the classroom: (1) as a means of recording classroom discussion; (2) as the only practical means I know of to let each student hear how his own reading and his own writing sound. If the tapes are not erased, a student can "objectively" judge his own progress.

[2] Francis Christensen, *The Christensen Rhetoric Program* (New York: Harper & Row, Publishers, 1968).

[3] Hart Day Leavitt and David A. Sohn, *Stop, Look, and Write* (New York: Bantam Books, 1964). This book provides a series of photographs around which a composition course can be developed.

it took about half an hour. It was as follows:

1. Jazz: Pharoah Sanders' "Japan" and Dave Brubeck's "Koto Song." Identify the country this music represents. How does the music tell you this?
2. James Brown's "Hot Mix." How does this make you feel or what does it make you think of?
3. Beatles' "Getting Better All The Time," and Steve Miller Blues Band's "Roll With It." What is the singer talking about?
4. Procol Harum's "Repent Walpurgis." Free. Write anything, but be sure to write.

In all assignments of this type I emphasized that I really did not care what they wrote as long as *they wrote* and kept writing as long as the music played. Having this much freedom was hard for them at first, since they seldom get it in school, but they caught on quickly once they found that they really could write whatever they *wanted* to write—in other words, what was important to them. I never censured anything anyone wrote for me in class. Any topic was fine provided they wrote as well as they could. I never had any written "breach of conduct" or decency.

Then the assignment shifted gears.

5. I gave them excerpts from two civil rights speeches, one by President Johnson, the other by Malcolm X. They had to paraphrase what each speaker said and pass judgment on the content of each excerpt, then compare the two speakers from their own standpoints.
6. Flip Wilson's "Cowboys and Colored People" was given them for discussion. This was mainly to relax them and give them respite from writing. (Everyone complained that they did too much writing in the class.)
7. Write a story to the following music picking a main character out of *SLW*: "My Girl" by Otis Redding; "Baby Please Don't Go" by the Chambers Brothers; Eric Satie piano music; "The End" by the Doors; "The Time Has Come Today" by the Chambers Brothers.

These seven exercises represent the various methods I used to stimulate creative writing with the help of a tape recorder.

After formal instruction in paragraphs and sentences, during which I did not use the tape recorder, we returned to music. The highlight of the last two weeks was a story students wrote to a prepared tape collage of music. The assignment was:

We are going to write a movie. I have the soundtrack and you are to listen to it and write the plot which you feel fits the music. Before you in *SLW* is a picture of a soldier. He is your hero, and is being sent on a secret mission to an island which is inhabited by cannibals. He has been brought there by the navy, which will cover for him and the regiment while they get ashore. This is the kind of soldier who is very likely to get lost.

The music was: Cannons from *Victory at Sea Volume II*; Marching music and island birds with suspenseful violins from the same album; the second movement from Symphony Number 3 by Gliere—scary violin music; the first part of John Antil's *Corroboree*—a symphonic replica of Australian Aboriginal tribal music; "Cure" from *Message to the Ancestors* by Big Black (congo drum and flute and some frantic verbal noises).

Evaluation

The music was very suggestive; and almost everybody's hero was tortured, but the written results—when compared with the work the students had done in June—were very gratifying. Appendices A and B include examples from the two students whom I felt made the most visible progress.

Appendices C and D are selections from the results of two questionnaires I presented to the class, one during the third week and one on the next to the last day of the course. From these it is clear that everyone enjoyed the class and came out of it with improved writing skill as well as with a better image of themselves as creative thinkers.

Suggestions

To duplicate this project, or to successfully motivate students through music, one should know what music they like, what the trends in music have been, and where they are likely to go. Such knowledge is not hard to obtain if you do not already have it. Most young people can tell you, in half an hour or so, the state of rock and jazz.

The main point is to always have a good reason for playing the music. Never let it become an end in itself. Using music is helpful because music is very important to young people. Normally young people do not think much about the music; they hear it incessantly and often are aware of it only as background. They seldom give thought to what a song might say to them personally, or what it means. Their response is emotional, yet paradoxically impersonal. It is geared to style, not content, and I believe this undifferentiated emotionalism is not confined to music. Therefore, by working through something so basic as the import of music in their lives you not only use a medium which they enjoy and which is totally relevant to them, but you are giving them training in skills which are almost as universal as music itself.

The following samples of student writing represent extremes within the class (Appendices A and B). The first is R. B.'s. R. B. was tall and cool, the "leader" of the black males in the class. His ability to express himself in writing seemed nonexistent. Although it became evident to me that R. B.'s ability in this area was truly inadequate, his final writing showed some dramatic improvement, and was personally very gratifying to him.

A. M.'s papers are another story. He was a very quiet white boy, slow in answering questions, seemingly dull. However, his initial writing was characterized by an active imagination which more fully revealed itself in the surprise ending of his final story. A. M.'s ability was higher than that of most of his classmates.

Appendix A

Composition—First Week: Student R. B.

I thing that the teacher should let the stuen take caer of ther on problem in school and if the stuen can't than the teacher should do something.

Composition—Last Week: Student R. B.

Hes move in on the iland hes all by himself—so now he going to chck the iland than all at once the enemy come out of the tree he run for cover they shoting at him he shot one and that jump him form the back now they caut him they tring to get him to talk he wont. So they tiey him up to a tree they got a long rod put in in the fir and put in on his back and then a gen agen. He can't stan it his in pain. He died.

The End

Appendix B

Composition—First Week: Student A. M.

There's picture here of a man dressed up in it looks like a world war i outfit like he all set to go to battle with the hat the gun the coffee pot the big boots canteen pots pans I even an egg butter and razor yip he all prepared to go to battle. There is a bomb shelter right behind him. He looks like Charlie Chaplyn with the phoney mustache he might just be and he is making a movie.

Composition—Last Week: Student A. M.

There this man let's call him Joe he isn't that smart but he is going to this Island for a secret mission and the navy is covering for him he hears the sound of the guns and he get down low and his whole tigetment [regiment] walks away while he down on the dirt so he can't find them. The mission is to blow up a bridge that the enemy uses. Without this one little bridge the enemy would have to give up it was this important. the only problem was he didn't and the rigetment didn't know wher it was. So he just started walking and he saw some of the enemy. He had to kill all four of them before they killed him so he shot and killed them all. Right about then he thought that if there were that many of them around they would probably have already have caught the whole redgement. The enemy was a group of canabels and they had to capture or destroy all of them so he started walking he saw a nother one he had a fist fight and he made him bring him to where the bridge was. He was think why would a bridge be so important and when he got there and he discovered it he didn't say because he was taken capture and they ate him and nobody found what happened in the jungle.*

Appendix C

English Composition   Mr. Ross   June 26, 1968

RESULTS OF THE FIRST QUESTIONNAIRE

Should last year's teacher have made you read more? If I didn't want to read it, it wouldn't make any difference what a teacher said. (Typical response.)

Do you write letters? yes 31, no 9

Which Radio stations do you listen to? KDIA 21, KSOL 8, KJAZ 7, KSAN 7, KMPX 10, KYA-KOIT 4, KFRC 4, KGO 1

What do you like about the class? like to write and want to learn to write creatively/I don't like strict ugly and mean teachers/blood's music/music and movies/teacher and work, its interesting/teaches the way the class likes/new experiences/its easy/we have fun/you learn what interests you/nothing/young teacher/teacher's method is good/how we discuss racial and political problems/things we do/general easy-going atmosphere/ freedom to write about what you want to say/freedom to speak freely/people in this class like to talk/you can let all the tension out of you and speak your piece.

How do you know when you have learned anything? when you find out something you didn't know at first/when I can relate something new to something. I just feel it/I think about it before I go to sleep/when someone asks me and I know/when it comes in need and I have it/when I do, act, say, or think someway differently/Later recall/I don't know/I remember it next day/When I go home and talk about it/when it stays in my brain/When I do a test right/

Appendix D

English Composition   Mr. Ross   July 25, 1968

RESULTS OF THE SECOND QUESTIONNAIRE.

This class interested me more than   24
                        the same as   1
                        less than   0   *other classes in English last year.*

In this summer school class I was able to learn
  better than   19
  as well as   2
  not as well as   1   *in the regular school year.*

Our class was split up into three parts. One was free writing. The second was learning how to write good paragraphs and sentences. The third was free writing after this learning.

Which did you enjoy most? one 10   two 3   three 9

Why? I couldn't write as well on the first/The second helped for the third/At first I didn't have the experience of writing and didn't like it, but now that I know, I enjoy it.

* ED. NOTE: While these compositions show some improvement, they also demonstrate the enormity of the challenge teachers face.

Did freedom in class help you to learm more and write better?
yes 21   no 2   I didn't feel pressured/I have time to think/

Do you think you are a better writer, thinker?
yes 10   no 4   I can sit down and write a story/Yes because of experience/
Because I can write better paragraphs/There is a lot of things I didn't know how to
do before this class/You told me to write what I think, so I try/I am learning about
what life in general is about/I've learned that my potential isn't bad/I put more
things in my sentences/I think I know what to be thinking of at the right time and
place/I think I write a little better because I was able to write what I wanted instead
of something out of a book/Maybe just a little better than when I came in because
no matter how much you teach me I can understand, but when it comes to the
actual writing I can't seem to work my ideas into work with my writing. After
I write it I can see what needs to be done. I learned to do something people have
been asking me to do since I can remember—proof read my work/I didn't think as
clearly and my writing was very sloppy and my sentences and paragraphs were all
wrong/Yes because I learned to write more about what I was writing on/It made
me think/I think I am a better writer by the grades you give/

JOSEPH D. FRIEDMAN **65**

An Experiment in Time

Introduction

Classroom Strategy: It is perhaps something of a commentary on the state of education today that we choose to refer to our classroom actions as strategy. Strategy connotes to my mind's ear visions of generals plotting battle plans, of coaches' half-time "chalk talks," of chess players' convoluted reasoning. All these instances imply adversary situations. Is it that the teacher-student relationship is of the same ilk? Unfortunately, that is how I often feel. I certainly do not yet have a solution for helping older and younger persons to work together for common, harmonious goals, but I cannot help expressing the feeling that so long as we have to think in terms of strategies public education is in a state of turmoil.

None of the above paragraph is to be construed as a boast that I do not think in terms of strategies vis-à-vis my classes. It merely expresses something which often pains me. I do not like fighting, especially when the odds are against me. Sour grapes, you say? Indubitably. The voice of incompetence? Without a doubt.

The Field of Battle

A small junior high school, 50 percent black, 50 percent white. Large gaps between the two groups. I am teaching Social Studies to eighth-graders. My successes have been few, and you know the rest. Motivation and control are the prime problems.

The Plan

After weeks of struggling with a largely unreadable text and spending hours teaching things I little enjoyed, I threw up my hands and said I must try another way. Which was to create a week's unit on what I feel is the essence of history—time. The vehicle for the basic content of the unit was popular records.

I introduced the unit by stating that "This

week we are going to study time." The rationale which I had earlier told myself was that we needed to do something different, that time was history, that records were attention-getters, that if I dittoed up the lyrics and asked some questions to be written, I might be able to get some people to read, write, and think who had never done so before.

The three basic approaches to time and history which I chose to concentrate on were largely limited by my own record collection. For a start, I played the Chambers Brothers' song, "The Time Has Come Today." This song expresses a sense of reacting existentially in time, a sense of now, a sense of revolution, of struggling against the confines of one's historical situation.

The class reactions to the first day's lesson were mixed. From my slowest group, an all-black class, the response was very positive. To them school is always a drag. Listening to records is fun. Therefore, listening to records is not school, so it's okay to relax and think a bit.

To come to school, listen to records, write a little bit, and get a good grade for it was novel to them. The top class, mainly white, didn't dig the music that much, but I think it was more than that. These are kids who are making it in the present system and crazy stuff like rock and roll records shake up the works. I mean what is this guy anyway, some kind of *hippie* (which, by the way, is worse than being a Communist).

The next day I switched gears and brought in Otis Redding's recording of "Sittin' on the Dock of the Bay," a profoundly pessimistic song. It is the song of a man who just sits "on the dock of the Bay/ Wastin' time." For Otis it "Look like nothing gonna change.../ So I guess I'll remain the same." The song is a slow tidal sort of song. It was a good musical contrast as well as philosophic contrast to the wild rhythms of the Chambers Brothers. The central idea I was trying to present was another way of dealing with life—the way of defeated accep-

tance. The kids said time seemed to have pushed Otis Redding rather than vice versa.

The last song I played was "The Fool on the Hill" by Lennon and McCartney of the Beatles. The black kids did not react as well to this particular song *qua* song because it was of a genre outside their experience. They said quite straight-facedly, "Mr. Friedman, this isn't music." And to some of them, it really wasn't. Still most people were able to listen and, directed by the questions on the lyric sheet, to see the different philosophy this song expressed. Rather than fighting time or being pushed around by it, the fool on the hill was simply above the hurly-burly of temporal society. Although "They don't like him.../ He knows that they're the fools," presumably because he has grasped some greater truth.

To wrap up the unit we spent one class period making collages of the three major themes of the records. I used butcher paper to cover three bulletin boards, brought lots of old magazines, etc. If you halve the class (in the case of a large class), you can let one half work on the collage for half the period, and the other half can work with something else while they wait their turn. Rather than making new collages each period, I let the three I started first period grow during the day. There was a great deal of enthusiasm, if not artistic ability expressed, and the room was certainly more alive at the conclusion of the day.

Conclusion

This unit on time was, in my estimation, a success for the following reasons: the class, on the whole, enjoyed it tremendously; the questions they had to answer coupled with the lyrics of the song tended to free them from the rote answering which too often spells school. They were feeling something; the material for many students was related to their lives, and they showed it; abstract concepts were learned in a painless way; I liked it.

SITTIN' ON THE DOCK OF THE BAY*
by Otis Redding and Steve Cropper

Sittin' in the morning sun
I'll be sittin' when the evening come,

* Copyright © 1968 by East/Memphis Music Corp., Time Music Co., Inc., and Redeval Music Co., Inc.

Watchin' the ships roll in
Then I watch them roll away again.

I'm sittin' on the dock of the bay
Watchin' the tide roll away,
I'm just sittin' on the dock of the bay
Wastin' time.

I left my home in Georgia
Headed for the Frisco Bay.
I had nothin' to live for,
Look like nothin' gonna come my way.

So I'm sittin' on the dock of the Bay
Watchin' the tide roll away.

Look like nothing gonna change
Every thing still remain the same
I can't do what ten people tell me to do
So I guess I'll remain the same.

(Chorus)

Sittin' here restin' my bones
And this loneliness won't leave me alone,
2,000 miles I've roamed
Just to make this dock my home.

1. How do you feel about this song? How did it make you feel?
2. How does the singer of the song seem to feel about his life? Why?
3. How is this song different from the one we heard yesterday? How is the way Otis Redding seems to feel about time different from the way the Chambers Brothers felt about time?
4. Maybe Otis is singing about more than himself. If he is, what else could this song be about?

USE OF ADVERTISEMENTS
IN AN ART CLASS

LOIS ATCHISON **66**

Commercial Art : Unit for Continuation High School Students

Introduction

Guitar rhythms, transistor radios, gold cigarette packs, boss tattoos, the art of the latest dance style, car designs, hair styles, teen-age clothes—all are art items in the teen-age world at Mission Continuation High School, a small school fed by the Mexican-American community of Hayward, California. A surprising number of the students both enjoy and do well in art.

My problem this year, then, has not been to stimulate students to produce and enjoy art, but rather to make them *conscious* of the art which fascinates them.

The art of Madison Avenue is the art which grips the students and sometimes leads them by "hidden persuasion" to buy or not to buy, to (ironically) steal or not to steal, occasionally to love or not to love. Engaging the interest of the class in a project on commercial art which would explore the techniques and effects of Madison Avenue's art was not the difficult part of the endeavor. It was encouraging the students to analyze their fascination that required the most patience.

The unit described here on commercial art has been pulled together from group discussions and related art projects which worked successfully (and sometimes not so successfully) with continuation high students. Because commercial art embraces so many design areas, the unit could be easily expanded to include activities not discussed here.

Specific goals for this unit on commercial art include the following:

1. Exploring the techniques and effects of commercial art in order to help educate the student to understand his environment
2. Helping the student increase his manual skills and visual perception and encouraging him to incorporate newly discovered art elements into his work
3. By studying the ways in which commercial art is used to persuade consumers to buy products, increasing the students' ability and willingness to think critically
4. Through requiring analysis of consumer motivation, stimulating the student to analyze his own motivation, not only toward buying products, but toward all daily activities
5. Ultimately helping the student to like himself better, to feel less hostile, depressed, and agressive—the traits that prevent the continuation high student from being a successful achiever in the public schools

The Unit: Commercial Art

Week One

To introduce the unit on commercial art, the first week was spent having students make collages from magazine cutouts. The assignment was phrased: "What would you buy if you had a million dollars? Cut out pictures of the items and arrange them on a page, keeping in mind the placement of shapes, colors, and contours." The collage project required little manual skill and no drawing ability. So it was relatively easy for the students to get involved with pictures. Consciously or unconsciously the students were responding to the art of advertising.

This project took four days. Although I did not show it at the time, I would recommend for viewing at the end of the first week the film entitled "A Trip Through the New York World's Fair"[1]—a gay and colorful tour of that funland of advertising.

Week Two

On Monday of the second week the collages were analyzed by the students. Dominant themes were picked out (for example, cars, girls, food, underwear, liquor). Having a tape recorder going during the discussion helped to upgrade the tone of the responses, I think. After dominant themes had been cited, specific questions about each theme were posed. For example: (1) Why is the car such an appealing item? (2) What exactly does a car do for a guy? (3) Describe what you think the man is like who drives a '67 Chaparral with a 327. In this manner a foundation was established for an understanding of existing attitudes toward some objects.

During the next three days we approached the topic of symbols. First the students discussed "status symbols," and long lists were made on the board of items that might indicate status. I brought into the discussion a few striking examples of how status symbols might be involved in the selling of products. (For example: "The car we drive tells others who we are and what we think we want to be. Our

car is the clearest way we have of telling people our exact position in life."[2]) On the overhead projector we looked at a few examples of magazine ads containing status symbols such as yachts, motorcycles, resorts. The symbols were identified and discussed.

An impressive list of items resulted from the discussion the next day on "sex symbols." Such things as hair styles, miniskirts, and even the guitar were included. The following day "power symbols" were discussed in the same manner. Heated discussion arose over the question of whether or not an automobile needed horsepower enough to go 140 miles per hour. It was suggested that perhaps there were reasons other than "transportation" for buying fast cars.

A film which could be shown at this point in the unit is "Symbols and Signatures."[3]

The next step which seemed logical to me at the time was to have the students choose an appealing product and create an advertisement to sell it. But the idea was a flop. The students didn't respond at all. Although they had begun to understand basic concepts of advertising (products may appeal to people on more than one level; products may be made to appeal by the symbol or image they project, etc.), they lacked the facility and ingenuity to create their own designs. To bridge the gap I decided to have the students work first on a project that would increase their skill at handling two-dimensional design. Then I would try to find other exercises that would increase their inventiveness.

Week Three

"Op" art proved to be the successful vehicle for getting the students involved in abstract two-dimensional design. Examples of "Op" art abound in the teen-age world—on record covers, in clothes, in the patterning of cosmetic cases, vibrating on billboards—and from these the students got inspiration to make their own bold, mostly black and white designs. The results were impressive. At the end of the week two films on formal poster design were shown

---

[1] This film is available free of charge at Association Films, Hayward, California.

[2] Vance Packard, *The Hidden Persuaders* (New York: David McKay Co., Inc., 1957), p. 85.

[3] Also available through Association Films, Hayward, California.

to demonstrate how the bold "Op" art designs could work in a poster that had to advertise something.[4]

Week Four

Monday we had a clinic on "sensory perception." The idea was to rekindle interest in commercial products. The girls and then the boys were asked to respond to the soap package they would buy in the supermarket—the orange one with the red swirls or the blue one with the yellow-orange vortex. (Presumably females respond to one color and males to another.) Other packages were tested. Then students were blindfolded to see if they could distinguish between two similar brands of cigarettes, butter and margarine, two popular brands of potato chips, etc., the point being that many products are sold, not because of their unique quality, but because they project an image which inspires brand loyalty.[5]

The next day the technique of "brainstorming" was explained and different products, including the automobile, were "brainstormed" in an effort to get the students to come up with advertising ideas freely and quickly.

The last step in the bridge consisted of a blank form of a car or a person which the students were to embellish by drawing or cutting out and pasting on those particular design features which they thought would make the product (car or dress) salable. Here the student was able to incorporate commercial art concepts into a two-dimensional design. He was able to describe the environment without actually having to create the whole work himself.

The film "Follow It All the Way,"[6] which describes the steps in the manufacture and sale of a product, was shown at the end of the week.

Week Five

The final assignment in this unit entailed having the students create their own advertisements using one of the things they would like most to have in the world. The object (product) could be drawn, copied, traced, or cut out of a magazine. But it had to be incorporated into an original layout and it had to appeal to a particular urge or desire in the consumer. Special attention had to be paid to the overall design of the advertisement and to the impact of the color.

Summary

As suggested in the introduction, there are numerous activities which could broaden this unit on commercial art. Offhand, I think of car design, a trip to the Chevrolet plant in Fremont, making and designing packages, visiting an advertising agency, etc. Also, there are intermediary exercises that would increase the students' two-dimensional design skills—for example, lettering, making stencils, silk-screening, practicing with scratchboard, shading sheets, and other materials of the advertising artist. However, it is the beginning of the unit, the discussion of symbols and the analysis of ads to determine their motivational effect, that requires the most careful planning and presentation. Symbols, images, motivational forces are all very personal phenomena. But even if it cannot be done in an entirely objective way, an attempt to understand more fully the techniques of commercial art and the effects of advertising on our lives is, I feel, worth the effort.

Whether or not the concepts presented have had any effect on the behavior or attitudes of my students this year, I cannot say. One positive result, I feel, from the commercial art unit is this: the students understood that I was interested in the designs and objects that form their reality, and this helped open the door for communication between us. Recent projects calling for the design of a travel poster and a traffic poster, in effect commercial art, have produced some very striking results, so striking, in fact, that I am not discouraged.

[4] "Poster Making—Design and Technique" and "Poster Making—Printing by Silk Screen" were both available in the district film library.
[5] The ideas in this paragraph come out in Vance Packard's *The Hidden Persuaders*.
[6] Available through Association Films, Hayward, California.

Bibliography

Books

1. *Art Directors Annual of Advertising Art.* New York: Art Directors' Club, 1958.

2. Britt, Stewart H. *The Spenders*. New York: McGraw-Hill Book Company, 1960.
3. Gentry, Curt. *The Vulnerable Americans*. Garden City, N.Y.: Doubleday & Company, Inc., 1966.
4. Herdeg, Walter. *Packaging*. Zurich: Graphis, 1959.
5. Packard, Vance. *The Hidden Persuaders*. New York: David McKay Co., Inc., 1957.

Periodicals

1. *Artforum*—provided good examples of painting and graphics using "Op" art principles.

Films

1. Association Films, Inc., 25358 Cypress Avenue, Hayward, Calif. Association has many good films available free that can be used in the art classroom.
2. Alameda County Schools Film Library, 224 Winton Avenue, Hayward, California.

Brochures

1. San Francisco Museum of Art—the nicely designed advertisements from the museum provide good examples of design to use in the classroom.

STUDENT-PRODUCED FILM

KENNETH ROSENBERG AND EDWARD TROY **67**

Guide to Filmmaking in the Schools

Introduction

Movies are very much a part of the life of today's student. Recent statistics point out that children, by the time they leave high school, have spent approximately 15,000 hours watching movies in the local theater and on television. They are truly a film generation.

Students in grade school, high school, and colleges are today turning to films as a form of artistic self-expression. Innovative educators are

ED. NOTE: This strategy provides technical information and practical suggestions both for class-produced filmmaking in any subject and for school programs in cinematography. Mr. Rosenberg (an intern in 1966–1967) developed many of these approaches during his first year of teaching.

beginning to realize and provide for this interest. Many American schools offer at least a rudimentary course in film as a creative medium, while more and more colleges and universities include filmmaking as an accredited part of the curriculum.

Teachers have begun to realize that a student produced film can serve several purposes. First, the production of the film can lead the students to a deeper appreciation of film as an artistic form, and second, teachers can have more control over the type and scope of the visual aids they use. Third, the film itself can serve as an instructional tool not limited to the particular class or school making it. Most important, the class that conceives, writes, and produces a film is engaged in a creative process of far greater value than the contents of the film.

In response to the needs of this film generation, the authors, Kenneth Rosenberg, an English teacher, and Edward Troy, a social studies teacher at Davidson Junior High School in San Rafael, California, have introduced into their school district a continuing cinematography program.

Starting in the eighth grade, we have introduced a two-semester course open to all students as an elective. The first part of the course is a basic introduction to cinematography, which includes the history of the cinema, film appreciation, and film theory. The second part involves the actual production of a film through a film workshop, starting with plot selection and adaptation, followed by filming and editing.

The cinematography classes have produced many feature films such as *The Lottery,* adapted from the short story by Shirley Jackson; *My Cool Lady,* adapted from the play *Pygmalion* by G. B. Shaw; and *The Glorious Whitewasher* adapted from *Tom Sawyer* by Mark Twain.

The cinematography classes have created a wide interest in many school districts. The authors have gone to other classes and have helped other teachers' students make films, such as dialogues in foreign language classes, instructional films for industrial arts classes, animated cartoons for science classes, and documentary films with social studies classes.

This growing demand for information has led the authors to consolidate their ideas and prepare information that will enable any teacher to lead a class in the production of a film. In Part One we will discuss the activities involved in filming. Part Two provides more technical information about format, equipment to purchase, and production of sound to accompany the film.

Part One: Setting Up to Film

This guide could not possibly cover all the creative ways of capturing ideas on film. There is only one real way of learning to be a good filmmaker: get yourself a camera and do it. After you have the equipment that you are going to use in your class (see Part Two), experiment with a few rolls. Use the recommended camera settings that come with the film.

After you have shot some footage, check the results. You should purchase an editing machine (prices start at less than fifteen dollars) and try cutting and splicing the film to obtain the desired results. Use only "magnetic splicing tape" made especially for 8mm sound film. Hints on improving your films can be found in the leaflet normally returned with each roll of processed film.

Filming

Once you know what you are going to do and how to do it, make a script. Even the best filmmakers shoot from a script which should indicate exactly where everyone is supposed to be at any time and what they have to do. Go over the script with the class until they can visualize the film. Try to let the students do most of the work. Only if it is their film will they feel the pride of accomplishment.

The older and more mature your students are, the less you need to do. However, we suggest that in the beginning the teacher be the cameraman. In this way you are able to maintain control over the production. Later as students learn and develop good judgment, you can pick the most responsible ones to work the camera.

Besides the cameraman, you can appoint a soundman, propman, etc. Everyone should have a job, even if this requires manufacturing many moviemaking jobs such as "Recorder Knot Watchman" or "Light Meter Keeper" or "Time Keeper." Take a look at the credits on a movie and you will get an idea of the many jobs you can create to keep everybody busy and happy. Besides, there are many legitimate jobs that students must do to produce a movie. The film is a classroom project and should be the work of everyone. The spirit of professionalism will play an important part in maintaining classroom discipline. Never let the students believe that they are amateur moviemakers—*they are professionals.*

The most important rule to follow when filming is to keep the camera steady. Avoid panning. Use a tripod if possible. Animation, titles, and other unusual effects can be created by taking a few frames at a time while someone moves the object or letters between frames. Action can be reversed to obtain a desired effect by turning the camera upside down. Later this footage is cut and righted in the editing process. Disappearing or reappearing objects require a tripod to keep the camera still while the action changes between frames. Shooting faster than the projector's speed causes the action to slow down. Fewer frames per second cause an "old time movie effect" of fast motion. Fade-ins or fade-outs are made by turning the aperture setting on the lens of the camera. All sorts of tricks can be added to the film during editing. There are many books dealing with the operation of the camera for the professional. Avoid most of these techniques until you have mastered the basic art of filming.

Adding the Soundtrack

There are two ways of adding a soundtrack to film: simultaneous recording (adding the sound while the picture is taken) and post-recording (adding the sound after the film has been processed and edited.)

For most films, the teacher will find post-recording the most practical. The film is shot and later edited. Errors are cut out, and the footage assembled. Then the students reassemble for the recording session. While the movie is projected on the screen, the students lip-sync in the sound and sound effects on the recorder part of the projector. Again, a script aids immeasurably to this procedure.

Simultaneous recording requires excellent equipment, including the tape recorder. There must be a means of starting and stopping the tape recorder at the same time as the film. A "Clacker-board" can be used to set up an image/sound reference point at the beginning of the film. Since the sound is 56 frames ahead of the picture, editing is very difficult. The simultaneous recording procedure is not recommended unless the scene is a one time affair, not to be edited, such as a film of someone who cannot return to put in the sound.

Projection

When the film is ready for projection, the class can prepare invitations and programs for other classes and parents who may wish to see the movie. There are numerous film festivals where students can enter their 8mm films for prizes and awards. A possible source for money to support school moviemakers is the student films. If the money can be advanced for a 8mm sound projector, the profits from a noontime showing of cartoons and selected shorts can be used to repay the money and purchase movie-making equipment. In this way, many limited budget districts have been able to develop programs. A selection of commercial sound or silent films for 8mm can be obtained from 8mm dealers ranging in price from $1.50 up.

Film Libraries

Once your school starts making movies, it is possible to start a library of films that can be shared by other classes or schools. Science classes can use a close-up lens and time-lapse photography to explore the wonder of a growing plant. Biology classes can use slow motion to capture the bee's motion in a flower, and English classes can film a play.

Extra prints from an original 8mm film can be obtained through any photographic dealer or company for about ten cents per foot.

Part Two: Technical Information— Format, Equipment, Sound

Choosing the Format

Sixteen millimeter films are widely shown in the public schools, but their production in the classroom is virtually nonexistent due to the extremely high cost of film and processing. A 16mm sound camera equals the cost of some of the video tape machines, and a sound color print can cost upward of six dollars per minute.

Recently with the advent of improved films and magnetic sound coatings, the amateur's 8mm movie camera has taken on new importance as a means of producing quality sound moving pictures at a nominal cost. Because of its different size and makeup, 8mm color sound movies cost less than one dollar per minute. The low cost of 8mm equipment has made these small versatile cameras and projectors ideal tools for the teacher.

Among the 8mm formats there are four choices: regular 8, super 8, single 8, and double 8. This guide will limit itself to regular and super 8 where equipment and film are readily available. Contrary to wide belief, regular 8mm is probably the better choice than the newer format, super 8mm. The heavily advertised super 8 usually costs more than comparable regular 8's. Film costs more for super 8 than regular 8. Regular 8 gets more film running time per foot because of the smaller picture. Super 8 sound recording is more expensive than 8mm. Regular 8 offiers a wide variety of film ranging up to 1000 ASA black and white for use where little light is available to color film from 25 up to 160 ASA; further, all film is labeled as for use so the teacher can select the exact film for every filming situation. Because super 8 film is encased in a metal cartridge, the teacher is limited in the techniques he can use. Since good, used regular 8mm equipment is widely available, we recommend this choice for a film format.

The Principle of 8mm Sound

Regular 8mm film is made from twenty-five feet of 16mm film which is run through the camera twice, slit down the middle, and spliced end to end, forming a standard roll of fifty feet. Each foot of regular 8mm film contains eight small individual picture frames of 5mm × 4mm.

At the standard projection speed of eighteen frames per second (FPS) a fifty foot roll's running time is 220 seconds. These fifty foot rolls can be spliced together to make a continuous show of any length.

There are various devices on the market which attempt to synchronize a tape recorder with a movie projector. These devices do not use sound recorded on the film itself, and are therefore not suited for simplified showings one now has with sound-on-film equipment. Because separate sound systems are both complex and expensive, this guide will only discuss the standard sound-on-film system for 8mm, as approved by the Society of Motion Picture and Television Artists (SMPTA).

Sound-on-film can be added to 8mm film with the addition of a magnetic soundtrack, which is usually added to the sprocket side of the film after processing. This sound track is a strip of magnetic oxide coated on the edge of the film. The film is passed through an 8mm sound projector where live or prerecorded sound is taped on the film 56 frames ahead of the picture. The projector's recorder head serves as a playback head and the sound can be recorded and erased as often as desired. Standard recording speeds are 18 and 24 FPS. There is a shorter running time at 24 FPS, but the sound fidelity is slightly better.

Choosing Equipment

CAMERA. Most 8mm cameras may be used since the sound is recorded on a separate tape recorder. However, there are some features that one might look for in a camera:

1. An electric drive is an advantage. The camera may shoot an entire scene without stopping. Also, when scenes are shifted, there is no time wasted for windup.
2. A variable speed control allows the camera to adjust for 18 FPS or 24 FPS. Prices of suitable 8 mm cameras range from about ten dollars up.

SOUND PROJECTORS. There are a number of sound 8mm projectors on the market. These play silent and sound films and conform to the SMPTA standards. These projectors also have a "still position" for projecting single frame images similar to a slide or strip film projector. Most sound 8mm projectors sell new for under $250.

SCREENS. The type of room light will determine the type of screen. Normally the best all-around classroom screen is of the silver lenticular type. For best results, extra care must be taken with 8mm to insure that the projection room or auditorium is completely lightproof and dark.

CAMERA LIGHTS. When filming indoors with color film, additional light is normally required. A separate light meter or built-in meter will determine if there is sufficient light. If not, follow the film manufacturer's recommendations for photoflood illumination. A suitable 600 watt movie light sells for under seven dollars.

TAPE RECORDER. The quality of your sound film will depend on the quality of the tape recorder. A tape recorder with capstan drive to keep the speed steady is necessary. Use speed 7½ IPS for best fidelity.

FILM. Any 8mm film can be used and the sound track put on by the processing laboratory. Simply specify "Magnetic Soundtracking," and the film will be returned with a magnetic coating ready for recording. This service usually costs about four cents per foot in addition to the processing charge, which costs about $1.50. Special sound track film is available at Sears for about $2.70 per fifty foot roll. Price includes processing, and soundtracking. Kodak film with "Sonotone Tracking" is available at dealers for $4.60 complete.

Another way of soundstripping film is to purchase a soundstripping machine and do it yourself at less than one cent per foot. These machines are available for under fifteen dollars and they are easy to operate.

RESOURCES. All the above mentioned equipment is available from Superior Bulk Film Company, 450 North Wells Street, Chicago, Ill.

This company specializes in 8mm film and equipment and their catalog is filled with information for the person who wishes to set up a film program. Another company, Abbe Films of 417 West 44th Street, New York, has a wide selection of 8mm sound equipment. The best magazine on 8mm film production is the British magazine *8MM Magazine,* available at some book stores.

Conclusion

This guide, while not complete as far as the many technical possibilities of class filmmaking, should serve as a helpful guide to the teacher who desires to make his classroom a place of creative expression through the medium of film.

VII: TEACHING FOR VALUES, CONCERNS, ATTITUDES

Student at Martin Luther King Junior High School, Berkeley, California. What is he thinking? Feeling? How can a teacher help?

...In youth the tables of childhood dependence begin slowly to turn: no longer is it merely for the old to teach the young the meaning of life, whether individual or collective. It is the young who, by their responses and actions, tell the old whether life as represented by the old and as presented to the young has meaning; and it is the young who carry in them the power to confirm them and, joining the issues, to renew and to regenerate, or to reform and to rebel....[1]

From one end of the nation to the other, we see portentous protests and confrontations daily. Not only the schools, but all institutions are under attack. Perhaps, more than ever before, adolescents need to know what to affirm and what to reject.

Until some sweeping social and educational changes are made to meet old promises and new demands, what can concerned teachers do in their classrooms? How can they deal helpfully with pressing social problems and value conflicts? How can they avoid "inert" ideas from the past and achieve the "relevance" that today's students demand?

Perceiving that academic performance is directly related to one's self-image, ability to relate to others, and a sense of connectedness with the environment, our incoming committed teachers *do* try, in whatever school setting they are placed, to help their students gain greater self-respect and a deeper understanding of the urgent issues facing us all.

The strategies in this section are illustrations of several ways such motivated teachers connect with the key concerns of adolescents, and even in this difficult period, help their students explore and strengthen personal and social values.

The strategies we have included here are placed in the following five categories: (1) Developing Self-Image; (2) Personalizing School Learning; (3) Career Preparation; (4) Developing Social Values and Awareness; (5) Dealing with Race Problems and Issues.

Developing Self-Image

We begin with Linda G. Davis's strategy, "Illustrate Who You Are." Instead of the usual autobiographical assignment, she asked her students to describe themselves either in a collage or notebook as a composite product of the significant external influences—the music, poetry, art, drama, heroes, movies, magazines, books, etc.—that had helped shape their unique personalities. Next, in a strategy which combines contemporary with traditional approaches, through reviving the practice of the old "Commonplace" books—a compilation of useful quotations—Eliene Bundy illustrates another way to help students develop a sense of themselves and their heritage.

Personalizing School Learning

The genius of the interesting teacher consists in sympathetic divination of the sort of material with which the pupil's mind is likely to be already spontaneously engaged, and in the ingenuity which discovers paths of connection from that material to the matters to be newly learned....[2]

[1] Erik H. Erikson, *The Challenge of Youth* (Garden City, N.Y.: Doubleday & Company, Inc., Anchor Books, 1965), p. 24.
[2] William James, *Talks to Teachers* (New York: W. W. Norton & Co., Inc., 1958), p. 82.

Working with unmotivated students, Nancy S. Harms describes some simple techniques for "Personalizing Earth Science," for demonstrating how one can take students from an interest in their immediate neighborhood to an understanding of man's cosmic environment.

Next, Brownlee Shirek, despairing at first of ever motivating his tuned-out students in a continuation high school, describes how he maneuvered them from the pool table to intramural sports and finally to newspaper writing about these events. Willie L. Williams, drama and music teacher also teaching at a continuation school, in his strategy, "Teaching by Discovery," describes his own discovery of a few methods which really "turned on" his classes. Hoping at first to teach the music and drama he loved, he came to realize how much more motivating popular music and improvisational drama could be for his disaffected students. In "Does It Relate, Man?" Margaret Bentley demonstrates various ways to make traditional literature and drama significant for her students. For example, by relating the tragic death of President Kennedy to a unit on drama, she discovered that Shakespeare's *Julius Caesar* could be genuinely appreciated, even by a lethargic class of below average students.

Career Preparation

In the last few decades, the laudable effort to offer all high school students the opportunity to go on to college has resulted, unfortunately, in the virtual neglect and downgrading of programs preparing students for the everyday world of work—the world which the majority of students will have to face. Presently, far too many high school seniors graduate without any clear sense of their next step. If they do not go on to higher education, they are generally left floundering. Even those who are college-oriented have little knowledge about the types of colleges and career preparation available to them.

Some of our incoming teachers are especially sensitive to students' concerns about the future. We have included here a few samples of the directions such teachers take with their students.

First, Robert E. Keller, business teacher, in "Toward a Contact Curriculum," describes how the lack of job readiness he discovered in noncollege-bound students prompted him to join the high school's curriculum committee. His paper also offers a few specific suggestions for structuring a more appropriate curriculum for the vast numbers of students who will not go on to four-year colleges.

In another paper, Mary S. Thomas, social studies teacher and counselor, reports her students' desire to know about their own job possibilities. Her strategy, "The Present and the Future," describes the five-day unit she developed for acquainting her pupils with jobs for the summer and after graduation. The unit she developed, including practice in role-playing of job interviews, could easily be reproduced in many high school classes.

Robert Latham, science teacher, working with high ability college-preparatory students, discovered that his students also were woefully uninformed about careers appropriate for their needs and abilities. His strategy paper, "Career and College Guidance in the Classroom," details a unit he devised to provide his class with the kind of concrete and practical information about career possibilities in science which overworked school counselors cannot possibly provide.

Developing Social Values and Awareness

In the last analysis, what the school is uniquely equipped to do, given the range of agencies that educate, is to make youngsters aware of the constant bombardment of facts, opinions, and values to which they are subjected; to help them question what they see and hear; and ultimately, to give them the intellectual resources they need to make judgments and assess significance. . . . The importance of radio and television, and the common experiences they provide, cannot be overestimated. . . .[3]

Moving to more controversial areas, we have included a set of instructional strategies which wrestle with the formation of social values. We start with the efforts of two teachers in different schools, but in similar white, suburban settings. First, Frederick W. Brock's "Experiences in Teaching for Values" explains the kinds of written materials and taped speeches he found useful in leading his "advantaged" but protected students toward thoughtful inspection of their assumptions and beliefs about education, authority, and race. Social studies teacher Richard C. Raines, working with similarly "advantaged" students, in "Functional Democracy: Historic, National, and Personal," recounts a three week unit containing several strategies for making both ancient and modern history relevant and illuminating—including an inquiry into group dynamics and the democratic process operating within the classroom itself.

Burton H. Greene, an English teacher in a metropolitan setting, focused on *The Grapes of Wrath,* a novel of the thirties, for his strategy, "Teaching the Social Novel." Drawing on the mass media, community resources, and present-day problems—such as the grape pickers' strike in California—he shows a wide range of methods and materials which English teachers can employ to promote sympathetic social awareness in their students. In "An Approach to Africa," Karen Dorn, history teacher in an all white school, details the various techniques and resource materials (filmstrips, guest speakers, readings, group projects) which she used to help her students develop an appreciation of cultural differences and some insight into the racial problems besetting the United States.

Dealing with Race Problems and Issues

If our democracy is to survive in years to come, the schools and local communities, as well as the national government, will need to create ambitious programs to help solve interracial tensions and minority group problems. Some communities and school districts have already begun to create special school programs to meet these needs. (Note the black studies and Mexican-American interdisciplinary programs in Part Three.) Meanwhile, concerned classroom teachers are seizing the opportunity to improve interracial understanding and minority group self-images wherever and however they can.

[3] Lawrence A. Cremin, *The Genius of American Education* (New York: Random House, Inc., A Vintage Book, 1966), pp. 22–23.

For example, a biology teacher, Rochelle Esterle, in "Biological Aspects of Race," illustrates a way to help a predominantly black class of students to understand and appreciate the biological advantage of certain racial characteristics. Drama teacher Richard Jones, in his strategy, "Black History Week," recounts the rationale, the joint planning, and the success of his school's one week program of black history, black psychology, and black art, including an original dramatic adaptation of *Black Rage,* by psychologist Price Cobbs and W. H. Grier. Mr. Jones believes that the series of events which he and his classes devised could serve as a model for more extensive Black Studies Programs.

Minerva Barranco, history teacher at a racially troubled inner-city school, reveals some of the the problems that she, a Panamanian, had to face in teaching a Black History class, and describes the various community trips to school agencies which she arranged to develop greater rapport with the students and to make the course more relevant to their daily lives.

We complete this group of strategies with Burton H. Greene's review of the books, materials, and procedures used in a "Black Literature" course which he and his black and white students pioneered together at the JFK Experimental Summer School, 1968.

In Part Three there will be descriptions of schoolwide programs designed to help students with their values, attitudes, and concerns. The strategies included in this particular chapter of Part Two are examples of what individual teachers can make possible in most present-day school settings.

DEVELOPING SELF-IMAGE

LINDA G. DAVIS **68**

Illustrate Who You Are

The Project

This strategy came about as an attempt to begin the year with my sophomore English students—heterogeneous classes of about thirty students taking a two-semester course called English II. Their language skills varied greatly. I wanted to avoid assigning the usual autobiography or report of summer activities. Instead, I asked students to do a project, one that would be limited only by their imagination and creativity. Their task: using pictures from magazines and newspapers, using lyrics from songs, lines from poetry, using material (quotations, prints, selections) from music, philosophy, religion, history, psychology, sociology, art, and drama, *illustrate* who you think you are now, what's happening to you, what's important to you. In other words, try to illustrate the "happening" that you are now. This can be a light show on paper that says something about you. *Show* you.

Students graded themselves on this project. Self-evaluation is, I believe, a meaningful experience for these students, and it is an area in which they, although white and middle class, are underprivileged. They have had very little opportunity to decide how to regard something they have created. Having worked their way through nine years of a system in which authority figures gave approval or disapproval, they were reluctant to grade themselves, saying they did not know how to decide; they wanted me to do it.

This kind of response helped me see again that self-evaluation is one small beginning way in which students can be made more responsible for themselves and their learning. My students need to trust themselves more; they need to trust their feelings, their creativity. Responsibility, self-direction, and trust do not grow in an environment where the student never develops the skill and the strength to evaluate his own work.

Students were given a week and a half to complete this assignment. After the projects were turned in classwork was such that it allowed me to take some time during the period and sit down with each student and page through his project. The collages and notebooks were meeting places and springboards. And since I was new to the school, the conferences were an excellent way for me to get to know each student. We talked about what the assignment meant to him and where it took him. Since I was not able to see all the students during classtime, I met with the remainder before and after school. This took about two weeks.

Results

During the conference the student told me how many points he was giving himself. Since

I use a point system, students were given a range of points and could grade themselves according to how much this assignment meant to them, how much time they spent on it, and whether or not it was a learning, exploring venture for themselves.

The student response was positive. Rather than presenting a word-by-word account, they enjoyed "showing" themselves. So many of these projects were beautifully, sensitively done, they were put on display in the library. There were collages, notebooks, photographic essays, a carpentry creation, other three-dimensional collage constructions, a sewn piece, and from one young man a shoe box with a broken mirror in it. Many students affirmed that one of the most significant parts of the assignment was not the final product but the process of looking for pictures, quotations, and collage material that "said *them*." In this they discovered they had to make new decisions about who they feel they are.

Future Plans

The final part of this strategy is another creative project, one that is the last assignment for the year, due in June. Their task will be slightly different, more encompassing. But by that time they will have more to bring. They know now about this assignment and have begun collecting material.

Their task: illustrate the forces, events, philosophies, ideas, people, and happenings that have affected you, both positively and negatively, and helped to make you the person you are in June. In the final part of this project, say something about hope—what kind of hope you see for yourself and for our world. Again, for all of this, draw from as many sources as you can: magazines, newspapers, lyrics from songs, poems, quotations, art prints, music, philosophy, religion, history, psychology, sociology, drama.

They will grade themselves in the same way, and I will sit down with them and chat about their projects.

Among other positive results, the "Illustrate Who You Are" assignment was effective in my classroom situation because it gave everyone, even those with low ability language skills, a chance to start off well; and it should give everyone the opportunity to finish the year in a strong and individual way.

ELIENE BUNDY **69**

Commonplace Books

Although the word *commonplace* now refers to an ordinary topic, a trite remark, or an everyday occurrence, it did for a long time mean a general theme or argument applicable to many particulars. And a Commonplace Book was a collection of ideas applicable to many particulars, a store of usable or striking ideas.[1]

In a suburban school in which my middle-track, eleventh-grade English students had "done" journals, English notebooks, and stream-

[1] See Appendix.

of-consciousness or random writing, it seemed that, to go smoothly through their last required year of English, something new—maybe just a gimmick—was needed. I wanted something that would encourage sustained writing, something in which students could feel some pride, a product, but something that did not necessarily depend on their originality.

The commonplace book appeared to be an attractive package into which I could put the benefits to be had from several devices. It has become many things to various students in these junior English classes. Much more "mileage" than I had supposed can be had from it. I find that it allows the freedom of random writing, the structure of an English notebook, and is a broader product than a journal. And, very important, it helps to break down the traditional subject boundaries of English classes. It helps to blend the outside world with the study of form, content, and articulation.

On the first day of class I asked students to bring a new, thick spiral notebook. It was to be, I said, a special book called a commonplace book, in which they would collect things all year. Some brief history of the commonplaec had to be given, but such rather esoteric stuff about a quaint subject had to be fed out very sparingly and judiciously for several weeks.[2]

Students should write in it what and when they pleased, copying ideas, facts, quotations into the book from any source. If they liked recordkeeping, they might find it interesting to date things collected. The important things to remember—there were two—are, first, that the book should truly reflect what interests the student keeping it and not in any way be an English notebook. Some people may even use pictures, cartoons, diagrams to express ideas in other than the usual written ways. One student, for example, filled his book with elaborate drawings of motors and wrote about motorcycles and quoted from magazines on racing. Another student was interested in illusion and included many optical illusions, photos, and also riddles and complex problems to figure out. He wrote about them occasionally, but mostly just collected them. Another student wrote constantly and at length about everything, in chatty journalistic style, under such headings as *Girls, Boys, Pets, Books,* and *Where My Head Is At.* This last heading contained her most serious ruminating.

The second important thing to remember is that commonplace books should have headings: topic or category designations. The student should write at the top of each page what he considers the subject therein to be. His headings, again, should reflect what is important to him. For example, when Fielding wrote about Alexander the Great in his commonplace book, the heading for it was not war or history or great generals, but "drunkenness."

2 See Appendix.

To get students started requires some writing time in class. Also, I put pithy quotes on the board occasionally, with only the suggestion that they could copy these or any other ideas, from whatever source, into their books if they found them interesting—and comment on them or not. Students need to be encouraged periodically to continue adding to their books: by the end of the year they can look back on the history of what their education really was during that time, on what had really caught their fancy. It may be very different from the usual school fare and more important to them. Also, it will probably surprise them to see the direction their thought took during that time. Many students don't even notice what they notice, and recording ideas can be a start at constructive self-awareness. I would like to see students take pride in their own intellectual development. Keeping a commonplace book can serve to direct their attention to it.

By the end of the semester, I have found that many students have enjoyed keeping the book. They like the way it releases them from "English," and it has encouraged them to do more creative writing. Several books are literally full of poems. And one girl who seems quite dull in class spent a long time discussing with herself the problem of political and police authority. This was the result of a class discussion in which she had not said a word.

An unexpected benefit has been to the maverick student who disapproves of and refuses most of the work the class does. He can "make up" a fair amount by reading and writing about whatever he pleases in his commonplace book. It has proved the salvation of several such students, who were able to learn something about articulating and structuring ideas without being confined by teacher prescriptions.

No emphasis, by the way, was placed on neatness or grammar. If the student got an idea while sitting in the park, he should write it on the back of an envelope—or scrap of bark—and then later merely staple or tape it onto a page of his book, check it for legibility, and put a heading on the page. The book is strictly an idea collection, original or not original, to which the student gives some minimal organization.

Many teachers find it necessary, today, to

defend the prescriptive education that has been accepted so long. Students suddenly resent models, seem to admire originality and "creativity" alone—too often at the expense of both reason and form. At such a time, using the commonplace book might provide one tool for the teacher struggling for order and reason, and still provide comfort to the egocentric adolescent, bent on his own "thing." Whatever the student chooses from the world around him to collect into his book is a model he has picked out for himself. Although his teacher has not gotten him to accept her models, she has moved him in the direction of defining what he himself finds admirable, and therefore choosing a model. The book provides a way for the student to gradually put his "thing" into specific and meaningful language. Only at the end of several months, though, will he see results. By the end of a year, with luck, he may be able to tell the teacher, and himself, what his "thing" is—at least for that year.

Even though "original" and "creative" are terms sometimes generously applied even to complete gibberish, I believe these terms are threatening ones for many young people. They set a very high standard for performance. In a commonplace book the student can legitimately copy as much as he pleases from any source, is encouraged to collect all bits of wisdom that attract him. He can plagiarize freely and without remorse if he wishes. He doesn't do this long, I find, because as he gains respect for his own ideas, he wants them separate and labeled as his own. Meanwhile there's originality and creativity in his choices and headings. These will form a pattern after a time, reflecting the student's concerns.

I have had little success, so far, in asking students to use the headings to categorize their material. One student, however, did write a charming little parable about an odd teacher who went frantically about requiring all students to label everything, until the whole world had become nothing but a classification system. Amusing it was, but his and most of the students' problem with the headings was akin to a problem that they have with exposition. They are reluctant to, or cannot, commit themselves to a resolute position. It does require a bit of plain courage to take a definite stand on a subject, certainly in a composition where the stand must be supported or defended—must ultimately prove to *be* defensible. Hopefully, putting headings in one's commonplace book (with more encouragement than I gave) could provide an exercise in pinning oneself down: Just what *was* the subject that the paragraph I wrote last night was about? or, How do I explain why I put that cartoon and that quotation on the same page? What heading shall I give it? Such questions should help, since teachers of composition are constantly trying to get students to address a specific subject without wobbling about, to identify and define ideas.

Bibliographical Note

There is apparently not a good body of research on commonplace books, the reason often given being that the subject is too unwieldy, takes too many forms, and is naturally full of repetition, plagiarisms, and plain dull writing. The commonplace books of many well-known writers have been preserved and usually are published with monotonous, scholarly commentaries. But information and comments turn up in books written on the development of Medieval and Renaissance thought.

The sketchy information in this brief paper has come from:

1. Lechner, Sister Joan Marie. *Renaissance Concepts of the Commonplaces.* New York: Pageant Press, 1962.
2. *The Oxford English Dictionary.*
3. Lecture notes from a University of California course on seventeenth-century English literature given by Professor O. Hehir, Berkeley, 1966.

Appendix

Historically, the concept of commonplaces goes back to Aristotle, to whom a "place" meant a place—a pigeonhole in the mind—where one finds arguments or recorded bits of rhetoric and logic that could contribute to constructing an argument. As the medieval world carried out the classical idea, there evolved commonplace books in which commonly used ideas, topics, arguments were categorized under subject headings: serious "heads," ethics or metaphysics; and whimsical "heads," blushes, gnomology, and the like.

The medieval preacher used these topics or arguments in constructing his sermons after classic rhetorical forms. A sermon would have an introduction, theme—with divisions—and a moral exhortation. For each part, he would have many ready-to-go formulae: introductions from nature, from art, or from history, etc., all collected under headings, as usable commonplaces.

Commonplace books were in part responsible for the invention of conventional character types. A book would contain models for describing a virtuous woman, a politician, a prince. Very specific characteristics were included in each. Although moderns are offended by "commonplace" thinking that tended to reduce individuality to types, still the emerging commonplace book was a basic part of the education of Western man. Education in the Middle Ages was largely a matter of collecting, in commonplace books, virtuous models to imitate, both people and ideas. Originality was not so important as categorization and classification.

Used selectively and interpreted freely, there is a good deal in this early history which can add touches of tradition and background to the teaching of composition and literature. For example, the topics taken from ancient rhetorical "places" to signify the cycle of a man's life were used as the basis of a sixteenth-century biography of Chaucer, and have been a usable formula for biography ever since. They are: "Country, Parentage, Education, Marriage, Children (so much as we can find by records, etc.), Revenues, Service, Reward, Friends, Bookes, Death."[3]

Besides sermons and biography, there emerged formal letter writing with commonplace book models and examples of formulaic salutations, introductions, and conclusions. It is important that students learn the formulaic nature of much of literature: the preamble, the catalogue, etc. Whether one is talking about the list of ships in the *Iliad* or the list of guests in *The Great Gatsby,* it is the same kind of literary catalogue, one of several formulae an author uses as rhetorical devices. Recognizing the formula adds further connotative dimension to the passage one is reading. Familiarity with early "commonplace" thinking, with its types, models, and categories, is one way to get at the subject.

But through the following centuries commonplace books changed character many times, were so freely adapted to whatever use the writer put them that they are difficult to define. Every schoolboy began early using one as a simple copybook. As he grew older he added from his own thoughts. When he fell in love he was apt to fill a commonplace book with love sonnets. Most of English men of letters kept commonplace books all their lives. Bobby Burns discovered himself to be a poet from observing what he'd been putting in his commonplace book the first time he fell in love. Bacon's essays sometimes came straight out of his commonplace book with little change. Thomas Jefferson kept a commonplace book of only political ideas from his reading and thinking. He kept another as a running commentary on the Bible, of which he was a careful student. Jonathan Swift said, "Whatever in my small reading occurs, concerning this our fellow-creature I do never fail to set it down by way of Commonplace."

[3] See Bibliographical Note, above.

NANCY S. HARMS 70

Personalizing Earth Science

Background

Having a novice teacher devise strategies to be used upon forty-odd culturally and intellectually deprived students is somewhat comparable to having a premed student run a psychiatric ward. The basic problem is one of containment, and any device toward this end should be deemed successful. Somewhere along the way, however, is the requirement to teach the subject matter and it becomes obvious, even to a beginner, that containment and teaching do not always go hand in hand.

The forty-odd students of whom I speak are in two C track Earth Science classes. Each class includes four EH (Educationally Handicapped) students and a full range of C track. Several were borderline mentally retarded.

The problem of containment was lessened substantially when my mind became firmly fixed about what I could reasonably expect from these youngsters. I could not expect an "orderly" classroom, for I always seemed to have table sitters, standees, and wanderers. Private conversations would constantly interfere with what I wanted to say to the class. Petty thievery and malicious destruction were so common that it almost became easier to overlook them. Yet, with their many failings, the students were extremely sensitive and many were charmingly

open. Few of them really accepted the position they were in, and not far down underneath most of them did want to accomplish something.

It would be most comforting to think that in one fell swoop these antisocial, anti-intellectual, anti-everything students could be turned into vigorous, inquiring, enthusiastic pupils. Alas, this is not the game we are playing. The situation becomes a problem in gradual acceptance: they accept you and your standards; they and their standards must be at least tolerated. There must be give and take, swapping favors, attrition, and—as one pundit described it, in a way particularly appropriate to earth science—a matter of erosion.

The overwhelming problem at the beginning of the year finally evolved into one of putting science on a sufficiently personal basis so that most of the students could become interested and any who tried to do the work could not fail. I have found two areas which seem to have almost universal appeal. They are as usable in general science as earth science and could be used in grades seven through twelve. These are (1) earthquakes—particularly the study of the San Andreas fault, and (2) topographic maps of the local area. (A third topic of special interest has been fossils, but if they are not available locally it is of questionable value to expand the regular work with them.)

Anyone who lives in California can expect to experience an earthquake sooner or later. People who have already felt a quake almost always recall precisely what they were doing at the time. They are a natural happening but maintain an aura of the supernatural. The San Andreas fault receives a great deal of publicity as does the Hayward), and much new information is being brought to public attention on an almost regular basis. Stories of the 1906 earthquake are pulled out every April in commemoration of the devastation of San Francisco.

These are the things that make the study of earthquakes a natural subject in either general or earth science. Earthquakes are: (1) apt to happen again; (2) probably quite local in origin—most will be within the state; (3) highly publicized; and (4) extremely personal.

It might also be noted that the study of earthquakes provides a natural prelude for other areas of geology—sedimentary, metamorphic, and igneous rocks; landforms—basin and range structure, drowned valleys; geosynclines; topographic maps; fossils; etc.

Most textbooks make some mention of California's San Andreas fault and the destructive 1906 earthquake, but few give any detail. The best reference by far is Robert Iacopi's *Earthquake Country*.[1] The text is, of course, technically accurate but it is written for the lay reader. It is far more palatable and understandable than anything I have ever seen. It is replete with over two hundred photographs, maps, and sketches. Any student who merely looks at these and reads the captions will have gained tremendously. Anyone who delves into the text will be amply rewarded. While Iacopi's book deals primarily with the San Andreas fault, there is also much information on other California faults and recent activity along them. There are many photos of the 1925 Santa Barbara, the 1933 Long Beach, and the 1952 Tehachapi-Bakersfield earthquakes. Other large California quakes can be detailed from historical documents.

My basic approach to this inquiry was "What would you look for in recognizing a fault line?"

[1] (Menlo Park, Calif.: Lane Publishing Company, 1964).

Students were quick to say (and incorrectly) "Knocked down buildings." Leaning heavily on *Earthquake Country* and *Geology of Northern California* (Bulletin 190, California Division of Mines and Geology), we took up fault scarps, offset sedimentary layers, truncated mountain spurs (vertical movement); offset streambeds, offset rows of orchard trees, and rift valleys (horizontal movement). Both references cited have numerous illustrations of these features. Transparencies made for the use of an overhead projector are particularly effective. However, blackboard sketches, using colored chalk, are more than adequate.

Topographic maps of the Point Reyes, Painted Rock, and McKittrick Quadrangles are extremely useful in illustrating a rift valley and offset streambeds.

Sufficient interest was generated in this unit that students voluntarily brought in newspaper and magazine articles. Several did unsolicited written reports. One of the most impressive results was a model of the Tomales Bay-Olema-Bolinas Lagoon area done in damp sand (120 mesh Del Monte—$1.30/100 lbs.). The relief model was taken from the Point Reyes Quadrangle and was complete with an "active" San Andreas fault.

Topographic Maps

The local topographic map is a far better place to start with than the maps usually recommended in textbooks. During the fall I had used the local quadrangle as a Friday filler. The students were fascinated to see their own homes as sixteenth of an inch black squares on such an official document. I was delighted to see my own home. Interest was extremely high.

After Christmas, when I really needed something to recapture the students, I started a unit on topographic maps. Reading these maps, which on first glance can seem very confusing and complicated, is primarily a matter of experience. There is no better way to gain this experience than to hunt for familiar landmarks.

After a few general introductory remarks about map reading (scale, contour lines, color coding, etc.) I gave the following assignment:

1. How far do you live (in a straight line) from school?
2. At what altitude do you live?
3. At what altitude is the school?

Two days later some of the students were still working on the assignment. Our maps were issued in 1959, which means, of course, that much of Contra Costa County's "progress" is not shown. No freeways, few housing tracts, no flood control channels are shown. Our own school does not appear, nor does the street the school is on. Without such landmarks some students had to struggle—but struggle, they did.

The second assignment was only:

1. What is the highest altitude on the map?
2. What is the lowest?
3. Give a general description of the entire area on the map.

I was pleased with the quality of the area descriptions.

On the fourth day of the map work I put out as many adjoining quadrangles as we had. This gave good coverage of the central county area, an area with which the students were thoroughly familiar.

The last three days of the unit were spent drawing profiles from topo maps. There are few maps which are suitable to work from and I found it best to prepare my own. These were extremely simplified landforms (hills, valleys, mountains with craters, mesas, sand bars, etc.) and used either a ten, fifty, or one hundred foot contour interval. Once the mechanics of making the profile had been taught (scale and dropping perpendiculars), the students needed time to develop their techniques. Many profiles were done three or four times and a substantial supply of quadrille paper is essential.

Preparation of the profiles seems to drive home the real meaning of the topographic maps. It is difficult for many (as it is for me) to visualize the third dimension as it is represented by contour lines. Things fall into their proper place by means of this simple, mechanical technique.

A valuable adjunct to the topographic map is the geologic map. Unfortunately these are not available for all quadrangles, but when they are they should be used. There is so much information available from these maps that it is best to limit the students to kinds of rock, their geologic ages, and where the exposures are located. Field trips to exposure sites are highly desirable.

When the students have become familiar with their own area they are in a position to appreciate the landforms, peculiarities, and subtleties of other areas. I found I could show any map at random (Mt. Ranier, Grand Canyon, Mt. Morrison, Point Reyes, etc.) and get an immediate, quite accurate description of the landform. By this time the work had become a game to many.

While I spent about two weeks on the local topographic maps, this unit could be cut to one week or expanded into three or four. Any teacher who wishes to dwell on physical geography (physiography) or intends to do a great deal of work in geology would be wise to run this unit as early as possible in the year.

I have found that my students return to topo maps of their own volition whenever they have free time. They are able to pick out things of interest to themselves and are able to use this information in many class pursuits.

References, Aids, and Recommendations

1. *Earthquake Cards:* Issued biweekly, listing the preliminary determinations of epicenters. No charge. Write on school letterhead to:
   Director, Coast and Geodetic Survey
   Environmental Science Services Administration
   Coast and Geodetic Survey
   Rockville, Maryland 20852
2. *Earthquake Watch Kit:* Pacific centered Mercator world map, 50 × 30 inches. 100 each of three colors of map pins. Used in conjunction with USGS earthquake cards (see above). The circum-Pacific belt of activity is vividly and graphically developed. Available from most supply houses.
3. *ESSA Earthquake Information Bulletin:* Approximately 16 pages of current information. Issued monthly at no charge. Write to above address and ask to be put on their mailing list.
4. *Geology of Northern California.* Bulletin 190, California Division of Mines and Geology, Ferry Building, San Francisco, 1966. Chapter VIII—The San Andreas Fault. Good general reference but written in technical language. Excellent photos. It also details several Bay Area field trips, complete with mileage log.
5. Iacopi, Robert. *Earthquake Country.* Menlo Park, Calif.: Lane Publishing Company, 1964. Written in lay language but technically accurate, this book could be used as the sole source for studying earthquakes. No index.

Pool, Papers, and Volleyball: A Cooperative Strategy

Problems at a Continuation High School

Churchill High is a so-called continuation school. Its sixty-one students comprise but a small percentage of the almost 46,000 continuation students in the state of California. At Churchill, a one room schoolhouse, the students range in age from fifteen to eighteen years. Located in Newark, a middle to low income suburban town of 20,000 in the San Francisco Bay Area, the ethnic balance is approximately 80 percent Anglo-American and 20 percent Mexican-American at the school. In the minds of the school authorities and/or court authorities, most of these students have failed to fit into the standards of conventional adult behavior.

The basic problems confronting the staff at Churchill High are two; first, how to achieve a community of learning; and second, how to improve the self-image of the students.

There are forty-five courses offered at the secondary level. A modified contract system is used, with each student progressing at his own rate with the aid of tutoring whenever necessary. It is an adaptive education system. Contracts can be changed from day to day as the students' needs and abilities are revealed. The principal-teacher, the two classroom teachers, and the school secretary are dedicated to non-authoritarianism. To state that anything which goes on in the school is a single teacher's strategy would not only be presumptuous, it would be misleading. All strategies are developed cooperatively in daily conferences.

As a result of such daily conferences, it became obvious to us after a few weeks of the semester that we had a one room school physically, but emotionally we had sixty-one separate units—the students. This, then was our problem: the students hated themselves and each other almost as much as they hated the adult world as represented by the school system and the courts of law.

Our Attempted Solutions

1. First, we proposed a school paper. We found one student willing to take a course in journalism. We then produced a ditto sheet for all students asking for opinions, articles, and art designs. Nothing was submitted.

2. At about the same time, we initiated a physical education program. Since we had no regular facilities for P.E., our principal received permission to use the community playground which had basketball and volleyball courts. We played both basketball and volleyball, with the teachers participating. At first the play was vicious and antagonistic. There was no team play, only a great deal of hostility, four letter words, and accusations when a point was made or lost. Gradually, however, the play settled down. When the students became angry, the principal would admonish, "It's only a game." After about the third week of recreation the students began to form teams in a friendly rivalry. It should be noted here that more than 75 percent of these students had failed P.E. in conventional high school.

A problem arose in the use of the community center. On rainy days there was no place to play. This was solved when permission was granted for us to use the pool hall in the community center. Thus pool, ping pong, and checkers were added to the curriculum. One sidelight of interest occurred when our woman teacher trimmed the students at pocket billiards.

Some Results

Over the weeks the students began to relate to each other in a more positive way, both in the recreation center and in the classroom. Some interstudent tutoring developed, providing an exchange of knowledge of familiar material.

The most positive aspect of the P.E. periods came about when articles about sports began to be submitted for the moribund paper project. These articles left much to be desired in the way of "journalese" finesse, but they were the first public expression by these students. Furthermore, once the idea was established that they could submit their own opinions, other articles were submitted. Two additional students decided they wanted to be "journalists" and began writing for the paper. The self-image of the students was beginning to improve, and when the local press, through the school, conducted a survey of attitudes about the eighteen-year-old vote, ten students readily expressed their opinions and were featured in the local press.

The first edition of the school paper finally came out and received favorable comments from the community. As a result of finding that they had somethnig to say, the students began submitting their opinions about the school system, the society in which they lived, and about the schools which they had attended and were now attending. Most significant among the contributions was the recurring admonition to try harder since they were in a "good school" with "good teachers."

A corollary of the beginnings of a school community feeling were two Christmastime projects developed by the students themselves. The first of these was a committee formed by the students to collect from among themselves a basket of toys and food for a needy family, the family to be chosen by the student committee. Needless to say, these students at Churchill know about need. The second project was the organization of a choral group to entertain the oldsters in the many rest homes in the area during the Christmas season.

A further proof that the school is meaningful to the students is that they come early and stay late. Many of them also visit during the hours they are not required to be in class.

We feel that at Churchill High we are beginning to learn, and that we are not a continuation school but a beginning school for a community of learning, a community image, and a sense of self-respect.

And all this from a silly little game of volleyball, a game of pool, and a paper.

WILLIE L. WILLIAMS **72**

Teaching by Discovery

_____ High East Campus is a unique school. That is, there is much experimentation here with new ideas on how to teach turned-off kids in our society today. It is a school with so-called open enrollment. Some students are sent here because they failed to function in normal schools. Others are here because they became involved with the law—smoking marijuana cigarettes, incorrigible in class, fighting, etc. Still others are here because they wanted to find themselves in a way that regular classroom structures do not meet. Ninety percent of the black students are sent here against their will for misbehavior or misunderstanding, or whatever. Ninety percent of the white students are here because they come from broken homes or refuse to try to live up to middle-class ideas.

I teach music and drama at East Campus. Teaching these subjects became a problem for me. Why? In my four music classes mostly black students enrolled. In my two drama classes mostly white students enrolled. My music classes were very large at first, I tried to teach them basic principles of music. They responded for about a week and soon became bored as hell. About the fourth week, I had only about ten students per class. I decided to have a confrontation with them. I turned the classes into "rap" sessions. The purpose of these sessions was for students to talk to each other about music and for me to find out what students really want to do in the way of music. Their reply was, "Man, we want to play music of today. Later for all that Bach, Beethoven, and Brahms jazz." They wanted to do "Rock and Roll" Rhythm and Blues. Another reply was, "Man, we been so poor all of our lives until that classical stuff you have been teaching means nothing to us. We never heard a classical piece of music until you played a record last week and made us listen to it. We can't dig it, man."

One kid stated, "My old man left my ma' ten years ago. She listened to 'soul' music six days a week and on Sunday she played church music. She would go to church and come home crying, 'The Lord will provide.' The Lord never provided anything and we were both still hungry on Monday morning. Like, if I could just learn enough about music to sing and play 'soul' music, I might get some job in a nightclub to support her a little. Who knows, I may even become a Ray Charles or Lou Rawls. They never went to college and learned all that theory stuff you are trying to teach us." I had a headache and dismissed the class. I lay in bed that night and all kinds of questions went through my mind. What could I do to help them? My mind was blank. Finally I decided to junk the "good stuff" in music for a while. I would let my kids do their kind of music in a classroom situation. I didn't have the faintest idea about how to teach it.

I began to bring in my own records of the top artists of today and to teach students to sing along with the record. I divided the girls in groups of five and the boys likewise. This worked for a while and the class began to get back together. But some students could not sing and wanted to play drums and guitars instead. The school department had no such instruments. After another "rap session" they wanted to know why the school couldn't purchase such instruments. I went home with another headache and couldn't sleep.

The next day I had a talk with some Afro-American students at the University of California at Berkeley. (Some funds had been allotted to them for special projects.) I persuaded them to buy electric guitars and amplifiers and drum sets so that my students could form groups that might eventually help them earn a living without mastering all the paraphernalia of formal learning. They agreed to give me the money for my purposes, and about December we had our instruments.

The students became so excited that they often stayed late after school trying to play. There was one drawback during the day. Too many students from other classes would come over and listen to our rehearsals, until my job became doorman. That is, I had to send non-music students back to their regular classes. Needless to say, they didn't go; they just milled around outside.

Playing musical instruments was not the only thing I worked on. I would stop occasionally to talk about music and what it did to help "greats" get where they are. Like, all great stars did study music one way or another. They listened but all the while they were eager to play. I soon discovered that there wasn't much need for talking any more. I only had to pick a record they wanted to learn and teach them the basic chords and the rest was theirs. They did all kinds of crazy things in arranging the songs their own way. I must admit that I was skeptical at first but the kids really "dug" hearing music they were familiar with. By so-called musical standards it wasn't the music one would write about, but it was enjoyed by all except maybe a few uptight teachers. I did receive letters of appreciation from teachers who really understood what I was trying to do.

I must also tell of my discoveries in teaching drama. My school had no music or drama program until I arrived last year. I didn't know I could reach such turned-off students in a drama situation. (I had learned the art of teaching improvisational drama from my master teacher, Linda Fisher. She used the "Spolin technique of Improvisational Drama"[1] which was devised for teaching drama to anyone— even the hardcore turned-off student.) I used the improvisational exercises to let students see what drama is all about. My students would never respond to learning a three act play by any of the great playwrights. I knew this from the beginning. Drama had to be taught without long scripts to be memorized. The improvisational method was the ideal thing for these students. It can be used in any classroom situation. One can always role-play any situation and ad lib the rest. It is like improvisations in jazz. You say what you want to say as long as it is in the context of a controlled situation.

The class responded in all kinds of ways. Most of the students didn't have any idea of what drama was all about. I used simple exercises, such as everyone walking around on the stage and observing each other. Then I had them say anything they wanted to say about our school. Later I had them answer questions about themselves and use any kind of gesture to implement the story of their life. I used the exercises from the Spolin book for the next four to six weeks.

Some of the improvisational exercises can be varied to fit all teaching situations, if the teacher has imagination. For example, the blindfold exercise was used by grouping the students in pairs. One would be blindfolded and the other would lead him around the school playground and up on Telegraph Avenue. About halfway back, they would change over and the other partner would become blindfolded. When all returned, they would relate to each other what they had felt and what fears came upon them. To make this into a dramatic experience, let the student state his reactions on the stage to his classmates.

Another exciting exercise is to have the students walk as a group during the lunch hour

about the school grounds doing unusual things —such as looking under a car and becoming excited by something underneath it. Then when other students mill around to see what is going on, the drama students leave abruptly as though nothing was happening. We soon had a mob following us. These are only a few of the drama techniques that can be used to turn kids on to drama.

In getting hostile kids to work together, it is very important to have them do group things at first. They must feel the need to depend upon each other. Some days, we would just talk about conditions in society and role-play what should be done about getting people to live together without hating one another.

Out of the "rap" sessions, I began to let the students play the roles of the persons we talked about. For example, about this time the strike at San Francisco State and U. C. Berkeley was the big thing in the news media. One student played Governor Ronald Reagan, another played Chancellor Heyns, one played the representative of the Black Student Union, and still another played the leader of the Third World Liberation Front. The scene was a meeting to discuss the issues. There were all kinds of fireworks going on. They did solve the problem and I explained to them how this was real life drama. Unfortunately, their elders didn't listen.

I soon discovered that the students were ready to create their own scenes. When a student had an idea, we all worked on it together and when we felt it was ready we would perform the scene for students in another classroom and listen to their criticism until the scene was ready for another school performance.

Meanwhile I attended shows of the "Committee" in San Francisco[2] and took courses in the techniques of teaching improvisational drama at the University of California in the Extension Program. Therefore, I had a basic idea of what would work and what would not. The class and I wrote two original plays and we eventually performed them at elementary schools.

Our first performance was at an elementary school where our students discovered for the

[1] See Viola Spolin's *Improvisation for the Theater* (Evanston, Ill.: Northwestern University Press, 1963).

[2] ED. NOTE: The "Committee" is a repertory group of "improvisational" performers in San Francisco. Their forte is social satire.

first time in their lives that someone really appreciated them. At the next class session they had numerous ideas for scenes to do at the next school. We had very simple props and most of the scenes were done with a small table and a telephone prop. Speaking of the telephone, there are a thousand ways to use the telephone as a prop for improvisational drama. Everyone uses the telephone—everyone from one to sixty to a hundred. There are so many ideas that one can use with a telephone. Just get a simple telephone prop and you can teach a drama class for weeks on this alone, with a little imagination.

Teaching by discovery can be fun but you must be at a school where success is not a must—and where failure can be tolerated without the risk of being replaced in your job.

The teacher must be patient and have the desire to start again when students are not responding. Our present educational system is not suitable to all kids, and we as teachers must find new ways to reach students. I believe our old system was based on family and social togetherness; today, the family is disintegrating, society is crumbling, and many kids are too lost to fit into the present system.

I agree that it is hard to alter old approaches, but if we are to try to reach kids of today we must discover their way of learning. Kids are more expressive than we usually realize; and I am convinced that students will let the teacher lead them only if the teacher lets them have their say. Then the teacher can begin to make use of his own experience, work from that point, and go on to tomorrow.

MARGARET ANDERSON BENTLEY 73

Does It Relate, Man?

When *Lysistrata* by Aristophanes was performed in San Francisco in 1965, the prologue to the play consisted of three "type" characters speaking in turn. The first was the Professor who explained the historical facts about Greece when Aristophanes wrote the play. He was interrupted by Mrs. Club Woman, self-appointed Preserver of Morals, who charged, "It's a dirty play! I've seen it three times, and it's a dirty play!" A third character, a bearded Nonconformist, casually regarded the two and then asked quietly, "But does it relate, man, does it relate?"

Abstract

The purpose of this paper on "relating" is twofold: first, my own discovery of being able to wake up a sleepy sixth-period tenth-grade English class of slightly below average ability by relating the tragic death of President Kennedy to a unit on drama and *Julius Caesar*.

Essentially, "relating" should require the student (1) to recognize his own subjective experience, (2) to look out into the immediate world with increasing recognition of "same" and "different," and (3) to use both the subjective and objective understanding in meeting a new experience, such as "the study of drama as a literary type." The success of this strategy in making relationships depends on the genuine "immediate" nature of the assignments, on the way they make a grab into the "now." When current newspapers, magazine articles, television, and the students themselves are the sources, there is a built-in spontaneity. As a teaching device it is not time-consuming, but does demand a quick recognition and seizing of the opportunity. In my classroom, a large section of the classroom bulletin board is labeled "Happenings" and is used for posting clippings. Occasional copies of the *Berkeley Barb* serve as bait to draw attention to the board.

In approaching a unit on drama which ends with *Julius Caesar,* I decided that I wanted to direct the study in such a way that the students could begin to grasp the relationship between "literature" and "life": that the short story, drama, poetry, and the novel (types covered in tenth-grade English) emerge *from* life, but have particular form and shape. Before starting on *Julius Caesar* the class spent two days discussing the "Death of a Leader" from their own experience. The first assignment was to write the details of where they were, how they heard the news, how they felt, and whatever else they remembered about the assassination of President Kennedy. This was a "natural" for remembering specific details. One of the papers was written by a student who has had considerable psychiatric treatment for behavior problems beginning in the first grade, is potentially a paranoid schizophrenic, and is sometimes so absorbed in making a chain out of staples that he appears completely withdrawn and unaware of anything going on around him. This is one of the few assignments that he completed during the first semester. In reading portions of the papers back to the students, special note was made of those who were able to articulate their feelings in some way other than "everyone was sad."

The second assignment was to bring in newspaper clippings, articles, etc., on Kennedy to post on the bulletin board. I made use of all the publicity which was coming out on the William Manchester book, and the Report of the Warren Commission. This continued throughout the reading of *Julius Caesar,* with the lucky "happening" of the local paper carrying a banner headline, "Kennedy Warned: Stay Out of Dallas" just as we were finishing Act II in which Caesar is warned not to go to the Forum. The various clippings included "The Grim Who Killed Kennedy Game," "Assassination: Lincoln and JFK," a story which says "Oh, I know you will say the Kennedy boys were born to rule...," and others.

The third step was reading *Julius Caesar,*

---

1 ED. NOTE: Obviously dated by the event of President Kennedy's death, this strategy has been rendered more dramatic by the subsequent assassinations of Robert Kennedy and Martin Luther King. It now appears both historical and relevant.

unfortunately interrupted by Christmas vacation after the first act, and my forced reliance on recordings because I had a cold and lost my voice. When the plot and characterization seemed well in hand, I divided the class into five groups of five or six, giving each group the same list of questions to talk over and pool ideas. The next day representatives from each group formed a panel in front of the class to "give back" the combined results of their thinking.

QUESTIONS

A. 1. Compare the sequence of events in Kennedy's death and the events surrounding the assassination of Caesar. How are they alike, and how are they different?

2. When Mrs. Kennedy heard the news that Lee Harvey Oswald, a lone man acting on reasons peculiar to himself, killed Kennedy, she is reported to have said, "It can't be... then it has no meaning...." What might she have meant?

3. Do you think her statement has anything to do with the number of books that are coming out now on the death of Kennedy?

4. Do you think Shakespeare's *Julius Caesar* (or the historical facts on which it was based) makes a better "story" than Kennedy's death? Why or why not?

B. What is the difference between the "facts" of history and a drama using these facts?

1. What is the purpose of a newspaper story?

2. What is the purpose of a play?

After class discussion, the last assignment was to write a definition of drama as a literary form, drawing on their knowledge of *Julius Caesar, The Glass Menagerie* (which the class had read and used for writing characterization and to get experience reading a play in familiar language), and an "outside reading" play of their own choice. They had only fifteen minutes to write their ideas in class time. I purposely did not have them write the assignment for homework because I did not want a definition from a dictionary which they might use to find a "safe" answer. Reading quickly through the papers, I picked out interesting comments, observations, and individual expressions of ideas, made up a ditto of the following, and gave it back to the students. From these ideas we added up the various aspects of "drama." The following are some of their definitions of drama.

Drama works more on the emotions and feelings than just reciting the facts. In a play the dramatist focuses on a certain person or group of persons. It shows more why something was done and how it affects the people involved than how it was done or what was done.

Drama is something which brings together things in life. It shapes it together in a story with a beginning and an ending, and brings out the hardships and heartbreak in life.

A drama is a story about life, about the things that happen to people, places, and things. It shows what other people are like, and how they act.

History in real life is all done and said at the same time. In real life history is one great suspense and is not really expected. In a play you expect something to happen. It is written in sections and puts you in curiosity and suspense to find out what happens.

Drama is the thrill of something and the moment of happening.

Drama is a group of facts twisted around with emotions to make it meaningful.

Drama is focused on one thing. Newspapers tell the facts. Drama brings out the questions and answers. It shows emotions, and it tells why things happen the way they do.

Drama is an enlargement on the real picture of something that has happened. It is a look in depth at something that has happened. The writer takes the action from something, then adds detail, exaggeration, and enlargements. He interprets the happening in a form so that it is exciting and entertaining.

I feel that this kind of individual formulation of "drama" from the student's own experience with it is more valuable than learning a definition. It is certainly more fun for the teacher to read, and it gathers together the individual ideas of the group. In terms of specific content of the plays read, half the slower students regularly fail the examination. I'm not satisfied with this result, but performance on an objective test is not all that counts. One student made a grade of 37 on *The Glass Menagerie*. Two months later, in connection with another assignment on "Twenty Facts About Yourself," she described her own self-consciousness about bands on her lower teeth (which nobody else had noticed until she mentioned it) as "just like Laura and her brace in *The Glass Menagerie*." She had learned something of value.

CAREER PREPARATION

ROBERT E. KELLER 74

Toward a Contact Curriculum[1]

As a first-year teacher, only five months removed from the business world, I was somewhat

[1] See Mario D. Fantini and Gerald Weinstein's pamphlet *Towards a Contact Curriculum* (New York: B'Nai B'Rith Anti-Defamation League, 315 Lexington Ave., New York, 10016, n.d.)

overwhelmed when asked to serve on my school's curriculum committee. In accepting this position, I would be involved in formulating new course offerings, and would be in a prime position to help initiate a new secondary education program. (Our high school is in its first year, in a rapidly growing suburb.)

The one factor which influenced me most to accept this challenge was the knowledge that our school, because of the area it serves, could, perhaps, become more vocationally oriented than most. During the last ten years, while managing a family-owned business, I had constantly employed part-time students from the district's older high school. Our business, as it expanded, was so starved for promising talent, that I had often been in close contact with the school's counselors, vice principal, and principal, in a continuing search for students with enough sense of responsibility and background in basic subject areas who could, after a six-month orientation period, start apprenticeship programs with the various unions involved in my business. I felt I could make a contribution to the area of vocational preparation. And after my experience in teaching the traditional curriculum offered to noncollege-bound students, I knew something had to be done.

What I Had Encountered in My Classes

These last few months I have been teaching four classes of Introduction to Business and one class of General Math. In this group of one hundred and sixty students, almost all of whom are ninth-graders and two thirds of whom are girls, I found a general reading level of approximately sixth grade, a math proficiency of fifth grade, and behavior patterns typical of those which might be expected from a fourth-grade group. At present, I would have a difficult time finding ten pupils who might conceivably get through the first semester at a junior college four years from now.

My general math class, made up of students in the school's bottom twenty percentiles, further deepened my concern. Several of them have to count on their fingers to perform basic whole number subtraction and addition. Many still do not know either simple or long division. Discipline problems manifest themselves frequently. On one occasion while seeking help from an administrator in charge of discipline, I was told, "Don't worry with this bunch. If you just keep them in their seats and get them to open the book just once in a while and do a few problems, you're doing a whale of a job."

This is *not* what I thought teaching would

be like, and I am not at all satisfied with the prospect of having these kids complete their education with so poor a foundation in math. In a little over three years they will be out looking for jobs, and possibly becoming heads of households and parents of children whom it will be our responsibility to educate fourteen or fifteen years from now.

At first, in an effort to increase my students' motivation to learn math, I had brought in several games, special books, and other "fun" type aids. These were not enthusiatically accepted. In fact, they were met at best with disdain. Spitwads, chalk erasers, candy, and all sorts of other missiles continued to find their way into orbit in Room D-6. (Of course, no one ever admitted to throwing them. They just found their way into the atmosphere from their own launching pads.)

I discovered that these kids had all been exposed to basic math areas at least six or seven times in their past schooling. They had not gained even the simplest concepts of problem solving, and with the type of textbook we are using, despite the various games I had attempted, for them it was still the same old boring numbers. I am now convinced that these pupils will continue to be "turned off" to math until it can be shown to their satisfaction that math is relevant to their future—and that some knowledge of basic math is important for earning a living and finding one's rightful place in society. As for me, I insist on becoming a teacher, not a baby-sitter for the teen-agers in my charge.

The reader might ask at this point, "How does all this tie in to membership and active participation in one's school curriculum committee?" I would answer that question by quoting a well-respected, nationally syndicated author whose articles appear daily in the "Business World" section of the *San Francisco Chronicle*, Sylvia Porter. On November 25, 1968, in an article entitled "The Vocational Education Gap," she wrote:

Today, at least 25 million Americans should be receiving vocational training. Yet only 8 million are enrolled in vocational education courses, 4 million of them of high school age.

This translates into a vocational educational gap of an awesome 17 million.

Today, only one of five high school students goes

on to get a four-year college degree. Yet our high schools continue to center on the college-bound rather than on the overwhelming percentage who are bound for careers in the trades and technical professions.

This means we are failing to get to the heart of the problems...for at this heart is the need for education and training both younger and older Americans to fill the jobs which are and will be open for them.

I, too, am deeply concerned. Fortunately, there are other teachers on the curriculum committee, from such departments as Arts and Crafts, Industrial Arts, Business, and Home Economics, who are also dissatisfied with our present methods of educating the noncollege-bound, especially in the basic skills of math and English. We feel that a change has to come about if we are going to achieve any degree of success in truly educating the majority of our high school students.

First of all, what can we do for the bulk of our students who may go on to a junior college, but will never get through the first semester? Second, how are we preparing those students who will pursue a terminal or vocational program in junior college? What kind of job can we do at the high school level to prepare these students for their future?

Some of us on the committee feel we have at least some partial answers to those questions. We realize that a vocational type program will be an expensive program to operate, both in capital outlay and in arranging optimum class size. But we also realize that it is desperately needed.

Our first change in disturbing the status quo would be to make the ninth grade primarily an exploratory year for prospective vocational students. They could take introductory courses designed to give them some idea of what the various industrial arts courses encompass, what business or homemaking is all about, and what the fields of art and mechanical drawing might have in store for them. Some could be full year courses; others would be only one semester in length. Such courses might also help to orient students to high school. Many of our current problems in the transition from grade or intermediate school could thus be more easily resolved.

By the end of the first year, if these courses are well structured, most students should have found some which interest them, and in which they believe they could achieve a reasonable degree of success. In the tenth grade, then, they could take math and English oriented toward their vocational objectives. Such courses as math for business, math for mechanics, math for printers, math for home economics, and their counterparts in English would then have more relevance for these students. They could see why some skills in math and English are so important to their future lives. For those remaining students too immature, unable, or insufficiently motivated to choose a vocationally oriented program at the end of their freshman year, a math requirement for graduation could be fulfilled in their senior year, in a course entitled consumer math, preferably tied in with a course in consumer education and family finance. After all, they are going to have to manage their own personal affairs very soon after graduation.

What we are saying is that noncollege-bound students would still be taught the decimals, fractions, percents, and other math, as well as English skills, but the subject matter would be approached and structured to meet the students' readily apparent needs.

I am appalled that at present we are losing contact with the very students who need our help the most. I have therefore decided to continue on as a member of the curriculum committee, hoping, in some way, to influence our existing school institutions "Toward a Contact Curriculum" for all our students.

The Present and the Future

Earlier this year several students had discussed the possibility of obtaining summer jobs. They had also expressed a desire to know more about occupations or careers in the future—in other words, what they would do after high school.

I would like to digress a moment to give you a few background facts. I am a freshman social studies teacher and advisor at Hayward High School, California. In our district the social studies teacher is also the advisor to the students in the four classes he teaches. My present class size and advisory group numbers 130 students. Although this arrangement has its advantages and disadvantages, the philosophy of the program is a positive one. In most schools, given a larger case load, counselors do not get an opportunity to see their counselees often enough to really know them as individuals. In our district it is felt we can best serve our advisees by seeing them each day. Consequently, the teaching and advising roles have been combined.

Each teacher-advisor is assigned to a group of students and remains with them throughout their high school career. In this manner the teacher-advisor is in a unique position to encourage an individual student and help him daily in his effort to achieve his highest educational goal. Because of this opportunity, it is possible to plan group guidance units more successfully.

Now, back to our subject. Hayward High School is a four-year high school located in a suburban bedroom city of the greater Bay Area. For this paper, I would like to concentrate on one particular class, a typical heterogeneous freshman group.

The thirty-three students in this class represent all economic groups. It is equally divided between both sexes, and is racially balanced.

My objective was to satisfy their need for immediate knowledge of possible summer jobs for fifteen-year-olds. My long-range objective was to stimulate their interest in the future. Through this unit I expected to give my students information about the possibility of part-time jobs; the information necessary for them to plan their future programs in high school and for their future beyond high school.

The unit I am about to describe was completed in five days. It began with a discussion of the possibilities of summer jobs for fifteen-year-olds and of possible future part-time jobs. Most of the students already held small part-time jobs—generally baby-sitting for the girls and some typing in family firms. A few of the boys had paper routes, some were part-time gardeners or worked in service stations or small shoe stores. Generally, their vocational outlook was limited.

The first day we saw a filmstrip with a recording, *Part-Time Jobs for High School Students,* which generated enthusiastic discussion about summer jobs. The second day we extended our discussion into the qualities necessary for obtaining part-time jobs, and we role-played interviews. The students had been informed the day before that we would role-play certain jobs. To prepare for it, each student had been given a homework assignment to complete sample job applications and read a pamphlet, *Preparing for a Job Interview.*

The next day students took turns as interviewers, potential employees, and critics. The class gave valuable suggestions about dress, manner of sitting, strength of voice, and what should or should not be said in an interview. The class voted on the most effective performance. The distinction was given to a student previously of low achievement. In this case, she came fully prepared for her role. She was well groomed, spoke in a delightful, positive manner, and had a good background for her potential position. She explained she was applying for a volunteer job as a nurse's aide. Her experience included working with her grandmother in a geriatric hospital. (For once, at least, she was able to excel in the classroom.)

The third day we saw a second filmstrip and recording entitled *Preparing for the World of Work*. Our discussion included a look at which courses in high school could be useful for future careers.

A final filmstrip and recording was viewed the fourth day. *Jobs of the Seventies* provided the basis for a meaningful discussion of high school programs and education beyond high school. Many of the students indicated they had been thinking of their future and had gained information that could help them plan a more realistic program for their sophomore year.

The fifth day of the unit gave each student an opportunity to become more familiar with a particular field. The occupations handbook was divided into thirty-five sections of related positions—e.g., the clerical field, the service fields, etc. Each section gave information about occupations related to the general topic.

For each occupation listed, there was information regarding job opportunities, job requirements, salary schedules, and future possibilities. As a class assignment, each student was asked (1) to choose an occupation of interest, (2) to read the handbook's description of the selected occupation, and (3) to write an essay based upon the information he had gathered. The essay was to include a knowledge of the requirements for getting the position desired, the kind of high school courses which could be beneficial for obtaining this goal, and finally, a self-appraisal by the student, indicating why he felt he was suited to the particular occupation.

I was not sure that this approach to the future would be successful until their enthusiastic responses on the first day encouraged me to complete the assignment with great energy. I explained that summer jobs were not plentiful for high school freshmen; thus they should assume that many of them could not secure positions this year.

The class stated that they wanted to know what the possibilities were for the present summer as well as what they might consider for the future. Several students who had not known what to expect after high school indicated they had gained important knowledge about possible future occupations. Following this unit I spoke with a number of students individually and helped them complete applications for summer jobs. At this time, one student has secured a summer job as stock boy for a supermarket, and another has a position as a shoe salesman.

All students agreed they should begin thinking now about the future. Each had found that an occupation involves preparation, whether it be for a licensed vocational nurse or a highly trained attorney. Thus, they had already taken their first step into the future world of work.

Annotated Bibliography

1. Brokenshire, John R., ed. *Directory of Occupation Centered Curriculums in California: Junior Colleges and Schools for Adults.* California State Department of Education, 1965 edition. This directory is designed to help youths and adults obtain occupational training that will qualify them for beginning employment. This listing is primarily designed as a counselor's tool. It gives essential information in readily accessible form about the programs offered in the Junior College System. (For teacher use.)

2. Bureau of Labor Standards. *Handbook for Young Workers.* U.S. Department of Labor, Bulletin No. 271, 1965. Booklet written for youth in readable form. Information covers labor laws, training opportunities, and sources of help.

3. ———. *Job Guide for Young Workers.* U.S. Department of Labor. Gives highlight information on 110 entry jobs frequently held by young beginners entering the labor market from high school.

4. Bureau of Labor Statistics. *Jobs for College Graduates.* U.S. Department of Labor. Booklet contains information for over seven hundred occupations and thirty major industries for which college graduates may qualify, including jobs for those who have graduate degrees. Information covers nature of work, training and other qualifications necessary for entry, where employment opportunities are found, employment outlook to 1975, earnings and working conditions, and where to obtain additional information.

5. ———. *Jobs for Which a High School Education is Necessary or Useful.* U.S. Department of Labor. Booklet contains information for over seven hundred occupations and thirty major industries. Information covers nature of work, training and other qualifications necessary for entry, where

employment opportunities are found, employment outlook to 1975, earnings and working conditions, and where to obtain additional information.

6. ——. *Occupational Outlook Handbook: Career Information for Use in Guidance.* U.S. Department of Labor, Bulletin No. 1450, 1966–1967 edition. This bulletin evaluates the effects of automation, new technology, and recent economic developments upon the occupations covered. It is primarily designed for guidance workers. The information given represents an effort to define the modern world of work. Each occupation listed discusses job opportunities in the particular occupation, nature of the work, and earning and working conditions. (For teacher use.)

The following are pamphlets that may be used in the classroom. They are distributed through the Youth Opportunity Center, California State Department of Employment Service.

1. *Choosing Your Occupation.* Includes important facts on interest areas; aptitudes, and a self-inventory that gives a student an idea where his interests may lie.

2. *Employment Interview.* Sample fact sheet that gives students an opportunity to write a brief resumé.

3. *How to Prepare Yourself for Job Interviews.* Gives pertinent hints on preparing for job interviews.

4. *You're Already Old Enough.* Gives pertinent information to begin to build a successful career.

*Filmstrips and Recordings:
Guidance Associates, Inc.*

1. *Jobs of the Seventies.* Gives information to a student regarding how he should prepare himself for a job that does not exist today.

2. *Part-time Jobs for High School Students.* Gives information that is necessary for those students who may need or wish to find part-time jobs or summer jobs.

3. *Preparing for the World of Work.* Invaluable information that will stimulate interest in courses in high school that are needed for future careers.

ROBERT LATHAM **76**

Career and College Guidance in the Classroom

Subject matter is not necessarily the most important part of any course, even in a physics class of high ability seniors. In fact, the week that we spent discussing science careers, colleges, and scholarships in physics was probably of greater benefit to the students than any other week in the course. The students definitely appreciated the unit because it was useful to them.

The reason for the unit's success can be summarized as follows:

1. *Student need* for the information presented was obvious.
2. *Teacher interest* in each student's future was demonstrated.
3. *Student involvement* was paramount since the students themselves gave the reports on either

careers or colleges in which they were interested. Concrete, practical information was required. (Guidelines given the students for their reports are included in the Appendix.)

Our school does, of course, have counselors whose job it is to give vocational and college guidance. However, each counselor has approximately five hundred students in his charge. Most of his time is taken up by program changes, problem students, and assorted clerical work. Any teacher who can offer vocational and college guidance in the classroom to supplement the "official" offering will be doing his students a big favor. In the process the teacher can learn much about his students. In most cases the student's academic motivation will also be increased.

The class in which I used this strategy was physics. All of the students are graduating seniors interested in science, most of whom maintain a high level of academic achievement. However, the community which this high school serves is neither science- nor college-oriented. The parents of most of the students are non-professional and did not attend college. Many of the students have low aspirations in spite of their ability and academic achievement. I hoped to raise their aspirations.

For a graduating class I believe a unit on career and college guidance should be given in the early fall to allow time for students to apply for scholarships and college entrance.

To anyone planning to provide vocational and college explorations by the students in the classroom, I recommend the following:

1. Consult the counselors. Make sure that you are aware of all of the vocational and college programs that are currently available or planned. The counselors can probably be of help in providing career pamphlets, college catalogues, etc.

2. Give definite guidelines for career and college talks. (See examples given in the Appendices.)
3. Let the students pick their own topics as much as possible.
4. As an introduction to the unit give an inspirational talk about the many scholarships that are available. Stress the fact that college tuition is *not* a consideration for a student with good grades and financial need.
5. Have the students form panels to prevent overlapping. For example, we had a panel of five students on medicine. Included were careers as physician, nurse, veterinarian, medical researcher, biological researcher. Use some class time to organize and coordinate the presentations.
6. An enrollment questionnaire (see Appendix for an example) is useful to provide information on the students' interest and background. It can also indicate whether or not vocational and college guidance is needed.

The week spent in the classroom discussing careers, colleges, and scholarships was well received by the students. Most of the students made excellent presentations. The students felt that the time was well spent. So did I.

Appendix A

ENROLLMENT QUESTIONNAIRE

Chemistry
Mr. Latham
Period_____

Last,   First   (Nickname, if any)
Name_____

How long have you
Age_____Grade_____lived in this area?_____

Please indicate the semester marks you received in all of the following courses which you have had:

Algebra I_____   Science 9_____   Physics_____
Geometry_____   Earth Science_____   Physiology_____
Algebra II_____   Biology_____   _____

What other math and science courses do you have this year?_____

What school activities did you participate in last year?_____

What special interests or hobbies do you have?_____

What are your career plans?_____

For seniors planning to attend college: To what colleges are you planning to apply?

_____

Do you plan to apply for scholarships? _____

What do you want out of this class? _____

_____

_____

Appendix B

GUIDELINES FOR CAREER REPORTS

The following information should be included:
Description of career
    Type of work
    Opportunity for self expression, variety, independence, working with people, etc.
Education and training required
Starting salary, average salary
Opportunity for advancement
Other benefits
Disadvantages

Appendix C

GUIDELINES FOR COLLEGE REPORTS

The following information should be included:
Specialties of the college
Entrance requirements
Any special undergraduate programs
Tuition and living costs
Special scholarships
Admission and scholarship deadlines
Placement services
Location description (if not near by)
Regulations and policies
Other special features

Appendix D

CAREERS AND COLLEGES COVERED

Careers		*Colleges*
Architecture	Military	Harvard
Astronautics	Oceanography	Stanford
Electronics	Science Research	Massachusetts Institute of Technology
Engineering	Teaching	nology
Electrical	Elementary	California Institute of Technology
Chemical	Secondary	University of California, Berkeley
Mechanical	College	University of California, Davis
Civil	Zoology	University of California, Santa Cruz
Technicians		University of California, San Diego
Medicine		State Colleges
Physician		DeVry Technical Institute, Chicago
Nurse		
Medical Technologist		
Veterinarian		
Biological Researcher		

DEVELOPING SOCIAL VALUES
AND AWARENESS

FREDERICK W. BROCK ## 77

Experiences in Teaching for Values

Viewed in terms of my own education, the first year of teaching proved its worth in the final month. It was not until this point, or shortly before, that I was able to crystallize even a small part of my "teaching philosophy." As an extension of this speck of philosophy I decided to teach the things which are revealed in this paper.

The aim here—an almost embarrassingly simple one—was to encourage questioning. The simplicity of my aim, however, was complicated by an approach I had used during the entire year. To wit: questioning of a student's casually accepted *"a priori"* truths results at first in defense, and then in some gradual inspection of the worth of those ideas. If the teacher is willing to introduce topics and to carry discussions to some fruition, this demanding process can be an exciting one.

The three classes I used this approach in were ninth grade English "A" (denoting "college prep") at a suburban high school of about 2600 students. The school is located in a very homogeneous environment of middle- and upper middle-class, 99.9 percent white, tract homes several miles east of Berkeley. These facts are included only to reinforce an important point about the situation. Given the environment and the ability level placement of these particular kids, chances were excellent

that a concensus of them could be aroused by the challenge of "playing the game." By this, I mean acting out the pattern so familiar in a number of classrooms: listen to the teacher, take down what he says, tell him what he "wants" to hear, get the grade. The exercises below are part of an attempt to get away from such academic puppet shows and to move toward an atmosphere of greater individual responsibility. Such an atmosphere, it would seem, leads students to more honest consideration of their own values.

The first exercise dealt with an article which appeared in *Track and Field News* (March 1, 1968) entitled "College Track Uptight" by Jack Scott. Scott expresses the opinion that the American college track coach, almost without exception, is a man who has been raised to a position of authority which prevents him from treating athletes as human beings. For example, the coach becomes a purveyor of an institution's image, demanding short haircuts, clean shaves, and red blazers, while often ignoring the need for consideration of athletes as individuals.

One of the letters to the editor which followed the Jack Scott piece was written by Bob Giegengack, track coach at Yale University (*Track and Field News*, March 11, 1968). Giegengack's opening remark was "Just who or what is Jack Scott?" Here was ample inspiration for the discussion of a semantic pearl: the *ad hominem* fallacy, which tends to hang up people who won't listen to an argument made by someone below the rank of Duncan Hines. Conversely, Herb Caen's[1] byline becomes for them a positive sanction. At any rate, Giegengack proved to be more of a godsend than I had reckoned, for he also became an example of unquestioned authority trying to justify itself.

Instead of calling for immediate oral discussion of the article and the response, I had the class write answers to four or five questions—e.g., "What approach does Giegengack take in responding to the Scott article?" or "What is an argument?" or "Should people on either side of an argument reveal certain prejudices which they may bring to the argument?" (Credit should be given here to Raths, Harmon, Simon, *Values and Teaching*, specifically pp. 109–11. Moreover, the entire book is a veritable gold mine of ideas and techniques.)

Student reactions, both written and oral, were varied, yet one recurrent statement could be paraphrased. "Giegengack's approach is a meaningful one, because he is a track coach and knows what's right. Jack Scott is not a coach of a college team, so what does he know?" Here again was a made-to-order entrée for *ad hominem*.

In response to the "prejudice" question, many said that nobody who wanted to "win the argument" would ever tip his hand in the direction of his opponent. This led eventually to a discussion of whether winning the argument was as important as understanding and carefully evaluating another person's attitudes or opinions.

The second exercise dealt with an article which appeared in the San Francisco *Chronicle* entitled "Super Students Blasts Grades." The article told of a speech given by the highest ranking graduate in the College of Letters and Science at the University of California. In the speech he condemned the present grading system as a stagnant and impersonal approach to evaluating human beings. It is interesting to note here that the kids paid very close attention to the "super student's" argument, not only because he was talking on a familiar topic but also because of his prowess as a student.

[1] Herb Caen is a columnist in the *San Francisco Chronicle*.

The article served two main purposes:

1. It led to a genuine inspection of values, one which was initiated by pure perplexity. The notion of a high-ranking student looking his transcript in the mouth raised unsettling questions among many students. Any C+ student could be expected to cry "foul," but why on earth should a four-pointer do such a thing?

2. The article proved to be an excellent sequel to the Scott-Giegengack issue, broadening the view of the *ad hominem* fallacy. Toward the end of the discussion, members of the class were able to catch others falling into the trap of dealing with the *man* rather than with what he had said. (To be sure, several students are probably still convinced that the super student was not a super student at all, but rather the fabrication of the *Chronicle's* news editor, who was no doubt the dupe of some Communist-Zionist-Basque-Afro-Asian Conspiracy which daily plots the overthrow of the entire American Way of Life.)

My third vehicle was a twenty-minute tape of a speech given by Harry Edwards. Edwards was the leader of the Olympic Project for Human Rights, more commonly known as the boycott-protest of the 1968 Olympic Games. Edwards' speech habits are alien to the students I teach, and I was therefore obliged to transcribe the entire speech onto ditto sheets. By itself, the written speech (originally given *ad lib*) is probably the best teaching aid I have ever used, and its beauty is enhanced by the sounds of Harry Edwards' funky delivery.

My treatment of the speech did not involve any writing assignment, as did the two previous exercises, but there was adequate material for students' oral participation. Here again was an opportunity to consider a radically new value structure as an avenue to learning about one's own values. (Can a black man reconcile running for the U.S. in Mexico City with returning to West Oakland to witness ill-treatment of his brothers?) This was also a good test of the students' own abilities to deal with the *ad hominem* fallacy. I was encouraged by the overall reception to such a threatening figure as Edwards must have seemed to them. In greater numbers than I had expected, the kids were willing to consider his *argument*.

In terms of a suggested "method for teaching values," I would hope that this paper reveals this partly by the way of *what* was being taught. In addition to this, the teacher's responsibility includes, to echo Raths, *teaching a means of arriving at values rather than imposing values.* Central to this notion are the principles of challenge and question in the face of established, old ideas, to see whether those ideas are indeed worth the respect of the young (or anyone else).

Teaching for values is exciting. There is no way to predict a student's reaction to a particular "hot" issue or question, and as the teacher improves his skills in obtaining responses, there is no end to students' questioning—a questioning which leads to greater understanding for all involved. The teacher and the student agree to meet each other on common ground, the impor-

tant cards are placed on the table, and neither hand has to win. That's not the point.

Selected Bibliography

Raths, Louis E., Merrill Harmin, and Sidney B. Simon, *Values and Teaching.* Columbus, O.: Charles E. Merrill Publishing Company, 1966.

Possibilities for further source material are infinite. In this paper I have mentioned the use of *Track and Field News,* The San Francisco *Chronicle,* and a private tape. One can easily see that there is no formula for the selection of material. No doubt original vignettes by the teacher could be used, as well as any of the suggestions offered by Raths and company. With so much to choose from, my only guideline would be to choose something you can be enthusiastic about.

RICHARD C. RAINES **78**

Functional Democracy: Historic, National, and Personal

Philosophy of the Unit

Whether one decided to teach world history by beginning in the present and picking up the relevant past, or by beginning with a past proven relevant to the present, the primary concern is relevancy. I suggest three levels of relevancy; first, relevancy to the personal history of the student and the class; second, relevancy to the present experience of our nation and our world; third, relevancy to the historical development of the past as proven by its present significance and endurance.

Relevancy as applied to the three areas of the personal and communal, the present external history, and the enduring presentation from the past is cast, in this strategy paper, into a unit on Greece. The unit was designed to last about three weeks. The first week dealt with Ancient Greece and its development of a democratic form of government. The second week dealt with democracy as it takes shape in the

United States. The third week dealt with democracy in interpersonal relationships at home and in the classroom. Unknown to the class, two students volunteered (without my encouragement) to evaluate the students and the teacher during the entire unit to see if there was any growth in the way we listened to one another and handled ourselves in the class. What follows is a day-by-day outline of the unit, with a special commentary on the last week and the final evaluation raised by the volunteer students and responded to by the class as a whole.

The First Week

MONDAY. A filmstrip on the Geography of Greece (from the series entitled *Ancient Greece*[1]) and some Greek dances by a student who happened to be Greek in origin.

[1] *Ancient Greece.* SVE Educational Filmstrips.

TUESDAY. Assignment: *Men and Nations:*[2] Chapter 6, "Greece Dominates the Mediterranean World." Discussion: Steps toward a Democratic Government.

WEDNESDAY. Assignment for Wednesday and Thursday: *Men and Nations:* Chapter 7, "Athens: The Golden Age." Classroom: Film *Athens: The Golden Age.*[3]

THURSDAY. Discussion of Greek Democracy in its flower. The essentials of democracy: (1) division of power, (2) the franchise (3) written law and the judicial system, and (4) freedom of thought and dissent.

FRIDAY. Is any democracy complete? *32 Problems in World History:*[4] (Fenton) "A dissection of Pericles Oration."

ACCOMPLISHED: An historical appreciation of Greek democracy. An appreciation of the essentials of any democracy, and the relationship between democracy and geography, democracy and the implicit or explicit "view of human nature."

The Second Week

MONDAY. Assignment: The Bill of Rights (classroom copies). A discussion of the implications of American Democracy as shown in the Bill of Rights.

TUESDAY. Assignment: American Government, Checks and Balances (civics chart and class discussion[5]).

WEDNESDAY. Assignment: Fill in work sheet on democracy.[6] Define and explain *compromise, conflict, dissent, democracy, totalitarianism.* Explain how the first three terms function in a democracy.

THURSDAY. Assignment: Worksheet in rating societies.[7] Here a worksheet was taken from a paperback on totalitarianism which pictured six possible societies graded from anarchy to dictatorship. This worksheet asked the students to create their own society by ranking various listed attitudes and statutes in a scale from 1 to 6 depending on how much they wanted each statement to exist in the society they created. The results were tabulated and saved for the next class.

FRIDAY. No assignment: A graph and picture of the varying societies created showed the students how various the individual points of view were as to what was ideal and "democratic" to each one. They were surprised to find some democracies bordering on anarchy and some verging on authoritarianism in one class of "American youth." Discussion: The meaning of conflict and compromise and dissent (after tabulating and exposing the many different societies).

The Third Week

MONDAY. Film: *The Oxbow Incident*[8] (a film clip from movie of same name).

TUESDAY. Assignment: Describe your reactions to this film in terms of our study of democracy. Make a list of the rights violated, and describe how such a thing could happen in a "democratic nation." Classroom: A discussion of the film and an emphasis on how democracy has to be defended and rewon in each generation.

WEDNESDAY. Assignment: A ditto on Justice Fortas and Dissent.[9] Classroom: Debate on the place and role of dissent in a democracy.

THURSDAY. Assignment: A ditto on Socrates and dissent. Film: *The Death of Socrates.*[10] Discussion: Socrates and Martin Luther King and Jesus of Nazareth and Ghandi.

FRIDAY. No Assignment: Continued discussion on "the great dissenters." Three classroom reports and a mock conversation between Socrates, Jesus, and Martin Luther King on how to gain and maintain human freedom.

The Fourth Week

MONDAY. Mr. Ronald Lepke, District Psychologist and Counselor. "Democracy in

---

[2] Anatol G. Mazour, *Men and Nations,* rev. ed. (New York: Harcourt Brace Jovanovich, 1968).

[3] *Athens: The Golden Age.* Encyclopedia Britannica Films, 1962.

[4] Edwin Fenton, *32 Problems in World History* (Chicago: Scott, Foresman & Company, 1964).

[5] Frank Abbot Magruder, *American Government* (New York: Allyn and Bacon, Inc., 1967).

[6] Richard Raines, "Worksheet on Democracy." Teacher-prepared; each can do one of his own.

[7] Howard Mehlinger, *Totalitarianism: An Inductive Approach* (Washington, D.C.: National Council for Social Studies, No. 27, NEA), pp. 19 and 20.

[8] *Due Process of Law Denied,* film clip of the *Oxbow Incident,* 1943, Twentieth Century Fox Studios.

[9] Abe Fortas, *Concerning Dissent and Civil Disobedience* (New York: Signet Books, 1968).

[10] *Death of Socrates,* CBS-TV "You Are There Series," 1955.

interpersonal relationships." Role playing of authoritarian and anarchical and democratic relationships between parents and youth, between youth and youth, between teacher and students.[11]

TUESDAY. Mr. Ronald Lepke. Continued role playing on all three situations above, all with students playing the roles, except the teacher, who played the role of a student.

WEDNESDAY. Absence of the teacher. Class election of two students to guide class for twenty-five minutes each without the teacher's presence on the subject of a nonauthoritarian classroom relationship. Subject for debate: Law and Order versus. Law and Dissent (election year issue for 1968).

THURSDAY. Review for the full period test on Democracy. The essential constituents of a democracy. The essentials of democratic interpersonal relationships. The essentials of how creative growth takes place in a democracy (self-renewal of democracy).

FRIDAY. Test on Democracy.

The Fifth Week

MONDAY. Evaluation by two students who took on the project of looking at the class and the teacher in terms of growing experience with

---

[11] Thomas Gordon, *Parent Effectiveness Training* Pasadena, Calif., 1968 (Parents' Manual).

democracy. The evaluators noted a considerable growth in capacity to listen and hear differing opinions in the class. They also noted growth in the teacher's ability to keep from dominating the class or administering classroom discipline. It was the students' task to relieve themselves of the presence of a monitoring authority figure. They decided the class proceeded better when they handled the problems that arose in the class themselves.

The class voted to ask the two evaluating students to continue their project throughout the semester, giving their evaluation in very frank terms about every three weeks. They agreed to do so.

This classroom strategy frankly had as its main purpose the development of a real atmosphere of community within this particular class. The unit on Greece came at a time in the fall when the class had been together just a month and was getting to know itself and the teacher. It came at a time when both teacher and students wanted more order and better listening among us. It was thus devised to place lengthy emphasis on the theme for the year, which was "democracy starts in the classroom." The strategy was effective, and it has remained so. The teacher now hands discussion leadership over to the students, sits in a different place almost every day, and is regularly advised by the students to maintain this posture.

BURTON H. GREENE **79**

Teaching the Social Novel

Introduction

On my desk is a yellowing newspaper headline: "SCHOOLS RUIN KIDS." Learning becomes less than enjoyable. Novels become bookish, narrow, vacuous, unrelated to anything, and unexciting. A classroom can become a place where a teacher paces off a monotonous

monologue in which the grand concept of "littra-ture" is expounded along with the idea that the skill of critical reading is more important than dialogue concerning relevant issues. Students sink into their traditional roles and the teacher gives them what they expect: chapter by chapter analysis, constant repetition of stock critical phrases, and final exchange of a grade for some well sorted-out, packaged, lifeless information.

The Unit

I was about to embark on a four week unit in high school junior English on *The Grapes of Wrath*. We had just finished a unit on *The Glass Menagerie* and although the unit was successful in its group work, acting, and role playing areas, the general concensus of opinion was that the people were "unreal," flimsy, and too easily shattered. Thematic and background material were not especially meaningful to most students and although students could identify with some of the characters in the play, their participation was separate from their lives and only a pleasant flight into fantasy.

For *The Grapes of Wrath* a more "relevant" approach, I felt, was necessary. The classroom could be a very self-limiting place. Prior to this book, the class and I had come to the conclusion that although reading had its place, it was often no more important than other media when they are used to their fullest potential. We also found that, generally, students had very good visual and audio vocabularies. These vocabularies needed expanding and were the avenue for motivating students to enjoy and learn from a novel. They gained more information from films and sound than from reading, and when all methods of gathering data were combined, the result was superior to simply reading alone. Learning was *not* a very exclusive, selective process, but a "shotgun barrage" of all kinds of media, reality, and concepts. In other words, education is not synonymous with critical reading, and the teaching of English need not be restricted to literature.

There are further things I would have liked ideally for this unit on *The Grapes of Wrath*. First, I would have preferred to take my students out of the classroom to spend a summer reading Steinbeck and traveling through "Steinbeck Country," and then spend time working alongside migrant workers. Since the real experience was not available to motivate the students, the reality had to be simulated.

A novel taught in a vacuum of isolation supports the dichotomy between school learning and life. The concept that Charles Dickens created works of art while Bob Dylan only writes "popular" music; that Woody Guthrie's name should not be mentioned in the same sentence with T. S. Eliot's, is not accepted by students. Hand in hand with outdated concepts goes the idea that the student is preparing to become an "adult," and is not a human being *now*.

My "strategy" contained the following facets:

1. Rather than dealing with this novel by concentrating on the work of art, the novel was a starting point for a larger experience.
2. As often as possible the "outside world" was brought into the classroom.
3. The classroom methods were inundative rather than selective.
4. The students' concerns were uppermost in the classroom.
5. The teacher acted as a resource and gave way to the student and machines whenever profitable for learning.

Laying the Groundwork

The students and I approached this unit with enthusiasm. I had just read the book for the first time and had thoroughly enjoyed it. The book had a good reputation from the previous year, the first year it had been taught. Two weeks were spent on various other projects and an introduction to the book while the students were reading it. They were assigned approximately thirty pages a night and were to be halfway through the book (page 300) by the end of two weeks, at which time a factual test was given on that part of the book. Some of the two weeks was spent on the following aspects of the unit:

1. *John Steinbeck and his other works.* Most students had read *The Pearl* in their previous semester of English and were still familiar with it. Others had read *Of Mice and Men,* one student had given a report on *In Dubious Battle.* Still others had read *East of Eden, Tortilla Flat,* and *Cannery Row.* Students asked their parents and other people about the 1930s, and we discussed their findings. Others knew about Steinbeck's support of the war in Vietnam, the accusations that he was a Communist in the 1930s, and most knew of his son's return from Vietnam and his exposé of the plentitude of marijuana smoking among the servicemen there. If students did not know any of the above, they did have a great deal to say about their parents' attitudes and the lingering ma-

laise in their lives as children of depression parents. They also had much to voice about the war, "pot," Communists, and much more. Sometimes these discussions carried over into the next day of class to the point where "formal" debates were set up.

2. *Woody Guthrie's life and works.* The song "Tom Joad" was distributed on ditto when the students received their books. This song, from the album "Jack Elliot Sings Woody Guthrie," was written, so the story goes, to tell the message of Tom Joad to everyone who could not afford to buy the book or who could not read it. It is a fine distillation of the book and gave the students a working outline. At the students' request, the song was played in class quite often. I even heard a student humming it in the hall during change. (The words of the song are in the Appendix.) Other Guthrie songs such as "Talkin' Dustbowl," "Talkin' Columbia," and "Pretty Boy Floyd," were excellent background material.

3. *The songs of Arlo Guthrie* (Woody's son), especially "Alice's Restaurant," a full side of an LP dealing with the draft. Many students knew the song well and excited others about it. There was happy laughter in the classroom. What a joyous sound and not an uncommon one during this unit. (Schools make kids unhappy.)

4. *Bob Dylan,* particularly his "Tribute to Woody."

5. *The grape boycott.*

To summarize this section of the unit I would say the major accomplishments were these: my students and I got to know each other better; we shared and talked about issues that concerned the students: the war, "Pot," the draft, the grape boycott, their parents, music and poetry of two of America's finest folksingers, Guthrie and Dylan, and *The Grapes of Wrath,* which was still very much of interest to us. In fact it became important. Students were able to budget their time and feel quite free in the classroom, while the onus of "required work" was taken off the book. Without the restrictions and drudgery of day-to-day explication or analysis, the students were motivated to read the novel.

Parts of the unit remained ongoing and the "world" was often in the classroom. On the heels of the Eldridge Cleaver controversy, new rules on the use of outside speakers were drafted by the administration. Although these restrictions did not close out the possibility of speakers, they did form a deterrent. Speakers from VISTA, California Rural Legal Assistance, and the California Growers' Association were considered but not contacted. Instead, an after-school speaker from the grape boycott movement was part of the unit and although this activity was not mandatory, many students attended. Some became involved in active support and others are collecting toys and canned goods for the grape pickers. (Some students who had been involved to the point of working in Delano [California] this summer are the vanguard of a planned picket on a neighborhood supermarket.) Although these social activities were not part of the "strategy," they brought a great deal of energy into the classroom.

The Final Push

Visual stimuli and the past, present, and future were involved in our next subunit. Library books containing photographs from the 1930s, especially those of Dorothea Lange, were circulated during the class. There was some discussion of the film *Bonnie and Clyde* and the revival of fashions from that era.

Films were shown when available and techniques of film and filmatic language were often part of the discussion. A filmstrip and recording, "Folksongs of the 1930s" was of minor excitement. (Had I been a singer, a guitar would have been at home in the classroom.) We did a little singing with this record, but the school atmosphere restricts singing to the music room and that barrier inhibited us all.

Four films followed. They comprised a fine survey of the documentary film. First there was the classic documentary, *The River,* which we analyzed, dissected, and got good mileage out of. Next came a typical history class education film, *The Boom of the 1920s and the Depression of the 1930s.* There were some fine pictures in this film, but generally the students decided it was dry and poorly executed propaganda. The third film was an Edward R. Murrow documentary on migrants from the 1950s, *Harvest of Shame.* It was originally shown prior to Thanksgiving, and as luck would have it, we received a timely message that the people who pick "the bountiful blessings" may not always share in them. We also talked quite a bit about television, responsible journalism, and Murrow (and parenthetically, smoking). A fine National Educational TV program, *The World of Piri Thomas,* was aired at this time and many students brought their observations on poverty into the classroom with this viewing experience.

The final film was entitled *Huelga,* a very good film not because of the issues it raised, but in the film techniques it used. Along with this film came discussion of Cesar Chavez, "charisma," "guerilla" theater—particularly Teatro Campesino—and religion. Students interested in Christianity traced down Biblical parallels in *The Grapes of Wrath;* others saw mysticism and Zen Buddhism in Preacher Casey, and one student saw the novel in relation to classical Hinduism and Emersonian Transcendentalism.

Two recent articles about the 1930s from *The New York Times* and *The Saturday Review* were presented to the class. They were both "difficult" by high school standards, but the students were involved in the unit and wanted to bring as much to the classroom as they could. Since they could not but help by this time having a great deal of information on the book and the historical period and its relevance to the present day, they worked hard to understand these articles.

Another article by Buckminster Fuller on "Goddesses of the 21st Century" led us into a discussion of the role of men and women in the novel and in the present, and the students wrote essays on what they thought the roles of men and women would be in the future. (Too often schools do not deal with relevant issues. They deal more with the past than with the present or future.)

From the class library, Marshall McLuhan's and Quentin Fiore's *The Medium Is the Massage* became a popular "comic book." It was read by most of the students in class or at home. ("Marshall McLuhan, what are ya doin'?")

Conclusions

At the end of the unit, the students took a test made by another teacher, who was teaching the book in the traditional way. The test consisted of matching questions, true and false, sentence completions, and essay questions. Most students exceeded their usual grades and my classes performed considerably better than the other teacher's. We exchanged a set of papers and the results of the same level classes were quite complimentary to the "enrichment" method I had used.

The novel as a self-contained unit is a highly personal experience. Expansive teaching can counteract the message of the constricting schools. Students can be treated as human beings, and treat each other and themselves as such. Knowledge is not something that should be put on a pedestal, out of reach of the students. The drifting student can be brought back into the classroom if it is stimulating enough. Important personal matters can open and bloom in a classroom. Students can comprehend that there must be changes in a society that did not hear Rose of Sharon's still-born message. A dead baby is a ghastly foreboding and students grasp that from *The Grapes of Wrath.* In many ways the full weight of the society comes down on them and they are strong enough to accept it and go on and perhaps produce something better.

Selected Bibliography

Articles

1. Aaron, Daniel. "The Radical Humanism of John Steinbeck," *Saturday Review,* September 28, 1968. A perceptive critical article on *The Grapes of Wrath* thirty years later.
2. Fuller, Buckminster, "Goddesses of the 21st Century," *Saturday Review,* March 2, 1968. A trenchant analysis of the role of men and women.
3. Hutchings, Robert M. "In the Thirties, We Were Prisoners of Our Illusions. Are We Prisoners in the Sixties?" *New York Times* Magazine Section, September 8, 1968. A rambling piece that raises some interesting questions.

Films

1. *The Boom of the 1920s and the Depression of the 1930s,* an economic snow job on prosperity and bust.
2. *The River,* a New Deal documentary poetically exposing the squandering of human and natural resources in the early twentieth century and possible, glib solutions.

Television

1. *Harvest of Shame*, CBS Reports by Edward R. Murrow. A fine documentary of migrant conditions in the fifties.
2. *Huelga*, a film on the grape strike and subsequent boycott. California migrants. Also shown on N.E.T. and available from The National Farmworkers Organizing Committe, Delano, Calif.
3. N.E.T. Journal on the migrants in a camp at Cutchogue, N.Y., an exposé on east coast migrants, 1967.
4. N.E.T. Journal. *The World of Piri Thomas,* an excursion with a Puerto Rican American down the "mean streets" of Spanish Harlem in New York and his road from heroin to prison to emancipation, 1968.

Filmstrip and Recording

1. *Folksongs of the 1930s,* available from the U.C. Media Lab.
2. The 1940s feature film of *The Grapes of Wrath,* starring Henry Fonda as Tom Joad, Jane Darwell as Ma Joad, and John Carradine as Preacher Casey would be an excellent addition to this unit.

Appendix

TOM JOAD*
by Woody Guthrie

Tom Joad got out of the old McAlester pen,
Was there that he got his parole,
After four long years on a man-killin' charge,
Tom Joad come a-walkin' down the road, poor boy,
Tom Joad come a-walkin' down the road.

Tom Joad, he met a truck drivin' man,
Was there that he caught him a ride,
He said I just got loose from the McAlester pen
On a charge called homicide,
On a charge called homicide.

The truck rode away in a cloud of dust,
Tom turned his face toward home,
He met Preacher Casey and they had a little drink,
And he found that his family, they were gone, poor boy,
Found that his family they were gone.

He found his Mother's old-fashioned shoes and he found his daddy's hat,
They found ole Muley and Muley said:
I've been tractored out by the cat, Tom,
I've been tractored out by the cat.

Went down to Uncle John's farm and he found his family there,
Took Preacher Casey and loaded in the car and his Ma said:
We've gotta get away, Tom,
And his Ma said we've gotta get away.

The twelve of the Joads made a mighty heavy load,
But Grandpa Joad did cry,
He picked up a handful of land in his hand and said:
I'm staying with the farm 'til I die;
I'm staying with the farm 'til I die.

They fed him short ribs and coffee and syrup,
But Grandpa Joad did die,

* Words and music by Woodie Guthrie. TRO-Copyright © 1960 and 1963 by Ludlow Music, Inc., New York, N.Y. Used by permission.

They buried Grandpa Joad by the side of the road,
And buried Grandma on the California side;
And buried Grandma on the California side.

Stood on a mountain and they looked to the West,
And it looked like the promised land,
The big green valley with the river running through,
There was work for every single hand, they thought,
There was work for every single hand.

The Joads rode in to a jungle camp,
It was there that they cut down the stew,
And the hungry little kids in the jungle camp said:
We'd like to have some too, Yes,
We'd like to have some too.

The Deputy Sheriff fired loose at a man,
And he shot a woman in the back,
But before he could take his aim again,
It was Preacher Casey dropped him in his tracks, good boy,
Preacher Casey dropped him in his tracks.

They handcuffed Casey and they took him to jail,
And then he got away,
And he met Tom Joad by the old river bridge
And these few words he did say, Preacher Casey,
These few words he did say.

I've prayed for the Lord a mighty long time,
Preached about the rich and the poor,
Us working folks have got to get together
Cause we ain't got a chance anymore, God knows,
We ain't got a chance anymore.

And the Deputy come and Tom and Casey run,
To the bridge where the water runs down,
And the vigilantes forces hit Casey with a club
And they laid Preacher Casey on the ground, poor Casey,
They laid Preacher Casey on the ground.

Tom picked up that Deputy's club,
And he hit him over the head,
And Tom Joad took flight in the dark rainy night
And left a Preacher and a Deputy lying dead, Amen,
Left a Preacher and a Deputy lying dead.

Tom ran back where his Mother was asleep,
And he woke her up out of bed,
And he kissed good-bye to the Mother that he loved,
And he said what Preacher Casey said, Tom Joad,
He said what Preacher Casey said.

Everybody must be just one big soul,
Well, it looks that-a-way to me,
So everywhere that you work in the day and the night,
That's where I'm gonna be, Ma,
That's where I'm gonna be.

Wherever the children are hungry inside,
Wherever the people ain't free,
Wherever men are fighting for their rights,
That's where I'm gonna be, Ma,
That's where I'm gonna be.

KAREN DORN **80**

An Approach to Africa

The Swiss historian Jacob Burckhardt maintained that history is "the record of what one age finds worthy of note in another." The historian who takes this concept to heart has a triple task: to understand the past, to recognize that his perception of history is a function of his opinions and experiences, and to try to *communicate* the message which he thinks the past holds for his age. I stress the latter because it may be the central task of the teacher of history in both the university and the high school. Order and meaning must be imposed upon an infinity of facts and occurrences; this has been my central goal this year in the teaching of world history. A gradually evolving approach to African history is an example of my attempts to create order and meaning for my students out of an extremely complex subject.

My first attempts to teach African history at the beginning of the year were largely unsuccessful for two reasons. First, since I had not really decided on what main concepts I wanted to concentrate, the resulting message was too diffuse. Second, the approach I used did not generate much enthusiasm. Each student gave an oral report on a specific country, all too often expounding at length upon the annual rainfall of Mali or the most prevalent crops in Gabon—material which, needless to say, did not inspire the captive audience. (My average, medium track freshmen have greatly improved since then in their oral delivery; I was wrong at that time to expect them to distill the significant out of the sea of trivia.) Some class dis-

cussions were stimulating, but I did not feel, at the end of four weeks, that my classes had found much significance in African history. Fortunately, I had the opportunity to try again the second semester with a new class.

By this time, I knew much better the needs, abilities, and limitations of my students. Our high school serves an all-white community of small tract houses; a homeowners' association attempts to preserve the homogeneity of the community. Most of its residents have lower middle-class or working-class occupations. Generally, parents have high school educations; newspapers and magazines are scarce in many homes. The effect of an intellectually impoverished environment showed up in class in many of my students. The fears and prejudices of the "white ghetto" were often voiced or implied. Racial prejudice was part of a larger problem—a suspicion and intolerance toward many other cultural differences, and a painful parochialism. (Who'd ever want to visit Africa or any of *those* places?) My earlier unit on Africa had not touched very directly on these attitudes and values. I decided to direct my teaching toward them. My broadest aims became the fostering of tolerance and curiosity, as well as an understanding of racial problems in the United States and the world today.

The Africa unit I initiated lasted six weeks. The first week was spent in lecture-discussions of Africa's geography and peoples, aimed at a simple understanding of the complexity of the continent. Background reading for students was from our basic paperback text, *Emerging Africa*. A worksheet served as an introduction to the peoples of Africa. The purpose of this exercise was for students to discover for themselves some relationships between environment and social organization, and also to get them thinking of each group in its *own* terms. We talked at length about "Frames of reference," or how one group's views of another group are colored by their presuppositions. Witchcraft was discussed as an example of a custom totally misunderstood by the Europeans; in forbidding its practice, they undermined the basis of legal decision-making in many tribes. I tried to get students to think about the *functions* performed by customs, so they would not pass judgment on them as being "queer" or "primitive." At the end of the week I showed the excellent filmstrip-record combination, "Exploding the Myths of Prejudice." This filmstrip defines prejudice, discusses how prejudices are learned, and proceeds to disprove several myths, including ideas of "pure" races, Negro cultural inferiority, racial blood types, and racial intelligence. Man is shown as having a common African origin, branching out from East Africa to various parts of the world, and there developing physical traits in response to his environment. This presentation turned out to be an excellent stimulant for discussion.

At the beginning of the second week, I had students pick from the following topics for group research:

1. Tribes versus the Twentieth Century (tradition and change)
2. Contact with Europe (colonialism, slavery, imperialism)
3. Independence and Nationalism
4. Race Relations in Africa
5. Africa and the American Negro
6. The Peace Corps in Africa.

This topical approach generated much more interest than had my original country-by-country assignment. Our school library had many good sources on Africa; if it had not, topical approach would not have been possible. Each group made up a list of questions about its topic before starting to do research; these questions formed the basis for their individual reading. Each group kept a news file in the room,

bringing in articles each week to supplement the library materials. My class subscription to *The New York Times Student Weekly* was invaluable, for it contained many features on Africa. Several groups wrote to the two African consulates in San Francisco (Ethiopia and South Africa), and to the African embassies in Washington. For three weeks we spent a great deal of time in the library; in the classroom, we continued to discuss tribal customs, and read chapters in *Emerging Africa* to discuss European involvement in Africa.

In approaching the relationships of Europeans and Africans, I stressed three time periods in African history: early contacts (twelfth through sixteenth centuries), which were on a basis of equality; slavery and imperialism (seventeenth through ninteenth centuries), when relations were between conqueror and conquered; and the twentieth century, once again a period of equal relationships between Africa and the white outside world. While discussing the earliest period, we examined the early African kingdoms of Ghana, Mali, and Songhay to see that Negroes had indeed produced rich cultures at times when Europe was much less advanced. We spent several days on the subject of the slave trade's destructive impact on the European-African relationship. Harold Spear's book on the slave trade is horribly vivid, giving a sense of the inhumanity of the trade. Borrowing an idea from another intern teacher, I allotted to each student the space allowed a slave on the Atlantic voyage, and made them stand and crouch packed together for ten minutes. The point was made.

There exists a great deal of good African literature which expresses the African view of the European, especially in the anthology, *African Heritage*. (Langston Hughes' anthology of black literature came to the library after this unit was completed. It should also be used.) We contrasted black images of the white man with the European view of Africa. Another worksheet was designed for students to conclude how slave traders, merchants, and missionaries treated Africans. Kipling's smug poem "The White Man's Burden" is an excellent statement of Victorian assumptions. For extra credit, in anticipation of the group reports, a list of books on Black Americans was handed out; students could read one and report to me orally after school.[1]

The fifth week was devoted to group presentations, panel discussions of the topics. In order to lend a sense of reality to the projects, to prove that some people did indeed want to go to Africa, I invited two teachers to speak that week. One had set up an entire school system for Monrovia, Liberia, for an Agency for International Development project. His slides of eager students crowded into tiny classrooms emphasized the eagerness of Africans to attain an education—an important message for suburban teenagers. The other teacher related her experiences as a Peace Corps volunteer in Nigeria. Both these talks were quite successful, and I would suggest using as many resource people as you can find.

After the group presentations, for which each group received a grade for oral presentation and the written report, the groups each summarized their reports in one page. These summaries were dittoed and handed out to the class to use as study sheets for the tests on the reports. The sixth week of study was devoted to discussing black Americans in relation to their African experience, and race relations in America today. A good film was used at the beginning of the week, around which our discussions were based. Called *Walk in My Shoes,* it shows the black man's own views of the white man, of fellow blacks, of his identity with Africa and with America. For many of my students, who talk glibly about Negroes but who have never seen the ghetto ten miles away, the scenes of poverty and dejection had a real impact. It is a major step forward in an all-white school to give students even a glimpse of the reality of Negro life today. They must be shaken out of the assumption, shared by many, that it is the fault of the black man that he has not availed himself of all the opportunities that lie waiting at his doorstep. This film sparked some good discussions about *why* the ghetto is a trap.

As well as discussing race relations in the U.S., we spent several days on race conflict in Africa, focusing on apartheid in South Africa. With our text as background, I used the Fenton series, *Race Relations in the Republic of South Africa.* Articles in this pamphlet contrast the life of the Bantu in the village and in the city slum; there is good material for preparing debates and panel discussions on apartheid, which I will do when I teach this unit again.

At the end of six weeks my students had acquired a partial background for understanding the racial tensions in the world today. They had been introduced to the problems of Africa, and their viewpoints on race and tolerance had been aired in the classroom. Six weeks is not enough time to change prejudices deeply held, but it was a beginning.

Bibliography

Books

1. Bernheim, Marc and Evelyne. *From Bush to City—A Look at the New Africa.* New York: Harcourt, Brace & World, Inc., 1966. Tradition and social change—many excellent pictures.
2. Bohannon, Paul. *Africa and Africans.* New York: Natural History Press, African history in perspective of social change.
3. Cameron, James. *The African Revolution.* New York: Random House, 1961.
4. Chu, Daniel, and E. Skinner. *A Glorious Age in Africa.* Garden City, N.Y.: Doubleday and Co., 1965. Ancient African kingdoms. Geared for high school students.
5. Davidson, Basil. *African Slave Trade: Precolonial History.* Boston: Little, Brown, 1961. Originally published under the title *Black Mother.* A history of the relationships between Europe and black Africa, mostly about the deteriorating effects of the slave trade on African society.
6. ———. *A Guide to African History.* London: George Allen & Unwin, 1963. Survey of history from beginning to modern times. Very readable for students.
7. Drachler, Jacob. *An African Heritage.* New York: The Crowell-Collier Publishing Co., 1963. An anthology of African literature, and of black Americans' views of Africa. Explores attitudes toward the white man, independence, and identity in poetry, short stories, and essays.
8. Duberman, Martin B. *In White America.* New York: Signet Books, 1964. Drama based on historical documentation; about the Negro in America from the days of the slave trade.

[1] Titles included *Black Like Me* (Griffin), *Black Boy* (Wright), *Yes I Can* (Sammy Davis, Jr.), *Manchild in the Promised Land* (Brown), *Stride Towards Freedom* and *Why We Can't Wait* (King), *To Kill a Mockingbird* (Lee), *In White America* (Duberman), *Go Tell It on the Mountain* (Baldwin).

9. Fenton, James. *Studies in the Non-Western World,* "Race Relations in the Republic of South Africa." New York: Holt, Rinehart & Winston, Inc., 1967.
10. Ferkiss, Victor C. *Africa's Search for Identity.* New York: George Brazillier, Inc., 1966.
11. Isaacs, Harold R. *The New World of Negro Americans.* New York: The Viking Press, 1963. The impact of world affairs on the race problem in the U.S. and particularly on the Negro, his view of himself, his country, and of Africa. See especially section III, "Negroes and Africa."
12. Lincoln, C. Eric. *The Negro Pilgrimage in America.* Chicago: University of Chicago Press, 1965. Negro history, including African beginnings.
13. Scholastic Multi-Text. *Emerging Africa.* New York: Scholastic Book Services, 1966. Good basic text; readable by average students. Teacher's guide.
14. Spears, John R. *The American Slave Trade.* New York: Bickers and Son, 1960. Detailed documentation of the slave trade—*very* powerful material.
15. Stavrianos, L. S. *Readings in World History.* Boston: Allyn and Bacon, Inc., 1967. Entire section of readings on Africa, including a good short story, "Peter Learns Respect," about the effects of the apartheid mentality on a young Bantu boy.

Movies

1. *Black and White in South Africa,* McGraw-Hill, Text-Film Division, 628 8th Avenue, New York, N.Y. 10036. Rental film. Good presentation of problems of apartheid.
2. *Buma,* Alameda County Audio-Visual Dept., West Winton Ave., Hayward, Calif. (Hereafter referred to as "County.") Short (10 min.) film on African use of masks and statues to cope with fear of the unknown. Good for discussing taboo, voodoo, and superstitions in all societies.
3. *Giant People,* County. Movie on Watusi tribe.
4. *Walk in My Shoes.* Attitude of the Negro toward himself (middle class versus poor Negroes, problems of prejudice and identity); traces the history of the early civil rights movement; explores the impact of African independence movements on Afro-Americanism in the U.S. Not recent enough to include SNCC, Panthers, etc., but still quite useful.

Records

1. "Exploding the Myths of Prejudice," County. Filmstrip-Record combination. Excellent discussion of myths about race and religion. Used to start African unit.

2. "The Negro," part of "Immigrants Have Made America Great" Series, WASP, Pleasantville, N.Y. I was not able to get this, but it was recommended as being good.
3. "Negro Music of Africa and America," Folkways Scholastic Records, 906 Sylvan Ave., Englewood Cliffs, N.J. 07632.

Filmstrips

1. "Africa: Cairo to Capetown," County. Series of six filmstrips on people and geography. Individual titles include: Oasis in Libya; The Nile; The Congo; Contrasts in Nigeria; The Bantu in South Africa; The Highlands of Kenya.
2. "Africa: Explosive Continent," County. Problems of nationalism and independence. Usual problem of being outdated.

Other Sources

1. Afro-American Student Union, University of California, Berkeley.
2. All African Embassies in Washington, D.C.
3. Anti-Defamation League of B'nai Brith, 40 1st St., San Francisco. Good materials on race relations, prejudice, community relations, religion. Rental movies and records, books for sale, some materials free.
4. Consulates in San Francisco. Ethiopian Consulate General, 450 Sutter, S.F. South African Consulate General, 360 Pine, S.F. Good for official policy of apartheid—debate material!
5. *The New York Times Student Weekly;* published weekly for high school students, with format of the regular paper.
6. American Geographic Society, Broadway & 15th St., N.Y.C. 10032. Publishes monthly *Focus,* on various countries.
7. American Society of African Culture, 401 Broadway, N.Y.C. 10013.
8. Civic Education Service, 1733 K St., N.W., Washington, D.C. 20006. Chart on "The New Africa"—statistics. Maps of Africa.
9. Foreign Policy Assn., World Affairs Center, 345 East 46th St., N.Y.C. 10017. Bimonthly Headline Series; *South Africa: The End Is Not Yet* (1966).
10. Population Reference Bureau, Information Service, 1755 Massachusetts Ave., N.W., Washington, D.C. 20036. Publishes *Population Profile: The New Africa—Diversity and Change.* (1 copy free)
11. World Affairs Council, 105 Newbury St., Boston, Massachusetts 02116. Offer study kits on various countries, at a fee.

A SAMPLE HOMEWORK ASSIGNMENT

Pretend that you are an African writing a history of imperialism.

A. What would your history say about merchants, slave traders, and missionaries?
B. How would your history differ from one written by a European?

Student Paper

(A) If I was an African I'd tell that the slave traders were the worst of the bunch because if they were the one that captured the slaves. They sold them for cheap merchandice of little value knowing that about half would reach the ports alive. The traders put all of them they could into the hull of the ship. The hull was unsanitary and the slaves couldn't move enough to stretch for three mounths. They had food throwen down upon them from deck and if a patrol ship came they tied them to the anchor and let it pull them over board to get rid of evidence. The missionarries brought their customs with them and tried to teach them their customs and religion. Some were even involved in the slave trade.

(B) The slaves are animals and only fit for the purpos of serving civilized men. They live in the jungl like dogs and hunt like pigs. They had no empire or great civilization. All the people or countries were trying to get power, so we tried to come in and civilize the natives and tell them abut Christ and education. This is what a European would say.

DEALING WITH RACE PROBLEMS
AND ISSUES

ROCHELLE ESTERLE **81**

Biological Aspects of Race

The Teaching Situation

1. Biology
2. Grades ten through twelve (racially mixed)
3. Ability level low to high
4. Most of the students (twenty-two of the twenty-eight) had taken biology before, and failed due to a general lack of interest in school, absences, conflicts with teachers, and discipline. I don't think any were incapable of passing for academic reasons.

Description of the Project

The project I wish to describe is a unit on the subject of heredity, through a study of the races of man: what features characterize each race, and one theory of *why* these certain features are present. The underlying theme is adaptation to one's environment.

What I Hoped to Achieve

Through a study of the genetics of race, I hoped to specifically achieve an understanding of *why*, on a biological level, some people are black, others white, others yellow, *why* some have flat noses, *why* some lack body hair—in short, *why* our features are exactly the way they are. I hoped that this understanding would lead to a sense of pride in one's race, plus a knowledge that no race is superior, and each race has certain characteristics which are better adapted to specific environments than other races. In addition, I hoped that this study would give the students a "feeling for" the concept of adaptation and natural selection—or survival of the fittest.

Plan of Attack

I planned to introduce the subject of genetics by first arousing their interest with a unit on adaptive coloration. After the students began asking "how," we turned to some of the cellular aspects of genetics—chromosomes, DNA, genes. Then we focused specifically on certain traits which were relevant to these students:

1. Hair, eye, and skin color
2. Ability to taste PTC paper
3. Blood types
4. Eye shape
5. Nose structure

6. Amount of body hair
7. Texture of hair
8. Shape of lips
9. General body structure and size
10. Disease immunities

Account of Project

The subject was introduced through a unit on adaptive coloration—how the colors of various animals make them better suited to their environments through camouflage, mimicry, sex identification, territoriality, etc. The natural result of such a discussion was the question of *how* such changes in the colors can happen (genetics and natural selection.) A further question arose: Why are different colors present in humans? First we studied the mechanisms of natural selection—mutations, selection, survival of the fittest, gene replication, chromosome structure—and saw the movie, *The Thread of Life*. This technical discussion was more meaningful at this time because they now cared about the traits that were affected by these mechanisms. From this discussion we came at last to the question of the color of man. We began this unit by listing all of the characteristics which we associate with the various races of man, with an emphasis on the Caucasoid, Mongoloid, and Negroid races. There is an excellent and very effective illustration of this in the last chapter of Moore's book *Evolution*. The list that the students came up with themselves consisted of seven or eight characteristics for each race, as follows:

Mongoloids	*Negroids*	*Caucasoids*
1. Yellow skin	1. Little body hair	1. Straight nose with high bridge
2. Folded eyelids (tight eyes)	2. Black, curly hair on head (thick)	2. Many shades of hair and eyes
3. High cheek bones	3. Thick lips	3. Lots of body hair
4. Straight, black hair	4. Wide nose	4. Lots of skin problems
5. Small body	5. Large eyes with long lashes	5. Curly and straight hair
6. Short eyelashes	6. Athletically inclined	6. Thin lips (wider than mongoloids)
7. Thin lips	7. Natural rhythm	
8. Wide nose	8. Black skin	

From here we proceeded through each of the characteristics and discussed *why, or what advantage* these characteristics might give an individual in a particular environment. For example, what would be the advantage of having a longer heel bone (Negroids)? Why do more Negroes get sickle cell anemia than people of other races? What is the advantage of having a wide nose in warm climates? Each race has certain characteristics which make it more adapted to its environment than other races, and it is important for Negroes, for example, to know why they are black. This discussion, supplemented by the quiz on race in the October 1966 issue of *Science Digest,* seemed both fascinating and relevant to the students. The discussion lasted throughout the period (two hour periods in summer school).

After the students had a fairly good understanding of the mechanisms and the characteristics involved, we delved further into the subject of skin color with a movie called *The Color of Man.* This movie described the adaptive value of having a dark skin near the equator and a lighter skin color in areas farther north. It also discussed the function of skin color in allowing the correct amount of ultraviolet light and Vitamin D to penetrate the skin.

The unit on race was concluded with a question and answer period which primarily dealt with the issue of race superiority, origin of the races, and fossil records. The time span of the unit was about one week (ten hours).

Summary and Evaluation

I feel that this was one of the most successful units that I attempted this summer. The subject came up quite naturally and was approached from a genetic and biological theory instead of a moralistic or sociological one. I would have been happier with the unit had I had more time to deal with it. I could see that the preliminary work on adaptive coloration was premature without a genetic approach given first; however, the genetics wouldn't have been as interesting without the introduction of coloration. I suggest that these two activities be taught simultaneously, so as to hold the interest of the students. The unit on race was not approached as being any different from the other units that we covered; the students seemed to fall upon the subject naturally. However, their understanding of it would have been improved if the sequence of study had been (1) cell structure, ending with a focus on the nucleus of the cell and the heredity material; (2) heredity and genetics, using adaptive coloration for examples; (3) color of man. All along, the underlying theme should be the theory of natural selection and adaptation. I realize that for any unit to be a success, the most important thing is for the students to be prepared for it. For example, it might have been a fiasco for students to have seen the film on the color of man without an explanation of its relevance to the course of study.

Bibliography

Movies

1. *The Color of Man.* U.C. Extension Media Center. (Describes adaptive value of dark skin and eyes, requires discussion in class before movie.)
2. *The Thread of Life.* Free from Bell Telephone. (A good introduction to cellular aspects of heredity; excellent photographs of chromosomes.)

Books

1. Howell, Francis Clark. *Early Man.* New York: Time, Inc. (*Life Magazine* Nature Series), 1965.
2. Moore, Ruth. *Evolution.* New York: Time, Inc. (*Life Magazine* Nature Series), 1964.
3. Scheinfeld, Amram. *The New You and Heredity.* Philadelphia: J. B. Lippincott Co., 1967.
4. Stern, Curt. *Principles of Human Genetics.* San Francisco: W. H. Freeman, 1960.

Magazine

1. *Science Digest* (October 1966).

Appendix

THE "WHY" OF SOME SUGGESTED TRAITS WHICH CAN BE DISCUSSED

Skin color: Dark skin is found near the equator, lighter skin farther north or south. At the equator the rays of the sun are most direct and their effects are most harsh. Dark skin not only prevents burning but also allows less penetration of vitamin D, overdoses of which can be harmful. Light skin allows for more vitamin D to enter the skin, for a lack of this vitamin will cause rickets (brittle bones). Dark eyes also resist the glare of the sun.

Width of nose: The nose functions not only to smell and to breathe, and to prevent dust particles from entering the nose, but also to warm the air before it enters the lungs. There is a theory that flat noses have shorter nasal passages for warming the air, while noses with high bridges have an elongated warming passage. Therefore, a higher-bridged nose would be better adapted to and necessary in colder climates, away from the equator.

Malaria resistance: The condition of sickle cell anemia produces a side effect of malaria resistance. Although this type of anemia has no beneficial effects in the United States, in Africa it is positively selected because the malaria is a greater handicap there than is the anemic condition. Sickle cell anemia is most common in the black population, but also may occur in Caucasians.

Ability to digest cow's milk: It has been found that certain tribes in Africa react adversely to the lactose in cow's milk. This has been a genetic change brought about by the lack of cattle in certain parts of Africa over a long period of time, which allowed this trait to appear with no apparent effects on the population.

Blood type frequencies: A, B, AB, and O blood types are all found in Negroid, Caucasoid, and Mongoloid peoples, but in different ratios among each population. These frequencies break down even further with geographical areas. American Indians have only Type O blood, unless they have interbred with other people.

Eyelids: The shape of the eyelids of oriental (Mongoloid) people may have been an adaptation to resist the glare of the sun.

American Negroes: By testing the relative proportions of different blood types, PTC tasting abilities, and other objective features, it has been estimated that the Negroes of the United States (not recent immigrants, however) are 30 percent "impure"— that is, on a scale of traits characteristic of Negroids and Caucasoids, they would fall somewhere in between. This is due to both interbreeding and different selection pressures.

RICHARD JONES 82

Black History Week

As the drama teacher at Fremont High School in Oakland, the task of preparing a series of programs celebrating "Black History Week" fell on my shoulders. The planning and rationale behind this program series may serve as a sample approach to implementing a Black Studies Program.

The first problem I had to work out was to choose a format which would draw from as many areas of black life as possible. I decided on a series of three presentations covering black history, black psychology, and black art.

All materials used were carefully selected in an effort to achieve immediacy, a prime requisite for communication with today's students. One thinks of the generation gap and corresponding credibility gap as referring to the difference between, for example, parent and child. I have discovered, however, particularly among blacks in my drama classes, a marked suspicion and rejection of even a playwright such as James Baldwin, who wrote *Blues for Mr. Charlie* in 1958.

The first assembly was a documentary-type affair patterned after the old "You Are There" television program. I strove to use characters who would hold audience interest because of their previous obscurity. Thus, while we had such people as Booker T. Washington and Malcolm X, we also had Matt Henson,[1] Nat Love,[2] and Suzie King.[3] The students playing these roles stood in darkness at the rear of the stage and responded when called upon by a narrator.

During rehearsals it became obvious that many students were uptight about playing "Toms" like Booker T. Washington, George Washington Carver, and even Martin Luther King. One must be aware of the pressure the vociferous militant blacks have upon their brothers. This pressure creates a great amount of self-deprecation and paranoia in the student who so fears being called a "Tom." As a teacher of drama it was my job to show such fearful students that being a "Tom" was first of all a state of mind. Furthermore, as actors my students had to be helped to realize the intellectual distinction between playing a role on stage and playing one in life.

Fortunately, players from ACT (The American Conservatory Theater Company) had come to Fremont two weeks before our scheduled series and had performed *In White America*. Their performance was a smashing success and, in particular, the acting of one man stole the show. This man was black, about 6'3" and 230 pounds, with a deep basso voice. He portrayed a slave in the Old South, a blatantly stereotyped Stepin Fetchit character. At another point he played W. E. B. Du Bois. Both characterizations were successful and my students recognized them as such. I pointed out that his success derived from the power of his concentration, which allowed him to play a role probably very far removed from his own life. Thus my students had a case in point with ramifications both immediate (as to resolving their emotional hang-ups about "Toms") and theoretical (as to the relationship between man the actor, and the role he plays).

This difficulty overcome, the first assembly went smoothly. Yet I felt that the "You Are

1 With the Peary expedition, actually the first American at North Pole.
2 Famous cowboy, popularly known as "Deadwood Dick."
3 Courageous nurse who served with Clara Barton.

There" format dealing with historical figures speaking quotable quotes was too stilted, almost too academic—in other words, not where it's at experientially. The second assembly was to get away from the history book approach and assume a more "nitty-gritty" psychological, or guts approach to race relations.

I must own up to three weeks of failure in preparation for this second assembly. I tried various approaches: comic one-acts, satiric "minstrel shows." But none said what I wanted to say. Then it dawned on me that it was probably impossible for a white man to write about black experience—condescension might automatically be involved one way or another. Thus my presentation needed to be a dramatic adaptation of something written by a black man.

I foresook any black plays in favor of *Black Rage* by W. H. Grier and P. M. Cobbs. This study based on psychoanalysis of black people was exactly the material I wanted. Furthermore, the "drama" in the analyst's room was a natural for holding an audience.

I feared that the white students at Fremont (roughly 60 percent of the total student body) might begin to tire of and become alienated by presentations about black people in such a concentrated dose (three in one week). Thus the problem in this second assembly was to combine enough black ethnocentricity to relate to the black students, and enough universality of situation to correlate with the white experience.

The authors of *Black Rage* pull no punches. The book hits hard at white society and ultimately indicts it. Okay, all we white liberals can dig that, but can a white student body that had gone through three separate incidents of violence during the year? And is an indictment going to be rejected by the white kids because it alienates them? Realizing that my white students come from blue-collar families and that, as such, they probably were feeling the greatest pressure from racial tensions for obvious socioeconomic reasons, I decided to dramatize the psychoanalysis of two people in the book who weren't in rebellion against anyone; they just wanted to lead successful lives."

The play was divided into two case studies, the first about a man, the second about a woman. The man was failing because he felt the pressure of competition in the white middle-class world of biological research that he had tried to enter. The woman was failing in love relationships because of her view of herself as black, ugly, and a slut—an opinion which had been reinforced by childhood and adolescent experiences.

Because of the heavy and profound message of the play, I realized that the staging technique had to be both startling and diverting. The technique I used not only met these requirements but also related to white students because of its similarity to psychedelic "light shows" at the rock ballrooms. As a character recounted an experience to the analyst, he moved to another part of the stage and acted this experience out. To dramatize the dreamlike quality of these scenes, I used in them music from the movie *2001: A Space Odyssey* and an unusual cut from an album by the Iron Butterfly. The more nightmarish recollections were also accompanied by a high-intensity stroboscopic light which, when flashed on a moving person, makes him appear to float. These lights are also typical of the modern rock concert and lent a mystical and contemporary mood to the presentation.

The response to this assembly was so over-poweringly positive that it completely over-shadowed the final assembly, which was a purely aesthetic presentation of black art forms, such as music, fashion design, and dance. Perhaps this last assembly was weak because the technique was that of the rather ordinary "variety show."

What started out as a project for a Black Studies curriculum turned into a learning and creative experience for all students, and particularly myself. I learned that, as a drama teacher, my greatest ally is contemporaneity, and my greatest foe is banality; that is, the pseudo-Hollywood, pseudo-Golddiggers-of-1938 bag that many of my drama colleagues are still suffocating in.

MINERVA BARRANCO 83

Black History

Teaching Situation

Mission High School is located in the city of San Francisco. The school operates on a tracking system, and this year I teach four U.S. history classes (one "remedial," three "average") and one black history class.

I was pleased with my three classes of U.S. history students. They were eager to work after I explained to them the ways in which I approach history. We all agreed that facts and details were not the most important things in history; concepts and problems in U.S. history were more significant and easier to learn.

My black history class was different. It was different for many reasons:

1. The students were from grades low ten through high twelve.

2. Some students could read and write, others could do neither.
3. Some students were interested in the subject and willing to work; others were taking the class just for curiosity.
4. This class was in the curriculum of the school for the first time. It was offered because of a student sit-in the semester before.
5. The unrest that existed in San Francisco, and all over the nation, in regard to the subject of black history and who was to teach it, made this class tense and different.

Description of the Problem

The first few days of the semester were very routine because of essential clerical duties. I was quite eager to start with the subject of black history, but because of my Spanish accent

I knew that I was not completely accepted by my black students. (I am a native of Panama, dark skinned, and with a completely Spanish background.) I knew if I wanted to succeed that semester and the following ones, I had to be accepted by my students in this particular class.

After the first two days of classes I had changed my mind about how to begin. I had planned to start with the history of the black man in Africa, how he came to America as a slave, and so on. But this was not what the students wanted. My last unit was to have been the black man and San Francisco, but I decided to start with this unit instead, because the topic would give me more interaction with the students and might help to solve my problem of being accepted by them.

Account of Project

My project had two objectives:

1. I wanted the students to be aware of the community around them; and
2. I wanted to find out more about my students and to gain their trust.

First of all, I wanted to know how much they knew about San Francisco. The first day we had a class discussion in which we only exchanged ideas; no real learning took place; it was a gripe session, in which the black students complained about how badly they were mistreated in San Francisco. I am aware of this, but I am also aware that there are some facilities for the black people in this city, and I learned that day that my students didn't know what kind, or where the facilities were.

The next day I presented my project. The students were to choose a topic from the following list: Employment, Neighborhood Centers, Recreation, Educational Opportunities, Law Enforcement, Health Facilities, Economic Conditions, and Housing.

I explained to them that in order for this project to be successful we had to have some students working in all the different areas. We ended up with five students in each group.

The next plan was to visit some of the public agencies and to arrange for speakers to come to our class. Before this could take place, we tried to formulate questions that would enable us to get the information we wanted.

After the students had made a list of questions and we had arranged our visit to a Neighborhood Center, we started our trip into the city. I have to mention that I could not get a special bus to take us because I had to give notice of a field trip at least three weeks in advance. Since the black students that come from Hunter's Point to Mission High School have to take *three* different buses, each way, every day, the students and I decided to go through all these transfers. We sat together in the back of the bus, exchanged ideas, and they began to see me as a human being.

The afternoon visits were very short to get the information we needed. The next day was a day to write letters to different agencies and ask for more information. In the days that followed we discussed the results of our investigations. One flattering result was an invitation to the students to become resource persons themselves.[1]

Summary and Evaluation

The class began to see the teacher in a different role. They also saw the various roles the teacher has to play inside and outside the classroom. The students learned to accept me first as a teacher; and later on as a member of the black community but with a different background, and of course, with a foreign or "latino-american" accent. And most important of all, they learned that it doesn't matter who you are as long as you are willing to accept people as people.

It was a wonderful experience for the students as they had a chance to reappraise the situation in regard to being black in San Francisco. They not only appraised the extent of discrimination against blacks in the community; they also learned about resources and facilities available to black people. And they became involved in community problems, resources, and programs as a result of their experiences.

[1] See Appendix for a letter written to one of the students requesting that our black history students serve as resource persons for the Bayview Adult Opportunity Center.

Dear Miss Pearoon,

We have been told that the Bayview Youth Opportunity Center has been in touch with your instructor in Black History regarding your request for information about job opportunities. So that we do not duplicate or confuse the efforts, the Adult Opportunity Center will bow out and let our YOC friends take over.

May we reverse our roles? Since we are not to become a "resource" for you, will you become one for us in "Black History"? Many of the adults in the Bayview-Hunters Point Area never have had the chance to study this subject. Do you suppose that some of the students in your class would be willing to share their knowledge with a group of our applicants one evening a week? If you do find willingness, please talk to your instructor because we know there would be a great deal of interest here.

Yours very truly,

BARBARA ENO ROOT
Branch Supervisor
Bayview Adult Opportunity Center

BURTON H. GREENE **84**

Black Literature Course

Planning

The Teaching Situation

1. Subject: Black Literature.
2. Grades: Nine through twelve.
3. Ability Level: A wide range of ability from students who read at third- and fourth-grade level to those entering college with very high abilities.
4. Other Factors: The racial make-up was approximately 50 percent black, 45 percent Caucasian, and 5 percent Mexican-American, Philippino, Japanese. The wide range of abilities did not follow racial or ethnic lines.

Description of the Project

The project was to teach a black literature summer course to students of varying abilities, using all forms of literature—i.e., novels, plays, speeches, letters, poems, autobiographies, essays, film, tapes, and records. In addition, the course was to utilize groups, student-directed activities such as a class magazine, student choice of their own outside reading, and student-led discussions.

What I Hoped to Achieve

1. A better understanding of literature and its many forms.
2. An appreciation of literature written by black Americans.
3. An appreciation of black and white for each other, and of the positive values in each culture, from working together on various activities.
4. An involvement of students not usually involved in a tangible successful activity.

Plan of Attack

Generally, my idea was to start by exploring racial barriers and mutual fears by pointing them out in literature. At the end of two weeks after much of this had been exposed, my attitude shifted to the idea "that we all understood cultural problems and at this point we were together." Generally the students accepted this and we started working "together" on a magazine, in assigned groups and as a class.

Account of the Project

The First Week

Grouping was random. Students separated according to where they chose to sit. The first lesson was to work on various aspects of culture from *The Family of Man* and complete a ditto on it. As a total class we worked on James Baldwin's "My Dungeon Shook: Letter to His Nephew on the 100th Anniversary of the Emancipation." Very little pressure was put on the students this first week, but the emphasis was to get them to relax with each other.

The Second Week

The autobiographical novel by Richard Wright, *Black Boy*, was used. As a class we wrestled with the meanings of his experiences. Supplementing *Black Boy* were poems that thematically tied in: "Defeat" by Witter Brynner; "Personal" and "Merry-Go-Round" by Langston Hughes; "Kid Stuff" by Frank Horne; "Refugee" by Naomi Long Witherspoon; "Incident" by Countee Cullen; and "A Boy's Need" by H. C. Johnson. A class period was spent on a recording of *The Autobiography of Frederick Douglass* with the Herbert Clark Johnson poem, "Frederick Douglass." During this week we discussed the possibility of publishing a class literary magazine.

Note that the activities and the materials were structured so that a nonreader would not be left out of discussions. Even if he had not read the assigned book, he could understand what was going on by listening to a poem, record, or tape which was germane to the assignment. Also used this week was a record by Godfrey Cambridge. The main emphasis was on grasping the Southern segregationist reality and understanding how to move away from it, laugh at it, but understand its seriousness and the importance of its being communicated in literature.

The Third Week

By this point I felt the class was ready for grouping. I used as my criteria racial balance with a corresponding ability balance (as I perceived it.) There were now work groups that were assigned and magazine groups that were voluntary (editorial, music, poetry, prose, and art.) Some students were reluctant to participate at first, but I insisted that they do so in some way. Because the groups were relaxed and student-run, they joined in after this initial push. Editors were elected. With a minimum of help from me, students went to work on the magazine, formulating its goals and focus. Also at this point the class was "together" and much of the early tension had eased. (During the trouble which resulted in bringing the police to the school, discussions led by the students dealt with the facts, rumors, attitudes, and solutions of the incident. Somehow these open discussions had brought the class closer together.) Assignments were made for the magazine by the student editors. The title "Premeditated Soul" was chosen and the dedication: "An attempt by black and white students to put forth the feelings and thoughts surrounding the black environment."

The Fourth Week

The next two weeks were devoted to a unit entitled "The Times They are A-Changin.' " The Dylan lyrics were given to the students on ditto and sung by Odetta on record. Individual books and reports were chosen by students from newspaper articles, *Ramparts* Magazine, *Life, The Reporter,* etc. The reading material included a wide selection of current books, the most popular being *Pimp* by Iceberg Slim, *And Then We Heard the Thunder* by Killens, *Nigger* by Dick Gregory, etc. Note that not all these books were black literature, leaving an outlet for students to read what they wanted.

The anthology *Way Out* was used, including the following: "Toward Black Liberation" by Stokely Carmichael, a difficult essay on Black Power stressing the intellectual content rather than the emotional reactions to it; a short story, "Autumn Leaves" by Sam Greenlee, which raises the question of self-image and whether the hero is black or white; poems used were: "Status Symbol" and "The Rebel" by Mari Evans, "Black, Bourgeousie" by Leroi Jones, and "No Images" by Waring Cuney. Classes were kept varied with at least three separate activities during the two-hour class. A typical day might have been whole class discussions on assigned reading, groups working on dittos, silent reading, and magazine groups, or student reports, lectures by the teacher, etc.

The Fifth Week

The Huey Newton trial[1] was just starting at this time. Students were asked to keep their ears, eyes, and minds open, producing some enlightening discussions. In addition to the Newton trial, the wealth of television shows (Xerox and ABC Specials and two series on the Educational station about Black problems) started off the class period with student reactions to the various programs. The magazine was taking shape and would be ready soon. The book for this week was *The Autobiography of Malcolm X*. Students were not required to read it and were told if they did not read it there would be other materials to draw from in class. Materials used were speeches by Malcolm X, "From the Grassroots" and "To Mississippi Youth," and Malcolm's "Letter from Mecca." At the beginning of the week, students were asked to write everything they knew about Malcolm X on a piece of paper. At the end of the week this assignment was repeated and it was evident to the class that they had learned a great deal.

The Sixth Week

During this week the magazine was run off and distributed by the students. There was a class meeing with the school superintendent of curriculum. He communicated to the class why he would not allow an "anti-white" poem to be published in the magazine and the students debated why they thought it should be.[2] Other materials this week included the film *Walk in My Shoes,* and hearing, reading, and performing the play *In White America*.

[1] Huey Newton, Minister of Defense for the Oakland Black Panthers, was on trial for the shooting of a policeman.
[2] The superintendent volunteered to come to the class and explain his position. Although the students still maintained their original position, the visit was significant and gave them more insight into the unit on "Change" and the complexities involved.

Summary and Evaluation

I am not exactly sure what I did, but I feel it worked. Students were exposed to a great deal of material and enjoyed much of it. The Baldwin letter and Carmichael essay were quite difficult for the class but worthwhile. Discipline was not a significant problem. White and black students came together, not so much through the materials (although this gave them a good intellectual grasp of the situation), as through their joint activities. All students learned in the class because the activities allowed them to give of themselves and to better understand each other. Empathy was created. Students who would not normally participate because of lack of reading skills were often on equal footing with better equipped students.

One Philippino student, who had rarely participated in groups or even conversed with other students previously, was often a group leader. Several nonreaders wrote for the magazine and drew some inspiration from the lives of Richard Wright and Malcolm X.

If this course were to be replicated I would suggest that the teacher emphasize the ability of youth to change the society, rather than stress the ills of society and white guilt. Discussions should be oriented toward the subject matter with the teacher quietly maintaining control and directing expressions away from personal attacks on fellow students, and directing minds toward openness rather than vindictiveness.

In summary, the class was an attempt to extrapolate all the positive aspects of black literature and life in order to understand the saying "Black is Beautiful," which really means that each student is beautiful and that he must believe that for it to be true. To a certain extent this was accomplished in six weeks, but negative self-image seems to go hand-in-hand with being a teen-ager, and a more concerted effort on the part of the schools seems in order. Another way of saying this is: the more students learn, the better they feel about themselves, sometimes in spite of themselves.

Recommendations

In conclusion, I must say that I believe black literature should not be taught in the schools only *as a separate course*. All English classes should be varied and include contributions from all literature, and *all* students and teachers must understand that American (or world) literature has not been "lily white." Any of the literature I used in my class would be valuable because each work stands on its own merits and would be equally valuable to a "white" suburban school. In my summer class, the value of "over-compensating" toward black contributions was not detrimental to those nonblacks in my class, but rather quite beneficial, since the literature they read had application to their lives, and to the most significant issue facing our society.

Bibliography

In addition to the films, records, tapes, and paperbacks mentioned in the essay, I should like to stress the usefulness of the anthology *Way Out,* edited by Lois Michener (New York: Holt, Rinehart & Winston, Inc., 1968). I enthusiastically recommend it for wide use in English classes. I also used many of my own personal books, and I recommend to other English teachers that they might start gathering their own class libraries.

PART THREE

Developing
New School Programs and
New Public School Models

For the past decade we masculinized the schools with mathemetics, physics, and with a variety of new toughminded curricula. Educational criticism in the next decade may well concern itself more with the soft side of things—with non-cognitive approaches.... There are a number of people who are talking seriously about a 'curriculum of concerns,' educational programs that begin with the interest and experience of kids, not with predetermined sets of skills to be learned.... These things, too, can be carried to undisciplined extremes. None is a cure-all, but nothing in education ever is. The very nature of the enterprise is unsettling and troublesome. Education and maturation mean change, and that in turn, means dealing with new problems, new elements every day....[1]

How do you change schools from ineffective holding operations into places young people want to attend? How do you create the feeling of a community within a large, impersonal institution? What kinds of counseling can be most beneficial for difficult students? How can we meet the growing demands of minority group students for school programs that will enhance their self-respect and improve their academic performance? What kinds of new school models will better meet the problems of today's disaffected or value-conflicted adolescents?

The strategy papers we have included in this last part describe the beginning attempts of several Graduate Internship Program teachers to find answers to such questions through (1) formulating new school programs, and (2) developing new public school models. Attempting first to accomplish their instruc-

[1] Peter Schrag, "Why Our Schools Have Failed," *Commentary* (March 1968); p. 37.

tional aims in their own classrooms, each of these teachers later felt compelled to expand individual efforts into more comprehensive educational strategies—to include other teachers, other subject matter, more students, and whenever possible, the school district and the community. Like the classroom strategies, these innovative programs and new public school models represent preliminary ventures. Undoubtedly they will change as new needs and circumstances dictate. Meanwhile, we offer these more ambitious strategies to the reader in the hope that they may suggest possibilities for others to explore more fully.

1. New School Programs

We begin with descriptions of four school programs that have been introduced into ongoing comprehensive high schools.

A Cooperative Counseling Program

Myrna Walton (Intern '64, Master teacher '67, '68) in her paper "Student-Teacher Relations: An Experiment in Cooperative Counseling," delineates a special kind of school "Halfway House" which she devised for problem students and their perturbed teachers at John F. Kennedy's Experimental Summer School, 1968.[2] The purpose of the summer school was to "give success experiences to nonachievers," and through this success to improve the self-image of a predominantly black "turned-off" student body. (See "SPAN: A Strategy for Reaching the Untaught," pp. 7–11.) Mrs. Walton's efforts were aimed particularly toward setting up a "Counseling Cooperative in which: (1) classroom teachers and their disruptive students might jointly explore the ways in which the behavior and attitudes of each of them might be subverting the purposes of the school, and (2) teachers and students might together help change these attitudes and behaviors. After watching its operation during the summer of 1968, we believe that the teacher-pupil counseling cooperative which Mrs. Walton pioneered could serve as a useful model from which the understaffed and overworked counseling programs in most schools could benefit.

A Drug Education Program for
School and Community

We move next to another area of urgent need for contemporary youth—the problem of providing effective education about drug abuse. Gene G. Davis, biology teacher at Albany High School, in his paper on drug education tells how he and the administrators of Albany High joined forces with the PTA, the Albany Adult Evening School, and other community agencies to help students, teachers, parents, and other concerned citizens to deal with student drug abuse more wisely. They did this by looking at drug-taking both from the viewpoint of a student's personal needs and problems and by taking into account the external pressures on youth in the contemporary scene. We suggest

[2] See also Marcia Perlstein's description of the youth-tutor-youth program she coordinated at JFK the same summer (Strategy 44). In some areas, the two programs overlapped.

that this many-pronged psycho-sociological approach—involving key elements in both school and community—is worthy of study by other school districts.

Ethnic Studies Programs

Our next two strategies deal with a burgeoning new program in many schools—the ethnic studies approach to working with educationally disadvantaged and unmotivated high school students.

Convinced that the usual U.S. history courses she was asked to teach failed completely to place the role of the American Negro in any correct or helpful perspective, Samantha H. Lee (Intern '62), history teacher and counselor at Berkeley High School, Berkeley, California, in her paper "Evolution of a Black Studies Program," explains the particular circumstances which gave rise, first to a black history course, and then to an interdisciplinary Black Studies Program at her school. She sees the present program as one which, if properly taught and supported, can become a basic step toward the real integration of black students into American society.

Gini Matute (Intern '68), another history teacher and counselor, working mainly with Mexican-American students, similarly felt a strong need to devise a comprehensive interdisciplinary ethnic studies program at her school. We have included here her original proposal for "An Interdisciplinary Seminar in Mexican-American Studies"—which, after some heroic efforts, was adopted by the Hayward, California, Unified School District, as a pilot project in the regular school program for 1969–1970.[3]

In the years to come, it will be important for all educators to watch the effects of such evolving programs, to see if, in fact, ethnic studies will improve the academic performance and self-respect of minority group students.

2. New Public School Models

The new schools described in this section are parts of existing public school systems. Other limited alternatives to the traditional school exist today in the form of private, experimental, and "free schools." The competition introduced by such alternatives—whether inside or outside the school system—may well provide, as sociologist Kenneth Clark suggests, the very stimulus needed to shake public schools out of their "inefficient and monopolistic hold on American education."[4]

The teacher who elects to foster improvement from within the system faces a set of hard problems: How *can* important changes be made from within encrusted institutions? Can the advantages of a small community school be included in large comprehensive high schools? Can smaller units, or schools-within-schools function to keep benefits of both small and large institutions? Can a city school sponsored by a big city system offer its disaffected, low socio-economic students the same kind of nurture and individual attention usually

---

[3] We recently heard that Miss Matute is serving as Hayward's District coordinator of Mexican-American programs.

[4] See, for example, Kenneth Clark's statement "Alternative Public Schools Systems," *Harvard Educational Review* (Winter 1968), 100–113.

reserved for students at costly private schools? Most important, how can the new models best influence older school patterns?

Opportunity High School, San Francisco

We begin with Marcia Perlstein's description ("Opportunity High: Getting it Together") of her dreams and vision about a new type of inner-city school for continuation and dropout students; of the careful planning that she and an inspired group of fellow teachers and cooperating school personnel undertook to "get it together"; and finally, of the eventual Opportunity High School that resulted from these efforts—an inner-city school with a voluntary student body, gifted and compassionate teachers, and an imaginative yet practical curriculum.[5]

Philadelphia Cooperative Summer Schools Program

Terry Borton (GIP intern in 1963, later a consultant to the Philadelphia public school system) ran a pilot summer workshop in Philadelphia in the summer of 1965, which became the model for subsequent summer programs in Philadelphia as well as for several intern-originated school programs in the Bay Area.[6]

In his paper, "What Turns Kids On?" Mr. Borton describes the "curriculum of concerns" which he and his colleagues devised in their quest for "schools that students want to attend because their education is important to them...as human beings."

Community High School, Berkeley, California

Jay Manley, and Peter Kleinbard, faculty members of Berkeley High, piloted a Berkeley High Summer Workshop in 1967 based in good part on the Philadelphia Summer Program reported in "What Turns Kids On?" They sought to incorporate and expand several of its key features—improvisational drama, experience-based learning, student-centered curriculum—in a year-round school-within-a-school. They stated their goal as follows:

> We seek to create in our school an environment which will encourage a sense of community among its members. Through such an environment we hope to help the individual student and teacher to establish a secure sense of who each is and a faith in his own ability to become the person he wishes to be.

[5] See earlier strategies of Marcia Perlstein's "A Suggestion for the Constructive Use of Grades" (No. 7) and "Introducing Success: High School Tutors in an Urban Setting" (No. 44).

[6] With Mr. Borton's permission we have reprinted in this collection the article "What Turns Kids On?" which first appeared in *Saturday Review* (April 15, 1967), pp. 72–80. Terry Borton has since written a book, *Reach, Touch, and Teach* (New York: McGraw-Hill Book Company, 1970), in which he describes at greater length the various programs he has helped set up. We have included Mr. Borton's article here because Mr. Borton was a Graduate Program intern, and two other interns—Anne Hornbacher and Peter Kleinbard—who participated with him in the Philadelphia summer program introduced some of its important features into a Berkeley High Summer Workshop in 1967.

We have included here a description by Mr. Manley and Mr. Kleinbard of the evolution of the Community High School from the first summer workshop in Berkeley into its present reality—a school-within-a-school at Berkeley High.

In the years to come undoubtedly many more schools—both private and public—will be started in response to the growing restlessness of today's students, the increasing demand for "relevance," the growing militancy of minority groups demanding full educational opportunity, the insistence of teachers on smaller class size and better working conditions, and countless other educational needs as they emerge. With all these pressures toward change, it is indeed hard to predict what our schools will be like even in the early seventies, much less beyond that. The only thing we can be sure of is that they will change, somehow.

It is the hope of the Graduate Internship Program that these future schools will incorporate some of the inventive and compassionate spirit contained in the interns' strategies. We would feel well rewarded for our efforts in assembling this collection if it should trigger improved instruction for today's students, and inspire brighter visions for the schools of tomorrow.

I: NEW SCHOOL PROGRAMS

Black studies at Berkeley High School summer school, 1970, Berkeley, California.

MYRNA WALTON **85**

Student-Teacher Relations:
An Experiment in Cooperative Counseling

What I Hoped to Achieve

I should start by stating that my personal aims in organizing a counseling cooperative were somewhat different from the goals of the summer school, "to give success experiences to nonachievers" and "to improve their self-image." I do not believe that one can "give success" to black students unless one is willing to examine one's own honesty, understanding, and behavior toward the black community. I do believe the lack of respect and understanding frequently shown by the school has a great deal to do with creating alienated and nonachieving students. In this summer school I saw teachers and counselors who told students they were lazy, when in fact the students were not and the teacher had made no effort to find out if the students had been working. I saw a teacher tell students they were not trying to better themselves or get an education when in fact these students had come to summer school for that very reason. Such behavior helps to create alienated students. I do not believe that all black students possess a poor self-image. Nowadays, black students may be more likely than whites to have a very powerful and positive self-image. The school has had very little to do with the change. The black nationalist movement (in particular the Black Panthers) has instilled in students a very great pride in themselves and a belief in their potential. This improved self-image often comes in conflict with the school, because teachers fail to recognize this improvement for what it is; they see it as a threat. Out of these thoughts I forged my *first goal*. I hoped to develop a program that

would help teachers to explore their own attitudes and begin to change.

As I began to plan, other goals appeared. I wanted to establish some viable alternatives to the present school structure of classes on one hand, and deans and counselors on the other. Our democratic society has taken great care to provide alternatives because we value freedom and the dignity of the individual. If a man dislikes his employer, he can quit and find another job. If he fights with his neighbor, he can move. If he has been wronged, he has various ways of obtaining justice. But few alternatives have been provided in most schools. A student either conforms to whatever his school considers acceptable behavior, or he does not. Often, in order to retain his dignity he chooses not to conform. But unless the student has a teacher or counselor who will pull strings or fight for him, he has no power to make changes —no matter how dull, inept, humorless, provincial, or rude the teacher, no matter how boring, mindless, or meaningless the lessons. Sometimes, alternatives actually exist, but the student or his teachers do not see them. I planned to use the Counseling Cooperative to explore which alternatives were possible.

When we started seeing students, a third goal appeared. We wanted to explore what the behavior of students in class was, and how the student's attitudes toward school influenced his behavior. When desirable, we would try to help the student to change his behavior. Usually, this is the function of teachers, students, and deans. But teachers lack time; they must aim their efforts at the class as a whole. Deans and counselors carry a heavy work load also. Because we were acting outside the usual framework of the school and had no particular position to protect, and no precedents to uphold, we felt we had a better chance of reaching students on terms meaningful to them.

Account of Project

Organization

I recruited the staff informally by discussing my ideas and asking for volunteers. Seven teachers and five intern teachers joined me. Although most of us lacked professional training in counseling, we felt that teachers are closer to the reality of the classroom than are most counselors or deans. Any teacher interested in his students spends a great deal of time, inside class and out, in what might loosely be called counseling. We called ourselves the Teacher-Student Counseling Cooperative and were known as the Co-op. Our principal provided a classroom and a typewriter; we arranged tables and chairs informally, installed two dictaphones, magazines, and lots of scrap paper.

We invited teachers to send us students who were preventing their class from learning or the teacher from teaching, or who were making no effort to learn. Any teacher who wanted to use our services would have to commit himself to a follow-up conference, either with the student or our staff. Teachers could make an appointment for a student during class time by filling out an appointment request and describing the problem.

This plan for follow-up conferences with teachers had problems at first. Many teachers wanted nothing to do with follow-up conferences. Their feeling was that they were not paid for such conferences. We would not have seen any students of such teachers except that the regular counselors, who were very cooperative, often sent us their overflow of problem students. Several teachers sent us students without making appointments, and were not eager for follow-up conferences. Most teachers cooperated fully, and naturally our greatest success was achieved with their students. Without exception, intern teachers were very cooperative and eager to profit from our observations and suggestions.

The chart below shows what kinds of students came to us (during four weeks).[1]

Race	Male Junior High	Female Junior High	Male Senior High	Female Senior High	Total
Black	10	37	16	13	76
White	1	1	3	1	6
Mexican	0	0	2	1	3
Total	11	38	21	15	85

Activities

Each day in the Co-op was different. When a student came in we wrote his name in the log and introduced him to an available staff member. The staff member tried to establish exactly what had happened in the class (an extremely long process), why the student and teacher acted as they did, what alternatives had been available, what was the student's responsibility now and for the future. Usually the student decided what the next step would be. Sometimes he simply returned to class. Often the staff member agreed to explain to the teacher what had been discussed. Sometimes we set up a conference between the teacher and the student, mediated by a staff member in the neutral environment of the Co-op. We also conducted conferences with groups of students, with parents, with tutors, or with whoever happened to be sitting in the Co-op at the moment. Oddly enough, students welcomed having other students or teachers hear their problem, and very often, these bystanders contributed a lot to the discussion. Two student tutors assigned to us were very helpful in drawing the other students out.

If a student wished, he could draw, type, or speak into a dictaphone, which helped him to cool off or express his feelings. Some students preferred to sit in a corner alone; others would not talk about themselves but would join in on informal discussions, which were always occurring, with or without the staff. The main topic of conversation was education; what made a good teacher, what kind of punishment worked best, what was wrong with school, what teachers were really like, etc.

Occasionally we put through a change of

_____

[1] The principal has estimated that 80–90 percent of the population was black. There were thirty-two junior high classes and sixty-one senior high classes. Note the reversal of female and male referrals from junior high to senior high.

program if the student felt strongly against the class or if a mistake had been made in scheduling. We tried to introduce new reading material to students, we took them to the library, to previews of movies for classroom use, to other classes as a visitor. We also permitted several students to use the Co-op as a workroom. Their teachers felt they were too disruptive in class, but could work well alone or with some help from the staff. For a few students we devised a special course of study taught by a tutor.

We visited classrooms to observe the behavior of students who came to us, and to offer advice, particularly to new teachers who were having problems with the class as a whole. Finally, we allowed students to drop in on us during breaks, and many did, just to talk or see what was happening.

Students were sent to us for a variety of reasons: tardiness (4), failure to bring work materials to class (2), student feels work is too hard (3), student didn't want this course (5), personality conflict with teacher (8), fighting (4), not working (4), home problems (3), conflict with other students (4), boredom (2), student is high on drugs (1), insubordination (4), mistake in scheduling (6). The greatest problem of junior high students (30) was what the staff called "age" or immaturity—i.e., restlessness common in twelve to fourteen year olds. They talked, ran around the class, refused to work, defied the teacher, showed hostility to the teacher and to each other, giggled, ate in class, were tardy, threw things, shouted, and left class on impulse. This type of behavior changes as students move on to high school, from restlessness to deliberate "cutting up." Twenty-one high school students were sent to us for this reason, mainly talking too much or talking to the teacher. Some students were sent out for more than one reason and by more than one teacher. More than half were counseled two or more times.

Atmosphere

We encouraged an informal atmosphere for discussion and constructive problem solving, rather than deciding upon a penalty for a student already condemned. Students could openly express their feelings, in whatever language they chose, without fear of punishment. We took great pains to treat the student in a respectful and interested manner.

Evaluation of Progress toward Goals

First Goal: Helping Teachers to Examine and Change Their Attitudes

The teachers on our staff felt they had learned a great deal about the individual needs of students. By talking to a student from another class, a staff member could gain a new perspective on his own students. He could see how other teachers had handled various situations. The teachers whose students we counseled often benefitted by learning more about the students' feelings, and in some cases, realized that they might have responded in more positive ways. Teachers learned by observing the way in which staff members spoke to students and by hearing our observations of their class. One teacher had not realized how rude her voice and manner had been. She changed, and as a result we saw fewer of her students in Co-op.

We would have been much more effective if we had had time for more follow-up conferences. There are many teachers who feel no need to change and who resent an effort such as the Co-op. Any future Co-op should plan more effective ways to educate such teachers without threatening them.

Originally I had planned to set up meetings between teachers and a psychologist who specialized in communication. At these meetings so much material was uncovered that we decided to work toward a long-range program. The "Get Hip" program is being planned now by students who intend to explore with teachers mutual language barriers, differences in culture, and how teachers could be more effective in reaching black students.

Second Goal: Alternatives to the Present System

The Co-op functioned in several different ways, all of which would be valuable if expanded in the regular school. First, we provided a talk center, where students could discuss anything they chose with interested and sympathetic adults. Often, the only contact students have with teachers is formal and rigid. Students showed a great thirst for contact on a person-to-person level, to question and be questioned on equal terms.

In a very superficial way we provided some group therapy.[2] Many, many students could profit from such help, both those with serious problems and those who wish to learn more about themselves. We also provided an individual study center. Much more should be done to individualize study programs, both on a long- and short-term basis, for students with serious adjustment problems.

Finally, we helped to cut red tape, to aid the inarticulate students who could not make their needs known to counselors, and to defend students against a few unjustified actions on the part of teachers and counselors.

Third Goal: Changing Students' Attitudes and Behavior

At the end of the term we sent questionnaires to all the students who had come to us. Some had left school or were absent that day. We asked the fifty available students, "Are regular counselors and deans for or against students?" Twenty-five said "against." Eight said "for." Seven said "sometimes for and sometimes against." The overwhelming majority said that the Co-op was *for students.* Most believed the Co-op to be more helpful than deans and counselors. Here are some of their comments:

They [deans or counselors] would have called my mother without even talking to me.

The Co-op was interested in what I said.

The counselor doesn't listen to the student. They just read what the note says, what the students have done, and home you go.

The counselor would have made me mad.

When we go to the counselor we get swats or suspended. We should talk.

I think regular counselors aren't really against students, just sick of them. They have so many and they have so many other things to do.

[2] One student asked if we could organize an encounter group.

The counselor would not have had the time to discuss the problem, only time enough to punish.

Co-op understands students better.

You can't teach a person by swatting them.

Co-op helps teachers and people and children. People who come here change.

Some students felt we were not sufficiently strict, that we talked too much, were too trusting. Students sometimes felt our activities in Co-op were unimportant, "just talk, that's all." We tried to educate them to the importance of talking things over.

Fourth Goal: To Change Students' Attitude toward Teachers

Too often teachers have difficulty in revealing the person behind the role. As one student implied, there are teachers and there are people. In Co-op we tried to explain what pressures caused teachers to act as they did. Students and teachers were encouraged to speak as people, rather than as role players. As a result, many students saw teachers in a new light. One student said, "Co-op helped my teacher to understand my point of view and for me to understand his."

One teacher wrote,

Sally was sent to the counseling center to cool off. She wasn't sent home as she expected to be, and this left her in a state of shock, receptive to just about anything. She found that the teachers were not only interested in her, but were also frank and open in return. Her newfound respect for teachers made her very concerned with what they thought of her, and her performance in class improved. She became more introspective about why she disliked school and what she could do to make it more meaningful.

Fifth Goal: To Change Student Behavior in Class

In some cases student behavior may have improved because the class as a whole improved, the teacher adapted his methods, the student tired of making trouble, or parents put on pressure. On our final questionnaire, we asked students and teachers to evaluate Co-op's success in changing behavior. Of eighty-one teacher responses, only twenty felt there had been no change. Sixty-one saw a change, ranging from very slight to very great, since the time we had counseled the student. Of forty-two student responses, six said we had not helped, but thirty-six said we had. In many instances, we might have made a real difference if we had worked more often with the student, but we, like the counselors, ran out of time.

GENE G. DAVIS 86

Drug Education: Community Education for a Community Problem

Most drug educators today agree that the use of scare techniques and antidrug propaganda is the most ineffective way to teach about drugs. As an alternative, a totally clinical approach is being used by some—possibly accompanied by suggested alternatives to drug use which, it is hoped, will convince students that drug taking is a "cop-out."

Both these methods attempt to supply a rationale for abstinence from drugs; a rationale which avoids the basic issues—that drug taking is a part of our culture, and that the decision to take drugs is based upon the total personality and history of the individual student. I believe that until we begin to examine drug taking as part of a total behavior pattern and as a response to conditioning imposed by the drug industry, our attempts to limit drug taking in the teen-age groups are doomed to failure. Already, teen-agers are calling our attention to the fact that we approve of some drugs (alcohol and tobacco) while condemning others (marijuana) which may do less harm.

The educational task is, then, twofold. First, we must make our young people the most judicious and critical of drug *users*—drug users who are aware that drug abuse (use of drugs in a way which limits one emotionally or physically) is symptomatic of more deep-rooted problems. Secondly, we must educate their parents and the community to the nature of the drugs being used, some of the reasons for their use, and some of the attitudes young people have about them. We must also attempt to dispel some of the parental fears resulting from obsolete drug education.

To Help Students Discriminate

The first goal, to make students judicial and critical drug users, I think bears some explanation. At no other time in the history of man have so many drugs been available for the treatment of sickness. A great deal of money is required to support the research which has led to the discovery of many of the so-called wonder drugs. This money comes partially from the sale of over-the-counter drugs—drugs which as the result of the zealous efforts of the advertising companies, even have new diseases created for them (Excedrin headaches #1-35, the "blahs," "tired blood," etc.).

As a result, our young people are much more drug-oriented than their parents, and could even be called drug seekers rather than simply drug takers. This type of orientation is, I think, impossible to reverse. I prefer to try to make this group of young people into drug critics who demand their right to know about whatever drug is offered to them, people who are also aware that behavior can affect health and that such behavior indicates a great deal about how you feel about yourself and the world in which we live.

To accomplish this in class, a "total person" approach to health is essential. That health-affecting choices of behavior are made by everyone, and that the type of choice made may have permanent physical and emotional consequences are basic elements in this approach. Finally, behavior choices can be called symptoms of the background and circumstances leading to the choice made. Thus, drug abuse is symptomatic rather than a disease in itself.

I do not isolate drugs from any other behavior-oriented health problems that affect teenagers. They are included with other problems (symptoms) such as obesity, alcoholism and tobacco addiction, and are examined from three points of view. *First, the clinical aspects of the problem are examined.* Psychological and physiological effects are presented as completely as current information allows. When there is no real information, I do not try to fabricate some —there is every little available about marijuana so I can't say very much, clinically, about it.

Second, the symptom is defined and discussed. Obesity—simple; alcoholism and nicotine—a snap; but when it comes to drug abuse, each type of drug must be discussed separately. I usually talk about "ups" and "downers," hallucinogens, and opiates separately, with great emphasis upon the difference between addicting and nonaddicting effects. Where there may be great physiological changes, as with speed, these are pointed out.

Finally, we try to address ourselves to the question of why. I try to develop a pattern of evaluation by starting with the rationale for smoking or drinking, and then applying the same evaluation pattern to drug taking.

It is most important that the students be able to see that the *real* reason a person does something that may be bad for him can be complex. The transfer of this understanding from topic to topic is also of great importance. The students may be able to understand that obesity may result from behavior based on more complex reasons than simply the desire to eat— that other feelings are involved. But if the same understanding isn't applied to the question of drug use, then the student will lack a critical attitude when he makes his choice about drugs. If my students can be aware that the rewards of turning-on are commensurate with their own needs and expectations, then at least some rational element will be present when they make their choice of behavior.

It is this rational element that I consider to be essential for achieving one of my most impor-

tant goals—critical evaluation of any and all drugs used, from aspirin to heroin. I want my students to be prudent enough not to trust to luck that the material they choose to swallow, or smoke, or inject is pure and will have the desired effect. They will become this demanding only if they feel they have a right to be concerned about their own well-being.

The most poignant part about drug education is that in so many instances a student may say in so many words, "What if I don't care what happens to me?" It seems that this type of drug user is always envious of the relative ease with which the user with a good self-concept has in functioning with no difficulty— a feat all but impossible for him.

The only way I see to influence a student to care why he chooses what he does, is by example. But I wonder how much a person who is told by his parents, his teachers, and his peers that he is *not* desirable can get from someone telling him that his choices are so important because he is so important.

Program for Parents

It became clear to us that the new wave of drug use and attitudes was of such a nature that the school could choose to render only minimal service and teach what drugs were and how they may harm you, or we could seek to try to treat drug usage as a signal of other problems which only an involved family and community could affect. Our school chose to offer a program for parents as well as for our students.

The parents' class meets at night once a week for six weeks. It runs concurrently with the health problems block offered in the high school, and all of the materials and techniques used in the day class are used in the night class. This allows the parents to experience the program in about the same way as their children.

The parents are generally more eager to begin discussing drugs than the high school people are, and as a result, the parents are talking about drugs far in advance of the high school students. This allows me some time to introduce drugs as a topic for discussion to the parents. This is sometimes harder than it sounds because there are always some who refuse to accept the idea that "anything like that could happen here." Sometimes the best convincers are other parents.

I try to identify the drug use situation as I can assess it at our school and to keep the discussion from dwelling upon the more glamorous hip subculture of the Berkeley Telegraph Avenue area. It is too simple to perceive that all drug situations are the same. They are not. My students are middle-class kids who watch television, eat at home, and have warm beds and material goods. They may try to emulate the hip community but this does not mean that behavior ascribed to the hip is also ascribable to them.

It is hard to convince some parents that even the kids with short hair and clean clothes take drugs. It is equally hard to convince them that some of our best looking, most academic, and most popular people occasionally turn on.

After the topic has been introduced, the parents are most eager to talk to students. Three forms of communications have evolved. I may carry direct questions and answers between groups, students may visit the night class (this is not very successful unless the students' parents are absent), or we may exchange tapes between the two groups. (Both groups have suggested the same sinister thing—that I bug the others' room to get the "real" comments of the groups.)

The parents themselves assume responsibility for the class discussions, and as time passes I find that they are are most receptive to information from the student group. They are used to dealing with situations in a direct problem-solving manner and seem very eager to propose ways to handle the drug situation. These range from the simple suggestion that we "Build more basketball courts" to the complex attitude of despair: "We all need psychiatrists."

But I feel that they are doing the most useful thing by simply discussing drugs with the students and trying to understand the nature of current drug use. For if the parent class offers no simple solutions or proposes no social reforms, it does help develop dialogue between parents and students on a subject that may not have been open for discussion before.

As encouragement to discussion I try to use only materials that make no final statements but leave plenty of room for class discussion. Such films as David Smith—San Mateo Unified School Districts' *LSD–25* and *Escape to No-*

where are examples of this type of open-ended film. Tapes of class discussions of the films may be played for the parents and students to stimulate further discussion. Other resources are used —speakers visit class and can be taped for the parents. I have found that my students always want to hear a police officer. This always opens up the area of greatest parental concern, "What happens if my kid gets busted?"

The classes are all as unstructured as possible and this, I hope, encourages discussion. Some parents and students think that this is wrong. They have told me that it would be better to use scare tactics. Students have said that it would be better to show people freaking out and having withdrawal symptoms. Besides being a teaching technique that I am uncomfortable with, there are other reasons I can't do this.

To begin with, it's not honest. The persons I have observed having a bad drug response usually are not doing sensational things which would supply the dramatic impact hoped for. Next, I think that such overly dramatic presentations perpetuate the myth that drug users are "other people." A mystique certainly exists about drug takers, but this mystique is somewhat dispelled when one considers that it is people who take drugs, and people who respond to them.

Community Activities

One final observation. The community in which I teach is not happy to find out some of these things that are part of their children's lives. But they are concerned enough to want to know the realities involved. For this reason, the community must be considered the greatest resource available to the drug teacher.

As a result of a desire to learn more about the drug scene, our PTA sponsored an evening drug conference with educators, ex-users, police, and drug experts. It also sponsored a series of six evening lectures by David Smith of the Haight-Ashbury Clinic in San Francisco. At the present time, it is considering groups where both students and parents can discuss problems.

I was reflecting on all that I have learned from this course and think that the most important thing was that when an issue emerges which so critically needs understanding, it is the community which facilitates the presentation of a truly meaningful program of education. If as a drug teacher you feel slightly paranoid as the result of dealing with a topic which is such anathema in the community, maybe you should go to that very community and seek help in presenting your program. It is there.

Resource, Reading, and Materials List

Resources

1. State of California Department of Public Health, 2151 Berkeley Way, Berkeley, California 94704 (films, pamphlets)
2. U. C. School of Pharmacology, U. C. Medical Center, San Francisco, California—Speakers Bureau (pharmacology students with drug experience)
3. The Committee for Psychedelic Drug Information, Mrs. Paula Gordon—Chairman, 2605 Haste, Apt. 104, Berkeley, California (speakers—youth groups)
4. Haight-Ashbury Medical Clinic, 558 Clayton, San Francisco, California (general information)
5. Langley-Porter Youth Drug Clinic, 401 Parnassus, San Francisco, California (general information and referrals)
6. Talk to local people. You may be surprised at the experience and abilities of local people.

Reading

1. "Thinking About Using Pot" by Tod Uilsuriya, M.D., The San Francisco Psychiatric Medical Clinic, 1840 Grove Street, San Francisco, California 94117 ($1.00 per copy—one of the best investments a district could make)
2. *Drug Abuse Papers 1969,* by David E. Smith,

M.D., Dept. B., University of California Extension, University of California, Berkeley, California 94720 ($5.50—excellent!)
3. *Drugs: The Children are Choosing* K.Q.E.D. Educational Services, 525 Fourth Street, San Francisco, California
4. Pamphlets from U.S. Department of Public Health, Public Information Branch, National Institute of Mental Health, Chevy Chase, Maryland, 20203 (pamphlets #1827–1830)
5. Pamphlets from State Department of Public Health, 2151 Berkeley Way, Berkeley, California 94704

Films

1. *LSD–25.* San Mateo Unified School District (Should be in county school film library. Quite a good film. Topic is not so current, though.)
2. *Escape to Nowhere.* San Mateo Unified School District (Great for opening discussions.)
3. *The Mask.* California State Department of Public Health (Used in alcohol instruction. Very real, sometimes shocking, but it opens kids up for discussion.)
4. *The Mind Benders—LSD and Hallucinogens,* P.H.S. Audio Visual Facility, Chamblee, Georgia 30005 (*very straight* film about LSD)
5. *LSD—Insight or Insanity.* County School film libraries (Quite good—except that the film tries to make a moral appeal without developing enough reason for such an appeal.)
6. *FDA Special Report: Drug Abuse—Bennies and Goofballs,* Public Health Service Audio Visual Facility, Atlanta, Georgia 30333 (very authoritative)

These are materials that are useful in the class to elicit discussion. There are many more materials available of a general interest nature.

SAMANTHA H. LEE **87**

Evolution of a Black Studies Program

In an interview for a teaching position as a graduate intern teacher at Berkeley High School, the personnel director assured me that in two years I could be considered for a counseling position. This factor weighed heavily in my decision to accept the offer at Berkeley, as my ultimate goal in becoming an intern and obtaining teaching experience was to become a counselor. However, that dream was deferred for six years because I became so involved in the problems of teaching history that my efforts were concentrated on curriculum development instead of preparation for counseling. Therein lies the tale of my experience with a pioneer course—at least for the high school level—related to the black experience.

Even during my intern year (1962), students were asking for a course in Negro history, the popular terminology in the early 1960s. For several years, I agreed with the prevailing attitude of the history department that Negro history should not be a separate course, but for entirely different reasons than they. Many members of the department were saying that they would have to be very careful not to overemphasize the role of the Negro in America because that role was comparatively minor. My reasons were that I felt the role of the Negro was highly significant, that every teacher should be made to study the material and be forced to include the information in all required United States history courses, and that every student should be assured the opportunity to learn about a segment of history that had never been included in textbooks.

Proceeding under this assumption, I set about gathering as much information as I could by being involved in the Intergroup Education Project of the Berkeley Unified School District (now the Human Relations Department), by attending lectures and taking courses at the University, by planning and participating in conferences on history and on minority youth. I asked to teach as many history classes as possible about the period which would include the Civil War and Reconstruction; and I concentrated on trying to develop materials that would put that period in new perspective—relate it to the current civil rights movement nationally, at the state level, and locally. Some of my colleagues did the same; but many did not. Black students continued to complain, and we continued to say to them that we were including information about Negroes in all history classes—and, of course, we knew this was true because we did have some references to the Negro in the curriculum guide, didn't we?

Still the students and members of the com-munity pressed the issue. Students even organized study groups during lunch periods and after school to which community persons were invited to speak on Afro-American history, a more acceptable term than Negro in the mid 1960s. As some of us in the department talked with students, it became more and more apparent that few of us were dealing with the subject matter in any significant manner. It became obvious that if we were to be effective, we would have to develop a separate course as a pilot project. The materials from that course could be used by other teachers and eventually the courses could become truly representative of all the peoples of the country—an altruistic point of view. After several confrontations with members of the Afro-American Students Association who expressed what seemed to be an extreme view—that only Afro-Americans could teach Afro-American history—the department finally agreed that a separate course should be developed. Not really believing the Afro-Amercan students' contentions, and yet half believing it, too, the department decided that the two "Negroes" on the staff should develop curriculum during the summer of 1967 and begin teaching two sections of the pilot course on The Negro in America in the fall of 1967. Mr. Clarence Hampton and I worked the entire summer, but Mr. Hampton accepted a fellowship for advanced graduate study at Syracuse, and I was left to flounder with the new course in the fall semester of 1967. Oh, happy day! What an experience!

The goals for this course included not only a consideration of subject matter but also experimentation in interracial relations and in heterogeneous grouping, as well as student involvement in curriculum development. Remember, these were not the only sections of history I was to teach. From the more than two hundred applications received for the course, a committee selected fifty students to participate in setting up two classes of twenty-five persons each, racially balanced according to the school population percentages and ability-grouped so that there would not be a disproportionately high number of slow learners. A type of lottery was used to effect these goals. It looked beautiful on paper until counselors hit snags in scheduling which destroyed our well laid plans. Nevertheless, the course must have worked fairly well because the demand for admission continued; class size was doubled for the second semester. I must admit that I felt better about the outcome of the second semester. Although there continued to be more blacks (a more acceptable term now) enrolled, the best courses were those in which races were mixed, providing opportunity for interchange of ideas. The very best section, I felt, was one in which the ratio was fourteen blacks, thirteen whites, and one oriental. Also during that semester, I served as sponsor for the Black Students Union which was responsible for several cultural programs.

With Mr. Hampton's return in the fall of 1968, I was granted half-time leave, so that he taught two and I taught three sections of Afro-American history. I enrolled in more courses on counseling at Cal State. The BSU assumed new leadership and decided to press for an extension of courses on the black experience to other departments. The Board of Education agreed to implement the demands of the BSU. It established the position of Curriculum Associate for Black Studies to coordinate courses in the history, English, music, business, and physical education departments at the secondary level as well as subjects at the elementary level. Although there were several applicants, Mr. Hampton was appointed to the position. Additional black counselors were hired, and I became one of them. My original goal to counsel has been realized via a circuitous route.

But what of my intermediate goal of an effective course in Afro-American history? Out of a modest beginning has emerged a creditable program, the success of which depends heavily on the personnel available for planning and teaching. Is this separatism a form of segregation? I do not think it is. I see Black Studies as a basic step toward total integration. On the other hand, if courses are not taught well, Black Studies could become a vehicle for promoting the worst possible racism—to prove the blacks inferior. I'm not talking about the black racism of which the "Black is Beautiful" concept is often accused; rather, I'm referring to the reinforcement of the old stereotype of the racial inferiority of the black man which would result from failure of the program to operate at optimum efficiency and effectiveness.

A positive aspect of Black Studies is the interest it has generated in other ethnic studies. Perhaps the GIP and other teacher education institutions could assume leadership in providing knowledgeable, motivated personnel who would be dedicated to developing similar programs where needed,[1] and in implementing the inclusion of ethnic studies into secondary curricula in proper perspective.

1 See the strategy on Mexican-American Studies which follows.

GINI MATUTE **88**

An Interdisciplinary Seminar in Mexican-American Studies

Origins of the Proposal

In our high school of almost two thousand students, more than five hundred claim a Spanish-speaking background. Most of these students hover together in the hallways and at lunchtime in markedly segregated small groups.

Mexican students present an important problem in our school because they are here in large numbers, and because they are members of a larger cultural group that has consistently and traditionally failed to make it both in the public schools and in society. Generally, Chicano students have been segregated, isolated, and programed into a set of academic experiences that have conditioned them to repeated frustration, failure, and lack of self-confidence.

In their attempts to cope with the system, they carry on a variety of defenses. Some desperately try to become as Anglo, as "student-activities-cheerleading"-oriented as their skin color or ability will let them. Others become the school toughies, the "bad men," the frequent visitors to the deans' offices, the dropouts. They have given up trying to fit into the system because they know that they'll get batted down again somehow. Then there are those who can laugh, joke, and prattle endlessly with their clique in the halls, but turn silent, withdrawn, and afraid once they enter their assigned classrooms. I see all these students on campus; I have many of them in class. Their resistance to the traditional curriculum has been too blatant to be ignored. In essence, our students have been pleading, "give me something in school that speaks to me and that lets me be me."

The idea for a Mexican Studies course evolved out of several afterschool MAYA (Mexican-American Youth Association) meetings. We knew we wanted a Mexican history course and from there we added on the art, music, and homemaking complements. The problem then was to find interested and qualified teachers for each area. At Sunset High, we are fortunate to have three talented and enthusiastic fine arts and homemaking teachers. We sat down together one afternoon with each of us presenting our own ideas, hopes, and schemes for the course. It was an exciting afternoon. One idea would create, expand, and touch another and another.

Finally, we outlined the broader perspectives and designs of the course, wrote a proposal, and presented it to our principal. He in turn had us present the course to our school's administrative council. After their approval, the proposal was passed on to various curriculum and district councils. *It was approved.* And now, in preparation for next fall, we have begun scheduling Mexican-American students into the program. We still face many problems before then, mostly financial. We don't know if each participating department will contribute matching funds or whether a separate fund will be scrounged from some already meager sources. Despite the problems, we are looking forward to beginning our new program in September. Undoubtedly as we proceed there will be several changes made, but we will base our program on the proposal which follows.[1]

I. Introduction

The question with which we are confronted has long been a vital one. It has to do with the education and progress of the students of Mexican-American descent enrolled in our schools. As we all know, the educational progress for most of our Mexican-American students has been slow over all. If the school is conceived as a bridge between these students and the adult world which they will subsequently enter, we must address ourselves to the critical dropout and failure rates of these students in our schools today. This adult world will sometimes be Anglo in character but usually it will combine elements of the Anglo and Mexican cultures. Our purposes are directed toward developing the concept that Mexican-Americans can be both American and Mexican, that they can live happy and useful lives, that many choices are open and possible to them.

While it is true that greater numbers of Mexican-American youth are attending high school and enrolling in college than ever before, it is also true that the dropout rate among this segment of our school population is disproportionately high. According to recent statistics cited by the California Fair Employment Practices Commission, 48.5 percent of the male and 52 percent of the female Mexican-American population over fourteen years of age had completed one or more years of high school. This stands in stark comparison to the total population: 72.1 percent and 75 percent, respectively, and even to the nonwhite population, 63.2 percent and 67.5 percent. These statistics suggest that for too long the public schools serving these students may have remained irrelevant to their background, language, and interests. For too long the typical school serving Mexican-Americans has made insufficient use of the Mexican heritage, the Spanish language, or the resources of the Mexican-American com-

[1] This proposal was submitted to Dr. Nels Nelson, Principal of Sunset High School, by Rosemarie Harrington, Gini Matute, Ron Quintanal, and Frank Wright.

munity. Characteristically, the schools teach, counsel, encourage, and treat Mexican-American students as if their distinctive cultural patterns and life style are unimportant or non-existent. That is, the schools have been operating largely on the assumption that the Mexican-American child comes from a white middle class set of experiences and conditioning. Often, the schools have failed to see that the cultural patterns which constitute the life style of the Mexican-American student are sufficiently different from those of the dominant culture to require special educational consideration.

Mexican-American students tend to live in two cultures, each with its respective demands on the individual. On the one hand are the demands of the home and the behavioral expectations of its distinctive cultural background; on the other hand are the middle-class demands usually encountered in the schools. Unfortunately, the schools seem unaware that the lives of their Mexican-American students are molded by the stark reality of living in two worlds. Their cultural dichotomy has not yet been touched or tapped by the content or methods of instruction used in most high schools. More seriously, the schools have failed to recognize the key areas of serious conflict for the Mexican-American. They have assumed that the usual high school education would lead Mexican-Americans toward complete and normal participation in the mainstream of American life. Unfortunately, the records show that Mexican-Americans are lagging behind both economically and academically. Apparently, effective education for the Mexican-Americans will not be accomplished until the particular needs and strengths of the Mexican-American community are taken into account.

Given the disproportionate number of Mexican-American dropouts, it seems clear that we can no longer accept the usual procedures for English-speaking students as a viable approach with the Mexican-American student without considering the following factors:

1. The bicultural community in which he resides.
2. The lack of his acceptance in the society at large.
3. The consequent isolation and segregation which produces the unassimilated individuals.
4. The subsequent low socio-economic status endemic to this lack of social acceptability.

5. The inherent cultural lag brought on by barriers which impede normal participation in community living.

The impact of these conditions has produced an arena of cultural confusion and ambiguity for the Mexican-American. The result is that he is left helpless to cope with the expectations of two equally demanding cultures. The outcome of this confusion and ambiguity is that many children feel they must make a single choice and select one culture over another in which to succeed, thereby refusing to accept the other. Regardless of the culture selected, the decision is painful since both cultures exist. Other Mexican-American children try to succeed in both cultures, yet in spite of it all, remain foreigners, strangers, and "Mexicans," with the complete stereotypical connotations brought on by the years of cultural conflict. Additionally, the partial disintegration of the Mexican culture and the fact that social pressure has taught the Mexican to disown and be ashamed of his distinctive heritage has made the Mexican-American a figure of insecurity, confusion, and frustration.

II. Objectives for an Interdisciplinary Seminar in Mexican-American Studies

The underlying assumption of our interdisciplinary seminar is an understanding that one cannot run away from himself or what he is or from what he believes in. To do so is to prevent the realization of self-esteem and self-confidence and to stunt the development of broad ambitions and hopes. Our purposes for the seminar in Mexican-American studies are:

1. For the students to gain dignity from their distinctive past
2. For the students to gain an understanding and perspective of the present
3. For the students to gain a hope for the future, with as many choices as possible
4. To motivate the Mexican-American student to *all* school learning

There is an important relationship between educational opportunities and the economic and social well-being of cultural minorities. If there is to be significant progress against those barriers which prevent and obstruct a more useful citizenship, the Mexican-American must be given the chance to retrieve his dignity and worth as a person with a specific ethnic heritage, possessing a positive contribution to civilization. The school as a social institution is in a position to provide a different kind of opportunity to learn, and to improve the Mexican-American child's own self-image. One who is ashamed of himself or his people is alone, helpless, and without true expression.

The questions, then, are: What can be done to improve the self-concept of the Mexican-American student? What must be done in order to better guide and direct our Mexican-American students and fulfill their complex needs arising from a bicultural life? The interdisciplinary seminar is not conceived as a total solution. It is simplistic to assume that improving the Mexican-American's self-image is an all-inclusive solution to the problems of social lag resulting from longstanding cultural and social isolation. Rather, the interdisciplinary seminar has grown out of the need to establish within the existing educational objectives *a positive reinforcement* through which the Mexican-American's social integration and cultural assimilation in American society can be made a smoother and more stable process.

While the major purpose of the seminar is to provide greater self-respect and motivation to learn for the Mexican-American students, all students could benefit from it in the following ways:

1. Students studying Spanish could profit from an understanding of Spanish and Mexican-American culture.
2. Students from diverse cultural backgrounds could enlarge their perspectives, gain deeper understanding of themselves and of others through a study of the Mexican-American culture (perhaps this course could include, at some point, a look at each ethnic or cultural group in the school).
3. The course should impart useful knowledge to all students from the contributing disciplines: art, music, history, and homemaking (foods, costumes, holidays, customs).

If we are to utilize our community and its needs to formulate our school's program, elements of history, art, food, music, language, and clothing of the rich Mexican tradition should be included in the curriculum. The seminar places the school in a strategic position to assume its complete role and function as an educational institution for the community. If we are to be a truly pluralistic society, our goals should be to facilitate our living together harmoniously, each in our own way.

III. Course Description

The course is conceived as an interdisciplinary elective two-semester seminar for the junior and senior levels. The cooperating departments are:

1. Social Studies
2. Art
3. Home Economics
4. Music

Appendix: Course Descriptions

Course Title: *Interdisciplinary Seminar in Mexican-American Studies*

Grade Levels: *11th–12th*

Subject: _____ ART _____   Suggested time allotment: 1 period daily

Content	Suggested Approaches	Materials
An introduction to the arts and crafts of the Americas with a special emphasis on the Latin-American cultures. Subject areas would include: 1. Pre-Columbian arts and crafts 2. Colonial period 3. Modern Mexico	Activities to include: 1. Field trips 2. Lectures 3. Art activity 4. Craft activities 5. Exhibitions and demonstration of native crafts	1. Art supplies 2. Craft supplies 3. Slides of Mexico and Guatemala (personal) and commercial slides of other Latin-American countries.

Course Title: *Interdisciplinary Seminar in Mexican-American Studies*

Grade Levels: *11th–12th*

Subject: SOCIAL STUDIES   Suggested time allotment: 1 period daily

Content	Suggested Approaches	Materials

1. An introduction to the Mexican-American community in the United States, with emphasis on California.
2. The History of Mexico:
  a. Pre-Columbian
  b. Colonial Spanish period
  c. War of Independence
  d. Early republic
  e. La Revolution
  f. Modern Mexico and its place in hemispheric and world affairs
3. The heritage of the Mexican in the United States
4. The twentieth century Mexican-American community and its internal development (with emphasis on California)
	1. Field Trips
	2. Studies of the community
	3. Lectures and discussions
	4. Selected readings
	5. Group and individual study projects
	6. Guest speakers
	7. Resource persons
		Recommended texts:
		Simpson's *Many Mexicos*
		Samora's *Forgotten Americans*
		
		Selected reading from a variety of sources
		
		Films

Course Title: *Interdisciplinary Seminar in Mexican-American Studies*

Grade Levels: *11th–12th*

Subject: MUSIC   Suggested time allotment: 1 period daily

Content	Suggested Approaches	Materials
An introduction to an understanding and appreciation of: 1. Indian 2. Hispano-Mexican 3. Modern Mexican musical styles and contribution of Mexican composers to music.	Comparison of Aztec, American Indian, and Inca music Study of the uses of music: festivals, religious, dances Study of the differences of Spanish and Mexican music Development of mariachi and bullfight music Study of Mexican music on the stream of classical music Field trips	Records Tapes Pictures

Course Title: *Interdisciplinary Seminar in Mexican-American Studies*

Grade Levels: *11th–12th*

Subject: <u>HOMEMAKING</u>   Suggested time allotment: 1 period daily

Content	Suggested Approaches	Materials
An introduction to the foods, customs, holidays, and costumes of the Latin-American cultures, beginning with the Pre-Columbian era to the present day.	Lectures Foods lab Student presentations Guest speakers Demonstration Field trips to community homes	Films Slides Artifacts Community resources

II: NEW PUBLIC SCHOOL MODELS

Jay Manley and students at orientation for Community High School (school within a school, Berkeley High School, Berkeley, California).

Opportunity High: Getting It Together

The Dream

I suppose that at some point every new teacher dreams of starting a school. I spent my preteaching days with fantasies of a Rousseauean utopia replete with its own wilderness, rustic huts, and a communal, natural atmosphere. After teaching for two years in Samuel Gompers High School, an urban continuation school in San Francisco, I decided that my fantasies didn't include the important problems or the important people. There were some exciting small schools in country settings in California which approached or moved toward Rousseau. The only problem, however, was that these schools, in order to survive, had to cater to middle- or upper-class kids. Lower-class kids were the exception and even those from the higher socio-economic groups attending these schools were relatively small in number. Although some of the learning models developed at these private schools could be useful (with modifications) in public schools, the aperture between the public school and the small private one is so deep that this kind of interchange is difficult. In general, the small schools tend to feel very estranged from "the establishment" and the public schools tend to be very suspicious of the "offbeat" learning situations. In a sense, I wanted to wed the two extremes by trying to determine what each had to offer the other; I wanted to help set up a small public school where learning would be all the things it could be in the wilderness. The people who would attend this visionary public school would be the students of all classes and colors who have opted out. They are the ones who register for school because their probation officer or social worker or parents force them to, but they spend most of their time in hallways or parks or roaming around town. At the ripe old ages of sixteen or seventeen they've decided that their formal learning has ended.

At Gompers, three other teachers and I had come to know many of these students. They could be "turned on" to learning, but not easily. We were still in a school which was too large for us to do the things we thought necessary. However, we had some very specific ideas and a real desire to start something new, something into which we could pour our enthusiasm and insights, something which would become part of the public school system. (See Appendix A.)

Help from Others

Although any large school district tends to be impersonal in many respects, there are always some people who are thinking along innovative directions. In San Francisco we felt that Dr. Lewis Allbee, Assistant Superintendent, was such a person. It was to him that we brought our idea. Simultaneously, the assistant principals were meeting to discuss pressing problems of cutting and truancy. Mr. Harvey Christensen, then dean at Lincoln High School, was instrumental in setting up these meetings. The deans also turned to Dr. Allbee. The element that Dr. Allbee, Mr. Christensen, and we (the four teachers) had in common was a view that part of the answer to some of the district's problems lay in a small, specialized school staffed by people who are particularly interested in and effective at working with students who have had difficulties in the larger schools. Dr. Allbee sifted through many of the ideas and drew up a proposal for such a school. (See Appendix B.) In August, the Board of Education appropriated funds for a mid-fall opening. I would like to talk a little about the planning and the actual functioning of what was initially termed Opportunity High. Although many of us were involved in this undertaking, I cannot speak for the entire group. However, I'd like instead to give a rather personal interpretation of our school and the emerging reality in the hope that somewhere in your dreams there are threads where connections can be made.

The Planning Period

Armed with Dr. Allbee's proposal, a nucleus of seven of us were selected to spend a portion of the first semester in setting up the school. Harvey Christensen, principal; Lillian Powell, assistant principal; the four teachers, and one other staff member comprised the initial planning team. We had the backing of the district and the board to move in the direction we felt would be most appropriate.

We tried to cover ground in as many areas as possible. Although we had listened carefully to students' complaints when we were teaching, we now were ready to hear them from a different perspective. We wandered around the hallways and the streets of the comprehensive high schools in the district. Our students would be coming from these schools. We also got to know the head counselors and deans who would be discussing our school with their students and processing the applications. It was essential that Opportunity High be presented as a positive alternative to the larger school and that the student and his parents *voluntarily* choose this alternative. We did not want the students we received to be sent to us as a punishment; choosing a new learning environment was to be, for many, the first step in altering a pattern of failure toward a new pattern of success. With this as one of our goals, we spent some of our time searching for schools which already had some success in working with alienated youth.

Planning Programs

There are a number of schools in the Bay Area which service "disaffected" students in

new and meaningful ways. We visited several. Based on what we saw, we decided to incorporate certain elements into our own situation. These ranged from ideas such as credit cards (indicating that a student had earned a single credit and thereby giving him immediate positive reinforcement), class calendar cards (a way for individual students to note their own attendance and academic progress and carry these achievements to new classes if they changed somewhere within the semester), to philosophical attitudes concerning relationships between students and staff, the possibilities of developing a happy yet productive atmosphere, etc. Toward these ends we also tried to use the resources in our own district.

We returned to San Francisco and met with the people who had initiated and followed through on innovative projects in our own schools. They shared with us methods, materials, and problems, and candidly spoke of both their successes and their problems. I feel that we gained some insight into what lay ahead for our own program.

Community Response

In addition to reaching out to our potential students and to other schools with promising programs, we decided to contact community civic, youth, and education groups. We wanted their advice and we also wanted to know ways in which we could be useful to them. We hoped that our school could be responsive to the needs of the community as translated by these leaders.

Most groups were very excited about the ideas we had in mind and offered helpful suggestions. In many cases they said that they would try to set up meetings for us to talk with students and parents in their particular areas. Some organizations maintained a watchful, waiting attitude. They seemed to want to believe in us, but so far they hadn't seen anything; they'd merely heard a good deal of talk. They were willing to watch us try.

The only group which opposed our school was a civil rights organization whose leaders felt that in effect Opportunity High was an indictment against a public school system; by the very nature of its existence it was saying that the comprehensive high schools were failures. Furthermore, it was a "tracked" school which skimmed off problem students and forced them to suffer irreparable indignities.

Although entirely unprepared for this response, we thought a good deal about their charges, and several things became clear. We did not intend to have our school operate in the manner which that group suggested, and we resolved to work carefully to prevent that from occurring. The measures we had already taken included a decision to ensure a racial balance which would mirror the proportions of various ethnic backgrounds of the school-aged population in San Francisco, emphasizing once again our intention to make entrance to Opportunity High voluntary, and continuing with our curriculum plans for nontracked, nongraded classes. In effect, we had planned all these things before that particular group had made its protestations; we were now looking at our plans as answers to their charges. If the school turned out to be a degrading, demoralizing experience for any students we would be the first to want to close it down.

On the supportive end, I would like to mention at this point that Horizons Unlimited, a group in the Mission district dealing primarily with Spanish-surnamed youth, was particularly helpful to us both in the early planning stages when they gave specific suggestions and since the opening of school when they continued to assist by helping us track down prospective students. They provided an ideal model for ways that school and community organization can work together for the maximum benefit of the students they both serve.

Thus we experienced an entire spectrum of responses from community groups, ranging from support to distrust. Almost every encounter caused us to examine carefully what we were doing and to make some decisions regarding the various suggestions. We discovered that there is no single community and no single group which speaks for all our potential students. I feel that working with community groups is not a panacea for all school ills; it is merely using another tool, with some concomitant difficulties as well as benefits. The education of students has to be the primary goal. I believe that some teachers are frightened of community groups, whereas many others feel that their training as teachers gives them a monopoly on working

with young people. I believe that if we as teachers are truly interested in our students, we will try to avail ourselves of all human resources in trying to meet their needs. We can still be very important to our students, but we must be willing to reach out and work through problems with other people who are also associated with our students. I think that this cooperative attitude prevails on our staff and is one of the more important facets of the school which finally emerged.

In the Beginning

By the end of October we were eager to get under way. We felt that we had planned all we wanted to alone; for any further organizing we wanted our students to be present. The only problem was that the facility we'd rented was not yet ready, nor had all the students' applications come in. In spite of these deterrents, we decided to open on a limited basis with a partial staff and a partial student body. Thus, November 3 we entered our building at 1480 Mission; along with the carpenters, plumbers, and electricians we welcomed our first forty students. Five of the seven small classes were held in separate sections of one large room, which was later to become the student lounge. There was at this time a unique spirit among teachers and students which still appears to be our most important quality. This atmosphere is the one which visitors most often point to as the truly significant thing about our school. The Human Rights Commission of San Francisco sent part of its education committee to speak with our students; when that group came out with its final report, titled "High Morale at John O'Connell and Opportunity Schools," on January 23, 1969, the following was said:

Throughout the fact-finding sessions, it was apparent that student and teacher morale was particularly high at John O'Connell and Opportunity Schools. Inadequate facilities and poor maintenance seemed less important than the perceived quality of teacher-student relationships. Students felt that they were treated as individuals and their courses were relevant to life as students found it. It is incumbent upon the San Francisco Unified School District to examine this "success" carefully and to duplicate this experience in other schools.

Opportunity High : As We Are

I think that the high morale at the school is due to a number of factors. These are inextricably bound to the structure and day-to-day operation of the school. I'd like to spend the remainder of the paper concentrating on a description of Opportunity High as it exists at the time of this writing; its limitations and some of my suggestions for the expansion and revision of San Francisco's opportunity program will comprise the final sections of this paper.

We currently have a staff of fourteen teachers, a job counselor, a principal and an assistant principal, four counseling interns, and about two hundred ten students. Half the students attend in the morning and half in the afternoon. They have a good deal of flexibility in choosing courses from our special selection of offerings.

Hyphenated Curriculum

We offer the courses students need with the emphasis they choose. For example, to satisfy the requirements for English 3, 4, 5, or 6, a student may take any one of our English offerings: Creative Writing, Drama, Journalism, Ethnic Studies in Literature, Photo-Journalism, Psychology, Reading Workshop, and Seminar in Teaching Reading. Most of our courses are those requested by students and of interest to them. Additions may be made at any point in the semester; it is not uncommon for an entire class to change focus for a week or two or for several individuals to spend some time on a project seemingly unrelated to the title of the course. For the most part, however, although a good deal of variation occurs with each individual within a course, the entire class will focus on the area discussed in the course description. (See Appendix C.)

In addition to variety within particular classes, there are interesting combinations offered. For example, we have cross-age experiment where our students tutor elementary school students who need to be brought up to grade level in basic skill areas. Our students travel to the elementary school, work with the younger children, and return to Opportunity High to prepare their lessons and discuss their "teaching problems." In the creative arts area, photography and journalism combine in Photo-Journalism so that both sets of students will gain experience in communicating both graphically and in writing. The Urban Problems class uses a Photographic approach to look with eyes which "tell it straight" and to record and share these perceptions with others. Psychology can combine with Creative Writing for a short unit to explore dreams and symbolism. The combinations are infinite, and those mentioned above are merely a sampling of those tried. I think that adaptability is central to our school and extends beyond the area of curriculum. Our counseling system is another case in point.

Counseling

Every teacher at Opportunity High also serves as a counselor. We spend at least one period each day exclusively working with our fifteen counselees. Since classes are in session eight periods per day and each teacher spends four in the classroom, he has four periods in which he can meet informally with counselees, make home visits, and spend time with community resources. As far as I know, we have both the smallest counseling loads in the San Francisco schools and the greatest amount of time to be with our students.

Rap Sessions

Rap sessions are another means for counselors to spend time with counselees. Perhaps a short history would be appropriate. Before we opened, when we were spending time visiting our students in their regular schools, one of the recurring problems from the students' point of view seemed to be the lack of real dialogue among students, teachers, and administrators. The students seemed to feel that nobody would listen to them until there was a crisis; then administrators came in droves. At these times, discussion situations were threatening and unreal to everyone involved; solutions were merely sought for immediate problems. We wanted to have a built-in mechanism in our school for listening to and talking with our students on a regular basis. Thus, every Tuesday we stopped school an hour early for what we called rap sessions. At first, this hour was used for small group discussions on a variety of problems ranging from those of a personal nature to those of a more societal emphasis.

These small group meetings weren't entirely successful for several reasons. Not all teachers were comfortable as group leaders; many students did not profit from this kind of interchange. Although the groups themselves left something to be desired, both the faculty and students were pleased with the idea of using unprogramed time for pure communication. The content of the discussions was less significant than the interchange itself. Students seemed to be seeking some large group activity since they never had an opportunity to spend time together as an entire school. Thus some of the rap sessions were converted into large group discussions.

Students confronted each other and tried to deal with the problems which they felt were most important to them. Although the range in the large group discussion was a little more limited in some respects (things of a very personal nature didn't tend to come up in meetings of one hundred students), these sessions proved useful. In a very real sense, some of these gatherings were the modern counterpart of the New England town meetings; direct democracy prevailed. The students decided that they didn't want student body officers; instead they chose seven representatives from each session (morning and afternoon), all of whom were to have equal status. Any other member of the group could substitute for these representatives whenever it was necessary. The students had a very natural, almost primitive notion of direct and moderately representative democracy. Although they didn't use the precise terms, they really took these concepts seriously. Most of them had had very bad experiences with token student governments; they weren't about to repeat that pattern at Opportunity High. Now the students are organizing to name their school. They plan to present their suggestion to the Board of Education. This may seem insignificant, but if they succeed, they will be the first student body in the city to have named their own school. I feel that it will be symbolic of the larger role which they play in most areas of our school policy. It seems appropriate to end this section on a symbolic note

and to move back to reality when discussing the school's limitations.

Problems and Projections

The discussion of our problems, by the very nature of the topic, must be the most subjective. I want again to underscore the point that although a number of people are responsible for Opportunity High, the following interpretation of its values and limitations is my own.

Philosophical-Operational Differences

The largest problem we have faced has been the philosophical differences among the faculty in terms of the degree of freedom and the degree of structure we wish to have for ourselves and for the students. Some of the staff feel that limitations are impositions which strongly prevent the students from learning. They do not want to repeat the patterns of the larger schools by setting up restrictions. They feel that in an atmosphere of trust students will no longer need to rebel and will eventually come around to working productively with the adults who have treated them with this kind of dignity. Others, including myself, feel that our students need some structure. However, every rule or requirement ought to be justified in terms of its purpose. Those which seem necessary ought to exist. Within this larger structure a good deal of flexibilty must occur. I think that at this point an illustration might be helpful.

Attendance Problems

When we first opened the school we never discussed our philosophical differences in terms of what they might imply. Thus we ran into difficulties on the question of class attendance. Some felt that students should not be required to attend their particular classes; if they were in the building working on some project, somewhere, that would be more than they'd have done previously. Others felt that they ought to be asked to attend their classes but within each particular room should have a good deal of flexibility. For example, they might choose to go to another class for a period of time, but that would be the exception rather than the rule. However, since the school was so small that anything one teacher did necessarily influenced other teachers, students were confused by our lack of unity; one teacher would encourage a particular student to attend other classes, while another might require that he remain in his own class. As a consequence, the student would be less able to handle the structure in the second class because it would seem arbitrary and unfair. This may seem insignificant, but at a certain point during the first term problems of this nature predominated. We couldn't proceed until we as a staff had honestly confronted each other and worked them through.

Counseling

The counseling system has many limitations. Although it is theoretically a good idea to have a large number of teacher-counselors, I do not think that everyone can necessarily function in this manner. I believe that for teachers who have never counseled before, some very specific in-service seminars need to be designed. This is difficult with the present two-session system because there is not enough time for lengthy open-ended seminars.

Two-Session System

The two-session system presents another problem. Although there is a large amount of un-programed time for each teacher and student (since students attend either the morning or afternoon session and teachers teach four periods out of eight), there are almost no blocks of un-programed time for the total student and faculty population. I think that this is sorely felt at the present time. During the first term, when we had only a morning session, the entire faculty met three afternoons a week. They used the other two afternoons for informal association with students who hung around the building, or for field trips, home visits, and community contacts. The lack of this time is, in my opinion, a serious problem of the current structure.

There are several other areas of concern, but we have been in operation too short a time to have dealt with all of them. I think that some problems have been identified well enough for us to turn our energies in the coming semester toward creative solutions. At the time of this writing, I am planning to present a list of specific suggestions (see Appendix D) to the entire staff. I hope that in areas where there is agreement we can get together and present these items in the form of a proposal to Dr. Allbee. He and other administrators have tentatively suggested two new schools for the coming year; this would seem to be the ideal opportunity for trying alternatives which seem feasible.

At our first evaluation session the team of administrators who sat down with the entire faculty seemed "cautiously optimistic." Apparently many dreams are finding partial fulfillment in our small, urban counterpart to schools in surrounding areas. I feel that in the short time we have been in operation some students have had experiences which have made significant differences in their lives, others have started attending school more frequently, some have begun developing skills in areas they'd shown little proficiency in before entering Opportunity High, and, frankly, some students have not been reached at all. We've made some inroads, but we still have a long way to go. I feel secure, however, in knowing that the direction is clear; mostly our own limitations bind us. I hope we can continue working through our problems to our satisfaction. Although we've had ample reinforcement (from our own district, the hundreds of educators who have visited us over the past few months, and most important, from our own students), I'm eager to move to a more sophisticated developmental stage. We've begun to help students see themselves as unique and important; we now must help them cope competently with their environment.

SAN FRANCISCO'S CONTINUATION PROGRAM: A VIEW AND A VISION*

A. Who is a continuation student?
   1. Student released from juvenile hall after beginning of term who couldn't be enrolled in neighborhood school

* This proposal was submitted by the four teachers at Samuel Gompers High School.

2. Sixteen-year-old ninth-graders
3. Ten-day suspensions from other schools
4. Students who have had babies and need an interim school before returning to other neighborhood school
5. Working students whose work obligations prevent them from carrying a full load
6. Students who have experienced continued academic failure in regular program

B. What broad program alternatives may he choose from?
1. One-half day of continuation school attendance
2. One-half day continuation attendance plus one-half day vocational school attendance (John O'Connell)
3. One-half day school attendance plus one-half day work
4. Full day attendance

C. Who will service the students in these programs?
1. At least fifteen teachers
2. At least four counselors (full-time)
3. One social worker
4. One school psychologist
5. Two deans
6. One head counselor
7. One principal
8. One attendance counselor
9. At least twenty New Careerists (para-professionals, paid community aides)

D. Within the setup prescribed above, and without additional funds, what can be done?
1. Clusters of self-contained classes with teams of teachers modeled upon Gompers W. E. (work experience) programs
2. Contract plan
3. Tutoring program with credits instead of money
4. Group counseling
5. Extensive home visits
6. Fully staffed counseling-study room (patterned on Sausalito idea)
7. Special, gradual class selection for students
8. Inclusion of minority group history course
9. Close contact with community groups such as Mission Rebels and Horizons Unlimited
10. Close contact with special college programs for high potential nonachievers (e.g., Upward Bound and San Mateo's College Readiness Program)
11. Student responsibility for maintaining and improving school site

E. With additional funding, possibly through foundations and special continuation funds,* after regular program (see section D) is underway, what can be done?
1. Store school—ten or fifteen students set up business in neighborhood. Class meets beind store. Curriculum based on skills students need to run business (e.g., math lessons center upon purchasing supplies, setting prices, etc.).
2. Storefront school. Modification of Sera Unobskey's Yeshiva University experiment.
3. New careerists—involved in every phase of school (classroom, home visits, counseling, etc.).
4. Library—in every classroom. Paperbacks provided in abundance.
5. Tutoring program (modification of Emeryville's Summer 1966 and McKinley's present programs): high school nonachievers teaching elementary school nonreaders.

* *Operation Reach*: "In addition to the reasons which provide advantages for the student in a continuation school, there are often administrative and financial advantages to providing a continuation program in a separate high school. State support is usually greater for the separate continuation high school than for continuation classes."

SAN FRANCISCO UNIFIED SCHOOL DISTRICT,
SENIOR HIGH SCHOOL DIVISION

May 2, 1968

MEMORANDUM
TO: Dr. Robert E. Jenkins, Superintendent of Schools
FROM: Lewis Allbee, Assistant Superintendent
SUBJECT: Proposal for a Small Continuation School,
              beginning September 1968

It is requested that consideration be given to the establishment of a small Continuation High School, beginning in September 1968, to provide a program of individualized instruction to more adequately meet the needs of some of our most difficult students.

General Plan
The plan is to take 210 of the most difficult students in the senior high schools and assign them to a small continuation school. These students would be identified by the administrations of the various schools, but those to be admitted to this school would be selected by the Principal. The reason for this is to ensure, so far as practicable, a well integrated school.

Students would be provided basic education (reading, writing, spelling, mathematics, science, and social studies) as well as some opportunities for occupational preparation.

There would be two four-hour sessions each day—one from 8:00 A.M. to 12:00 noon and the other from 1:00 to 5:00 P.M. Teachers will teach four classes of fifteen students each (or the equivalent) and have one period each day in which to advise students, follow up on their individual problems, help them with their homework, make home visits, check carefully on attendance, provide for their needs of security and belonging, and help them in every way to succeed in school.

This will be an integrated school—with both an integrated staff and an integrated student body.

Staffing
The following staff will be needed:

1. Principal. To select the students and teachers, and to organize and administer the school
2. Head Counselor or Student Advisor. To assist the Principal in the selection of students and teachers, and plan and coordinate activities of the teaching staff during their "guidance" periods.
3. Teachers. Seven for morning session, seven for afternoon session
4. Employment Advisor. To provide occupational orientation, to help students get part-time jobs, and to supervise them while they are getting their on-the-job training
5. Secretary. To assist the Principal and Head Counselor in the operation of the school
6. School Aide. To assist with the library and general supervision of the school

It is hoped that this school will attract some interested student-teachers who may wish to work with studens who have serious school problems.

Facilities
We will need the following:

7 small classrooms (15 students per classroom)—These will be used for 105 students in the morning and another 105 students in the afternoon.
7 teachers' offices, each large enough to accommodate 2 two-drawer files and desk

space for 2 teachers, so that while one group of seven teachers is teaching the other seven may be "counseling" or "advising" students.

1 teachers' lounge-workroom, equipped with small stove, sink, refrigerator, storage space, tables and chairs to use for their lunches, a work table, space for a duplicating machine, etc.

1 small library to house instructional materials

1 general occupational preparation room

1 student lounge—place where students can meet before school and during the nutrition periods for light snacks (from vending machines) and conversation. This might also double as the general meeting place of the school.

1 Principal's office with appropriate space for a secretary

1 Head Counselor's or Student Advisor's office

1 office space for the Employment Advisor

Restrooms for students and staff

Mr. Vestnys and Mr. Esherich from the Real Estate Board are now in the process of helping us to locate suitable facilities. Whatever may be found, it can be assumed that we will need to plan on some minor building alterations in order to make the facilities serve the needs of this continuation school.

Additional Materials, Supplies and Equipment
First of all, we will need furniture for this school. Then we will need funds for materials of instruction, supplies, and equipment. We should probably allocate the following:

Furniture for the school	$ 5,000
Additional materials of instruction	2,500
Additional school supplies	1,000
Additional equipment	1,000
Additional building supplies, equipment, custodial services	7,000

Total Additional Costs Involved
Staff

1 Principal	15,000
1 Head Counselor or Student Advisor	10,000
6 Teachers @ $8,000	48,000
(Seven teachers should come from the current staff needed to teach these youngsters in groups of thirty and one teacher should come from the plan to reduce class size to twenty-eight in the low achieving areas.)	
1 Employment Advisor @ $8,000	8,000
1 Secretary	6,000
2 School Aides	4,500
	$108,000

Rental of Space

12,000 sq. ft. @ 25¢ per sq. ft. per month $3,000 × 12 = $36,000	$ 36,000
Building alterations	20,000
Building furniture	5,000
Materials of instruction	2,500
School supplies	1,000
Equipment	1,000
Building supplies, equipment, and custodial services	7,000
Other:	
Mileage for teachers while visiting homes	700
Field trips	500
Library	500
Summer Workshops—1 week @ $150 for 16	2,500
Grand Total	$184,700

Dear Student:

The following course selections have been made with your needs in mind. You may have your required classes and at the same time choose the emphasis which interests you most.

For example, any course listed under English Seminars and Workshops will satisfy the requirements for English 3, English 4, English 5, or English 6. In like manner, completion of five units of Individual Studies in Math will enable you to satisfy the Basic Math requirement. In the area of Social Studies several choices are given for U.S. History 1 and 2 and also a few different types of Civics 1 and 2 classes are offered. We hope you will develop important skills by studying material which means something to you. These courses satisfy graduation requirements.

If a course which interests you does not appear on this list, then you have several options. You may choose individual studies in the subject area of your choice; you may make arrangements with a teacher who will help you plan independent research outside of school (this must be cleared with the Principal); you may submit a course description and ask that a particular class be offered the following semester. If you decide to try to set up a course, you may want to work with other students and teachers.

We hope that by having many choices your studies may begin to have some real meaning for you. This course list is revised often. We try, in each edition, to reflect your feelings, interests, and needs. We can best continue doing so by hearing from you. Read these offerings carefully and select those classes which really seem to "turn you on." Together we can get excited about learning. Let's get going.

Opportunity High Faculty

OPPORTUNITY HIGH SCHOOL EXCERPTS OF CLASS OFFERINGS

Ethnic Studies in Literature

Short stories, essays, poems, and novels written about members of minority cultures will be studied in a cultural context. Students will choose at least two groups of people upon which to concentrate their reading. They will then do individual and small group projects in order to share their findings with the class.

Model Business Office

Offered with the desire to provide a meaningful, concentrated model business world approach toward educating the student to educate himself. Frequently, resource people from outside businesses and volunteers will show how many types of machines and communication devices are used. Concentration will be on our young men and women playing job roles while developing skill, knowledge, business attitudes and aptitudes in typing, communication, clerical skills, independent studies, conduct, and appearance. (Admission by consent of teacher.)

Photo-Journalism
(Credit Given in English or Art)

Simultaneous instruction in the basics of photography (use of camera, darkroom equipment—developing, printing, enlarging) and creative communication skills. Students will write about what they film and film both what they and others have written. Each will be interpreted with relevance to the students' own experiences.

Psychology

We will view various novels and stories through the eyes of the characters. By doing so we will try to understand what is happening with these people. In addition, certain areas will be covered thematically—the psychology of violence and aggression, sensitizing ourselves to the needs of others, *et al.* Students will involve themselves with projects which will enable them to cover areas of particular interest in depth.

Seminar in Teaching Reading—Tutoring at Daniel Webster Elementary School

Each tutor will be enrolled in two class periods of tutoring seminar. After a preliminary training period, the tutor will begin meeting with an elementary school student three times a week to help him with his reading. During the remaining two days of the week the tutors will participate in a seminar in which they will discuss and evaluate their work, share effective techniques, and learn about child psychology and development. (Admission by consent of teacher.)

The Space Age and What It Means to You

We will explore the physical world and learn how it works; we will analyze the scientific principles and see how they are applied in a wide variety of industries; we will take field trips to natural museums, scientific and industrial laboratories; you will be able to choose from a number of individual projects to help you get started on an interesting career with a future.

Urban Problems

The major emphasis in this course will be upon issues confronting large cities today. Because the course content is current, much of our resource material will be newspapers and magazines. In many cases, in order to understand modern situations, we will have to do research on the roots of these problems, going back to certain areas of American history and before. A multi-media approach, involving the use of music, will be stressed.

Industrial Laboratory

This course will deal with structures, their construction and theory. Students will construct and test various structures. The student will be exposed to a variety of materials and will have an opportunity to use them. When the laboratory is completed, the students will be able to work in their own interest areas.

Appendix D

SUGGESTIONS FOR EXPANDED OPPORTUNITY PROGRAM

1. Ask that one of the two new schools cater specifically to students above 18 who would like to earn a high school diploma but are disaffected with adult school. Community youth groups could send us applicants from their own programs.
2. Search for larger facilities so that the entire school can be conducted in either a morning or an afternoon session (one session per new school) with the other session reserved for no less than three faculty meetings per week. One faculty meeting could be devoted to a potpourri agenda which would take in all areas of concern, another could be devoted exclusively to counseling, and the third to interpersonal relations on the staff. The third might be conducted by a trained leader who had no previous relationship to any members of the staff. The potpourri session would be open to students.
3. Use greater flexibility in offering students alternatives. Some may attend school one session and work the other. Some may attend school one session and go to John O'Connell for specific vocational training. Students whose attendance is fairly regular over a six week trial period may attend two Opportunity Schools for the

purpose of acceleration, and the last group may merely want to attend school for one session, with no additional activity scheduled.

4. Our faculty may split so that a portion remains at the present site and two other groups go to the other two schools. The student body, in like manner could split up and form the nucleus of each of the two new schools. Six students could then be on the planning committees for each of the new schools they'll be attending.

5. Hire a head counselor for each of the three schools. He would have at least a half-time clerk responsible exclusively for counseling work. He'd coordinate the counseling activities of the fourteen teacher-counselors, organize in-service training for the group, channel all referrals to outside agencies, supervise counseling interns, and work with individual students.

6. Arrange for an all-school weekend at a campsite outside the city for every student, faculty, and staff member associated with the school. This ought to be held early in the term so that areas discussed can be implemented and worked on throughout the school year.

7. Have faculty members and students participate on the committees which will hire new faculty members.

TERRY BORTON **90**

What Turns Kids On?

All teachers have pets. I don't mean that all teachers encourage the "kiss-ups" who try to get good grades through flattery, but every teacher has a special interest in a few students. These pets provide the personal impetus for the vast system of American education. A teacher's conviction that he has "made a difference," even with these few students, reassures him that education is something far more complex and fundamental than training students to know the phyla, solve differential equations, or speak Spanish. Mere training, teachers admit, may soon be done better by machines than by men, but education requires an attention to the student's personal concerns which programmed courses cannot give.

Reprinted from Terry Borton, "What Turns Kids On?" *Saturday Review* (April 15, 1967), 72–74, 80, by permission of *Saturday Review*. Copyright © 1967 by Saturday Review, Inc. [ED. NOTE: Terry Borton, an Intern in the Graduate Internship Program in Teacher Education, University of California, Berkeley, in 1963, is the author of *Reach, Touch, Teach* (New York: McGraw-Hill Book Company, 1970).]

Yet students hate pets—and not just the "kiss-ups." Their scorn for any of those who are "in" with the teacher is notorious. But their hatred of pets is only a symptom, like their hair styles, their music, their clothes, their language, and the fact that they drop out of school in such vast numbers. These things are symbols of their alienation from an educational system which, no matter what its teachers feel, has done little to "make a difference" in the things which concern most students.

My first years of teaching were spent trying to find ways to make my classes relevant to my student's concerns—to make all students pets. In spite of administrative support and the success I sometimes had, my efforts were often frustrating. I had no way of determining what student concerns really were, no clearly defined concept of what they could become, no planned sequence of activities which would develop them, and above all, no time in the hurly-burly of public school teaching to evolve the necessary curriculum.

I did have the opportunity to help organize

two summer programs to work on these problems. In each program the staff was developing curricula by trial and error and so it is impossible to describe here a complete curriculum of concerns, much less a plan of integrating such a curriculum with training in the basic skills. But by indicating what we taught in the limited setting of a summer school, I may be able to suggest what might be done on a larger scale and offer some speculations on the consequences.

Much of what we were trying to achieve in the two summer schools was clarified for me by a paper which I read in the middle of the second summer. Written by Gerald Weinstein and Mario Fantini of the Ford Foundation's Fund for the Advancement of Education and entitled "A Model for Developing Relevant Content for Disadvantaged Children," this paper outlined a theoretical model for developing courses around the basic concerns of students. Messrs. Weinstein and Fantini did a careful job of distinguishing between the progressive clichés about student *interests* and what they defined as *concerns,* the basic psychological and sociological drives of students. They pointed out, for intance, that a student might be *interested* in cars because he was *concerned* with his feelings of powerlessness, and that the proper approach to such a student was therefore not necessarily *Hot Rod Magazine* but some way of helping him explore his understanding of power. Weinstein and Fantini were also careful to emphasize that they did not envisage the classroom as a place for solving the emotional problems of individuals; rather they wanted to find a way to direct lessons toward the general, yet personal, concerns of an entire class.

The concepts on which Weinstein and Fantini built their model were basic to the curriculum of the summer school I will describe here, though we found that in practice their distinctions were not so easy to draw. Our first attempt at a curriculum of concerns began as a pilot project in 1965 and in 1966 developed into the Philadelphia Cooperative Schools Summer Program. This was an experimental six-week project sponsored jointly by the public, private, and parochial schools of Philadelphia and financed by the Philadelphia Board of Education and the federal government. There were two centers of sixty students each, one a high school and the other for grades five through

eight. Each student body was selected to represent an ethnic, racial, and economic cross section of Philadelphia, and attended morning classes in heterogeneous groups of fifteen. High school classes were art, drama, urban affairs, and communications; middle school classes were drama, music, and science. The afternoons were reserved for projects of the students' own design including play production, a newspaper, psychology and sociology clubs, trips, and sports.

The Cooperative Program's statement of purpose defined the kind of student we hoped the curriculum of concerns would generate:

We want to educate students so that they become larger, more open, more independent human beings, able to function effectively in a world of rapid social and moral change. We believe that a person struggles toward these goals through a process of integrating his *thoughts,* his *concerns,* and his *actions.* Our teaching will be directed toward the development of this perspective, this sense of an integrating self.

These were idealistic goals, and they embarrassed us a little because we were not at all sure that we knew any more about how to achieve them than did the thousands of other schools which put such generalities into their statements of purpose. We had several advantages, however, that most schools do not have. First, attendance was voluntary and we had no grades whatsoever, so there was no academic pressure on our students. Second, any individual class contained some students who had received the best and most expensive preparatory school educations, and some who could barely read. We were forced then to seek what was common to all of our students; no matter what their backgrounds; we were forced to teach toward generalized concerns. Third, we knew that the diversity of background, education, and belief would create tension among the students, and our previous summer's experience had taught us that this tension could be a constructive force when it brought basic student concerns to the surface.

The major concern which had arisen during the first summer was one of self-identity, and it was on this that we decided to concentrate the second year. We wanted to build a curriculum which would explore the students' own sense of the disparity between what they thought about in school, what they were concerned about in their own lives, and the way they acted. Though this dissociation of self was revealed in different forms in students of different backgrounds (e.g., the obsession with "soul," with "phonies," and with "commitment"), we believed it was a concern common to all our students and one that we could build a curriculum to meet.

Our curriculum outline consisted only of a series of questions designed to move the students from a generalized concern about man's identity as man to the personal sense of identity, and finally to an examination of the actions which would express that sense of self.

1. What is human about humans? What distinguishes humans from animals? Individually? In groups?
2. What masks do humans use to hide or express what is human or personal about themselves? Is race a mask? Who am I?
3. What happens when people don't hide themselves? Do we mean that we are afraid of being what we really are when we say we don't want to make a fool of ourselves?
4. What forms will express genuine human relationships? How is personal style developed? How can we find actions to express our thoughts and feelings, and yet be accepted by others?

To explore the first of these questions, "What is human about humans?" we contrasted humans with animals and worked out a number of particular questions in each subject area. The whole unit was built around a trip to the zoo. The students were equipped with a sheet which asked a range of questions running from the factual, "What foods does this animal eat?" to the more philosophical, "Are fur and feathers the same thing as clothing?" and "Describe the 'animal' in man."

When the high school students returned from the zoo another teacher and I put on an impromptu reading of Edward Albee's *Zoo Story* and classes the next week picked up the themes which emerged. In drama class the students tried to imitate the movement of the animals they had watched—the ponderous stumbling of the turtles, the grace of the swans. There followed a discussion about why humans characterized so much of their action with animal metaphors. One girl who had watched a swan was eager to speak of it but, though she seemed to be an extrovert, could not bring herself to demonstrate its grace in a drama improvisation. The swan, she wrote later, was part of her personal dream, locked away in her mental "jewel box" where no one could get at it:

> *I am like a crazy, complicated maze.*
> *I never cry, never love*
> *I am like egotistical egotists*

I am fear, constant fear that they might find out what I really am. I'm not really fear but fear is the blanket that protects and prohibits what I really am. I've locked it all away in a jewel box. I'm afraid that it might be hideous. I'm afraid that there won't be anything at all. I'll be disgusted if it's beautiful.

> *My only request is to know it.*
> *When I am dying. Or dead.*

During the session of improvisation in which she first spoke of her swan, she did not know what was in that jewel box. She was scared and uncertain about talking, but not disgusted and not dead. Her voice, which had been loud and tinny, became a soft contralto. She, who called herself a "project child" because she had brazened her way through so many special programs, began to take on the serenity of the swan she admired. She was not transformed— no miracle happened—but her response to that lesson convinced us that a curriculum of concerns could make a difference in students' lives.

In the urban affairs class the "zoo" curriculum was used in a different way. The students took turns sitting on the floor of a "cage" built of circling chairs while their classmates questioned them. "What district of the city do you live in? Do you feel caged in there? Do you ever hear people in your neighborhood refer to people in other parts of the city as 'animals'? Is it better to keep different animals in different cages so they won't hurt each other? What problems arise when people feel as through they're caged in? What can be done about it?" Classes in art and communications followed a similar curriculum of questions designed to lead students from their experience with animals to a better understanding of themselves as humans.

In a group discussion period that I led we got into a debate about animal and human groups. The class began by collecting a list of different kinds of animal groups (hive, herd, pack, school, etc.) and then I asked the students what animal group their own class was most like. I was unprepared for the answer I got but I was very impressed: they were like no animal group because no animal group was voluntarily composed of antagonistic animals, yet the diversity of people in the room had voluntarily come together to learn more about themselves and others. That answer struck me as extremely significant because it pointed so explicitly to the fact that man's self-consciousness allows him to utilize his own diversity for his own benefit. If a consciousness of self is one of the major differences between animals and men, then one of the most effective ways to make men more human, or more humane, would be to help them explore the significance of their own diversity. And if our curriculum of concerns was bringing students to that kind of realization perhaps we were on the track of a plan of classroom education which led to our goal of "more open, more independent human beings."

The other questions of the curriculum guide were not explored as fully as the one on "What is human about humans?" because we did not give ourselves adequate time to work out detailed curricula. As a result, the students' response to the program was not as clear-cut as we would have liked. Perhaps their combination of insight and frustration is best revealed in an interview between Gerald Weinstein, who wrote the paper mentioned earlier, and some of the program's students. The interview took place in October, after the students had been back in their regular school settings. Mr. Weinstein was posing as a school official.

FIRST STUDENT: I sat in school today and it was in geometry and I sat and I looked at everyone and I said, "Now they're really not like I am at all," because I was so angry. She was teaching geometry ...it was nothing. She was saying that this plane is this plane and that line runs that way and I'm feeling awful and I was looking at the people sitting there being their nice little selves...goody-goody girls sitting there, "Yes, teacher, you're right. I understand," and they didn't understand at all.
MR. WEINSTEIN: Well, what was it that made you feel bad? That they were responding that way?
FIRST STUDENT: No, that they weren't being themselves. They weren't feeling anything.
MR. WEINSTEIN: How do you know they weren't being themselves? Couldn't that have been themselves?
SECOND STUDENT: That could have been her six months ago.
MR. WEINSTEIN: Could it? Was that you?

FIRST STUDENT: That was me.
MR. WEINSTEIN: You mean that experience you had this summer made you so different from them? And now you're unhappy?
FIRST STUDENT: I'm not unhappy.
MR. WEINSTEIN: Well, you're uncomfortable.
FIRST STUDENT: I'm uncomfortable but I'm not unhappy because I think I'm more of a person. And, you know, I can accept myself.
MR. WEINSTEIN: You're more uncomfortable but you're not more unhappy. I don't understand.
SECOND STUDENT: It's not unhappy, it's just being aware of something. It makes you a little more unhappy but at least it gives you a feeling of knowing why you have this frustrating feeling of sitting there thinking, "There must be something wrong with me because I don't like this."...I've been going to this school since fourth grade and more and more and more, every year, I've felt there is nothing for me in this school. And yet six weeks [of the Summer Program] and I feel like I've learned something more than in all those ten years.

Formal research evaluation conducted by a team from Bryn Mawr is still under way. Attitude studies have produced ambiguous results which later follow-up should clarify. The results which emerged from other tests showed, interestingly enough, that the students' parents gave the program an enthusiastic rating. All but one thought there was a "change for the better" in their children and large numbers reported a substantial change for the better. Also, it was clear from research that the students formed friendships across racial and school lines to a much greater extent than occurs in regular school situations.

Whatever the final results of the program's evaluation, it would be foolhardy to generalize them into sweeping conclusions about the nature of education. Yet it would be equally foolhardy not to continue the experiment, both to benefit those students who attend and to refine the measuring tools. This will be done by the Cooperative Program planned for next year. It would also be foolhardly not to hypothesize about the implications of the past summer and to work on a theory that would help to explain such experiences. Mr. Weinstein is heading a national field group of educators who are considering the many problems involved in developing such a theory.

In the meantime the Philadelphia Board of Education is investigating several ways in which the Cooperative Program's philosophy and curriculum can be transferred to mass education: (1) by using a similar program as part of training designed to increase a teacher's ability to reach students who are unlike himself; (2) by using improvisational drama to develop awareness and self-confidence among a diverse student body; (3) by using subject matter more relevant to student concerns—by substituting an "urban affairs" class for "civics," by broadening English to "communication" which includes movies and other modern forms of expression; (4) by using a high school course in group dynamics as a way of helping students understand the concerns which motivate or block their progress in school; (5) by facing conflict openly and using tension to provide an educational stimulus; and (6) by experimenting with ungraded, unmarked, noncompulsory "discovery" classes for small groups of difficult or especially talented students.

All of these activities can be conducted without changing the present orientation of the school system in any major way. They supplement, or perhaps enhance, the commitment to teach all students the skills of reading, writing, and arithmetic. But perhaps it is not too early to speculate on what changes might occur in the operation of a school if a curriculum of concerns were developed for kindergarten through twelfth grade and if it were made to serve as the basis for integrating skills training, subject matter, and the students' personal needs.

Suppose at the high school level, where one of the primary concerns of students is self-identity, the curricula were completely revised so that most subject matter was related to questions of self. Suppose the biology course stopped the yearly ritual of chopping up pickled frogs and began exploring the brain, that tantalizing source of self-identity. Suppose, instead of memorizing theorems which they will forget immediately after the exam, math students learned the mathematical concepts of computer programing and the ways that systems analysis is being used to control much of their economic and political identity. Suppose history were

presented not as a series of battles and prime ministers but as the quest of man to establish his identity by religious, territorial, economic, political, and educational means.

One of the many complications of such a presentation is that the students would not graduate knowing the same facts they now know. But with the amount of knowledge doubling every ten years, selection is a necessity. If, as Jerome Bruner has suggested in *The Process of Education,* we can teach the structure of any subject to any child at any age, perhaps the structure which is directly related to a child's own concerns would stimulate a dramatic renascence in learning. At the elementary level there is evidence from programs all over the country that we have underestimated the potential of elementary children's concerns in almost every field.

If one of the major concerns of very small children is communication with the buzzing world around them, no wonder so many programs are preparing children to read at very early ages. In Philadelphia a local television station is even running an experimental program which hopes to teach three-year-olds to read as they watch TV. Similarly, in foreign languages, the millions of bilingual four-year-old Puerto Ricans and Mexicans are making educators wonder why they teach language in high school, when after four arduous years of Spanish most of the students will not be able to speak it adequately. Perhaps if we taught children *what* they are concerned with knowing *when* they are concerned with knowing it, they would graduate knowing more and understanding more.

The curriculum of concerns suggests the vision of a new function and meaning for schools—schools that face the questions all men have experienced. I believe we can create schools that students want to attend because their education is important to them not simply as economic or social climbers, but as human beings. I believe such schools may someday educate students for a society where people are not judged by money, class, or I.Q. but by their understanding of others and of themselves.

Community High School

The morning after Martin Luther King's death, school began with an assembly. A black member of the school board spoke. He appealed to the students to remain nonviolent "at least on this day, for this is what he would have wanted." Afterward, many black students, gathered in the school courtyard, while most white students returned to class.

It seemed to me that any speeches I made to my classes must appear irrelevant. So I read from the book by James Baldwin and Richard Avedon, *Nothing Personal*. Tense, whispering students entered my fourth-period class. Only about half of them appeared. Outside, some of the black students began to lead others to the shopping area of Berkeley. Several hundred students were strung in a long thick line between the school courtyard and the street. How many would go? What damage would occur? Would anyone be hurt? I read: "The sea rises, the light fails, lovers cling to each other and children cling to us. The moment we cease to hold each other, the moment we break faith with one another, the sea engulfs us and the light goes out."

Quiet.

And then the one black girl in the class spoke: "All my life I've had white friends, and played with the white kids on my block. There are many white people whom I love..." She paused, and her silence swept the room, emphasizing the color of her audience. "I went to class today and came in here. But I don't really feel I belong in here. I feel I belong somewhere else. But I can't go out there with them and do what they're doing." She paused again.

"Don't know where I should be. I don't know who I am." She lowered her head and cried.

There were a few titters of embarrassed laughter. Some students looked down or away, as if to avoid confronting themselves or others in this most personal moment. But no one spoke for a long time. It was as if students and teacher felt frozen, rigid, horrified, totally unable to act, to reach out, to support, to communicate.

Later, reflecting on that day, I can excuse, perhaps, our inability to speak. But our inability to act supportively and humanely is less easy to dismiss. It causes us to examine the nature of the institution and our roles within it which foster such coldness and separation.

A large city school such as Berkeley High School[1] is structured with the purpose of administering an "education" to a large number of students as efficiently and cheaply as possible, much as we administer vaccines to huge masses of people. Efficiency and economy become primary values. The school is a place where teachers "teach," students "learn," and courses and curriculum form a chart which, if followed, steer the student on toward the college of his choice. In such a structure, roles are of vital importance: the administrator is the executor of an order imposed from without. The teacher, his minister of state, is an expert, a fountainhead of fact. The student is the uninitiated—his experiences and concerns are removed from and irrelevant to the "great ideas" or themes of the curriculum. The range of human feelings and relationships in such a structure is limited. For a student or a teacher to admit to feelings (let alone show them) of boredom, anger, hurt, or affection simply does not fit such a structure. Pretending that such feelings do not directly affect the learning process, "we must proceed with the lesson!"

At Berkeley High School on the occasion

---

[1] Berkeley High has three thousand students.

343

of Martin Luther King's death, the "learning process" ground to a halt. That order we had come to depend upon proved impotent when it was tested and stretched. In that classroom and in that school no real community existed. Like the young girl, we did not know where we were, how we should act, or who we were.

The Berkeley Summer Project: A Prototype

While the situation on the day of King's death brought to a head many problems which are present in the large urban school, several of us had attempted to develop a program to deal with these problems the previous summer.

It was with the hope of remaking the high school into a place where identity and community could be affirmed and developed that we created the Berkeley Summer Project in 1967.[2] Each morning for six weeks an academically and racially mixed group of sixty students, ranging in grade level from eight to twelve, attended three one-hour classes in Art, Communications, and Dance-Drama. Each day, prior to the classes we held a brief organizational meeting, planned the day's schedule and special events, and discussed problems we were encountering in the project. That is, students and staff determined together how they would use their time and how they would make their summer experience work. After the classes, students and staff could lunch together in the student lounge and then spend the afternoon working on projects they had chosen to develop. They were also free to leave, but most students stayed and worked, producing some superb creative efforts in writing, dance, drama, music, painting, and sculpture. While the students worked, teachers were available primarily as resources.

Using the three classes as a scaffolding, the staff tried to plan the summer project in such a way that individual choice could take place within a meaningful context. We grappled with three arguments which seemed to have a crucial

bearing upon the idea of individual choice in a social context.

The first argument centered on the desirability of training the students to manipulate abstractions of experience as opposed to helping them to experience directly as fully as possible. A unit was begun with a trip to the zoo. Students were encouraged to imitate the animal postures in the dance-drama class. Improvisations were developed on the problem of being caged. Students acted out the experience of entrapment in a cage, a jail, or the psychological states of slum life, drug addiction, time addiction, etc. The focus of this class was, in part, to feel the experience of entrapment from within. This contrasted with the communications class where elaborate discussions of the state of being trapped were held. The results were poems, stories, readings, communications, exercises, and other attempts to abstract the experience in language.

A second argument concerned itself with absolute individual freedom versus the limitations resulting from the social context of a group. The concept of entrapment and the focus of the project on creating a community generated this second argument. In art, students chose their medium and went at their own speed. In contrast, most of the work in drama and dance required that individuals add positively to a scene or improvisation in progress. Because much of this work was nonverbal, it was somewhat frightening for many students, and participation demanded the willingness to take risks for the progress of the group. The communications class focused quite openly on the problem of the group versus the individual. Here the teacher chose not to be the initiator of activity for the group. The initial groping for a process which would be stimulating for all members of the group resulted in an intensive questioning of what individuals can contribute to a group.

The third argument revolved on the question of whether significant learning occurs when the primary purpose of that learning is the mastery of skills or the airing of personal feelings and concerns. The latter value was upheld primarily in the communications class where the students began openly to discuss themselves, to share descriptions of such experiences as "what had been the most beautiful moment of

[2] Jay Manley, director and drama instructor; Montford Cardwell, art instructor; Anne Hornbacher, communications instructor; Elizabeth Janssen, dance instructor; Peter Kleinbard, co-originator and director of the afternoon program; Barbara Glasser, intern teacher in drama.

their lives," or how they felt about individuals within their group of a different temperament or race or sex. In art, drama, and dance, the focus was on mastering the medium of the body or the mediums of clay or paint, in an outward expression of inner feelings and ideas.

The values contained in these "arguments" remained in continuous flux with respect to how we dealt with them in class. We often disagreed as individuals. Our aim, however, was not to sell ideas, but to use what we thought were valid and significant philosophical issues as the basis for developing relevant curricula and a dynamic program.

The Summer Project was intended as a prototype for the regular school. We studied it carefully to determine what elements of the design could be reproduced during a school semester.

The Community High School Project

Our evaluation of the Summer Project pointed to means for revitalizing aspects of the larger school during the regular academic year. Additional impetus was given by the ominous events of the year, the death of Martin Luther King, the rising tension in the schools, and the complete desegregation of the Berkeley schools. Berkeley High School, with all the qualities of the big city school, was an ideal place to set up a laboratory school based in part on the model of the summer project. This model came to be called the Community High School Project.

Principles

We seek to create in our laboratory school an environment which will encourage a sense of community among its members. Through such an environment we hope to help the individual student and teacher to establish a secure sense of who each is and a faith in his own ability to become the person he wishes to be.

We intend to use the school as a laboratory to develop methods which cause students and staff from every origin and achievement level to share feelings, concerns, and knowledge. We want our student to have attitudes of tolerance and to value individual differences. We intend

to help the student learn processes to achieve change without violence. In order to do this, stress will be placed upon increased interpersonal sensitivity, communication skills, and self-respect.

Guided by these principles, the Community High School began in the spring semester, 1969, with 116 tenth-grade students. The students were selected to represent the precise racial and academic proportions of the regular school.[3] A teaching staff was gathered to represent the disciplines of English, history, physical education, science, art, dance, drama, and music.[4] These students and teachers began meeting together for half of each school day in one area of the high school plant. During the other half of the day, students were enrolled in elective courses which we were not equipped to offer, such as foreign language or shop courses.

Curriculum

Curriculum was developed to help students share experiences, values, and concerns from their varying backgrounds. Initially, we intended to utilize two basic approaches to curriculum to facilitate this process.

The first approach involved all students in arts courses which were intended to give an experiential basis to the more abstract formulations being dealt with in other courses. For example, our trip to a migrant labor camp gave rise to dramatic improvisations about the effect of environments upon people. The concrete experience of playing in improvisations provided the experiential basis for discussions of man's control over himself, as opposed to man's being controlled by his environment or by other men.

A second approach involved what we have called a task-oriented curriculum. In this, the

[3] Sixty percent Caucasian; 40 percent Black; 10 percent others (Mexican-American, Oriental, etc.); 20 percent Track 1, 60 percent Track 2, 20 percent Track 3.
[4] Project Staff: Director and Drama Instructor, Jay Manley; Drama, Photography Teacher, Peter Kleinbard; English, Carl R. Brush; History, Susan Bement; Art, Ben Hazard; Dance, Evelyn Chiles; Music, Robert S. Pearson; Physical Education, Mike Spino; Science, John Rosenbaum; Student Assistants, Kevin Schafer and Mike Torrance; Black Studies, Dwayne Nunley.

student and staff were involved together in concrete projects (such as making a book or a film or recreating a microscopic model of the city) which require a variety of interests and skills.

We began to involve students in important decision-making processes, and in the future students will participate increasingly with the staff in the development and selection of curricula, selection of teaching staff and school government. Parents, too, are involved in the Community High School project, through regular informal evening discussions and the publication of a Community High School newsletter.

Service projects are encouraged in which students receive credit for activities such as tutoring their peers, teaching elementary school children, developing audiovisual materials on aspects of their own cultural heritage, and making presentations about the school for the community and the Board of Education.

Techniques and new curricula developed in the laboratory school will be available to the regular school through participation of Community High School staff members in regular school meetings and committees and through invitations to regular school personnel and students to observe and participate in the laboratory school.

At the time of this writing, we have completed the first six weeks of the Community High School Project. It is too early to generalize about the project. But we can describe what a student may have experienced to this point.

In the months before we began, we described the Project to the eleven hundred tenth graders at the high school. All were invited to apply. From the six hundred applicants, 120 were chosen by lot, once racial, academic, and sexual proportions were established to reflect those of the regular school. Our student is one of these.

Before the program begins, she is invited to a series of meetings. She and her parents meet the project staff and ask questions of them: "Will my child's chances of getting into college be hampered?" "What is the grading policy?" "You aren't going to try group therapy on these kids, are you? And they leave feeling the whole thing is a bit tentative, for the staff is committed to working out many of the answers with the students.

A second meeting is held. This time it is at the home of a staff member. Here she gets acquainted with him and six or seven other students.

Lastly, she is invited to a series of lunchtime meetings at school. Here the staff asks such questions as "What should happen the first week of school?" "What options should be available in Physical Education?" "How should grades be determined?" Knowing hardly anyone, she feels uncomfortable and hesitates to commit herself. Only a few people speak at length. She's never given much thought to this kind of thing in school. She begins to wonder whether the staff is really able to run a school if they don't *know* what's going to happen.

A week later the project begins. She is in a group twenty-seven other students from all tracks. The first two weeks are to be a "sampling" period. The students are asked to attend all the elective courses and later to choose the ones they wish to take. Her schedule is unlike any she has seen before. Some classes meet two two days a week for an hour and a half. Some meet three days. There is some free time when she doesn't have classes scheduled.

At the end of the two week sampling period there is a day of confusion. Students are given a list showing what classes are available when, and are asked to work out their own schedules. All students must take English, history, and P.E., and as many electives as they wish. Our student tries, at first, to write her schedule so that she has no free time. But finally, she decides to give herself two hours off three days a week. The free time still makes her uneasy. She's not quite sure what to do and feels that she should be doing something. But she's begun to get interested in photography and thinks that she might use the darkroom during this time.

The next week, she embarks upon her new schedule. She spends the first English classes playing communication games. In one, she is asked to leave the room while the rest of the class determines a simple activity which she must do (entering the closet and closing the door). When she comes back, the class claps, louder as she nears her task, softer as she moves away from it. Her excitement at the game is mixed with a feeling of discomfort about the control the group has on her. The game ends when she discovers what they wanted her to do. And then they talk. Now, the focus is on that second feeling—what it feels like to be controlled by a group. A student points out the similarity in dress among many of the girls in the room. Another notes that our student likes the same music as most of her friends. And the teacher observes that even groupings of students in the room reflect prevailing social patterns. The teacher asks the students for personal descriptions of their experience in being controlled by a group. At first, the discussion focuses on highly subjective experiences, some of which have been created in this classroom, and then moves out to interpretations of that experience. Reading and writing assignments are then based on this topic.

Interdisciplinary Approaches

The student is confronted with a similar problem in history, but with a different focus. She and her classmates are asked to determine their own organization for the class: "The teacher should do it. She knows more." "*We* should control what happens to us." The argument rages, and out of it comes the students' organization for the use of power in the class.

The drama teacher takes a similar idea, the relation of the individual to the group, and adds to it the point of view of his discipline. Our student is asked to forget all previous ideas of who she is, and then to enter an ongoing scene in which everyone knows who the new actor is but herself. She must discover from their nonverbal cues who she is. The scene causes a discussion about how individuals pick up cues about themselves from a group.

As our student becomes more involved in the activities of the project, she is able to articulate her criticisms. She is still uncomfortable with the free time. The staff continues to seem uncertain. Instructors constantly ask advice from the students about what should be happening—even what should happen in this class right now. Other students agree with her. There is too much uncertainty. Finally they speak to the staff members about this feeling. Their complaint results in an examination of the problem from the point of view of the various disciplines. In English, for example, poems are read on problems of anxiety, emptiness, and freedom. Drama improvisations are developed from the poems.

As a staff, we have been uncertain—at times, purposefully so. Often the day-to-day realities of the Project have caused us to change our original concepts of what we should do and of where the students are. Instead of imposing our own themes, we have listened and tried to pick up ones that the students have indicated concern about. Nonphysical sexual differences, the animal in man, the individual in the group, the problem of freedom are examples of general problems we have examined. Gradually, like our students, we are finding our way.

We have begun to develop a second way of relating the disciplines other than through problems treated by the entire class. Early in the English and history classes small groups and individuals chose books or topics of particular interest to them. Now they are developing projects on these.

The development of these projects has taken a great deal of staff time in individual conferences. But gradually students are beginning actively to use the resources at hand rather than depend on the teacher to give them information and direction. For example, students who are doing a small group project in Black History are using their art and photography classes to make photographic essays on the subject. They have asked the science teacher for assistance in developing measures for a test of racial attitudes of people in the project, and the drama and dance teachers for materials to dramatize their concern with racial problems. Several such crossdisciplinary projects are being developed. Another grew from a student's interest in planting a roof garden, and has now become an elaborate study of nutrition and its effects on people. Gradually the students are taking greater initiative, and now we look forward to some exciting small group and individual projects.

Since much of this work is in small groups, a task of the staff is to help the students master processes for dealing with each other in small groups. We are setting up exercises which teach such skills and help the students develop their ability to observe and resolve interpersonal problems.

As the initiative of the students in the curriculum has increased, they have also taken a larger role in running the school. At first, our numerous invitations to them were not received too actively. Now, more of our students attend and participate in morning staff meetings. At times they significantly alter our decisions in respect to curriculum, field trips, or schedules. And we look forward to the time when decisions will not be "staff" decisions, but result from action of the entire Community High School.

While most aspects of the Community High School are running smoothly, it is also important for us and for those contemplating similar projects to try to articulate some of the difficulties we have encountered.

The transition from the rigid program of the regular school to our own has been a difficult one for many of the students. These students feel uncomfortable with the large amounts of free time. Some feel that because we do not make them turn in traditional assignments and tests they will not be prepared for college or jobs. Many, unused to having choices in school, have not yet begun to exercise the control of their time which the program offers. We might have anticipated these problems by providing a more gradual transition into the freer atmosphere of our school. Secondly, we might have made more of an effort in the beginning to interpret the philosophy of our school to the new students so that they could see value in some of the uncertainty and anxiety they are suffering.

While the staff has gotten along well together, differences in philosophy have prevented us from reinforcing each other's work in the classroom to the extent that we had hoped. We needed, before the program began,

to make it clearer to each other where we stood in respect to educational philosophy and what we envisioned as the operational consequences of our philosophies.

As a staff we need to know more processes which will help our students make sense of their concerns and needs. We are speaking specifically of the adolescent's concern as an individual for how he appears in the eyes of another person, how he can choose what he wishes to gain competence in, and how he can express the intense feelings he experiences. Second, we speak of the adolescent's concern as a member of a group for learning how to listen, how to give or share, and how to request help.

Conclusion

The Project is stressing human values and relationships, . . . an interest in subject matter rather than set curriculum. The emphasis is very much more on the *now* and an interest in other people and learning for what it is worth rather than as preparation for college.

I'm more relaxed, not so tense. And I'm more honest and straightforward.

But my head is still spinning too fast to be clear in my thoughts.

These are some student reactions to the Project. The early stage of uneasiness at the new freedom seems to be fading. Students are helping each other, reaching out to their fellows, and penetrating more deeply into the work they are doing in class and on their own. The slow and sometimes painful gestation period seems to be ending for many.

Index *

Abot, Viviane, 105
  "A French Page for the School Newspaper," 114–15
Adolescent Society, 176
Advanced Composition: A Book of Models for Writing (Warriner), 116
Advertisements used in art class, 218–19, 244–47
African Heritage, An (Drachler), 290, 291
African Myths and Tales (Feldman), 186
Alamillo, Everardo, 178
  "Drama in Foreign Language," 207–8
Albee, Edward, 340
Algebra (*see also* Mathematics), **14,** 59–60; **32,** 129–31
Allbee, Lewis, 327
American Conservatory Theater Company, 297
Ancient Greece (filmstrip), 281
And Then We Heard the Thunder (Killens), 301
Andersen, Marion, xxviii
  "Clark Robinson: An Appreciation," xxi–xxii
Arithmetic (*see* Mathematics)
Art classes:
  advertisements used in, 244–47
  self-evaluation in, 44–45
Arts and crafts, 125–26
Assignments, samples of:
  in English, 32, 39, **68,** 257–58
  in mathematics, 54–55
  in social studies, 98–99
Atchison, Lois, 218
  "Commercial Art: Unit for Con-

* Strategy numbers are boldface.

Atchison (*cont.*)
  tinuation High School Students," 244–47
Athens: The Golden Age (film), 282
Attendance problems, 331–32
Autobiography of Frederick Douglass, 301
Autobiography of Malcolm X, 302
Avakian, Elizabeth, 105, 128
  "An Experiment in Grouping," 131–35
  "Teaching the Reading and Writing of Short Stories Concurrently," 119–23
Avansino, Kristin, 105
  "Dancing: The Joy of Discovering Together," 123–25

Baldwin, James, 301
Barahal, Anabel, 145
  "Strategies for a Seventh-grade String Orchestra," 154–55
Barlow, Janelle, 177
  "Game Simulation in U.S. History," 201–6
Barranco, Minerva, 256
  "Black History," 298–300
Bebelaar, Judy, 34, 40, 42, 104–5
  "The Soul Searchers," 107–10
Behavior standards, 22–23, 26–27, **3,** 29–31
Bentley, Margaret Anderson, 254
  "Does It Relate, Man?," 269–71
Bingham, Gretchen, 217
  "Heavy, Heavy Hangs Over Thy Overhead," 228–31
Biological Science for High School (Gregory and Goldman), 75
Biology (*see also* Science), **3,** 29–31;

Biology (*cont.*)
  11, 49–52; **18,** 74–78; **35,** 139–41; **81,** 293–96
Black Boy (Wright), 301
Black Rage (Grier and Cobbs), 256, 297
Black studies:
  evolution of program of, 318–20
  history in, 298–300
  literature in, 300–303
Block, Jeanne, 10
Bonnie and Clyde (film), 285
Bonnin, Robert, xxviii
Boom of the 1920s and the Depression of the 1930s (film), 285
Borton, Terry, 308
  "What Turns Kids On?," 338–42
Brand, Jacquelyn and Stephen, 218
  "Reaching the Nonreader," 233–35
Brock, Frederick W., 255
  "Experiences in Teaching Values," 279–81
Brown, Janet E., 145
  "Students Devise Homework Assignments," 152–53
Bruner, Jerome, 65, 201, 342
Brynner, Witter, 301
Bundy, Eliene, 253
  "Commonplace Books," 258–61
Burckhardt, Jacob, 289
Business classes:
  career preparation in, 271–73
  planning for Friday afternoon in, 45–47
  simulation techniques used in, 195–99
  students as teachers of, 156–59

Caen, Herb, 280
Cambridge, Godfrey, 301

Camera lights, 250
Cameras, 165, 250
Canobi, Paul, 145
  "Individualizing Instruction and Students as Teachers," 156–59
Career preparation, 254–55, 271–78
  materials used for, 274–76
Carmichael, Stokely, 301
"Catbird Seat, The" (Thurber), 120
Cather, Willa, 121
Chambers Brothers, 242
Chambers, Judy, 217, 222
  "The Visual Approach to Vocabulary," 220–21
Chance, Ruth, xx
Christensen, Francis, 237
Christensen, Harvey, 327
Clark, Esmer, xxviii, 9, 35, 36
Clark, Kenneth, 307
Classroom control (*see* Discipline)
Classroom newspaper, 107–10
Clerical duties performed by students, 26, 148, 156
Cloward, Robert D., 144
Cobbs, P. M., 297
Coglianese, Al, 65, 177
  "The Game," 188–94
  "Inventing Your Own Language," 68–71
Coleman, James S., 176
Collages, 224–25
Colleague cooperation, 47–49, **85,** 311–15; **86,** 315–18; **87,** 318–20; **88,** 320–25; **89,** 327–38; **90,** 338–42; **91,** 343–48
Color of Man, The (film), 295
Colorful Teaching of Mathematics (Walch and Cordell), 149
Commonplace books, use of, **69,** 258–61
Community High School, 308–9, 343–48
  curriculum for, 345–47
  interdisciplinary approaches of, 347–48
  principles of, 345
Concept-building, 67, 95–102
  mathematics and, **21,** 90–91; **22,** 92–94
  processes and, 100–102
  unit on government for, 96–97
Contests (*see also* Games), 209, 213
Continuation high schools:
  Berkeley High School East Campus (Berkeley, California), **72,** 266–69
  Churchill High School (Newark, California), **71,** 265–66
  definition of, 16n
  Mission Continuation High School (Hayward, California), **66,** 244–47
  Opportunity High School (San Francisco, California), **89,** 327–38
  Samuel Gompers High School (San Francisco, California), **7,** 39–44; **25,** 107–10; **62,** 233–35
Cooperative counseling program, 306, 311–15
  activities of, 312–13
  atmosphere of, 313
  evaluation of progress toward goals of, 313–315
  organization of, 312
Cooperative Program, 338–42
Counseling (*see also* Career preparation), 274, 330–332
  cooperative program of, 306, 311–15
Course individualization, 156–58

Creative class projects, 105–6, 113–14, 301–2
  in arts and crafts, 125–26
  in dance, 123–25
  in film, 248
Creative teaching, 104
Creative writing, 104–5
  in classroom newspaper, 107–10
  in foreign languages, 114–15
  remedial reading and, 110–14
    form of evaluation, 112–13
    form of expression, 112
    topics, 111–12
  of short stories, 119–23
  workshop in, 115–19
Critical thinking process, **77,** 279–81
Crossman, Lee, xxx
Crow, Wayne, 177
  "State versus Santa Claus," 199–201
Cullen, Countee, 301
Cuney, Waring, 301
Cunningham, Al, 10
Current Events (magazine), 211
Curriculum:
  Community High, 345–47
  of concerns, **90,** 338–42; **91,** 343–48
  Graduate Internship Program, 4–6
  hyphenated, 330
  interdisciplinary ethnic studies, **87,** 318–20; **88,** 320–25
  Opportunity High, 336
  process-oriented, 24
  SPAN, 9

Dance, 123–25
Darwin, Charles, 75
Davis, Gene G., 306–7
  "Drug Education: Community Education for a Community Problem," 315–18
Davis, Linda G., 253
  "Illustrate Who You Are," 257–58
Davis, Robert, 217
  "Look and Write," 226–28
Death of Socrates, The (film), 282
Debates, 38
Dice games for mathematics, 209
Dick, Thomas, 122
Dictaphones, 234–35
Discipline, 14, 20–25, 29–30, 31
  advice to new teachers on, 21–22, 182–83
  consideration of students and, 23
  consultation with other teachers on, 23
  counseling and, **85,** 311–15
  developing responsibility and, **12,** 52–56; **49,** 195–99
  establishing order and, 22, 26
  Friday afternoons and, **54,** 210–12
  improvisational drama and, 181–83
  recurrent discipline problems, 373
  rules and behavior standards and, 22–23, 26–27
  team learning and, 137
Discovery:
  concept-building in social studies and, 67, 95–102
    processes and, 100–102
    unit on government, 96–97
  language and, 65–66, 68–74
    foreign, 71–74
    invention of, 68–71
  mathematics and, 66–67, 90–94
    function machine, 92–94
    devising number systems, 90–91
  science and, 66, 74–90
    laboratory science, 79–87
    taxonomy, 74–78
  teaching and, **72,** 266–69

Discussion, 15, 35–39, **77,** 279–81
  debates and panels as stimulators for, 38
  interviews as stimulator for, 32
  problems in, 35–41
  small groups and, 130, 134
  use of individual projects and, 37–38
Dorn, Karen, 255
  "An Approach to Africa," 289–93
Drachler, Jacob, 290, 291
Drama:
  black history and, 296–300
  personalized learning of, 266–69
Dramatizing devices, 176–215
  games as, 178, 208–15
    contests, 209
    dice, 209
    materials for, 211–12
    mathematics laboratory, 208–9
    think sheets, 209
  improvisation as, 176–77, 179–88
    change of emotion, 185
    literature and, 187–88
    mechanics of, 182–83
    object exercise, 185
    opening and closing lines, 185
    orientation games, 183–84
    play ball, 185–86
    for teachers, 179–81
    transformation of relationships, 185
  role playing as, 177–78, 199–206
    current problem, 203–5
    daily work activities, 200–201
    historical, 202
    institutional, 202–3
    political convention, 203
    preparation for, 199–200
    requirements for groups in, 200
  simulation techniques, 177–78, 188–99
    grouping, 189
    input, 189–90
    materials, 189
    method, 190
    modifications, 191
    site, 189
    social institutions, 189
Drug education program, 306–7, 315–18
  community activities for, 317–18
  program for parents in, 316–17
Dylan, Bob, 285

Earthquake Country (Iacopi), 263
Edwards, Harry, 280
Emerging Africa (Scholastic Multi-Text), 290
English (*see also* Creative writing):
  developing rapport and, 31–33
  discovery and, 68–71
  discussion and oral work in, 35–39
  games for, 210–12
  improvisational drama and, 186–88
  individualized teaching of, 159–62
  organization and, 25–29
  personalized learning of, 269–71
  pictures used in teaching, 220–21
    collages, 224–25
    films, 227–28
    photographs, 222–23, 226–27
    popular music and, 235–41
    self-image and, 257–61
  social values and, 279–81, 283–88
  team learning and, 136–49
English for the Rejected (Holbrook), 104, 111, 113
Erikson, Erik H., 196, 253
Escape to Nowhere (film), 317

Esterle, Rochelle, 128, 256
  "Biological Aspects of Race," 293–96
  "Grouping for a Final Exam," 139–41
Ethnic studies programs, 307
  evolution of 318–20
  interdisciplinary, 320–25
Evaluation (*see also* Grading):
  of a course, 240
  of creative writing, 112–13
  of democratic classroom behavior, **78**, 281–83
  of a grouping project, 135
  of improvisational drama, 187
  in laboratory science, 81
  problems of, 15–16, 39–41, 201
  self, 44–45, 192, 257–58
Evans, Mari, 301
Evolution (Moore), 294
Examinations (*see* Testing)
"Exploding the Myths of Prejudice" (filmstrip), 290

Fader, Daniel N., 16–17, 222
Family of Man, The, 301
Fantini, Mario, 271, 339
Feldman, Susan, 186
Fenton, Edwin, 282, 291
Fielder, Marie, xxviii
Field trips, 49–52, 199, 299, 340
Film libraries, 249
Films, 227–28
  student produced, 219, 247–51
    film libraries and, 249
    filming of, 248–49
    projection of, 249
    soundtrack of, 249
    technical information on, 249–50
  use of:
    in drug education, 317–18
    in English, 227–28, 285–86
    in science, 294–95
    in social studies, 282, 291–92
Filmstrips, use of:
  in career guidance, **75**, 274–76
  in social studies, 281, 290, 292
Fiore, Quentin, 286
"First Confession" (O'Conner), 120
Fisher, Andrea, 16
  "Self-evaluation in Art Class," 44–45
Fisher, Linda, 268
Folders, 28, 42
Forcada, Judith, 145, 175
  "Student Involvement in Math," 147–50
Ford Foundation, xx, 9
Foreign languages:
  discovery and, 71–74
  dramatizing devices in, 207–8
  games, 213–15
  imagination in teaching, 71–74
  overhead projectors for, 228–31
  students as teachers of, 150–51
    devising homework assignments, 152–53
  team learning of, 141–42
Freeman, Warner, 66
  "My Use of the Discovery Method in Teaching Junior High School Science," 88–90
French (*see* Foreign languages)
Friday afternoons, problems of, 15, 45–47
Friedman, Joseph D., 218
  "An Experiment in Time," 241–43
Fuller, Buckminster, 286
Function machine, 92–94
Game simulation (*see* Role playing)

Games, 178, 208–15
  dice, 209
  in geometry, 232
  improvisational drama and, 185
  materials for, 211–12
  in mathematics laboratory, 208–9
  team learning and, 137–38, 142
  think sheets and, 209
  in typing class, 46
Gangwer, Susan, xxviii
Geology of Northern California (California Division of Mines and Geology), 263
Geometry (*see* Mathematics)
German (*see* Foreign languages)
Giannini, Winifred, 14
  "In the Beginning," 20–25
Giegengack, Bob, 279–80
Glasser, Barbara, 176–77
  "Improvisational Drama in an Urban Junior High," 181–87
Goldman, Edward H., 75
Goodlad, John, 65
Graded Spanish Readers, Books I–V (Heath), 207
Grading:
  constructive use of, 39–44
    fallacious assumptions, 40–41
    new assumptions, 41
    notion of quality, 43–44
    strategy, 41–43
    student responses, 41
  mathematics and, 55, 57, 148
  planning and, 28–29
  by students, 148
  by students and teachers, 120
Graduate Internship Program, 1–6, 104, 309
  curriculum of, 4–6
    principles of, 4–5
    structure and content, 5–6
    supervision, 6
  screening and selection for, 2–4
Grapes of Wrath, The (Steinbeck), 285–87
Greene, Burton H., 255–56
  "Black Literature Course," 300–303
  "Teaching the Social Novel," 283–88
Greenlee, Sam, 301
Gregory, William H., 75
Grier, W. H., 297
Gross, Michael, 128
  "A Grouping Project in Math," 129–31
Grouping, 57, 128–42
  in black literature course, 301–2
  at Community High, 347
  in English class, **58**, 224–25
  for examinations, 139–41
    rules for, 140
  in French class, 195
  in mathematics laboratory, 149
  for research, 290
  for discussing short stories, 120
  in speech course, 200
  students as teachers and, 161–62
  team learning as system of, 136–39, 141–42
    activities, 137–38
    discipline, 137
    games, 142
  voluntary, 102, 129–35, 189
    group meetings, 130
    objectives, 131–32
    optional daily lectures, 130
    procedure, 132
    project assignment, 129–30
    project design, 129
Guthrie, Arlo, 285
Guthrie, Woody, 285

Gutierrez, José, ii, 67
  "The Function Machine," 92–94

Haikus, use of, 116, 118–19
Halfway House, 306, **85**, 311–15
Hall, Anita, 178
  "How to Spice Up an Old Enchilada," 213–15
Hall, Mike, 17
  "Skill in Reading Math," 52–56
Hampton, Clarence, 319–20
Harms, Nancy S., 254
  "Personalizing Earth Science," 262–64
Harvest of Shame (film), 285
Hauser, Elaine, 104–5
  "Writing Yields Reading," 110–14
Hawkes, Geoffrey, 177
Herndon, James, 21
Hershdorfer, Marilyn Johnson, 14
  "Handbook for the Disorganized," 25–29
Hiatt, Mary, 121
Hicks, Mary, 15, "The Art of Discussion," 37–39
Holbrook, David, 104, 111, 113
Holland, Nancy, 145
  "Spanish Teaching by Spanish Students," 150–51
Homework assignments, 26
  devised by students, 152–53
  student board for answers and discussion of, 147–48
Hooked on Books (Fader), 16–17, 222
Horizons Unlimited, 329
Hornbacher, Anne, 10, 176–77, 183, 308*n*
  "Improvisational Drama for Teachers," 179–81
Horne, Frank, 301
Huckleberry Finn (Twain), 96
Huelga (film), 286
Hughes, Langston, 290, 301
Human Rights Commission of San Francisco, 329
Hume, David, xix

Iacopi, Robert, 263
Ilium (literary magazine), 115, 116, 118
Imagawa, Janet, 66
  "Identifying Living Organisms," 74–78
Improvisation for the Theater (Spolin), 176, 179, 183
Improvisational drama, 176–77, 179–88, 268–69
  literature and, 187–88
  mechanics of, 182–83
  methods of, 183–86
    change of emotion, 185
    object exercise, 185
    opening and closing lines, 185
    orientation games, 183–84
    play ball, 185–86
    sculpture exercise, 184–85
    transformation of relationships, 185
Individualizing instruction (*see also* Personalized learning), 128, **33**, 131–35; **37**, 147–50; **40**, 154–55; **41**, 156–59; **42**, 159–62; **43**, 163–65; **44**, 166–74; **89**, 327–38
  for gifted students, **52**, 207–8; **53**, 208–10; **54**, 210–12, 226; **76**, 276–78
Individual prescription, **42**, 159–62

In White America (play), 297, 302
Interdisciplinary approaches, 340, 347–48
in ethnic studies, 320–25
Intradepartmental coordination, 47–49
Introduction to Mathematics (textbook), 152
Introduction to Secondary School Mathematics (School Mathematics Study Group), 53

James, William, 253
Jersild, Arthur T., 14
Jobs of the Seventies, 275
Johnson, Herbert Clark, 301
Johnston, Marcia, 217
"Using Collages with Literature," 224–25
Johntz, Marjorie, xxviii
Johntz, William, 66
Jones, Leroy, 301
Jones, Richard, 256
"Black History Week," 296–300
Julius Caesar (Shakespeare), 270
Junior high school strategies:
"Concepts and Processes in Social Studies," **24**, 100–102
"Devising Number Systems," **21**, 90–91
"An Experiment in Time," **65**, 241–43
"A French Page for the School Newspaper," **27**, 114–15
"Games for Math," **53**, 208–10
"Gamesmanship, or How to Survive Friday Afternoons," **54**, 210–12
"Getting Kids to Follow Directions," **15**, 61–62
"Guide to Filmmaking in the Schools," **67**, 247–51
"Heavy Heavy Hangs Over Thy Overhead," **60**, 228–31
"Helping Slow Eighth-graders to Understand U.S. History," **23**, 95–100
"Improvisational Drama in an Urban Junior High," **46**, 181–87
"In the Beginning," **1**, 20–25
"Look and Write," **59**, 226–28
"Math for the Disadvantaged," **13**, 56–58
"My Use of the Discovery Method in Teaching Junior High School Science," **20**, 89–90
"Photographed Vocabulary," **57**, 222–23
"Popular Songs and Poetry," **63**, 235–36
"Spanish Teaching by Spanish Students," **38**, 150–51
"Strategies for Seventh-grade String Orchestra," **40**, 154–55
"Student-Teacher Relations: An Experiment in Cooperative Counseling," **85**, 311–15
"Team Learning: The Only Way to Fly," **34**, 136–39
"Warm-up Activities in a Foreign Language Class," **36**, 141–42

Keller, Robert E., 254
"Toward a Contact Curriculum," 271–73
Kennedy, John F., 270
King, Martin Luther, 343–45
Kipling, Rudyard, 290

Kleinbard, Peter, 177, 183, 308–9
"Community High School," 343–48
"Improvisational Drama and Literature," 187–88

Lange, Dorothea, 285
Language experience approach, **25**, 107–10; 234
Latham, Robert, 254
"Career and College Guidance in the Classroom," 276–78
Lee, Samantha H., 307
"Evolution of a Black Studies Program," 318–20
Lepke, Ronald, 282–83
Lepore, Margaret, xxviii
Lippincott, Ray, xxviii
Listening posts, 218, 233–35
language experience approach and, 234
dictaphones and, 234–35
LSD-25 (film), 317
Luebbert, Jeff, 17
"Algebra for Nonachievers," 59–60
Lurie, Carole, 14–15
"The Interview," 31–33

McClosky, Mildred G., xxiii–xxviii, 9, 13–18, 63–67, 104–6, 128, 144, 176, 217, 253, 305
McLuhan, Marshall, 217, 286
Magazine, The, 113
Malcolm X, 302
Mandelbaum, Ruth W., xix–xx, xxvi, xxvii, 17*n*
"SPAN: A Strategy for Reaching the Untaught," 7–11
Manley, Janet, 67
"Concepts and Processes in Social Studies," 100–102
"Helping Slow Eighth-graders to Understand U.S. History," 95–100
Manley, Jay, 183, 308–9
"Community High School," 343–48
Marine biology, **11**, 49–52
Marking, Elizabeth, 105
"Stitchery Project for an Arts and Crafts Class," 125–26
Masters, June, 14, 19, 31
"Discipline Problems?," 29–30
Mathematics:
basic, 272–73
discovery and, 66–67, 90–94
devising number systems, 90–91
function machine, 92–94
games for, 208–10
nonachievers and, 59–60, **12**, 52–56; **13**, 56–58; **37**, 147–50
overhead projector and, 232
skill in reading, 52–56
structure and, 56–58
avoidance of excessive lecturing, 57–58
grouping, 57
use of textbook, 58
weekly work schedule, 56–57
students as teachers of, 147–50, 157
devising homework assignments, 152–53
use of grouping in, 129–31
Mathematics (McSwain), 58
Mathematics laboratory, 208–9
students as teachers in, 149
Mathisen, Bonnie, 178
"Games for Math," 208–10
Matute, Gini, 307

Matute, Gini (*cont.*)
"An Interdisciplinary Seminar in Mexican-American Studies," 320–25
Mearns, Hugh, 107
Medium Is the Message, The (McLuhan and Fiore), 286
Men and Nations (Mazour), 282
Mexican-American studies, 320–25
Mexican-American Youth Association (MAYA), 321
"Model for Developing Relevant Content for Disadvantaged Children" (Weinstein and Fantini), 339
Moore, Ruth, 295
Morrison, Charles, 10
Motivation (*see also* SPAN), 253–56
in English class, **28**, 115–19; 119–20
in foreign language classes, **36**, 141–42; **55**, 213–15; **60**, 228–31
in science, **11**, 49–52; **19**, 79–87; **20**, 88–90; **70**, 262–64
in social studies, **65**, 241–43
for students to become teachers, 159
through tutorial programs, **43**, 163–65; **44**, 166–74
Motivation of nonacademic students, 49–52
Murrow, Edward R., 285–86
Music (*see also* SPAN, strategies):
in black studies, 320
in Mexican-American studies, 324
personalized learning of, 266–69
popular, 218, 235–43
in teaching the social novel, 285, 287
in teaching Spanish, 213–14
students as teachers of, 154–55
use of in writing workshop, 118
Muska, Carolyn, 16
"Planning for Friday Afternoons," 45–47

New public school models, 307–9, 327–48
Community High School as, 343–48
curriculum, 345–47
interdisciplinary approaches, 347–48
principles, 345
Cooperative Program as, 338–42
Opportunity High as, 327–38
attendance problems, 331–32
class offerings, 336–37
community response, 328–29
counseling, 330, 332
curriculum, 330
philosophical-operational differences, 331
planning programs, 328
rap sessions, 330–31
two session system, 332
New York Times, The, 286
New York Times Student Weekly, The, 290
Newton, Huey, 302
Nigger (Gregory), 301
Nonacademic students (*see also* SPAN, strategies):
appeal of high status subjects for, 59–60
motivation of, 49–52
with reading problems, 52–56
structure and, 56–58
teaching and, 16–17
test taking by, 61–62

Norris, Karen Drury, "Getting the Teacher to Shut Up," 35–37
Norton, Suzy, 128
  "Warm-up Activities in a Foreign Language Class," 141–42
Norvelle, Annette, 128
  "Team Learning: The Only Way to Fly," 136–39
Notebooks:
  English, 259
  science, 80
Number systems, devising of, 90–91

O'Conner, Frank, 120
Opportunity High, 327–38
  attendance problems of, 331–32
  community response to, 328–29
  counseling in, 330, 332
  course offerings at, 336–37
  curriculum of, 330
  origins of, 327–29, 332–35
  philosophical-operational differences in, 331
  planning programs for, 328
  rap sessions in, 330–31
  two session system of, 332
Oral work, problems in, 15, 35–41
Organization, 14, 25–29
  planning and, 27–29
  folders, 28
  grading, 28–29
  in weekly blocks, 27–28
  rules for, 26–27
Overhead projectors, 217–18, 228–32
Oxbow Incident, The (film), 282

Pairing, 160–61
Panel discussions, 38
Part-Time Jobs for High School Students (film), 274
Patterns and Processes (Biological Science Curriculum Study), 79
"Paul's Case" (Cather), 121
Pearl, Arthur, 132
Perlstein, Marcia, xxviii, 16, 34, 107, 146, 309
  "High School Tutors in an Urban Setting," 166–74
  "Opportunity High: Getting It Together," 327–38
  "A Suggestion for the Constructive Use of Grades," 39–44
Personalized learning (*see also* Individualizing instruction), 253–54, 262–71, **89**, 327–38; **90**, 338–42; **91**, 343–48
Photo stories, 165
Photographs, 217
  for teaching English, 113, 222–23, 226–27
  films, 227–28
Physical education, **71**, 265–66
Physical science (*see also* Science), **19**, 79–87
Physical Science, A Laboratory Approach (Marean and Ledbetter), 79
Pictures (*see also* Collages; Photographs), 217
  for teaching short stories, 119–20
  for teaching vocabulary, 220–21
Pimp (Iceberg Slim), 301
Planning, 27–29
  colleagues and, **10**, 47–49
  folders and, 28
  for Friday afternoons, 45–47
  grading and, 28–29
  students as teachers, 158
  in weekly blocks, 27–28, 82–87

Plato, games and, 178
Poetry, teaching of, **28**, 115–19; **47**, 187–88; **63**, 235–36
Poirier, Gérard, xxviii, 128*n*, 136*n*, **34**, 136–39; **36**, 141–42
Popular music, 218, 235–43
  English and, 235–41
  social studies and, 241–43
Porter, Sylvia, 272–73
Practical English (magazine), 211
Preparing for a Job Interview (pamphlet), 274
Preparing for the World of Work (filmstrip), 275
Process of Education (Bruner), 65, 342
Programmed reading, 165
Projection of student films, 249
Projects:
  in business class, **49**, 195–99
  in English, **58**, 224–25; 248; **68**, 257–58; **69**, 258–61
  individual, 37–38
  in mathematics laboratory, **32**, 129–31; 149
  in social studies, 203–4
Psychology, simulation techniques and, 188–94
  drama and, **82**, 296–98
  drug education and, **86**, 315–18
  group dynamics and, **78**, 281–83
  student-teacher relations and, **85**, 311–15

Quibell, Kati Lydon, xxviii, 66, 71–74

Race problems and issues, 255–56, 280, **80**, 289–93; **81**, 293–96; **82**, 296–98; **83**, 298–300; **84**, 300–303; **87**, 318–20; 343–44
  biological aspects of, 293–96
  black history and, 298–300
  black literature and, 300–303
  dance and, 123
  dramatization of, 296–98
  teaching and, **1**, 20–25; **3**, 29–31; **60**, 228–31; **87**, 318–20; **91**, 343–48
Race Relations in the Republic of South Africa (Fenton), 291
Raines, Richard C., 255
  "Functional Democracy: Historic, National and Personal," 281–83
Randall, Julie, 105
  "An Eight-day Creative Writing Workshop for High School Seniors," 115–19
Rap sessions, 330–31
Rapport, establishment of (*see also* SPAN, strategies), 14–15, 31–33, **78**, 281–83; **91**, 343–48
Reach, Touch, Teach (Borton), 338*n*
Read Magazine, 211
Reading, 24–25, **57**, 222–23
Reading problems (*see* Remedial reading)
Redding, Otis, 242–43
Reflection sheets:
  games and, 209
  tutorial programs and, 169–70
Relevance, 228, **73**, 269–71; **74**, 271–73; **78**, 281–83; **79**, 283–89; **82**, 296–98
  teaching and, 181
  new school programs and, **86**, 315–18; **87**, 318–20; **88**, 320–25; **89**, 327–38; **90**, 338–42; **91**, 343–48

Remedial reading, 17, 52–56
  creative writing and, **25**, 107–10; **26**, 110–14
  form of evaluation, 43, 112–13
  form of expression, 112
  topics, 111–12
  language experience approach to, **25**, 107–10; 129, 233–35
Reports, 50, 129, 149, 278, 291
River, The (film), 285
Robinson, Clark, xxi–xxii, 7, 11
  "Graduate Internship Program in Teacher Education," 1–6
Role playing, 177–78, 199–206
  of current problems, 203–5
  daily work activities and, 200–201
  historical, 202
  institutional, 202–3
  of political convention, 203
  preparation for, 199–200
  requirements for groups for, 200
  social values and, 283
Rosenberg, Kenneth, 219
  "Guide to Filmmaking in the Schools," 247–51
Ross, Steven, 218
  "Incorporating Music into the English Curriculum," 237–41
Rules (*see also* Discipline), 22–23
Ruskin, John, xii

San Francisco Chronicle, 272, 280
Sarason, Seymour B., 14
Saturday Review, The, 286
Schaefer, Robert J., 13
Scheer, Abbot M., 177
  "The Mock Corporation," 195–99
Schlaudt, Rita, 178
  "Gamesmanship, or How to Survive Friday Afternoons," 210–12
Scholastic Book Club, 211
"School-within-a-School" (*see* Community High School)
Schrag, Peter, 306
Scholastic Scope (magazine), 211
Schwartz, Tobey, 145
  "Individualized Teaching," 159–62
Science:
  career preparation in, 276–78
  discovery and, 66, 74–90
    laboratory science, 79–87
    taxonomy, 74–78
  discipline and, 29–30
  group for tests in, 139–41
  motivation of underachieving students in, 49–52
  race issues and, 293–96
Science Digest, 295
Scott, Jack, 279–80
Sears, Robert, 104
Self-evaluation, **7**, 39–44; **8**, 44–45; 169
Self-image, development of (*see also* SPAN, strategies), 253, 257–61, **71**, 265–66; 302; **87**, 318–20; **88**, 320–25
Senior high school strategies:
  "Algebra for Nonachievers," **14**, 59–60
  "An Approach to Africa," **80**, 289–93
  "The Art of Discussion," **6**, 37–39
  "Biological Aspects of Race," **81**, 293–96
  "Black History," **83**, 298–300
  "Black History Week," **82**, 296–98
  "Black Literature Course," **84**, 300–303

Senior high·school strategies (*cont.*)
 "Career and College Guidance in the Classroom," **76**, 276–78
 "Commercial Art: Unit for Continuation High School Students," **66**, 244–47
 "Commonplace Books," **69**, 258–61
 "Community High School," **91**, 343–48
 "Concepts and Processes in Social Studies," **24**, 100–102
 "Dancing: The Joy of Discovering Together," **30**, 123–25
 "Developing Intradepartmental Coordination," **10**, 47–49
 "Discipline Problems?," **3**, 29–31
 "Does It Relate, Man?," **73**, 269–71
 "Drama in Foreign Language," **52**, 207–8
 "Drug Education: Community Education for a Community Problem," **86**, 315–18
 "An Eight-day Creative Writing Workshop for High School Seniors," **28**, 115–19
 "Evolution of a Black Studies Program," **87**, 318–20
 "Experience in Teaching for Values," **77**, 279–81
 "An Experiment in Grouping, **33**, 131–35
 "The Function Machine," **22**, 92–94
 "Functional Democracy: Historic, National and Personal," **78**, 281–83
 "The Game," **48**, 188–94
 "Game Simulation in U.S. History," **51**, 201–6
 "Getting the Teacher to Shut Up," **5**, 35–37
 "Grouping for a Final Exam," **35**, 139–41
 "A Grouping Project in Math," **32**, 129–31
 "Guide to Filmmaking in the Schools," **67**, 247–51
 "Handbook for the Disorganized," **2**, 25–29
 "High School Tutors in an Urban Setting," **44**, 166–74
 "How to Spice Up an Old Enchilada," **55**, 213–15
 "Identifying Living Organisms," **18**, 74–78
 "Illustrate Who You Are," **68**, 257–58
 "Improvisational Drama and Literature," **47**, 187–88
 "Improvisational Drama for Teachers," **45**, 179–81
 "Incorporating Music into the English Curriculum," **64**, 237–41
 "Individualized Teaching," **42**, 159–62
 "Individualized Instruction and the Use of Students as Teachers," **41**, 156–59
 "Interdisciplinary Seminar in Mexican-American Studies," **88**, 320–25
 "The Interview," **4**, 31–33
 "Inventing Your Own Language," **16**, 68–71
 "Math for the Disadvantaged," **13**, 56–58
 "The Mock Corporation," **49**, 195–99
 "Motivating Underachieving Students in a Biology Class," **11**, 49–52

Senior high school strategies (*cont.*)
 "Opportunity High: Getting It Together," **89**, 327–38
 "Personalizing Earth Science," **70**, 262–64
 "Planning for Friday Afternoons," **9**, 45–47
 "Pool, Papers, and Volleyball: A Cooperative Strategy," **71**, 265–66
 "Popular Songs and Poetry," **63**, 235–36
 "The Present and the Future," **75**, 274–76
 "Reaching the Nonreader," **62**, 233–35
 "Self-evaluation in an Art Class," **8**, 44–45
 "Skill in Reading Math, **12**, 53–56
 "The Soul Searchers," **25**, 107–10
 "Spanish Teaching by Spanish Students," **38**, 150–51
 "Stitchery Project for an Arts and Crafts Class," **31**, 125–26
 "State versus Santa Claus," **50**, 199–201
 "Strategy: Imagination," **17**, 71–74
 "Student Involvement in Math," **37**, 147–50
 "Students Devise Homework Assignments," **39**, 152–53
 "Student-Teacher Relations: An Experiment in Cooperative Counseling," **85**, 311–15
 "A Suggestion for the Constructive Use of Grades, **7**, 39–44
 "Teaching by Discovery," **72**, 266–69
 "Teaching Laboratory Science," **19**, 79–87
 "Teaching the Reading and Writing of Short Stories Concurrently," **29**, 119–23
 "Teaching the Social Novel," **79**, 283–89
 "Team Learning: The Only Way to Fly," **34**, 136–39
 "Toward a Contact Curriculum," **74**, 271–73
 "Use of the Overhead Projector for Teaching Geometry," **61**, 232
 "Using Collages with Literature," **58**, 224–25
 "Visual Approach to Vocabulary," **56**, 220–21
 "Warm-up Activities in a Foreign Language Class," **36**, 141–42
 "What Turns Kids On?," **90**, 338–42
 "Writing Yields Reading," **26**, 110–14
Shapiro, Elliott, 10
Sheffield, Joan James, 17
 "Motivating Underachieving Students in Biology," 49–52
Shirek, Brownlee, 254
 "Pool, Papers, and Volleyball: A Cooperative Strategy," 265–66
Short stories, writing of, **25**, 107–10; 119–23
Siegelman, Ellen, xxviii
Silberman, Charles E., 63
Simulation techniques, 177–78, 188–99
 grouping for, 189
 materials for, 189
 method of, 190
 modifications of, 191
 site for, 189
 social institutions and, **23**, 95–100; 189; **51**, 201–6
Smith, Anne, 66

Smith, Anne (*cont.*)
 "Teaching Laboratory Science," 79–87
Smith, David, 317
Social studies:
 career preparation and, 274–76
 concept building in, 67, 95–102
  processes and, 100–102
 unit on government, 96–97
 English and, **77**, 279–81; **79**, 283–89
 improvisational drama and, 186
 intradepartmental coordination in, 47–49
 popular music and, 241–43
 role playing in, 97, 201–6
 social values and, 281–83, 289–93
Social values, 255, 279–303, 305–48
Soul Searchers, The, 107–10
Sound projectors, 250
Soundtrack for student films, 249, 250
SPAN (School Programs for Academic Nonachievers), 7–11
 cross-age tutorial program of, 163–65
 curriculum for SPAN interns, 9–10
 experimental summer school programs:
  Emery High, 10, **43**, 163–65
  John F. Kennedy High, 10, **35**, 139–41; **46**, 166–74; **64**, 237–41; **84**, 300–303; **85**, 311–15
 preparation for, 9
 school tutorial program at John F. Kennedy High, 166–74
 selection for, 8–9
 strategies, **1**, 20–25; **3**, 29–31; **4**, 31–33; **7**, 39–44; **11**, 49–52; **13**, 56–58; **15**, 61–62; **20**, 88–90; **21**, 90–91; **25**, 107–10; **26**, 110–14; **28**, 115–19; **29**, 119–23; **33**, 131–35; **35**, 139–41; **44**, 166–74; **46**, 181–87; **47**, 187–88; **57**, 222–23; **59**, 226–28; **60**, 228–31; **62**, 233–35; **64**, 237–41; **65**, 241–43; **66**, 244–47; **71**, 265–66; **72**, 266–69; **74**, 271–73; **76**, 276–78; **79**, 283–89; **81**, 293–96; **82**, 296–98; **83**, 298–300; **84**, 300–303; **88**, 320–25; **89**, 327–38; **91**, 343–48
 techniques and materials of, 9–11
Spanish (*see* Foreign languages)
Spear, Harold, 290
Speech classes, role playing in, 199–201
Spolin, Viola, 176, 179, 181, 183
Sprechen and Lesen (textbook), 152
Standards of behavior (*see also* Discipline), 22–23
Stanley, Jessica, 217
 "Photographed Vocabulary," 222–23
Steinbeck, John, 284
 "Studies in Tutoring" (Cloward), 144
Stop, Look and Write (Leavitt and Sohn), 109, 122, 226–28, 237
Story and Structure (Perrine), 121
Strategies, in this volume:
 assignment for, xxiv
 cautions for use, xxvii
 criteria for selection, xxv
 suggested uses, xxvii
 unique features, xxv
Structure:
 in the classroom, 25, **13**, 56–58
 in the Graduate Internship Program in Teacher Education, 5–6
Student-produced films, 219, 247–51
 setting up to film, 248–49
 film libraries, 249

Student-produced films (*cont.*)
    filming, 248–49
    projection, 249
    soundtrack, 249
  technical information for, 249–51
    equipment, 251
    format, 249–50
    principle of 8mm sound, 250
Students as teachers, 144–74
  classroom procedures for, 144–45, 147–62
    in art class, 126
    clerical duties, 148
    course individualization, 126, 156–58
    devising homework assignments, 152–53
    grading, 148
    grouping, 161–62
    maintaining interest, 155
    mathematics laboratory, 149
    pairing, 160–61
    reviewing homework, 151
    student board for homework answers and discussion, 147–48
    technique building, 154–55
  in tutorial programs, 145–46, 163–74
    evaluation of, 164–65
    group activities, 165
    machines and gadgets, 165
    objectives of, 163
    orientation for, 163–64
    photo stories, 165
    programmed reading, 165
    reflection sheets, 169–70
    results of, 170
    selection process for, 166–67
    seminar, 169
    teaching assignments, 167–68
    videotaping, 168
Studying Teaching (Raths, Pancella, and Van Ness), 128
Suchman, J. R., 57
Sullivan, Robert M., 218
  "Use of the Overhead Projector for Teaching Geometry," 232
Sullivan programmed readers, 165
Sweet, Raymond, 148

Taba, Hilda, 101
Tape recorders, 21, 218, 233–35, 237*n*
  for making soundtracks, 250
Taxonomy, 74–78
Teaching problems, 15–18, 35–62
  classroom management (*see* Discipline; Organization)
  colleague cooperation as, 47–49
  discussion and oral work as, 35–41
  evaluation as, 39–43
  Friday afternoons as, 45–47
  with nonacademic students, 16–18, 49–62

Teaching problems (*cont.*)
  appeal of high status subjects, 59–60
  motivation, 49–52
  reading problems, 52–56
  structure, 56–58
  test taking, 61–62
Team learning, 136–39, 141–42
  activities for, 137–38
  discipline and, 137
  games and, 142
  Poirier, Gérard, and, xxviii, 128*n*, 136*n*
Testing:
  comparative, 286
  following directions in, 61–62
  grouping for, 139–41
  oral discussion test, 130
  pop quiz in mathematics, 53
  of vocabulary, 221
Thatcher, Michael D., 218
  "Popular Songs and Poetry," 235–36
Think sheets, 209
32 Problems in World History (Fenton), 282
Thomas, Mary S., 254
  "The Present and the Future," 274–76
Thread of Life, The (film), 294
Thurber, James, 120
Todd, Doris, 66
  "Devising Number Systems," 90–91
"Tom Joad" (Woody Guthrie), 287–89
Track and Field News, 279
Troy, Edward, 219
  "Guide to Filmmaking in the Schools," 247–51
Tutorial programs, 166–74
  group activities in, 165
  machines and gadgets for, 165
  photo stories used in, 165
  programmed reading in, 165
  orientation for, 163–64
  reflection sheets and, 169–70
  results of, 170
  selection process for, 166–67
  seminar in, 169
  teaching assignments in, 167–68
  videotaping and, 168

Underachieving students, motivation of (*see also* SPAN, strategies), 49–52
Units:
  art, **66,** 244–47
  earth science, **70,** 262–64
  English, 27, **29,** 119–23; **73,** 269–71; **79,** 283–89
  marine biology, **11,** 49–52
  physical science, **19,** 79–87

Units (*cont.*)
  race and adaptive coloration, **81,** 293–96
  social studies and, **23,** 95–100; **65,** 241–43; **78,** 281–83

Values, 252–70, 293–300, 305–48
Values and Teaching (Raths, Harmon and Simon), 280
Videotaping, 168
Vocabulary development, **56,** 220–21; **57,** 222–23
Volmert, Cheryl, 16
  "Developing Intradepartmental Coordination," 47–49
Voluntary grouping, 102, 129–35
  assignment for, 129–30
  group meetings and, 130
  procedure for, 132
  project design for, 129
  objectives of, 131–32
  optional daily lectures and, 130

Wagner, Gary, 17
  "Math for the Disadvantaged," 56–58
Walk in My Shoes (film), 291, 302
Walton, Myrna, 306
  "Student-Teacher Relations: An Experiment in Cooperative Counseling," 311–15
Way It Spozed to Be, The (Herndon), 21
Way Out (Michener), 301
Weidoff, Paul, xxviii
Weinstein, Gerald, 271, 339, 341
  "White Man's Burden, The" (Kipling), 290
Whitehead, Alfred North, 67
Williams, Willie L., 254
  "Teaching by Discovery," 266–69
Witherspoon, Naomi Long, 301
Wittenburg, Diane, 18
  "Getting Kids to Follow Directions," 61–62
Wong, Harry, 79
Work experience program, **25,** 107–10
World of Piri Thomas, The (film), 286
Wright, Penny, 145–46
  "A Cross-age Tutorial Program," 163–65
Wright, Richard, 301, 302

Yeats, William Butler, 187

Zahn, Jane (Edises), xxviii
Zoo Story, The (Albee), 340

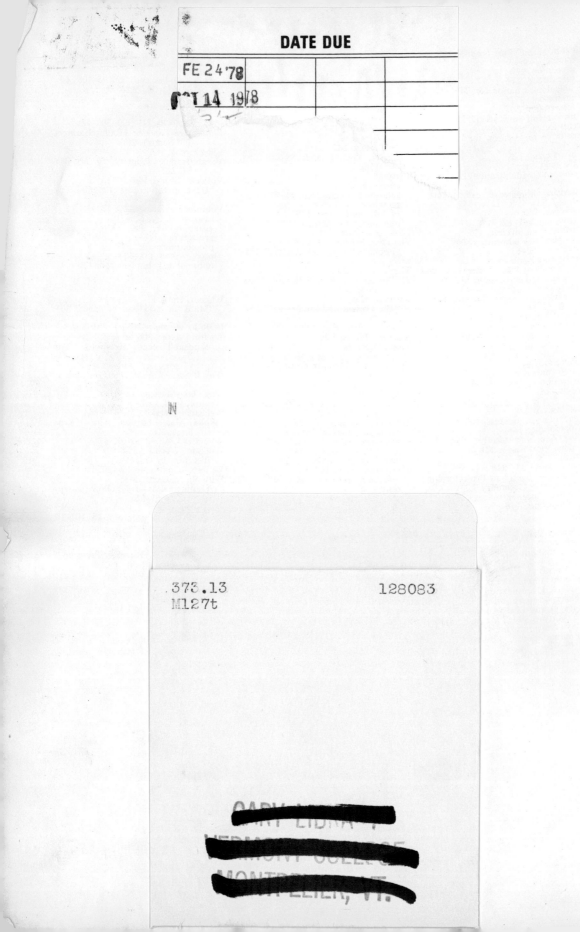